M000249538

HMH | into Math™

Advanced 2

Copyright © 2020 by Houghton Mifflin Harcourt Publishing Company

All rights reserved. No part of this work may be reproduced or transmitted in any form or by any means, electronic or mechanical, including photocopying or recording, or by any information storage or retrieval system, without the prior written permission of the copyright owner unless such copying is expressly permitted by federal copyright law. Requests for permission to make copies of any part of the work should be submitted through our Permissions website at https://customercare.hmhco.com/contactus/Permissions.html or mailed to Houghton Mifflin Harcourt Publishing Company, Attn: Rights Compliance and Analysis, 9400 Southpark Center Loop, Orlando, Florida 32819-8647.

Common Core State Standards © Copyright 2010. National Governors Association Center for Best Practices and Council of Chief State School Officers. All rights reserved.

This product is not sponsored or endorsed by the Common Core State Standards Initiative of the National Governors Association Center for Best Practices and the Council of Chief State School Officers.

Currency and Coins Photos courtesy of United States Mint, Bureau of Engraving and Houghton Mifflin Harcourt

Printed in the U.S.A.

ISBN 978-0-358-11584-7

5 6 7 8 9 10 0607 28 27 26 25 24 23 22 21

4500819460 C D E F G

If you have received these materials as examination copies free of charge, Houghton Mifflin Harcourt Publishing Company retains title to the materials and they may not be resold. Resale of examination copies is strictly prohibited.

Possession of this publication in print format does not entitle users to convert this publication, or any portion of it, into electronic format.

© Houghton Mifflin Harcourt Publishing Company

Dear Students and Families,

Welcome to *Into Math*, Advanced 2! In this program, you will develop skills and make sense of mathematics by solving real-world problems, using hands-on tools and strategies, and collaborating with your classmates.

With the support of your teacher and by engaging with meaningful practice you will learn to persevere when solving problems. *Into Math* will not only help you deepen your understanding of mathematics, but also build your confidence as a learner of mathematics.

Even more exciting, you will write all your ideas and solutions right in your book. In your *Into Math* book, writing and drawing on the pages will help you think deeply about what you are learning, help you truly understand math, and most important, you will become a confident user of mathematics!

Sincerely,
The Authors

© Houghton Mifflin Harcourt Publishing Company

Authors

Edward B. Burger, PhD
President, Southwestern University
Georgetown, Texas

Matthew R. Larson, PhD
Past-President, National Council
of Teachers of Mathematics
Lincoln Public Schools
Lincoln, Nebraska

Juli K. Dixon, PhD
Professor, Mathematics Education
University of Central Florida
Orlando, Florida

Steven J. Leinwand
Principal Research Analyst
American Institutes for Research
Washington, DC

Timothy D. Kanold, PhD
Mathematics Educator
Chicago, Illinois

Consultants

English Language Development Consultant

Harold Asturias
Director, Center for Mathematics
Excellence and Equity
Lawrence Hall of Science, University of California
Berkeley, California

Program Consultant

David Dockterman, EdD
Lecturer, Harvard Graduate School of Education
Cambridge, Massachusetts

Blended Learning Consultant

Weston Kiercshneck
Senior Fellow
International Center for Leadership in Education
Littleton, Colorado

STEM Consultants

Michael A. DiSpezio
Global Educator
North Falmouth, Massachusetts

Marjorie Frank
Science Writer and
Content-Area Reading Specialist
Brooklyn, New York

Bernadine Okoro
Access and Equity and
STEM Learning Advocate and Consultant
Washington, DC

Cary I. Sneider, PhD
Associate Research Professor
Portland State University
Portland, Oregon

© Houghton Mifflin Harcourt Publishing Company

Unit 1

Transform and Construct Geometric Figures

MODULE 1 Transformations and Congruence

Build Conceptual Understanding | Connect Concepts and Skills | Apply and Practice

© Houghton Mifflin Harcourt Publishing Company • Image Credit: © Jim West/Alamy

MODULE 2 Draw and Analyze Two-Dimensional Figures

MODULE 3 Transformations and Similarity

© Houghton Mifflin Harcourt Publishing Company

Unit 2

Equations and Inequalities in One Variable

MODULE 4 Solve Linear Equations

Build Conceptual Understanding   Connect Concepts and Skills   Apply and Practice

© Houghton Mifflin Harcourt Publishing Company • Image Credit: ©gpflman/E+/Getty Images

MODULE 5 Solve Problems Using Inequalities

© Houghton Mifflin Harcourt Publishing Company • Image Credits: (dog) ©GK Hart/Vikki Hart/Getty Images; (house) © irina88w/iStock/Getty Images Plus/Getty Images; (cat) © Stockdisc/Getty Images

Unit 3

Similarity, Slope, and Linear Functions

MODULE 6 Angle Relationships

MODULE 7 Proportional Relationships

© Houghton Mifflin Harcourt Publishing Company

Build Conceptual Understanding | Connect Concepts and Skills | Apply and Practice

MODULE 8 Understand and Analyze Functions

MODULE 9 Systems of Linear Equations

© Houghton Mifflin Harcourt Publishing Company

Unit 4

Data Analysis and Sampling

MODULE 10 Scatter Plots

MODULE 11 Proportional Reasoning with Samples

Build Conceptual Understanding | Connect Concepts and Skills | Apply and Practice

© Houghton Mifflin Harcourt Publishing Company • Image Credit: ©ewastudio/iStock/Getty Images Plus/Getty Images

© Houghton Mifflin Harcourt Publishing Company • Image Credit: ©amwu/iStock / Getty Images Plus/Getty Images

Unit 5 Applications of Real Numbers and Exponents

MODULE 14 Real Numbers

© Houghton Mifflin Harcourt Publishing Company • Image Credits: (t) ©Betsy Hansen/Houghton Mifflin Harcourt; (b) ©Monty Rakusen/Alamy

Build Conceptual Understanding   Connect Concepts and Skills   Apply and Practice

MODULE 15 The Pythagorean Theorem

MODULE 16 Exponents and Scientific Notation

© Houghton Mifflin Harcourt Publishing Company • Image Credit: © Betsy Hansen/Houghton Mifflin Harcourt

Unit 6

Area and Volume

MODULE 17 Analyze Figures to Find Circumference and Area

MODULE 18 Cross Sections, Surface Area, and Volume

© Houghton Mifflin Harcourt Publishing Company • Image Credit: ©Todd Gipstein/Corbis Documentary/Getty Images

Unit 7

Probability

MODULE 19 Understand and Apply Experimental Probability

MODULE 20 Understand and Apply Theoretical Probability

Build Conceptual Understanding   Connect Concepts and Skills   Apply and Practice

© Houghton Mifflin Harcourt Publishing Company • Image Credit: ©Michael Burrell/iStock/Getty Images Plus/Getty Images

My Progress on Mathematics Standards

The lessons in your ***Into Math*** book provide instruction for Mathematics Standards for Advanced 2. You can use the following pages to reflect on your learning and record your progress through the standards.

As you learn new concepts, reflect on this learning. Consider inserting a checkmark or inserting a question mark if you have questions or need help.

Standards	Student Edition Lessons	My Progress
Domain: THE NUMBER SYSTEM		
Cluster: Know that there are numbers that are not rational, and approximate them by rational numbers.		
Know that numbers that are not rational are called irrational. Understand informally that every number has a decimal expansion; for rational numbers show that the decimal expansion repeats eventually, and convert a decimal expansion which repeats eventually into a rational number.	14.1	
Use rational approximations of irrational numbers to compare the size of irrational numbers, locate them approximately on a number line diagram, and estimate the value of expressions (e.g., π^2).	14.3	
Domain: EXPRESSIONS & EQUATIONS		
Cluster: Solve real-life and mathematical problems using numerical and algebraic expressions and equations.		
Solve multi-step real-life and mathematical problems posed with positive and negative rational numbers in any form (whole numbers, fractions, and decimals), using tools strategically. Apply properties of operations to calculate with numbers in any form; convert between forms as appropriate; and assess the reasonableness of answers using mental computation and estimation strategies.	4.2, 4.3, 17.1, 17.2, 17.3, 18.2, 18.3, 18.4, 18.5, 18.6, 19.4, 20.3	
Use variables to represent quantities in a real-world or mathematical problem, and construct simple equations and inequalities to solve problems by reasoning about the quantities.	4.1, 5.2 *See also below.*	

© Houghton Mifflin Harcourt Publishing Company

• Solve word problems leading to equations of the form $px + q = r$ and $p(x + q) = r$, where p, q, and r are specific rational numbers. Solve equations of these forms fluently. Compare an algebraic solution to an arithmetic solution, identifying the sequence of the operations used in each approach.	4.2, 4.5	
• Solve word problems leading to inequalities of the form $px + q > r$ or $px + q < r$, where p, q, and r are specific rational numbers. Graph the solution set of the inequality and interpret it in the context of the problem.	5.1, 5.3	
Cluster: Work with radicals and integer exponents.		
Know and apply the properties of integer exponents to generate equivalent numerical expressions.	16.1	
Use square root and cube root symbols to represent solutions to equations of the form $x^2 = p$ and $x^3 = p$, where p is a positive rational number. Evaluate square roots of small perfect squares and cube roots of small perfect cubes. Know that $\sqrt{2}$ is irrational.	14.2	
Use numbers expressed in the form of a single digit times an integer power of 10 to estimate very large or very small quantities, and to express how many times as much one is than the other.	16.2	
Perform operations with numbers expressed in scientific notation, including problems where both decimal and scientific notation are used. Use scientific notation and choose units of appropriate size for measurements of very large or very small quantities (e.g., use millimeters per year for seafloor spreading). Interpret scientific notation that has been generated by technology.	16.3	
Cluster: Understand the connections between proportional relationships, lines, and linear equations.		
Graph proportional relationships, interpreting the unit rate as the slope of the graph. Compare two different proportional relationships represented in different ways.	7.2, 7.3	
Use similar triangles to explain why the slope m is the same between any two distinct points on a non-vertical line in the coordinate plane; derive the equation $y = mx$ for a line through the origin and the equation $y = mx + b$ for a line intercepting the vertical axis at b.	7.1, 7.2, 8.2	

© Houghton Mifflin Harcourt Publishing Company

Cluster: Analyze and solve linear equations and pairs of simultaneous linear equations.		
Solve linear equations in one variable.	4.3, 4.4, 4.5 *See also below.*	
• Give examples of linear equations in one variable with one solution, infinitely many solutions, or no solutions. Show which of these possibilities is the case by successively transforming the given equation into simpler forms, until an equivalent equation of the form $x = a$, $a = a$, or $a = b$ results (where a and b are different numbers).	4.4, 4.5	
• Solve linear equations with rational number coefficients, including equations whose solutions require expanding expressions using the distributive property and collecting like terms.	4.3, 4.4, 4.5	
Analyze and solve pairs of simultaneous linear equations.	9.1, 9.2, 9.3, 9.4, 9.5, 9.6 *See also below.*	
• Understand that solutions to a system of two linear equations in two variables correspond to points of intersection of their graphs, because points of intersection satisfy both equations simultaneously.	9.2	
• Solve systems of two linear equations in two variables algebraically, and estimate solutions by graphing the equations. Solve simple cases by inspection.	9.3, 9.4, 9.5	
• Solve real-world and mathematical problems leading to two linear equations in two variables.	9.6	
Domain: FUNCTIONS		
Cluster: Define, evaluate, and compare functions.		
Understand that a function is a rule that assigns to each input exactly one output. The graph of a function is the set of ordered pairs consisting of an input and the corresponding output.	8.1	
Compare properties of two functions each represented in a different way (algebraically, graphically, numerically in tables, or by verbal descriptions).	8.4	
Interpret the equation $y = mx + b$ as defining a linear function, whose graph is a straight line; give examples of functions that are not linear.	8.2	

© Houghton Mifflin Harcourt Publishing Company

Cluster: Use functions to model relationships between quantities.		
Construct a function to model a linear relationship between two quantities. Determine the rate of change and initial value of the function from a description of a relationship or from two (*x*, *y*) values, including reading these from a table or from a graph. Interpret the rate of change and initial value of a linear function in terms of the situation it models, and in terms of its graph or a table of values.	8.3, 8.4, 10.3	
Describe qualitatively the functional relationship between two quantities by analyzing a graph (e.g., where the function is increasing or decreasing, linear or nonlinear). Sketch a graph that exhibits the qualitative features of a function that has been described verbally.	8.5	
Domain: GEOMETRY		
Cluster: Draw, construct, and describe geometrical figures and describe the relationships between them.		
Solve problems involving scale drawings of geometric figures, including computing actual lengths and areas from a scale drawing and reproducing a scale drawing at a different scale.	2.5	
Draw (freehand, with ruler and protractor, and with technology) geometric shapes with given conditions. Focus on constructing triangles from three measures of angles or sides, noticing when the conditions determine a unique triangle, more than one triangle, or no triangle.	2.1, 2.2, 2.3, 2.4	
Describe the two-dimensional figures that result from slicing three-dimensional figures, as in plane sections of right rectangular prisms and right rectangular pyramids.	18.1	
Cluster: Solve real-life and mathematical problems involving angle measure, area, surface area, and volume.		
Know the formulas for the area and circumference of a circle and use them to solve problems; give an informal derivation of the relationship between the circumference and area of a circle.	17.1, 17.2	
Use facts about supplementary, complementary, vertical, and adjacent angles in a multi-step problem to write and solve simple equations for an unknown angle in a figure.	4.5	
Solve real-world and mathematical problems involving area, volume and surface area of two- and three-dimensional objects composed of triangles, quadrilaterals, polygons, cubes, and right prisms.	17.3, 18.2, 18.3, 18.6	

© Houghton Mifflin Harcourt Publishing Company

Cluster: Understand congruence and similarity using physical models, transparencies, or geometry software.		
Verify experimentally the properties of rotations, reflections, and translations:	1.1, 1.2, 1.3, 1.4 *See also below.*	
• Lines are taken to lines, and line segments to line segments of the same length.	1.1, 1.2, 1.3, 1.4	
• Angles are taken to angles of the same measure.	1.1, 1.2, 1.3, 1.4	
• Parallel lines are taken to parallel lines.	1.1, 1.2, 1.3, 1.4	
Understand that a two-dimensional figure is congruent to another if the second can be obtained from the first by a sequence of rotations, reflections, and translations; given two congruent figures, describe a sequence that exhibits the congruence between them.	1.5	
Describe the effect of dilations, translations, rotations, and reflections on two-dimensional figures using coordinates.	1.2, 1.3, 1.4, 1.5, 3.1, 3.2	
Understand that a two-dimensional figure is similar to another if the second can be obtained from the first by a sequence of rotations, reflections, translations, and dilations; given two similar two-dimensional figures, describe a sequence that exhibits the similarity between them.	3.3	
Use informal arguments to establish facts about the angle sum and exterior angle of triangles, about the angles created when parallel lines are cut by a transversal, and the angle-angle criterion for similarity of triangles.	6.1, 6.2, 6.3	
Cluster: Understand and apply the Pythagorean Theorem.		
Explain a proof of the Pythagorean Theorem and its converse.	15.1	
Apply the Pythagorean Theorem to determine unknown side lengths in right triangles in real-world and mathematical problems in two and three dimensions.	15.1, 15.2	
Apply the Pythagorean Theorem to find the distance between two points in a coordinate system.	15.3	

© Houghton Mifflin Harcourt Publishing Company

Cluster: Solve real-world and mathematical problems involving volume of cylinders, cones, and spheres.		
Know the formulas for the volumes of cones, cylinders, and spheres and use them to solve real-world and mathematical problems.	18.4, 18.5, 18.6	
Domain: STATISTICS & PROBABILITY		
Cluster: Use random sampling to draw inferences about a population.		
Understand that statistics can be used to gain information about a population by examining a sample of the population; generalizations about a population from a sample are valid only if the sample is representative of that population. Understand that random sampling tends to produce representative samples and support valid inferences.	11.1	
Use data from a random sample to draw inferences about a population with an unknown characteristic of interest. Generate multiple samples (or simulated samples) of the same size to gauge the variation in estimates or predictions.	11.2, 11.3	
Cluster: Draw informal comparative inferences about two populations.		
Informally assess the degree of visual overlap of two numerical data distributions with similar variabilities, measuring the difference between the centers by expressing it as a multiple of a measure of variability.	12.1, 12.2, 12.3	
Use measures of center and measures of variability for numerical data from random samples to draw informal comparative inferences about two populations.	12.1, 12.2, 12.3	
Cluster: Investigate chance processes and develop, use, and evaluate probability models.		
Understand that the probability of a chance event is a number between 0 and 1 that expresses the likelihood of the event occurring. Larger numbers indicate greater likelihood. A probability near 0 indicates an unlikely event, a probability around 1/2 indicates an event that is neither unlikely nor likely, and a probability near 1 indicates a likely event.	19.1	
Approximate the probability of a chance event by collecting data on the chance process that produces it and observing its long-run relative frequency, and predict the approximate relative frequency given the probability.	19.2, 19.4, 20.1, 20.3	

© Houghton Mifflin Harcourt Publishing Company

Develop a probability model and use it to find probabilities of events. Compare probabilities from a model to observed frequencies; if the agreement is not good, explain possible sources of the discrepancy.	20.1 *See also below.*	
• Develop a uniform probability model by assigning equal probability to all outcomes, and use the model to determine probabilities of events.	20.1, 20.3	
• Develop a probability model (which may not be uniform) by observing frequencies in data generated from a chance process.	19.2	
Find probabilities of compound events using organized lists, tables, tree diagrams, and simulation.	*See below.*	
• Understand that, just as with simple events, the probability of a compound event is the fraction of outcomes in the sample space for which the compound event occurs.	19.3, 20.2	
• Represent sample spaces for compound events using methods such as organized lists, tables and tree diagrams. For an event described in everyday language (e.g., "rolling double sixes"), identify the outcomes in the sample space which compose the event.	19.3, 20.2	
• Design and use a simulation to generate frequencies for compound events.	19.3, 20.4	
Cluster: Investigate patterns of association in bivariate data.		
Construct and interpret scatter plots for bivariate measurement data to investigate patterns of association between two quantities. Describe patterns such as clustering, outliers, positive or negative association, linear association, and nonlinear association.	10.1	
Know that straight lines are widely used to model relationships between two quantitative variables. For scatter plots that suggest a linear association, informally fit a straight line, and informally assess the model fit by judging the closeness of the data points to the line.	10.2	

© Houghton Mifflin Harcourt Publishing Company

Use the equation of a linear model to solve problems in the context of bivariate measurement data, interpreting the slope and intercept.	10.3	
Understand that patterns of association can also be seen in bivariate categorical data by displaying frequencies and relative frequencies in a two-way table. Construct and interpret a two-way table summarizing data on two categorical variables collected from the same subjects. Use relative frequencies calculated for rows or columns to describe possible association between the two variables.	13.1, 13.2	

© Houghton Mifflin Harcourt Publishing Company

Unit 1

Transform and Construct Geometric Figures

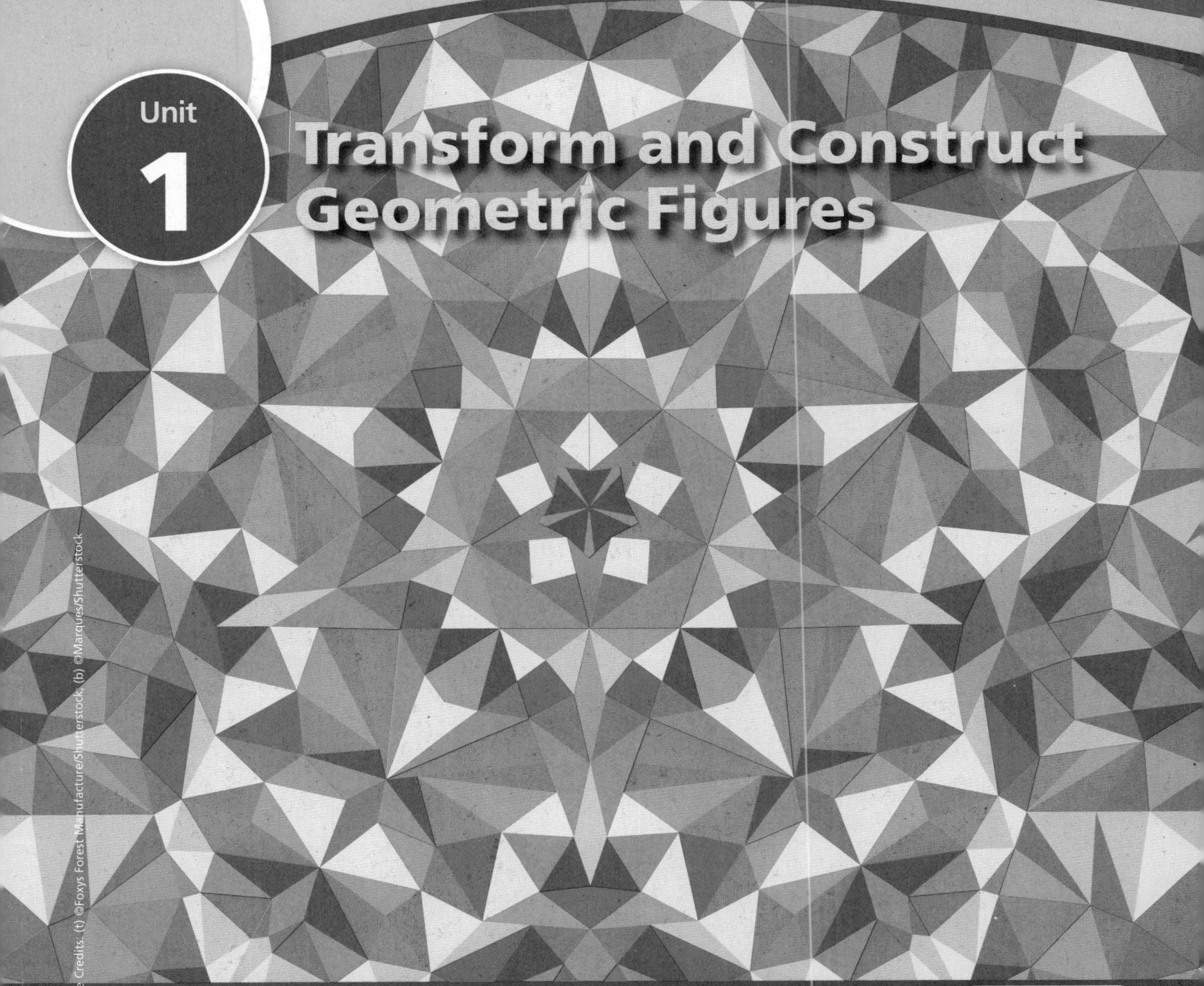

Puzzle Designer

STEM POWERING INGENUITY

A puzzle designer combines creativity and imagination with logical reasoning to produce challenging and entertaining puzzles. From three-dimensional puzzles to jigsaw puzzles to mazes to crossword puzzles, puzzle designers have something to intrigue just about everyone.

STEM Task:

Starting with 12 toothpicks arranged as shown each time, perform each task:

- Remove 4 toothpicks to form exactly 1 square.
- Remove 4 toothpicks to form exactly 2 squares.
- Move 3 toothpicks to form exactly 3 squares.

© Houghton Mifflin Harcourt Publishing Company • Image Credits: (t) ©Foxys Forest Manufacture/Shutterstock; (b) ©Marques/Shutterstock

Learning Mindset

Challenge-Seeking Builds Confidence

© Houghton Mifflin Harcourt Publishing Company • Image Credit: ©John Robertson/Alamy

Have you ever been asked to do something that you didn't know how to do? This happens to everyone at one time or another. Sometimes, people back away from a challenge because they are afraid of making a mistake. But taking on a challenge can be a rewarding growth experience. Here are two suggestions that can help you overcome a challenge when your confidence is fading.

- Build your confidence by trying simpler versions of the task. Think of levels in a video game. Succeeding at simpler levels give you confidence that you can complete the next levels.
- Don't give up. Remember, you are learning and growing through this process. If you got it right on the first try, it wasn't very challenging. A positive attitude will make this and future challenges easier to meet.

Reflect

Q **Did you feel confident as you worked on the STEM Task?**

Q **How does self-confidence affect your ability to successfully complete tasks or meet challenges?**

Module

1 Transformations and Congruence

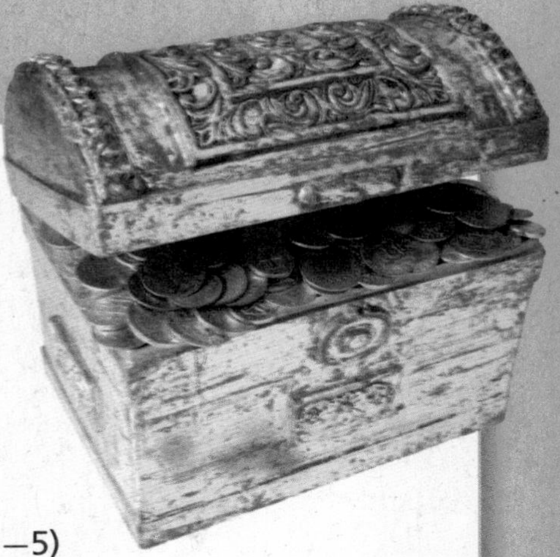

TREASURE Hunt

A treasure is on a remote island represented by the coordinate plane.

Graph the following polygons.

A. *ABCD* with *A*(1, 6), *B*(7, 6), *C*(7, −5), *D*(−4, −5)

B. *FGHJ* with *F*(−1, 3), *G*(6, 3), *H*(6, −4), *J*(−1, −4)

C. *KLMN* with *K*(−6, −3), *L*(3, −3), *M*(0, −9), *N*(−9, −9)

D. *STUV* with *S*(−9, 2), *T*(−3, 2), *U*(−3, −6), *V*(−9, −6)

E. Clues: The treasure is at a point with integer coordinates. The treasure is buried inside a trapezoid that is not a parallelogram, outside any squares or rectangles, and inside a parallelogram.

Where is the treasure buried? Explain how you know.

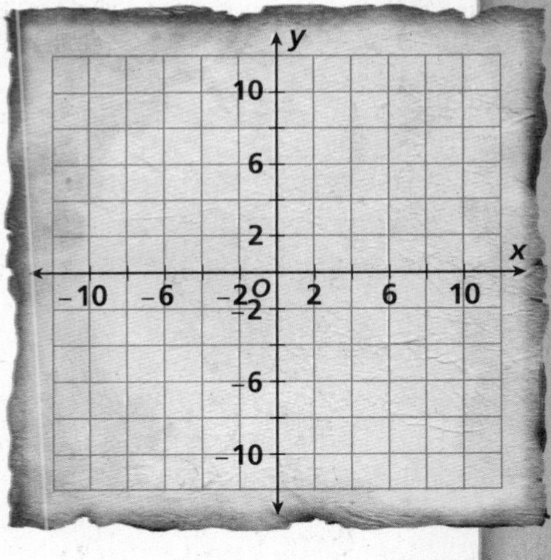

____

____

____

____

Turn and Talk

How did you use the clues to find the treasure?

© Houghton Mifflin Harcourt Publishing Company • **Image Credits:** (t) Brand X Pictures/Getty Images; (b) ©caesart/Shutterstock

Are You Ready?

Complete these problems to review prior concepts and skills you will need for this module.

Polygons in the Coordinate Plane

Draw each polygon in the coordinate plane.

1. Triangle *ABC* has vertices $A(-4, 3)$, $B(3, 1)$, and $C(1, -3)$.

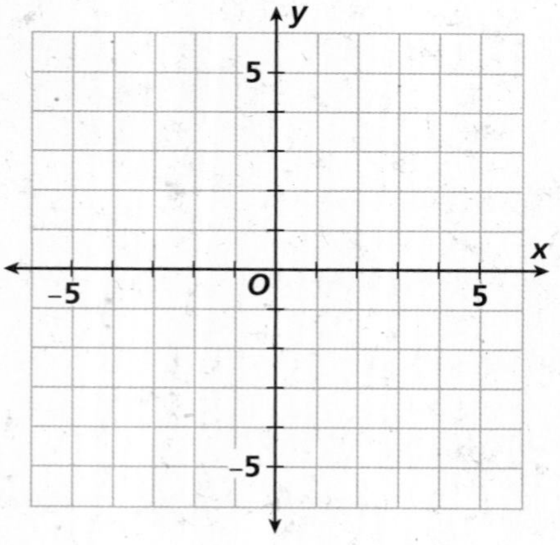

2. Quadrilateral *FGHJ* has vertices $F(-2, -3)$, $G(-2, 4)$, $H(1, 4)$, and $J(5, -3)$.

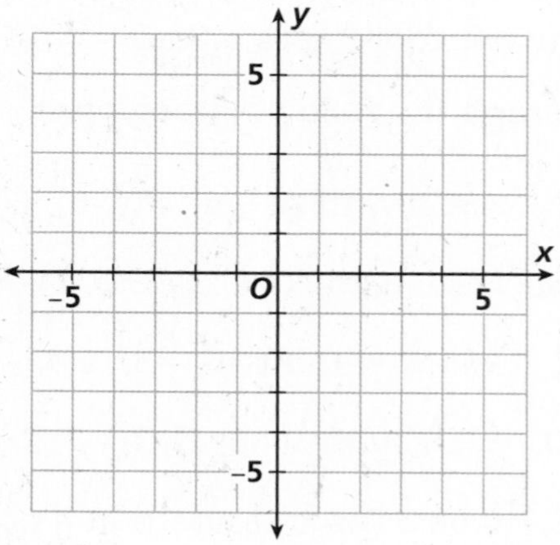

Draw Shapes with Given Conditions

Use a ruler and protractor to draw a quadrilateral that matches each description. Label the sides or angles described.

3. a square with a side length of 2 centimeters

4. a parallelogram with two angles that measure 65° and two angles that measure 115°

Use a ruler and protractor to draw a triangle that matches each description. Label the sides or angles described.

5. a right triangle with sides that measure 3 centimeters, 4 centimeters, and 5 centimeters

6. a triangle with two angles measuring 70° and the side between them measuring 3 centimeters

© Houghton Mifflin Harcourt Publishing Company

Name ______________________________

Investigate Transformations

I Can describe what happens to the sides and angles of a figure when it is transformed.

Spark Your Learning

SMALL GROUPS

Rachel is tiling a rectangular floor using triangles. Draw a triangle and cut it out. Move the triangle in different ways, and trace those shapes to draw a rectangular pattern using triangular tiles. Experiment with different shapes of triangles and different ways of moving the triangle to tile the whole floor with no gaps or overlapping tiles.

Turn and Talk Describe multiple ways you could move the original triangle to tile the floor.

© Houghton Mifflin Harcourt Publishing Company • Image Credit: ©trainman111/Shutterstock

Build Understanding

1 On graph paper, draw a quadrilateral that has exactly one pair of parallel sides. Remember, parallel sides are sides that would not intersect even if extended indefinitely. Cut out the shape and trace it in the center of the box.

Connect to Vocabulary

A **transformation** is a change in the position of a figure.

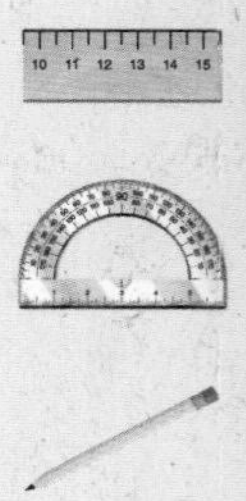

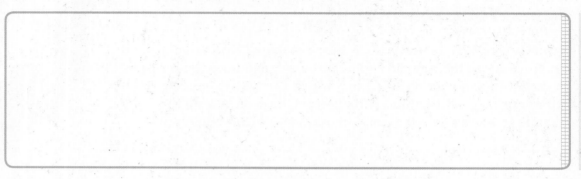

A. Slide the quadrilateral to a new location in the box and trace it. Describe the direction and length you slid the shape.

____

B. Use a ruler to measure the sides of each quadrilateral. Use a protractor to measure the angles of the original shape and the new shape. What has happened to the length of the sides, the size of the angles, and the relationship between the parallel sides of the two shapes?

____

____

____

____

C. When you slid the shape, did anything change besides its position?

____

D. Draw a horizontal line near, but outside, your second quadrilateral. Flip the second quadrilateral in Part A over the horizontal line and trace it in the box as your third shape. Measure the lengths of the sides and the angles of both quadrilaterals. How have the relationships between the sides and angles of the original shape changed or stayed the same compared to the flipped shape?

____

____

Turn and Talk Describe a way to move the third quadrilateral back to the original location of the first quadrilateral.

© Houghton Mifflin Harcourt Publishing Company

Name ____________________

2 On graph paper, draw a polygon that has at least six sides and one pair of parallel lines. Cut out the shape and trace it in the center of the box.

A. Place the tip of your pencil on the center of the shape and turn the shape. Trace the shape in its new location.

B. How do the sides and angles of the original polygon compare to the polygon you drew after turning the original?

____

____

____

____

C. Trace the shape again. Then, place the tip of your pencil on one corner of the shape and turn it. Trace the shape in its new location.

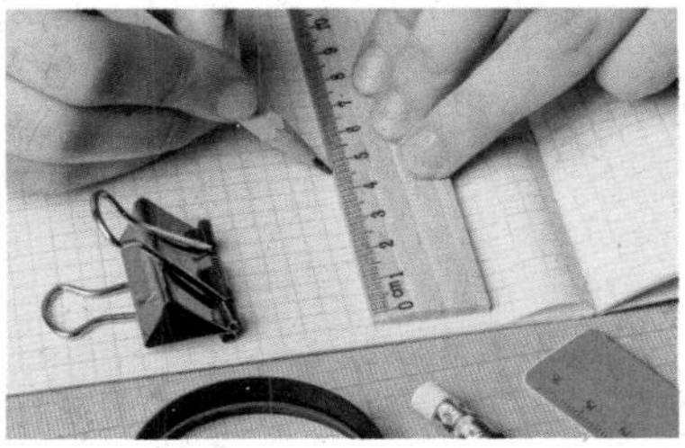

D. Draw an X on one angle of the original shape and on the same angle of the turned shape. Describe how the angle has been moved.

____

____

____

E. Based on these two examples, what do you think stays the same and what changes when a shape is turned?

____

____

____

Turn and Talk Two students use two different transformations on the same shape. One student slides it up. The other student flips it. What is true about the side lengths and angle measures of both transformed shapes?

© Houghton Mifflin Harcourt Publishing Company • Image Credit: ©Zhukov Oleg/Shutterstock

3 Dakota has a mirror in the shape of a **trapezoid**. She started by hanging the mirror in one location. Then she decided to hang the mirror in a different location.

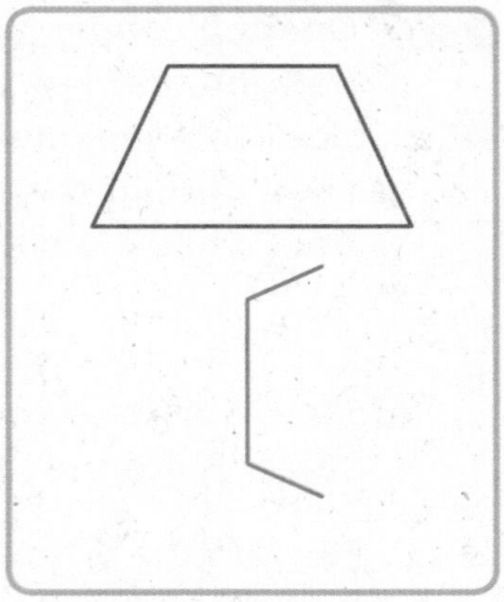

A. Complete the drawing of the mirror in its new location.

B. How could Dakota move the mirror from the first location to the second location?

C. How have the parallel sides of the mirror changed?

D. Describe how the side lengths and angle measures were affected when Dakota moved the mirror.

Check Understanding

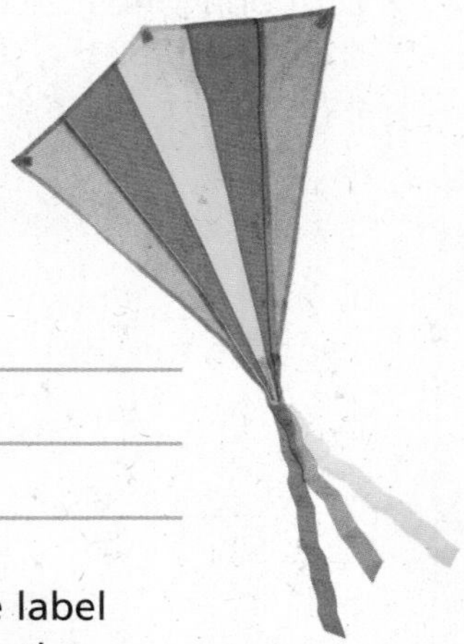

1. Darby hung a kite on the wall. Then she slid the kite higher on the wall to a better position. What is true about the size and shape of her kite? Explain what happened to the side lengths and angle measures after she made the move.

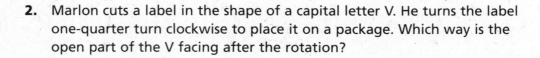

2. Marlon cuts a label in the shape of a capital letter V. He turns the label one-quarter turn clockwise to place it on a package. Which way is the open part of the V facing after the rotation?

3. Rachel tells Jonah that she can turn a square, but he won't be able to tell that it was turned after she is finished. How can she do this?

© Houghton Mifflin Harcourt Publishing Company • Image Credit: ©Hurst Photo/Shutterstock

Name ___

On Your Own

4. Tarik is working on a photo album and moved a photo as shown. What transformation did he use?

Before After

Use the information to answer Problems 5–6.

Ryan lays a pentagonal pattern on a piece of fabric.

5. If Ryan slides the pattern two inches to the right, what happens to the measure of the angles of the pentagon?

6. Ryan decides to rotate the pattern one-fourth turn clockwise. What happens to the lengths of the sides of the pattern?

7. MP **Reason** Beckie cuts out a piece of paper in the shape of a trapezoid with only one pair of parallel sides. The parallel sides are 2 inches apart. Then she flips the shape over. What is the distance between the parallel sides of the flipped shape? Explain how you know.

8. MP **Reason** Is Figure B a transformation of Figure A? Why or why not?

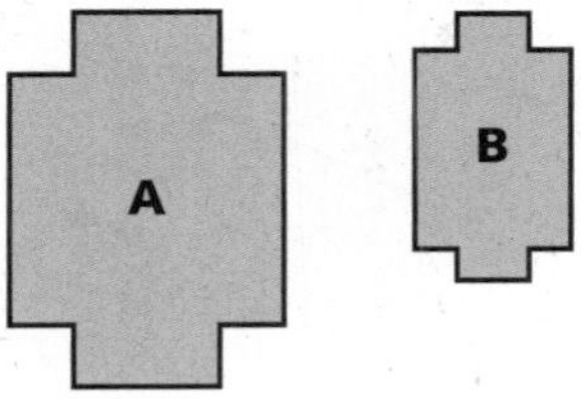

9. MP **Reason** Is Figure Y a transformation of Figure X? Why or why not?

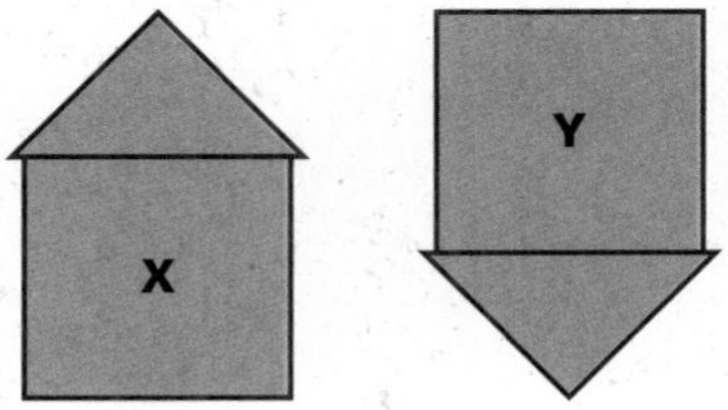

© Houghton Mifflin Harcourt Publishing Company • Image Credit: ©Ryan McVay/Photodisc/Getty Images

10. Bailey has a sheet of plywood with four right angles. She saws off one of the angles and turns the plywood one-half turn clockwise. How many right angles are there on the plywood now?

____

Use the information to answer Problems 11–12.

Margot draws a shape with one pair of parallel lines that are four centimeters apart. She then flips the shape across a horizontal line.

11. How many pairs of parallel lines are on the flipped shape?

____

12. How far apart are the parallel lines on the flipped shape? How do you know?

____

____

13. Complete each transformation of the given figure.

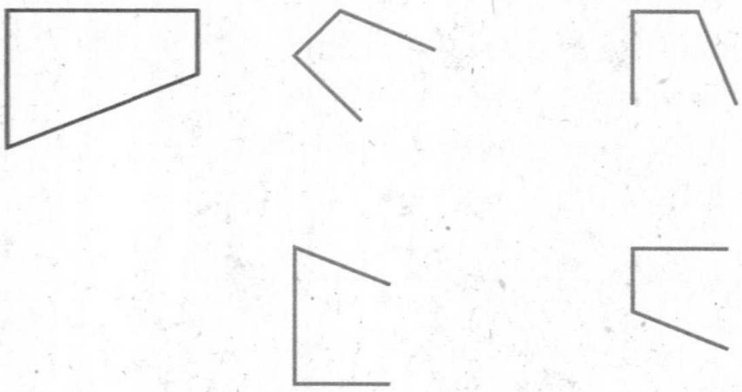

14. Complete the drawing of the parallelogram after a slide to the right.

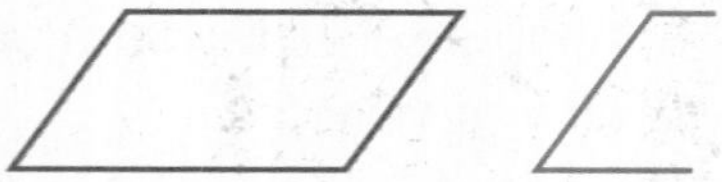

15. Open Ended Perform a transformation on the shape. Draw the result and describe the transformation you performed.

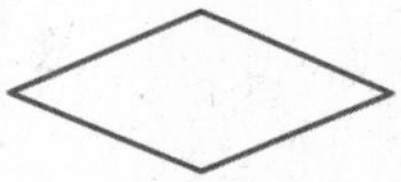

____

I'm in a Learning Mindset!

Did I have confidence in my answer to Problem 15? What specific evidence do I have that I performed a transformation correctly?

____

____

© Houghton Mifflin Harcourt Publishing Company

Name

ONLINE
Video Tutorials and Interactive Examples

Investigate Transformations

1. **Social Studies** Nautical flags are used by ships for signaling. Flipping a flag vertically can be a sign of distress. The flag representing the number 7 is shown. Where is the yellow side if the flag is flipped vertically? Explain.

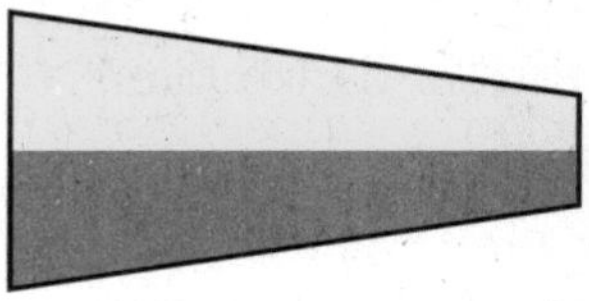

2. A quadrilateral has a pair of vertical parallel sides on the left and right of the figure. Ryan turns the quadrilateral one-half turn clockwise. Where are the parallel sides on the turned figure?

3. Does each pair of shapes show a flip, slide, or turn? If so, identify which.

A.

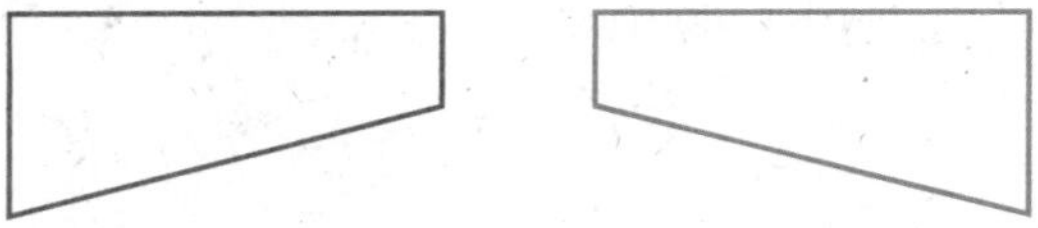

B.

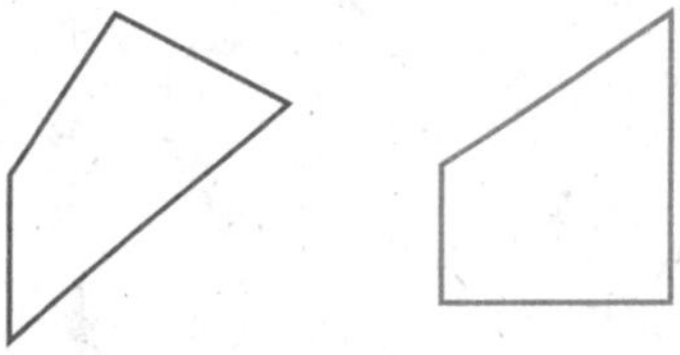

4. **Attend to Precision** Complete the drawing of the shape slid to the right.

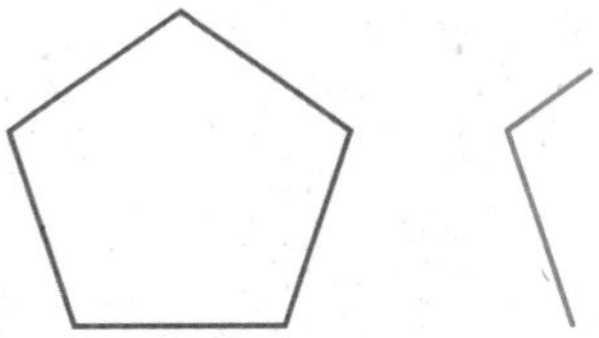

5. **STEM** A biologist is studying leaves with *line symmetry*. Complete the biologist's sketch of the leaf by flipping the shape across the vertical line.

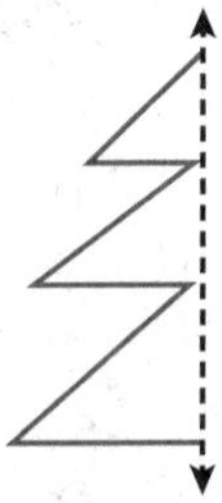

6. **Attend to Precision** Complete the drawing of the shape after it has been turned.

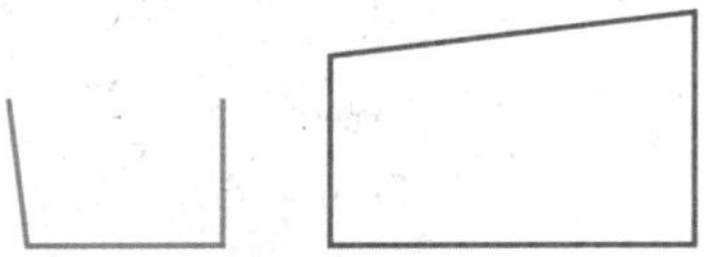

© Houghton Mifflin Harcourt Publishing Company

Test Prep

Use the information to answer Problems 7–9.

Daniel is babysitting his little sister. He makes her a sandwich and then uses a cookie cutter to cut the sandwich into the shape of a rhombus. Then he flips the sandwich over.

7. What shape is the flipped sandwich? ______________________

8. Determine the number of pairs of parallel sides for the flipped sandwich.

_____ pairs of parallel sides

9. Are the side lengths of the flipped sandwich longer, shorter, or the same size as the side lengths of the unflipped sandwich?

____

10. Select the description of the transformation of the given figure.

		Slide	Flip	Turn
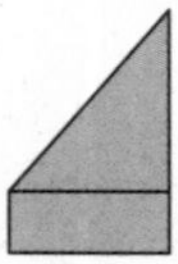	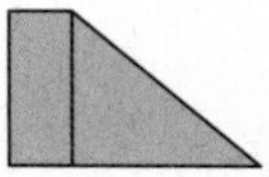	☐	☐	☐
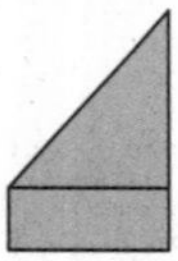	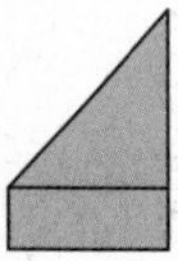	☐	☐	☐
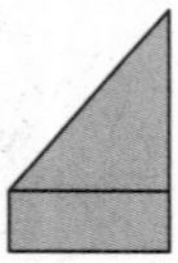	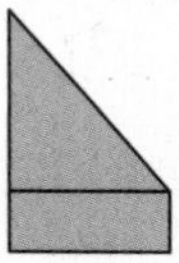	☐	☐	☐

Spiral Review

11. A store sells a bicycle tube for $21.00 and a tire patch kit for $9.00. The tax rate is 7%. How much would it cost to purchase both?

____

12. Tell whether the following relationship is a proportional relationship. Explain why or why not. If it is, identify the unit rate.

Time (min)	3	5	8	10
Words Typed	120	200	320	400

____

____

____

© Houghton Mifflin Harcourt Publishing Company

Name ______________________________

Explore Translations

(I Can) translate figures, describe the translations using words and mapping notation, and determine an algebraic rule for translating a figure on a coordinate plane.

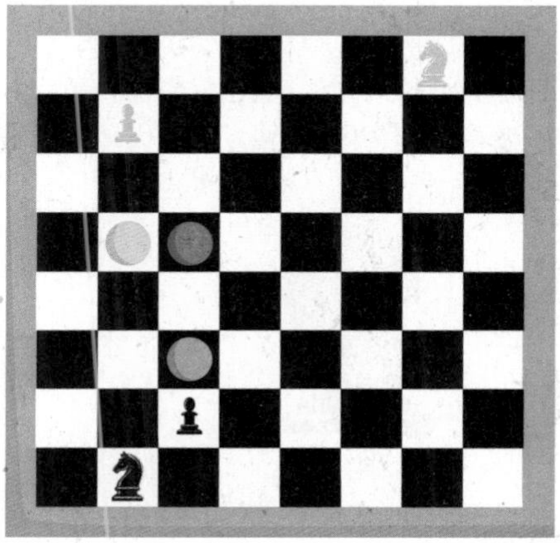

Spark Your Learning

SMALL GROUPS

The objective of chess is for one player's pieces to capture the other player's king. Each chess piece moves according to special rules.

Piece	Movement
	Pawns can move forward 1 or 2 squares on the first move and 1 square thereafter. They can also move diagonally to capture another piece.
	Knights can move 2 squares horizontally and 1 square vertically, or 2 squares vertically and 1 square horizontally.

Which move(s) will get any piece to land on a yellow, a blue, or a red dot? Two of the dots?

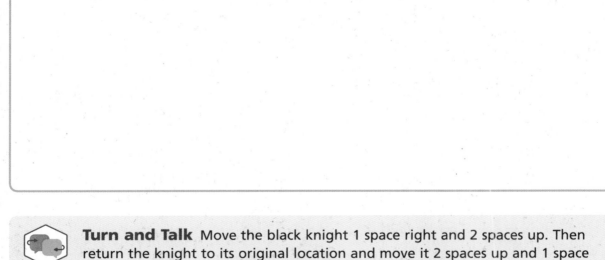

Turn and Talk Move the black knight 1 space right and 2 spaces up. Then return the knight to its original location and move it 2 spaces up and 1 space right. What do you notice? Is this always true? Explain.

© Houghton Mifflin Harcourt Publishing Company • Image Credit: ©JamesBrey/istock/Getty Images Plus/Getty Images

Build Understanding

The figure that results from a transformation, such as a translation, is called the **image**. The original figure is called the **preimage**.

> **Connect to Vocabulary**
>
> A **translation** is the movement of a figure along a straight line.

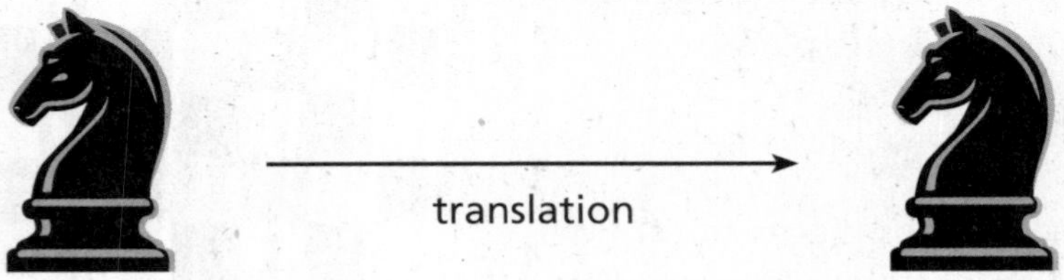

1 Aran says that if the pawn shown below is translated 2 inches right, the preimage and the image will have the same parallel line **segments** and will be the same height and width. Hiro says the parallel line segments will remain parallel but the height and width will not be the same. Who is correct?

A. Fill in the dimensions and angle measures. Are the dashed segments parallel? ________

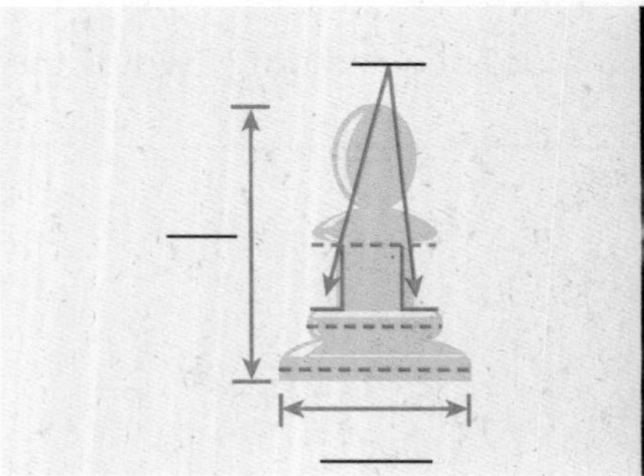

B. Trace the pawn. Translate your tracing 2 inches right. What is the relationship between the dimensions, angle measures, and parallel segments of the preimage and image?

____

____

____

C. Which student is correct? ______________________________

D. What translation must Aran perform on the image so that it returns to the exact location of the preimage?

____

> **Turn and Talk** Does the direction or distance a figure is translated affect the side lengths, relationships between sides, or angle measures of the figure? Explain.

© Houghton Mifflin Harcourt Publishing Company • **Image Credit:** ©Hero Images/Getty Images

Name ______________________________

Step It Out

ACTIVITY

2 Hiro draws a sketch of a game piece on a **coordinate plane**. Then he translates it 3 units right and 3 units up.

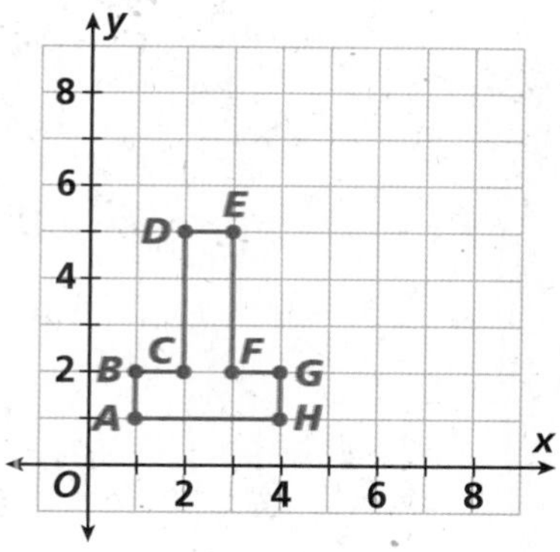

A. Draw the image of Figure *ABCDEFGH* on the coordinate plane after it is translated 3 units right and 3 units up.

B. Prime notation, adding apostrophes to each letter label, is used to label images. For instance, Point *A* in the preimage is labeled *A′* in the image and read as "A prime." Label the image you drew using prime notation.

C. Complete the table of ordered pairs.

Preimage	$A(1, 1)$	$B(1, 2)$	$C(2, 2)$					
Image	$A'(4, 4)$							

D. What do you notice about the relationship between the *x*- and *y*-values of each **vertex** of the preimage compared to the *x*- and *y*-values of each vertex of the image?

____

____

____

____

E. Translations in the coordinate plane can be described in mapping notation as $(x, y) \to (x \pm a, y \pm b)$ where *a* is the number of units the figure is translated horizontally and *b* is the number of units the figure is translated vertically. You read this notation as, "The ordered pair *x*, *y* is mapped to the ordered pair *x* plus or minus *a*, *y* plus or minus *b*."

Describe the translation of Figure *ABCDEFGH* using mapping notation.

$(x, y) \to (x + \_\_\_\_, y + \_\_\_\_)$

F. What do you notice about the size, shape, angle measures, and relationship between the sides in the preimage and image?

____

____

____

Turn and Talk If Figure *ABCDEFGH* is translated using the rule $(x, y) \to (x - 2, y - 4)$, how does the image of this translation compare to the image of the translation described in Task 2?

© Houghton Mifflin Harcourt Publishing Company

3 Triangle *DEF* is translated using the rule $(x, y) \rightarrow (x + 3, y - 4)$.

A. Use words to describe the distance and direction Triangle *DEF* is translated.

____

B. Draw the image. Label it using prime notation.

C. Complete the table.

Triangle *DEF*	Triangle *D′E′F′*
D(2, 5)	

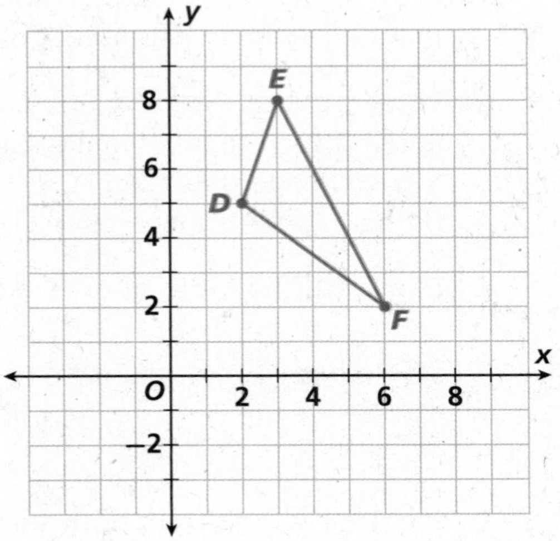

Check Understanding

1. The coordinates of a triangle's vertices are (2, 2), (4, 5), and (6, 1).

A. If the triangle is translated using the rule $(x, y) \rightarrow (x + 3, y - 5)$, by how many units and in what direction was the preimage translated?

____

B. What are the coordinates of the image's vertices?

____

C. Write a true statement about the relationship of the line segments and angle measures when a translation is applied to a preimage.

____

____

D. Will the line segment between (2, 2) and (4, 5) be parallel to its image?

____

2. The coordinates of the vertices of the preimage of a parallelogram are (1, 5), (3, 3), (3, 7), and (5, 5). The coordinates of the vertices of the image are (−5, 3), (−3, 1), (−3, 5), and (−1, 3). How far and in what direction was the parallelogram translated? Write your answer using mapping notation and practice reading your answer aloud.

____

© Houghton Mifflin Harcourt Publishing Company

Name ______________________

On Your Own

Solve Problems 3–5 using the graph of Buildings *A*, *B*, *C*, *D*, and *E*.

3. Shana translates Building *B* three units right and three units up. Draw the image of Building *B* in the new location.

4. (MP) **Model with Mathematics** Shana translates Building *C* to the location of Building *E*. Use mapping notation to describe the translation of Building *C*.

____

5. (MP) **Construct Arguments** The coordinates of the vertices of the image of Building *D* are (−7, 3), (−1, 3), (−1, −5), and (−7, −5). The coordinates of the vertices of the image of Building *A* are (1, 1), (3, 1), (3, 3), and (1, 3). Which of these is not a translation of the preimage? Explain by using the definition of a translation.

____

____

____

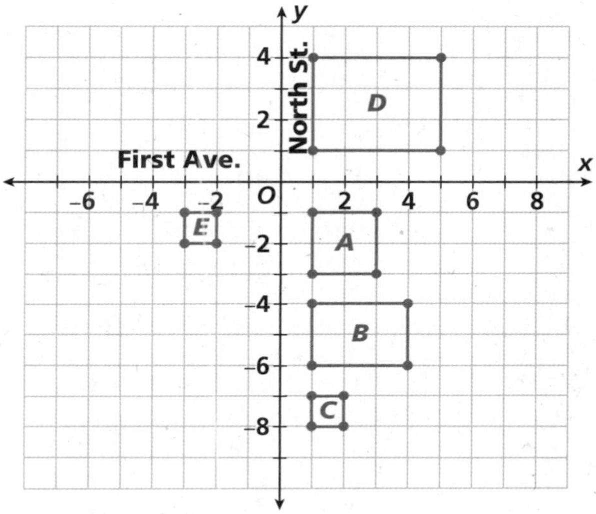

Use the triangles shown to answer Problems 6–7.

Triangle 2 is a translation of Triangle 1.

6. All the sides of Triangle 1 have a length of 3 inches. What is the length of each side of Triangle 2? ______________

7. All the angles of Triangle 1 have a measure of 60°. What is the measure of each angle of Triangle 2? ______________

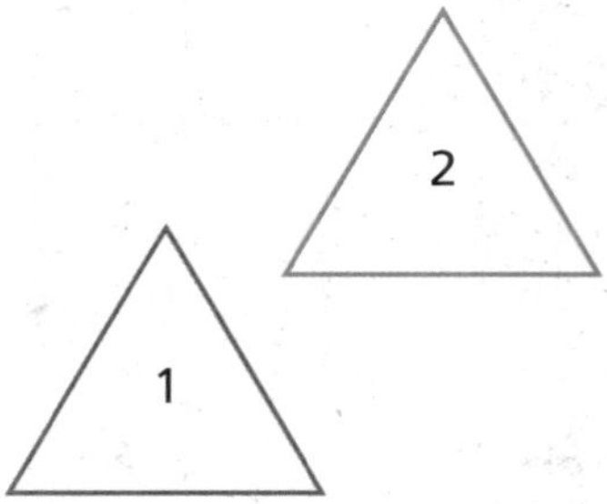

Use the description shown to answer Problems 8–9.

Square *P′Q′R′S′* is a translation of Square *PQRS*.

8. What is true about the angles of Square *PQRS* and Square *P′Q′R′S′*?

____

9. Opposite sides of Square *PQRS* are parallel and the same length. What is true about opposite sides of Square *P′Q′R′S′*?

____

© Houghton Mifflin Harcourt Publishing Company • Image Credit: ©JamesBrey/istock/Getty Images Plus/Getty Images

Solve Problems 10–13 using the graph of Houses *B*, *C*, *D*, and *E*.

10. (MP) **Attend to Precision** House *B* is translated using the rule $(x, y) \rightarrow (x - 3, y + 2)$. Draw House *B* in its new location.

11. (MP) **Model with Mathematics** The builder adds House *A* to her plan first with vertices at $(-1, 1)$, $(-5, 1)$, $(-5, 7)$, and $(-1, 7)$. Then she moves it so it has vertices at $(6, 2)$, $(2, 2)$, $(2, 8)$, and $(6, 8)$. Use mapping notation to describe how far and in what direction she translated the house.

____

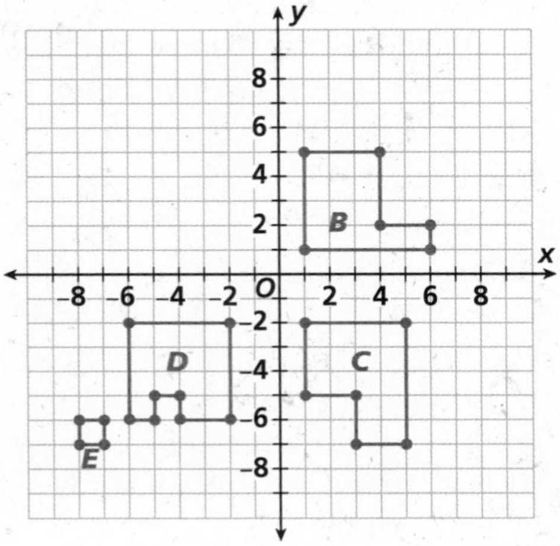

12. In its final location, House *C* has vertices at $(4, -2)$, $(4, -5)$, $(6, -5)$, $(6, -7)$, $(8, -7)$, and $(8, -2)$. In its final location, House *D* has vertices at $(-2, -2)$, $(-6, -2)$, $(-6, -6)$, $(-5, -6)$, $(-5, -5)$, $(-4, -5)$, $(-4, -6)$, and $(-2, -6)$. Which building represents a translation from its original placement? Explain.

____

____

____

13. Building *E* is a shed. It is translated 1 unit left and 2 units up. Draw Building *E* in its new location.

14. Explain whether Figure *B* is a translation of Figure *A* below.

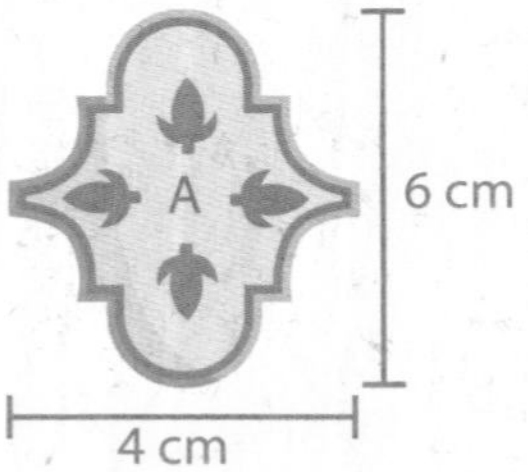

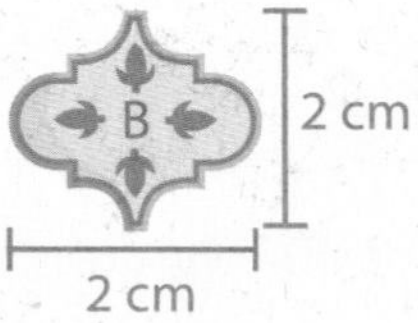

____

____

____

____

© Houghton Mifflin Harcourt Publishing Company • **Image Credit:** ©William Britten/iStock

I'm in a Learning Mindset!

How does my mindset affect my ability to successfully translate figures?

____

____

Name ______________________________

ONLINE
Video Tutorials and
Interactive Examples

Explore Translations

Use the graph to answer Problems 1–4.

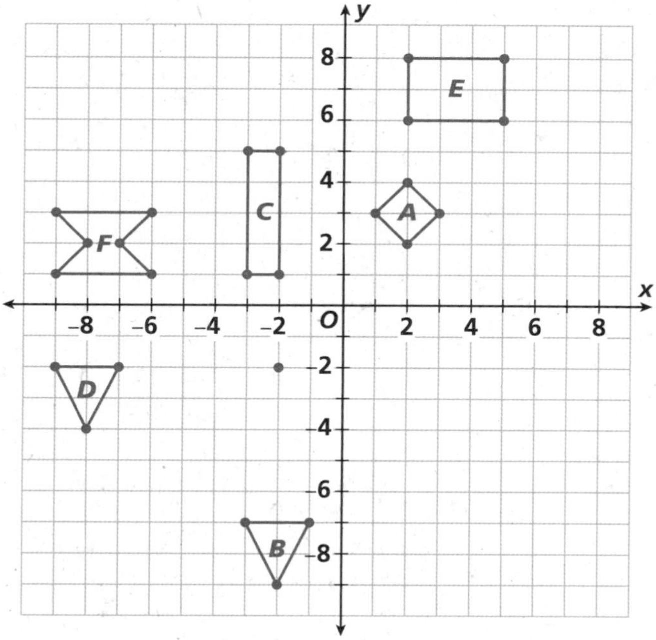

Elements in the pattern are translated.

1. Translate Figure *A* using the rule $(x, y) \rightarrow (x + 1, y - 4)$. Draw the image of Figure *A*. Practice reading the rule aloud.

2. (MP) **Model with Mathematics** How was Figure *B* translated to get Figure *D*? Write your answer using mapping notation.

____

3. (MP) **Construct Arguments** Why is Figure *E* not a translation of Figure *C*?

____

4. Figure *F* has vertices with coordinates at $(-6, 1)$, $(-9, 1)$, $(-8, 2)$, $(-9, 3)$, $(-6, 3)$, and $(-7, 2)$. If the figure is translated using the rule $(x, y) \rightarrow (x + 2, y + 5)$, what are the coordinates of the new vertices?

____

5. **Math on the Spot** Graph the translation of $\triangle XYZ$ 4 units right and 2 units down.

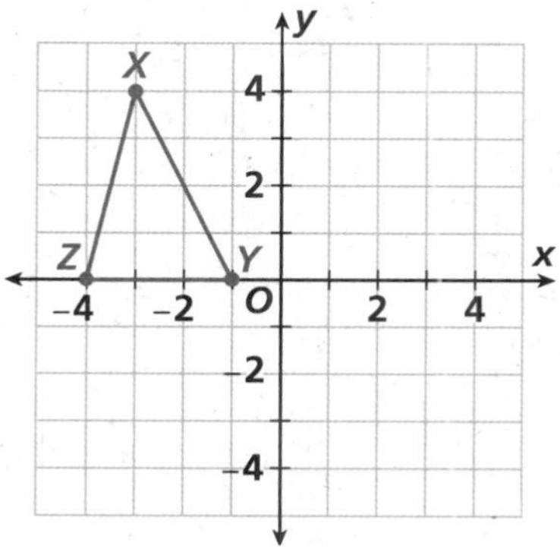

© Houghton Mifflin Harcourt Publishing Company • Image Credit: ©Corbis/Getty Images

Test Prep

6. Which figure is a translation of Figure *A*?

Ⓐ Figure 1

Ⓑ Figure 2

Ⓒ Figure 3

Ⓓ Figure 4

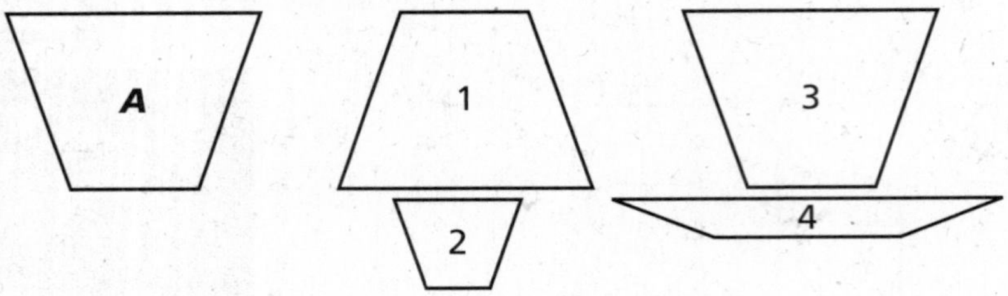

7. The coordinates of a triangle are given in the table. The triangle is translated using the rule $(x, y) \rightarrow (x - 3, y + 2)$. What are the coordinates of the image of the triangle?

Preimage coordinates	Image coordinates
(0, 1)	
(2, 3)	
(4, 2)	

8. A quadrilateral is translated 5 units right and 3 units down on a coordinate plane. Which expressions could be used to find one of the coordinates of the vertices of the image? Select all that are correct.

Ⓐ $x - 3$

Ⓑ $x - 5$

Ⓒ $x + 5$

Ⓓ $y - 3$

Ⓔ $y + 3$

Ⓕ $y + 5$

Spiral Review

9. What are the common factors of 6, 9, and 18?

10. Jovan is 15 years old. His sister is 6 years older than one-third his age. How old is Jovan's sister?

11. DeMarcus multiplies all the integers from −10 to −1 including −10 and −1. Should his answer be positive or negative? Explain your reasoning.

© Houghton Mifflin Harcourt Publishing Company

Name ______________________________

Explore Reflections

I Can reflect a figure over either axis in the coordinate plane and describe the reflection algebraically.

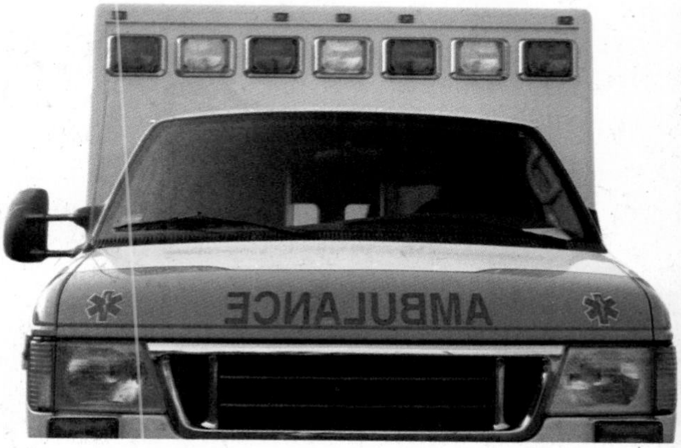

Spark Your Learning

The word "AMBULANCE" is often written backwards on the front of ambulances, so that it will appear forwards in the rear-view mirrors of cars.

Use tracing paper to trace the word as it is shown above. What can you do with your result to make the word readable?

What effect do your actions have on the order of the letters, and what effect do your actions have on the individual letters themselves?

Turn and Talk As you change the word "AMBULANCE" so that it is readable, which letters change their appearance and which do not? What is different about the letters that remain the same after the transition, as opposed to the letters that change?

© Houghton Mifflin Harcourt Publishing Company • Image Credit: ©zimmytws/Shutterstock

Build Understanding

1 How can you reflect a figure using tracing paper?

Draw the letter "N" on a piece of tracing paper, then fold the paper over the diagonal and trace the "N". Unfold the paper, and you should see the original "N" and its reflection:

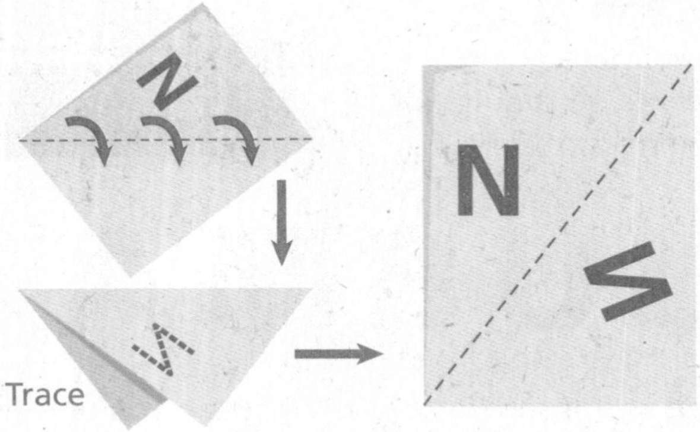

Connect to Vocabulary

A **reflection** is a transformation of a figure that flips the figure across a line, called the **line of reflection** so that each point on the preimage is the same distance from the line of reflection as the corresponding point on the image.

A. Find two line segments for the letter "N" that are parallel in the preimage. Are the corresponding segments in the image also parallel?

____

B. Use a ruler to measure the length of a line segment in the preimage. Then measure the length of the corresponding line segment in the image. What do you notice about the lengths of the two segments?

____

C. Use a protractor to measure an angle in the preimage and the **corresponding angle** in the image. What do you notice?

____

D. What can you conclude about the way reflecting a figure affects side length, angle measure, and parallel line segments?

____

____

E. Look again at the "N" and its image on the paper. Why do you think the word *reflection* is used to describe such an image?

____

____

Turn and Talk Two students perform a reflection of the same shape. One reflects over a vertical line. The other reflects over a horizontal line. How are their reflections the same? How are they different?

© Houghton Mifflin Harcourt Publishing Company

Name ______________________

Step It Out

2 How can you reflect a figure over the **x-axis** or **y-axis**?

A. Reflect the image shown over the *x*-axis. Remember to keep each point of the image the same distance from the *x*-axis as the corresponding preimage point. For instance, Point *C* is 12 units from the *x*-axis, so Point *C′* in the image must also be 12 units from the *x*-axis. Label the points using prime notation.

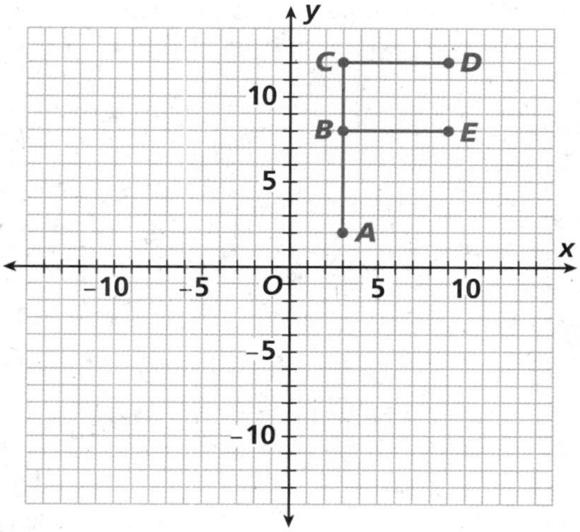

B. The preimage is upright. Is the image also upright, or has it changed?

____

C. Find the length of $\overline{AC}$ in the preimage (in units). What do you expect the length of $\overline{A'C'}$ to be? Find this length.

____

D. The original letter "F" faces to the right. Reflect the original image over the *y*-axis. Does the new image face the same direction? If not, how is it different? Label the points using double-prime notation (″).

____

E. What are the coordinates of the points on the images corresponding to the labeled points on the preimage? Complete the table.

Point	Preimage	Image after reflection over *x*-axis	Image after reflection over *y*-axis
A	(3, 2)	(3, −2)	
B	(3, 8)		
C	(3, 12)		(−3, 12)
D	(9, 12)	(9, −12)	
E	(9, 8)		

F. Look at your table. In general:

A point (*a*, *b*) reflected over the *x*-axis has the coordinates (☐ , ☐).

A point (*a*, *b*) reflected over the *y*-axis has the coordinates (☐ , ☐).

Turn and Talk On the grid, draw $\overline{DE}$ and $\overline{D'E'}$. Find the areas of Rectangle *BCDE* and Rectangle *B′C′D′E′*. What do you notice about these areas?

© Houghton Mifflin Harcourt Publishing Company

3 On a piece of graph paper, draw a **parallelogram** in the third **quadrant** of the coordinate plane with vertices at the points shown.

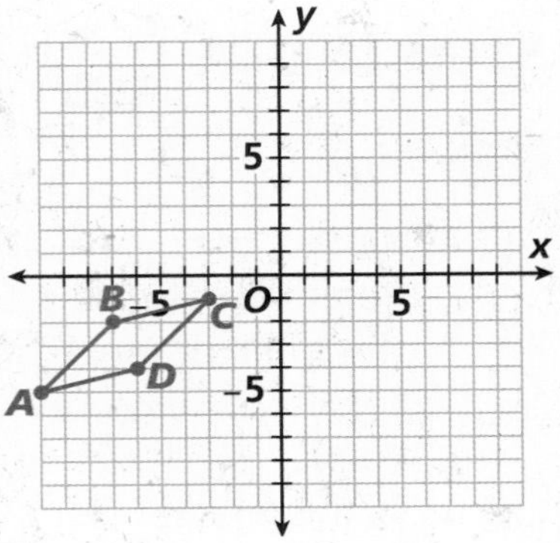

A. Reflect this preimage over the x-axis and describe the location of the image after reflection.

____

B. Reflect the preimage over the y-axis and describe the location of the image after reflection.

____

C. Fill in the table with the coordinates of the vertices of the images.

Point	Preimage	Image after reflection over x-axis	Image after reflection over y-axis
A	$(-10, -5)$		
B	$(-7, -2)$		
C	$(-3, -1)$		
D	$(-6, -4)$		
Any point	(a, b)		

Check Understanding

1. The coordinates of the vertices of a triangle are (2, 3), (5, 1), and (6, 4). After one reflection, the coordinates of the vertices of the triangle's image are (2, −3), (5, −1), and (6, −4). Over what line has the triangle been reflected?

____

2. The coordinates of the vertices of a square are (−10, −2), (−5, −2), (−5, −7), and (−10, −7). The square is reflected over the y–axis.

A. What are the coordinates of the vertices of the image?

____

B. Show that the image still has parallel sides and the same angles as the preimage: the image's sides are segments of the lines $y =$ ______, $y =$ ______, $x =$ ______, and $x =$ ______, which meet at ______ angles.

C. Does the image have the same side lengths as the preimage? Explain.

____

____

3. In your own words, describe the meaning of a reflection.

____

© Houghton Mifflin Harcourt Publishing Company

Name

On Your Own

Use the figures to answer Problems 4–7.

Figure *Y* is a reflection of Figure *X*.

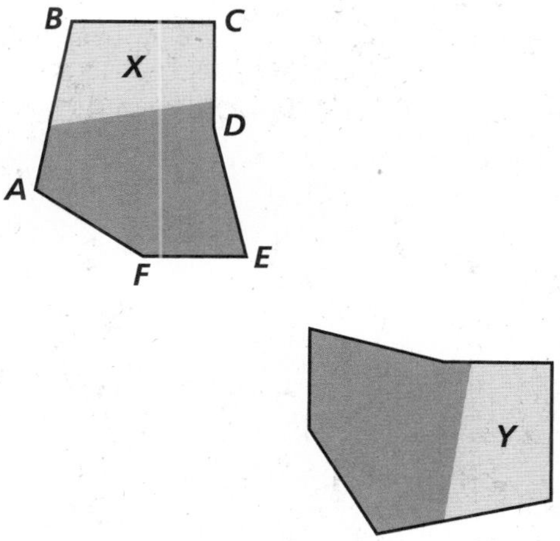

4. $\overline{AB}$ is 3 centimeters long. What is the length of the corresponding side of Figure *Y*? How do you know?

5. Angle *A* measures 115°. What is the measure of the corresponding angle in Figure *Y*?

6. $\overline{FE}$ is parallel to $\overline{BC}$. Are the corresponding sides in Figure *Y* also parallel?

7. Draw the line of reflection between Figures *X* and *Y*.

8. Draw a reflection of the preimage over the line shown.

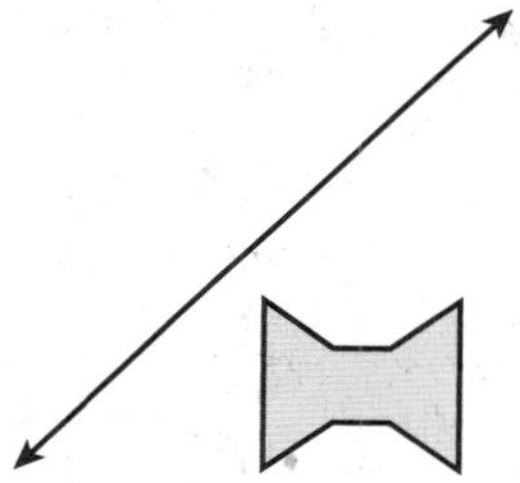

9. Marie is practicing her reflections on graph paper.

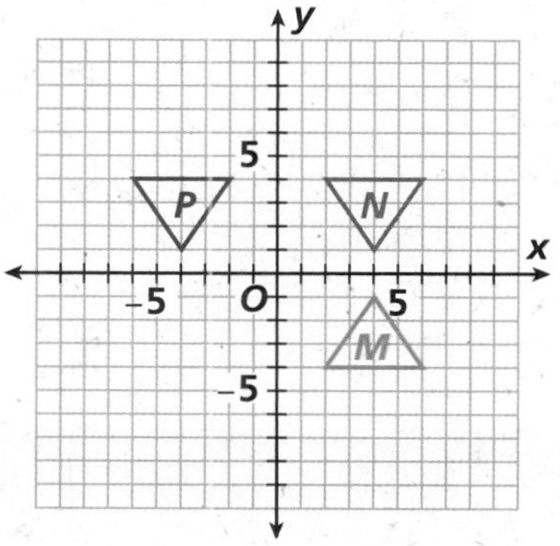

A. Is Figure *P* a reflection of Figure *N* over the *y*-axis?

B. Is Figure *P* a reflection of Figure *M* over the *y*-axis and then over the *x*-axis?

C. Is Figure *P* a reflection of Figure *M* over the *x*-axis and then over the *y*-axis?

© Houghton Mifflin Harcourt Publishing Company

10. Figure *ABCD* is a trapezoid in the second quadrant.

A. (MP) **Attend to Precision** On the given graph, draw the image of Figure *ABCD* reflected across the *y*-axis. What are the coordinates of the vertices of *ABCD* and *A′B′C′D′*?

ABCD	*A′B′C′D′*

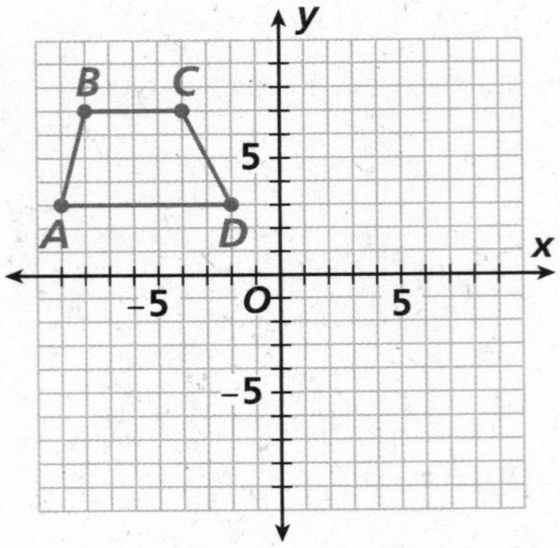

B. (MP) **Model with Mathematics** Given any point (*x*, *y*) on *ABCD*, what are the coordinates of the corresponding point on *A′B′C′D′*?

$(x, y) \rightarrow (\square, \square)$

C. Is *A′B′C′D′* facing the same direction as *ABCD*? Explain.

____

11. Draw a square with sides that are horizontal and vertical on a piece of paper.

A. If you reflect the square over a vertical line, does it look any different? If you reflect the square over a horizontal line, does it look any different?

____

B. In your original square, draw a right-angle mark in one corner. Reflect this square over a horizontal line. Does it look any different? If so, what is different?

____

C. If you reflect the square from Part B over a vertical line, does it look any different? If so, what is different?

____

I'm in a Learning Mindset!

How does my mindset affect my confidence with performing reflections?

____

____

© Houghton Mifflin Harcourt Publishing Company

ONLINE
Ed
Video Tutorials and
Interactive Examples

Name ______________________________

Explore Reflections

(MP) **Construct Arguments** **Use the tiger images to answer Problems 1–3.**

1. Could Tiger 2 be an image of Tiger 1 after one reflection? Explain.

____

____

____

____

2. Could Tiger 3 be an image of Tiger 1 after one reflection? Explain.

____

____

3. Could Tiger 4 be an image of Tiger 1 after one reflection? Explain.

____

____

4. The grid shows Figure R, a pair of arrows forming a right angle. On the grid, draw a reflection of R so that any point (a, b) on the preimage becomes $(-a, b)$ on the image, R'.

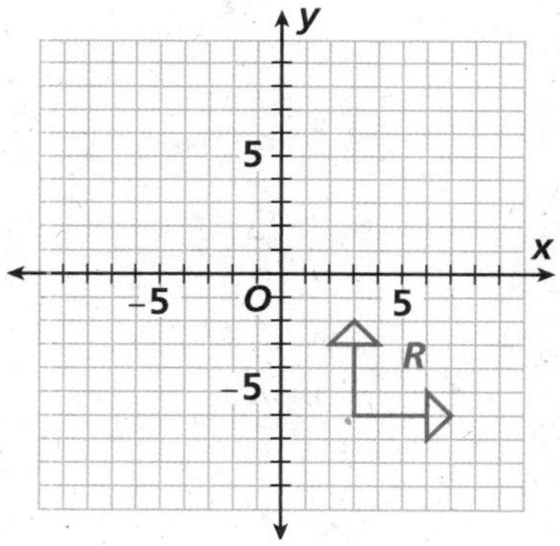

A. Over what line did you reflect R?

____

B. Both arrows in Figure R are 4 units long. How long are the arrows in Figure R'?

____

C. What are the coordinates of the tips of the arrows on R'?

____

D. On the same grid, reflect R' over the x-axis to arrive at Figure R''. In which quadrant is R''?

____

E. What are the coordinates of the point at which the arrows intersect in R''?

____

F. In which directions do the arrows point in Figure R''?

____

© Houghton Mifflin Harcourt Publishing Company

Test Prep

5. Select all the figures that could represent an image of the given figure after one reflection over a horizontal or vertical line through its center.

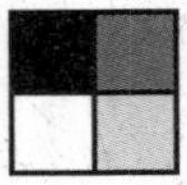

Ⓐ 

Ⓑ 

Ⓒ 

Ⓓ 

Ⓔ 

6. A triangle with vertices at (−6, 5), (−5, 1), and (−8, 2) is reflected over the *y*-axis. What are the coordinates of the vertices of the image?

Preimage coordinates	Image coordinates
(−6, 5)	
(−5, 1)	
(−8, 2)	

7. Which of the following is a rule that represents what happens to the coordinates of any point on a figure after it is reflected over the *x*-axis and then the *y*-axis?

Ⓐ $(x, y) \rightarrow (x, -y)$

Ⓑ $(x, y) \rightarrow (-x, y)$

Ⓒ $(x, y) \rightarrow (y, x)$

Ⓓ $(x, y) \rightarrow (-x, -y)$

Spiral Review

8. Can a graph of a horizontal line represent a proportional relationship? Explain why or why not.

____

____

____

9. A recipe calls for $2\frac{3}{4}$ cups of flour. Thomas is making $2\frac{1}{2}$ batches of the recipe. How many cups of flour does he need?

____

10. A diamond figure has vertices with coordinates at (−5, −4), (−3, −2), (−1, −4), and (−3, −6). If the figure is translated 3 units right and 8 units up, what are the coordinates of the vertices of the image?

____

© Houghton Mifflin Harcourt Publishing Company

Name ____________________

Explore Rotations

I Can **identify and perform rotations, and describe a rotation on a coordinate plane algebraically.**

Spark Your Learning

PAIRS

Use tracing paper to trace a copy of this recycling symbol.

Place the tip of your pencil in the center of the symbol and turn the paper about that point. You'll see that the original design reappears three times in every full turn.

In the space provided, sketch a design that reappears every quarter of a full turn. Trace the shape on tracing paper, then turn it to check your work.

© Houghton Mifflin Harcourt Publishing Company • Image Credits: (t) ©photka/Shutterstock; (tr) ©Olex Kmet/Shutterstock

Turn and Talk If the preimage and image of a figure look identical after being turned one-fourth turn clockwise or one-fourth turn counterclockwise, what must be true about the figure?

Build Understanding

ACTIVITY

1 Trace the hexagon and Points P, Q, and R on tracing paper.

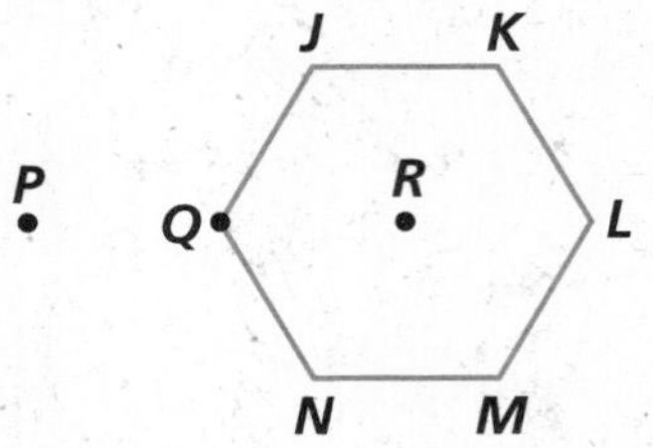

Connect to Vocabulary

A **rotation** is a transformation in which a figure is turned around a point. That point is called the **center of rotation**.

A. Use a ruler and protractor to complete the table.

Length of $\overline{JK}$	______ mm
Measure of $\angle JQN$	______ °

B. Place the tip of a pencil on Point R and rotate the hexagon 90° (one-fourth turn) clockwise about that point.

- What happens to the measure of $\angle JQN$?

  ____

- What happens to the length of $\overline{JK}$?

  ____

- Name a pair of parallel sides in the shape. What happens to the pair when the shape is rotated?

  ____

  ____

C. Move the center of rotation by placing the tip of your pencil on Point P. Rotate the shape about Point P. Describe the rotation. How is it different from the rotation in Part B?

____

____

____

D. Draw an arrow inside your hexagon that points to the top of the shape. When you rotate the shape 180° (one-half turn), what happens to the direction of the arrow in the image, and why?

____

____

Turn and Talk Can you make your hexagon change its shape using a rotation? Why or why not?

© Houghton Mifflin Harcourt Publishing Company

Name ______________________

Step It Out

2 You can rotate the letter "N" and get the letter "Z." Figure 2 was formed by rotating Figure 1 90° clockwise about the **origin**.

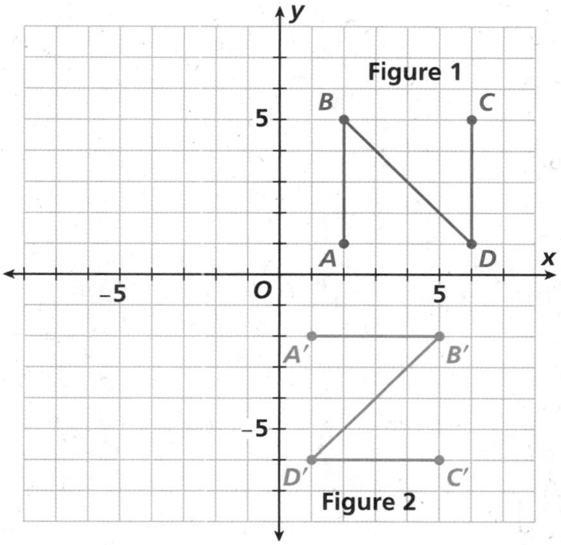

A. Use a ruler and protractor to measure the line segments and angles of both figures. What is the relationship between the side lengths and angle measures of the image and preimage?

____

B. In Figure 1, $\overline{AB}$ is parallel to $\overline{DC}$. What is the relationship between $\overline{A'B'}$ and $\overline{D'C'}$ in Figure 2?

____

C. Fill in the coordinates for each point.

Figure 1	$A(2, 1)$			
Figure 2	$A'(1, -2)$			

D. Look at the relationship between the coordinates of the vertices of Figure 1 and Figure 2. Write a rule to find the coordinates of the vertices of any figure rotated 90° clockwise about the origin.

$(x, y) \rightarrow (\square, \square)$

E. Rotate Figure 2 180° counterclockwise about the origin. Label the result as Figure 3. Then fill in the table.

Figure 2	$A'(1, -2)$	$B'(5, -2)$	$C'(5, -6)$	$D'(1, -6)$
Figure 3	$A''(-1, 2)$			

F. Write a rule that represents the change in coordinates of any figure rotated 180° counterclockwise about the origin.

$(x, y) \rightarrow (\square, \square)$

G. If you rotate the letter "W" 180° clockwise, what letter does it resemble?

____

Turn and Talk Identify which uppercase letters look the same after a 180° rotation.

© Houghton Mifflin Harcourt Publishing Company

3 Figure 1 is rotated to form Figure 2.

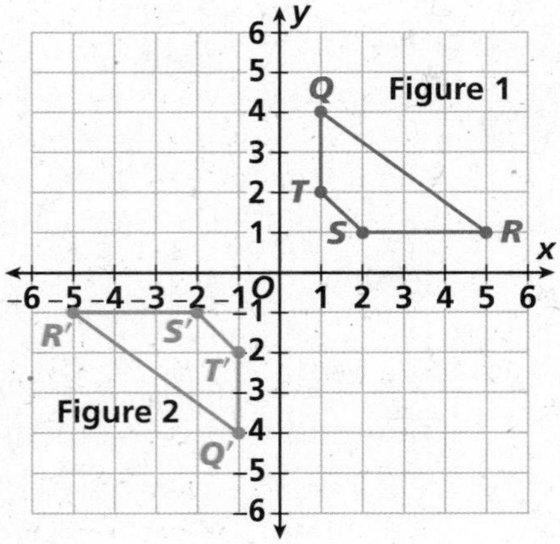

A. Describe the rotation.

____

B. Fill in the table of vertex coordinates.

Q(1, 4)			
Q′(−1, −4)			

C. Write a rule that represents the change in coordinates of any figure rotated 180° about the origin.

$(x, y) \rightarrow (\square, \square)$

4 **A.** $\triangle EFG$ has vertices (2, 4), (5, 1), and (1, 2). Graph the triangle and label it *Figure 1*.

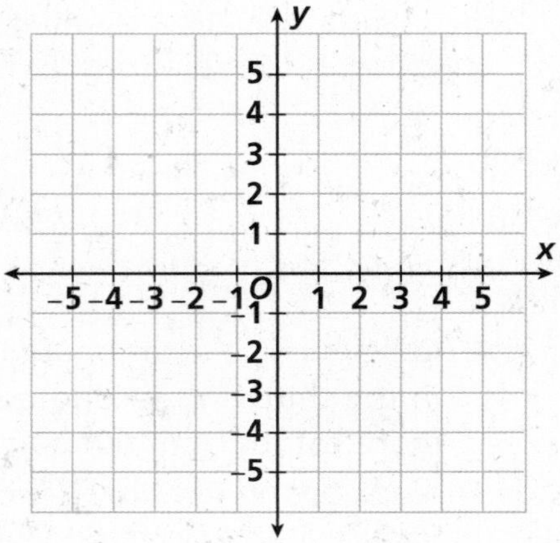

B. Rotate *Figure 1* by the rule $(x, y) \rightarrow (y, -x)$ and label the image *Figure 2*. Complete the sentence about the rotation:

To form Figure 2, Figure 1 underwent a rotation of 90° ________________ about the origin.

C. Rotate *Figure 1* by the rule $(x, y) \rightarrow (-y, x)$ and label the image *Figure 3*. Complete the sentence about the rotation:

To form Figure 3, Figure 1 underwent a rotation of __________ counterclockwise about the origin.

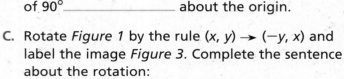

Check Understanding

1. Antoine and Bobby each rotated a pentagon about Point *P*, but they each got a different image. Which rotation is correct? Why?

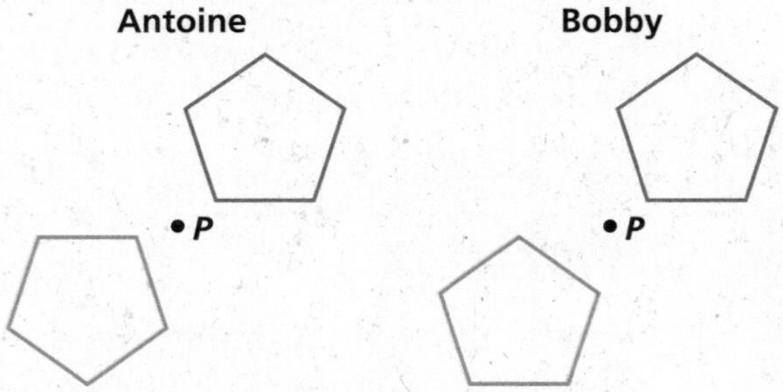

____

____

____

2. **A.** Draw rotations of Rectangle *STUV* 90°, 180°, and 270° clockwise about the origin.

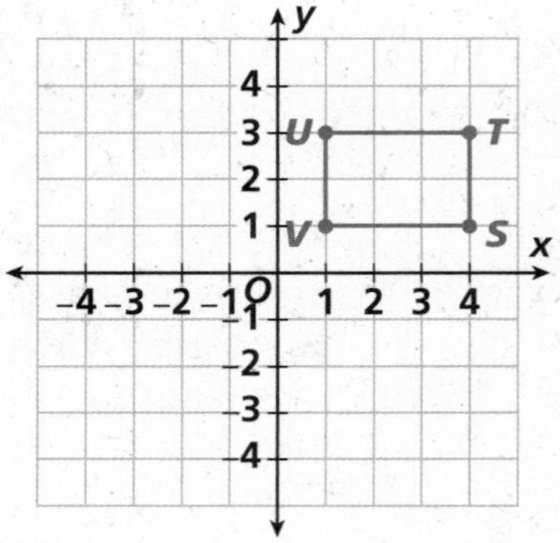

B. What do all four figures have in common? They all have ____________ side lengths and ____________ angle measures, and their ____________ sides are parallel.

© Houghton Mifflin Harcourt Publishing Company

Name ______

On Your Own

3. Victor rotated his initial, V, about Point *P*. What stayed the same between the preimage and image? What changed?

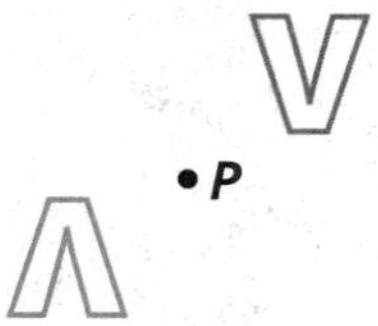

______

______

4. Sketch a rotation of the Figure *WXYZ*. Use Point *W* as the center of rotation.

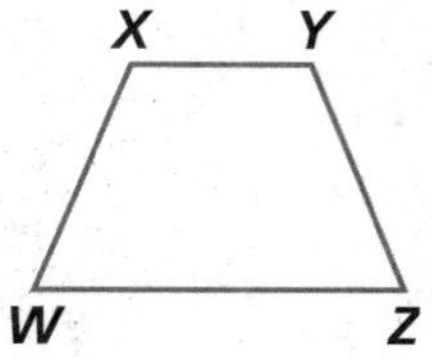

A. What is the same about the two images?

______

______

B. What is different about the two images?

______

5. Elias graphed the movement of one quarter-turn of a ceiling fan.

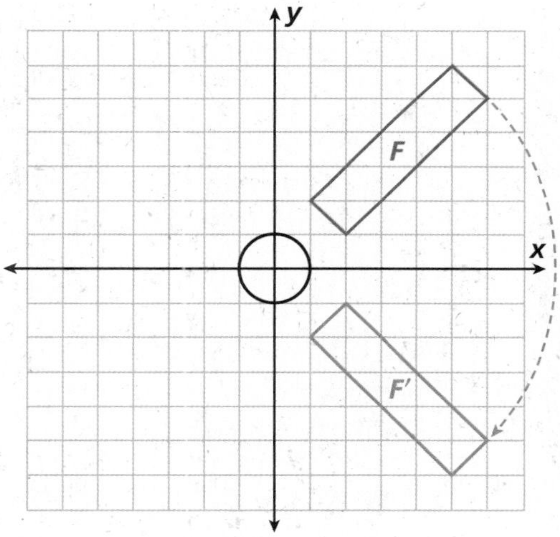

A. Continue the rotation and draw the fan blade in the third and second quadrants after two more rotations of 90° each.

B. Describe the rotation of the fan blade from *F* to *F*′.

______

______

C. (MP) **Model with Mathematics** Describe the rotation from *F* to *F*′ in mapping notation.

______

6. (MP) **Attend to Precision** Rotate each figure 180° about the origin.

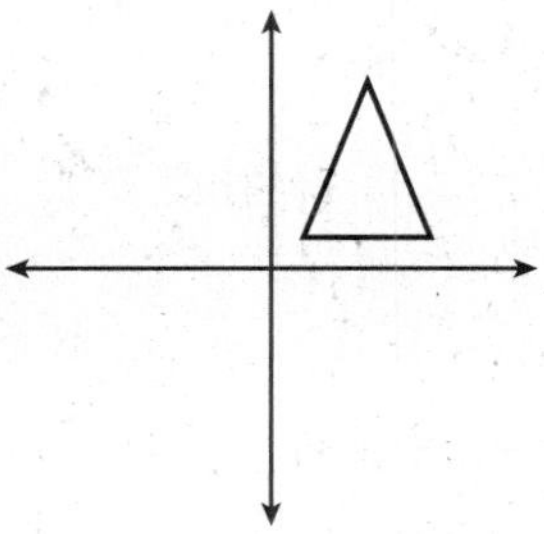
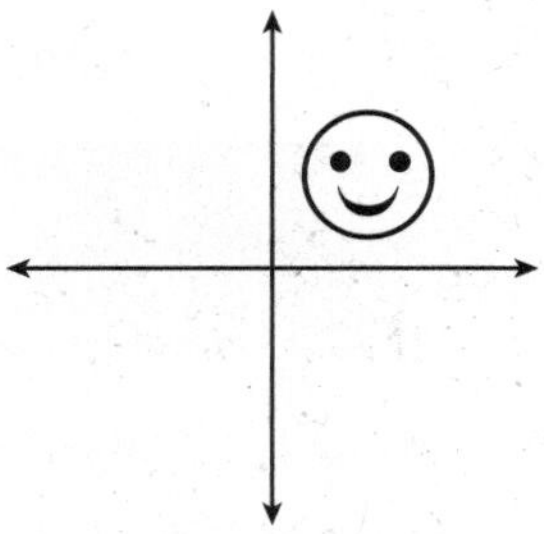
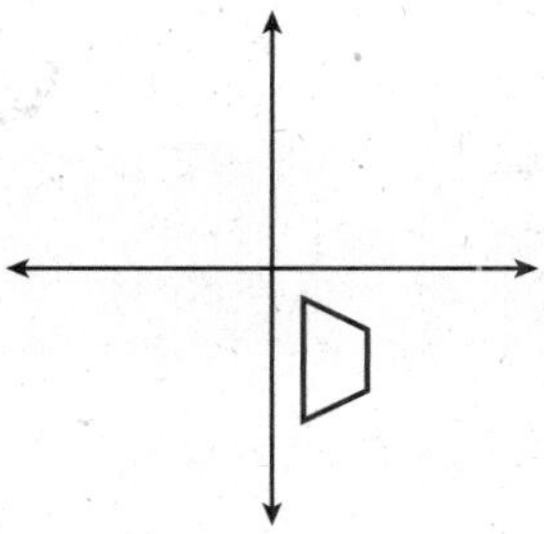
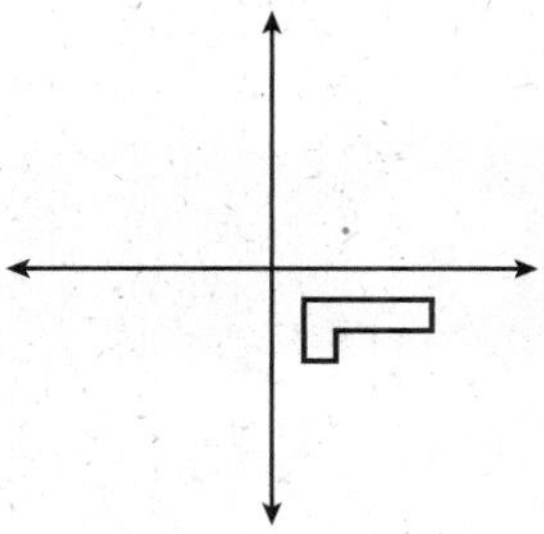

© Houghton Mifflin Harcourt Publishing Company • Image Credit: ©Prasanth.s/Shutterstock

7. Describe the transformation of Figure 1 to Figure 2 using mapping notation.

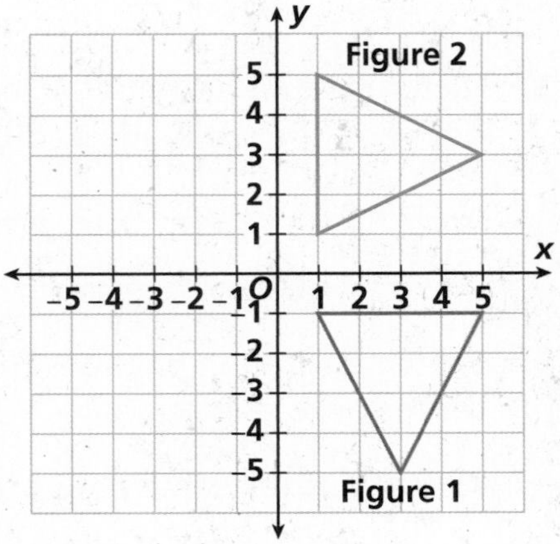

8. $\triangle JKL$ has an area of 3.25 square units. What happens to its area when it is rotated 180° about Point J?

9. The vertices of the preimage of a triangle are (−2, 1), (−5, 2), and (−3, 6). The triangle is rotated and its image has vertices at (1, 2), (2, 5), and (6, 3).

   A. Describe the rotation that resulted in the image.

   B. If the image is then rotated 90° clockwise, what are the coordinates of the new image?

10. MP **Attend to Precision** Rotate the shape by the rule $(x, y) \rightarrow (y, -x)$. Then rotate the new image according to the rule $(x, y) \rightarrow (-x, -y)$.

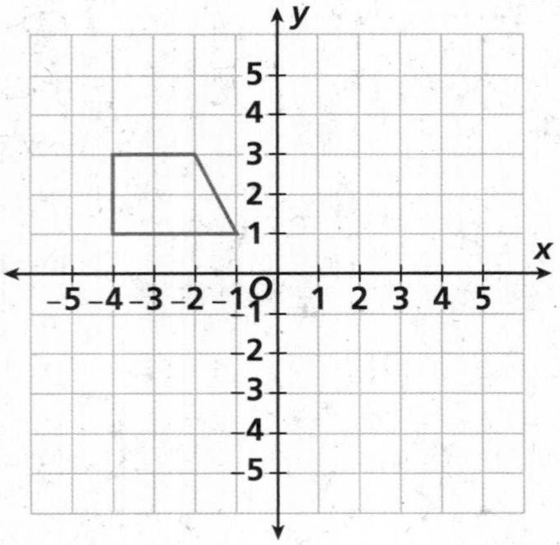

© Houghton Mifflin Harcourt Publishing Company

I'm in a Learning Mindset!

Do I have a fixed-mindset voice or growth-mindset voice in my head when I'm working with rotations? How can I tap into my growth-mindset voice?

ONLINE
Video Tutorials and
Interactive Examples

Name ______________________________

Explore Rotations

1. Which shape shows a rotation of the shaded figure following the rule $(x, y) \rightarrow (-x, -y)$?

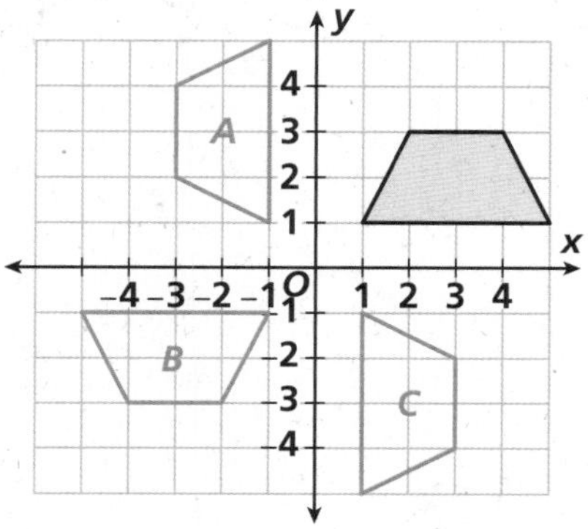

____

Windmill blades are a good example of rotation.

2. Sarika uses rotations to make designs. What characteristics of the design indicate it is a rotation?

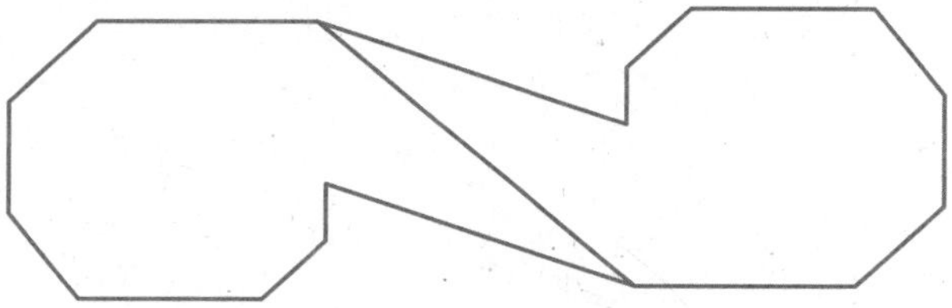

____

____

3. A triangle has vertices at (−3, 4), (−1, 0), and (−4, 0). What are the coordinates of the vertices after it is rotated 180° about the origin?

____

4. **A.** Graph Rectangle *ABCD* with vertices at *A*(1, 5), *B*(3, 6), *C*(5, 2), and *D*(3, 1). Then draw a rotation of the rectangle 90° counterclockwise about the origin and list the coordinates of the vertices of the result.

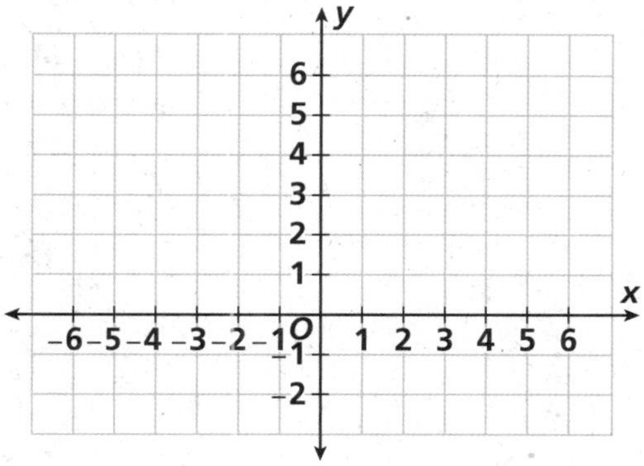

____

B. (MP) **Model with Mathematics** Describe the rotation in mapping notation.

____

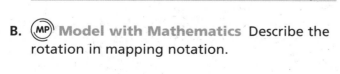

© Houghton Mifflin Harcourt Publishing Company • Image Credit: ©Slavko Slavcic/Fotolia

Test Prep

5. Draw a rotation of the parallelogram 90° counterclockwise about the origin.

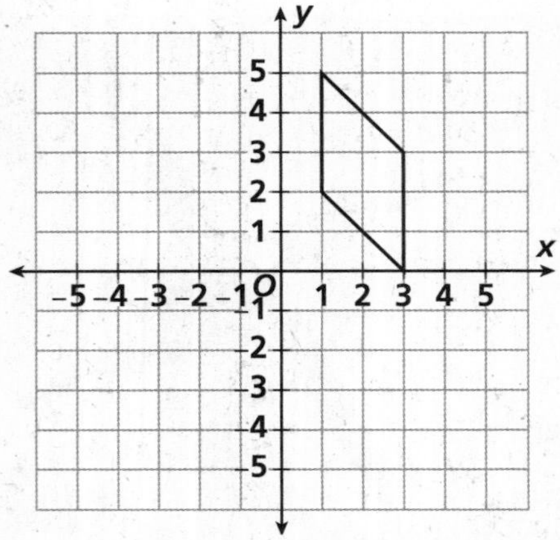

6. What rotation of $\triangle MNP$ about Point P could have produced $\triangle PQR$?

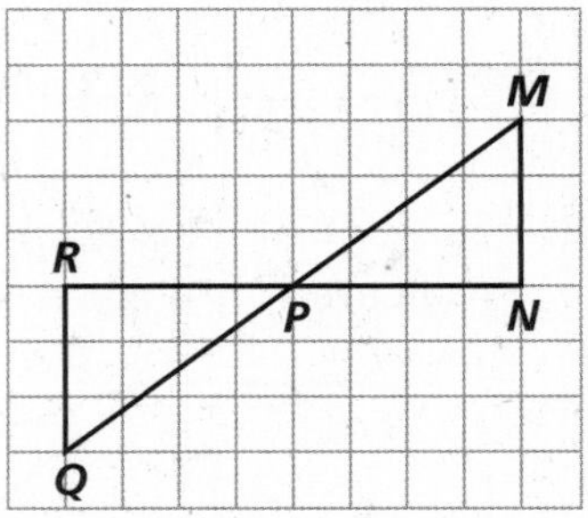

Ⓐ 90° clockwise

Ⓑ 180° clockwise

Ⓒ 270° counterclockwise

Ⓓ 360° counterclockwise

7. A pentagon has vertices at (−1, −1), (−5, −2), (−6, −4), (−4, −7), and (−2, −3). If the pentagon is rotated 180° clockwise about the origin, what are the coordinates of the vertices of the image?

____

Spiral Review

8. A figure has two pairs of parallel sides and four right angles. The figure is translated 4 units down. How many parallel sides does the image have?

____

9. Which figure is a reflection of Figure A?

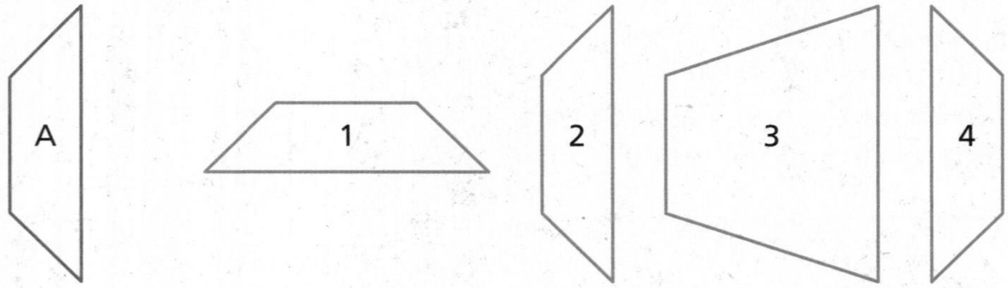

____

© Houghton Mifflin Harcourt Publishing Company

Name

Understand and Recognize Congruent Figures

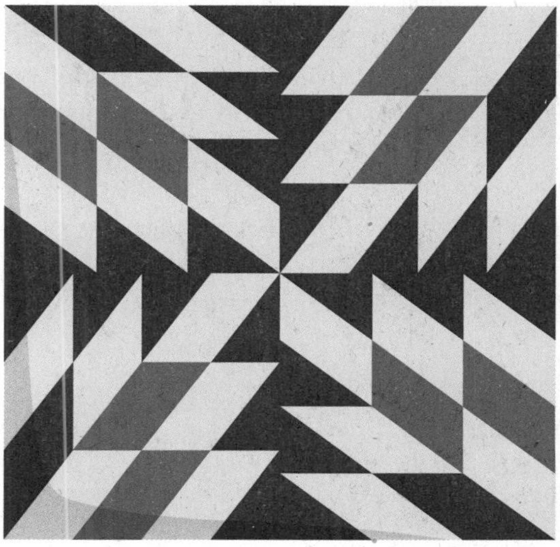

I Can determine congruence by performing or describing a sequence of transformations that maps one figure onto another.

Spark Your Learning

PAIRS

Maribel wants to make a quilt like this one. She has quilt pieces that are triangles and quilt pieces that are parallelograms. Describe ways she can transform the shapes to match the pattern in the quilt.

Turn and Talk Design a second quilt using parallelograms and triangles. Exchange your design with a partner and have him or her describe the transformations you used to design your quilt.

© Houghton Mifflin Harcourt Publishing Company

Build Understanding

1 Maribel needs to cut shapes out of fabric to prepare for a different quilt. Trace Figure 1 on a piece of paper and cut it out. Lay your cut-out on top of Figure 1 to make sure it is the same size and shape.

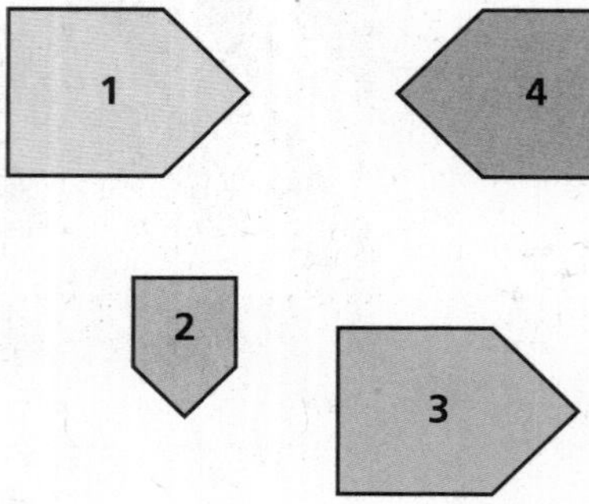

A. Experiment with transformations to move the cut-out shape on top of Figure 2. What transformations did you use? Explain how the figures are the same and how they are different.

____

____

____

B. Experiment with transformations to move the cut-out shape over Figures 3 and 4. What transformations did you use?

____

____

C. What do you notice when you compare Figure 1 to Figures 3 and 4?

____

____

D. A figure is congruent to another if and only if a series of rotations, reflections, and translations can map one onto the other. Which figures are congruent?

____

Connect to Vocabulary

Congruent figures are the same size and shape.

Turn and Talk Is there a series of rotations, reflections, or translations you can perform on Figure 2 to produce Figure 1, 3, or 4? Explain.

© Houghton Mifflin Harcourt Publishing Company • **Image Credit:** ©Lev Dolfachov/Alamy Stock Photo

Name ______________________________

Step It Out

2 While preparing fabric for quilting, Maribel lays a grid over her fabric. She wants to cut out five congruent triangles. She draws the triangles on the coordinate grid below.

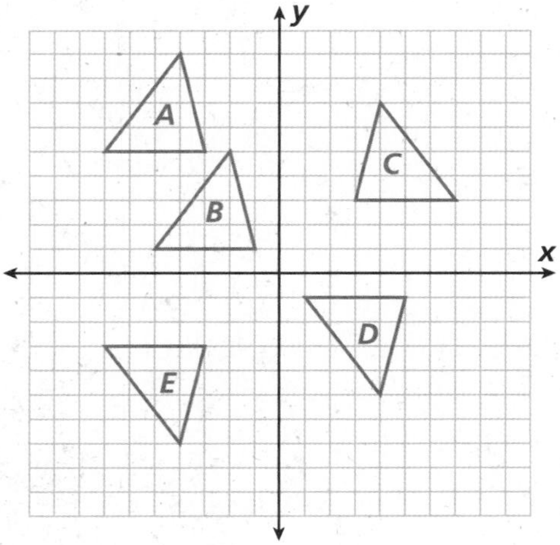

A. Triangle A is translated 2 units down and then reflected across the y-axis. Which triangle is the image of this sequence of transformations?

____

B. Are the two triangles congruent? Explain how you know.

____

____

____

C. Which two transformations can you perform on Triangle B to show that it is congruent to Triangle D?

____

____

D. Record the vertices of Triangle A and Triangle B. Use mapping notation to show how the vertices of Triangle A changed, and read the mapping notation aloud to another student. Explain how you know the shapes are congruent.

Triangle $A \rightarrow$ Triangle B

$(x, y) \rightarrow (x + \_\_\_\_, y - \_\_\_\_)$

____

____

____

© Houghton Mifflin Harcourt Publishing Company • Image Credit: ©Ailime/E+/Getty Images

3 Maribel wants to cut a new shape. She will reflect Figure *A* across the *x*-axis and translate the image 5 units left. She claims that the order in which she performs the transformations matters. Is she correct?

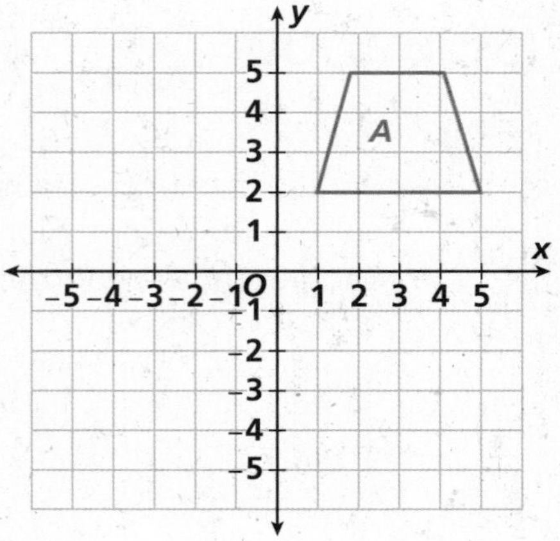

A. Reflect Figure *A* across the *x*-axis and then translate the figure 5 units left. Draw the final image.

Reverse the order of the transformations and draw the image again. How did the order you performed the transformations change the final image?

B. The vertices of Figure *B* have coordinates shown in the table. Figure *B* is rotated 90° clockwise about the origin, then reflected across the *x*-axis to form Figure *C*. Figure *B* is also reflected across the *x*-axis, and then rotated 90° clockwise about the origin to form Figure *D*. Complete the table.

Figure *B*	(0, 0)	(0, −3)	(2, −3)	(1, −1)	(2, 0)
Figure *C*		(−3, 0)			
Figure *D*		(3, 0)			

C. How did the order you performed the transformations on the figure change the final images, Figures *C* and *D*?

Check Understanding

Use the figures to answer Problems 1–2.

1. Which of these figures are not congruent to Figure 1? Why?

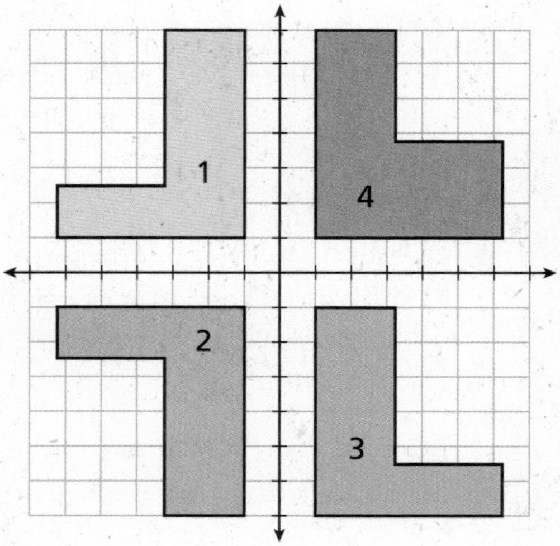

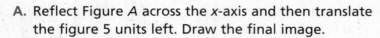

2. A. What sequence of transformations can you perform on Figure 1 to produce Figure 3?

B. Use mapping notation to describe this sequence of transformations.

© Houghton Mifflin Harcourt Publishing Company

Name

On Your Own

3. Can a square ever be congruent to a pentagon? Explain.

Use the graph to answer Problems 4–10.

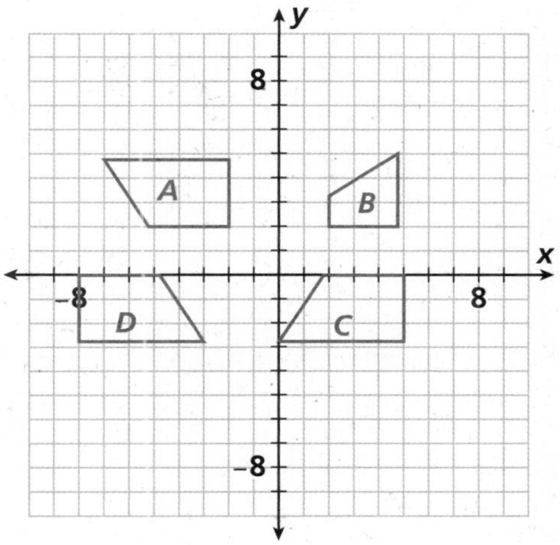

4. Open Ended What sequence of transformations can you perform on Figure *C* to produce Figure *A*?

5. Figure *D* is translated 3 units right and reflected across the *y*-axis. Which figure will this sequence of transformations produce?

6. Which figures are congruent to Figure *A*? How do you know?

7. Figure *B* is translated 3 units up and then reflected across the *y*-axis to form Figure *E*. Draw Figure *E* on the coordinate grid.

8. (MP) **Critique Reasoning** Nathan claims Figure *B* is congruent to Figure *A*. Is he correct? Explain.

9. Without performing a transformation on Figure *A*, how can you use tools to be sure it is congruent to Figure *D*?

10. Without performing a transformation on Figure *A*, how can you use tools to be sure that it is not congruent to Figure *B*?

© Houghton Mifflin Harcourt Publishing Company

Use the figures to answer Problems 11–13.

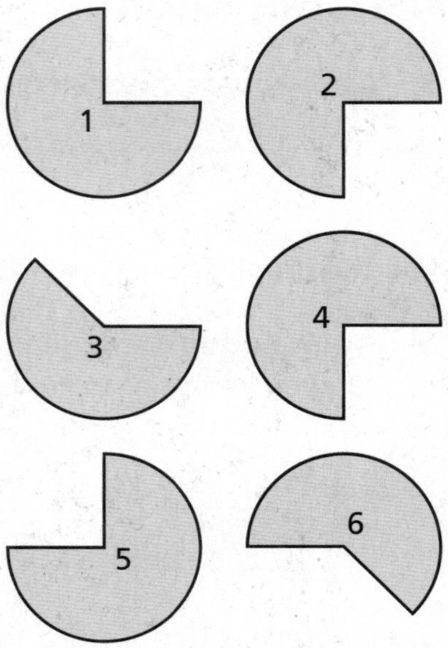

11. Which figures are congruent to Figure 1? Which are not congruent to Figure 1?

12. What sequence of transformations can be performed on Figure 4 to produce Figure 1?

13. Kailee reflected Figure 5 across a vertical line and then translated it up. Which figure is the result?

Use the graph to answer Problems 14–17.

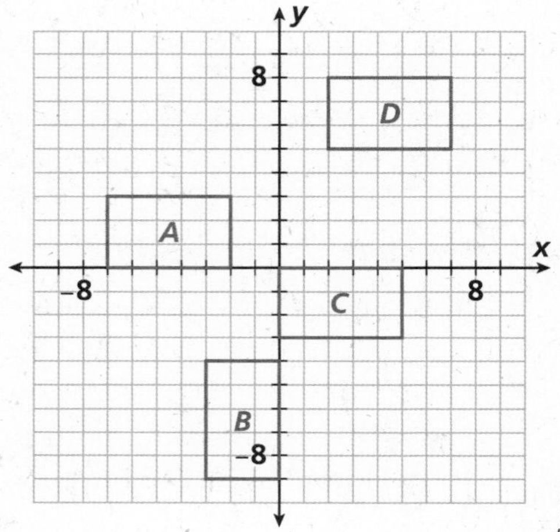

14. Henrietta claims that Figure *B* can be transformed into Figure *A* by translating it 2 units right and rotating it 90° clockwise about the origin. Is she correct? If not, find and correct her error.

15. Figure *C* is rotated 90° clockwise about the origin and translated 4 units down. Which figure will this sequence of transformations produce?

16. How can you prove that Figure *A* is congruent to Figure *C*?

17. Figure *B* is translated 5 units left and then reflected across the *x*-axis to form Figure *E*. Draw Figure *E* on the coordinate grid.

© Houghton Mifflin Harcourt Publishing Company

I'm in a Learning Mindset!

How did I support the strategy I used to identify congruent figures?

Name

ONLINE
Video Tutorials and
Interactive Examples

Understand and Recognize Congruent Figures

Use the kites shown to answer Problems 1–3.

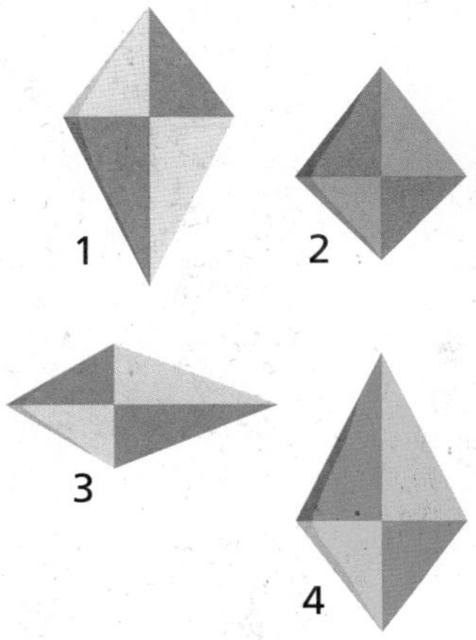

1. Draw a figure that is congruent to Figure 3. How can you prove that your figure is congruent using tracing paper?

2. Mirai transforms Figure 1 into Figure 4. What sequence of transformations did Mirai perform?

3. (MP) **Reason** Can you perform a series of transformations on Figure 1 to form Figure 2? Explain.

Use the graph to answer Problems 4–7.

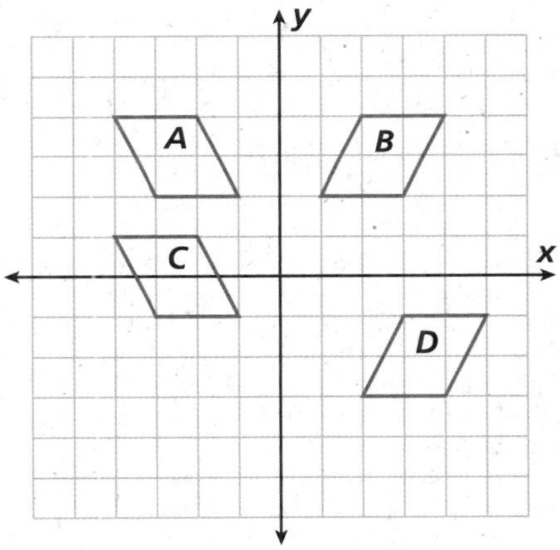

4. **A.** Figure *B* is reflected across the *x*-axis and translated 2 units left to form Figure *E*. Draw Figure *E*.

B. Ricardo translates Figure *B* 2 units left and then reflects it across the *x*-axis. What is the same about Ricardo's drawing and your Figure *E*, and what is different?

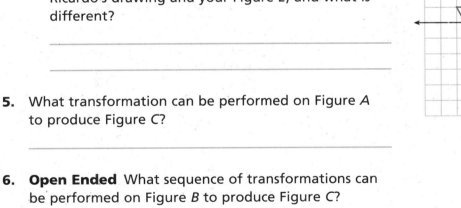

5. What transformation can be performed on Figure *A* to produce Figure *C*?

6. **Open Ended** What sequence of transformations can be performed on Figure *B* to produce Figure *C*?

7. Is Figure *A* congruent to Figure *D*? Explain.

© Houghton Mifflin Harcourt Publishing Company

Test Prep

8. Select all figures that are congruent.

Ⓐ Ⓑ Ⓒ Ⓓ Ⓔ

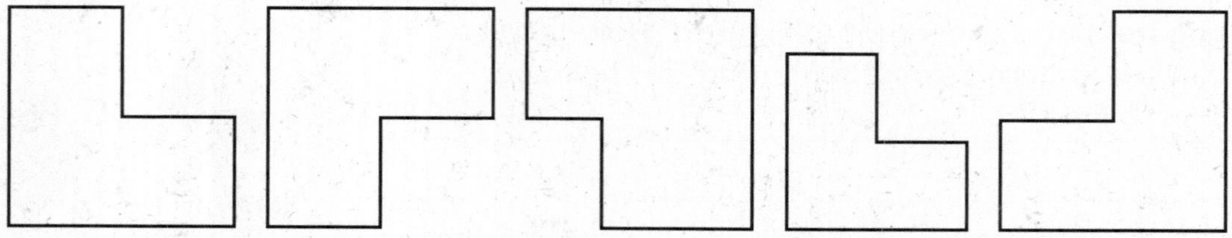

9. Figure *A* and its transformation Figure *B* are shown.

What transformations can be performed on Figure *A* to produce Figure *B*?

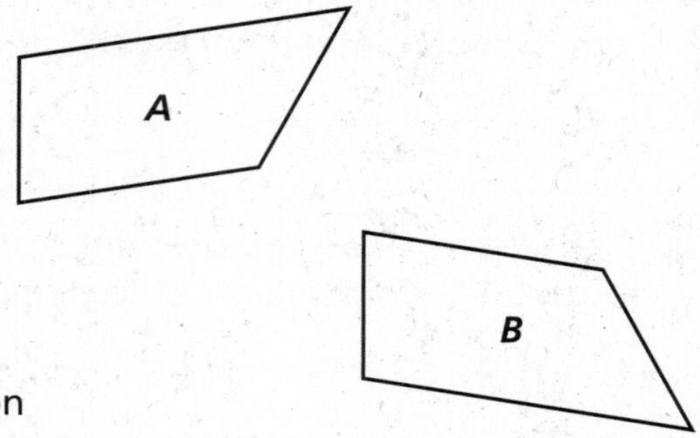

Ⓐ reflection across a vertical line followed by a translation to the right

Ⓑ reflection across a vertical line followed by a translation to the left

Ⓒ translation to the right followed by a reflection across a horizontal line

Ⓓ translation down followed by a reflection across a horizontal line

10. Triangle *ABC* is translated 2 units right and then reflected across the *y*-axis. Draw the image.

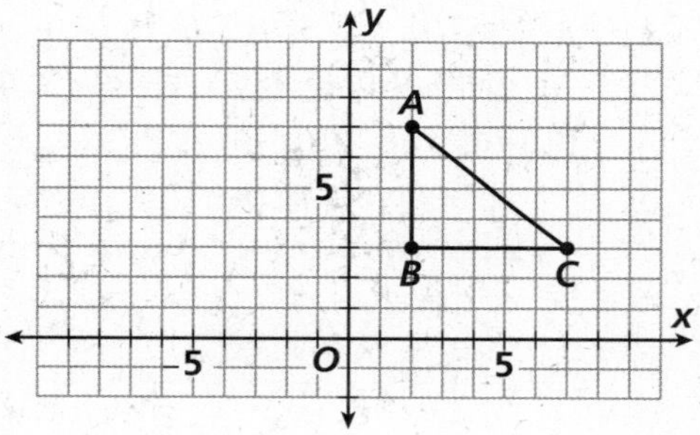

Spiral Review

11. Jose draws a triangle with vertices (4, 7), (4, 3), and (9, 3). He reflects the triangle across the *x*-axis. What are the vertices of the new image?

____

12. Figure *A* is translated 2 units right and 4 units up. Use mapping notation to write a rule for this translation.

____

13. The average cost of a gallon of gas in January 2014 was $3.42 and was $2.36 in December 2014. What was the percent change in the average cost of a gallon of gas in 2014? Round to the nearest percent.

____

© Houghton Mifflin Harcourt Publishing Company

Module

1 Review

Name ______________________________

Vocabulary

For Problems 1–5, choose the correct term from the vocabulary box.

1. A(n) ______________ is a transformation that slides a figure.

2. A(n) ______________ is a transformation that flips a figure across a line.

3. A(n) ______________ is a transformation that turns a figure about a point.

4. A(n) ______________ is the original figure in a transformation.

5. A(n) ______________ is the resulting figure in a transformation.

Vocabulary
image
reflection
rotation
translation
preimage

Concepts and Skills

6. Figure *ABCD* and its image, Figure *FGHJ*, are shown. Which transformation of Figure *ABCD* produced Figure *FGHJ*?

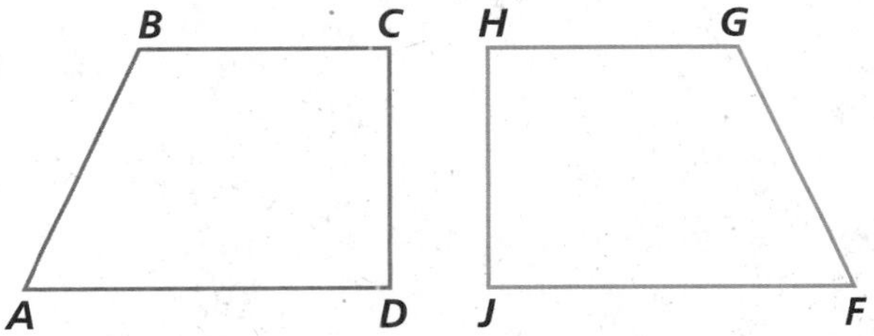

Ⓐ vertical translation

Ⓑ horizontal translation

Ⓒ reflection across a vertical line

Ⓓ reflection across a horizontal line

7. MP **Use Tools** Describe a sequence of transformations you could use to show that Triangle *DEF* is congruent to Triangle *JKL*. State what strategy and tool you will use to answer the question, explain your choice, and then find the answer.

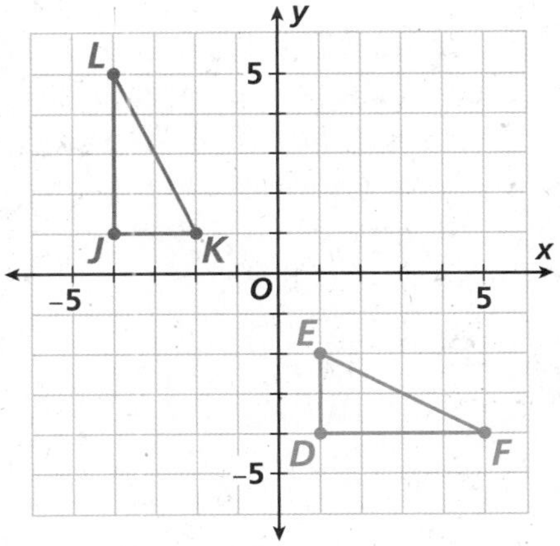

____

____

____

____

____

8. Triangle *PQR* has vertices *P*(2, −4), *Q*(4, −5), and *R*(7, −2). Triangle *PQR* is translated 6 units left and 3 units up to produce Triangle *P′Q′R′*. Complete the table.

Vertex	*x*-coordinate	*y*-coordinate
P′		
Q′		
R′		

© Houghton Mifflin Harcourt Publishing Company

For Problems 9–10, draw the image of each transformation.

9. Rotate Triangle RST 180° about the origin.

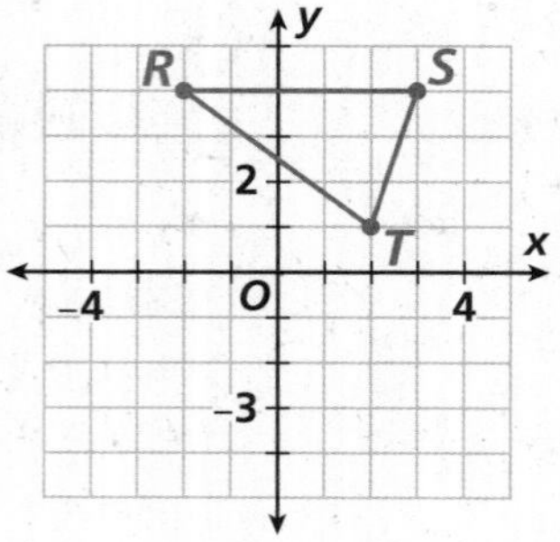

10. Translate Quadrilateral $WXYZ$ 5 units right and 2 units down.

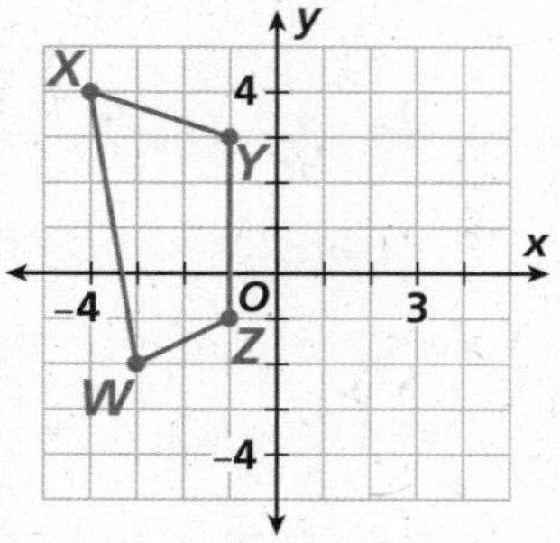

11. Side KN of Figure $KLMN$ is parallel to Side LM. Figure $KLMN$ is rotated 90° clockwise about Point P to produce Figure $RSTU$. Based on this information, select all statements that are true.

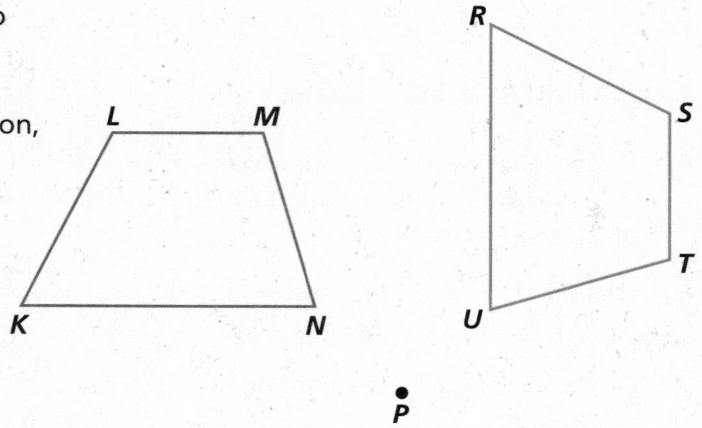

Ⓐ $\overline{ST}$ is parallel to $\overline{RU}$.

Ⓑ $\angle R$ has the same measure as $\angle N$.

Ⓒ $\overline{RS}$ is the same length as $\overline{MN}$.

Ⓓ Figure $RSTU$ is congruent to Figure $KLMN$.

Ⓔ $\angle T$ has the same measure as $\angle M$.

12. An artist is designing a logo for a new company by reflecting Triangle ABC across a vertical line and then translating it up and to the right to produce Triangle DEF. Find each measure.

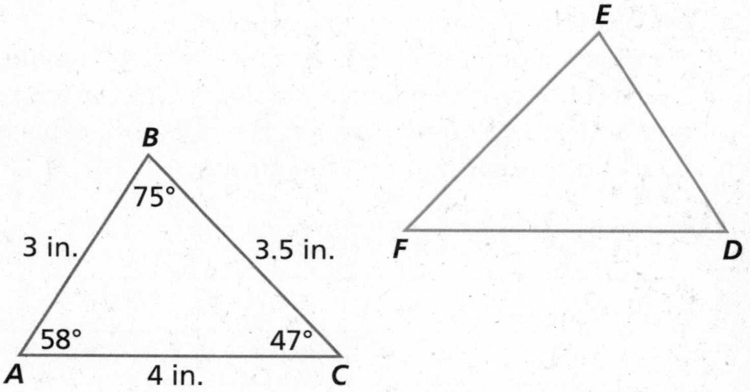

measure of $\angle D$: ________°

length of $\overline{EF}$: ________ in.

length of $\overline{DF}$: ________ in.

13. The point (a, b) is reflected across the x-axis and then translated 4 units to the right. What are the coordinates of the image of the point?

Ⓐ $(-a, b + 4)$

Ⓑ $(-a + 4, b)$

Ⓒ $(a, -b + 4)$

Ⓓ $(a + 4, -b)$

14. How many types of transformations did you study in this module? Name and define each of them.

____

____

© Houghton Mifflin Harcourt Publishing Company

Module

2 Draw and Analyze Two-Dimensional Figures

MOUSETRAP ON THE COORDINATE PLANE!

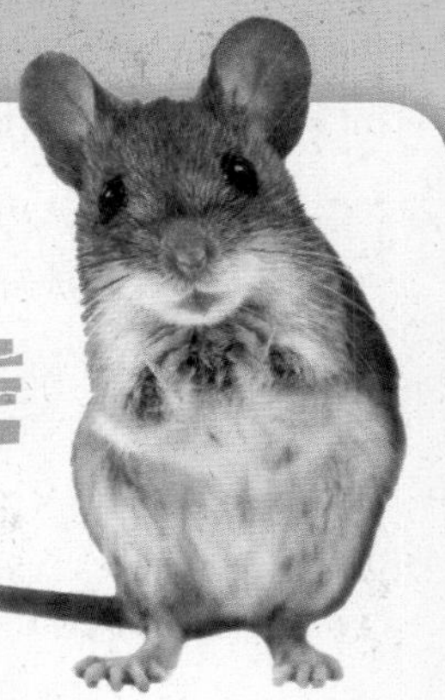

There is a mouse on the coordinate plane shown here. The mouse is at a location that has integer coordinates.

To find the mouse, first graph the following polygons.

A. Triangle *ABC* with vertices $A(-7, 7)$, $B(3, 7)$, and $C(-2, 2)$

B. Parallelogram *EFGH* with vertices $E(-3, 5)$, $F(6, 5)$, and $G(3, 1)$. Where is vertex *H* located? ________

C. Square *KLMN* with vertices $K(-1, 4)$, $L(6, 4)$, and $M(6, -3)$. Where is vertex *N* located?

____

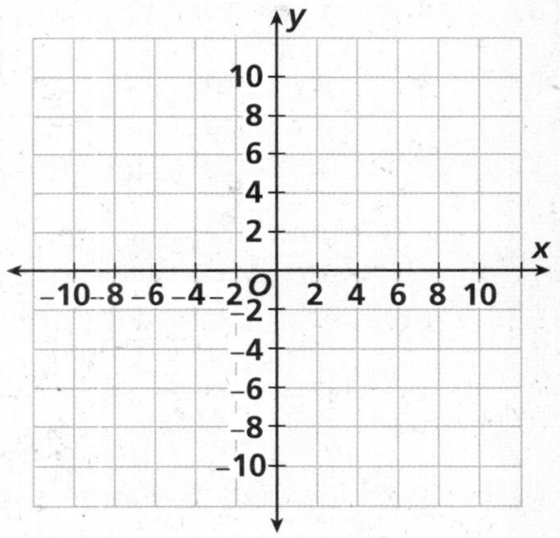

D. Trapezoid *PQRS* with vertices $P(-3, 4)$, $Q(2, -1)$, $R(2, -6)$, and $S(-3, -9)$

E. Now use these clues.

The mouse is located inside Triangle *ABC*.

The mouse is located inside Parallelogram *EFGH*.

The mouse is located outside Square *KLMN*.

The mouse is located outside Trapezoid *PQRS*.

Turn and Talk

What are the coordinates of the location of the mouse? Explain how you know.

© Houghton Mifflin Harcourt Publishing Company • Image Credits: (tr) ©CreativeNature_nl/iStock/Getty Images Plus/Getty Images; (tl) ©Yevgen Romanenko/Moment/Getty Images

Are You Ready?

Complete these problems to review prior concepts and skills you will need for this module.

Quadrilaterals

Classify each quadrilateral in as many ways as possible. Write *parallelogram, rectangle, square,* or *trapezoid*. If the figure is a quadrilateral only, write *quadrilateral*.

1. 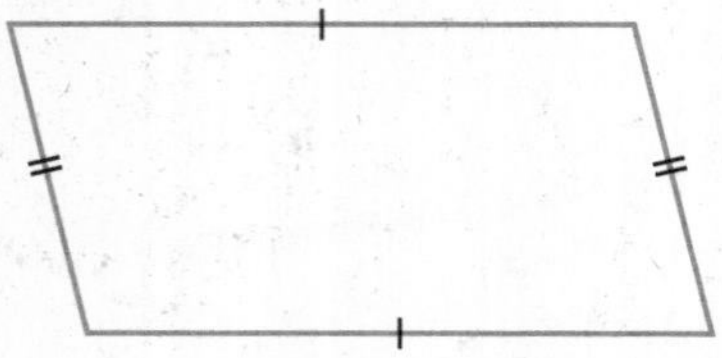

____

2. 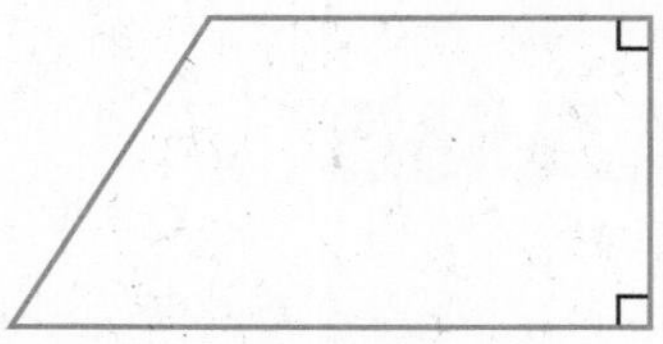

____

3. a four-sided figure with four right angles and four sides of equal length

____

4. a four-sided figure with no parallel sides

____

5. a four-sided figure with one pair of parallel sides

____

Polygons in the Coordinate Plane

Determine the length of each side of Quadrilateral *ABCD*.

6. Side *AB* ________

7. Side *CD* ________

8. Side *AD* ________

9. Draw triangle *FGH* with vertices *F*(−4, −4), *G*(−5, 2), and *H*(−1, −4) in the coordinate plane.

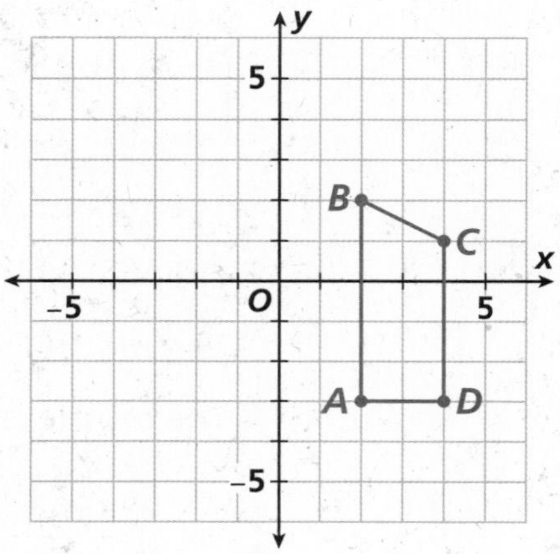

© Houghton Mifflin Harcourt Publishing Company

Name ____________________

Draw Shapes with Given Conditions

I Can **inscribe triangles in circles and draw geometric figures meeting given conditions.**

Spark Your Learning

SMALL GROUPS

Parker plans to build a circular fire pit in a square area. He is drawing a model on paper to confirm his plans before he starts to build. How can Parker use paper folding and a compass to draw the largest possible circular fire pit in the space he has staked off? Trace Parker's square to a piece of paper and draw the circle for the fire pit.

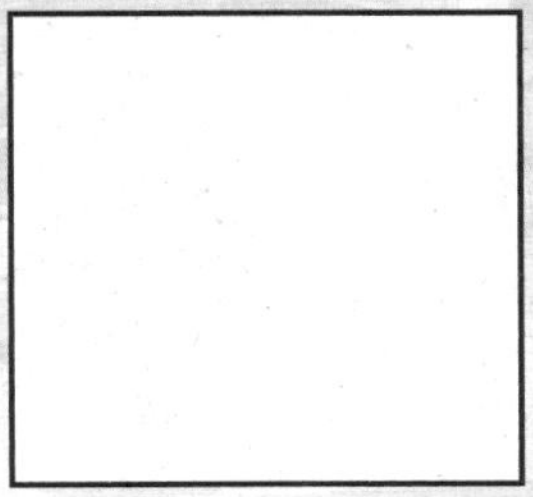

Turn and Talk Brainstorm a list of characteristics specific to squares and circles.

© Houghton Mifflin Harcourt Publishing Company • Image Credit: ©1Photodiva/E+/Getty Images

Build Understanding

1 A polygon is inscribed in a circle if every vertex of the polygon is on the circle. To investigate the kinds of triangles that can be inscribed in a circle, begin Parts A and B by using a compass to draw a circle with a radius of 0.5 inch. The **radius** of a circle is the distance from the circle's center to any point on the circle.

A. Draw a circle and inscribe a triangle in it. Inscribe more than one if you can.

B. A **diameter** is a segment that passes through the circle's center and has endpoints on the circle. Draw a circle and a diameter. Use the endpoints of the diameter and a third point on the circle to inscribe a triangle in the circle.

C. Draw three circles, each with a diameter of 1 inch. Can you inscribe each triangle in one of the circles? If so, draw it. If not, justify your answer.

a triangle with a 50° angle
a triangle with a side of length 1.25 inches
a triangle with a 30° angle and a 60° angle

Turn and Talk How many triangles can you draw in each of Parts A–C: none, only one, or more than one? Explain.

© Houghton Mifflin Harcourt Publishing Company

Name ______________________________

Step It Out

2 Draw a hexagon with side lengths 2, 3, 4, 5, 6, and 7 units. The two longest sides are perpendicular. The longest side and the third-longest side are parallel.

A. Begin by drawing the two longest sides perpendicular to each other. How can you draw two perpendicular segments?

____

B. Draw the third-longest side parallel to the longest side and connected to the second-longest side. How can you draw two parallel segments?

____

C. Use a ruler or compass to draw the last three segments, or cut thin strips of paper. Use the segments to complete the hexagon.

The figure [does / does not] have at least one line of symmetry.

3 Kaylee has a square piece of wood with a side length of 48 inches. She wants to use it to build the largest circular tabletop that she can.

A. Draw a square to model the piece of wood and label the square's side length. Then draw the diagonals to find the center of the square, which will also be the center of the circle, and draw the circle.

B. What is the diameter of the tabletop? How do you know?

____

____

____

© Houghton Mifflin Harcourt Publishing Company

Check Understanding

1. Draw a circle. Can you inscribe an obtuse triangle? If so, inscribe an obtuse triangle and tell how many you can draw. If not, explain why not.

2. A square has a side length of 2.5 meters. What is the radius of the largest circle that fits inside the square? ______________

On Your Own

3. (MP) **Use Tools** Draw a quadrilateral with two pairs of opposite sides that are parallel and equal in length, no right angles, and no lines of symmetry. What is the quadrilateral?

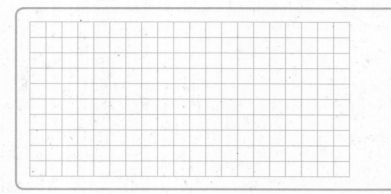

4. (MP) **Use Tools** Draw a circle and one of its diameters. Can you inscribe a triangle that has the diameter as a side and includes an obtuse angle? If so, draw the triangle. If not, justify your answer.

5. Use tools to draw a quadrilateral with exactly one pair of parallel sides. What is the quadrilateral?

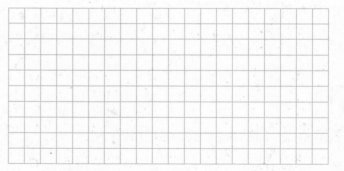

© Houghton Mifflin Harcourt Publishing Company • Image Credit: ©Tammy Venezia/Shutterstock

I'm in a Learning Mindset!

Am I confident in my answer for Problem 4? What evidence do I have that I solved it correctly?

Name ______________________________

ONLINE
Video Tutorials and Interactive Examples

Draw Shapes with Given Conditions

1. (MP) **Use Tools** Draw a decagon with eight sides of length 2 units and two sides of length 4 units. Any two sides that meet should be perpendicular, and the figure should contain parallel segments.

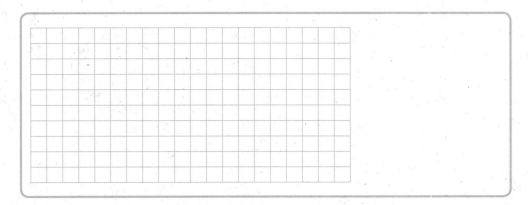

2. (MP) **Use Tools** Draw a quadrilateral with two pairs of congruent sides, no parallel sides, and one line of symmetry. What is the quadrilateral?

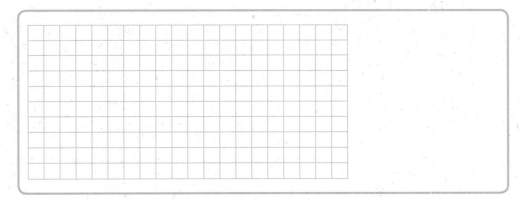

3. (MP) **Use Tools** Draw a circle with a radius of $\frac{3}{4}$ inch and a horizontal diameter. Inscribe a triangle that has the diameter as a side and a vertical line of symmetry.

© Houghton Mifflin Harcourt Publishing Company

Test Prep

4. Match each figure with its description.

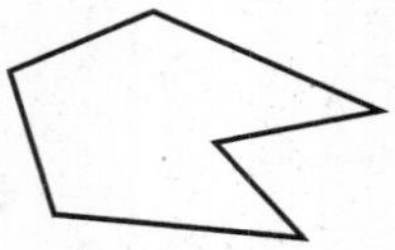

• hexagon with no symmetry

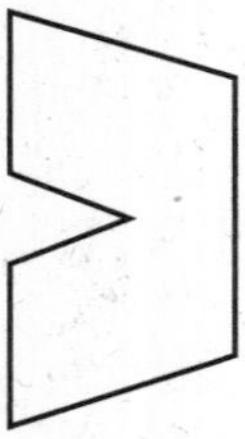

• hexagon with opposite sides parallel

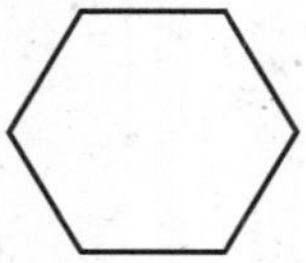

• heptagon with one line of symmetry

5. **A.** Use tools to draw a quadrilateral with four sides of length 3 units, two pairs of parallel sides, and four lines of symmetry. What is the quadrilateral?

____

B. What is the radius of the largest circle that fits inside your quadrilateral from Part A?

____

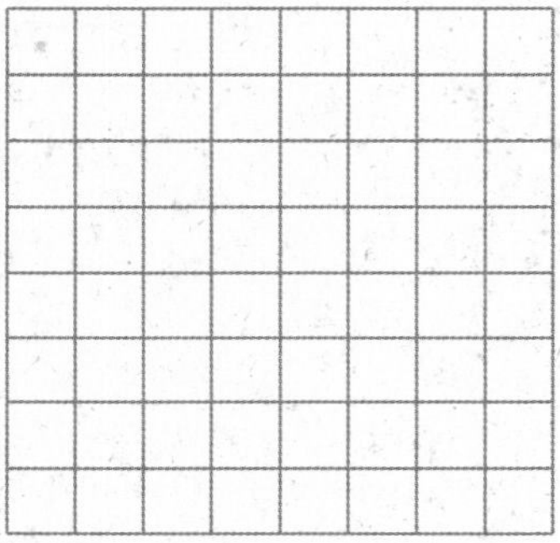

Spiral Review

6. This week, a department store is having a sale where everything is discounted 20%. A ski jacket originally sells for $185. How much will the ski jacket cost during the sale?

____

7. What sequence of transformations can be performed on Figure 1 to produce Figure 2?

____

____

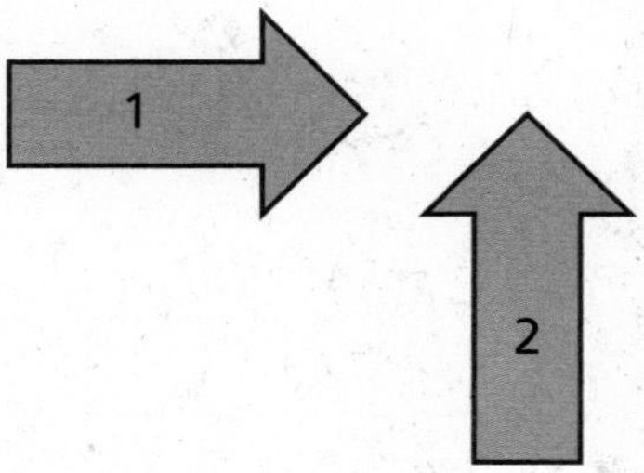

© Houghton Mifflin Harcourt Publishing Company

Name ______________________________

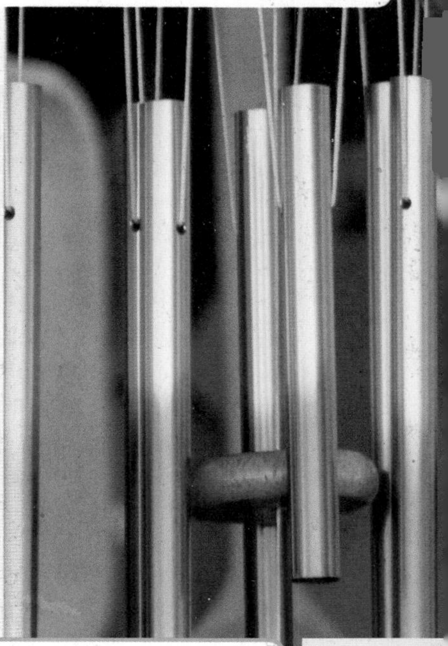

Draw and Construct Triangles Given Side Lengths

I Can determine whether three lengths could be side lengths of a triangle, and, given two side lengths, I can find the range of possible lengths for the third side.

Spark Your Learning

PAIRS

Martina is building a wind chime. She has pieces of metal pipe 2, 3, 4, and 5 inches long that she will use to make a triangular top for the wind chime. Which combinations of three lengths will **not** work for the top?

Turn and Talk What do you notice about the set of lengths that did not make a triangle?

© Houghton Mifflin Harcourt Publishing Company • Image Credit: ©Graphicbyake/Shutterstock

Build Understanding

1 Can you draw a triangle with side lengths of 3, 4, and 8 units? There are different ways to model the situation and investigate. You can use thin strips of paper cut to the correct lengths, or you can use tools such as a ruler and compass or geometry software.

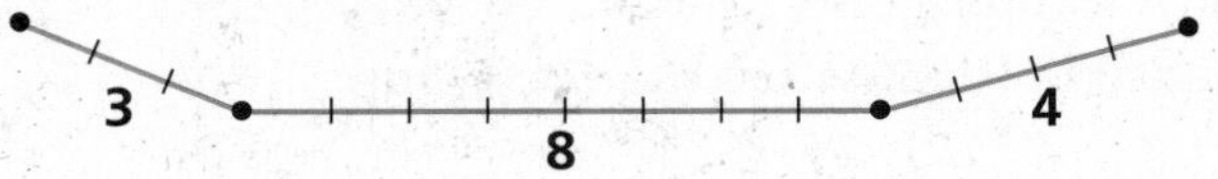

A. Use the longest side of your model as the possible base. Use your model to view the shorter sides in different positions. Can you draw a triangle? If so, draw one. If not, explain why you cannot.

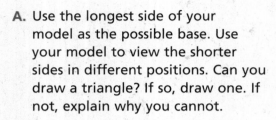

B. Repeat Part A using the shortest segment as the possible base. Can you draw a triangle? If so, draw one. If not, explain why you cannot.

C. Complete the statements describing the relationships among the three side lengths that do **not** form a triangle. Use *less than, equal to,* or *greater than.*

The sum of the lengths of the two shorter sides is ____________ or equal to the length of the longer one.

2 Can you draw a triangle with side lengths of 3, 4, and 6 units?

A. Use the 6-unit segment as the possible base. Can you make a triangle? If so, draw it. If not, explain why you cannot.

____

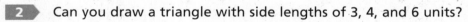

B. Use the 3-unit segment as the possible base. Can you make a triangle? If so, draw it. If not, explain why you cannot.

____

C. Use the 4-unit segment as the possible base. Can you make a triangle? If so, draw it. If not, explain why you cannot.

____

© Houghton Mifflin Harcourt Publishing Company

Name

D. How are the triangles you made in Parts A–C alike?

____

E. Complete the statements describing the relationships between the three side lengths that form a triangle. Use *less than, equal to,* or *greater than*.

The sum of the lengths of the two shorter sides is __________ the length of the longest side.

F. Complete the summary of what you have discovered so far for three segments with lengths a, b, and c, where c is the greatest length.

If $a + b$ is equal to or __________ than c, the segments cannot form a triangle. If $a + b$ is __________ than c, the segments form one triangle.

3 Can you draw a quadrilateral with side lengths of 2, 3, 4, and 5 units?

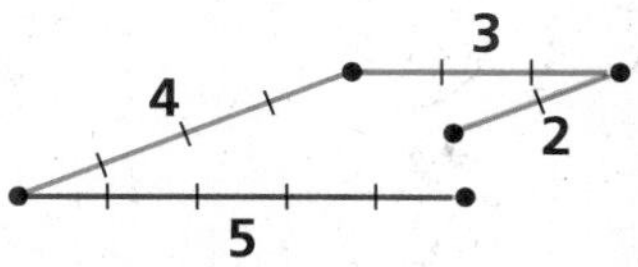

A. Make and use a model. Can you connect the endpoints to form a quadrilateral? If so, draw a quadrilateral. If not, explain why you cannot.

B. Using the same side lengths, can you make a quadrilateral that is different than the one you drew in Part A? If so, draw it. If not, explain why you cannot.

C. Make a conjecture about the number of quadrilaterals that can be made using four different segment lengths. Support your conclusion.

____

____

____

____

____

____

____

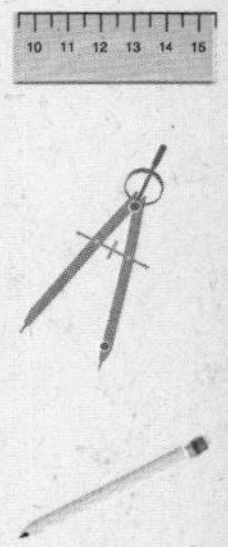

Turn and Talk Is it possible that four segments cannot form a quadrilateral?

© Houghton Mifflin Harcourt Publishing Company

Step It Out

4 In Parts A–C, let a and b be the shorter lengths and c be the longest length. Compare $a + b$ to c to determine if a triangle can be made. Write $<$, $=$, or $>$.

A. Nia wants to make a triangular picture frame from strips of wood that are 9 centimeters, 11 centimeters, and 15 centimeters long.

$9 + 11$ ☐ 15

Since the sum of the lengths of two shorter strips is ________ the length of the longest strip, Nia can / cannot make a triangle.

B. Gerard has pieces of string 6 inches, 5 inches, and 11 inches in length that he plans to use as a border for a collage.

$6 + 5$ ☐ 11

Since the sum of the lengths of two shorter pieces is ________ the length of the longest piece, Gerard can / cannot make a triangle.

C. Olivia gives her niece leftover pieces of ribbon from her art supplies. They are 12 inches, 10 inches, and 24 inches long.

$12 + 10$ ☐ 24

Since the sum of the lengths of two shorter ribbons is ________ the length of the longest, Olivia's niece can / cannot make a triangle.

D. Amil is making a bamboo frame. Given the side lengths shown for the first two sides, what is one possible side length that will form a triangular frame?

$5 + 8 =$ ________, so one side length that will make a triangle is ________ inches.

Check Understanding

1. Max has three pieces of oak trim that are 7 inches, 11 inches, and 18 inches long. He wants to use them to make a triangular base for a candleholder. Will the pieces make a triangle? Explain.

____

____

2. Bella is making a sculpture for her garden. She has pieces of copper pipe that are 4 centimeters long and 13 centimeters long. What is a possible third length of copper pipe that will make a triangle? Justify your answer.

____

© Houghton Mifflin Harcourt Publishing Company

Name

On Your Own

3. Horace is making a shadow box in the shape of a triangle to hold his homerun baseballs. He has pieces of wood 12 inches, 12 inches, and 26 inches long. Show whether these pieces will make a triangle.

4. **Art** An artist is going to make triangle earrings from glass rods with the lengths shown. Show whether these rods will make a triangle.

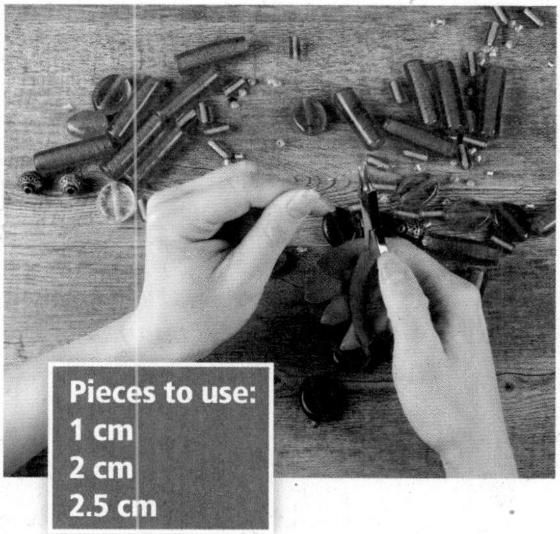

5. Alan makes triangular potholders and sews edging around the outside. He has pieces of edging 5 inches, 5 inches, and 10 inches long. Show whether these pieces will make a triangle.

6. **Open Ended** The volleyball team is making a triangular banner for their last home game. They want two of the sides to be 4 feet long each. Determine one possible length for the third side. Justify your answer.

7. (MP) **Reason** Dante is constructing a quadrilateral with four sides, each 2 inches long. How many different quadrilaterals can he make? Explain.

Determine whether each set of numbers could be lengths of the sides of a triangle.

8. 17, 13, 11 ______ **9.** 11, 19, 35 ______ **10.** 6, 7, 13 ______

Two side lengths of a triangle are given. Find a possible third length.

11. 5 meters, 12 meters **12.** 3 feet, 9 feet **13.** 23 miles, 31 miles

© Houghton Mifflin Harcourt Publishing Company • Image Credit: ©Helen Hotson/Alamy

14. A craftsman makes stained glass crafts. He has metal strips of lengths 5 inches, 8 inches, and 11 inches. Show whether these strips will make a triangle.

15. Karissa is building a triangular landscape border around her mailbox. She has logs 4 feet, 5 feet, and 10 feet long. Show whether these logs will make a triangle.

16. Pierce is developing his own board game. The border of the board is going to be 3 pieces of cardboard, each 17 inches long. Show whether these lengths will make a triangle.

17. (MP) **Construct Arguments** Risa has four sticks measuring 2 inches, 2.5 inches, 3 inches, and 8 inches. She wants to connect the sticks end to end to make a quadrilateral. Can she do it? Explain why or why not.

Determine whether each set of numbers could be lengths of the sides of a triangle.

18. 8.5, 6, 10 ______ **19.** 2.5, 2.5, 4 ______ **20.** 5, 12, 18 ______

Two side lengths of a triangle are given. Find a possible third length.

21. 5 inches, 10 inches

22. 6 yards, 18 yards

23. 9 meters, 21 meters

© Houghton Mifflin Harcourt Publishing Company • Image Credit: ©kali9/E+/Getty Images

I'm in a Learning Mindset!

How does my mindset affect my confidence in determining whether a set of side lengths could form a triangle?

Name ____________________

ONLINE
Video Tutorials and
Interactive Examples

Draw and Construct Triangles Given Side Lengths

1. Haley is making a triangle-shaped box garden. She has wooden pieces of lengths 6 feet, 8 feet, and 13 feet. Show whether these pieces will make a triangle.

2. Students are making shapes with string in an art class. Ben has pieces of string measuring 4 inches, 2 inches, and 1.5 inches long. Show whether these lengths will make a triangle.

3. (MP) **Construct Arguments** The Culinary Club is making a triangle-shaped sign showing a piece of pie for their pie-eating competition. Two of the sides measure as shown. Determine a possible length for the third side. Justify your answer.

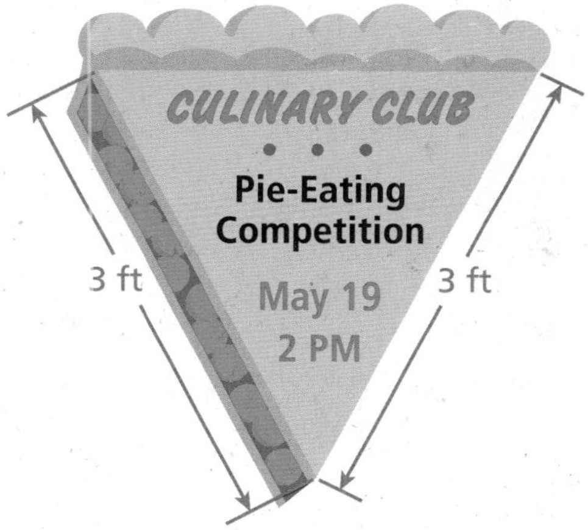

4. Seth wants to make a quadrilateral charm for a necklace. He has wire pieces with lengths 1 centimeter, 2 centimeters, 4 centimeters, and 5 centimeters. How many possible quadrilaterals are there with those side lengths?

© Houghton Mifflin Harcourt Publishing Company

Determine whether each set of numbers could be lengths of the sides of a triangle.

5. 2, 4, 6 ________ **6.** 16, 21, 33 ________ **7.** 1, 3, 3 ________

Two side lengths of a triangle are given. Find a possible third length.

8. 6 meters, 8 meters ________ **9.** 4 feet, 5 feet ________ **10.** 4.5 yards, 7 yards ________

Test Prep

11. Lorelei is making decorative boxes in the shape of triangles. Which of the following could be the lengths of the sides of the boxes?

Ⓐ 12 cm, 13 cm, 24 cm

Ⓑ 12 cm, 13 cm, 25 cm

Ⓒ 10 cm, 10 cm, 24 cm

Ⓓ 10 cm, 10 cm, 22 cm

12. Lhu builds dollhouses with triangle-shaped roofs. Which of the following could be lengths of the edges of the roof of a dollhouse?

Ⓐ 10 in., 10 in., 20 in.

Ⓑ 10 in., 12 in., 24 in.

Ⓒ 11 in., 12 in., 24 in.

Ⓓ 11 in., 11 in., 20 in.

13. Select all the sets of numbers that could be lengths of the sides of a triangle.

Ⓐ 2, 7, 9

Ⓑ 4, 11, 13

Ⓒ 6, 9, 12

Ⓓ 6, 6, 14

Ⓔ 8, 15, 21

Ⓕ 9, 17, 27

14. An artist gets strips of metal from a salvage yard to make decorative wall art. The artist finds strips that are 2.5 feet and 3.5 feet long. Determine one possible length for the third strip if the artist wants to make a triangle.

____

Spiral Review

15. Use geometry software to draw a quadrilateral with two pairs of parallel sides and four right angles. What is the most specific name that applies to the quadrilateral?

____

16. Complete the inequality with the correct comparison symbol.

$-4 \ \square \ |-4|$

© Houghton Mifflin Harcourt Publishing Company

Name ______________________________

Draw and Construct Triangles Given Angle Measures

I Can use tools to construct triangles when given angle measures and determine if no triangle or many triangles can be formed.

Spark Your Learning

SMALL GROUPS

A town is designing triangular flower beds for a park. Is it possible to choose three angle measures that will **not** form a triangle? If so, draw several examples.

Turn and Talk Pick one of your examples above and describe how you could revise your drawing to form a triangle.

© Houghton Mifflin Harcourt Publishing Company • **Image Credit:** ©swedewah/E+/Getty Images

Build Understanding

1 You can use tools to determine whether you can construct a triangle with three given angle measures.

A. Is it possible to construct a triangle with angle measures of 25°, 75°, and 80°? If so, draw the triangle.

B. Is it possible to construct a larger or smaller triangle with those same angle measures? If so, draw an example. If not, explain why not.

C. Is it possible to construct a triangle with angle measures of 45°, 60°, and 55°? With angle measures of 45°, 60°, and 95°? If so, draw the triangles.

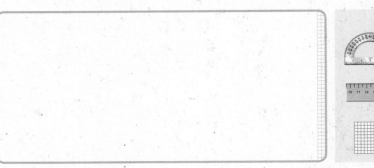

D. You have examined the number of unique triangles that can be formed using three given angle measures and the number of unique triangles that can be formed using three given side lengths. How do the numbers compare?

____

____

____

Turn and Talk What appears to be true about the sum of the measures of the angles of a triangle?

© Houghton Mifflin Harcourt Publishing Company • **Image Credit:** ©Tereza Tsyaulouskaya/Shutterstock

Name

Step It Out

2 Jenny draws a triangle that includes one angle that has a measure of 30°, one angle that has a measure of 90°, and one side that has a length of 1 inch. Without seeing her triangle, can you draw it?

A. Can the given side of Jenny's triangle be a side of both given angles of the triangle? Can it be a side of only one of the angles? ________

B. Think about how the given side and the given angles might be positioned. Draw all the triangles you can using the information given for Jenny's triangle. Label the known measures on your drawings.

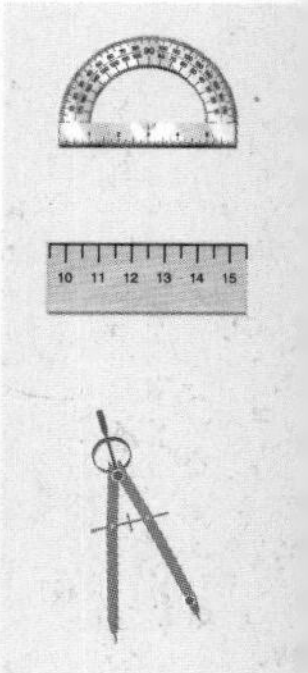

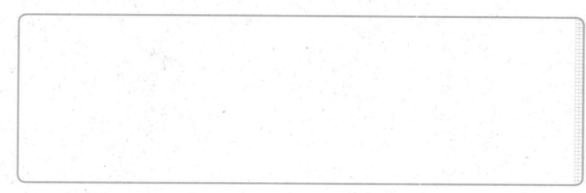

C. Can Jenny's triangle be found among your drawings? Explain.

D. Can you draw a triangle with one 90° angle and one 100° angle so that the side between the angles is 2 inches long? Why or why not?

Check Understanding

1. Cliff wants to draw a triangle with a 30° angle and a 60° angle so that the side between them is 2 inches long. How many triangles can he draw?

2. **A.** If possible, construct a triangle with angle measures of 45°, 65°, and 70°.

B. How many triangles are possible: none, one, or many?

© Houghton Mifflin Harcourt Publishing Company

On Your Own

3. Kara is making a picture out of tiles. One tile will be triangular with angle measures of 25°, 25°, and 130°.

   A. (MP) Use Tools Sketch a triangle with those angle measures.

   B. Do you have enough information to make Kara's triangle? Explain.

(MP) Use Tools **For Problems 4–5, determine whether it is possible to draw a triangle with the given angle measures. If it is possible, use tools to draw a triangle.**

4. 55°, 60°, 70°

5. 30°, 40°, 110°

6. (MP) Use Tools Kate is drawing a house. For the top of the house, she wants to make a triangle with angle measures of 30°, 30°, and 120°. Can Kate make a triangle with these angle measures? If so, use tools to draw the triangle. If not, explain why not.

7. Eduardo is building a triangular sandbox for a playground. He wants the triangle to include a 65° angle, a 50° angle, and at least one side that is 12 feet long. Draw at least one possible triangle on a separate piece of paper and estimate possible lengths of the other two sides of the triangle.

I'm in a Learning Mindset!

How does my mindset affect my confidence in determining whether it is possible to draw a triangle with given angle measures? How did I use tools to support my conclusion?

© Houghton Mifflin Harcourt Publishing Company

Name

ONLINE
Video Tutorials and
Interactive Examples

Draw and Construct Triangles Given Angle Measures

1. (MP) **Use Tools** Vanessa wants to build a triangular table. Can she build a table with angle measures of 15°, 55°, and 110°? If so, draw the triangle.

2. Carlos wants to draw a triangle with angle measures of 55°, 60°, and 65°. How many different triangles can Carlos draw: one or more than one?

For Problems 3–6, determine whether it is possible to draw a triangle with the given angle measures. If it is possible, use tools to draw a triangle.

3. 25°, 40°, 115°

4. 15°, 15°, 120°

5. 60°, 70°, 70°

6. 30°, 55°, 95°

7. (MP) **Construct Arguments** James sees a floor made of triangular tiles of different sizes. He notices that two triangles each have one angle with a measure of 35°, another with a measure of 45°, and one side with a length of 6 inches. Are the two triangles the same? Explain.

© Houghton Mifflin Harcourt Publishing Company • Image Credit: ©Compassionate Eye Foundation/Steven Errl/Digital Vision/Getty Images

Test Prep

8. How many different triangles can be made with the angle measures 30°, 60°, and 90°?

Ⓐ none

Ⓑ one

Ⓒ exactly two

Ⓓ more than two

9. Each set of angle measures and/or side lengths can be used to form a triangle. Which conditions produce only one triangle? Choose all that apply.

Ⓐ 35° angle, 55° angle, 90° angle

Ⓑ 3-inch side, 4-inch side, 5-inch side

Ⓒ 30° angle, 60° angle, 2-inch side joining the angles

Ⓓ 28° angle, 80° angle, 1-meter side

Ⓔ three 60° angles, three $\frac{3}{4}$-inch sides

10. Seamus draws a triangle with angles of measures 40°, 60°, and 80°. Edwina draws a triangle with these same angle measures. Which statement **cannot** be true?

Ⓐ Edwina's triangle is not the same size as Seamus's triangle.

Ⓑ Edwina's triangle is not the same shape as Seamus's triangle.

Ⓒ The perimeter of Seamus's triangle is greater than the perimeter of Edwina's triangle.

Ⓓ The area of Edwina's triangle is less than the area of Seamus's triangle.

Spiral Review

11. The vertices of a triangle are (5, 3), (−2, −5), and (0, −6). The triangle is rotated 180° about the origin. What are the coordinates of the vertices of the image?

____

12. Draw an octagon with six sides of length 3 units, one side of length 4 units, and one side of length 10 units. Every pair of sides that meet are perpendicular. The figure should have symmetry.

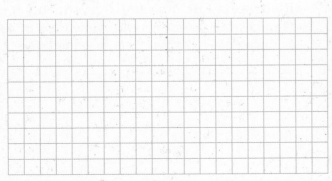

© Houghton Mifflin Harcourt Publishing Company

Name ______________________

Draw and Analyze Shapes to Solve Problems

I Can **draw and analyze shapes, including circles and triangles, to solve real-world problems.**

Step It Out

1 Lucas is using strips of wood to construct a triangle. The first two strips are 4 feet long and 7 feet long. When Lucas nails them together, the two pieces of wood form a 50° angle.

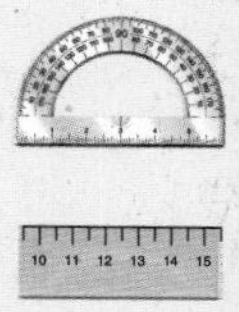

A. Draw a model of the two strips after Lucas nailed them together.

B. Can he use a third strip to construct a triangle? If so, complete the model.

____

C. How many triangles can be formed?

____

Turn and Talk What if the third strip were 12 feet long? Would Lucas still be able to construct a triangle? Explain.

2 In this task, you will draw triangles given the lengths of two sides and the measure of an angle that is **not** between them.

A. Side *AB*: 8 units; Side *BC*: 6 units; Angle *A*: 40°

To construct Triangle *ABC*, you need to draw Side *BC*. Because Side *BC* is 6 units long, put the point of the compass at Point *B*, and draw part of a circle with radius 6 units. You can use this segment to help you open your compass to the correct radius.

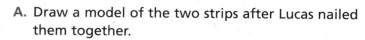

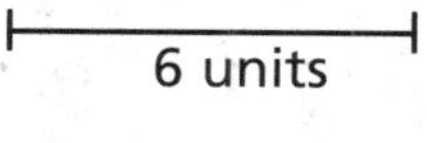

The circle intersects the other side of $\angle A$ in ______ point(s). You can draw ______ triangle(s). Draw the triangle(s).

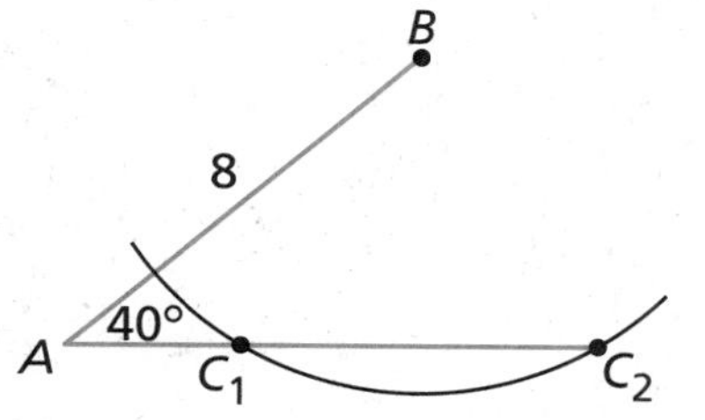

© Houghton Mifflin Harcourt Publishing Company

B. Side *AB*: 5 units; Side *BC*: 7 units; Angle *A*: 90°

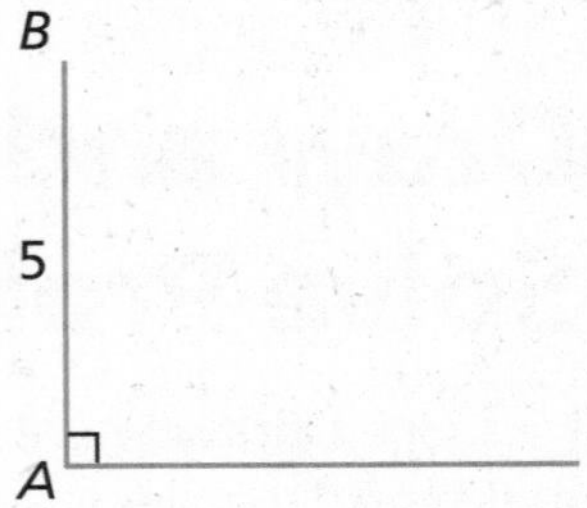

To draw Side *BC*, put the point of the compass on Point *B*, and draw part of a circle with radius 7 units. Use this 7-unit segment to open your compass to the correct radius.

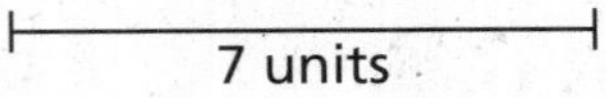

The circle intersects the other side of ∠*A* at _____ point(s).

You can draw _____ triangle(s). Draw the triangle(s).

C. Side *AB*: 6 units; Side *BC*: 9 units; Angle *A*: 120°

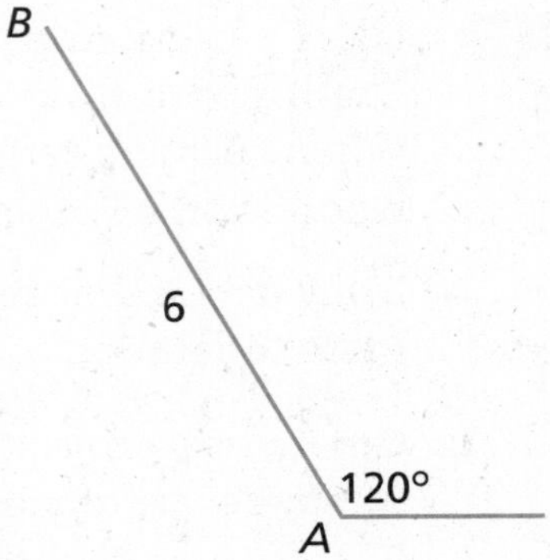

Use this segment to help you draw Side *BC*.

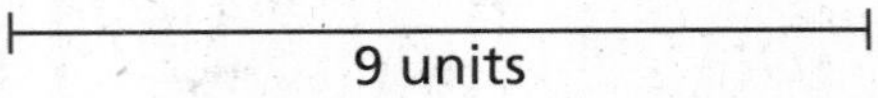

The circle intersects the other side of ∠*A* at _____ point(s).

You can draw _____ triangle(s). Draw the triangle(s).

D. How many triangles did you draw in Parts A–C given two sides and the measure of an angle that is not between them?

____

____

Turn and Talk How are the situations in Step It Out 1 and Step It Out 2 different? How are they the same?

Check Understanding

1. Draw a right triangle with two sides of lengths of 4 units and 5 units and the 90° angle between them.

2. Draw a right triangle with two sides of lengths 4 units and 5 units with the 90° angle not between them.

© Houghton Mifflin Harcourt Publishing Company

On Your Own

3. A triangle with the largest possible base is drawn inside a circle. What part of the circle must coincide with the base of the triangle?

4. (MP) **Use Tools** Use the diagram shown. Construct two different triangles that each have Side *AB* with a length of 8 units, Side *BC* with a length of 5 units, and a 35° angle that is not between them. Use the segment below to help you draw Side *BC*.

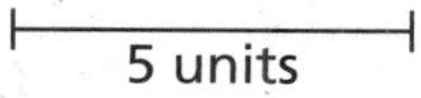

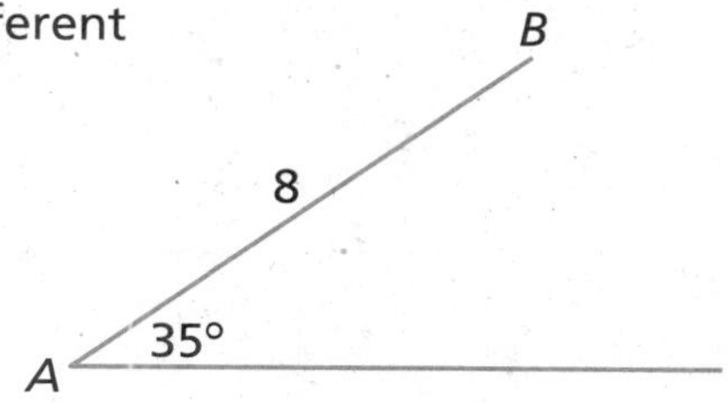

5. **STEM** An ethologist is a scientist who studies animal behavior. One ethologist studied the play behavior of a group of infant lowland gorillas and measured the portion of play time given to three types of play. Draw a circle graph to show the portion of the day for each type. The measure of the angle between the sides of the section for each behavior is given.

Solitary play: 150°
Social play: 195°
Mother-infant play: 15°

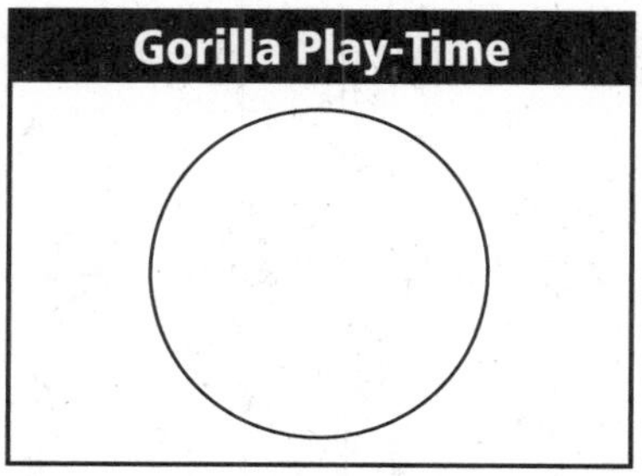

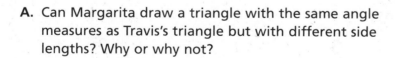

6. Travis draws a triangle with three 60° angles and three sides of length 5 inches.

   A. Can Margarita draw a triangle with the same angle measures as Travis's triangle but with different side lengths? Why or why not?

   B. Can she draw a triangle with the same side lengths as Travis's triangle but with different angle measures? Explain.

© Houghton Mifflin Harcourt Publishing Company • Image Credits: ©FLPA/Alamy

7. (MP) **Use Tools** Students were surveyed about the number of siblings they have. Draw a circle graph to show the part of the group surveyed that each has a given number of siblings. The table shows the measure of the angle between the sides of the section for each number of siblings.

Siblings	0	1	2	3	4	5 or more
Angle measure	40°	85°	95°	50°	50°	40°

Numbers of Siblings

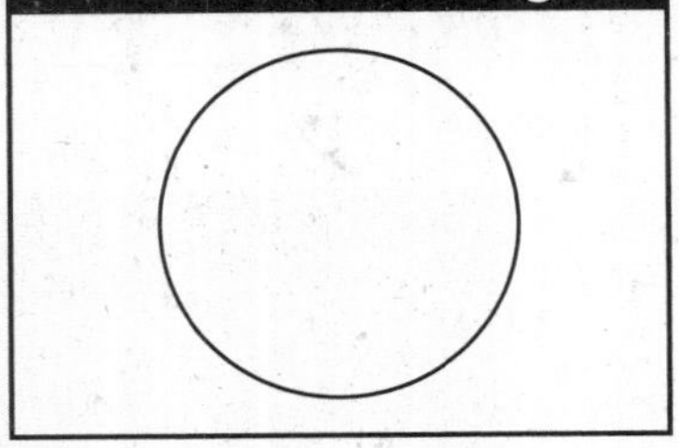

8. (MP) **Use Tools** Draw a triangle that has sides of length 7 units and 5 units with a 42° angle between them. Can you draw more than one triangle?

9. **Open Ended** Draw a figure that has at least one pair of parallel sides and at least one side that is 6 units long. The figure should also have at least one line of symmetry.

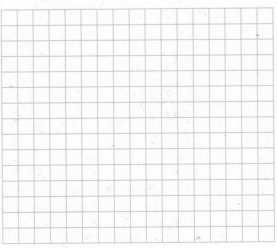

© Houghton Mifflin Harcourt Publishing Company • Image Credit: ©Steve Debenport/Getty Images

Name ______________________________

Draw and Analyze Shapes to Solve Problems

1. **Open Ended** Draw a figure that has at least one pair of perpendicular sides, at least one side that is 4 units long, and at least one line of symmetry.

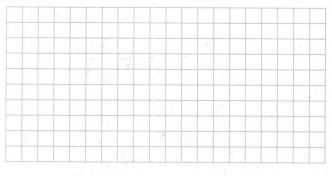

2. (MP) **Use Tools** How many triangles can you draw that have two sides of lengths 5 units and 2 units and a 68° angle between them? Draw the triangle(s).

3. A. (MP) **Use Tools** Complete the drawing to make Triangle(s) *ABC* with Side *AB* of length 9 units, Side *BC* of length 7 units, and Angle *A* with measure 45°. Use this segment to help you draw side *BC*.

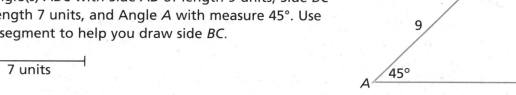

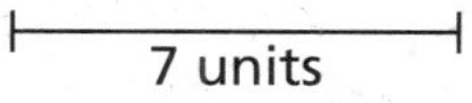

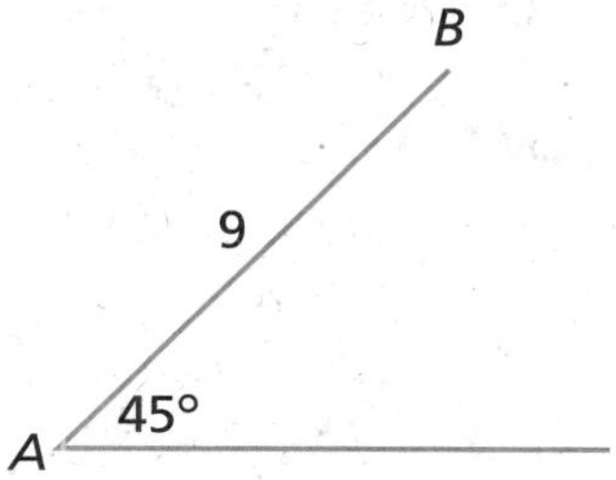

B. How many triangles with these measurements can you draw?

____

4. (MP) **Reason** The two longest sides of a triangle are 7 inches and 10 inches long. Describe a possible length for the shortest side. Explain your reasoning.

____

____

____

© Houghton Mifflin Harcourt Publishing Company

Test Prep

5. Indicate whether one, none, or many triangles can be drawn with the given side lengths and/or angle measures.

	None	One	Many
6 feet, 6 feet, 8 feet	☐	☐	☐
40°, 40°, 112°	☐	☐	☐
68°, 22°, 90°	☐	☐	☐
7 meters, 6 meters, 12 meters	☐	☐	☐
6 inches, 10 inches, 45° angle between	☐	☐	☐
3 feet, 5 feet, 10 feet	☐	☐	☐

6. A triangle has two sides of lengths 20 centimeters and 8 centimeters. Which can be the length of the third side of the triangle? Select all that apply.

Ⓐ 30 centimeters

Ⓑ 22 centimeters

Ⓒ 14 centimeters

Ⓓ 8 centimeters

Ⓔ 6 centimeters

7. A road worker wants to place a circular map on a square sign that has a perimeter of 240 inches. What is the greatest possible radius of the circular map?

Ⓐ 15 inches

Ⓑ 30 inches

Ⓒ 60 inches

Ⓓ 120 inches

Spiral Review

8. Write an inequality to compare the integers −5 and −6.

____

9. How many unique triangles can be made with sides of lengths 4 cm, 7 cm, and 12 cm: none, one, or many?

____

© Houghton Mifflin Harcourt Publishing Company

Name ______________________________

Practice Proportional Reasoning with Scale Drawings

I Can use a scale to make a scale drawing of a rectangular object.

Step It Out

ACTIVITY

The scale on a scale drawing can be shown in the same unit or in different units.

Connect to Vocabulary

A **scale** is a ratio between two sets of measurements.

A **scale drawing** is a proportional two-dimensional drawing of an object.

1 Mario's school is building a basketball court from the scale drawing.

Drawing length (in.)	Actual length (ft)
0.6	12
2.1	42

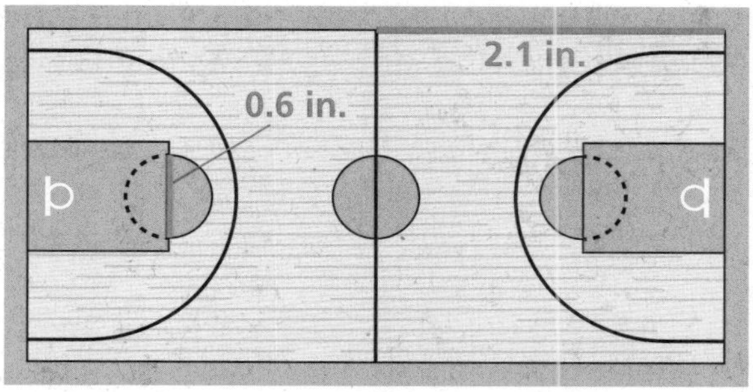

A. The table shows some lengths from the drawing and the corresponding lengths on the actual court. How can you tell this is a scale drawing?

____

____

B. What is the scale of the drawing in inches to feet? ____________

C. Write an equation for the **proportional relationship** between the actual length in feet x and the drawing length in inches y. ____________

D. Use your equation from Part C to find the actual length represented by a scale drawing length of 1.5 inches, and to find the scale drawing length that represents an actual length of 70 feet.

$\square = \frac{1}{20}x$, so $x = \square$

1.5 inches represents an actual length of $\square$ feet.

$y = \frac{1}{20}\square = \square$

70 feet represents a drawing length of $\square$ inches.

© Houghton Mifflin Harcourt Publishing Company

2 What is the relationship between area in the scale drawing and area on the actual basketball court?

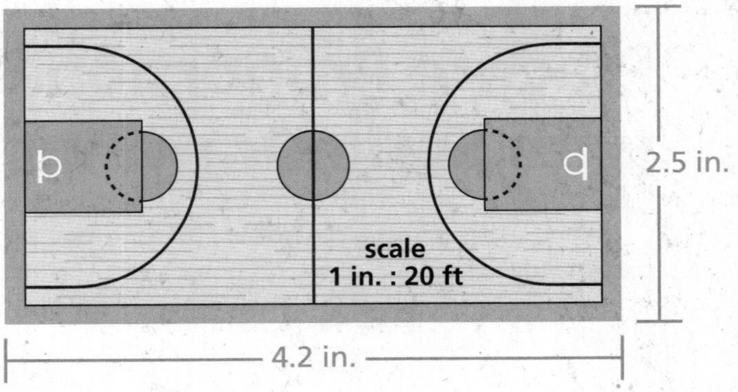

A. Show how to find the area of the court in the scale drawing.

____

B. Show how to find the length and width of the actual court.

____

C. What is the area of the actual basketball court? Show your work.

____

D. Is the ratio of actual area to drawing area the same as the ratio of actual lengths to drawing lengths? Explain.

____

____

____

Turn and Talk Is there a relationship between the scale for area and the scale for length? If so, describe the relationship.

3 Mario's school is also planning to make a rectangular garden 60 feet wide by 70 feet long. On the grid provided, make a scale drawing of the rectangular garden using the scale given.

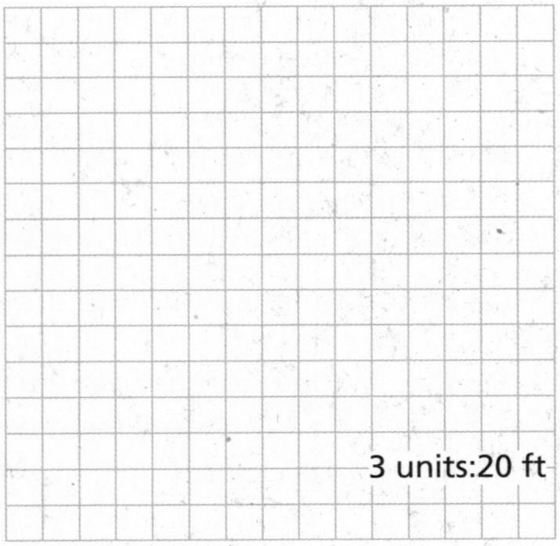

A. Write an equation for the actual length y based on a drawing length x.

____

____

B. Use the equation you wrote in Part A to find the scale drawing lengths. Then make the scale drawing.

____

____

Turn and Talk How could you write an equation for the drawing length y based on an actual length x?

© Houghton Mifflin Harcourt Publishing Company

Name ______________________

4 Mario's school is also planning a smaller rectangular area as a sitting spot. A scale drawing of the sitting spot is shown. Redraw the sitting spot on the grid at a scale of $\frac{\text{1 grid unit}}{\text{4 feet}}$.

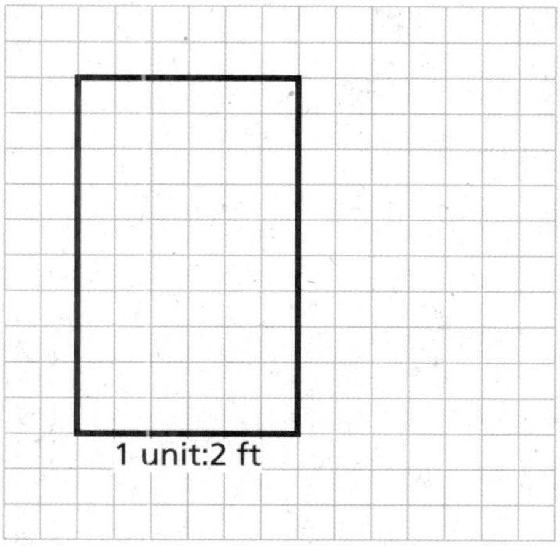

A. Write and simplify the ratio of the new scale to the original scale.

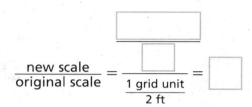

$$\frac{\text{new scale}}{\text{original scale}} = \frac{\frac{\square}{\square}}{\frac{\text{1 grid unit}}{\text{2 ft}}} = \square$$

B. Each side of the new drawing will be [longer / shorter] than the **corresponding side** of the original drawing.

C. Draw the rectangle for the new scale.

Turn and Talk What is another way you could have found the dimensions of your new scale drawing?

Check Understanding

1. The dimensions of an Olympic swimming pool are shown. A scale drawing of the swimming pool has dimensions of 50 centimeters by 100 centimeters and a diagonal that is about 112 centimeters long.

   A. What is the scale of the drawing in centimeters to meters? ______________

   B. What is the actual length of the diagonal of the pool? ______________

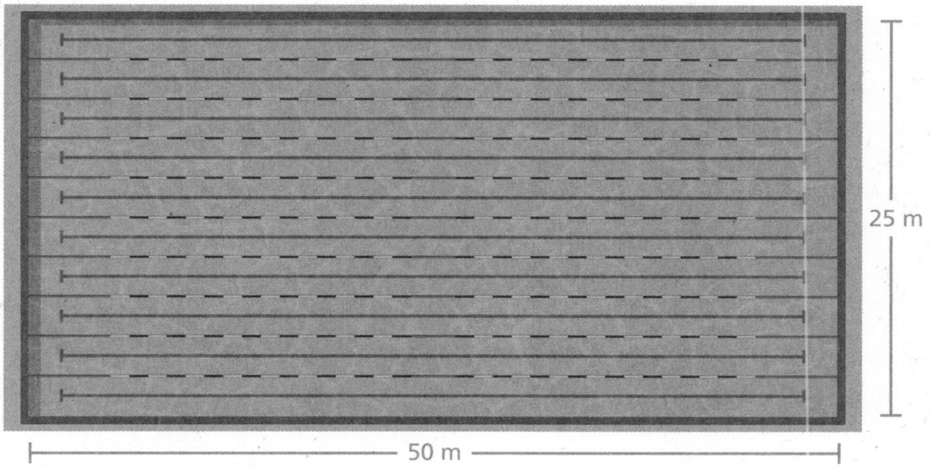

2. A different scale drawing of the same Olympic pool uses a scale of $\frac{5 \text{ cm}}{1 \text{ m}}$. What are the dimensions of the drawing? ______________

© Houghton Mifflin Harcourt Publishing Company

On Your Own

3. (MP) **Use Structure** Veronica's town is building a tennis court using the scale drawing shown. Find the scale between the drawing and the actual court. Then use the scale to show how a given length on the drawing represents a length on the tennis court, and how a given length on the tennis court is represented in the drawing.

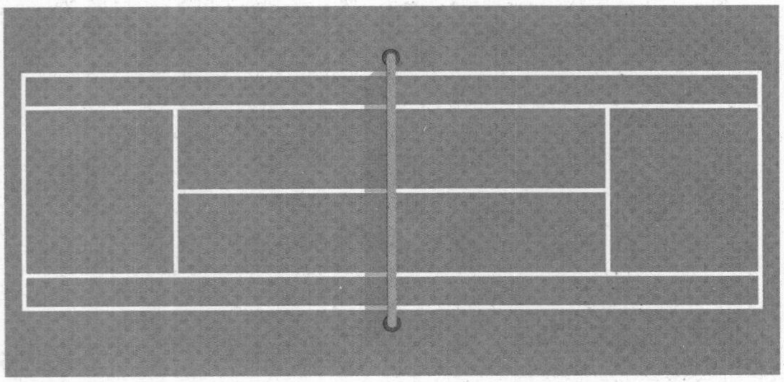

A. The table shows some lengths in the drawing and the corresponding lengths on the actual court. Explain how you can tell from the table that the drawing is a scale drawing.

Drawing length (in.)	Actual length (ft)
2	10
3	15
5	25
10	50

B. What is the ratio between the actual length and the drawing length as a unit rate?

C. Write an equation for the proportional relationship between the drawing lengths and the court lengths, where x is length in the drawing in inches and y is length on the court in feet.

D. Use your equation from Part C to find the actual length represented by a scale drawing length of 3.5 inches.

E. Use your equation from Part C to find the scale drawing length that represents an actual length of 40 feet.

© Houghton Mifflin Harcourt Publishing Company

Name

4. What is the relationship between area in the scale drawing and area on the actual tennis court?

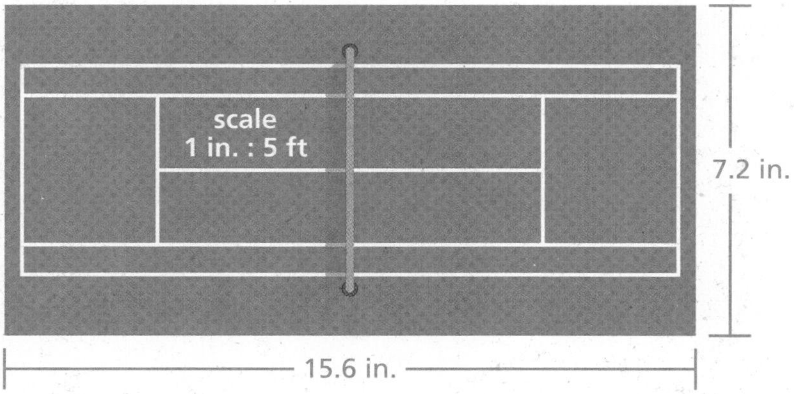

A. Show how to find the area of the scale drawing of the tennis court.

B. Show how to find the length and width of the actual court.

C. Show how to find the area of the actual tennis court.

D. (MP) **Attend to Precision** What is the ratio of the area of the actual court to the area of the drawing (as a unit rate)? Is it the same as the ratio of the length of the actual court to the length of the drawing? How do you know?

© Houghton Mifflin Harcourt Publishing Company

5. The students in Suzanne's school are painting a rectangular mural outside the building that will be 15 feet by 45 feet.

A. Write the unit rate for the proportional relationship between lengths on the mural *y* and lengths in the scale drawing *x*.

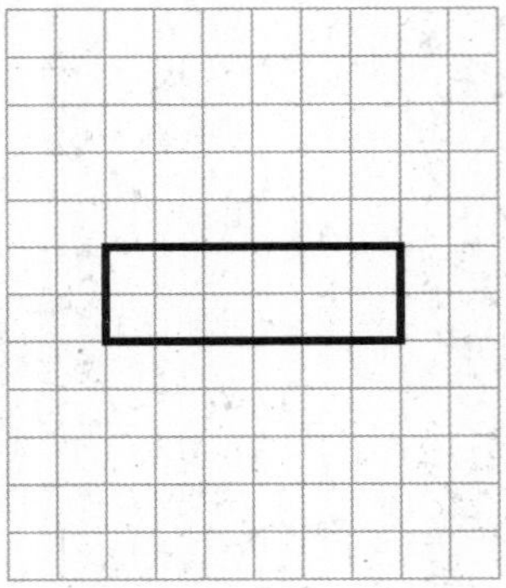

____

B. (MP) **Model with Mathematics** Write an equation that relates *x* and *y*. The diagonal of the scale drawing is approximately 6.3 units. Estimate the length of the diagonal of the mural.

____

6. The students at Suzanne's school are also going to paint a smaller mural inside the building. A scale drawing of the mural is shown on the grid.

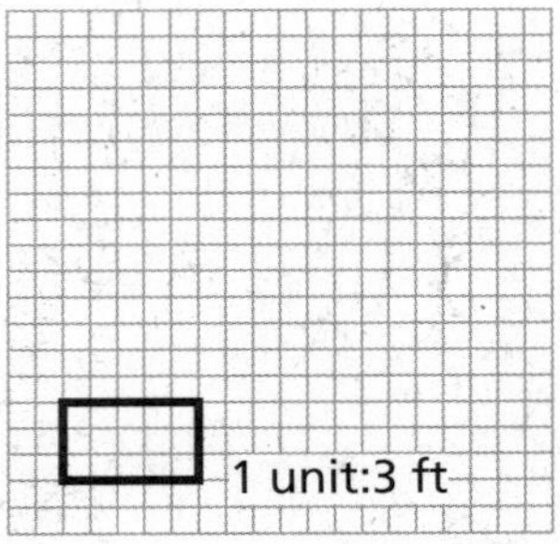

A. Redraw the inside mural on the grid using a scale of 1 unit:1 foot.

B. How many grid units are there for every 3 feet of mural in the original scale? How many grid units are there for every 3 feet of mural in the new scale?

____

C. What is the length of your scale drawing compared to the length of the original scale drawing?

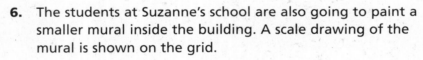

$$\frac{\text{your scale}}{\text{given scale}} = \frac{\dfrac{\square}{\square}}{\dfrac{1 \text{ grid unit}}{3 \text{ feet}}} = \frac{\square}{\square} = \square \text{ times as long}$$

D. How does the area of your drawing compare to the original area?

____

© Houghton Mifflin Harcourt Publishing Company • Image Credit: ©Jim West/Alamy

Name ______________________________

Practice Proportional Reasoning with Scale Drawings

ONLINE
Video Tutorials and Interactive Examples

1. Martine's town is building a volleyball court based on a scale drawing that is 40 centimeters by 80 centimeters and uses the scale 1 cm:22.5 cm.

A. (MP) **Model with Mathematics** Write an equation for the proportional relationship between drawing court lengths x in centimeters and court lengths y in centimeters.

B. What are the length and width in meters of the actual court? Show your work.

2. **Art** The students in Roberto's school are painting a mural that will be 8 feet by 15 feet. First they make a scale drawing of the mural with a scale of 2 feet:5 feet.

A. Write an equation for the proportional relationship between drawing mural lengths x in feet and mural lengths y in feet.

B. What are the length and width of the scale drawing in feet? Show your work.

C. What is the actual area of the mural? Show your work.

D. Is the ratio of actual area to drawing area the same as the ratio of actual lengths to drawing lengths? Explain.

3. **Geography** A map has a scale of 1 in.:10 mi. Find the distance on the map between two cities that lie 147 miles apart. Show your work.

© Houghton Mifflin Harcourt Publishing Company • Image Credit: ©Tetra Images/Mike Kemp/age fotostock

Test Prep

4. Ricardo draws a scale model of the floor plan of his house. His house is 60 feet long and 40 feet wide. He uses the scale $\frac{1 \text{ inch}}{4 \text{ feet}}$ to draw his model. Which statements are true? Select all that apply.

Ⓐ The equation $\ell = \frac{1}{4}(60)$ can be used to find the length of the scale model.

Ⓑ The equation $w = (4)(40)$ can be used to find the width of the scale model.

Ⓒ The width of the scale model is 10 inches.

Ⓓ The length of the scale model is 240 inches.

Ⓔ The scale means that 1 inch in the model represents 4 feet in the house.

5. A scale drawing of an elephant shows the animal as 6 inches high and 10.8 inches long. The scale used for the drawing was 3 in.:5 ft. What are the height and length of the actual elephant?

Height: ________ feet   Length: ________ feet

6. Town planners are planning a 500–foot by 700–foot parking lot by making a scale drawing that is 90 inches by 126 inches. What is the scale of inches in the drawing to inches in the actual object?

Ⓐ 3:200   Ⓑ 1:300   Ⓒ 2:30   Ⓓ 1:200

Spiral Review

7. A machine produces parts at a steady rate of 160 parts in 8 hours. Complete the table for this relationship.

Hours	2		5	8
Parts		60		160

8. The table shows possible numbers of basketball teams in a league and the number of jerseys needed for the number of teams.

A. Graph the relationship between the number of teams in the league and the number of jerseys made.

B. Is the relationship between the number of teams and the number of jerseys proportional? Explain.

Teams, x	Jerseys, y
3	36
4	48
5	60
6	72
7	84
8	96

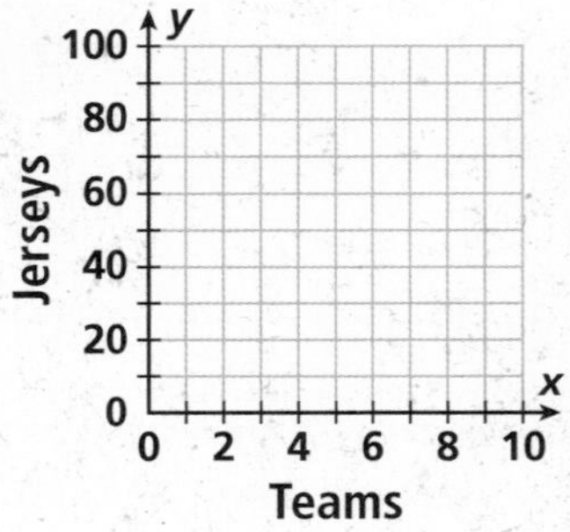

____

____

© Houghton Mifflin Harcourt Publishing Company

Module 2

Review

Name ____________________

Vocabulary

Choose the correct term from the Vocabulary box.

Vocabulary
corresponding sides
diameter
proportional relationship
radius
scale
scale drawing

1. The distance from the center of a circle to any point on the circle is the ____________________ of the circle.

2. A ratio between two sets of measurements is a ____________________.

3. A relationship between two quantities in which the ratio of one quantity to the other is constant is a ____________________.

4. A ____________________ of a circle is a line segment that passes through the center of the circle and has its endpoints on the circle.

Concepts and Skills

For Problems 5–6, draw a figure on the grid that matches each description.

5. A polygon with at least one pair of perpendicular sides, a side with a length of 8 units, and a side with a length of 6 units

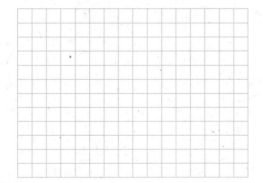

6. An acute triangle with exactly one line of symmetry and one side with a length of 4 units

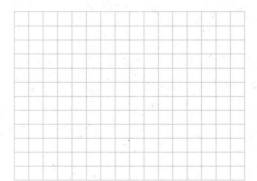

7. (MP) Use Tools Alisa drew the triangle shown. She claims it is the only distinct triangle that can be drawn with a 90° angle and two sides that measure 5 inches and 7 inches. Is Alisa correct? Why or why not? State what strategy and tool you will use to answer the question, explain your choice, and then find the answer.

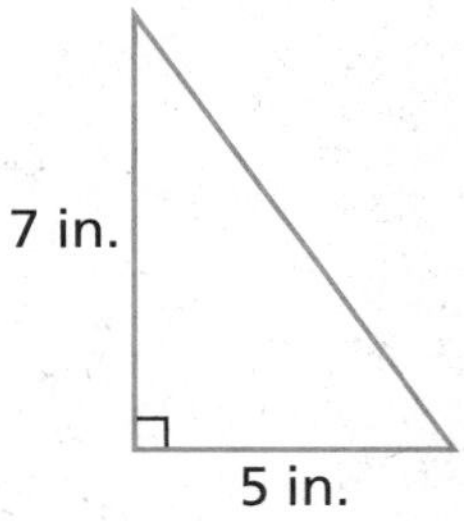

____

____

____

© Houghton Mifflin Harcourt Publishing Company

8. Ernesto drew a quadrilateral that has exactly one pair of parallel sides and exactly one line of symmetry. Which shape could he have drawn?

Ⓐ 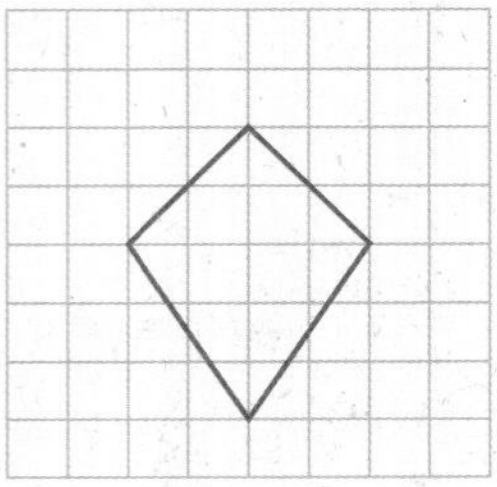

Ⓑ 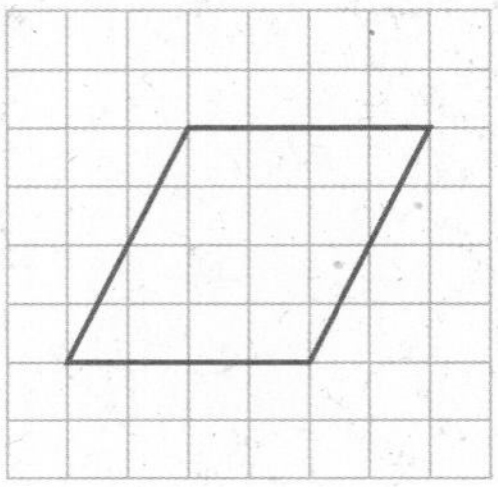

Ⓒ 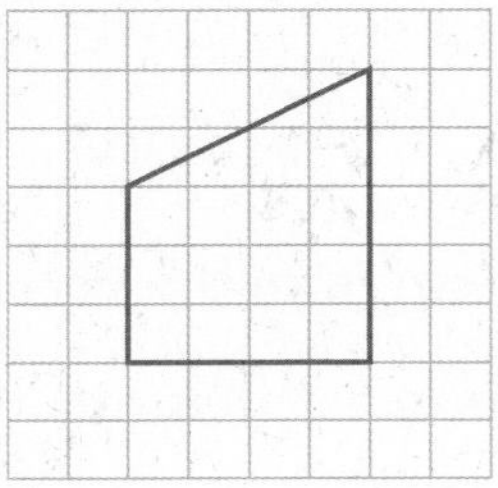

Ⓓ 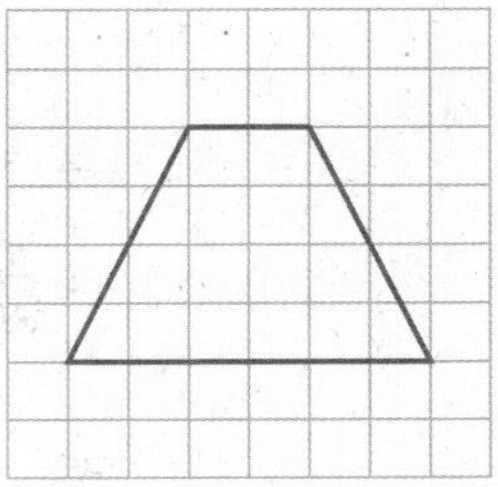

9. Two of the sides of a triangle measure 6 inches and 10 inches. Select all measurements that could be the length of the third side of the triangle.

Ⓐ 4 inches
Ⓑ 5 inches
Ⓒ 8 inches
Ⓓ 10 inches
Ⓔ 12 inches
Ⓕ 18 inches

10. The Pep Club is painting a banner based on a scale drawing that is 15 inches long by 5 inches wide and uses the scale 1 inch:2.4 inches. Write an equation for the proportional relationship between lengths x in the drawing and lengths y in the actual banner. What are the length and width of the actual banner in feet?

____

11. For each set of measurements, tell whether exactly one triangle, more than one triangle, or no triangle can be constructed.

	Exactly one triangle	**More than one triangle**	**No triangles**
Angles that measure 60°, 60°, and 60°	☐	☐	☐
Sides that measure 4 cm, 8 cm, and 9 cm	☐	☐	☐
Sides that measure 15 mm, 20 mm, and 35 mm	☐	☐	☐

12. An artist is designing a logo for a new business. She starts by drawing a rectangle with a length of 10 centimeters and a width of 6 centimeters. What is the radius of the largest circle the artist can draw inside the rectangle if points on the circle can touch the sides of the rectangle?

_____ centimeters

© Houghton Mifflin Harcourt Publishing Company

Module

3

Transformations and Similarity

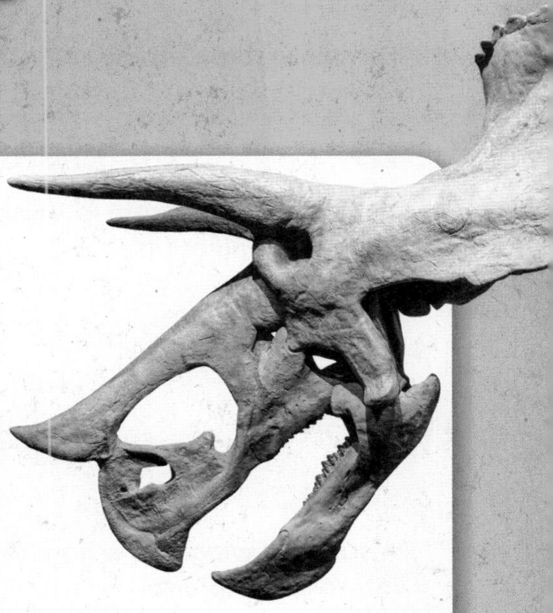

DO YOU HAUL BONES?

A museum received a crate containing a set of dinosaur bones. You need to move the crate from its current location to the location marked on the grid. Each unit on the grid represents 1 meter.

How could you use a sequence of transformations to haul the crate to its new location?

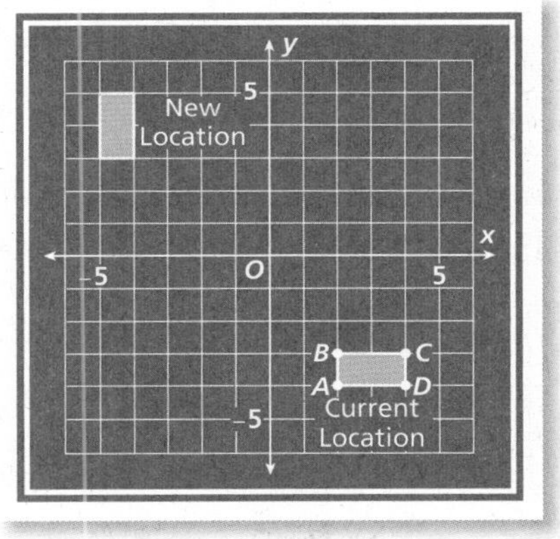

____

____

____

____

____

Turn and Talk

Why might the museum not want you to use a reflection to move the crate?

© Houghton Mifflin Harcourt Publishing Company • Image Credits: ©stockdevil/iStock / Getty Images Plus/Getty Images

Are You Ready?

Complete these problems to review prior concepts and skills you will need for this module.

Polygons in the Coordinate Plane

Determine the length, in units, of each side of the figure on the coordinate plane.

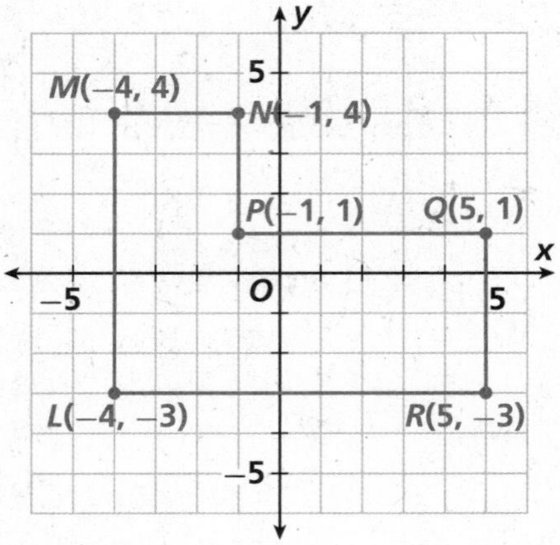

1. $\overline{LM}$ ________ **2.** $\overline{MN}$ ________

3. $\overline{NP}$ ________ **4.** $\overline{PQ}$ ________

5. $\overline{QR}$ ________ **6.** $\overline{LR}$ ________

Scale Drawings

A scale drawing of a school cafeteria has a scale of 1 inch : 4 feet. Use this information to answer each question.

7. In the drawing, the cafeteria dining room has a length of 18 inches. What is the actual length of the dining room?

____

8. The actual width of the cafeteria kitchen is 42 feet. What is the width of the kitchen in the scale drawing?

____

Translations, Reflections, and Rotations

Draw the image of each transformation on the coordinate plane.

9. Rotate Triangle *ABC* 180° about the origin.

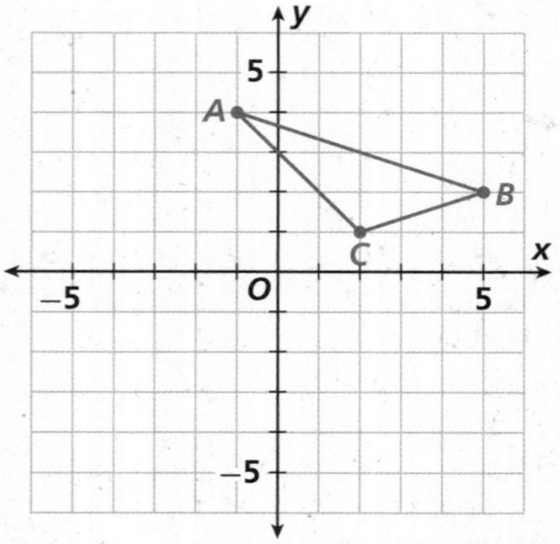

10. Reflect Triangle *DEF* across the *y*-axis, and then translate it 4 units down.

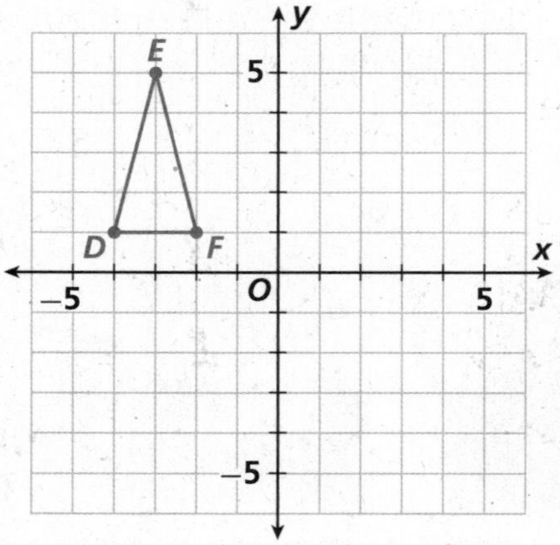

© Houghton Mifflin Harcourt Publishing Company

Name ____________________

Investigate Reductions and Enlargements

I Can identify and perform enlargements and reductions.

Spark Your Learning

SMALL GROUPS

Rachel wants to enlarge her company logo for a sign. Sketch an **enlargement** of the **Roofs by Rachel** logo. Use your protractor to make sure the angle measurements of your enlargement stay the same as the original.

How are the two images alike? How are they different? Describe your findings.

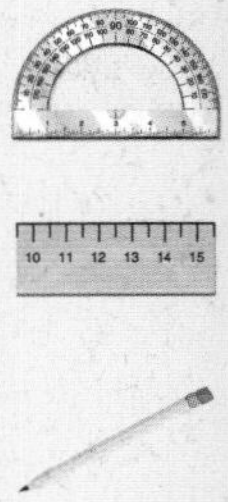

Turn and Talk Write ratios comparing the lengths of the short and long sides of the original parallelogram and also of your enlarged parallelogram. What do you find?

© Houghton Mifflin Harcourt Publishing Company

Build Understanding

Many computers and phones use reductions, called thumbnails, to represent images. **Reductions** are transformations that keep the proportions of the original image but are smaller in size.

1 **A.** Triangle ABC is a drawing of the side of a roof. Use a ruler and a protractor to measure $\triangle ABC$.

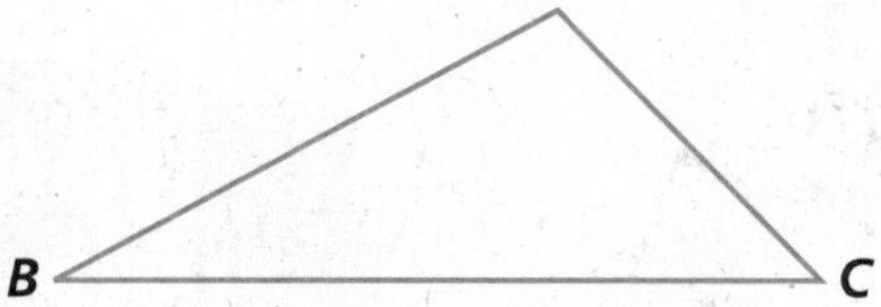

$\angle A$ measures ______°. $\overline{AB}$ measures ______ inch(es).

$\angle B$ measures ______°. $\overline{BC}$ measures ______ inch(es).

$\angle C$ measures ______°. $\overline{AC}$ measures ______ inch(es).

B. If $\triangle A'B'C'$ is a reduction of $\triangle ABC$ that results in $\triangle A'B'C'$ having a perimeter exactly half that of $\triangle ABC$, what are the measurements of $\triangle A'B'C'$?

$\angle A'$ measures ______°. $\overline{A'B'}$ measures ______ inch(es).

$\angle B'$ measures ______°. $\overline{B'C'}$ measures ______ inch(es).

$\angle C'$ measures ______°. $\overline{A'C'}$ measures ______ inch(es).

C. Draw $\triangle A'B'C'$ as a reduction.

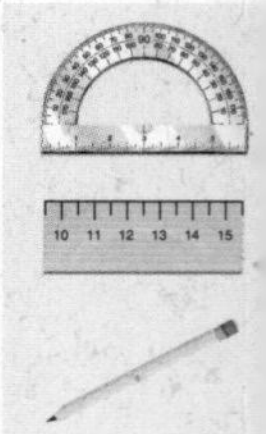

D. Explain how you know it is a reduction.

______

______

______

Turn and Talk What would happen if you enlarged $\triangle A'B'C'$? Could you make a new image that is congruent to the original figure $\triangle ABC$? If so, how?

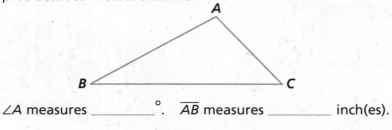

© Houghton Mifflin Harcourt Publishing Company • Image Credits: (all) ©ariwasabi/Getty Images

Name

Look at this photo. As the train tracks get closer to the front, they appear larger. A coordinate grid can help show how the tracks' apparent size changes.

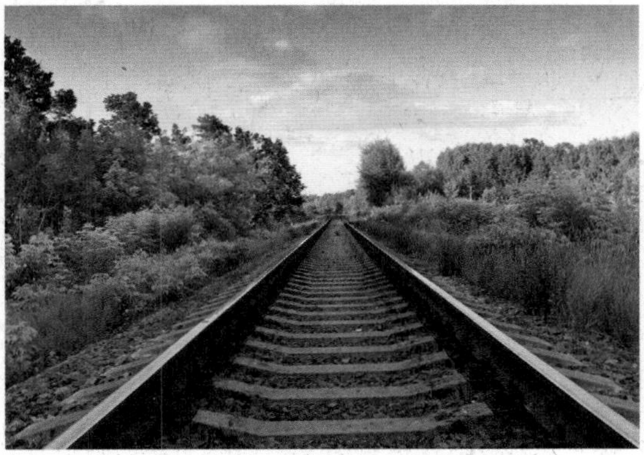

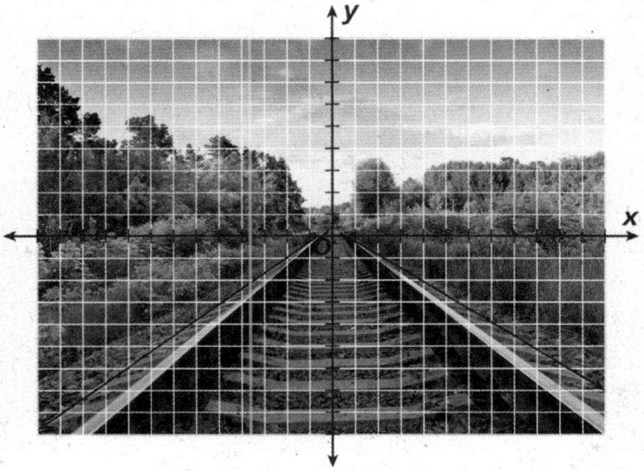

© Houghton Mifflin Harcourt Publishing Company • Image Credit: ©Raimundas/Shutterstock

2 Samuel wants to draw a railroad tunnel on a grid. First he draws the far end of the tunnel in blue as shown, then he decides to use rays to help him accurately enlarge the image.

A. Samuel draws two rays. Each starts at the origin and passes through a vertex of the blue preimage. He uses the rays to help sketch the floor of the tunnel closest to the viewer.

How do the rays help him draw the floor of the tunnel closest to the viewer?

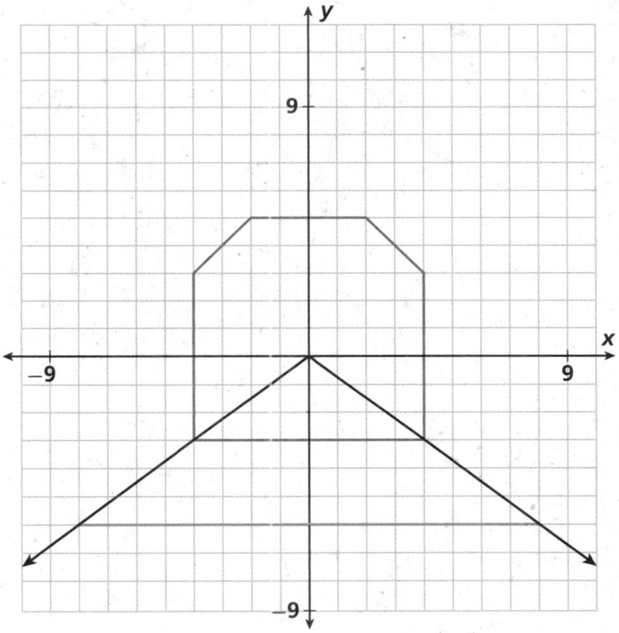

B. Draw additional rays from the origin through the vertices of Samuel's preimage. Use those rays to complete the enlarged image.

C. Look at your new image. Is it the same shape as the preimage? Explain how you know.

3 You can make reductions on a coordinate grid.

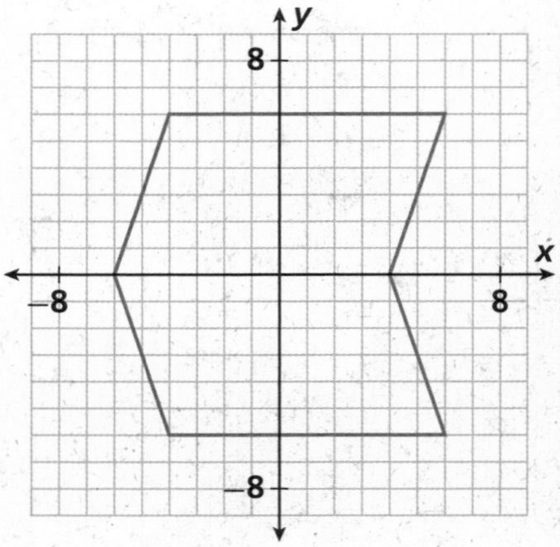

A. Draw rays from the origin through the vertices of the given shape. How can these rays help you reduce the shape?

B. Reduce the shape so the sides are half the original length. Use the grid to sketch your new image.

C. How can you be sure your image shows an accurate reduction?

Check Understanding

1. Does this pair show a reduction? Why or why not?

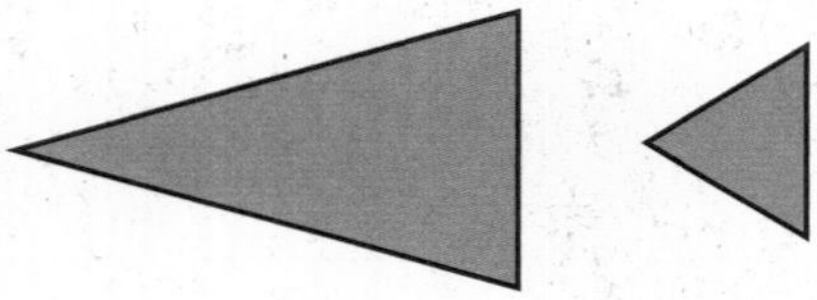

2. Sketch an enlargement of the shape. Explain how you know it's an enlargement.

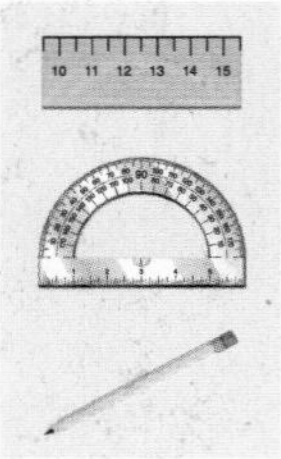

© Houghton Mifflin Harcourt Publishing Company • **Image Credit:** ©gnohz/Shutterstock

On Your Own

3. Identify whether the transformation from each blue Figure *A* to green Figure *B* is an enlargement or a reduction.

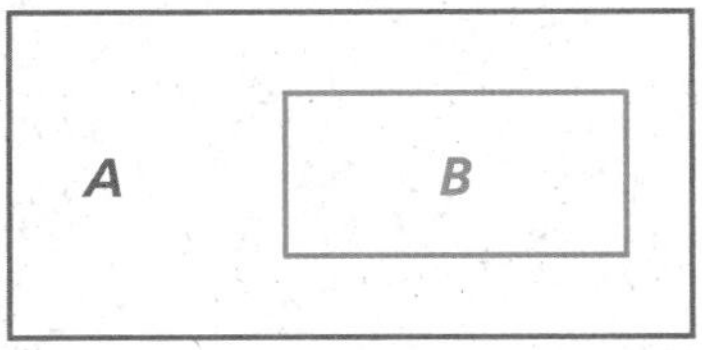

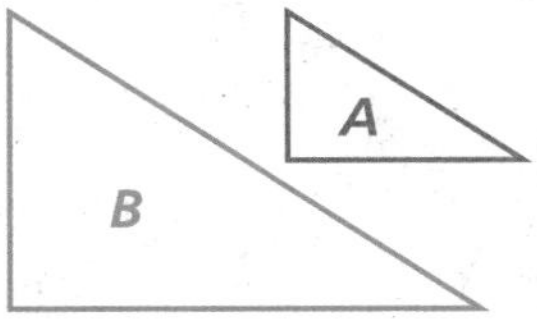

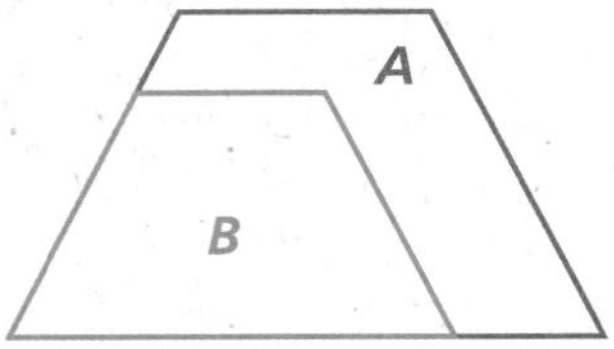

4. Use the coordinate plane to sketch an enlargement with side lengths twice those in the figure shown.

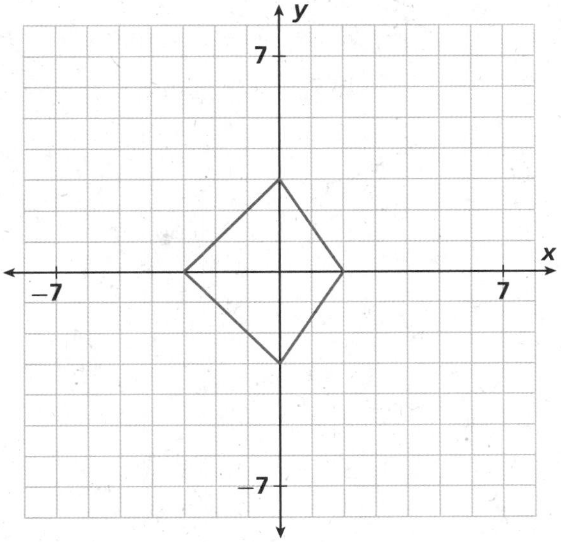

5. MP **Reason** Fredrick drew a reduction of a phone. Is the reduction accurate? Why or why not?

© Houghton Mifflin Harcourt Publishing Company • Image Credit: ©rangizzz/Shutterstock

6. MP **Use Tools** Draw a reduction of the figure with dimensions half those of the original figure.

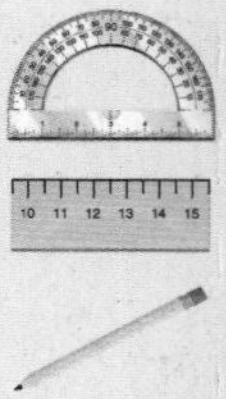

7. MP **Use Tools** Use the coordinate plane to reduce the side lengths of the figure by a factor of 2.

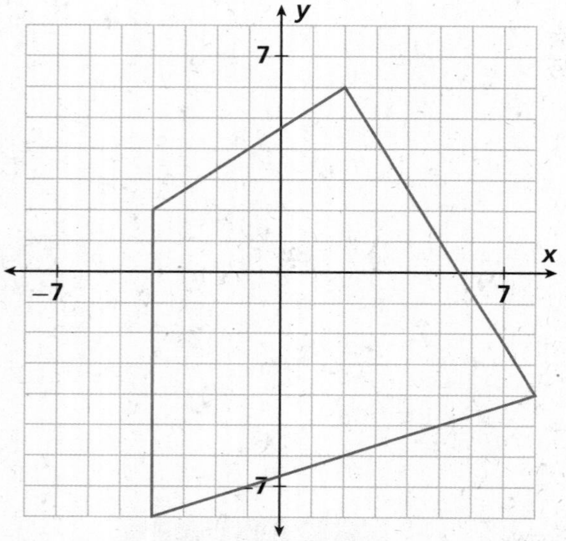

8. For each figure, determine if it is a reduction of Figure *S*.

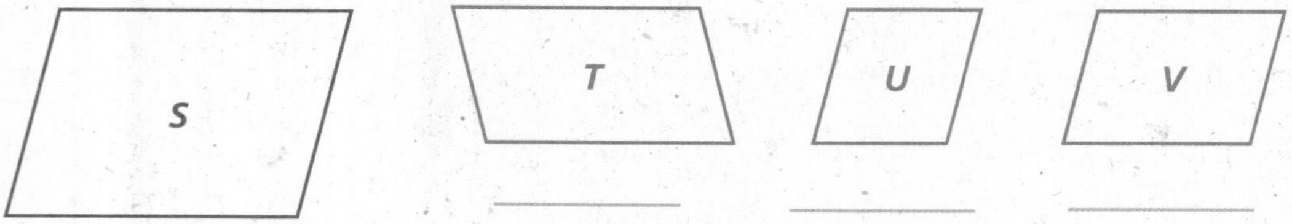

I'm in a Learning Mindset!

How does my mindset affect my confidence with reducing and enlarging figures?

© Houghton Mifflin Harcourt Publishing Company

ONLINE
Ed Video Tutorials and Interactive Examples

Name ______________________________

Investigate Reductions and Enlargements

1. (MP) **Use Tools** In the space provided, sketch an enlargement that has sides $\frac{3}{2}$ the length of each given figure.

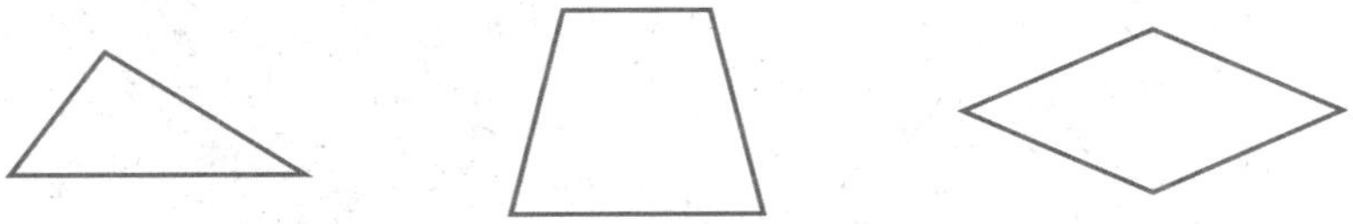

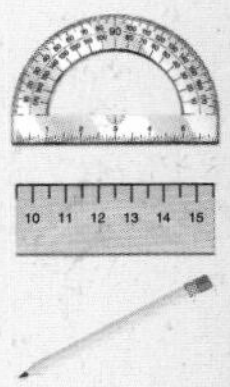

2. **A.** Use the coordinate plane to sketch a reduction of the irregular pentagon on the grid by any amount.

____

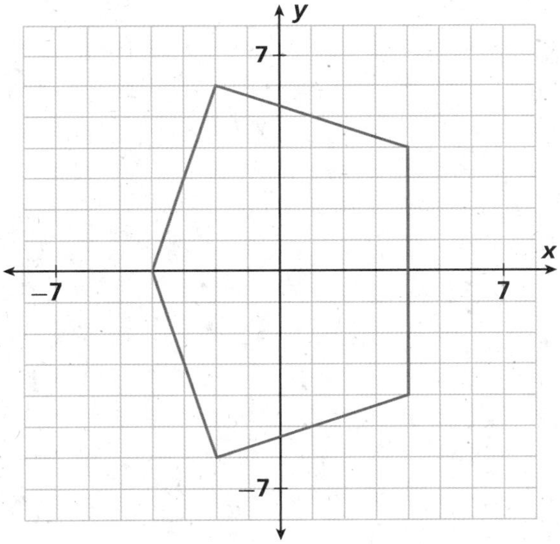

The Pentagon, in Washington, DC, is a regular pentagon.

B. Measure the angles of both figures with a protractor. Explain your findings.

____

____

3. A certain Figure *Q* is enlarged to form Figure *P*. Are Figures *Q* and *P* congruent? Why or why not?

____

____

© Houghton Mifflin Harcourt Publishing Company • Image Credit: ©Digital Vision/Getty Images

Test Prep

4. In which of the following has Figure 1 been enlarged to form Figure 2?

Ⓐ
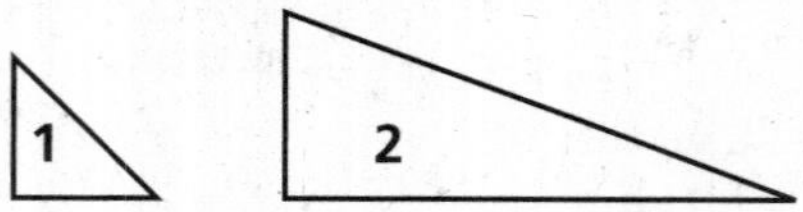

Ⓒ
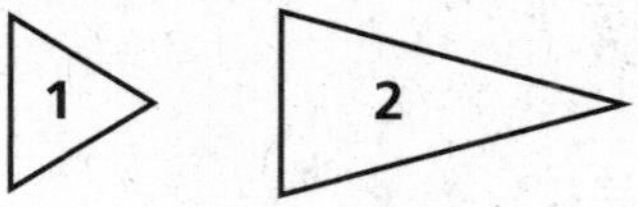

Ⓑ
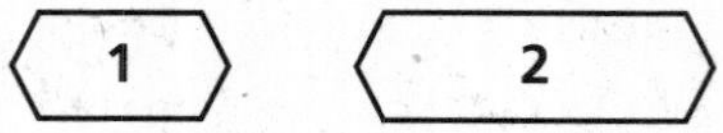

Ⓓ
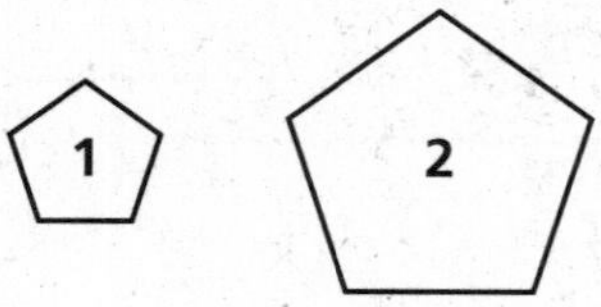

5. One of the shapes on the coordinate grid was transformed into the other shape. Which term could describe the transformation?

Ⓐ reflection Ⓑ enlargement Ⓒ translation Ⓓ rotation

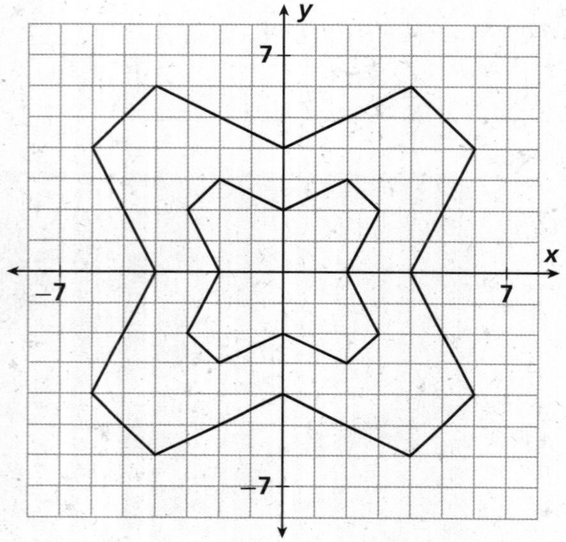

Spiral Review

6. Rotate △*ABC* 90° counterclockwise about the origin.

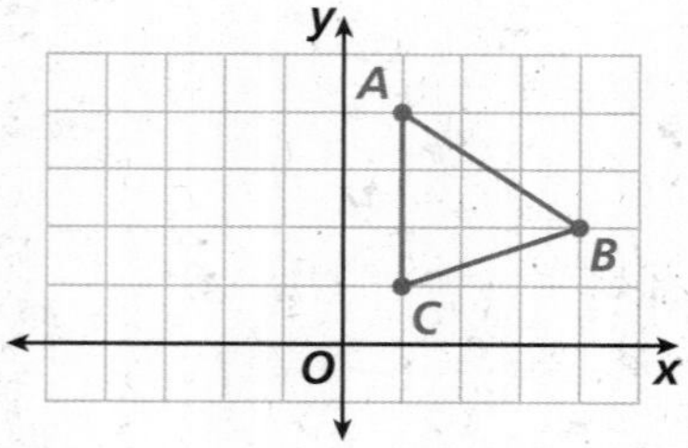

7. This design is made using only one type of transformation multiple times. Which one type of transformation is this?

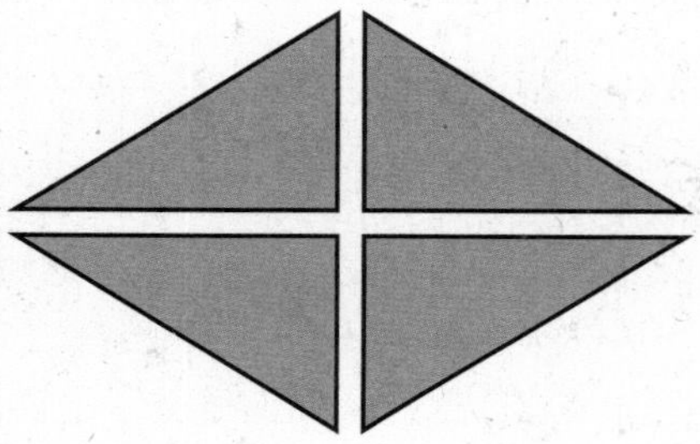

____

© Houghton Mifflin Harcourt Publishing Company

Name ____________________

Explore Dilations

I Can identify and perform dilations given a scale factor and center of dilation, perform a dilation on a coordinate plane, and identify an algebraic rule for the dilation.

Spark Your Learning

PAIRS

On a computer, Raquel uses polygons and a circle to make a model of the top of London's Big Ben clock tower. Then she reduces it.

Compare Raquel's image and reduction. What do you find?

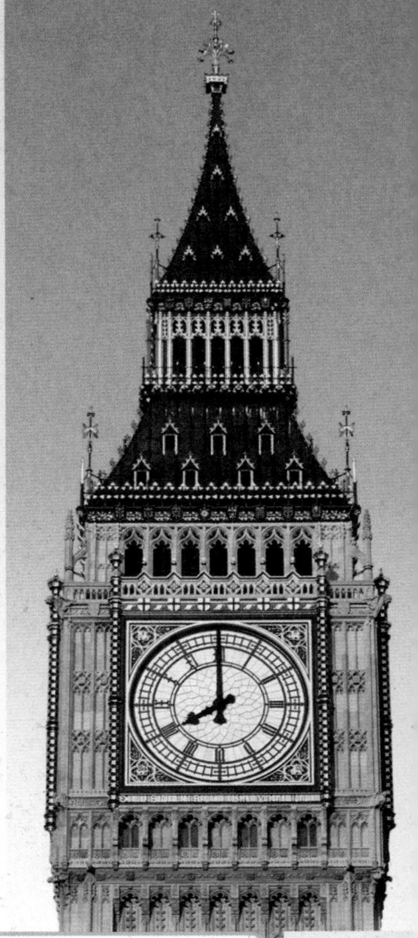

Turn and Talk What is the relationship between the perimeter of Raquel's original image and her reduction? How does this relate to the relationship between the side lengths?

© Houghton Mifflin Harcourt Publishing Company • Image Credit: ©Andrew Ward/Life File/Photodisc/Getty Images

Build Understanding

ACTIVITY

1 Rectangle *R′S′T′U′* is a dilation of Rectangle *RSTU*.

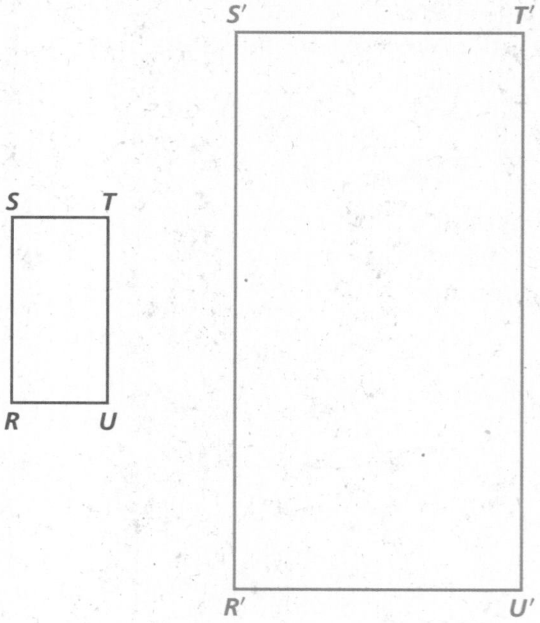

Connect to Vocabulary

A **dilation** is a transformation that produces an image that is proportional to its preimage.

A. Measure the sides of the figures, then fill in the table.

	RSTU	*R′S′T′U′*
Height (in.)		
Width (in.)		

What is the relationship between the measurements of the two rectangles?

____

____

B. What is the scale factor of this dilation?

____

C. Points *R* and *R′* are an example of corresponding vertices. Use a ruler or straight edge to draw four rays, each extending from a vertex of the image to the corresponding vertex of the preimage, and continuing through to the left. What do you notice?

____

D. Label the center of dilation for Rectangles *RSTU* and *R′S′T′U′* as Point *P*.

Connect to Vocabulary

The **scale factor** of a dilation is the ratio of the side lengths of the image to the preimage.
The point of intersection of lines through each pair of corresponding vertices in a dilation is called the **center of dilation**.

© Houghton Mifflin Harcourt Publishing Company

Step It Out

2

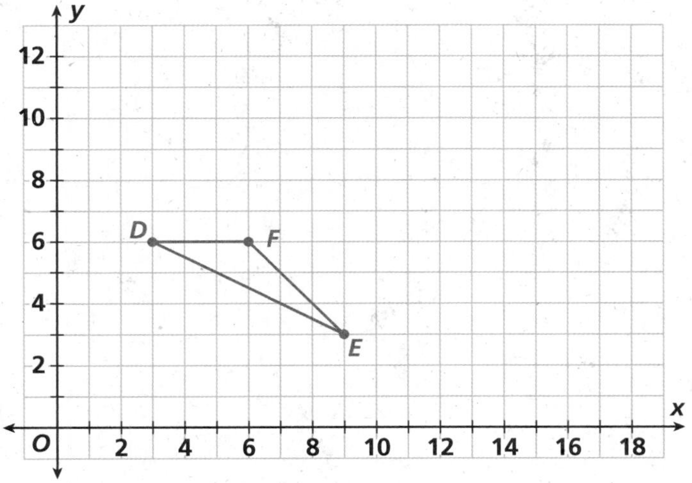

A. In order to dilate △*DEF* to form △*D′E′F′* with a scale factor of 2 and center of dilation (0, 0), first draw a ray from the center of dilation through Vertex *D*.

B. Find a point on the ray that is twice the distance from the center of dilation as Vertex *D*. Label it *D′*.

C. Give the ordered pairs for Vertices *D* and *D′*. How are these values related to the scale factor?

D. Predict the ordered pairs for Vertices *E′* and *F′*. Explain your reasoning.

E. Draw △*D′E′F′* on the graph. Use rays from the center of dilation to draw your dilation.

F. Using the ordered pairs of △*DEF*, how would you make a dilation △*D″E″F″* with a scale factor of $\frac{1}{3}$ and center (0, 0)?

G. Draw △*D″E″F″* on the graph. Use rays from the center of dilation to check your dilation. What are the coordinates of the vertices of △*D″E″F″*?

H. What happens when you dilate △*DEF* with a scale factor of 1? Describe the resulting image.

© Houghton Mifflin Harcourt Publishing Company

3 $\triangle G'H'J'$ is a dilation of $\triangle GHJ$. Find the scale factor and center of dilation. Represent the dilation algebraically.

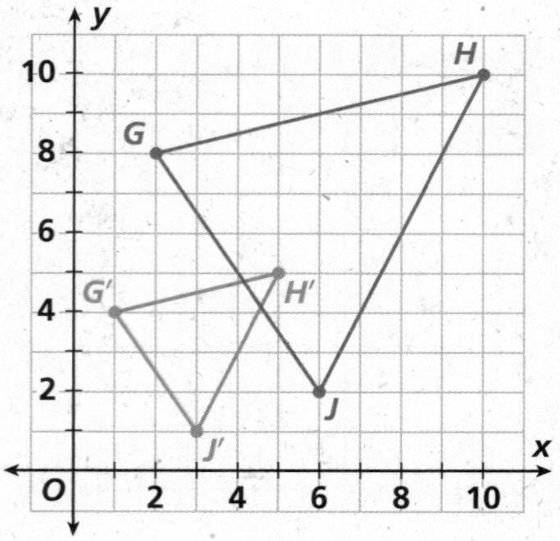

A. Complete the table.

G (2, 8)	→	G′ (1, 4)
H	→	H′
J	→	J′

B. How are the corresponding coordinates for the image and the preimage related?

____

____

C. What is the scale factor of the dilation? ________

D. Circle the algebraic representation that best describes this dilation. Explain your reasoning.

$(x, y) \rightarrow \left(x + \frac{1}{2}, y + \frac{1}{2}\right)$ $\qquad$ $(x, y) \rightarrow \left(x - \frac{1}{2}, y - \frac{1}{2}\right)$

$(x, y) \rightarrow \left(\frac{1}{2}x, \frac{1}{2}y\right)$ $\qquad$ $(x, y) \rightarrow (2x, 2y)$

____

____

E. Draw rays through corresponding vertices of both figures to find the center of dilation. What is the center of dilation?

____

Check Understanding

1. Does the pair of figures show a dilation with scale factor 4?

A.

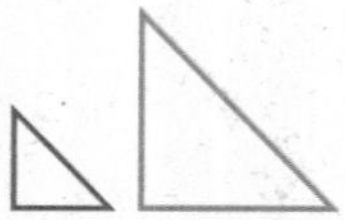

____

B.

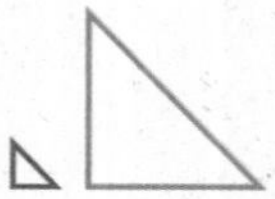

____

2. Polygon *BCDE* has vertices *B*(5, 1), *C*(5, 6), *D*(10, 6), and *E*(10, 1). If *B′C′D′E′* is a dilation of *BCDE* with scale factor 4 and center (0, 0), give the coordinates of *B′C′D′E′*.

____

© Houghton Mifflin Harcourt Publishing Company

Name

On Your Own

3. (MP) **Reason** Figure S' is a dilation of Figure S.

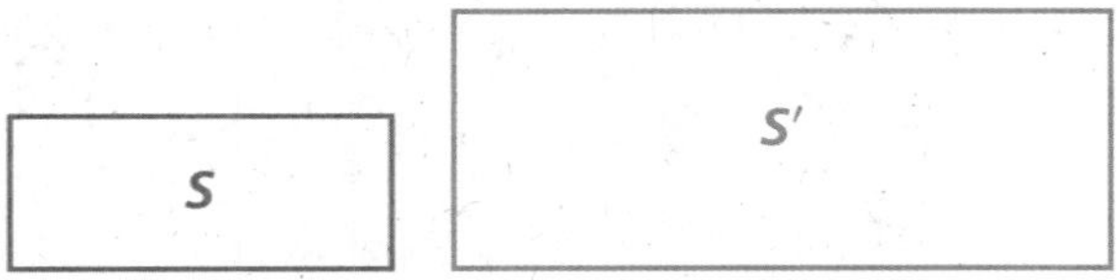

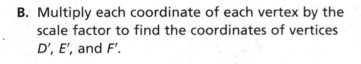

A. Is the scale factor greater than 1 or less than 1? ______________

B. Is Figure S congruent to Figure S'? ______________

C. Is the dilation a reduction? ______________

4. (MP) **Use Tools** Dilate $\triangle DEF$ with scale factor $\frac{3}{2}$ and center (0, 0).

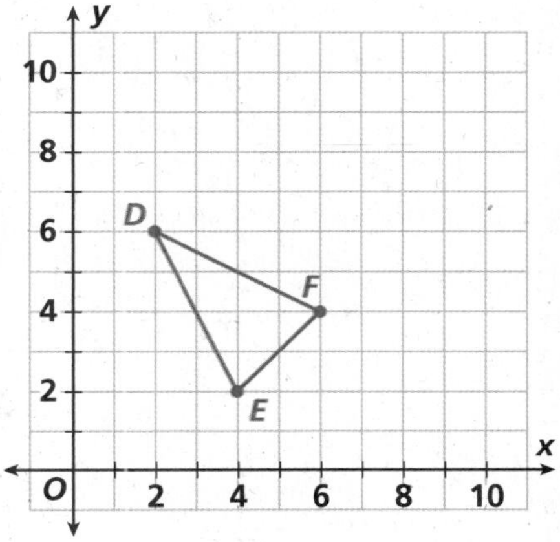

A. Find the coordinates of vertices D, E, and F.

____

B. Multiply each coordinate of each vertex by the scale factor to find the coordinates of vertices D', E', and F'.

____

C. Graph and label the vertices D', E', and F'. Draw rays to connect each corresponding vertex with the center of dilation.

D. Represent the dilation algebraically.

____

5. Figure $J'K'L'M'$ is a dilation of Figure $JKLM$. The center of dilation is the origin, (0, 0).

$J(3, 2)$	$\rightarrow$	$J'(9, 6)$
$K(7, 4)$	$\rightarrow$	$K'(21, 12)$
$L(7, 9)$	$\rightarrow$	L'
$M(2, 5)$	$\rightarrow$	M'

A. Given the coordinates of J, J', K, and K', what is the scale factor of the dilation?

____

B. Use the scale factor to complete the table for points L' and M'.

C. Represent the dilation algebraically.

____

© Houghton Mifflin Harcourt Publishing Company

6. Graph $\triangle TUV$ with vertices $T(4, 2)$, $U(2, 0)$, and $V(2, 4)$. Dilate the figure by a scale factor of $\frac{5}{2}$ with a center of dilation of $(0, 0)$. Graph $\triangle T'U'V'$.

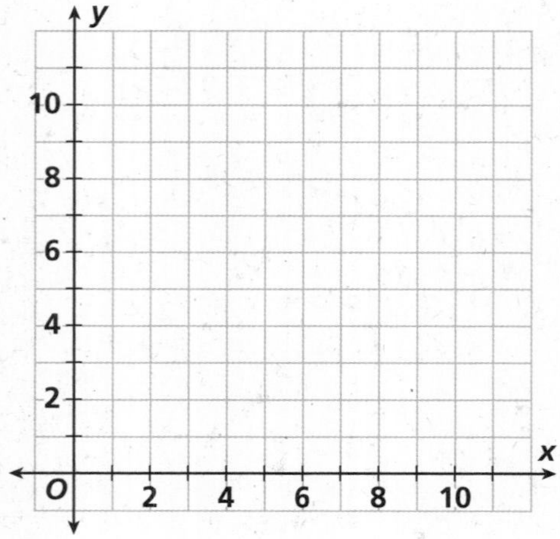

7. **STEM** An ophthalmologist is a doctor who studies the eye. The ophthalmologist records the effect of changes in lighting on the size of the pupil of the eye and graphs the results on a coordinate plane.

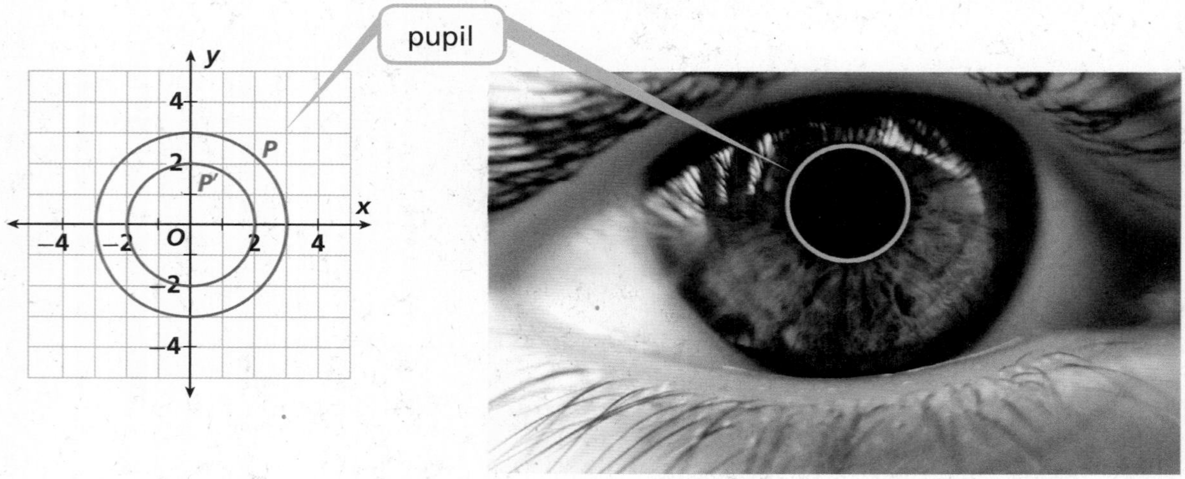

A. What is the scale factor of the dilation from P to P'? ________

B. Graph a dilation of P using scale factor $\frac{1}{3}$.

© Houghton Mifflin Harcourt Publishing Company • Image Credit: ©Miroslav Kyosev/EyeEm/Getty Images

I'm in a Learning Mindset!

Did I have confidence in my answer? What specific evidence do I have that I found a scale factor of a dilation correctly?

____

____

Name ______________________________

ONLINE
Video Tutorials and Interactive Examples

Explore Dilations

1. (MP) **Reason** Which shape shows a dilation of Figure *V*? Justify your reasoning.

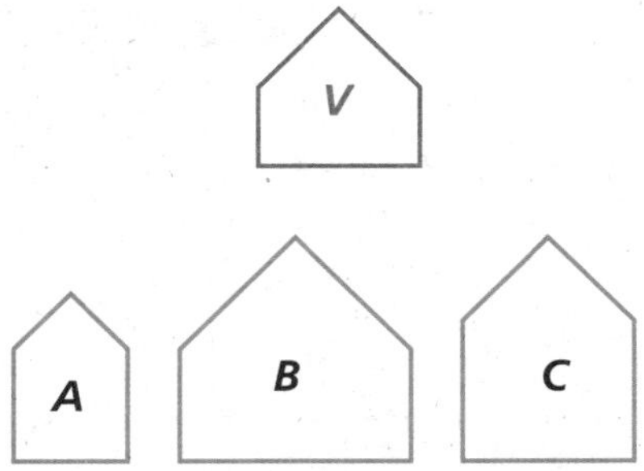

____

____

2. (MP) **Use Tools** What is the scale factor of the dilation from the smaller square to the larger?

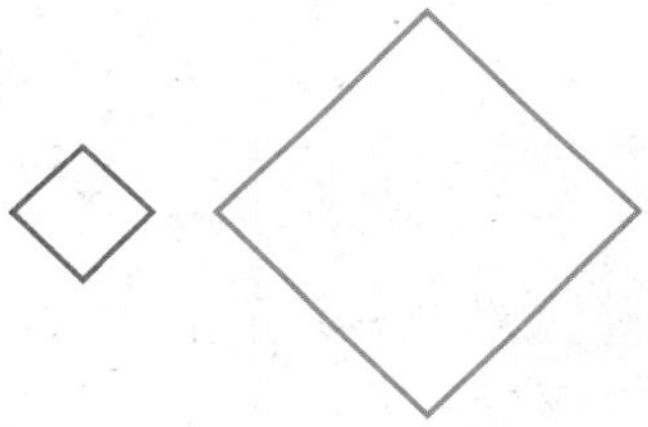

____

3. Identify the center of dilation for the given figures.

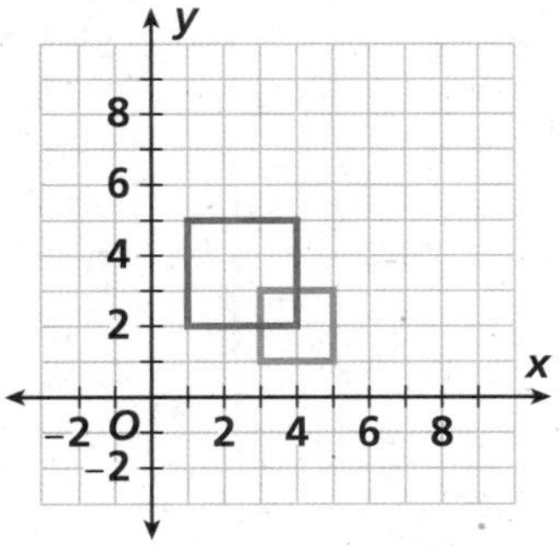

____

4. Polygon *WXYZ* has vertices *W*(4, 2), *X*(6, 4), *Y*(2, 3), and *Z*(4, 5). If *W′X′Y′Z′* is a dilation of *WXYZ* with center of dilation (0, 0) and vertex coordinates *W′*(2, 1), *X′*(3, 2), *Y′*(1, 1.5), and *Z′*(2, 2.5), find the scale factor.

____

© Houghton Mifflin Harcourt Publishing Company • Image Credit: ©Duane Osborn/Getty Images

Test Prep

5. Dilate *ABCD* with a scale factor of 2 and center (0, 0).

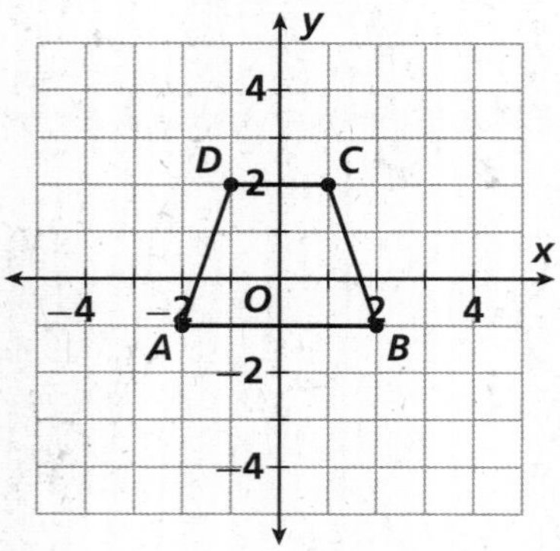

6. △*MNP* has vertices *M*(4, 8), *N*(12, 6), and *P*(2, 4). △*M′N′P′* is a dilation of △*MNP* with a scale factor of $\frac{1}{2}$ and center (0, 0). Select the coordinates of the vertices of △*M′N′P′*.

Ⓐ *M′*(1, 2), *N′*(2, 1), and *P′*(1, 2)

Ⓑ *M′*(2, 4), *N′*(6, 3), and *P′*(1, 2)

Ⓒ *M′*(4, 8), *N′*(12, 6), and *P′*(2, 4)

Ⓓ *M′*(8, 16), *N′*(24, 12), and *P′*(4, 8)

7. A triangle has angles of 30°, 60°, and 90°. It is dilated by a scale factor of 3. Give the angle measures of the dilation of the triangle.

____

Spiral Review

8. Translate the shape three units up and two units left.

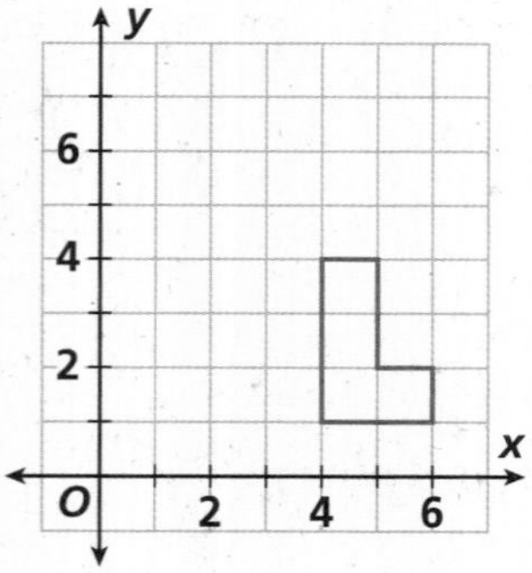

9. What single transformation is represented by the expression *P*(*x*, *y*) → *P′*(−*x*, −*y*)?

____

© Houghton Mifflin Harcourt Publishing Company

Name ______________________________

Understand and Recognize Similar Figures

I Can describe a sequence of transformations that exhibits the similarity between two figures.

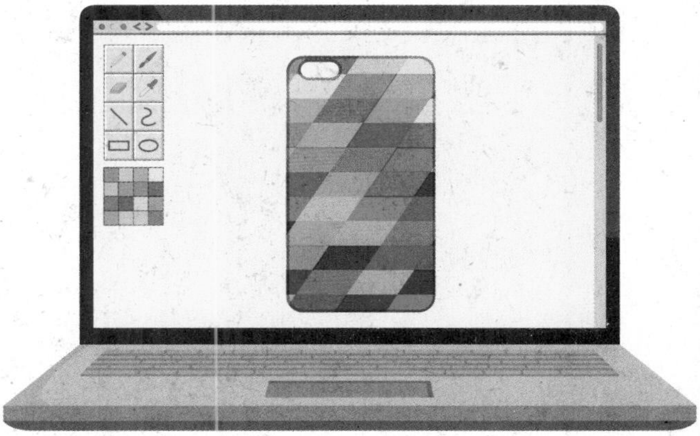

Spark Your Learning

SMALL GROUPS

Jamar is using a website to make a customized phone case. To make a design for the case, he starts by drawing Parallelogram *ABCD*. Then he dilates the parallelogram using a vertex as the center of dilation. Finally, he translates the dilated parallelogram. Draw a possible final image for the figure and label it *A′B′C′D′*. Show your work.

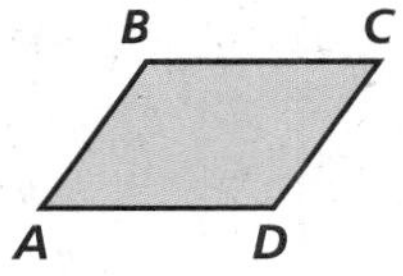

How are the sides and angles of *ABCD* and *A′B′C′D′* the same? How are they different?

____

____

Turn and Talk Suppose Jamar uses the same translation first, followed by the same dilation. Would the answers to the above questions be different? Explain.

© Houghton Mifflin Harcourt Publishing Company

Build Understanding

1 Bailey is going to use the shapes shown to make a customized phone case.

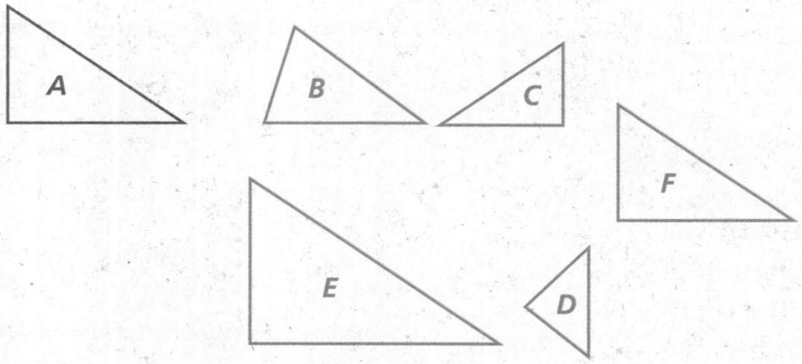

A. Which triangles are similar to Triangle *A*? You can use tracing paper, a protractor, and/or a ruler to help you decide which triangles are similar.

Connect to Vocabulary

Two figures are **similar** if one can be obtained from the other by a transformation or sequence of transformations that may include dilation.

B. For each of the similar triangles you identified, describe a transformation or sequence of transformations that takes Triangle *A* to the other triangle.

C. Is Triangle *A* similar to Triangle *B*? Why or why not?

D. Bailey decides to add another triangle to her design. She dilates Triangle *B* using a scale factor of 1 and then rotates the image to form Triangle *G*. How are Triangle *B* and Triangle *G* related? Explain.

Turn and Talk If two figures are congruent can you always conclude that they are similar? Why or why not?

© Houghton Mifflin Harcourt Publishing Company

Name ______________________

Step It Out

2 Brendan uses a coordinate plane to draw figures for his custom phone case. He includes several similar figures in the design, as shown on the graph.

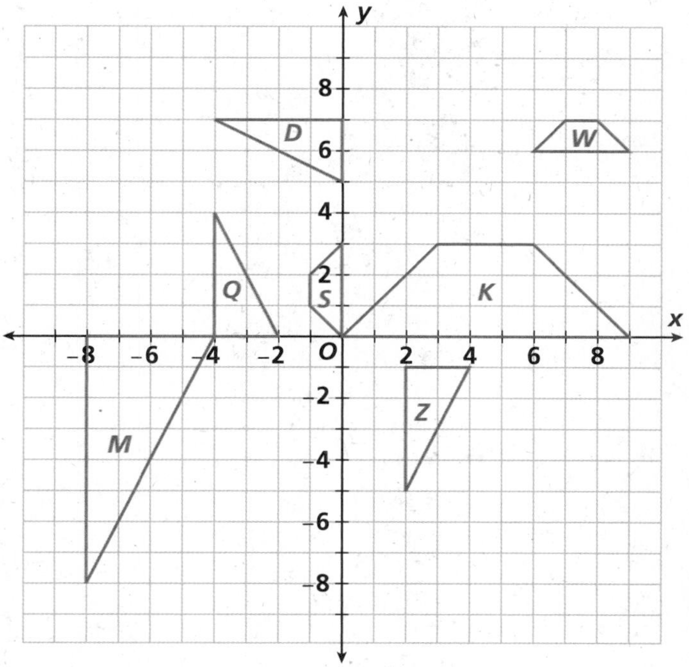

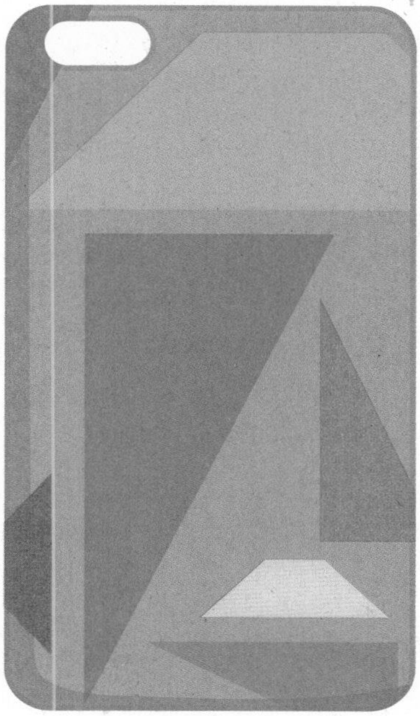

A. For each pair of similar figures, describe a sequence of transformations that can be used to map the first figure to the second figure.

Figure *K* to Figure *W*

____

____

Figure *S* to Figure *K*

____

____

B. Which pair of similar figures can be mapped from one to the other by the given sequence of transformations?

a dilation with scale factor $\frac{1}{2}$ and center of dilation (0, 0), followed by a reflection across the *x*-axis

____

the dilation $(x, y) \rightarrow (2x, 2y)$ with a center of dilation (0, 0), followed by a translation 12 units left and 2 units up

____

© Houghton Mifflin Harcourt Publishing Company

3 For his phone case, Brendan makes an additional shape $\triangle ABC$. He dilates the triangle using a dilation with a scale factor of $\frac{1}{2}$ and center of dilation (0, 0). Then he reflects the image across the *y*-axis.

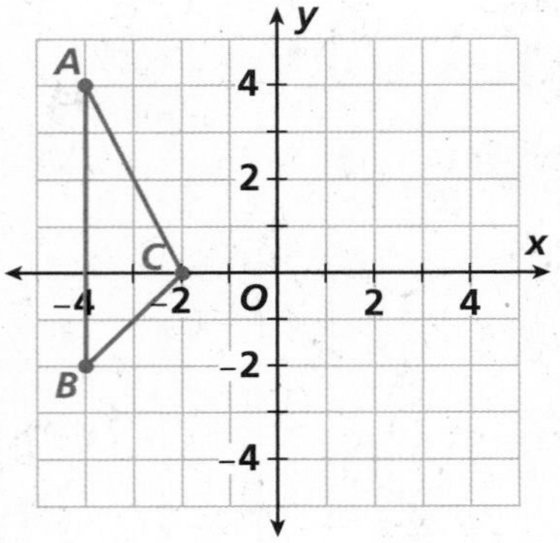

A. Draw the image of $\triangle ABC$ after the dilation.

B. Draw the final image after the reflection. Label the final image $\triangle A'B'C'$.

C. What can you conclude about $\triangle ABC$ and $\triangle A'B'C'$? Why?

D. Suppose Brendan uses a dilation with a scale factor of 1 instead of a scale factor of $\frac{1}{2}$. What can you conclude about $\triangle ABC$ and $\triangle A'B'C'$ in this case? Explain.

Check Understanding

1. Doretta is choosing tiles for a mosaic. She wants to choose two tiles that are similar but not congruent. Which pair of tiles could she use? Explain why she can only choose those tiles.

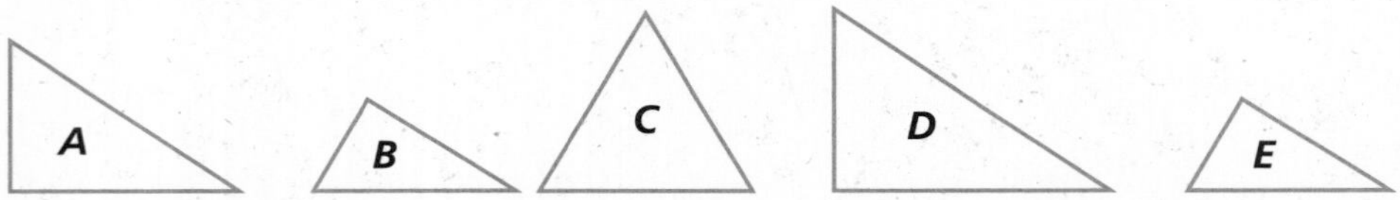

2. Identify all pairs of similar figures on the coordinate plane. For each pair, describe the sequence of transformations that maps one figure to the other.

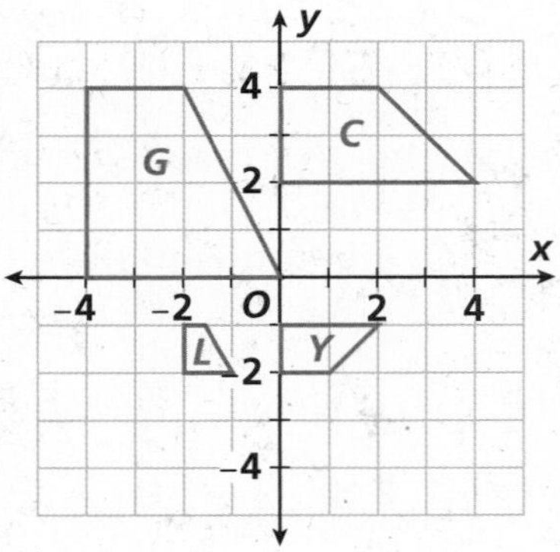

© Houghton Mifflin Harcourt Publishing Company

Name

On Your Own

3. Ryan is a landscape architect. He uses the coordinate plane shown to design flower beds at a mall.

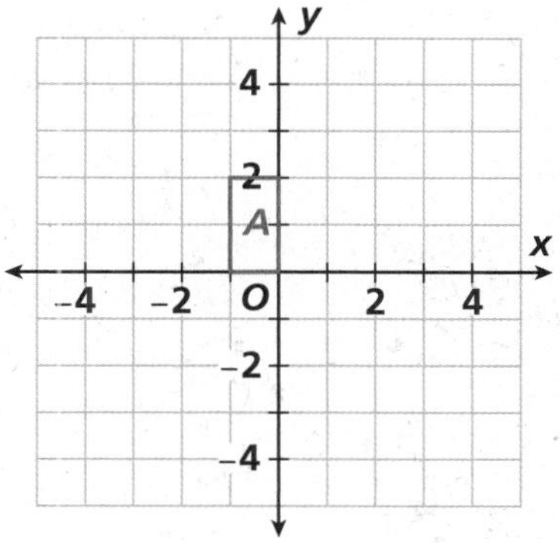

A. To draw flower bed *B*, Ryan reflects flower bed *A* across the *x*-axis. Then he applies the dilation $(x, y) \rightarrow (2x, 2y)$. Draw and label flower bed *B*.

B. To draw flower bed *C*, Ryan rotates flower bed *A* by 180° about the origin. Then he applies the dilation $(x, y) \rightarrow (2.5x, 2.5y)$. Draw and label flower bed *C*.

C. What can you conclude about the three flower beds?

____

4. **Art** A car show has advertising posters in different shapes and sizes. They are shown as they appear next to each other on a wall at the car show.

A. Circle all of the posters that are similar.

B. For the posters you identified, describe a sequence of transformations that takes one poster to the other.

____

Use the graph to solve Problems 5–7.

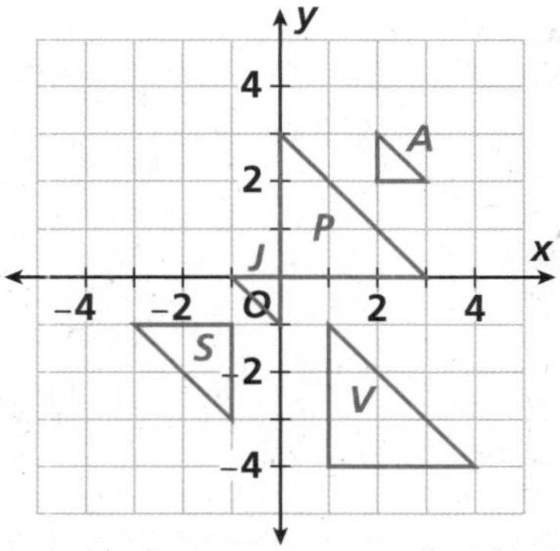

5. Which pair of similar triangles can be mapped from one to the other by a dilation with scale factor $\frac{1}{3}$ and center of dilation (0, 0), followed by a rotation of 180° clockwise around the origin?

____

6. Which pair of similar triangles can be mapped from one to the other by a dilation with scale factor 3 and center of dilation (0, 0), followed by the translation $(x, y) \rightarrow (x - 6, y - 6)$?

____

7. Describe a sequence of transformations that can be used to map Triangle *J* to Triangle *S*.

____

© Houghton Mifflin Harcourt Publishing Company

8. Glass laboratory flasks come in a variety of shapes and sizes. Different flasks have different purposes, such as heating, measuring, and mixing. Are any of the flasks shown similar? Explain why or why not.

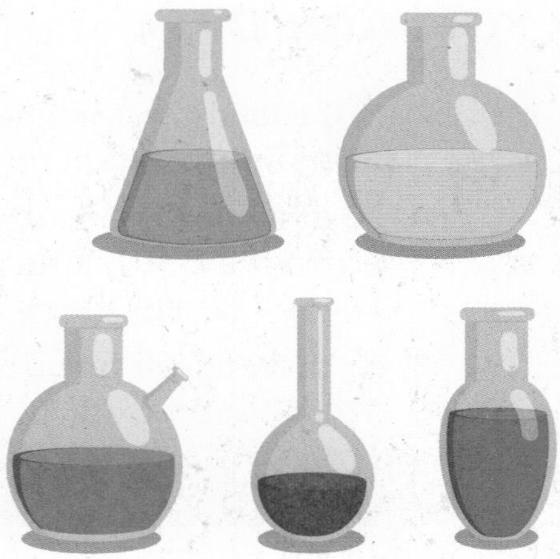

9. Describe a sequence of transformations that can be used to map $\triangle RST$ with vertices $R(-1, 0)$, $S(0, 1)$, and $T(1, 0)$ to $\triangle JKL$ with vertices $J(-4, 0)$, $K(0, -4)$, and $L(4, 0)$.

10. **Open Ended** The coordinates of the vertices of $\triangle ABC$ are $A(0, 0)$, $B(0, 4)$, and $C(-2, 0)$. Give the coordinates of the vertices of a triangle, $\triangle DEF$, that is similar to $\triangle ABC$ but not congruent to $\triangle ABC$. Then describe a sequence of transformations that maps $\triangle ABC$ to $\triangle DEF$.

11. (MP) **Use Repeated Reasoning** Jaycee draws a sequence of squares on the coordinate plane. First she draws the square shown and dilates it using $(x, y) \rightarrow (3x, 3y)$. Then she uses this same transformation to dilate the image. She continues dilating each image in this way to draw a total of six squares. What dilation could she use to map the first square she draws directly to the last square she draws?

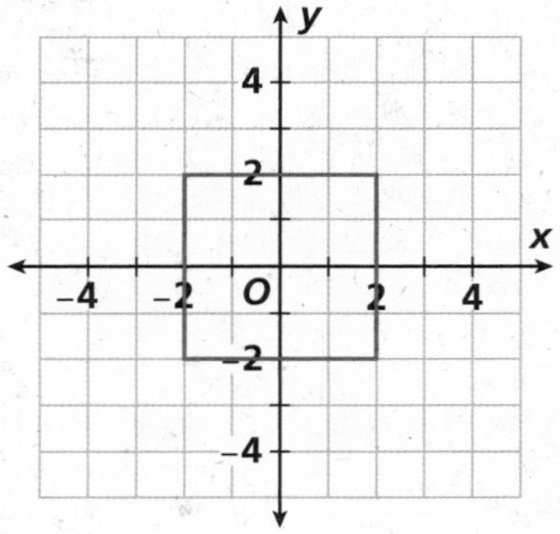

12. If Figure X is similar to Figure Y, and Figure Y is similar to Figure Z, can you conclude that Figure X is similar to Figure Z? Explain.

© Houghton Mifflin Harcourt Publishing Company

I'm in a Learning Mindset!

Do I have a fixed-mindset voice or a growth-mindset voice in my head when I'm finding similar figures? How can I tap into my growth-mindset voice?

Name ______________________________

ONLINE
Ed Video Tutorials and Interactive Examples

Understand and Recognize Similar Figures

1. MP **Use Tools** Keisha is using a coordinate plane to design the background image for a video game. She starts with $\triangle ABC$.

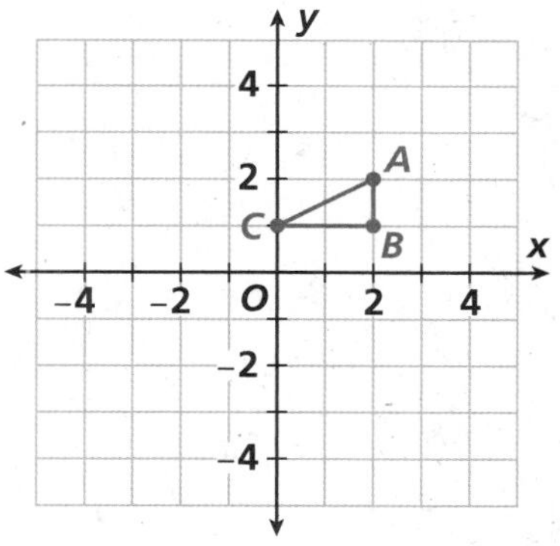

A. To draw $\triangle DEF$, Keisha translates $\triangle ABC$ using $(x, y) \rightarrow (x - 2, y)$. Then she applies the dilation with scale factor 2 and center of dilation (0, 0). Draw and label $\triangle DEF$.

B. To draw $\triangle GHJ$, Keisha reflects $\triangle ABC$ using $(x, y) \rightarrow (x, -y)$. Then she applies the dilation with scale factor 2 and center of dilation (0, 0). Draw and label $\triangle GHJ$.

C. MP **Critique Reasoning** Keisha claims that all three triangles are similar. Do you agree or disagree? Explain.

____

____

2. Marco is trying different designs for a business logo. Several of the logos are shown.

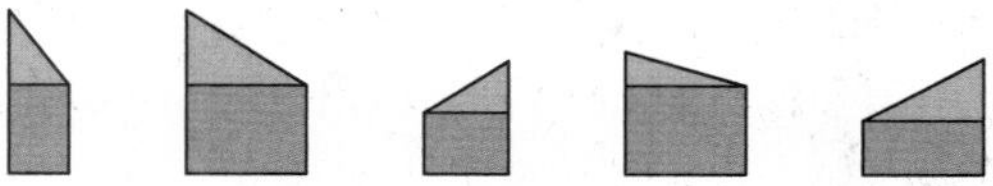

A. Circle all of the logos that are similar to each other.

B. For the logos you identified, describe a sequence of transformations that takes one logo to the other.

____

© Houghton Mifflin Harcourt Publishing Company

3. **Math on the Spot** Consider the pairs of figures on the coordinate planes.

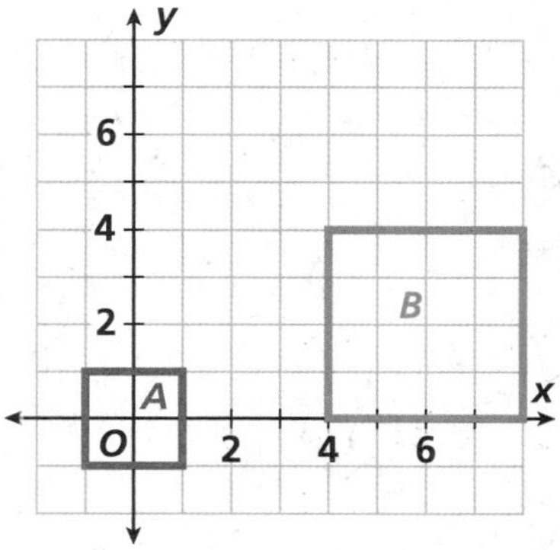

A. Identify a sequence of transformations that will transform Figure *A* onto Figure *B*. Tell whether the figures are congruent. Tell whether they are similar.

____

____

____

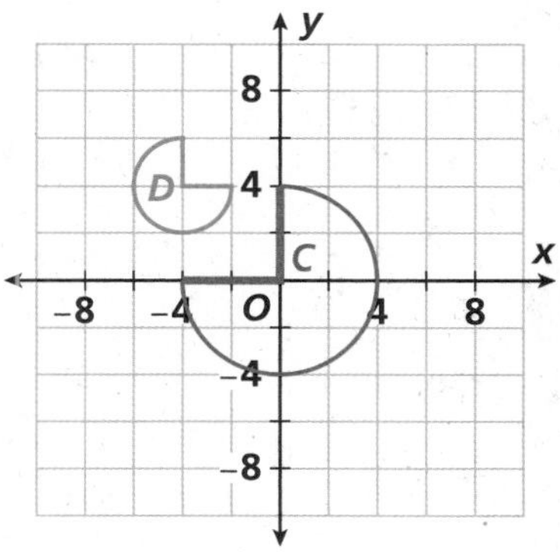

B. Identify a sequence of transformations that will transform Figure *C* onto Figure *D*. Tell whether the figures are congruent. Tell whether they are similar.

____

____

____

Test Prep

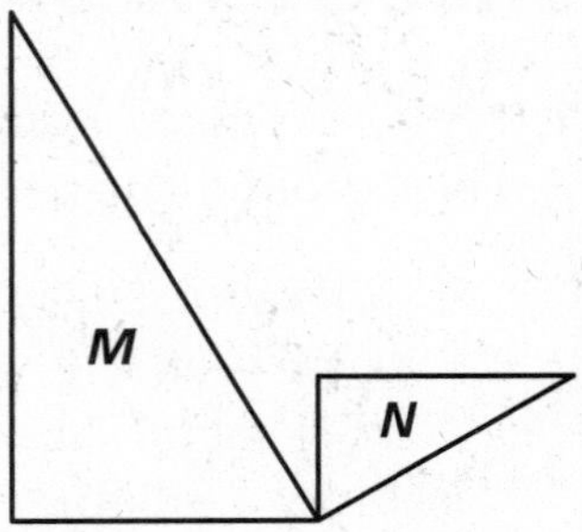

4. Figure *M* and Figure *N* are similar triangles. Which sequence of transformations can be used to map Figure *M* to Figure *N*?

Ⓐ a dilation followed by a reflection

Ⓑ a rotation followed by a dilation

Ⓒ a translation followed by a rotation

Ⓓ a dilation followed by a translation

5. Select all of the figures that are similar to Trapezoid *RSTU*.

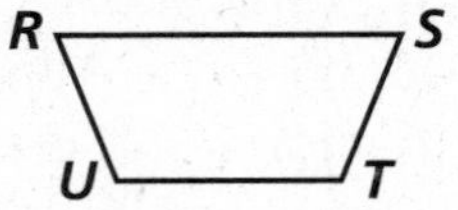

Ⓐ 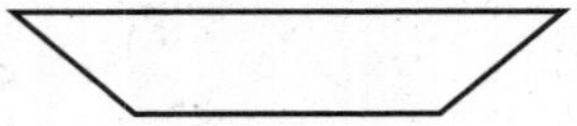

Ⓑ 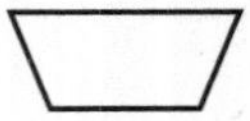

Ⓒ 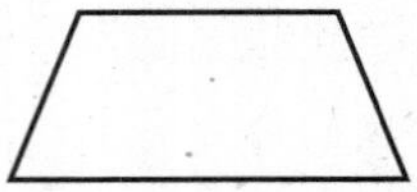

Ⓓ 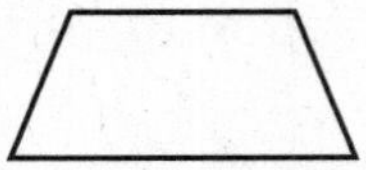

Ⓔ 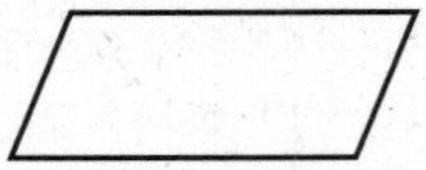

Ⓕ 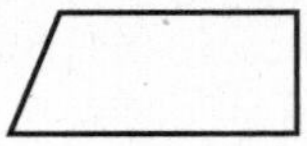

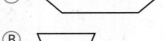

6. Maria draws $\triangle PQR$. Then she applies a dilation with scale factor $\frac{1}{3}$ and center of dilation *P* to the triangle. Next, she translates the image 2 centimeters up and 3 centimeters right. She labels the final image as $\triangle XYZ$. Which of the following must be true about $\triangle PQR$ and $\triangle XYZ$?

Ⓐ $\triangle PQR$ and $\triangle XYZ$ are congruent and similar.

Ⓑ $\triangle PQR$ and $\triangle XYZ$ are congruent but not similar.

Ⓒ $\triangle PQR$ and $\triangle XYZ$ are similar but not congruent.

Ⓓ $\triangle PQR$ and $\triangle XYZ$ are neither similar nor congruent.

Spiral Review

Use the graph to answer Problems 7–8.

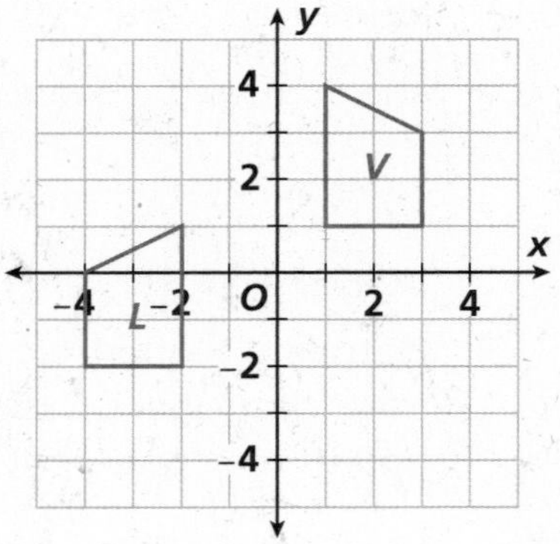

7. Justin makes a figure that is congruent to Figure *V* by reflecting Figure *V* across the *x*-axis and then translating the image 1 unit right. Draw this figure and label it Figure *F*.

8. Are Figure *V* and Figure *L* congruent? Explain why or why not.

____

____

____

9. $\triangle ABC$ has vertices $A(-2, -1)$, $B(1, 2)$, and $C(2, -4)$. If $\triangle A'B'C'$ is a dilation of $\triangle ABC$ with a scale factor of 2.5 and center of dilation (0, 0), give the coordinates of the vertices of $\triangle A'B'C'$.

____

© Houghton Mifflin Harcourt Publishing Company

Module 3

Name ______________________________

Review

Vocabulary

Tell whether each statement is true or false. If it is false, correct the underlined word to make the statement true.

Vocabulary
center of dilation
congruent
enlargement
reduction
similar
transformation
translation

1. The image of a dilation is always <u>congruent</u> to the preimage.

____

2. The preimage of a <u>reduction</u> is larger than the image.

____

3. Lines through each pair of corresponding vertices in a dilation intersect at the <u>center</u> of dilation. ______________________

4. A dilation is a type of <u>translation</u> that enlarges or reduces a figure.

____

Concepts and Skills

5. Triangle $R'S'T'$ is a dilation of Triangle RST.

A. What is the scale factor of the dilation? __________

B. What are the coordinates of the center of the dilation? (____, ____)

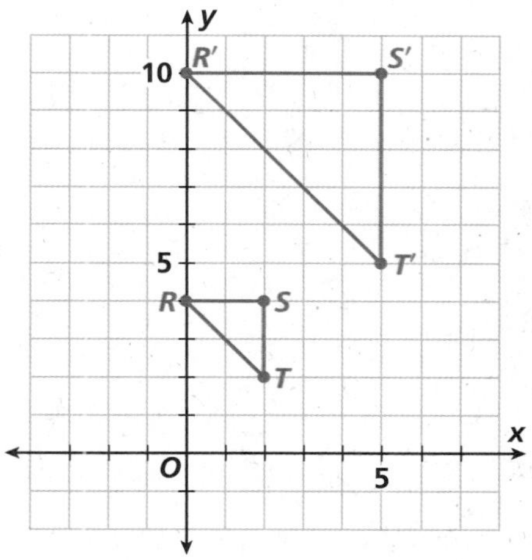

6. (MP) **Use Tools** Triangle JKL has vertices $J(-1, -3)$, $K(-2, 3)$, and $L(4, 1)$. It is dilated by a scale factor of 5, with the origin as the center of dilation, to produce Triangle $J'K'L'$. What are the coordinates of the vertices of $J'K'L'$? State what strategy and tool you will use to answer the question, explain your choice, and then find the answer.

____

____

7. Triangle DEF has vertices $D(-4, 0)$, $E(1, 3)$, and $F(3, -4)$. It is dilated by a scale factor of $\frac{3}{4}$, with the center of dilation at the origin. Use words from the box to complete the sentences about the dilation.

larger
negative
positive
smaller
x-axis
y-axis

The image of the dilation is __________ than the preimage. The image of Vertex D is on the __________. The image of Vertex F has a __________ x-coordinate.

© Houghton Mifflin Harcourt Publishing Company

Draw the image of each dilation in the coordinate plane. The center of each dilation is the origin.

8. Triangle ABC is dilated by a scale factor of 3 to form Triangle $A'B'C'$.

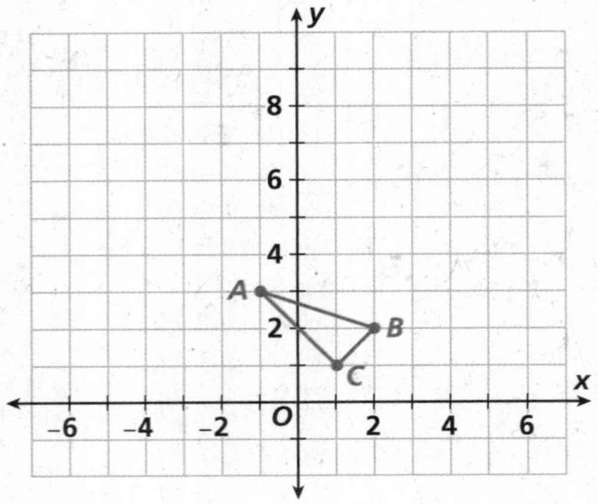

9. Quadrilateral $FGHJ$ is dilated by a scale factor of $\frac{1}{2}$ to form Quadrilateral $F'G'H'J'$.

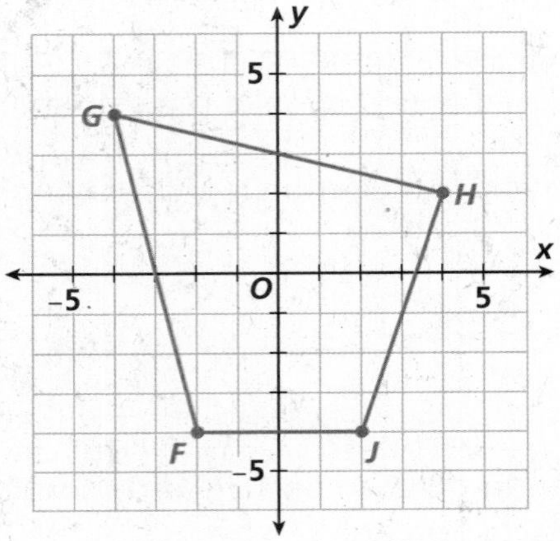

10. Quadrilaterals $LMNP$ and $WXYZ$ are similar. Which sequence of transformations could be used to obtain Quadrilateral $WXYZ$ from Quadrilateral $LMNP$?

Ⓐ 180° rotation, dilation

Ⓑ vertical translation, dilation

Ⓒ dilation, reflection across a horizontal line

Ⓓ reflection across a horizontal line, vertical translation

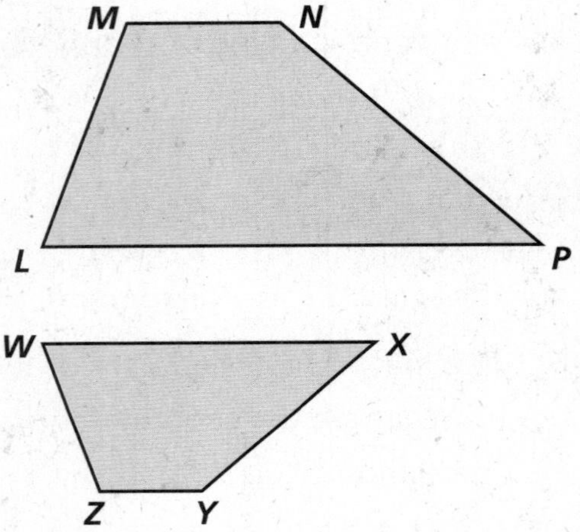

11. Which of these sequences of transformations result in figures that are similar but not congruent? Select all that apply.

Ⓐ 180° rotation, dilation with a factor of $\frac{1}{4}$

Ⓑ translation 3 units up, 90° clockwise rotation

Ⓒ dilation with a factor of 4, translation 1 unit down

Ⓓ reflection across the x-axis, translation 6 units right

Ⓔ 90° counterclockwise rotation, reflection across the y-axis

12. Are Triangles GHJ and LMN similar? Explain your reasoning.

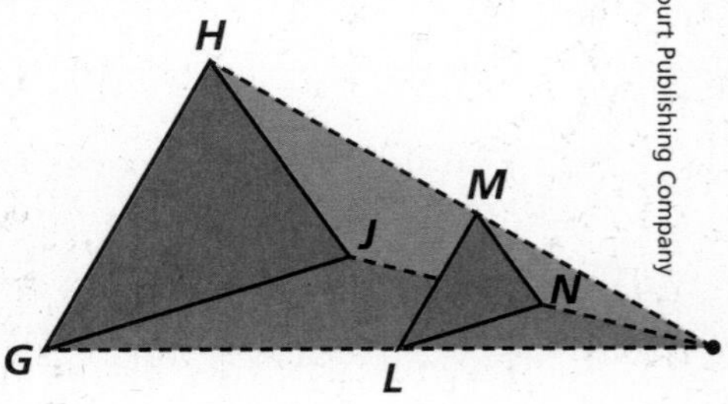

© Houghton Mifflin Harcourt Publishing Company

Unit 2

Equations and Inequalities in One Variable

© Houghton Mifflin Harcourt Publishing Company • Image Credits: (t) ©GeoEye/Science Source; (b) ©scorpion56/iStock/Getty Images Plus/Getty Images

Archaeologist

STEM POWERING INGENUITY

An archaeologist collects and analyzes data about past civilizations in order to learn about human life and cultures. Sarah Parcak is a space archaeologist who uses satellite images to identify ancient sites. Her wish is "for us to discover the millions of unknown archaeological sites across the globe" and to "find and protect the world's heritage."

STEM Task:

Volunteers often help archaeologists at excavation sites. At one excavation site, there can be no more than 8 volunteers for every field guide. If a total of 50 people are working at the site, what is the greatest possible number of volunteers? Explain your thinking.

Learning Mindset

Resilience Identifies Obstacles

© Houghton Mifflin Harcourt Publishing Company • **Image Credit:** ©John Elk III/Lonely Planet Images/Getty Images

Resilience is the ability to recover from a setback. Everyone encounters challenges or obstacles at some point. Resilience allows you to overcome them and continue moving forward. Next time you run into some difficulty completing a task or reaching a goal, try following these steps.

- Identify the problem or obstacle. What is holding you back from moving ahead?
- Develop a list of ideas for overcoming the obstacle. Visualize strategies you can apply to the problem and ways you can break the problem down into smaller steps. If you're still not sure what to do, think about where you can look for help.
- Choose an idea from your list and give it a try.
- Did you successfully overcome the obstacle? If not, try a different approach. And if that one does not work, try another one. Ask for help if you need it, but don't give up.

Reflect

Q **What challenges or problems did you encounter as you worked on the STEM Task? How did you address them?**

Q **Have you given up in the past when you encountered an obstacle or difficulty? What can you do to improve your resilience?**

Module

4 Solve Linear Equations

BALANCE Mystery

Jada has set up several balance mysteries for her friends. She has made stacks of 1, 2, or 3 blocks and hidden some blocks in cups. She is challenging her friends to figure out how many blocks are in each cup. If more than one cup is on a balance, there is an equal number of blocks in each cup. The cups are light enough that their mass does not impact the balance.

Write and solve an equation for each balance.

A.

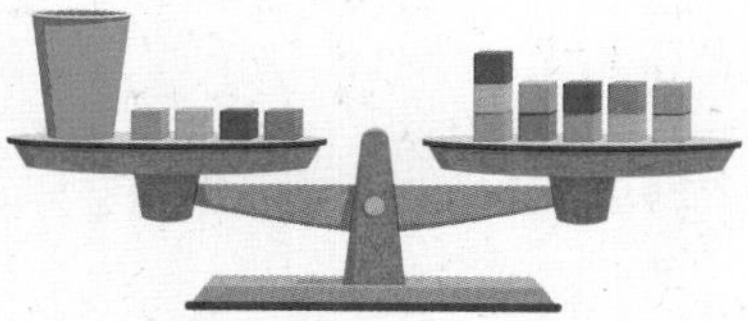

B.

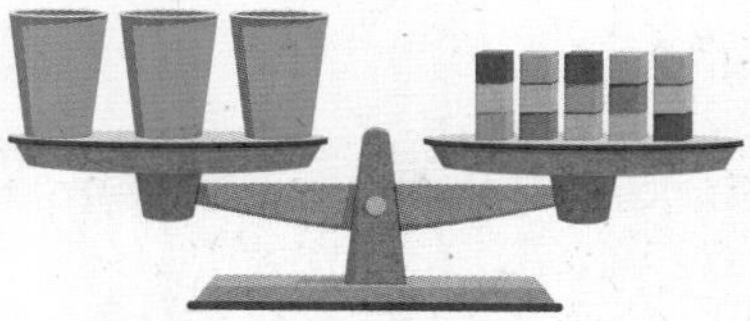

C.

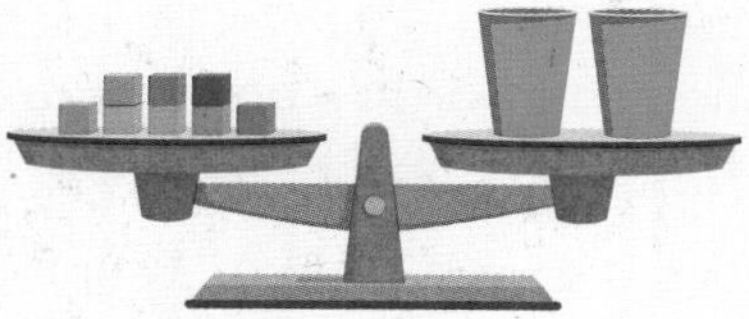

D.

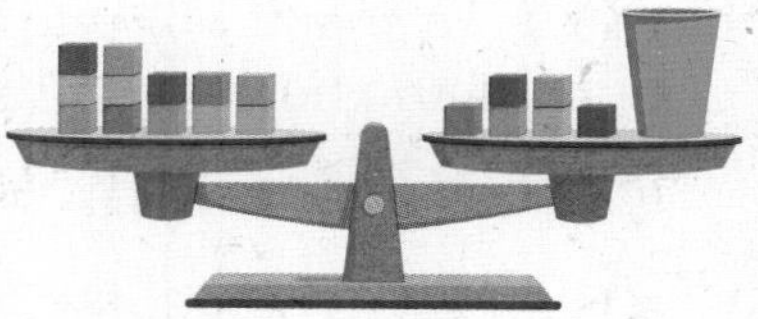

Turn and Talk

Darius says, "Balances A and D are both solved with the same operation." What pattern did Darius notice? Explain.

© Houghton Mifflin Harcourt Publishing Company

Are You Ready?

Complete these problems to review prior concepts and skills you will need for this module.

Solve One-Step Equations

Solve the equation.

1. $c + 27 = 68$ ________

2. $t - 1.5 = 7.9$ ________

3. $\frac{a}{3} = 21$ ________

4. $r + \frac{3}{4} = \frac{7}{8}$ ________

5. $4.2x = 25.2$ ________

6. $15b = 75$ ________

7. All tickets to a play have the same cost. A group bought 6 tickets and paid a total of $99.

A. Write a multiplication equation that can be used to determine the cost *c* in dollars for each ticket.

____

B. Solve the equation and tell what the solution represents.

____

8. It costs $0.80 to download a song from an online music store. Maxine has $6.00 to spend on songs. The equation $0.80s = 6.00$ can be used to determine the number of songs *s* that she can afford to download. Solve the equation, and interpret the solution.

____

Apply Properties of Operations

Use the given property to write an equivalent expression.

9. Commutative Property of Addition

$4(3x + 10)$ ________

10. Associative Property of Addition

$(16 + 4n) + 2n$ ________

11. Distributive Property

$2(a - b)$ ________

12. Associative Property of Multiplication

$\frac{1}{4}(12p)$ ________

© Houghton Mifflin Harcourt Publishing Company

Name ____________________

Write Two-Step Equations for Situations

I Can write two-step equations for various situations.

Spark Your Learning

PAIRS

Write an equation to represent each scenario.

Scenario 1: The cook at Sam's Diner made 19 quiches today. This is 1 more than 3 times the number of quiches he made yesterday. How many quiches did he make yesterday?

Scenario 2: Javier buys four dozen eggs. He saves $1.50 by using a coupon. The total he pays is $8.50. What was the cost of a dozen eggs without the coupon?

Scenario 3: Lina ate $\frac{1}{4}$ of a quiche for lunch. Her two sisters split another piece equally. The three ate a total of $\frac{7}{12}$ of the quiche. What fraction of the quiche did each of Lina's sisters eat?

A quiche is a pastry crust, like a pie crust, filled with a mixture of eggs and milk or cream with any variety of other ingredients, as desired.

Turn and Talk Choose one of the equations you wrote. Make up another scenario that the equation could represent.

© Houghton Mifflin Harcourt Publishing Company • Image Credit: ©bonchan/Shutterstock

Build Understanding

1 The perimeter of an isosceles triangle is 60 feet. The base is 12 feet long. Write an equation that could be used to find the lengths of the congruent sides.

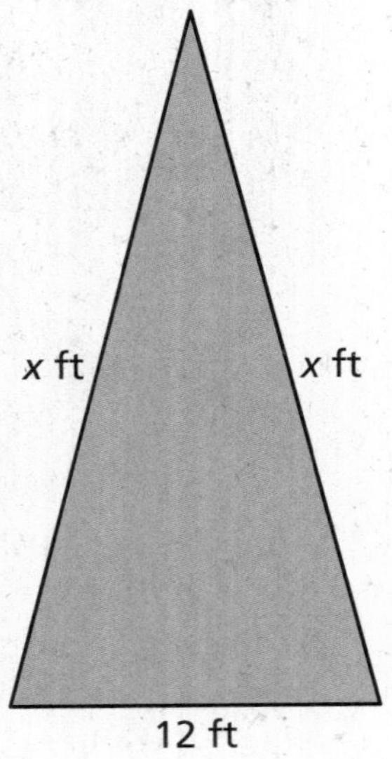

A. Write an **expression** for the perimeter (in feet) of the isosceles triangle. Use the variable x to stand for the unknown information.

☐ + ☐ + ☐

B. Combine any **like terms** in the expression.

☐ + ☐

C. What is the value of the expression you wrote?

____

D. Use your answers from Parts B and C to write an equation that can be used to find the length of each of the two equal sides.

____

E. How would your equation change if the perimeter were 80 feet?

____

F. What would your equation be if the perimeter were 80 feet and the base were 10 feet long?

____

Turn and Talk How is an equation like an expression? How is it different?

© Houghton Mifflin Harcourt Publishing Company

Name

2 Chelsea buys a shirt and shoes at the store with the coupon shown. The price of the shirt before the discount is \$22, and her total discount is \$18.55. Write an equation to find the price of the shoes before the discount.

A. What information are you trying to find? How can a variable help determine that information?

B. Write an equation that can be used to find the unknown information. Use x as the variable.

C. What does each side of the equation represent?

D. What does the variable x represent?

Turn and Talk Write a basic two-step equation, then have a partner make a real-world scenario that fits the equation.

Check Understanding

1. Each time Cheryl runs, she runs 3 miles. She rides her bike only on Saturdays and always for 10 miles. She exercises the same amount each week. She rides and runs for a total of 22 miles in a week. Write an equation that can be used to find out how many times Cheryl goes running each week.

2. Mrs. Wu uses a 25% off coupon to buy 1 adult ticket and 1 child ticket to a movie. She pays a total of \$9.00. A child ticket without the coupon costs \$4.00. Write an equation that can be used to find the cost of an adult ticket without the coupon.

© Houghton Mifflin Harcourt Publishing Company • Image Credit: ©Andrey Burkov/Shutterstock

On Your Own

Model with Mathematics For Problems 3–8, write an equation to represent the situation.

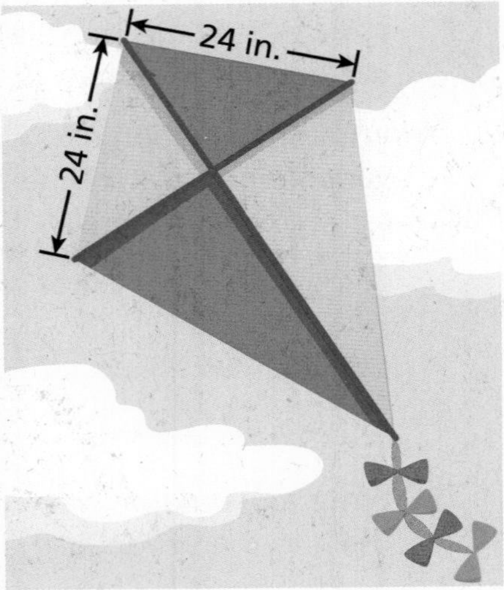

3. Carl is making the kite shown. It has a perimeter of 120 inches. The two longer sides of the kite are the same length. Write an equation that could be used to find the length of each of the longer sides.

4. Mrs. Malia bought a laptop with a 10% discount. She also bought a mouse for $13.99 and spent a total of $621.49 before taxes. Write an equation to find the original cost of the laptop.

5. Paolo is using his grandmother's breakfast bar recipe. He always doubles the amount of yogurt and oats. The recipe calls for $2\frac{1}{2}$ cups of yogurt. The total amount of yogurt and oats after doubling is $6\frac{1}{3}$ cups. Write an equation to find the original amount of oats in the recipe.

6. A square has side lengths as shown in the picture and a perimeter of 54.8 centimeters. Write an equation to find the value of x.

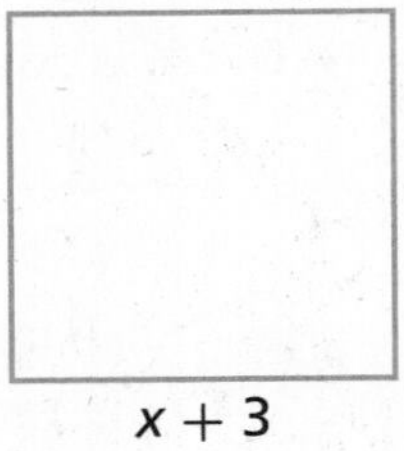

7. Ms. Emlyn buys a hat and gloves with a coupon for 30% off her entire purchase. The gloves cost $35 before the discount. Her bill before tax is $44.80. Write an equation to find the original cost of the hat.

8. Bo's sister Anna is $\frac{3}{4}$ his age minus 1 year. She is 11 years old. Write an equation to find Bo's age.

© Houghton Mifflin Harcourt Publishing Company

I'm in a Learning Mindset!

What barriers do I perceive to writing two-step equations for situations?

Name ______________________________

LESSON 4.1
More Practice/ Homework

ONLINE
Video Tutorials and Interactive Examples

Write Two-Step Equations for Situations

MP **Model with Mathematics** **For Problems 1–4, write an equation to represent the situation.**

1. Pierce is making a rectangular frame for a photo collage that has a perimeter of 72.2 inches. The length of the frame is 20.3 inches. Write an equation to find the width of the frame.

2. Kendra is 3 times her daughter's age plus 7 years. Kendra is 49 years old. Write an equation to find her daughter's age.

3. Mitchell orders a plain turkey sandwich and a drink for lunch. The drink is \$2.95. Instead he is served the super sandwich with lettuce, tomato, and mayonnaise. The restaurant manager takes 15% off the price of the sandwich. Write an equation to determine the original price of Mitchell's sandwich if his new bill is \$8.05.

4. Bianca and Meredith are sisters. Meredith's height is $\frac{2}{3}$ of Bianca's height plus 32 inches. Meredith is 60 inches tall. Write an equation to find Bianca's height in inches.

5. **Health and Fitness** Tyler does squats and pushups. He wants to increase the number of each type of exercise by 20% by the end of the month. He currently does 25 pushups. If Tyler meets his goal, he will do a total of 13 more squats and pushups than he does now. Write an equation to show how many squats Tyler does now.

6. MP **Model with Mathematics** An equilateral triangle has side lengths that measure $x + 4$ inches. The perimeter of the triangle is 18.6 inches. Write an equation to find the value of x.

7. MP **Model with Mathematics** Ms. Lynette earns \$19.50 an hour when she works overtime. She worked overtime twice this week. One day she worked 3 hours of overtime. Her total overtime pay for the week is \$146.25. Write an equation to find the number of overtime hours she worked on the second day.

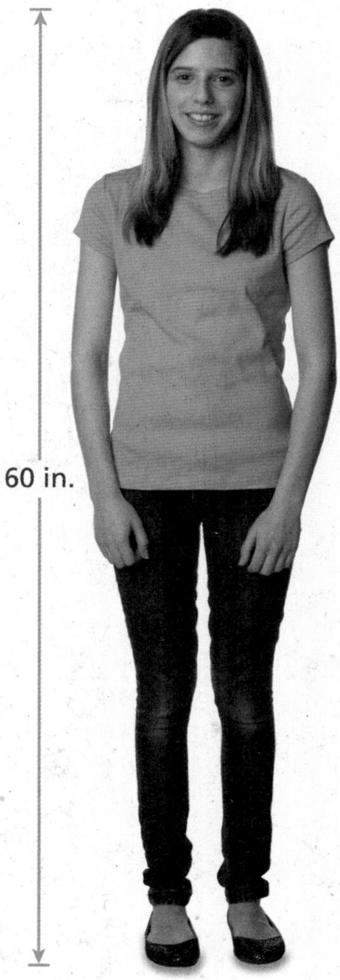

© Houghton Mifflin Harcourt Publishing Company • Image Credit: ©Blend Images/Shutterstock

Test Prep

8. A parallelogram has a perimeter of $50\frac{1}{2}$ inches. The two longer sides of the parallelogram are each $16\frac{1}{4}$ inches. Write an equation to find the length of each of the shorter sides.

____

9. A baby usually gains 10% of its birth weight plus 2 pounds in the first six weeks after birth. One baby gained 2.8 pounds during this time. Write an equation to estimate the baby's birth weight.

____

10. A rhombus has sides of length $x + 6$ inches and a perimeter of 49 inches. Which equation represents this situation?

Ⓐ $4x + 6 = 49$

Ⓑ $4(x + 6) = 49$

Ⓒ $x + 6 = 49$

Ⓓ $x + 24 = 49$

11. Mrs. Owens has a coupon for 40% off a pair of shoes. She pays $111.79 for a pair of shoes and a dress after using the coupon. The dress costs $64.99. Which equation can be solved for *x*, the retail price of the shoes?

Ⓐ $0.6x + 64.99 = 111.79$

Ⓑ $0.4x + 64.99 = 111.79$

Ⓒ $0.6(x + 64.99) = 111.79$

Ⓓ $0.4(x + 64.99) = 111.79$

Spiral Review

12. Sarah began the school week with $2.60 in her lunch account. She deposited $20 on Monday, and then spent $4.75 each day that week for lunch. What was the balance in her lunch account at the end of the day on Friday?

____

13. Mr. Alvarado goes shopping at the mall with $70. He buys a pair of pants for $33.76 and a shirt for $29.52. He also returns a hat he bought the previous week for $19.67. How much money does Mr. Alvarado have after he buys the pants and shirt and returns the hat?

____

© Houghton Mifflin Harcourt Publishing Company

Name ____________________

Apply Two-Step Equations to Solve Real-World Problems

I Can apply two-step equations to solve a variety of problems.

Spark Your Learning

PAIRS

A diagram of the rectangular sitting area in a botanical garden is shown. What is the length of the sitting area in the garden?

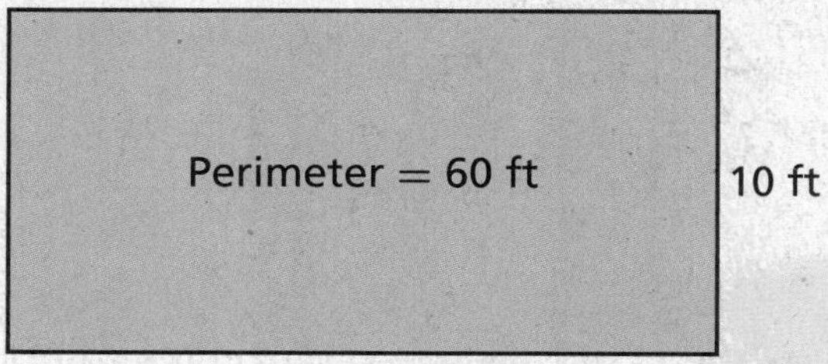

Turn and Talk Describe how you figured this out. Did you use a formula? Explain.

© Houghton Mifflin Harcourt Publishing Company • Image Credit: ©Corbis

Build Understanding

1 Lucy installs a towel bar $10\frac{3}{4}$ inches long in the center of a door $29\frac{1}{2}$ inches wide. How far is each end of the bar from the nearer edge of the door?

A. Estimate the distance from each end of the towel bar to the nearer edge of the door. Explain your reasoning.

B. Calculate the exact distance from each end of the towel bar to the nearer edge of the door. Is your answer reasonable? Explain.

C. Let x be the distance from each end of the bar to the nearer edge of the door. Write an equation of the form $px + q = r$ that you can use to find x.

D. To solve for x, you perform the same operations on each side of the equation until x is by itself on one side. What operation should you perform first on your equation from Part C? What new equation do you get?

Connect to Vocabulary

A **solution of an equation** is a number that makes the equation true when substituted for the variable (such as x).

E. What operation should you perform next on your equation from Part D? What is the solution of the equation?

Turn and Talk Compare the steps used to solve the equation you wrote in part C with the steps used to calculate the distance in part B.

© Houghton Mifflin Harcourt Publishing Company

Name ______________________

Step It Out

2 Tracy's fitness goal is shown on her planner. To meet her goal, she will need a total of 8 pushups more than her current daily total of morning and evening pushups. Tracy has been doing 25 pushups in the evening. How many pushups has she been doing in the morning?

Weekly Planner GOAL: 20% improvement on pushups

	Mon.	Tues.	Wed.	Thurs.	Fri.
AM	Pushups ✓		Pushups ✓		Pushups ✓
PM	Pushups ✓		Pushups ✓		Pushups ✓

A. Let x represent the number of pushups Tracy does in the morning. Write an expression for the current daily total of pushups.

$x + \square$

B. Write an expression for Tracy's desired increase in pushups.

$\square(x + \square)$

C. Write and solve an equation to find her current number of morning pushups.

$0.2(x + \square) = \square$

$0.2x + \square = \square$ ______________ Property

$-\square \quad -\square$

$0.2x = \square$ ______________ Property of Equality

$\frac{0.2x}{\square} = \frac{3}{\square}$ ______________ Property of Equality

$x = \square$

D. Check your solution.

$0.2(x + 25) = 8$

$0.2(\square + 25) = \square$ ✓

Check Understanding

1. Cookie Castle sells 8-inch cookies for $3 each plus a flat $5 delivery fee. Zach has $14 to spend on cookies. Write and solve an equation to determine how many cookies Zach can buy and have delivered.

____

2. Mr. Muñoz has a coupon for 15% off his entire purchase. He buys binoculars for $105 and boots. He spends a total of $170 before tax. Write and solve an equation to find how much the boots cost before the discount.

____

© Houghton Mifflin Harcourt Publishing Company

On Your Own

3. (MP) **Model with Mathematics** Geoff works at a warehouse, earning \$17.50 per hour plus a \$200 one-time hiring bonus. In Geoff's first week, his pay including the bonus was \$637.50.

A. Write and evaluate a numerical expression to find how many hours Geoff worked his first week. Explain your thinking.

____

____

____

____

B. Write and solve an equation of the form $px + q = r$ to find the number of hours x that Geoff worked his first week. Compare your solution with your answer from part A.

____

____

4. (MP) **Model with Mathematics** Mr. Burns takes a one-day trip and rents a car at the rate shown. The car rental costs \$68.25. Write and solve an equation to find how many miles he traveled.

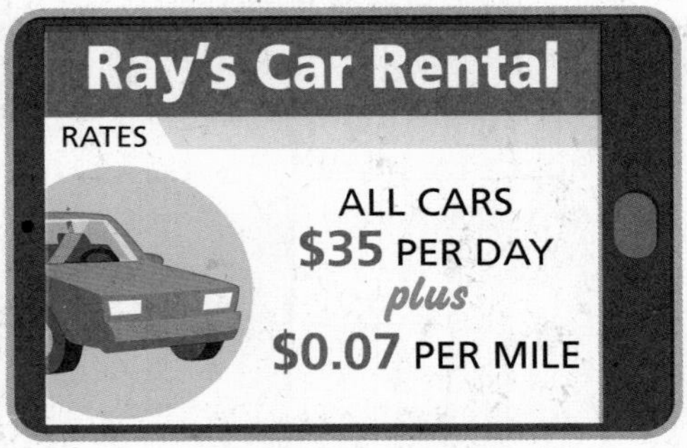

____

5. (MP) **Attend to Precision** A regular hexagon has sides of length $x + 5$ inches and a perimeter of 72 inches. Write and solve an equation to find x. How long is a side?

____

For Problems 6–9, solve each equation. Check your solution.

6. $-3(n + 5) = 12$

____

7. $-9h - 15 = 93$

____

8. $\frac{z}{5} + 3 = -35$

____

9. $3\left(y + \frac{2}{5}\right) = -\frac{1}{5}$

____

I'm in a Learning Mindset!

How do I keep myself motivated to solve problems with two-step equations?

____

© Houghton Mifflin Harcourt Publishing Company

Name ______________________

Apply Two-Step Equations to Solve Real-World Problems

1. (MP) **Model with Mathematics** Julie wants to buy tulip bulbs to plant. Each bulb costs \$0.50. There is a one-time \$4.50 shipping cost. She has \$22 to spend. Write and solve an equation to determine how many bulbs Julie can buy and have shipped.

2. **Math on the Spot** The total charge for a yearly Internet DVD rental membership is \$231. A registration fee of \$15 is paid up front, and the rest is paid monthly. How much do new members pay each month?

3. (MP) **Attend to Precision** Bev is making peanut butter–banana bread. She always doubles the amount of nuts and peanut butter chips. The total amount of chips and nuts after doubling is $4\frac{1}{2}$ cups. Write and solve an equation to find the original amount of nuts in the recipe.

$1\frac{1}{2}$ c peanut butter chips
? c nuts
3 very ripe bananas

4. Dirk sold 7 more than 2 times as many gym memberships this month than last month. This month he sold 43 memberships. Write and solve an equation to find the number of memberships Dirk sold last month.

For Problems 5–8, solve each equation. Check your solution.

5. $3 = 0.2m - 7$

6. $1.3z + 1.5 = 5.4$

7. $-3(t + 6) = 0$

8. $-8(1 - g) = 56$

9. **Open Ended** Write a two-step equation that involves multiplication and subtraction, includes a negative coefficient, and has a solution of $x = 7$.

10. **Open Ended** Write a two-step equation that involves division and addition and has a solution of $x = -25$.

© Houghton Mifflin Harcourt Publishing Company • Image Credit: ©margouillatphotos/iStock/Getty Images Plus/Getty Images

Test Prep

11. Leo started working for a new company that paid him \$25 per hour with a hiring bonus of \$100. During the first two weeks, he was paid \$1,200, which included the bonus. How many hours did he work during the first two weeks?

Ⓐ 40

Ⓑ 44

Ⓒ 48

Ⓓ 52

12. To convert to degrees Fahrenheit, use the formula $F = \frac{9}{5}C + 32$, where C is the temperature in degrees Celsius. From the choices below, which is the first step to solve for the Celsius temperature if the Fahrenheit temperature is 70 °F?

Ⓐ Add 32 to both sides.

Ⓑ Subtract 32 from both sides.

Ⓒ Divide both sides by $\frac{5}{9}$.

Ⓓ Multiply both sides by $\frac{9}{5}$.

13. Fred earns \$16.50 an hour for overtime. He worked overtime on Monday and Thursday this week. On Monday, he worked 4 hours of overtime. His total overtime pay for the week was \$123.75. Write and solve an equation to find the number of overtime hours Fred worked on Thursday.

____

14. Solve $\frac{1}{2}m - 5 = 23$.

Ⓐ 13.5

Ⓑ 27

Ⓒ 33

Ⓓ 56

Spiral Review

15. Apples at the farmers' market cost \$2.50 for 5 apples or \$0.70 for 1 apple. Which is the better buy if you want 5 apples? Explain.

____

16. Mr. Spencer drives 200 miles in 5 hours. What is his unit rate?

____

© Houghton Mifflin Harcourt Publishing Company

Name ______________________

Solve Multi-Step Linear Equations

I Can solve linear equations with integer and rational number coefficients.

Spark Your Learning

PAIRS

Jordan buys 2 new jerseys and a glove for softball. She pays the price shown for the glove and gives the clerk two fifty-dollar bills to pay the exact amount. How much does Jordan pay for each jersey? Write and solve an equation.

What would the equation and solution be if Jordan gives the clerk a single hundred-dollar bill? How are the equations alike or different? How is the process of solving the equations alike or different?

Turn and Talk Is there another equation that will solve the same problem? Explain.

© Houghton Mifflin Harcourt Publishing Company • Image Credit: ©C Squared Studios/Photodisc/Getty Images

Build Understanding

1 A batting machine uses an automatic baseball feeder. During baseball practice the feeder is $\frac{1}{6}$ full. An attendant fills it with 15 baseballs so that the feeder is now $\frac{2}{3}$ full. How many baseballs does the feeder hold when full?

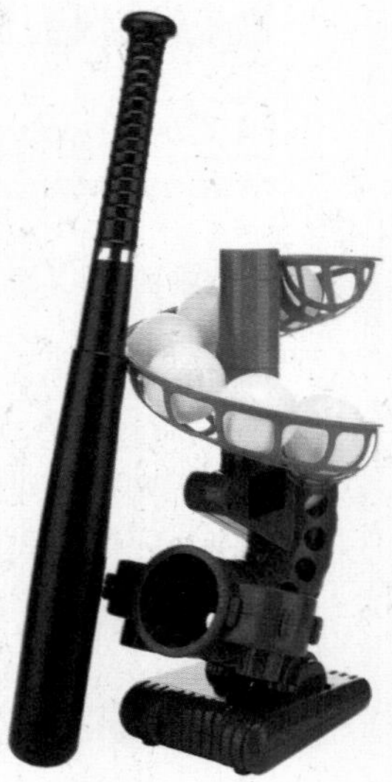

A. Write an equation to represent the problem.

$\frac{1}{6}x + \square = \square x$

B. In order to **isolate the variable**, all terms containing x need to be on one side of the equation. How can you isolate the variable in the equation? What is the resulting equation before simplifying?

____

____

C. Solve the equation for x.

D. Look back at the original equation. How could you use the least **common denominator** of the fractions to rewrite the equation with integer coefficients? A **coefficient** is the number multiplied by the variable.

____

E. Use your answer from part D to rewrite the equation. What is the new equation? Solve this new equation. Do you get the same solution?

This is an example of a linear equation with only one solution.

Turn and Talk Which equation did you prefer to work with? Why?

© Houghton Mifflin Harcourt Publishing Company • Image Credit: ©Michael Kraus/Shutterstock

Name ______________________

Step It Out

2 Lanie and Jen buy the same number of books at the used book sale. Lanie buys paperback books and Jen buys hardcover books. Lanie spends \$1.50 less than Jen. Solve the equation to find the number of books each of them buys.

$$1.2n - 1.5 = 0.45n$$

$$1.2n = 0.45n + \square$$

$$1.2n - \square = \square$$

$$\square = \square$$

$$n = \square$$

A. Look at the decimals in the equation and think about how you could rewrite the equation with integer coefficients. What is the least **multiple** of 10 you could multiply each term by to eliminate all the decimals?

____

B. Multiply each term of the original equation by your answer from part A to eliminate all the decimals. Solve the equation.

$$1.2n - 1.5 = 0.45n$$

$$\square(1.2n) - \square(1.5) = \square(0.45n)$$

$$\square n - \square = \square n$$

$$\square n = \square$$

$$n = \square$$

C. Do you get the same solution?

____

D. Which equation was easier to solve? Why?

____

____

Turn and Talk How is solving an equation that involves fractions similar to solving an equation with decimals? What methods can you use to solve each type of equation?

© Houghton Mifflin Harcourt Publishing Company • Image Credits: (tl) ©Kirsten Hinte/Shutterstock; (tr) ©JakeWalk/Alamy

3 Jackie has a coupon for \$8 off the price of a jacket. Then the clerk takes 25% off the discounted price, so she saves an additional \$10. Determine the original price of the jacket.

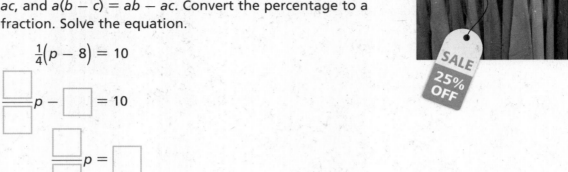

A. Write an equation using the **Distributive Property**, which states that for all real numbers *a*, *b*, and *c*, $a(b + c) = ab + ac$, and $a(b - c) = ab - ac$. Convert the percentage to a fraction. Solve the equation.

$$\frac{1}{4}(p - 8) = 10$$

$$\frac{\square}{\square}p - \square = 10$$

$$\frac{\square}{\square}p = \square$$

$$p = \square$$

B. Write the original equation, eliminate the fractions, and solve.

$$\frac{1}{4}(p - 8) = 10$$

$$4\left[\frac{1}{4}(p - 8)\right] = 4(10)$$

$$p - \square = \square$$

$$p = \square$$

4 Solve the equation $4(2.5x + 2) - x = 26.9$.

A. Use the Distributive Property to write an equivalent equation.

____

B. Combine like terms and solve.

____

Check Understanding

1. Anna spent \$2.75 at the school store. She bought two erasers and some pencils. How many pencils did she buy? Write and solve an equation.

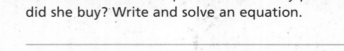

____

2. Solve the equation. Check your solution.

$\frac{1}{5}(n - 10) = 6 - 3\frac{1}{2}$

____

© Houghton Mifflin Harcourt Publishing Company • **Image Credits:** (tr) ©Brook Chen/Shutterstock; (br) ©Lane V. Erickson/Alamy

On Your Own

3. Three people participated in a free throw shooting contest. Glenna made x shots, Val made $2x - 10$ shots, and Kim made $x + 10$ shots. If a total of 180 shots were made, how many did each person make? Write and solve an equation.

4. (MP) **Reason** Jamie solved the equation $\frac{2}{3}x + 4 = 2 + \frac{1}{2}x$. Is his solution correct? Explain.

$$\frac{2}{3}x + 4 = 2 + \frac{1}{2}x$$
$$6\left(\frac{2}{3}x + 4\right) = 6\left(2 + \frac{1}{2}x\right)$$
$$4x + 24 = 12 + x$$
$$3x + 24 = 12$$
$$3x = -12$$
$$x = -4$$

5. Karinne hit 4 more home runs than half the number of home runs Lu hit. Together they hit 10 home runs. Let x represent the number of home runs Lu hit.

A. Write an equation to represent the situation.

B. Solve for x.

C. How many home runs did Lu hit?

D. How many home runs did Karinne hit?

E. How can you check your answer?

© Houghton Mifflin Harcourt Publishing Company • Image Credit: ©gpflman/E+/Getty Images

6. **Construct Arguments** Max and Corey solve the same equation but they use different methods. Which method would you use? Explain your answer.

Max

$$x + \frac{x}{4} = 14 - \frac{x}{2}$$
$$4\left(x + \frac{x}{4}\right) = 4\left(14 - \frac{x}{2}\right)$$
$$4x + x = 56 - 2x$$
$$5x + 2x = 56$$
$$7x = 56$$
$$x = 8$$

Corey

$$x + \frac{x}{4} = 14 - \frac{x}{2}$$
$$x + \frac{x}{4} + \frac{x}{2} = 14$$
$$\frac{4x}{4} + \frac{x}{4} + \frac{2x}{4} = 14$$
$$\frac{7x}{4} = 14$$
$$7x = 56$$
$$x = 8$$

7. What is a first step to solve the equation $0.3n - 15 = 0.2n - 5$?

Solve each equation. Check your solution.

8. $3(x - 2) + 6 = 5(x + 4)$

9. $2.2(4p + 2) = 13.2$

10. $\frac{m + 3}{2} = m - 5$

11. $2(11t + 1.5t) = 12 - 5t$

12. $\frac{7}{8}m - \frac{1}{2} = \frac{3}{16}m + 5$

13. $9(n + 1) = 2(n - 1)$

14. $\frac{4}{5}x - 3 = \frac{3}{10}x + 7$

15. $-4(-5 - b) = \frac{1}{3}(b + 16)$

16. $3.6w = 2(0.8w + 12)$

I'm in a Learning Mindset!

What about solving multi-step linear equations triggers a fixed-mindset voice in my head?

© Houghton Mifflin Harcourt Publishing Company • Image Credit: ©Klaus Vedfelt/DigitalVision/Getty Images

Name ______________________

ONLINE
Ed Video Tutorials and Interactive Examples

Solve Multi-Step Linear Equations

1. Elsie is planting a rectangular section of grass.

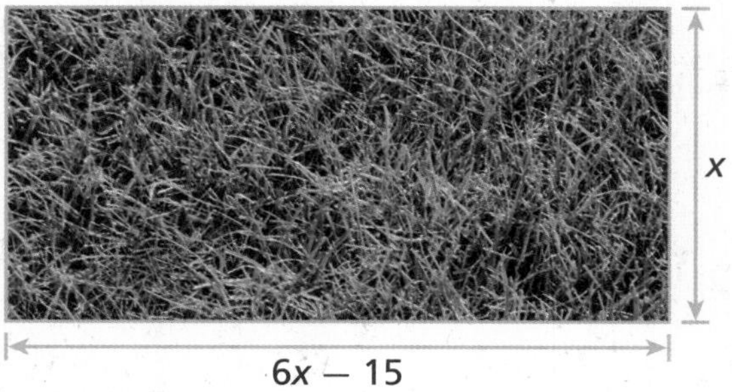

If the perimeter of the rectangle is 96 feet, what are the length and width of the rectangular section?

____

2. **Math on the Spot** Solve each equation.

A. $3n + 1 = 19$

B. $21 = -2p - 5$

3. (MP) **Reason** What step would you perform first to solve the following equation? Explain your reasoning.

$\frac{1}{4}(12 - 8x) = \frac{2}{3}(6x)$

____

____

4. Heather has a family phone plan. The monthly payment for the family plan includes a $70 charge for unlimited talk and text, a $20 line fee per phone, and a $22.91 equipment fee for each phone. Their total monthly bill is $241.64. Write and solve an equation to find how many phones are on the plan.

____

Solve each equation. Check your solution.

5. $a + 3(a - 1) = 3(2 + 1)$

6. $5y - 3(2 - y) = 10$

7. $1.2x - 2 = 7 + 0.9x$

8. $-k + 4(k + 1) = 2k$

9. $4\left(\frac{x}{6} + 5\right) = 2x + 10$

10. $3w + \frac{w}{2} + 1 = 10 - w$

© Houghton Mifflin Harcourt Publishing Company • Image Credit: ©Peter Dazeley/Photographer's Choice/Getty Images

Test Prep

11. Which could be the first step in solving the equation $0.05x + 3 - 0.02x = 4$?

Ⓐ Add 3 to each side of the equation.

Ⓑ Divide each side of the equation by 100.

Ⓒ Multiply each side of the equation by 100.

Ⓓ Subtract $0.02x$ from each side of the equation.

12. Solve the equation. Check your solution.

$\frac{3}{2}(x + 6) = 16 + \frac{1}{2}(x - 24)$

$x =$ ☐

13. Laurie earns $7.50 per hour at the fruit stand plus an extra $2.00 per hour on Sundays. One week in August, she worked on Sunday, Monday, and Wednesday. She worked the same number of hours on Monday and on Wednesday. On Sunday she worked 4 hours. If she earned a total of $83.00 for the week, how many hours did Laurie work on Monday? Write and solve an equation.

---

14. Which equation has the solution $x = 8$?

Ⓐ $x + 2x - 4 = \frac{1}{4}(3x + 4)$

Ⓑ $x + \frac{1}{2}(x + 8) = 4(1 + 3)$

Ⓒ $2(x - 4) = \frac{1}{4}(1 + 3) + x$

Ⓓ $x + 4(1 + 3) = \frac{1}{2}(2x + 4)$

15. Each year Rolando saves 8% of his income. This year he saved $3,000 and his salary was $2,000 less than in the previous year. What was his salary in the previous year? Write and solve an equation.

Spiral Review

16. Triangle *ABC* is dilated by a scale factor of 1.5 to form Triangle *DEF*. Are Triangles *ABC* and *DEF* congruent? Why or why not?

---

17. A triangle has angles measuring 45°, 55°, and 80°. It is dilated by a scale factor of 2. What are the angle measures of the dilated image?

© Houghton Mifflin Harcourt Publishing Company

Name ______________________________

Examine Special Cases

I Can recognize and solve linear equations that have no solution, one solution, or infinitely many solutions.

Spark Your Learning

SMALL GROUPS

Leah and Mai are taking a card-making class. The teacher has 4 packs of blank cards and an additional 8 cards. Leah buys 4 packs of cards that each come with an additional 3 free cards in the pack. Mai buys 4 packs of cards that each come with an additional 2 free cards in the pack.

How many cards would need to be in each pack of cards so that the teacher has the same number of cards as Leah? as Mai?

Leah and Teacher	Mai and Teacher
$4(x + 3) = 4x + 8$	$4(x + 2) = 4x + 8$

What do you notice when you solve each equation? What do you think this means?

Turn and Talk What do you think it means when an equation simplifies to a false statement? Why?

© Houghton Mifflin Harcourt Publishing Company • Image Credit: ©Monkey Business Images/Shutterstock

Build Understanding

You know that to solve an equation means to find the values for the variable that make a true statement. Sometimes an equation may have **no solution** or may have **infinitely many solutions**.

Just like a detective, you can gather clues to help you discover what will happen in each equation. Then you can record your clues in a table.

Solution	Meaning	Number of solutions
$x = a$	Only one value of x makes the equation true.	1

1 Solve the equation $2\left(\frac{x}{8} + 3\right) = 7 + \frac{1}{4}x$.

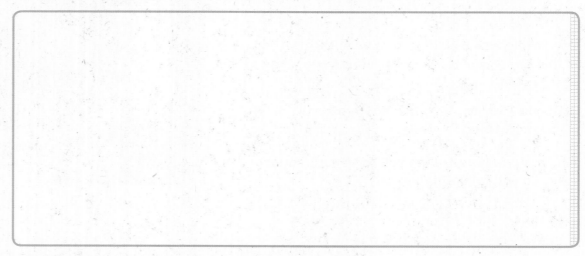

A. What do you notice about the final equation?

B. **Substitute** several different values for x into the original equation. Simplify. Explain what happens.

C. How many solutions does the equation have? Use what you have discovered to fill in the table.

Solution	Meaning	Number of solutions
$a = b$, where $a \neq b$		

Turn and Talk How can you write an equation with a variable x that uses addition on both sides of the equation and is never true?

© Houghton Mifflin Harcourt Publishing Company • Image Credit: ©Elnur/Shutterstock

Name

Step It Out

2 Solve the equation $x + 8 = 2(0.5x + 4)$.

$$x + 8 = 2(0.5x + 4)$$

$$x + 8 = \square + \square$$

$$x + 8 - x = \square + \square - x$$

$$8 = \square$$

A. Substitute several different values for x into the original equation. Simplify. Explain what happens.

B. How many solutions does the equation have? Use what you have discovered to fill in the table.

Solution	Meaning	Number of solutions
$a = a$ or $x = x$		

Turn and Talk What do you notice about equations that have no solution and equations that have infinitely many solutions? How are they alike or different?

Check Understanding

1. Brynne simplifies an equation and gets $2 = 3$. What does this tell you about the equation?

2. Simplify the equation and tell whether the equation has one solution, no solution, or infinitely many solutions.

$9(x + 5) = 20 + 9x + 25$

© Houghton Mifflin Harcourt Publishing Company

On Your Own

3. Lilly starts hiking along a trail at 3 miles per hour. Dave starts hiking the same trail from the same starting point at 3.5 miles per hour. If Lilly walked 2 miles before Dave started hiking, will he catch up to her? Write an equation to represent the situation and determine how many solutions the equation has.

4. Maria pays a yearly fee of \$3 to her swimming club and \$2 per lesson. Carmen pays a yearly fee of \$5 and \$2 per lesson. After how many lessons will Maria and Carmen have paid the same amount? Write an equation and explain your answer.

5. MP **Construct Arguments** Alex says that $3.2x - 5 = 3.2(x - 5)$ has infinitely many solutions. Is Alex correct? Explain why or why not.

6. **Open Ended** Write an equation that has infinitely many solutions. Prove that your equation is correct.

For Problems 7–8, solve each equation. Tell whether each equation has one solution, no solution, or infinitely many solutions. If there is only one solution, find it.

7. $\frac{1}{2}x + 3 - \frac{1}{4}x = 3 + \frac{1}{4}x$

8. $5.4x + 12 = 2(2.7x - 9)$

I'm in a Learning Mindset!

What strategy did I use to overcome barriers to writing an equation that has infinitely many solutions?

© Houghton Mifflin Harcourt Publishing Company

Name ____________________

ONLINE
Video Tutorials and Interactive Examples

Examine Special Cases

1. Denis orders a large pizza for \$16.50 plus \$2 for each topping. Sheng orders a medium pizza for \$13.25 plus \$2 for each topping. Can they both pay the same total amount if they get the same number of toppings? Write an equation and explain.

2. **Health and Fitness** Shara scored 34 points in the basketball game last night. She scored six 3-point baskets, and the rest were 2-point baskets. Write an equation to determine how many 2-point baskets Shara scored. Determine how many solutions the equation has.

3. (MP) **Construct Arguments** Blake says that $4(x - 1) = 12 - 4x$ has zero solutions. Is Blake correct? Explain why or why not.

Complete each equation so that it has one solution.

4. $-2(z + 3) - z =$ ______ $- 4(z + 2)$

5. $\frac{1}{4}x - 4(2) = -\frac{1}{2}\left(\frac{1}{2}x +\right.$ ______$\left.\right)$

Complete each equation so that it has infinitely many solutions.

6. $\frac{3}{4} + x = 2x - x +$ ______

7. $2h - 3(3 - h) +$ ______ $= 5h - 8$

Complete each equation so that it has no solution.

8. $6x + 5 = 3 +$ ______

9. $-k +$ ______ $(k + 1) = 2k$

For Problems 10–12, determine whether each equation has one solution, no solution, or infinitely many solutions. If there is only one solution, find it.

10. **Math on the Spot**

A. $x + 8x + 4 = 9x + 4$

B. $4(y + 5) = y - 10 + 3y$

11. $3.2(x - 1) = 2.2x + 1$

12. $3m - 2 = 25 - 6m$

© Houghton Mifflin Harcourt Publishing Company • Image Credit: ©monkeybusinessimages/iStock/Getty Images

Test Prep

13. What missing value would make the equation have infinitely many solutions?

$2(3 + 4x) = 8x + \square$

Ⓐ 1.5
Ⓑ 3
Ⓒ 6
Ⓓ $6x$

14. How many solutions does the following equation have? If there is only one solution, find it.

$3 + \frac{4}{5}x = \frac{9}{10}x$

____

15. Complete the equation so that it has no solution.

$10.5x - 4 = 5 + \square$

16. Complete the equation so that it has the solution $c = 4$.

$5(2c - \square) = 2(c + 11)$

17. How many solutions does the following equation have? If there is only one solution, find it.

$2x + 8 = 2(x + 3)$

Ⓐ one solution; $x = -5$
Ⓑ one solution; $x = 5$
Ⓒ no solution
Ⓓ infinitely many solutions

Spiral Review

18. Complete each figure so it is congruent to the figure shown.

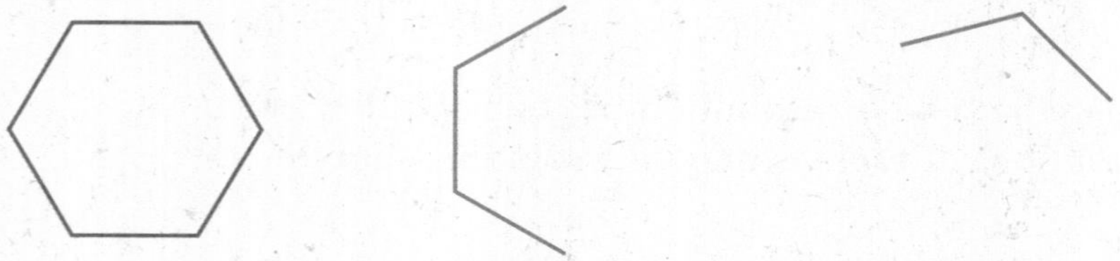

19. The coordinates of the vertices of the preimage of a triangle are (2, 1), (3, 4), and (4, 1). The coordinates of the vertices of the image are (3, 3), (4, 6), and (5, 3). How far and in what direction was the triangle translated?

____

© Houghton Mifflin Harcourt Publishing Company

Name ______________________

Apply Linear Equations

I Can solve equations and interpret solutions in context.

Step It Out

1 A student service club is raising money through a "Loose Change" competition among the grades. Jenaya brings in 20 coins, all of which are nickels and dimes, that have a total value of \$1.30 to put in her grade's bucket.

The equation $5(20 - d) + 10d = 130$ can be solved to determine the number of dimes in Jenaya's donation. How many dimes did Jenaya place in the bucket?

A. Apply the Distributive Property to the left side of the equation.

$\square - \square + 10d = 130$

B. Combine like terms.

$\square + \square = 130$

C. Solve the equation for d.

$100 \, \square + 5d = 130 \, \square$

$\square = \square$

$\frac{\square}{\square} = \frac{\square}{\square}$

$d = \square$

D. How many dimes does Jenaya place in the bucket? Write a sentence.

____

E. What if Jenaya brought 10 nickels and some dimes with a total value of \$1.30? How many dimes does Jenaya place in the bucket? Explain.

____

Turn and Talk Which variable or expression represents the number of dimes? Which variable or expression represents the number of nickels? Explain your reasoning.

© Houghton Mifflin Harcourt Publishing Company • Image Credit: ©Just Go Out There/Shutterstock

You previously learned that a right angle measures 90°. In this lesson, you will also work with pairs of angles called complementary angles and supplementary angles.

Connect to Vocabulary

Two angles whose measures have a sum of 90° are called **complementary angles**. Two angles whose measures have a sum of 180° are called **supplementary angles**.

2 Use the diagram for Parts A–D.

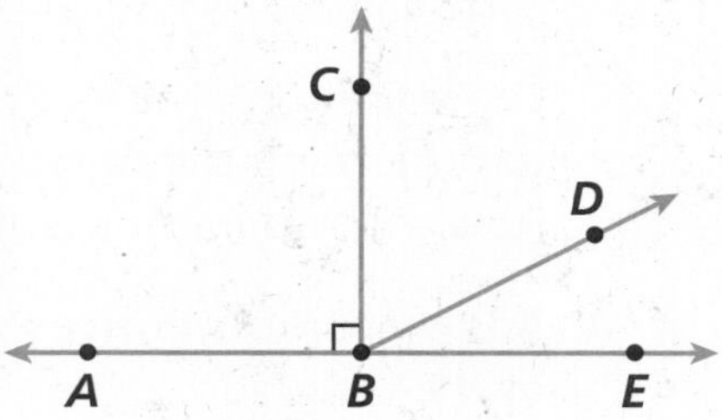

A. Name a pair of complementary angles.

$\angle$ ________ and $\angle$ ________

B. Name a pair of supplementary angles.

$\angle$ ________ and $\angle$ ________

C. If the measure of $\angle CBD$ is equal to $(5x)°$ and the measure of $\angle DBE$ is 40°, write an equation involving x. Then solve it.

[ ] + [ ] = [ ]

$x =$ [ ]

D. What is the measure of $\angle CBD$? ________

3 Use the figure for Parts A–E.

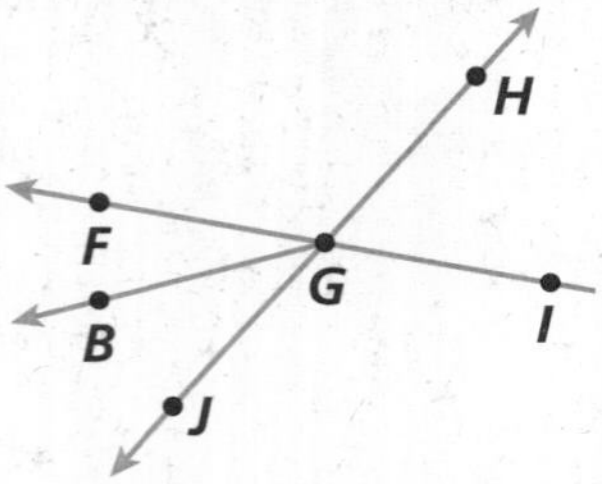

Connect to Vocabulary

Vertical angles are opposite congruent angles formed by intersecting lines.

A. Name two pairs of vertical angles.

$\angle$ ________ and $\angle$ ________

$\angle$ ________ and $\angle$ ________

B. Vertical angles [are / are not] congruent.

C. Given $\angle FGH$ measures $(6x - 24)°$ and $\angle JGI$ measures 96°, write an equation that can be used to determine the value of x. Solve for x.

[ ] = [ ] and $x =$ [ ]

D. Name a pair of adjacent angles.

$\angle$ ________ and $\angle$ ________

Connect to Vocabulary

Adjacent angles are two angles in the same plane with a common vertex and a common side, but no common interior points.

E. Given $m\angle FGJ = 84°$, $m\angle FGB = (4x)°$, and $m\angle JGB = (5x + 3)°$, write an equation that can be used to determine the value of x. Solve for x.

[ ] + [ ] = [ ] and $x =$ [ ]

© Houghton Mifflin Harcourt Publishing Company

Name

4 Pam and Rachel buy books at the bookstore where Rachel works. Each uses a coupon. After her coupon is applied, Rachel pays only 75% of the resulting price. How many books could each purchase and spend the same amount for the same number of books?

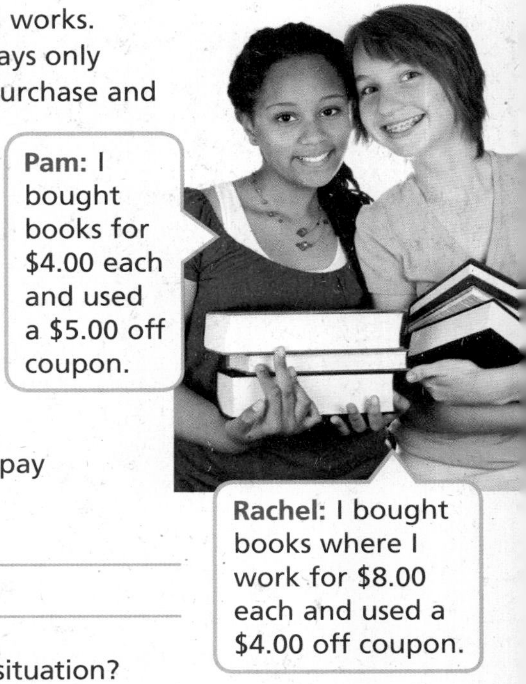
Pam: I bought books for $4.00 each and used a $5.00 off coupon.
Rachel: I bought books where I work for $8.00 each and used a $4.00 off coupon.

A. Complete the equation to represent Rachel and Pam buying x books each and paying the same amount.

$\square = 0.75\left(\square\right)$

B. Solve the equation.

$x = \square$

C. Is it possible for Pam and Rachel to purchase x books and pay the same amount? Explain.

____

____

D. What does the solution to the equation tell you about the situation?

____

____

Turn and Talk How would the solution be different if Rachel did not have a coupon?

Check Understanding

1. The equation $x + (75.3 - x) = 75.3$ represents the sum of the measures of two angles. How many possible combinations of angle measures satisfy the equation?

____

2. Two bicyclists on a 75-mile trail ride toward each other. One begins at the 45-mile marker. The other begins at the end of the trail. The expressions shown represent each cyclist's distance from the Parking Lot.

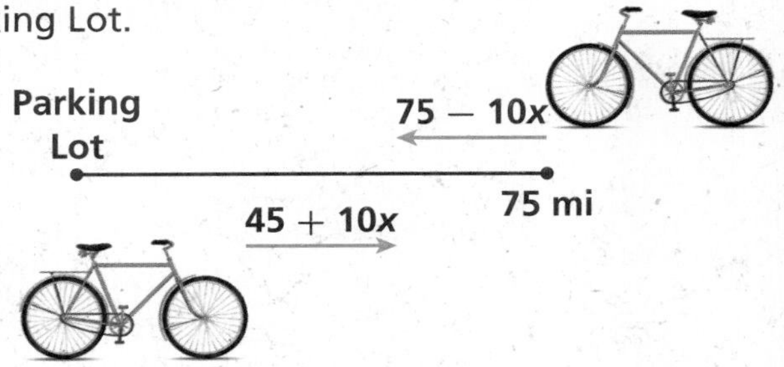
Parking Lot
75 − 10x
75 mi
45 + 10x

A. Write an equation to represent the bicyclists' meeting after x hours.

____

B. After how many hours do the bicyclists meet?

____

C. How far away are the bicyclists from the parking lot when they meet?

____

© Houghton Mifflin Harcourt Publishing Company • Image Credits: (tr) ©Elena Elisseeva/Shutterstock; (br) ©TroobaDoor/Shutterstock

On Your Own

3. James rides down an elevator that starts at a height of 120 feet. Brianne runs up the stairs from the ground floor.

Use the equation $120 - 2.5t = 1.5t$ to represent when James and Brianne are at the same height after t seconds.

A. Solve the equation.

____

B. What does the solution represent about James and Brianne's locations?

____

____

C. What is their height above the ground floor when they are at the same height at the same time? Explain.

____

4. The expression $100 - 2.5x$ represents the balance of Grace's account after x days. The expression $100 + 2.5(5 - x)$ represents the balance of Tim's account after x days. After how many days do the accounts have the same balance?

____

5. Josh is 3 years older than Lynette. The sum of their ages is 49. Write expressions for Josh's age and Lynette's age, and use the expressions to write an equation relating their ages. Use the equation to determine Josh's age and Lynette's age.

____

6. $\angle A$ is complementary to $\angle B$. The measure of $\angle A$ is $(8x + 12)^\circ$. The measure of $\angle B$ is half the measure of $\angle A$. Write an equation that can be used to determine the value of x. Then solve for x.

____

7. **Open Ended** A business *breaks even* when its production costs are equal to its revenue. The expression $120 + 4x$ represents the cost of producing x items. Decide on a selling price for each item, and write an expression for the revenue generated by selling x items. How many items would you need to sell at your chosen price to break even? Write an equation and solve it.

____

© Houghton Mifflin Harcourt Publishing Company • Image Credits: (tr) ©Dan Kenyon/Getty Images; (br) ©Hongqi Zhang/Alamy

Name

8. **STEM** A scientist conducts an experiment with two trees over many years. To the shorter tree, he applies a fertilizer, and to the taller tree, he does not. The shorter tree grows at an average rate of 8 inches per year. The taller tree grows at an average rate of 6 inches per year.

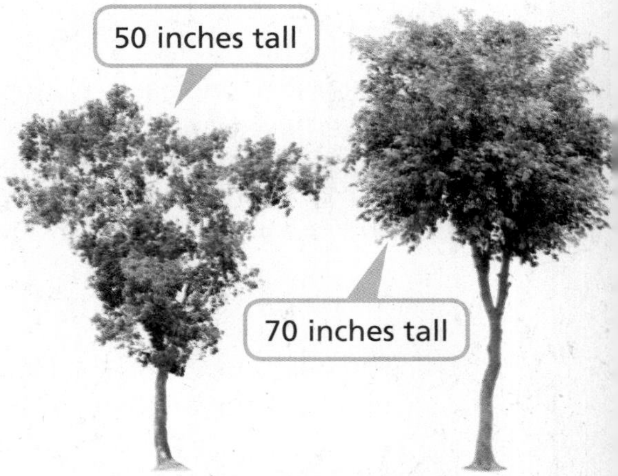

Starting Heights

A. Complete the equation to represent the trees having the same height after t years:

$$50 + 8t = \square$$

B. After how many years will the heights of the two trees be equal?

C. What will the height of the trees be when they are the same height?

For Problems 9–10, consider an angle with a measure of $(2x + 11)^\circ$.

9. What is the measure of an angle that is vertical to the given angle?

10. Write an expression to represent the measure of an angle supplementary to the given angle.

11. (MP) **Critique Reasoning** Ethan said $5x - 20 = 5(x - 20)$ has infinitely many solutions. Is he correct? Explain.

12. Abigail wants to find three consecutive even integers whose sum is four times the smallest of those integers. She lets n represent the smallest integer, then writes this equation: $n + (n + 2) + (n + 4) = 4n$.

A. Solve the equation.

B. What are the three integers?

13. Every year Aiden uses income from his job to pay for 75% of his college tuition. Next year's tuition will be \$720 more than this year's, and Aiden will pay \$2400. How much is this year's tuition?

© Houghton Mifflin Harcourt Publishing Company • Image Credit: ©Odua Images/Shutterstock

14. (MP) **Model with Mathematics** For Pool A, the water level is dropping 2.5 inch per minute. For Pool B, the water level increases 2.5 inch per minute. Starting water levels are shown. When will the pools have the same water level? Write an equation and solve.

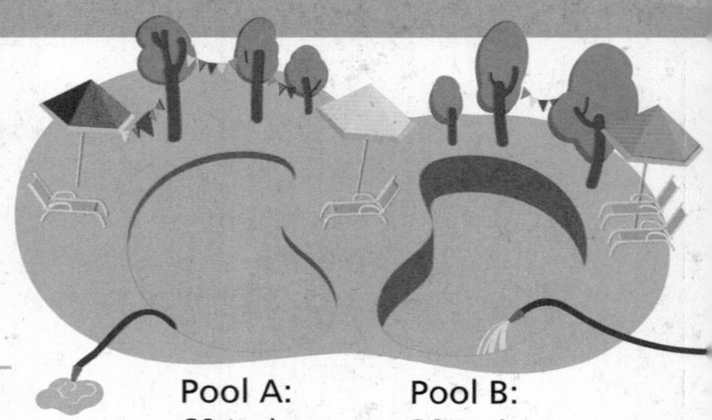

Pool A:
60 inches

Pool B:
20 inches

____

____

15. The diagram shows a right angle. What does x equal? What are the angle measures?

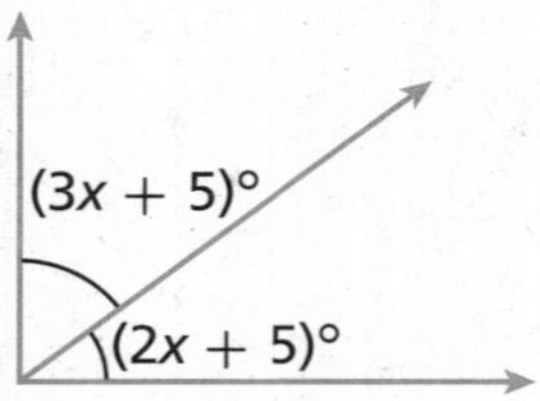

____

16. Determine whether each equation has one solution, no solution, or infinitely many solutions.

	No solution	One solution	Infinitely many solutions
$4x + 17 = 4(x + 9) - 12$	☐	☐	☐
$3.5 + 7.2x + 3.2x = x$	☐	☐	☐
$9x - 7x + 3x - 16 = 2x + 22 - x$	☐	☐	☐
$\frac{1}{2}x - x + 7 = \frac{1}{2}(14 - x)$	☐	☐	☐

17. STEM A rocket blasts off at a 90° angle from Earth. A second rocket launches at a different angle as shown in the diagram.

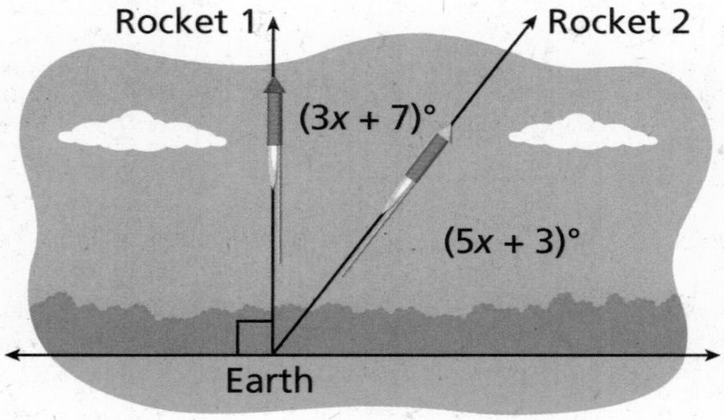

A. Write an equation that can be used to determine the value of x.

____

B. What is the value of x?

____

C. What is the measure of the angle of the second rocket launch in relation to Earth?

____

© Houghton Mifflin Harcourt Publishing Company

Name ______________________________

ONLINE
Ed
Video Tutorials and Interactive Examples

Apply Linear Equations

1. The expression $0.9(2x + 5)$ represents how much Stacy pays for x games of bowling at Lively Lanes. The expression $4.50 + 1.80x$ represents how much Parker pays for x games of bowling at Bowling and More. For how many games of bowling would they pay the same amount?

____

____

2. (MP) **Reason** Janesa has 24 coins in her pocket worth exactly \$1.00. She tells her younger brother Jackson that he can have the coins if he correctly guesses how many of each coin she has. She gives him the hint that there are only nickels and pennies.

A. Complete the equation that represents the total value of the nickels and p pennies:

$5(\square) + p = 100$

B. How many pennies does Janesa have in her pocket? __________

C. What is the total value of the pennies? __________

D. What is the total value of the nickels? __________

E. What should Jackson guess to get his sister's coins?

____

3. **Math on the Spot** Flex Gym charges a membership fee of \$150.00 plus \$40.50 per month to join the gym. A rival gym, Able Gym, charges a membership fee of \$120.00 plus \$46.75 per month. Find the number of months for which you would pay the same total fee to both gyms.

____

4. (MP) **Attend to Precision** Ms. Baumgartner draws a pair of supplementary angles and tells the class that the angle measures are $(4x + 30)°$ and $(2x + 6)°$.

A. Write an equation to determine the value of x. Solve for x.

____

B. What does the larger angle measure? What does the smaller angle measure?

____

© Houghton Mifflin Harcourt Publishing Company • Image Credit: ©Bessarab/Shutterstock

Test Prep

5. Consider adjacent angles that measure $(2x + 45)°$ and $(3x + 55)°$. The sum of the measures of these two angles is 135°.

A. Write and solve an equation to find the value of x.

____

B. Using the value of x, what is the angle measure represented by the expression $(2x + 45)°$? ______________________________

Use the information to answer Problems 6–7.

Riley is comparing cell phone plans. The table shows four options Riley is considering. The gigabytes of data used each month is represented by g.

Plan	Monthly fee	Charge per gigabyte of data	Total monthly cost ($)
1	$60	$5	$60 + 5g$
2	$40	$10	$40 + 10g$
3	$80	$0	80
4	$50	$5	$50 + 5g$

6. Which two plans will never cost the same amount for any amount of data?

Ⓐ Plans 1 and 3
Ⓑ Plans 2 and 4
Ⓒ Plans 3 and 2
Ⓓ Plans 4 and 1

7. Which plan should Riley get if he only uses 3 gigabytes of data each month?

Ⓐ Plan 1
Ⓑ Plan 2
Ⓒ Plan 3
Ⓓ Plan 4

Spiral Review

8. The segment with endpoints (0, 8) and (−6, 0) is dilated with the center of dilation at the origin to become a segment with endpoints (0, 6) and (−4.5, 0). What is the scale factor of the dilation?

____

9. For what value of m does $5 - 3x = m + mx$ have no solutions?

____

10. Frankie and Marcel are picking apples. Frankie has 18 apples, which is 4 times plus 2 more apples than Marcel has. How many apples does Marcel have?

____

© Houghton Mifflin Harcourt Publishing Company

Module 4

Name ______________________

Review

Vocabulary

Choose the correct term from the Vocabulary box.

Vocabulary
adjacent angles complementary angles supplementary angles vertical angles

1. a pair of angles with measures that add to 90°

____

2. a pair of angles with measures that add to 180°

____

3. a pair of opposite angles formed by two intersecting lines

____

4. a pair of angles that share a vertex and a ray but have no interior points in common ______________________

5. Underline the like terms in the equation in the box.

$-2x + 4 = 15x$

6. Which equation demonstrates the Distributive Property?

(A) $3(n - 2) = 3n - 6$

(B) $8(n + 7) = 8(7 + n)$

(C) $(n + 4) + 10 = n + 14$

(D) $12 + 3(n - 4) = 3(n - 4) + 12$

Concepts and Skills

7. (MP) **Use Tools** The box shows how Andrew attempted to solve the equation $\frac{1}{3}(n + 6) = -10$. His work contains at least one error. List the step(s) with an error and find the correct solution. State what strategy and tool you will use to answer the question, explain your choice, and then find the answer.

	$\frac{1}{3}(n + 6) = -10$
Step 1:	$\frac{1}{3}n + \frac{1}{3}(6) = -10$
Step 2:	$\frac{1}{3}n + 2 = -10$
Step 3:	$\frac{1}{3}n = -12$
Step 4:	$n = -4$

____

____

Solve each equation.

8. $-\frac{1}{2}d + \frac{5}{8} = \frac{3}{8}d - \frac{11}{16}$

$d =$ ______________

9. $0.4(p - 5) = 0.6p + 2$

$p =$ ______________

© Houghton Mifflin Harcourt Publishing Company

10. Select whether each equation has no solution, one solution, or infinitely many solutions.

	No solution	One solution	Infinitely many solutions
$2.5(n + 4) = n + 1.5n - 7$	☐	☐	☐
$2.5(n + 4) = 2n + 0.5n + 10$	☐	☐	☐
$2.5(n + 4) = 2.5n + 0.5n$	☐	☐	☐

Determine the measure in degrees of the angle indicated with an arc.

11.

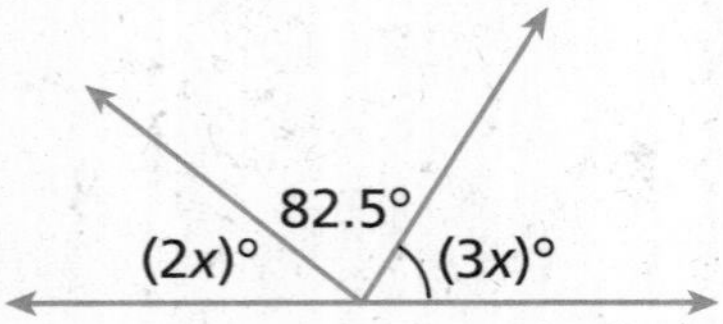

______

12.

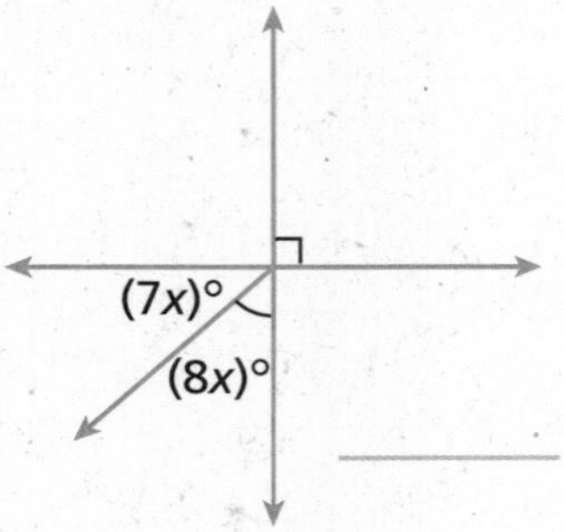

______

13. Use numbers from the box to complete the equation so that it has no solution.

2.5	3	5.5	9	12	15

$3x + 2.5 = 12x - \square\, x + \square$

14. A rancher uses 280 feet of fencing to build a rectangular corral for a horse. The length of the corral is 2.5 times the width. What is the area of the corral?

Ⓐ 112 square feet
Ⓑ 700 square feet
Ⓒ 4,000 square feet
Ⓓ 16,000 square feet

15. Two hikers walk on a trail in the direction of increasing mile marker numbers. Mandy starts at mile marker 1 and hikes at a rate of 2.5 miles per hour. At the same time, Rita starts at mile marker 2 and hikes at a rate of 3 miles per hour. The equation $2.5h + 1 = 3h + 2$ represents the number of hours h it will take Mandy to catch up with Rita.

A. What is the solution of the equation?

$h =$ ______

B. What does the solution of the equation indicate in this situation?

______

______

______

© Houghton Mifflin Harcourt Publishing Company

Module

5 Solve Problems Using Inequalities

The Suspect is Over There!

I believe the suspect is greater than or equal to four-fifths.

In your work with the Math Detective Agency, you have been asked to locate an integer suspect using witness reports given as inequalities. For example, the report $x \geq \frac{4}{5}$ means that the witness believes the suspect is greater than or equal to four-fifths.

Summarize each report by graphing the inequality on the number line.

A. $x \geq \frac{4}{5}$

B. $y < 6$

C. $n \leq 2.8$

D. $p > \frac{8}{5}$

Turn and Talk

If all the witness reports are correct, do you have enough information to determine which integer is the suspect? Explain.

© Houghton Mifflin Harcourt Publishing Company

Are You Ready?

Complete these problems to review prior concepts and skills you will need for this module.

Compare Rational Numbers

Compare. Write < or >.

1. -7 ☐ -3

2. 0 ☐ -1

3. $\frac{1}{3}$ ☐ $-\frac{3}{4}$

4. -2.10 ☐ -2.19

5. $-7\frac{2}{5}$ ☐ $5\frac{1}{2}$

6. $-\frac{2}{5}$ ☐ -0.35

Interpret, Write, and Graph Inequalities

For each inequality, circle the values in the box that can be substituted for the variable to make the inequality true.

7. $x + 2.4 < 8.6$

0	2.4	5.7	8.5	9.1

8. $\frac{1}{3}n > \frac{2}{5}$

$\frac{3}{4}$	1	$\frac{6}{5}$	$\frac{4}{3}$	2

Write an inequality to represent each situation.

9. The temperature t in a freezer must be at most -10 °F.

____

10. A person's weight w must be more than 110 pounds for the person to donate blood to a blood bank.

____

Graph each inequality.

11. $x < 16$

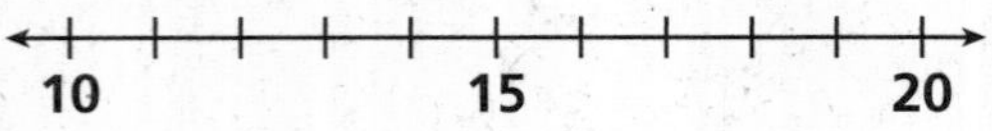

12. $n > 5.2$

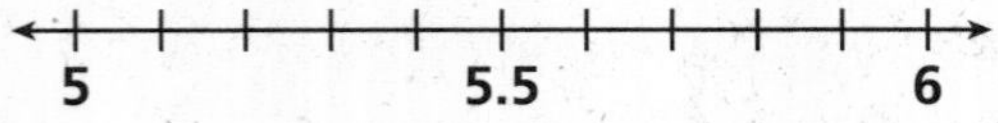

© Houghton Mifflin Harcourt Publishing Company

Name

Understand and Apply Properties to Solve One-Step Inequalities

I Can write and solve one-step inequalities.

Spark Your Learning

PAIRS

Suppose the lowest elevation to which the submarine shown has been tested is −490 meters. If it is currently at an elevation of −125 meters, how many meters more can it dive without going below the lowest elevation tested?

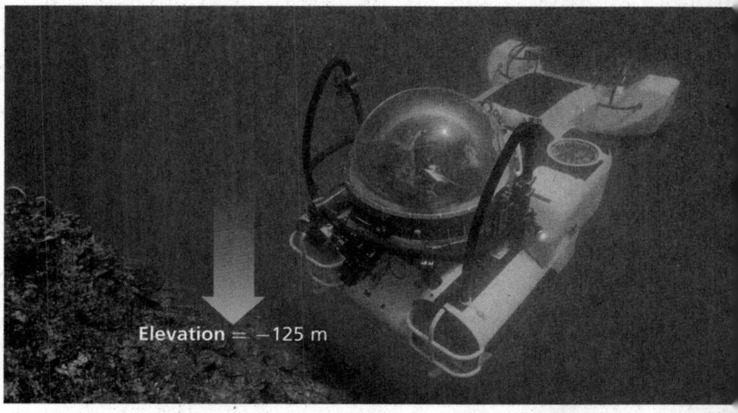

Turn and Talk Can the submarine dive 200 meters more without going below the lowest elevation tested? 400 meters more? How do you know?

© Houghton Mifflin Harcourt Publishing Company • Image Credit: ©Jeffry Rotman/Science Source

Build Understanding

Recall that an equation is a mathematical sentence showing that two quantities are equal, or equivalent. Likewise, an **inequality** is a mathematical sentence showing that two quantities are not equivalent. The meanings of the inequality symbols are shown in the table.

Connect to Vocabulary

The **solution of an inequality** is a value or values that makes an inequality true.

Greater than	$>$	Greater than or equal to	$\geq$
Less than	$<$	Less than or equal to	$\leq$

The **number line** shows $x \leq 365$. Note the closed circle represents "or equal to" in the inequality to indicate the inclusion of 365.

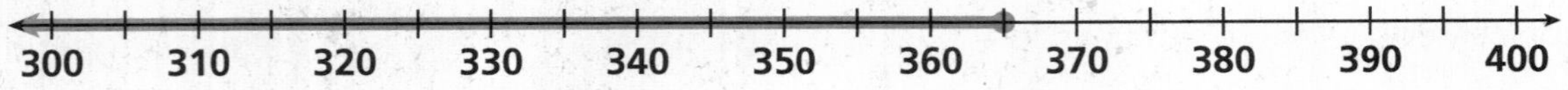

1 A submarine is at sea level, and it descends with a **rate of change** of −10 feet per second.

A. Write an inequality to represent the time t it takes the submarine to reach an elevation of −140 feet or deeper from sea level.

____

B. Write three values for t that will make the inequality from Part A true. Substitute each value in the inequality to check. Then describe the set of numbers that can make the inequality true.

____

____

C. Solve the inequality from Part A by writing a simple inequality that describes all of the numbers that will make the inequality true. Write an inequality symbol in the first box and a number in the second box.

t ☐ ☐

D. Graph the inequality from Part C. Can the submarine reach an elevation of −140 feet or deeper in less than 14 seconds? Explain.

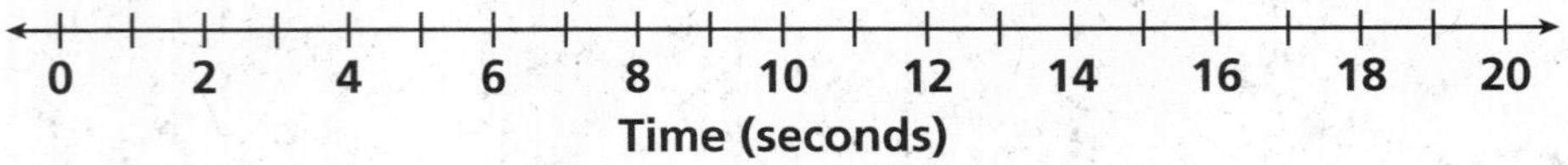

____

E. How are solving $-10t = -140$ and $-10t \leq -140$ alike? How are they different?

____

____

© Houghton Mifflin Harcourt Publishing Company

Name ______________________________

Step It Out

2 During the spring rains, the water level in a lake rises. Although the lake has a dam, when the water reaches the top of the dam, water will begin flowing over the top of the dam.

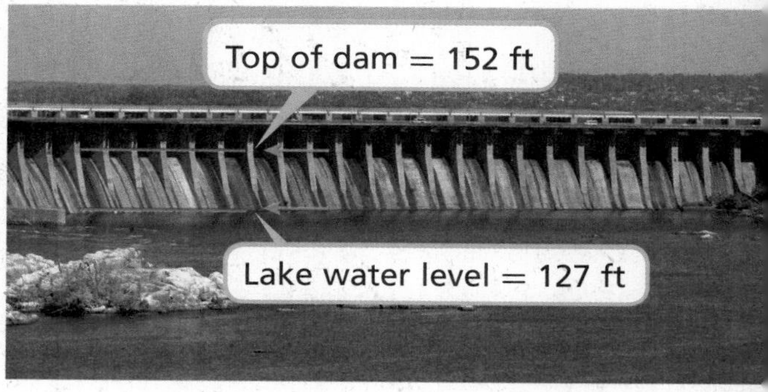

A. Write an inequality that expresses how much more the lake can rise *r* so that the water does not flow over the top of the dam.

____

B. Write three values for *r* that will make the inequality from Part A true. Then write and graph a simple inequality that describes all of the numbers that will make the inequality true.

____

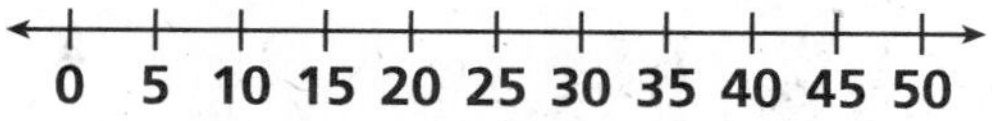

Turn and Talk How are solving $127 + r \leq 152$ and solving $127 + r = 152$ alike, and how are they different?

3 The properties of equality you used when solving equations hold true for inequalities, with one exception: when you multiply or divide by a negative number you must reverse the inequality symbol. Apply properties of inequalities to solve each inequality.

A.

$m - 0.3 > 1.45$

$+\square \quad +\square$

$m > \square$

B.

$3.5n \leq 7$

$\frac{3.5n}{\square} \leq \frac{7}{\square}$

$n \leq \square$

C.

$-2 \geq b + \frac{1}{8}$

$-\square \quad -\square$

$\square \geq b$

$b \leq \square$

D.

$-\frac{1}{2}y < 6$

$\square \cdot -\frac{1}{2}y > \square \cdot 6$

$y > \square$

E.

$-x < -4$

$\square \cdot -x > \square \cdot -4$

$x > \square$

F.

$\frac{-2a}{3} > 6$

$-\frac{2}{3}a > \square$

$\square \cdot -\frac{2}{3}a < \square \cdot \square$

$a < \square$

© Houghton Mifflin Harcourt Publishing Company • Image Credit: ©Lepsus/Shutterstock

4 Leila is designing a rectangular table. What is the range of values for x if the area of the table shown is to be 12 square feet or less?

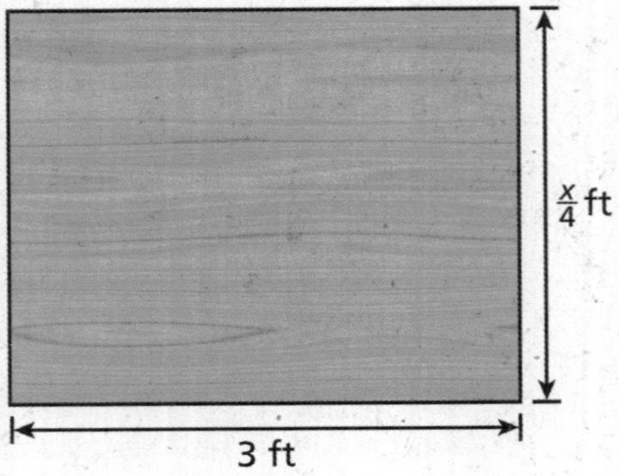

A. What is the inequality using the formula for the area of a rectangle?

____

B. Solve the inequality for x.

____

C. Give the range of values for x that are reasonable in the context of this problem and justify your answer. Graph the solution.

____

____

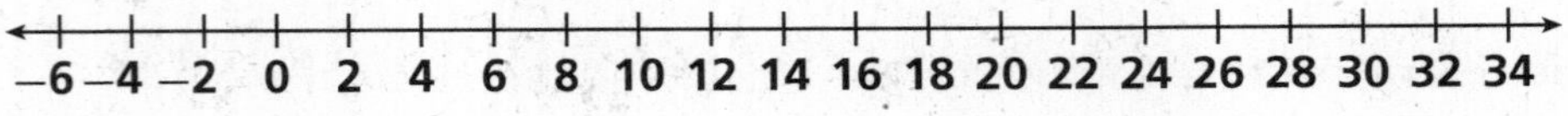

Turn and Talk What is the longest the unknown side of the table can be? Explain.

Check Understanding

1. The veterinarian told Hector that his 8-inch puppy would get no taller than 24 inches. Write and solve an inequality to find how much more his puppy, shown here, may grow.

____

____

For Problems 2–3, solve the inequality. Graph the solution.

2. $\frac{-2x}{3} \leq 2$ ____________

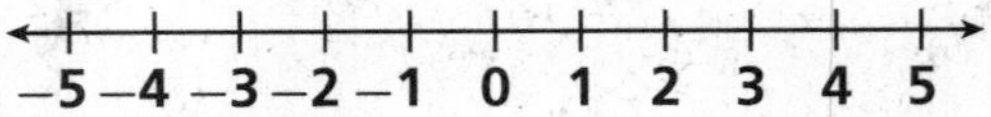

3. $x - 2 > -6$ ____________

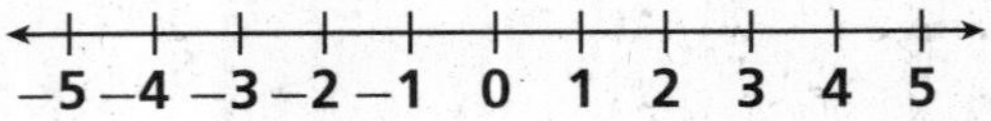

© Houghton Mifflin Harcourt Publishing Company • Image Credits: (t) ©Clearviewstock/Alamy; (b) ©GK Hart/Vikki Hart/Getty Images

Name ____________________

On Your Own

For Problems 4–5, use the given information.

Mr. Berg is designing a room addition to his home and wants a rectangular window with area that is more than 12 square feet but not more than 24 square feet. Mr. Berg knows he wants the window to be 4 feet wide.

4. MP **Model with Mathematics** Write and solve an inequality to find the length x that will guarantee that the window is not too small. Explain.

____

____

____

5. MP **Model with Mathematics** Write and solve an inequality to find the length x that will guarantee that the window is not too large. Explain.

____

____

____

6. MP **Use Structure** Emir is solving the inequality $-\frac{2}{3}x < 18$. What steps should he follow to find the solution?

____

____

For Problems 7–10, solve the inequality. Graph the solution.

7. $10 \leq x + 7$ ________

−7 −6 −5 −4 −3 −2 −1 0 1 2 3 4 5 6 7

8. $-x \geq -5$ ________

−7 −6 −5 −4 −3 −2 −1 0 1 2 3 4 5 6 7

9. $\frac{3x}{5} > -6$ ________

−12 −11 −10 −9 −8 −7 −6 −5 −4 −3 −2 −1 0 1 2

10. $2 < -\frac{x}{3}$ ________

−8 −7 −6 −5 −4 −3 −2 −1 0 1 2 3 4 5 6

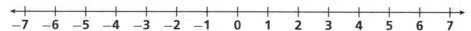

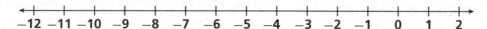

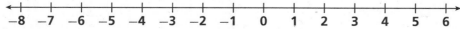

© Houghton Mifflin Harcourt Publishing Company • Image Credit: ©irina88w/iStock/Getty Images Plus/Getty Images

For Problems 11–13, use the given information.

Three friends are shopping at the garage sale shown.

11. (MP) **Attend to Precision** Ming has \$24. Write and solve an inequality for the number of shorts she can buy. Interpret the solution in the context of the problem.

____

____

12. (MP) **Attend to Precision** Camille can buy up to 5 shirts. How much money could she have?

____

13. (MP) **Construct Arguments** Juanita has \$24. Can she buy 5 shirts? Explain your answer.

____

14. (MP) **Model with Mathematics** Rudo has a target of at least \$150 in pledges for a walkathon. He currently has \$65 in pledges. Write and solve an inequality for the amount p Rudo has left to raise.

____

For Problems 15–17, solve the inequality. Graph the solution.

15. $x - 2.5 > 8.7$ __________

16. $1.8x \leq 13.5$ __________

17. $x + 1\frac{3}{5} < -2$ __________

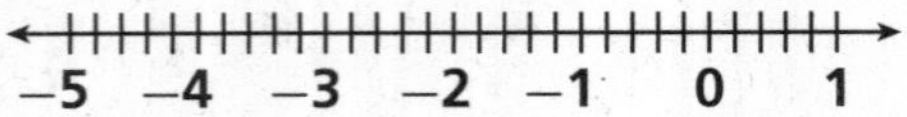

I'm in a Learning Mindset!

What part of solving one-step inequalities elicits a fixed-mindset voice in my head?

____

____

© Houghton Mifflin Harcourt Publishing Company • Image Credit: ©JulNichols/iStock/Getty Images Plus/Getty Images

Name ______________________________

Understand and Apply Properties to Solve One-Step Inequalities

1. (MP) **Model with Mathematics** Cara is designing the rectangular patio shown. She wants the area of the patio to be larger than 72 square feet but no greater than 156 square feet.

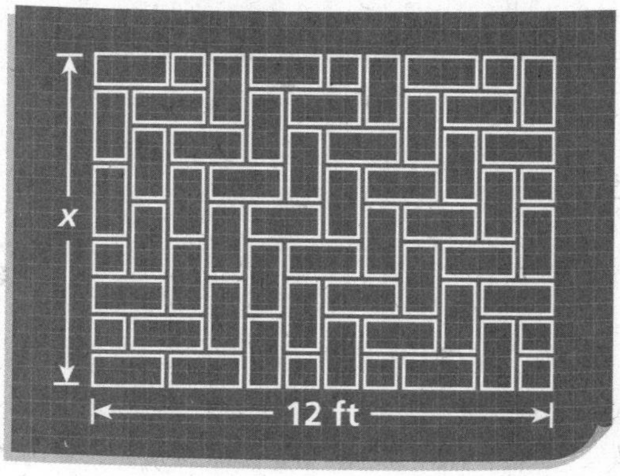

A. Write and solve an inequality representing a length that meets the requirement for the minimum area.

____

B. Write and solve an inequality representing a length that meets the requirement for the maximum area.

____

C. Describe the possible lengths for the unknown side.

____

2. **Math on the Spot** Solve the inequality. Graph the solution.

A. $-4x < 12$ __________

−10 −9 −8 −7 −6 −5 −4 −3 −2 −1 0 1 2 3 4 5 6 7 8 9 10

B. $-1 \geq \frac{w}{-4}$ __________

−10 −9 −8 −7 −6 −5 −4 −3 −2 −1 0 1 2 3 4 5 6 7 8 9 10

3. **STEM** In the science lab, Will is testing the freezing point of a substance, which should be −24 °C. He is changing the temperature at a rate of −3 °C per minute, starting at 0 °C. Write and solve an inequality for the time *t* before the temperature reaches the freezing point.

____

4. (MP) **Model with Mathematics** Tania has already saved \$25.75. She needs at least \$53.88 to buy a set of headphones. Write and solve an inequality that shows how much more she needs to save to buy headphones.

____

© Houghton Mifflin Harcourt Publishing Company

Test Prep

5. Chan is in a running club and needs to run at least 500 miles in a year to earn the gold level of achievement. He is presently at 220 miles. Which inequality can be used to determine the additional number of miles he can run and earn gold?

Ⓐ $x + 220 < 500$

Ⓑ $x + 220 \geq 500$

Ⓒ $x + 500 > 220$

Ⓓ $x + 500 \leq 220$

6. Select the number line that represents the solution of the inequality $7 - x \geq 4$.

Ⓐ
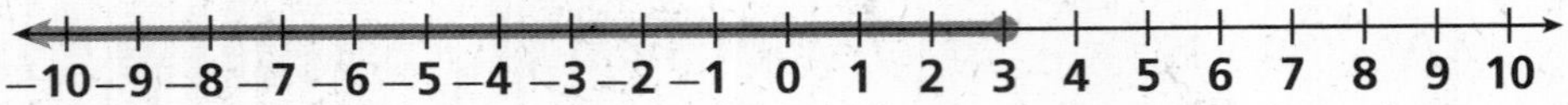

Ⓑ
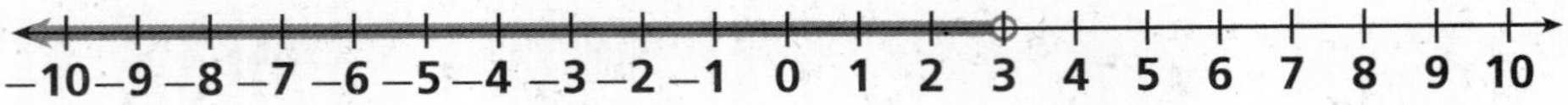

Ⓒ
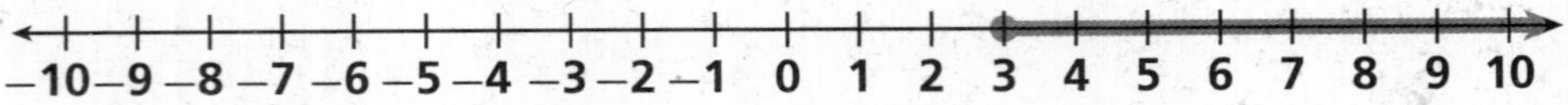

Ⓓ
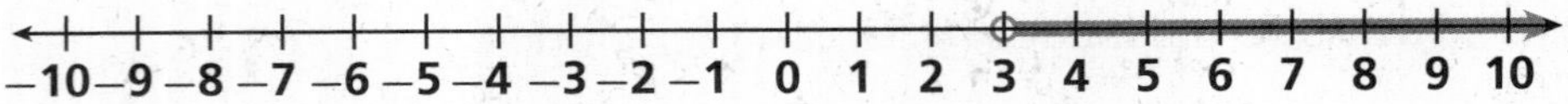

7. Shawna earns $12.75 per hour. How many hours does she need to work to earn $102 or more?

at least / at most / less than / more than ________ hours

Spiral Review

8. Francisco bought 2 theater tickets online. The total charge was $35 with an online booking charge of $5. If x is the price of the ticket, write an equation to solve for the ticket price.

____

9. Solve for x.

____

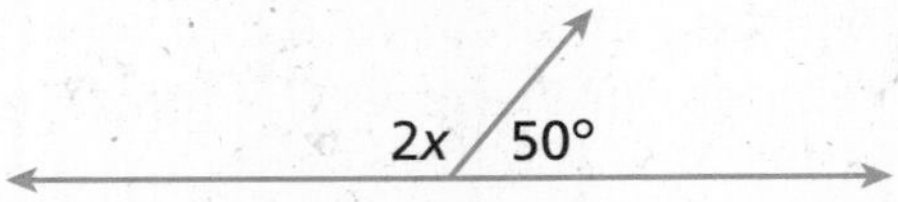

10. The perimeter of the table shown is 16 feet. Write an equation in the form $px + q = r$ to solve for x.

____

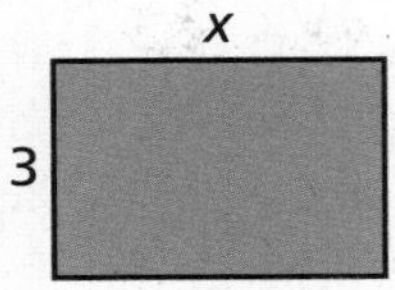

© Houghton Mifflin Harcourt Publishing Company

Name ______________________

Write Two-Step Inequalities for Situations

I Can write two-step inequalities to solve problems.

Spark Your Learning

SMALL GROUPS

A small business owner is planning to upgrade the computer system. A new system will cost \$1,200, but the total cost can be more with installation. The owner has saved \$300 and will continue to save \$30 from profits each day for the new system. How many days will it take the business owner to save enough money to purchase the new computer system?

Select the inequality that represents this situation. Describe what each part of the inequality represents.

$300 + 30x \geq 1{,}200$ $\qquad$ $300 + 30x \leq 1{,}200$

$300 + 30x < 1{,}200$ $\qquad$ $300 + 30x > 1{,}200$

Turn and Talk Describe a situation that could be represented by changing the direction of the inequality symbol in the inequality above. Explain.

© Houghton Mifflin Harcourt Publishing Company • **Image Credit:** ©andresr/E+/Getty Images

Build Understanding

As you have learned, a one-step inequality involves one operation. For example, $x + 1 > 3$ is a one-step inequality. In this example, 4, 40, and 4,000,000 are all solutions because they make the inequality true when substituted for x, but 1 is not a solution because it does not make the inequality true when substituted for x.

A two-step inequality involves two operations.

1 Caitlyn wants to buy sheets of trumpet music at the price shown. She has only \$25, and she first needs to pay back \$5 to her friend. How many sheets can Caitlyn buy?

A. Describe how this problem represents an inequality situation.

____

____

B. Describe the part of this situation that is a variable quantity.

____

C. What are all the costs that Caitlyn's money will cover?

____

D. Write an expression to represent all the costs that Caitlyn's money will cover.

____

E. Write an inequality for this situation.

____

F. State a possible solution for this inequality.

____

G. State a value for the variable that would NOT be a possible solution for this inequality.

____

Turn and Talk If Caitlyn wanted more than \$4 left over, how would you change the inequality? Explain.

© Houghton Mifflin Harcourt Publishing Company • Image Credit: ©Richard G. Bingham II/Alamy

Name

Step It Out

2 Kyle's family is renting a boat at a lake. The rental company initially charges $50 for the boat plus the hourly fee shown. The family plans to spend no more than $250 on the boat rental.

A. What are the values in the problem that cannot change?

B. What value in the problem can vary? How can this be represented?

C. Write an inequality for how many hours the family can rent the boat.

3 An office manager wants to buy headsets that cost $12 each. The budget allows $155, but the manager wants to leave more than $20 for an emergency. How many headsets can the manager buy?

A. Write an inequality for how many headsets the manager can buy while staying within the limits.

B. Explain why the inequality does or does not include *equal to* as part of the inequality symbol.

Check Understanding

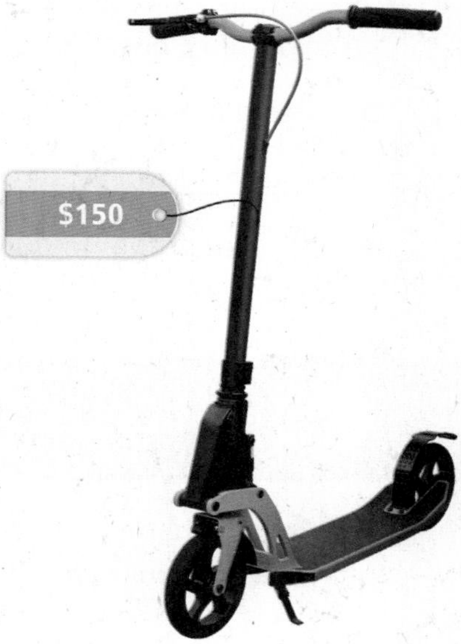

1. Gloria is saving for the scooter shown. She has $63 already. She earns $7 each week for doing chores around the house. How many weeks will it take for Gloria to save at least enough money to buy the scooter? Write an inequality to represent the situation. Do not solve the inequality.

2. Suppose Mario either wants to earn *no more than $500* or *more than $500* to afford his phone. How would the inequalities be different based on these two phrases?

© Houghton Mifflin Harcourt Publishing Company • Image Credit: © (t) Max Topchij/Getty Images (B) ©Lilkin/Shutterstock

On Your Own

3. **Model with Mathematics** Saleem is saving for a fish tank that costs \$140. He has \$20 and earns \$23 per day at a part-time job. What is an inequality he can write to find the number of days he has to work to have at least \$140?

4. **Open Ended** Consider the inequality $3x + 7 \geq 25$. Write a word problem that this inequality could represent.

For Problems 5–6, indicate whether each value of x is a *solution* or is *not a solution* of the inequality $33x + 55 > 17$.

5. $x = -2$

6. $x = 0$

7. **Model with Mathematics** The vet says that George's cat Milo has to lose weight, so George is going to portion out Milo's meals and stop giving Milo table scraps. If Milo loses 0.25 pound every week, write an inequality for how many weeks it will take Milo to drop below 18 pounds.

Model with Mathematics For Problems 8–9, write an inequality based on the statement.

8. Twice a number plus four is at most twelve.

9. Three less than a quarter of a number is less than six.

I'm in a Learning Mindset!

Do I recognize any obstacles to understanding two-step inequalities? Can those obstacles be changed? Why or why not?

© Houghton Mifflin Harcourt Publishing Company • Image Credit: Stockdisc/Getty Images

Name

LESSON 5.2
More Practice/ Homework

ONLINE
Video Tutorials and Interactive Examples

Write Two-Step Inequalities for Situations

1. **Music** Jason has already rapped a 40-word intro to a song and continues to rap 5 words per second. Write an inequality to represent how many more seconds t Jason will rap for the total song including the intro to be at least 500 words.

2. (MP) **Construct Arguments** A team can spend no more than \$300 on shirts. The team has already spent \$80. How many shirts for \$15 each can the team still buy?

   A. Write an inequality that represents the situation.

   B. Explain why you chose the inequality sign.

   C. Without solving, explain how you know that 20 is not a solution.

3. (MP) **Model with Mathematics** Felicia spends \$50 on materials to make jewelry, and she plans on selling the pieces for \$7 each. A friend donates \$5 to get her started. Write an inequality for the number of pieces of jewelry Felicia can sell and make a profit.

4. **Open Ended** Write a real-world problem that could be represented by $5x + 30 \geq 90$.

5. Write the inequality in words: $2n - 10 > 22$.

6. (MP) **Model with Mathematics** Rania is playing with her friend Arun, and they are setting up dominoes across the room. Each domino is 2 inches long. They have already placed 10 dominoes end to end. The room is 10 feet long and they want to know how many more dominoes they can set up before they reach all the way across the room. Write an inequality that models this situation.

© Houghton Mifflin Harcourt Publishing Company • Image Credit: ©Adrienne Bresnahan/Moment/Getty Images

Test Prep

7. A small plane can carry a maximum of 1,200 pounds of people and luggage. The people on the plane have a combined weight of 800 pounds. Each bag weighs 75 pounds. Write an inequality for the number of bags b that can be taken on board.

____

8. Select an inequality that represents *3 less than 5 times a number is no more than 63.*

Ⓐ $5n - 3 \geq 63$

Ⓑ $5n \geq 63 - 3$

Ⓒ $5n - 3 \leq 63$

Ⓓ $5n \leq 63 - 3$

9. Match the words with the inequality.

$4n - 4 > 10$ •	• 4 times a number is greater than 10.
$4n + 4 < 10$ •	• 4 less than 4 times a number is greater than 10.
$4n > 10$ •	• 4 less than 4 times a number is no more than 10.
$4n - 4 \geq 10$ •	• The sum of 4 and 4 times a number is less than 10.
$4n + 4 \geq 10$ •	• The sum of 4 and 4 times a number is at least 10.
$4n - 4 \leq 10$ •	• 4 less than 4 times a number is 10 or more.

10. Olivia's class is having a bake sale, and their goal is to raise at least $500. So far they have raised $210. If the items are all $5 each, which inequality represents how many more items they need to sell to meet their goal?

Ⓐ $5b + 210 \geq 500$

Ⓑ $5b \geq 500 + 210$

Ⓒ $b + 500 \geq 210$

Ⓓ $5b + 210 \leq 500$

Spiral Review

11. Max had d dollars and spent $31 but has at least $15 left. Write and solve an inequality to find d.

____

12. Write a simplified expression for the perimeter of the polygon shown.

____

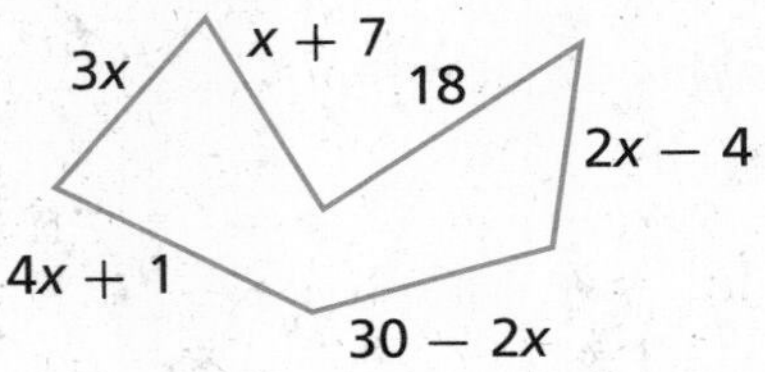

© Houghton Mifflin Harcourt Publishing Company

Name ____________________

Apply Two-Step Inequalities to Solve Problems

I Can write and solve two-step inequalities to solve problems.

Step It Out

ACTIVITY

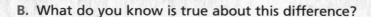

1 A study found that twice the number of deer in Maple Park is at least 20 more than the number of deer in Smith Park. The study found that there are 50 deer in Smith Park.

A. Write an expression to represent the difference between twice the number of deer in Maple Park and the number of deer in Smith Park. Use x for the number of deer in Maple Park.

____

B. What do you know is true about this difference?

The difference is __________ than or equal to ____.

C. Write and solve the inequality to determine the possible number of deer in Maple Park.

$\square \geq \square$

$+\square \quad +\square$

$2x \geq \square$

$\dfrac{2x}{\square} \geq \dfrac{70}{\square}$

$x \geq \square$

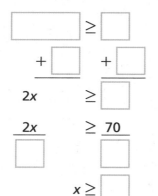

D. Graph the solution of the inequality. Do all the values make sense? Explain.

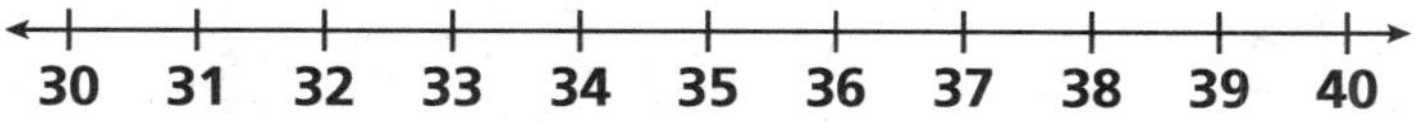

____

E. What does the solution of the inequality represent in the problem?

In __________ Park, there are __________ deer.

Turn and Talk Can you write the inequality for this situation differently and still find the same solution?

© Houghton Mifflin Harcourt Publishing Company • Image Credit: ©milehightraveler/iStock/Getty Images Plus/Getty Images

2 Rosina and Asia collect stamps. The number of stamps Rosina has is 7 more than 3 times the number of stamps Asia has. Rosina has less than 85 stamps. How many stamps can Asia have?

A. Asia has x stamps. Write an expression to represent how many stamps Rosina has.

____

B. What do you know about the number of stamps Rosina has in her collection?

Rosina has less / more than ____ stamps.

C. Write and solve an inequality to find the number of stamps Asia has in her collection.

$$3x + \square < \square$$
$$-\square \quad -\square$$
$$3x < 78$$
$$\frac{3x}{\square} < \frac{78}{\square}$$
$$x < \square$$

D. Graph the solution of the inequality. Do all the values make sense? Explain.

20 21 22 23 24 25 26 27 28 29 30

____

E. What does the solution of the inequality represent in the problem?

The number of stamps that Asia has is less / greater than ____.

3 Solve the inequality: $-3b - 2 \leq 13$.

A. $$-3b - 2 \leq 13$$
$$+\square \quad +\square$$
$$-3b \leq \square$$
$$\frac{-3b}{\square} \geq \frac{15}{\square}$$
$$b \geq \square$$

© Houghton Mifflin Harcourt Publishing Company • Image Credit: ©Lea Wood/Shutterstock

B. Graph the solution of the inequality.

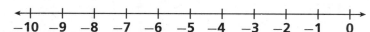

–10 –9 –8 –7 –6 –5 –4 –3 –2 –1 0

Turn and Talk Is −5 a solution of the inequality in Problem 3? Explain.

4 Monica and Lucy are participating in a scavenger hunt. The number of items Monica found is 7 more than $\frac{1}{2}$ the number of items Lucy found. The number of items Monica found is at least 17.

A. Lucy found x items. Write an expression to represent how many items Monica found. Then complete the sentence about the number of items.

________ The number of items Monica found is less / greater than or equal to ____.

B. Write and solve the inequality to find what you know about the number of items Lucy found.

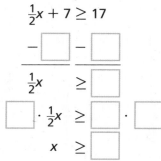

$$\frac{1}{2}x + 7 \geq 17$$

$$-\square \quad -\square$$

$$\frac{1}{2}x \geq \square$$

$$\square \cdot \frac{1}{2}x \geq \square \cdot \square$$

$$x \geq \square$$

C. Graph the solution of the inequality. Do all values make sense? Explain.

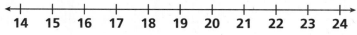

14 15 16 17 18 19 20 21 22 23 24

____

D. What does the solution of the inequality mean in the problem?

Lucy found less / greater than or equal to ____ items.

Check Understanding

1. Solve the inequality $-7m + 4 < -45$. Graph the solution.

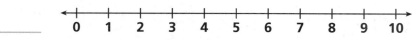

______ 0 1 2 3 4 5 6 7 8 9 10

2. The number of students using the cafeteria's healthy lunch line can be found by solving the inequality $\frac{1}{2}s - 51 \leq 20$. How many students use this lunch line?

____

© Houghton Mifflin Harcourt Publishing Company

On Your Own

3. **Attend to Precision** A warehouse has 2,100 tables packaged in boxes. The daily shipment is shown. After how many days will there be fewer than 1,500 tables in the warehouse?

A. Write and solve an inequality for this situation.

____

B. Graph the solution of the inequality.

20 21 22 23 24 25 26 27 28 29 30

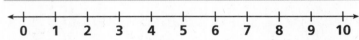

C. Do all the values make sense? What does the solution of the inequality represent in this context?

____

____

4. **Attend to Precision** Zachary and Dovante deliver packages. Dovante delivers 9 less than 4 times the number of packages Zachary delivers in one day. Dovante delivers no more than 11 packages in one day.

A. Write and solve an inequality to find the number of packages Zachary delivers each day. Graph the solution of the inequality.

____

0 1 2 3 4 5 6 7 8 9 10

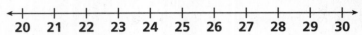

B. Do all the values make sense? What does the solution of the inequality represent in this context?

____

For Problems 5–8, solve the inequality. Graph the solution.

5. $6x - 11 > 67$

10 11 12 13 14 15 16 17 18 19 20

______

6. $3w + 1 \geq 19$

0 1 2 3 4 5 6 7 8 9 10

______

7. $-13d + 6 \leq 45$

−10 −9 −8 −7 −6 −5 −4 −3 −2 −1 0

______

8. $-8n - 4 < -60$

0 1 2 3 4 5 6 7 8 9 10

______

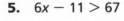

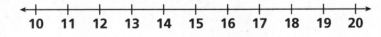

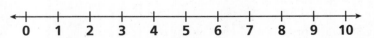

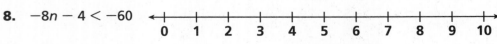

© Houghton Mifflin Harcourt Publishing Company • Image Credit: ©Acik/Fotolia

Name

9. Felipe is distributing discount coupons for a concert. He starts with 25 coupons. He gives 2 coupons to each person he sees. He will leave to get more coupons when he has fewer than 4 coupons left. How many people will Felipe give coupons to before he leaves to get more?

A. What is an inequality for this situation? What is the solution?

B. (MP) **Attend to Precision** What does the solution of the inequality mean in this context? Explain.

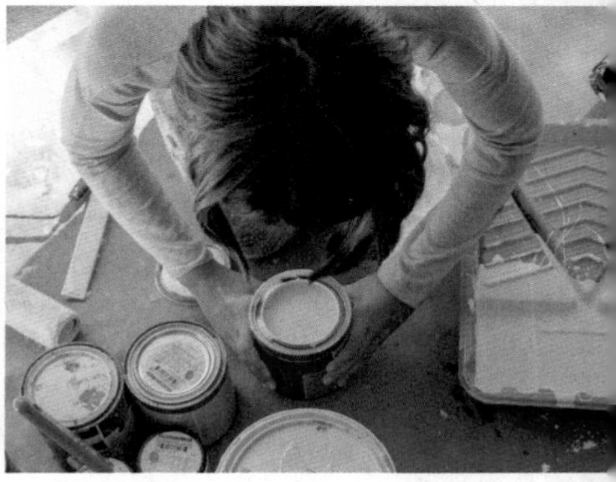

10. Alicia is mixing paint. She has a bucket that contains $5\frac{1}{2}$ pints of paint. She adds $\frac{1}{4}$-pint containers of paint to the bucket until she has at most $8\frac{3}{4}$ pints of paint in the bucket. How many containers of paint can she add to the bucket?

11. **Open Ended** Write a two-step inequality whose solution is represented by the number line.

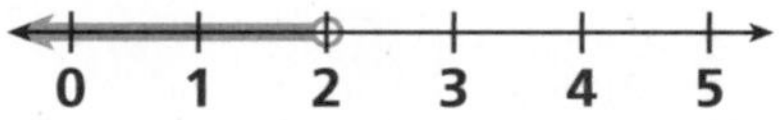

For Problems 12–17, solve the inequality. Graph the solution.

12. $\frac{2}{3}t - \frac{1}{6} \leq \frac{5}{6}$

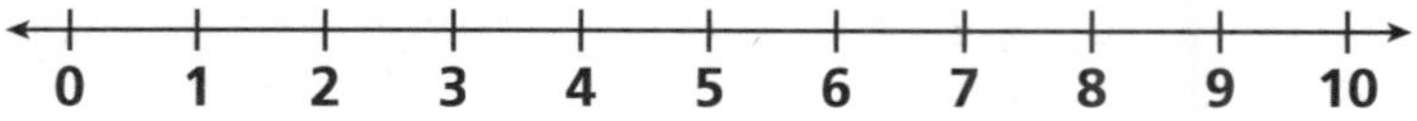

13. $-\frac{3}{4}m + \frac{1}{4} \geq 4\frac{3}{4}$

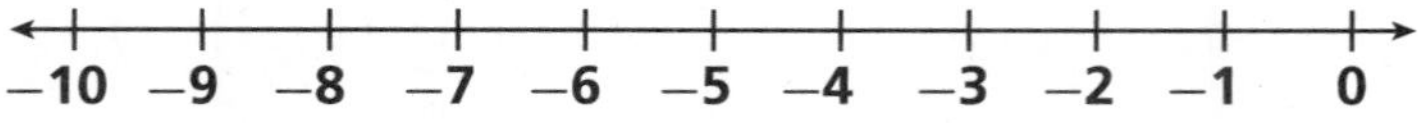

14. $-\frac{1}{10}a - \frac{2}{5} > \frac{3}{10}$

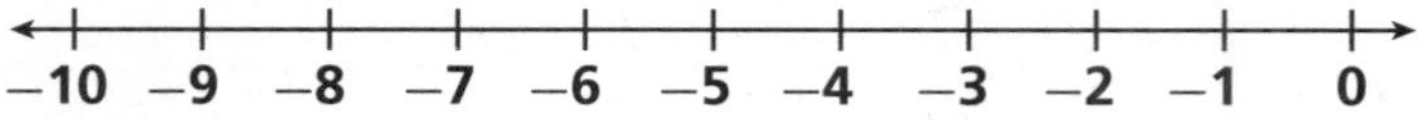

15. $\frac{3}{8}w + 5 < 11$

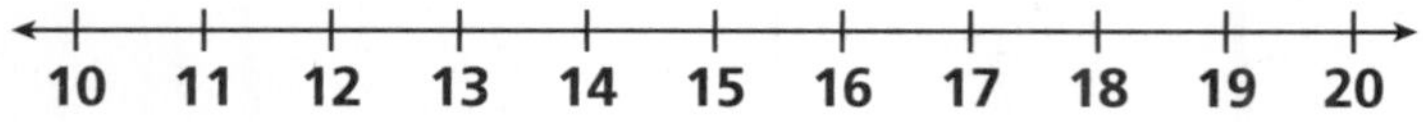

16. $\frac{3}{4}r + 5 \leq 17$

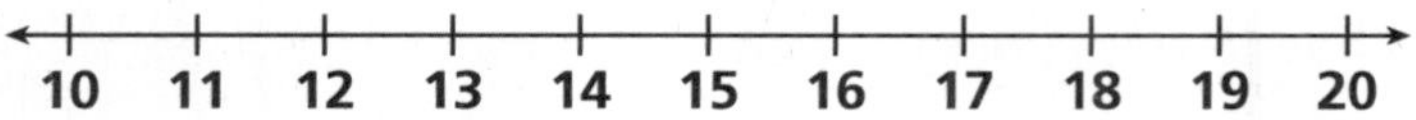

17. $2\frac{2}{3}b + 8 \geq 0$

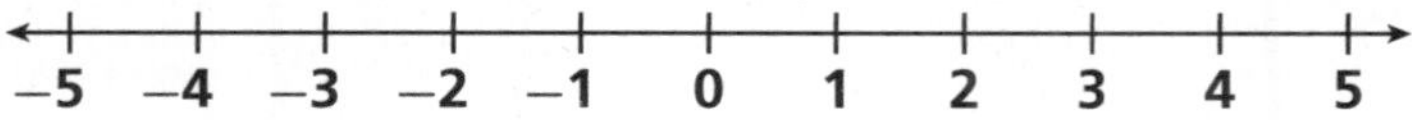

© Houghton Mifflin Harcourt Publishing Company • Image Credit: ©Celia Sanchez/Image Source/Getty Images

18. Financial Literacy Ariana started a savings account with $240. She deposits $30 into her account at the end of each month. She wants to know how many months it will take for her account to have a balance greater than $500.

A. (MP) **Model with Mathematics** Write and solve an inequality that represents this situation.

B. (MP) **Reason** How many months will it take for her account to have a balance greater than $500? Explain.

For Problems 19–22, solve the inequality. Graph the solution.

19. $-5y + 47 > -13$

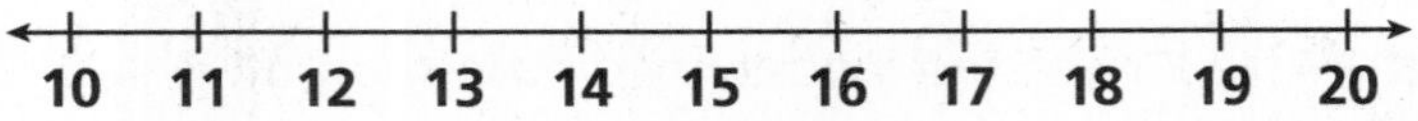

20. $18 - 4z \geq 26$

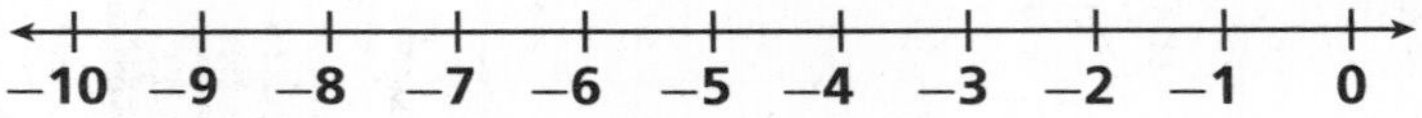

21. $8g + 30 < -2$

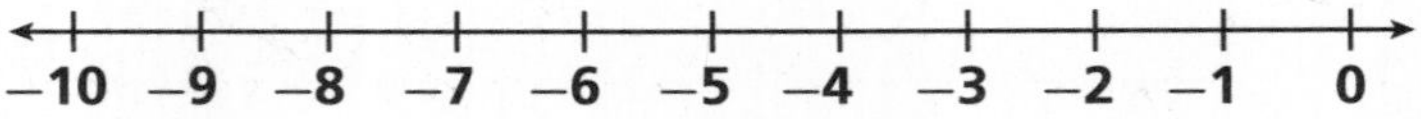

22. $-7s - 4 \leq 10$

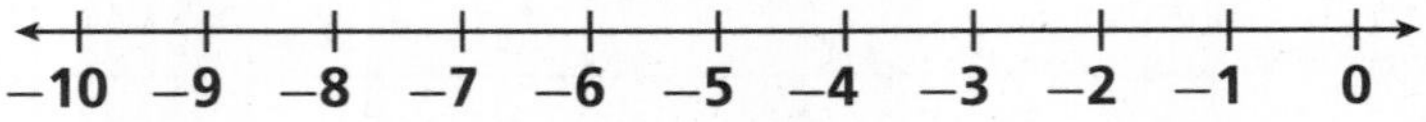

23. Colleen is attending a carnival. The price of admission into the carnival is shown. It costs $3 to play a game. Colleen has $35. What is the greatest number of games she can play?

24. A gift shop at an amusement park sells key chains. The gift shop has 55 key chains. When the number of key chains is below 10, the manager will reorder. If the gift shop sells 4 key chains each day, how many days will it take before the manager has to reorder?

© Houghton Mifflin Harcourt Publishing Company • Image Credit: © Steve Hamblin / Alamy

Name ______________________________

LESSON 5.3
More Practice/ Homework

ONLINE Ed Video Tutorials and Interactive Examples

Apply Two-Step Inequalities to Solve Problems

Solve the inequality. Graph the solution.

1. $5x + 13 \leq 48$

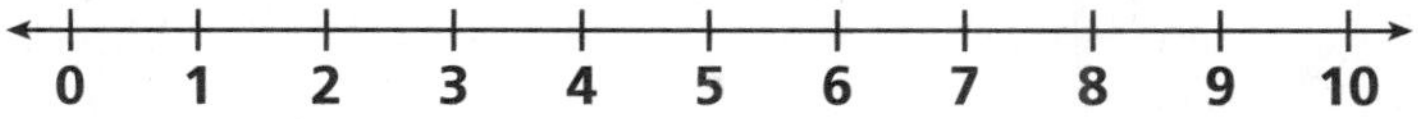

______

2. $16 - 7v < 2$

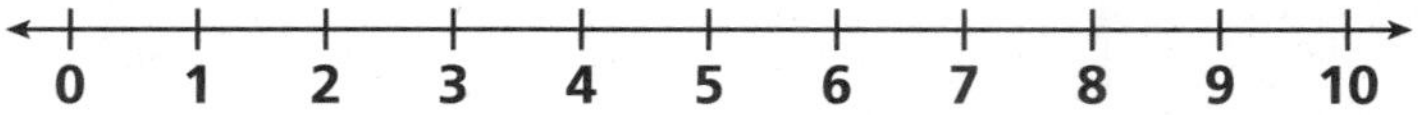

______

3. $9r - \frac{3}{5} > 3\frac{9}{10}$

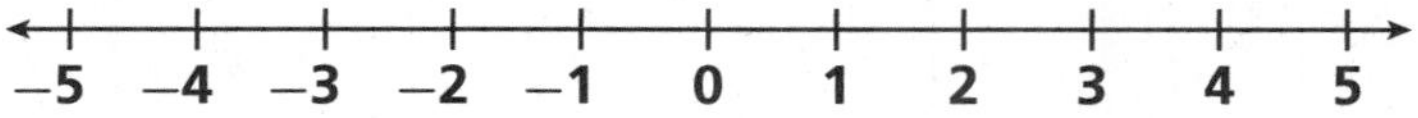

______

4. $-8c + 13 \geq 47$

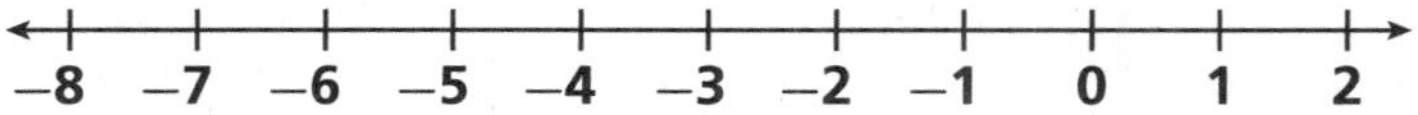

______

5. **Math on the Spot** Members of the drama club plan to present its annual spring musical. They have $1,262.50 left from fundraising, but they estimate that the entire production will cost $1,600.00. How many tickets at the price shown must they sell to at least break even?

______

Tickets: $6.75 each

6. (MP) **Model with Mathematics** Jenna has a collection of trading cards. She started her collection with 175 cards. She buys packs of cards that contain 15 cards each. Solve an inequality to determine how many packs of cards Jenna buys so that she will have over 400 cards in her collection.

A. What is an inequality that represents this situation? What is the solution?

______

B. How many packs of cards does Jenna buy?

______

7. (MP) **Model with Mathematics** Drew and Larry are working together on a jigsaw puzzle. Drew places 11 less than 3 times the number of pieces that Larry places. Drew places at least 10 pieces. How many pieces does Larry place?

______

© Houghton Mifflin Harcourt Publishing Company • Image Credit: ©Hill Street Studios/Blend Images/Getty Images

Test Prep

8. Dwight and Walt are building model cars. Dwight builds 7 fewer models than 4 times the number Walt builds. Dwight builds at most 9 models. Which inequality could be used to find the number of models Walt builds?

Ⓐ $4m - 7 < 9$

Ⓑ $4m - 7 \leq 9$

Ⓒ $4m - 7 > 9$

Ⓓ $4m - 7 \geq 9$

9. A truck rental company rents a truck for a one-time fee of $25 plus $1.50 per mile traveled. Kelly has $80 she can spend on the rental truck. What is the greatest number of miles that she can travel?

____

10. Ricardo measured the temperature in the morning. The temperature was −6 °C. The temperature is increasing $1\frac{1}{2}$ °C every hour. After how many hours will the temperature be at least 2 °C? Select the best answer.

Ⓐ more than $2\frac{1}{3}$ hours

Ⓑ $5\frac{1}{3}$ hours or more

Ⓒ less than 4 hours

Ⓓ less than $1\frac{1}{3}$ hours

Spiral Review

11. A football team earns 6 points for a touchdown and 3 points for a field goal. In one game, a team scored a touchdown and some field goals. The total points the team scored is 18 points. Write an equation that can be used to find the number of field goals the team scored.

____

12. Jean-Paul wants to make a triangular figure. He has side lengths of 2, 5, 8, and 18 centimeters. Could he make a triangular figure out of any combination of these pieces? Explain.

____

____

© Houghton Mifflin Harcourt Publishing Company

Module 5

Name

Review

Vocabulary

1. Complete the graphic organizer for the vocabulary term *solution of an inequality*.

Definition in your own words	Facts/characteristics
Example	Non-example

Solution of an Inequality

Concepts and Skills

2. (MP) **Use Tools** Water is pumped out of a 500-gallon tank at a rate of 2.5 gallons per second. The inequality $500 - 2.5t < 100$ can be used to determine the time t, in seconds, after which there will be less than 100 gallons of water remaining in the tank. Solve the inequality, then state what the solution represents. State what strategy and tool you will use to answer the question, explain your choice, and then find the answer.

3. Faith wants to run at least 7 miles this week. She already has run $2\frac{1}{2}$ miles. She plans to run an equal distance on each of the last 3 days of this week. Write and solve an inequality to represent this situation, where d represents the distance in miles that Faith must run on each of the last 3 days to reach her goal. Graph the solution set of the inequality on the number line.

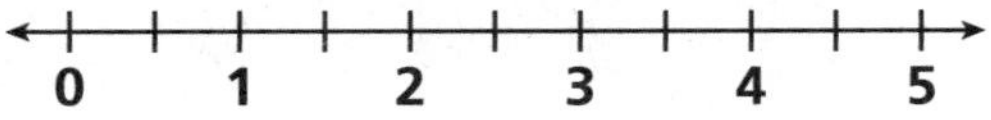

© Houghton Mifflin Harcourt Publishing Company

4. An airplane can carry a maximum of 36,600 pounds of cargo, passengers, and luggage. On the plane's next flight, it will carry 7,320 pounds of cargo. If each passenger with luggage weighs 220 pounds, what is the greatest number of passengers the plane can carry on its next flight?

Ⓐ 44 passengers
Ⓑ 133 passengers
Ⓒ 166 passengers
Ⓓ 199 passengers

5. At midnight, the outdoor temperature is 2 °C. The temperature is expected to drop by 0.5 °C per hour for the rest of the night. Select all inequalities that can be used to determine the number of hours h after midnight at which the temperature will be below 0 °C.

Ⓐ $0.5h < 2$
Ⓑ $0.5h > 2$
Ⓒ $0.5h - 2 < 0$
Ⓓ $0.5h + 2 < 0$
Ⓔ $2 - 0.5h < 0$
Ⓕ $2h - 0.5 < 0$

6. Winnie made headbands to sell at the school craft fair. She spent a total of \$22.50 on expenses, and she plans to sell the headbands for \$5 each. She wants to earn at least \$50 in profit. Write and solve an inequality to represent this situation, where h represents the number of headbands Winnie needs to sell to make a profit of at least \$50. Then state what the solution represents.

____

____

7. Marcus is ordering supplies online for his dog. He plans to order a collar for \$6.76 and some bags of treats for \$4.80 each. The total for his order must be more than \$25 to qualify for free shipping.

A. Write an inequality that Marcus can use to determine the number of bags of treats t he must order to get free shipping.

____

B. Marcus says that the minimum number of bags of treats he needs to order to get free shipping is 3. Do you agree? Explain your reasoning.

____

____

____

____

8. Sarah begins the week with \$21.55. A school lunch costs \$2.75. How many school lunches can she buy and still have at least \$10 left at the end of the week? Write and solve an inequality that Sarah can use to determine the number of lunches n that she can buy.

____

© Houghton Mifflin Harcourt Publishing Company

Unit

3

Similarity, Slope, and Linear Functions

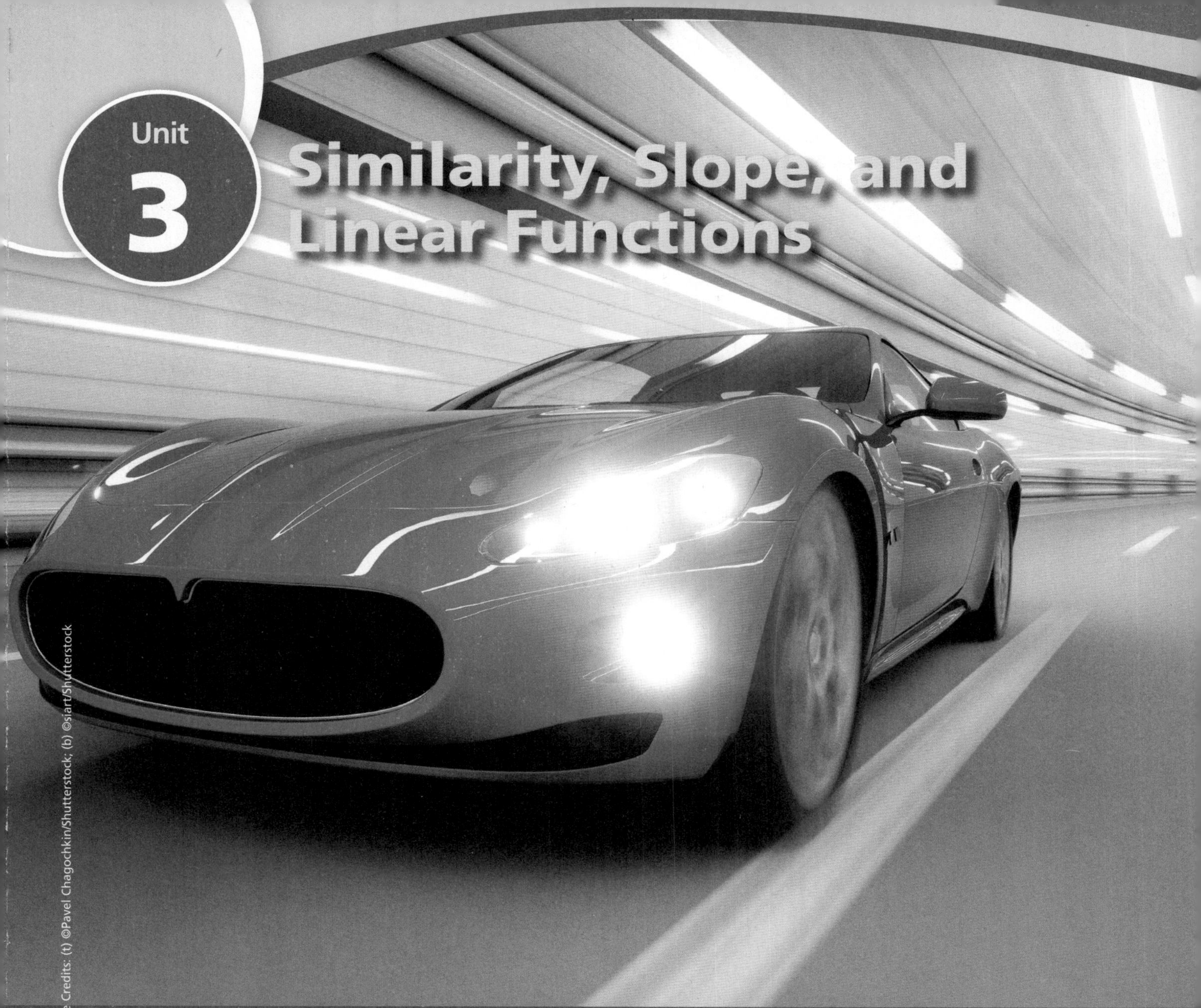

© Houghton Mifflin Harcourt Publishing Company • Image Credits: (t) ©Pavel Chagochkin/Shutterstock; (b) ©siart/Shutterstock

Auto Engineer

STEM POWERING INGENUITY

Auto engineers design new vehicles and improve existing vehicles. Some auto engineers work on improving a car's performance, fuel efficiency, or safety. Others specialize in certain components, such as brakes or electrical systems. Auto engineers must understand how some quantities, such as a car's braking distance, depend on other quantities, such as the car's speed.

STEM Task:

Three quantities related to a car engine's performance are torque, horsepower, and revolutions per minute (RPM). These quantities are related by the equation

$$\text{torque} = \frac{\text{horsepower}}{\text{RPM}} \cdot 5{,}252,$$

where torque is measured in pound-feet. How much torque is required to produce 300 horsepower at 2,500 RPM? At 5,000 RPM? How are the two related?

Learning Mindset

Challenge-Seeking Defines Own Challenges

As you grow, you discover the pleasure of setting your own goals and challenges, and designing ways to meet them. Maybe you want to learn a new language, write a book, or become more successful academically. Here are some things to keep in mind as you seek and define new challenges.

- Believe in your ability to improve skills that are a challenge for you now. Use positive self-talk to address any fixed-mindset voices telling you that you can't reach your goal. Believe in the power of "yet."
- Think about how you will handle unexpected difficulties. Don't become discouraged. Every failure can help you get closer the next time.
- Be flexible. You may find it necessary to adjust your plan or even redefine the end goal.
- Don't be afraid to ask for advice and assistance from content resources or people with more experience than you have currently.

Reflect

Q **How do you know whether a task is the right level of challenge for you?**

Q **Was the STEM Task an appropriate challenge for you? If not, what reasonable challenge would you set for yourself?**

© Houghton Mifflin Harcourt Publishing Company • Image Credit: ©Henrik Sorensen/Stone/Getty Images

Module

6 Angle Relationships

A Fox From Any Angle

The diagram shows the design for a fox made from folded paper.

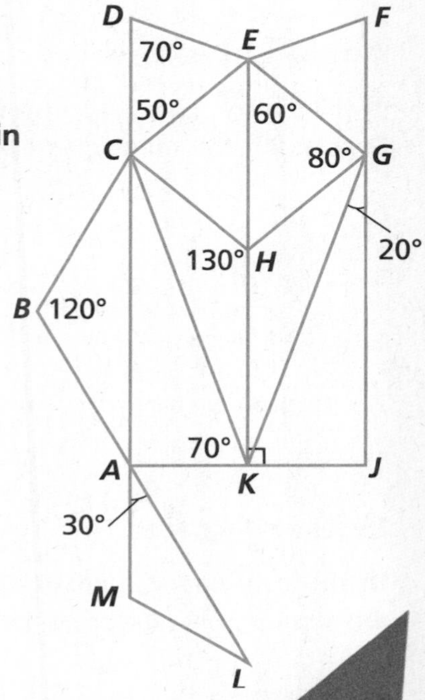

Give an example of each type of angle pair in the design.

A. Vertical angles

____

B. Adjacent supplementary angles

____

C. Non-adjacent supplementary angles

____

D. Adjacent complementary angles

____

E. Non-adjacent complementary angles

____

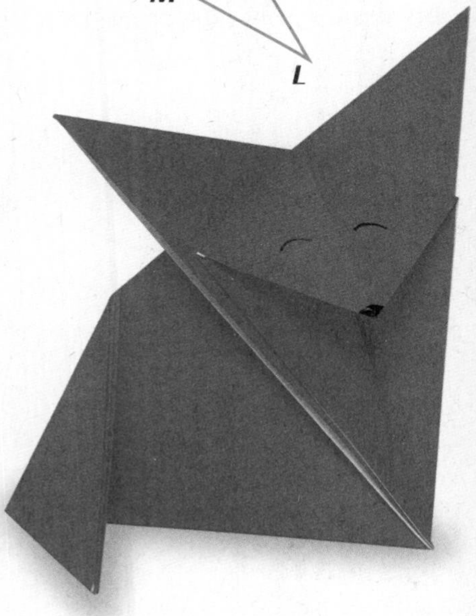

Turn and Talk

How did you identify a pair of non-adjacent supplementary angles?

© Houghton Mifflin Harcourt Publishing Company • Image Credit: ©Betsy Hansen/Houghton Mifflin Harcourt

ONLINE

Are You Ready?

Complete these problems to review prior concepts and skills you will need for this module.

Operations with Linear Expressions

Simplify each expression.

1. $x + 2x + 48$

2. $(n + 7) + 3(n + 1) + 90$

3. $180 - (68 + a)$

Angle Relationships

In the figure, Lines *AD* and *CE* intersect at Point *F*. Determine the measure of each angle.

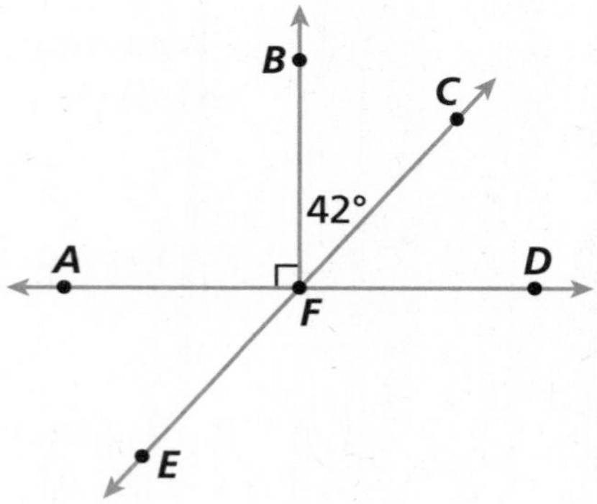

4. $\angle CFD$

5. $\angle DFE$

6. $\angle AFE$

7. Name a pair of vertical angles in the figure.

Similar Figures

Use tracing paper, a protractor, and a ruler to determine whether the triangles in each pair are similar. If so, describe a sequence of transformations that demonstrates the similarity.

8.

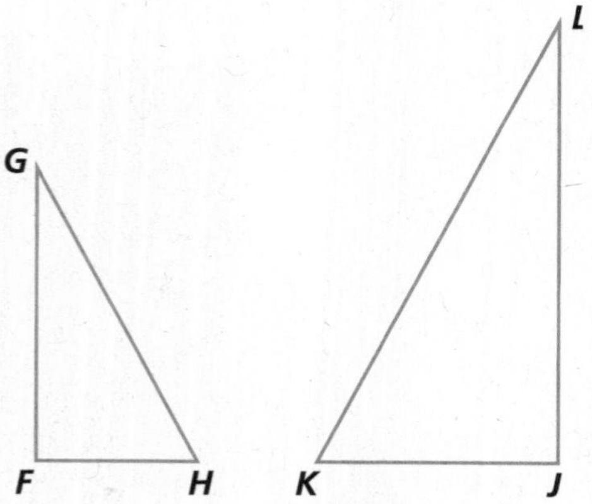

9.

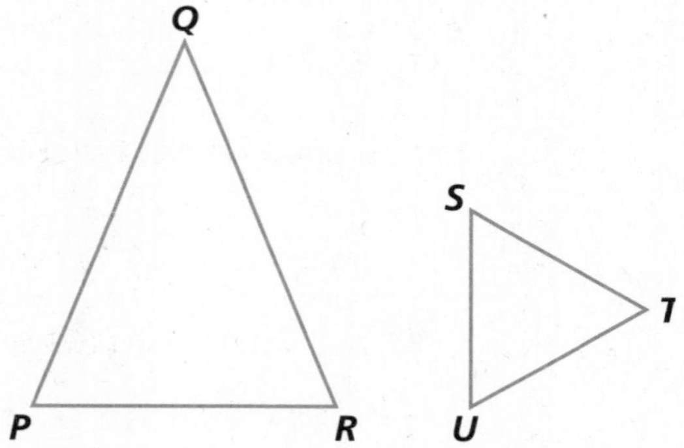

© Houghton Mifflin Harcourt Publishing Company

Name ____________________

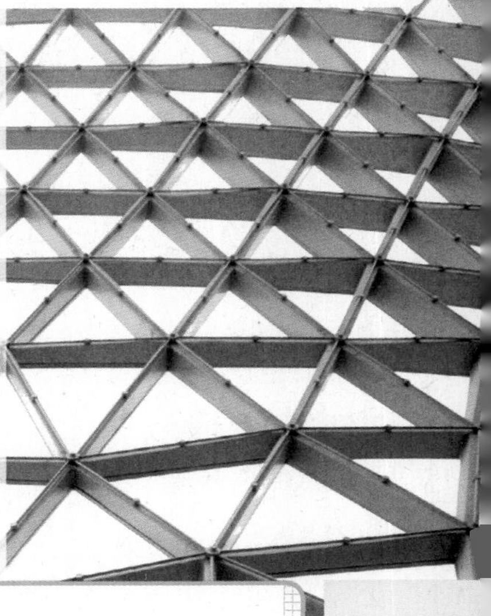

Develop Angle Relationships for Triangles

I Can find an unknown angle measure in a triangle.

Spark Your Learning

SMALL GROUPS

The angles of a triangle have a relationship with each other. Draw three unique triangles. What do you notice about the measures of the interior angles of the triangles?

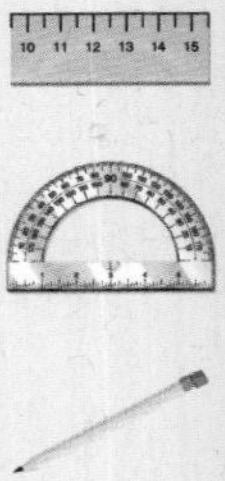

Turn and Talk What conjecture can you make about the sum of the measures of the angles of a triangle?

© Houghton Mifflin Harcourt Publishing Company • Image Credit: ©Ru Bai Le/Shutterstock

Build Understanding

1 What is the sum of the measures of the three interior angles of a triangle?

A. Find the sum of the measures of the angles in each of the three triangles.

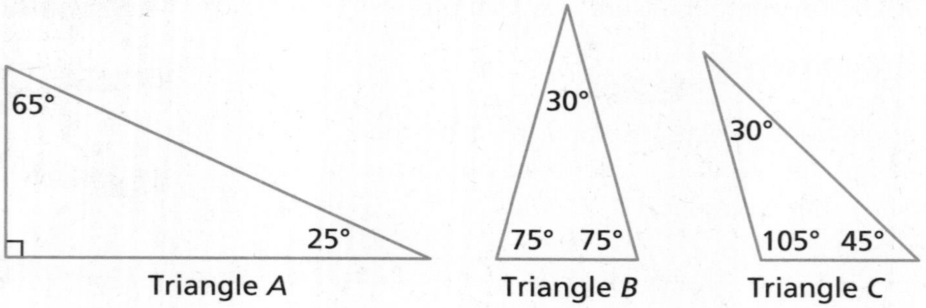

B. What do you notice about the sum of the measures of the three triangles?

____

C. Do you think this is true for all triangles? Explain.

____

____

The **Triangle Sum Theorem** states that the measures of the three interior angles of a triangle sum to 180°.

D. The angles in a triangle measure $2x$, $3x$, and $4x$ degrees. Write and solve an equation to determine the angle measures.

____

____

Turn and Talk Discuss how to find an unknown measure of an angle in a triangle when the other two angle measures are given.

© Houghton Mifflin Harcourt Publishing Company

Name ______________________________

Step It Out

The Triangle Sum Theorem can be used to draw conclusions about a triangle's interior angles.

2 The dashed line segment represents an extension of one side of the triangle. Together with the right side of the triangle, the segment forms an angle, ∠4.

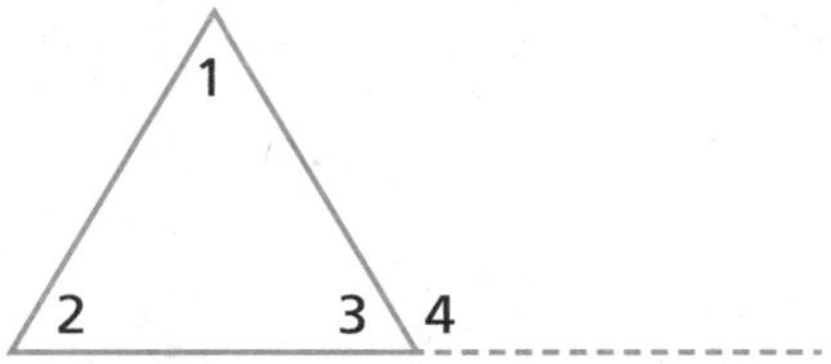

A. What is the sum of the measures of ∠3 and ∠4?

____

B. An **exterior angle** of a polygon is an angle formed by one side of the polygon and the extension of an adjacent side. Which angle in the diagram is an exterior angle?

____

C. If the measure of ∠3 is 60°, what is the measure of ∠4?

____

D. If the measure of ∠3 is 60°, what is the sum of the measures of ∠1 and ∠2?

____

E. Which angle has a measure equal to the sum of the measures of ∠1 and ∠2?

____

F. A **remote interior angle** of an exterior angle of a polygon is an angle that is inside the polygon and is not adjacent to the exterior angle. Which two angles in the diagram are remote interior angles in relation to Angle 4?

____

G. If the sum of the measures of ∠1 and ∠2 is 115°, what is the measure of ∠4?

____

Turn and Talk A triangle has exterior Angle *P* with remote interior Angles *Q* and *R*. Can you determine which angle has the greatest measure? Why or why not?

© Houghton Mifflin Harcourt Publishing Company • Image Credit: ©Huntstock, Inc/Alamy

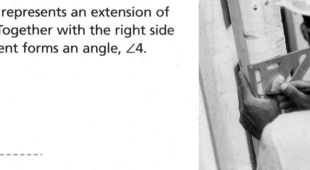

3 A machinist is drawing a triangular piece of an industrial machine.

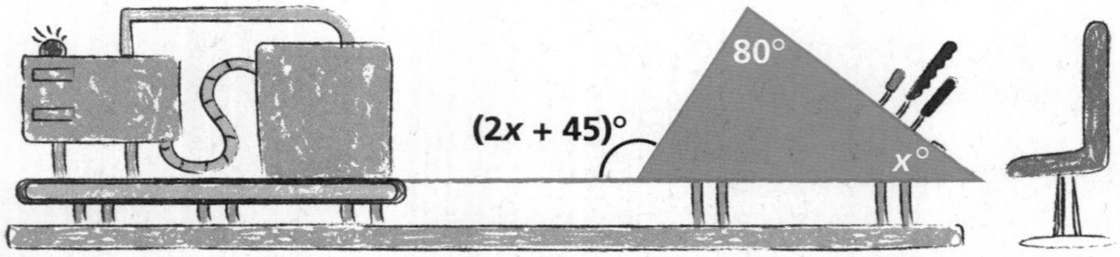

A. Write an equation and solve to find the value of x. Show your work.

$$\square x + \square = x + \square$$

$$\square x - x = 80 - \square$$

$$x = \square$$

B. What is the measure of the unknown remote interior angle?

____

C. Use the value of x from Part A to find the measure of the exterior angle.

$2x + 45 = 2(\square) + 45 = \square + 45 = \square$

D. What is the measure of the exterior angle?

____

> **Connect to Vocabulary**
>
> The measure of an exterior angle of a triangle is greater than either of the measures of the remote interior angles. This is the **Exterior Angle Theorem**.

Check Understanding

1. Two angles of a triangle have measures of 30° and 45°. What is the measure of the remaining angle?

____

2. Dana draws a triangle with one angle that has a measure of 40°.

A. What is the measure of the angle's adjacent exterior angle?

____

B. What is the sum of the measures of the remote interior angles for the exterior angle adjacent to the 40° angle?

____

3. An exterior angle of a triangle has a measure of 80°, and one of the remote interior angles has a measure of 20°. Write and solve an equation to find the measure of the other remote interior angle.

____

© Houghton Mifflin Harcourt Publishing Company

Name ______________________

On Your Own

4. A puppeteer is making a triangular hat for a puppet. If two of the three angles of the hat both measure 30°, what is the measure of the third angle?

____

5. (MP) **Construct Arguments** Can a triangle have two obtuse angles? Explain your answer.

____

____

____

____

____

6. **STEM** In engineering, equilateral triangles can support the most weight and so are commonly found in the design of bridges and buildings. Equilateral triangles are triangles with three congruent sides and three congruent angles. What are the measures of the angles of an equilateral triangle?

____

7. A triangle has one 30° angle, an unknown angle, and an angle with a measure that is twice the measure of the unknown angle. Find the measures of the triangle's unknown angles and explain how you found the answer.

____

____

____

____

____

For Problems 8–10, find the measures of the unknown third angles.

8.

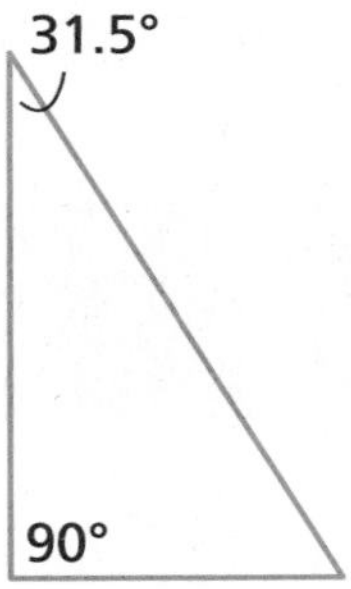

____

9.

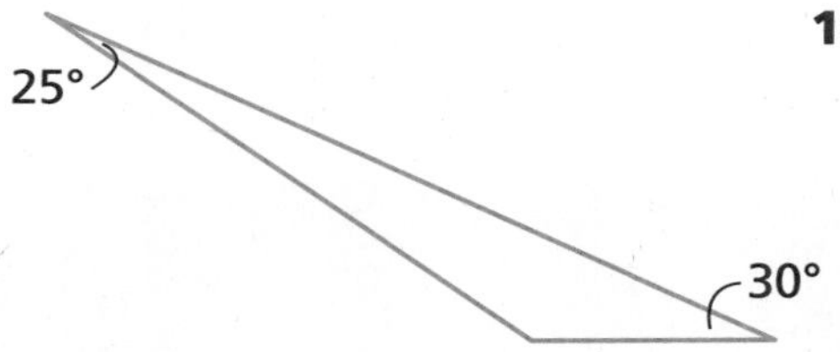

____

10.

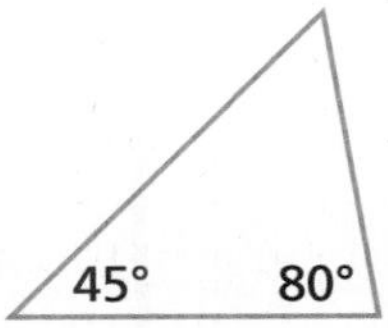

____

© Houghton Mifflin Harcourt Publishing Company

11. Open Ended The measure of an exterior angle of a triangle is $x°$. The measure of the adjacent interior angle is at least twice $x°$. List three possible solutions for x.

12. The measure of an exterior angle of a triangle is $40°$. What is the sum of the measures of the corresponding remote interior angles?

13. Steven is building a fin for a surfboard. In order to make the fin, he needs to know the value of x in the following diagram. Use your knowledge of triangle angle relationships to find the value of x.

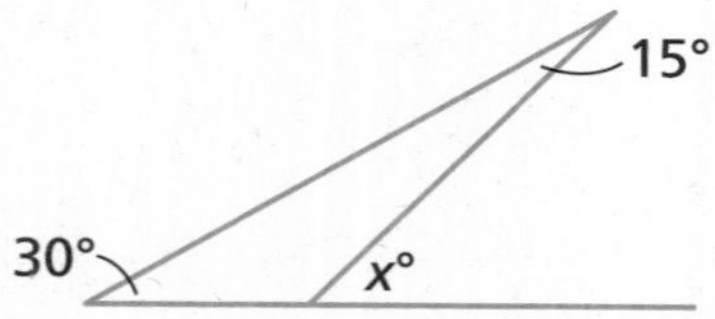

14. Find the value of x in the diagram. Explain how you found the answer.

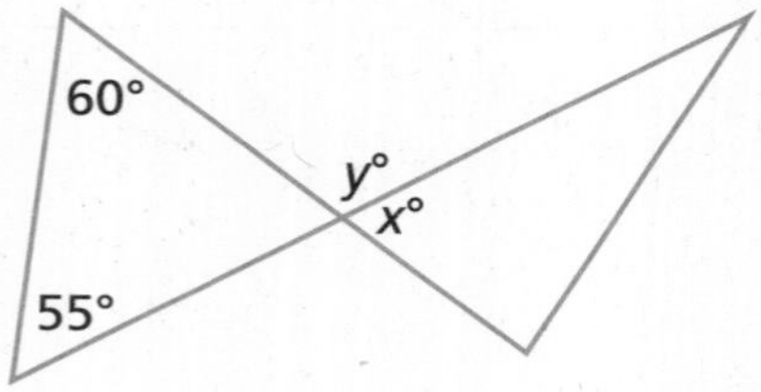

I'm in a Learning Mindset!

Was problem 13 an appropriate challenge for me? Why or why not?

© Houghton Mifflin Harcourt Publishing Company • **Image Credit:** ©Randy Duchaine/Alamy

Name ______________________

Develop Angle Relationships for Triangles

1. Find the value of x using your knowledge of the relationship between interior and exterior angles.

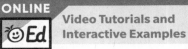

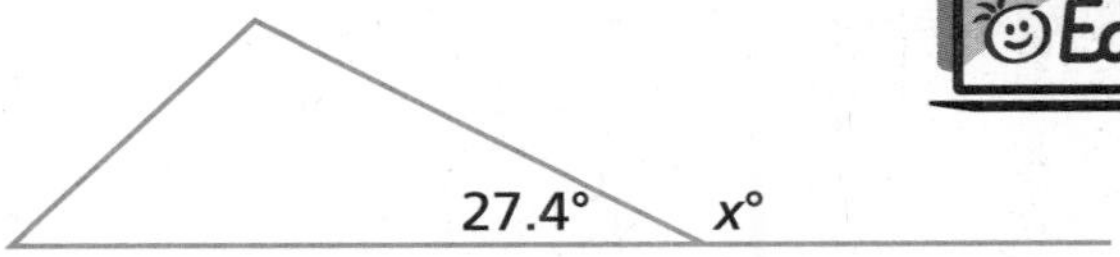

____

2. **Math on the Spot** Find the unknown measure in the triangle.

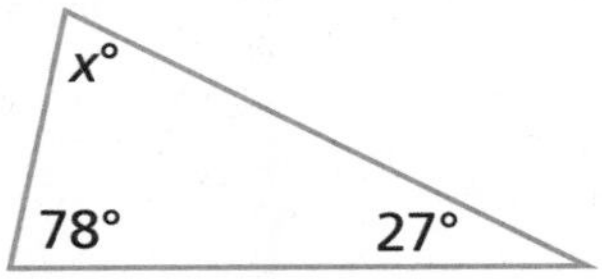

____

3. (MP) **Construct Arguments** Can the measure of an exterior angle of a triangle ever exceed 180°? Explain your reasoning.

____
____
____
____

4. **STEM** The measure of the angle formed at the center of an oxygen atom in a water molecule is about 105°. The angles formed at each hydrogen atom are congruent. What is the measure of the angle at each hydrogen atom?

____

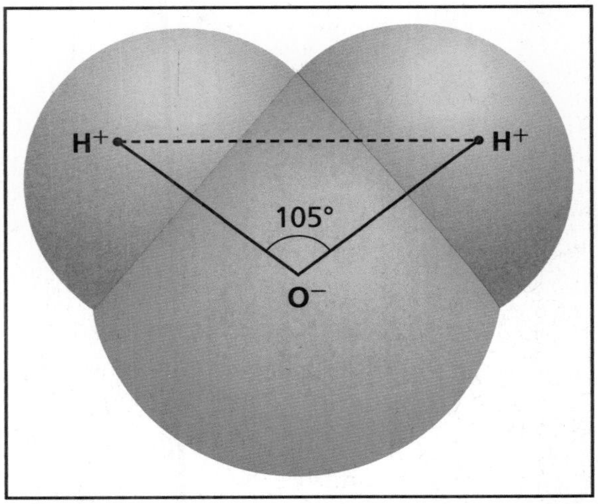

5. **Open Ended** One of the angles in a triangle measures 90°. Name three possibilities for the measures of the remaining two angles.

____
____

6. Find the value of x in the following diagram.

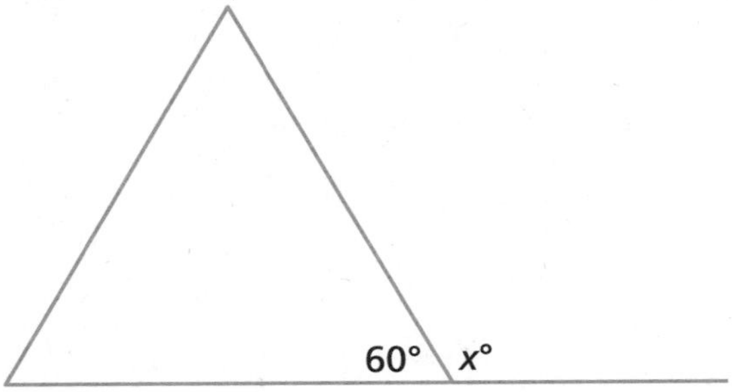

____

© Houghton Mifflin Harcourt Publishing Company

Test Prep

7. Complete the table by entering the measures of the unknown angles for the following two triangles.

Triangle	Angle 1	Angle 2	Unknown angle
1	30°	60°	
2	45°	20°	

8. If an exterior angle of a triangle has a measure of 35°, what is the measure of the adjacent interior angle?

____

9. Find the value of x.

$x =$ ☐

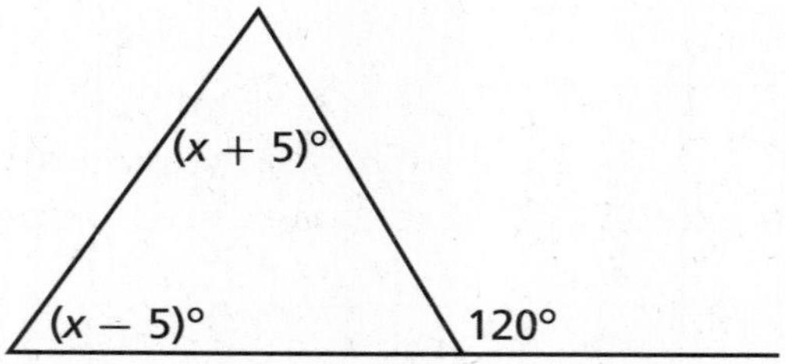

10. The measures of an exterior angle of a triangle and its adjacent interior angle add to what value?

Ⓐ 90°

Ⓑ 100°

Ⓒ 180°

Ⓓ 360°

11. The measure of an exterior angle of a triangle and the sum of the measures of the two remote interior angles are __________.

Spiral Review

12. Hayden and Jamie completed 20 math problems together. Jamie completed 2 more than twice the number that Hayden completed. Let p represent the number of math problems Hayden completed. Write an equation that can be used to find the number of math problems that Jamie completed.

____

13. Does the equation $5(x - 3) = 10x - 15$ have one solution, infinitely many solutions, or no solution?

____

14. Find the value of x, given that $4(3x + 2) = 44$.

____

© Houghton Mifflin Harcourt Publishing Company

Name ______________________________

Investigate Angle-Angle Similarity

I Can use angle-angle similarity to test triangles for similarity and find unknown angle measures.

Spark Your Learning

PAIRS

Asa is comparing the architect's model of a barn with the finished building. He looks at the triangle that forms the front of the roof in the model and in the completed barn. Are the triangles similar? Why or why not?

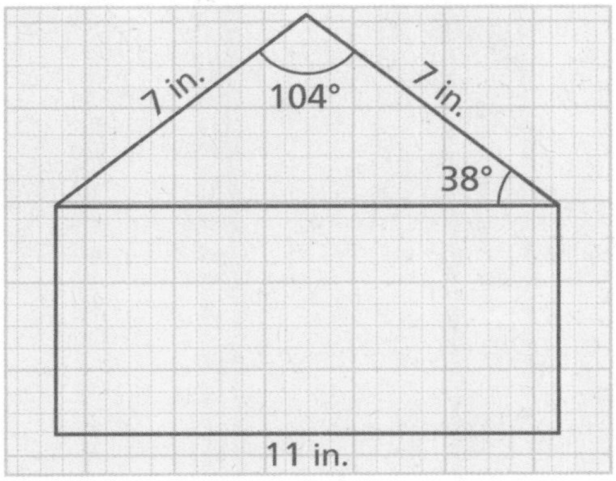

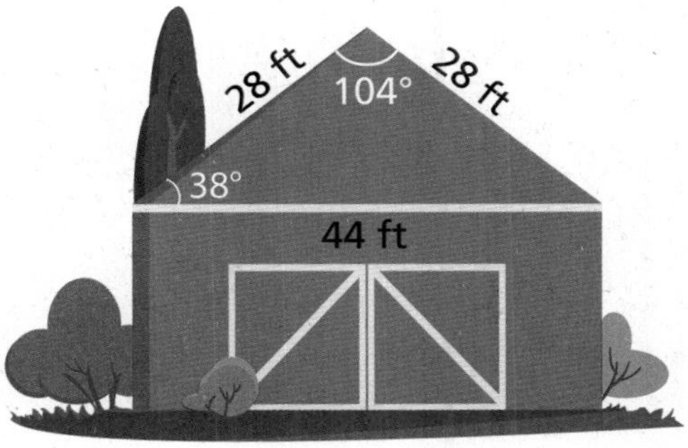

Turn and Talk Which is the easier way of deciding if the triangles are similar, comparing the angles or comparing the side lengths? Why?

© Houghton Mifflin Harcourt Publishing Company

Build Understanding

Two triangles are similar if all three pairs of corresponding angles are congruent. What if only two out of three pairs of corresponding angles are congruent?

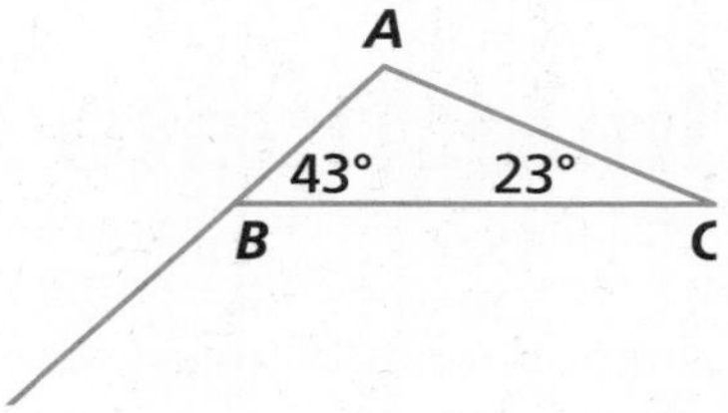

1 Using the given drawing by the set designer, Shawna is making a flag for a play. She has measured Angles *ABC* and *ACB* with a protractor, and they match Angles *E* and *F*, respectively, on the set designer's notes. Can she be sure that her flag is similar to the drawing without measuring the third angle?

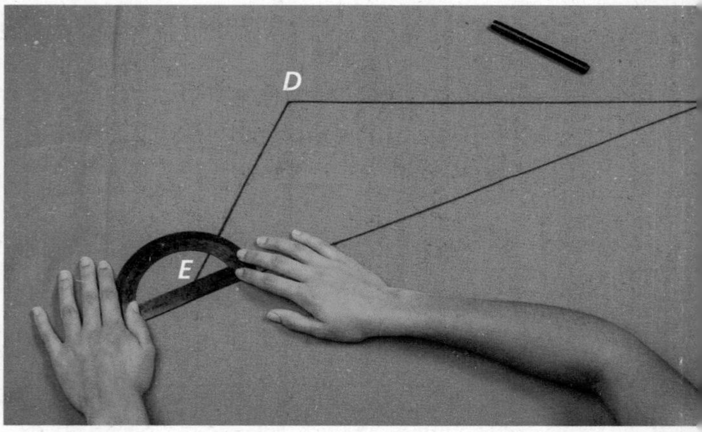

A. What do you know about the sum of the measures of the angles in a triangle?

B. How does knowing the sum of the measures of the angles in a triangle help you solve this problem?

C. Write and evaluate an expression to find the measure of the third angle of Triangle *ABC*, using the angle measures given.

D. Write and evaluate an expression to find the measure of the third angle of Triangle *DEF* using the angle measures given.

E. Based on your calculation of the measure of the third angle, can you now state with confidence whether Shawna's flag is similar to the drawing without measuring the third angle? Explain.

The **Angle-Angle Similarity Postulate** states that two triangles are similar if they have two pairs of corresponding angles that are congruent.

Turn and Talk When two triangles have two angle measures in common, will the third angle measure always be the same for both triangles? Explain.

© Houghton Mifflin Harcourt Publishing Company • Image Credit: ©Houghton Mifflin Harcourt

Step It Out

2 In the two triangles shown, $m\angle A = m\angle D$ and $m\angle C = m\angle F$.

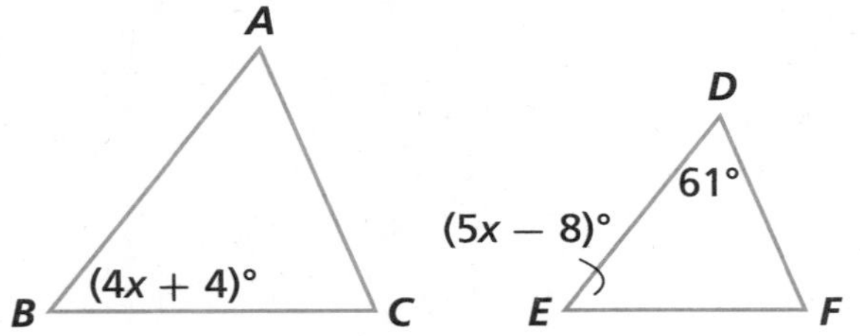

A. Do you know enough to say whether the two triangles are similar? Explain.

B. What does your answer to Part A imply about Angles *B* and *E*? Explain how you know.

C. What equation can you write relating the measures of Angles *B* and *E*?

D. Solve your equation from Part C for *x*. What are the measures of Angles *B* and *E*?

E. How can you find the measure of Angle *F*?

F. How can you find the measure of Angle *C*?

G. Fill in the measures of the six angles:

$m\angle A =$ ______ $m\angle B =$ ______ $m\angle C =$ ______

$m\angle D =$ ______ $m\angle E =$ ______ $m\angle F =$ ______

Turn and Talk If you were given the measures of Angles *A*, *C*, *D*, and *E* from Part G, how could you determine whether the triangles are similar?

© Houghton Mifflin Harcourt Publishing Company • Image Credit: ©Dave Reede/All Canada Photos/Getty Images

3 The illustration shows a wheelchair ramp from the side. The support at $\overline{BC}$ binds the ramp to the floor. Are Triangles *ABC* and *ADE* similar?

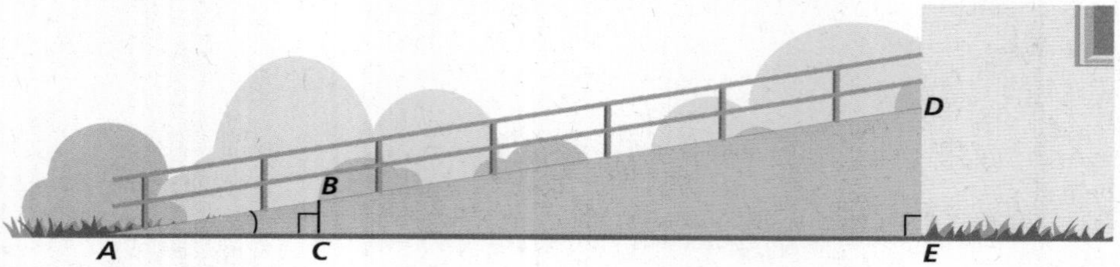

A. What do the little squares at Points *C* and *E* mean?

B. Do Triangles *ABC* and *ADE* both contain the same angle? If so, name it.

C. Does that mean both triangles have two pairs of corresponding congruent angles? If so, name the corresponding congruent angles.

D. Are Triangles *ABC* and *ADE* similar? Explain.

Check Understanding

1. Which two triangles are similar?

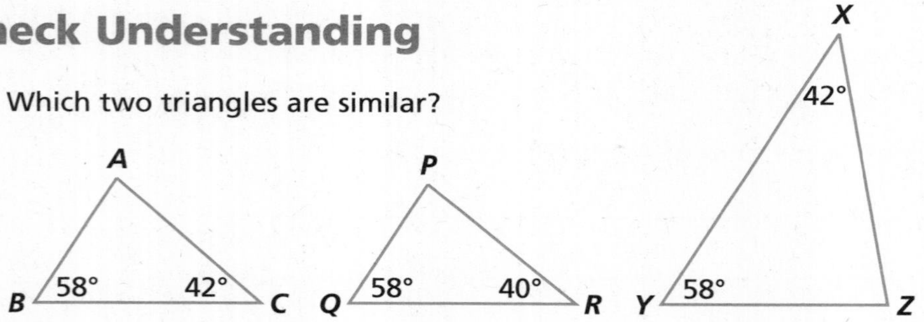

2. Explain why $\triangle XYZ$ is similar to $\triangle LMZ$.

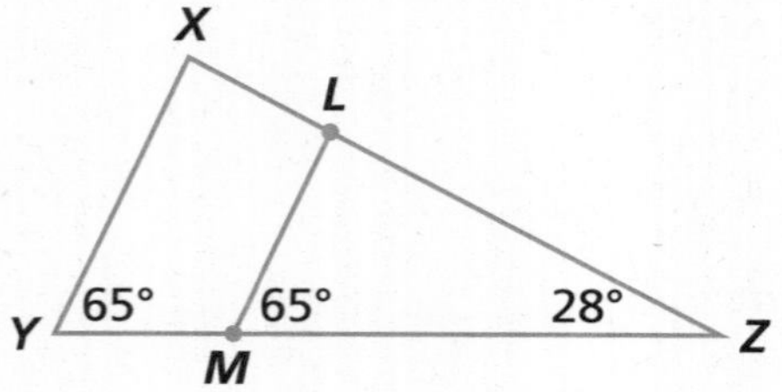

© Houghton Mifflin Harcourt Publishing Company

Name

On Your Own

3. (MP) **Reason** A graphic designer wants to reproduce the logo of a mountain-climbing club for some club stationery. The logo is a triangle with the angles shown.

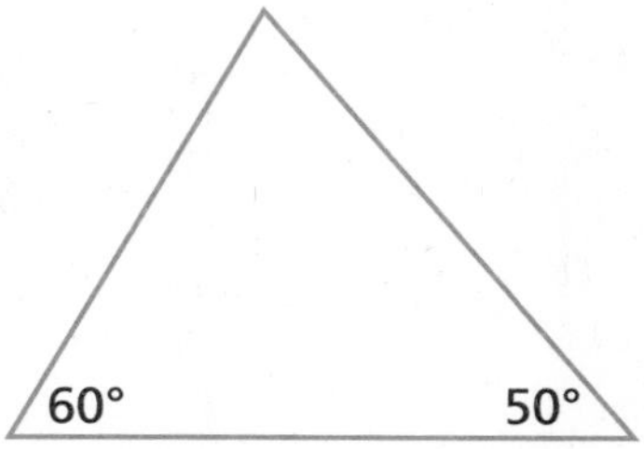

A. The designer wants the base to be 2 inches long. How should the triangle be drawn?

B. How can the Angle-Angle Similarity Postulate help the designer make sure the triangle is reproduced correctly?

4. Angles A, D, and G are congruent, and Angles C, F, and J are congruent.

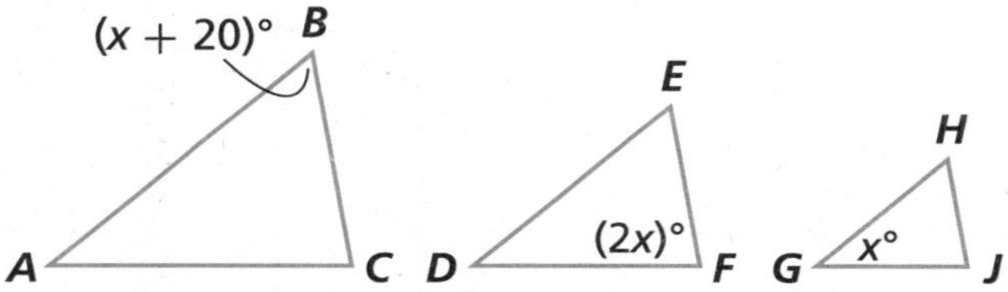

A. Write an equation to find the measures of Angles B, F, and G.

B. What is the measure of Angle E?

Use Triangles *QRS* and *TUV* to solve Problems 5 and 6.

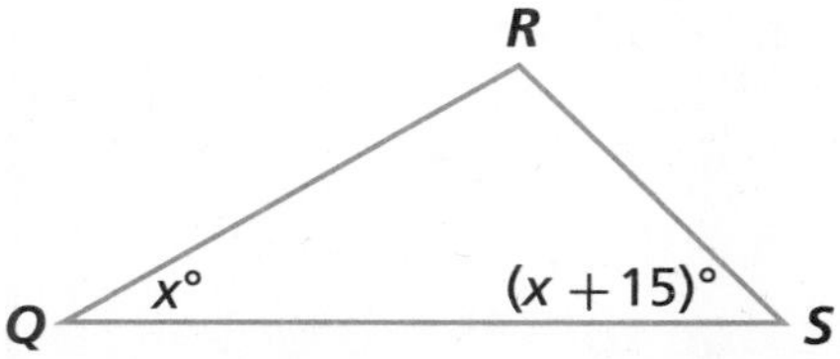

5. Are Triangles QRS and TUV similar? How do you know?

6. What is the measure of Angle R in terms of x?

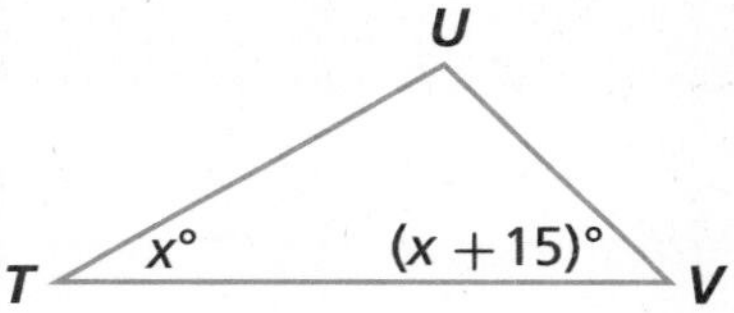

© Houghton Mifflin Harcourt Publishing Company • Image Credit: ©Paul Doyle/Alamy

7. **Reason** Are the triangles shown similar? Why or why not?

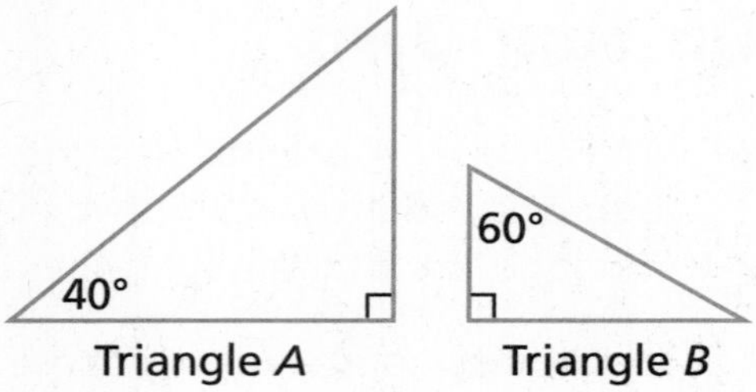

8. **Reason** Are the triangles shown similar? How do you know?

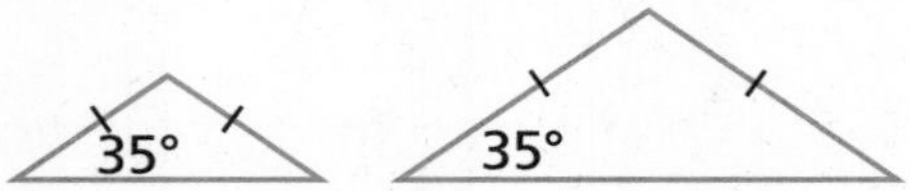

9. **Reason** Are the triangles similar? Explain.

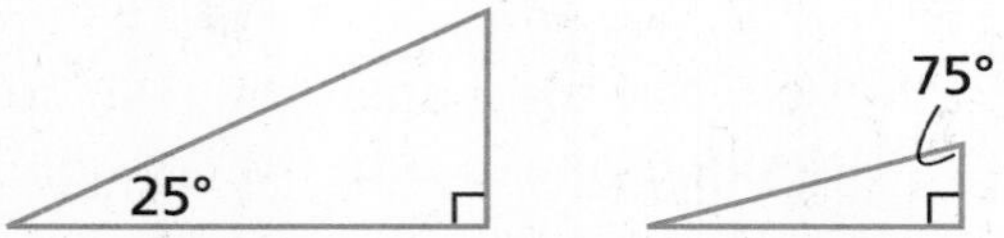

10. Angle *C* is congruent to Angle *F*. What is the measure of Angle *E*?

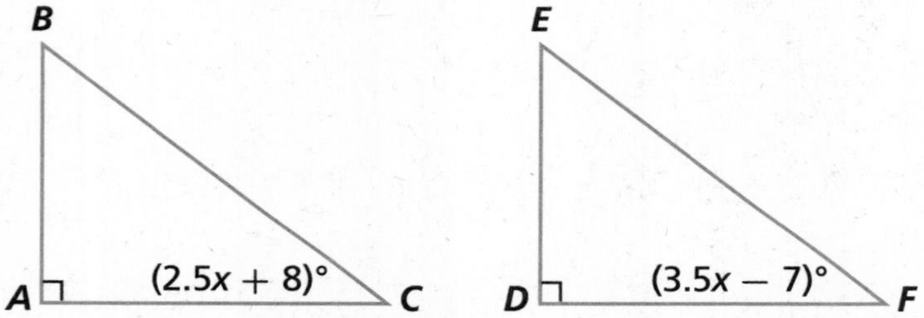

11. Does the diagram show similar triangles? Explain.

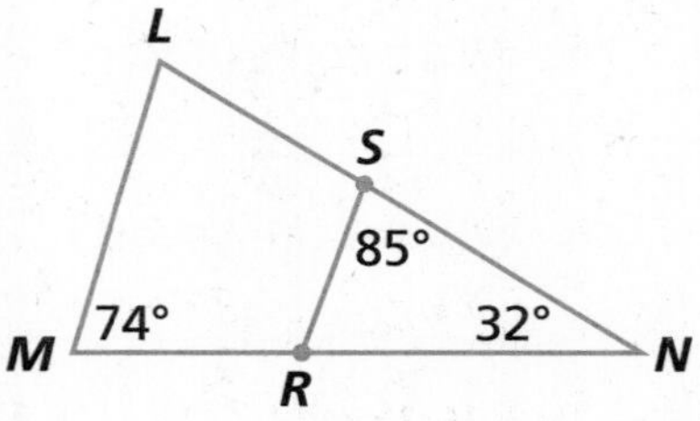

© Houghton Mifflin Harcourt Publishing Company

I'm in a Learning Mindset!

What challenges do I face trying to understand how to use angle relationships to determine whether two triangles are similar?

Name ______________________

Investigate Angle-Angle Similarity

1. One triangle shown is formed by the tree, its shadow, and a line of sight from the ground to the top of the tree. The other is formed by Manny, his shadow, and a line of sight from the ground to the top of his head.

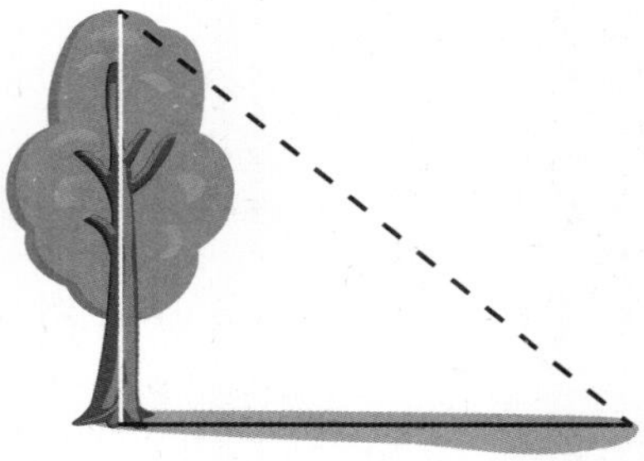

A. Are the two triangles similar? How do you know?

____

____

____

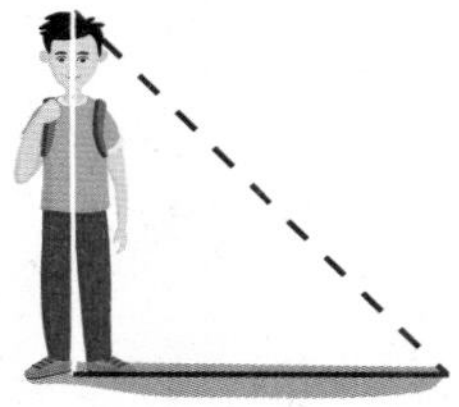

B. Manny is $5\frac{1}{2}$ feet tall, and his shadow is $4\frac{1}{4}$ feet long. The shadow of the tree is 17 feet long. Can you determine the height of the tree? If so, how?

____

____

C. What is the height of the tree?

____

2. MP **Reason** Explain whether the triangles are similar.

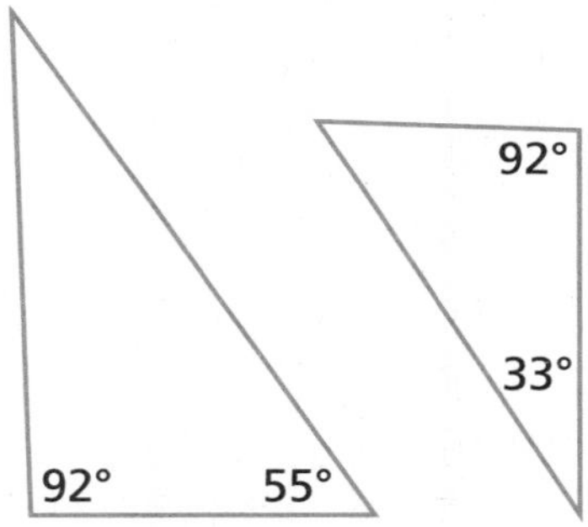

____

____

____

3. Consider the diagram for Parts A and B.

A. The value of *x* is ________.

B. The measure of Angle *A* is ________.

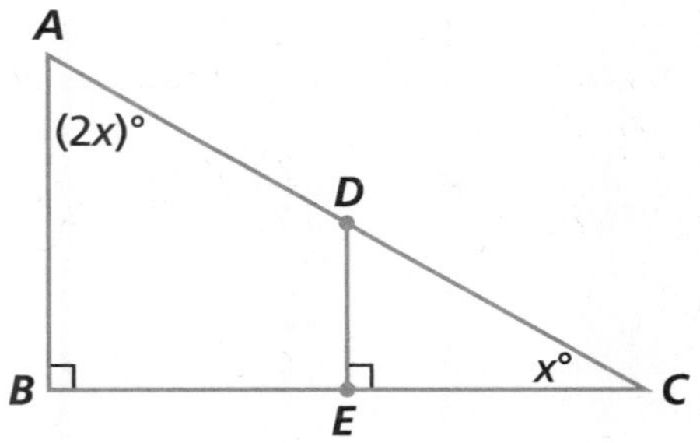

© Houghton Mifflin Harcourt Publishing Company

Test Prep

4. Angle L is congruent to Angle P, and Angle N is congruent to Angle R. What is the measure of Angle Q?

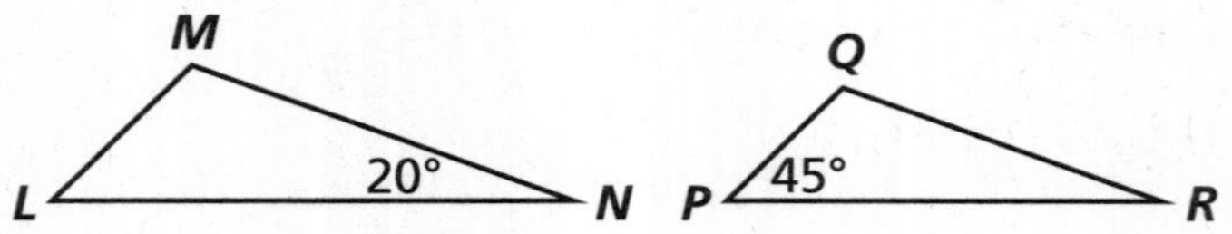

$m\angle Q =$ ______

5. Which triangles are similar?

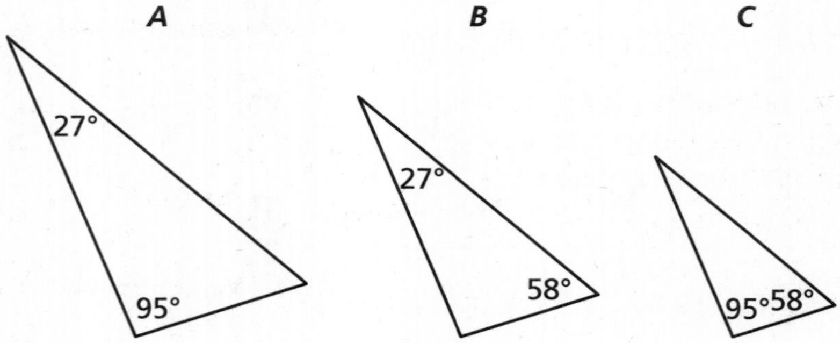

______

6. The measures of two pairs of corresponding angles of two triangles are 24° and 55°. Explain why the two triangles are similar.

______

______

Spiral Review

7. Mrs. Kato has 6 bags of dried beans and a 2-pound bag of rice in one shopping bag. In another shopping bag she has a 5-pound bag of flour. The two shopping bags weigh the same amount. What is the weight of each bag of dried beans?

______

8. A triangle is dilated with scale factor 4. Write a true statement about the image and preimage of the triangle.

______

______

9. Name a sequence of transformations that would map Figure A to Figure B.

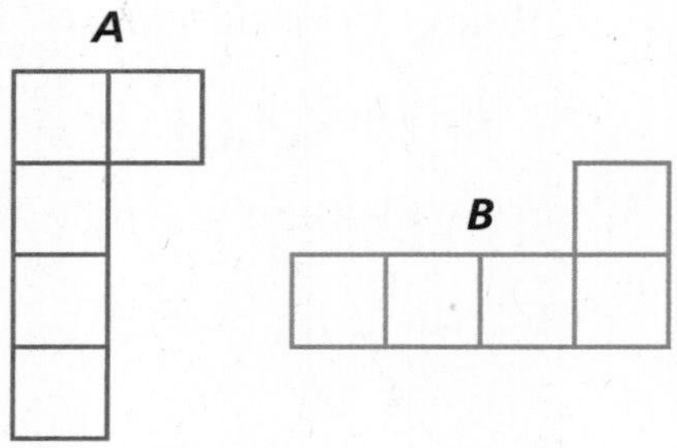

______

______

© Houghton Mifflin Harcourt Publishing Company

Name ________________________________

Explore Parallel Lines Cut by a Transversal

I Can identify the relationship between angle pairs as either supplementary or congruent.

Spark Your Learning

SMALL GROUPS

A walker sees these logs on a hike and notices that they make several angles.

Draw a representation of the logs and compare the lines and the angles in your drawing. How are the angles the same and how are they different?

Turn and Talk What pattern do you notice after measuring all the angles?

© Houghton Mifflin Harcourt Publishing Company • Image Credit: ©vilax/Shutterstock

Build Understanding

When two lines are cut by a third line, the third line is called a **transversal**. The intersections of the lines form eight angles, including five special types of angle pairs. When the two lines cut by a transversal are parallel, as shown, the angles in any of the special pairs will be either congruent or supplementary.

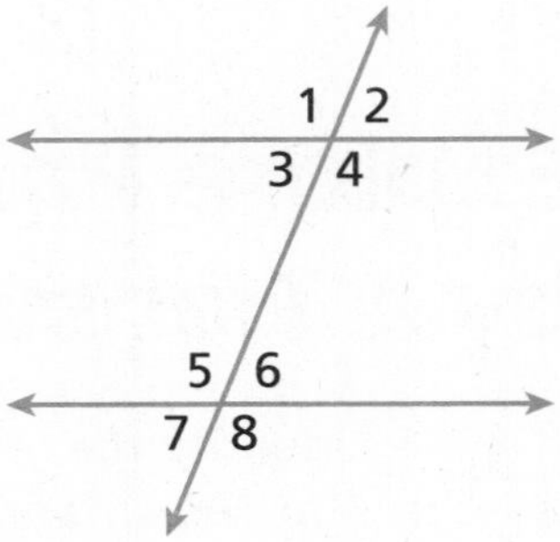

1 The term *alternate* means that two angles are on opposite sides of the transversal.

A. **Alternate interior angles** are angles on opposite sides of the transversal inside the parallel lines. Measure a pair of alternate interior angles with a protractor. Name the angles you found. Are they congruent or supplementary?

B. **Alternate exterior angles** are angles on opposite sides of the transversal outside the parallel lines. Measure a pair of alternate exterior angles with a protractor. Name the angles you found. Are they congruent or supplementary?

The term *same-side* means that two angles are on the same side of the transversal.

C. **Same-side interior angles** are on the same side of the transversal and between the parallel lines. Measure a pair of same-side interior angles. Name the angles you found. Are they congruent or supplementary?

D. **Same-side exterior angles** are on the same side of the transversal but outside the parallel lines. Measure a pair of same-side exterior angles. Name the angles you found. Are they congruent or supplementary?

E. **Corresponding angles** are angles in the same position formed when a third line intersects two parallel lines. Measure two pairs of corresponding angles. Name the angles you found. Are they congruent or supplementary?

© Houghton Mifflin Harcourt Publishing Company

Name ______________________________

Step It Out

2 The diagram shows two parallel lines cut by a transversal. Find the value of x.

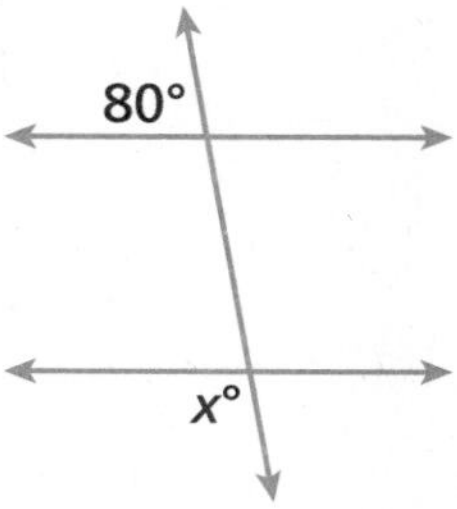

A. What kind of angle pair is formed by the two labeled angles?

____

B. How are the two angles related to each other?

____

C. Complete the equation to find the value of x.

$x + 80 = \square$

$x = \square$

3 The diagram shows two parallel lines cut by a transversal.

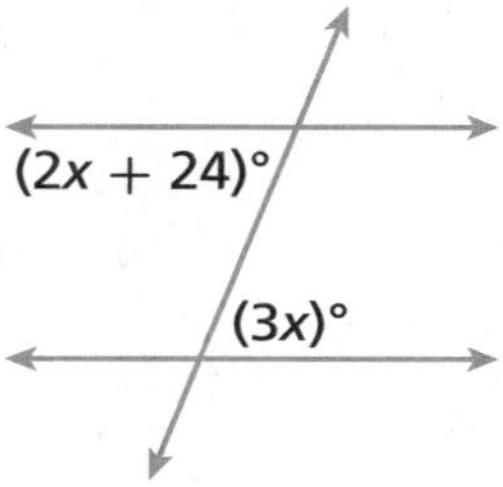

A. What kind of angle pair is formed by the two labeled angles?

____

B. What is true about the measures of the angles?

____

C. Complete and solve the equation to find the value of x.

$3x = \square$

$x = \square$

D. Find the measures of the angles.

$3x = 3(\square) = 72$

$2x + 24 = 2(\square) + 24 = \square + 24 = 72$

The angles both measure ____________.

Turn and Talk Consider the diagram in Task 3. What happens if it is rotated so the parallel lines are vertical? Explain how this affects the relationships of the angle pairs.

© Houghton Mifflin Harcourt Publishing Company • **Image Credit:** ©Baek Daehyun/Getty Images

4 You can use what you know about the angles formed by parallel lines and a transversal to prove the Triangle Sum Theorem. For any triangle, draw a line through a vertex parallel to the opposite side (in this case, through the vertex of $\angle 4$).

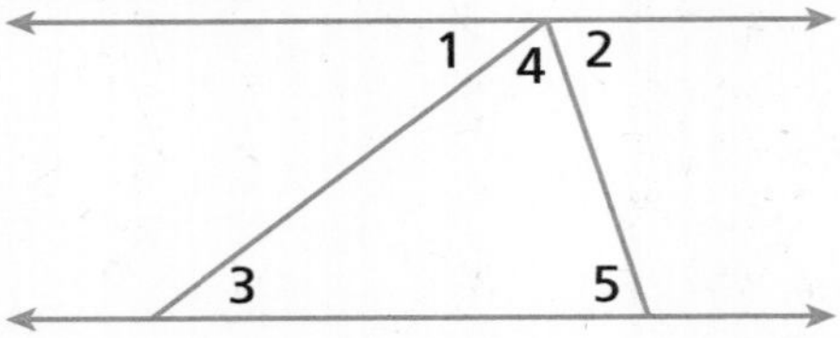

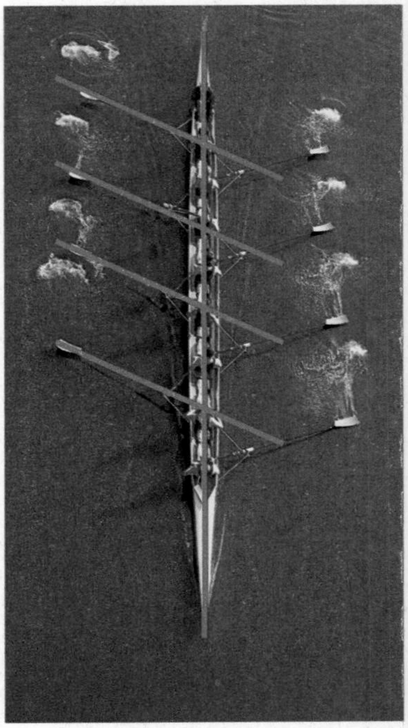

A. What is the sum of the measures of Angle 1, Angle 2, and Angle 4? How do you know?

____

B. How would you classify the angle pairs $\angle 1$ and $\angle 3$, and $\angle 2$ and $\angle 5$?

____

C. What does that tell you about their respective angle measures?

____

D. Complete this statement: If $m\angle 1 = m\angle 3$ and $m\angle 2 = m\angle 5$, then

$m\angle 3 + m\angle 4 + m\angle 5 = m\angle \square + m\angle 4 + m\angle \square = \square$.

E. Make three copies of the triangle and arrange them so the three angles form a line. Use parallel lines and transversals to explain how your figure proves the Triangle Sum Theorem.

Check Understanding

Problems 1–2 show two parallel lines and a transversal. Find the values of x.

1.

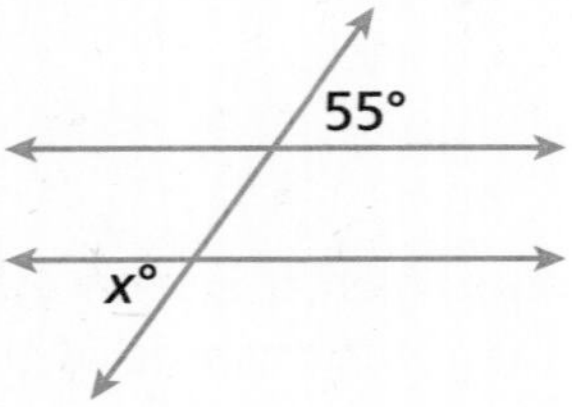

____

2.

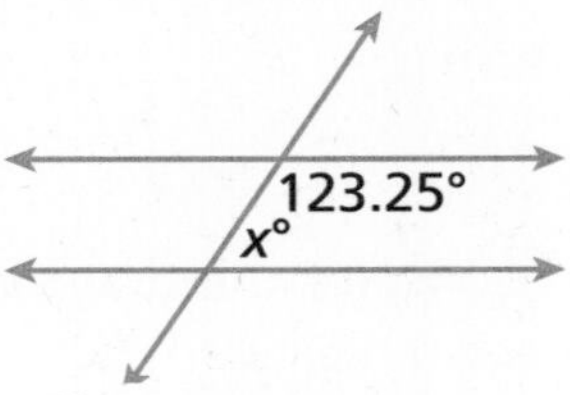

____

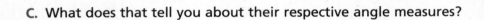

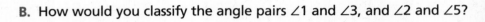

© Houghton Mifflin Harcourt Publishing Company • Image Credit: ©Robert Llewellyn/Photolibrary/Getty Images

Name

On Your Own

3. The picture shows a bridge between two parallel river banks. What angle does the driver's right turn make with the river after crossing the bridge to continue on Northbridge Road?

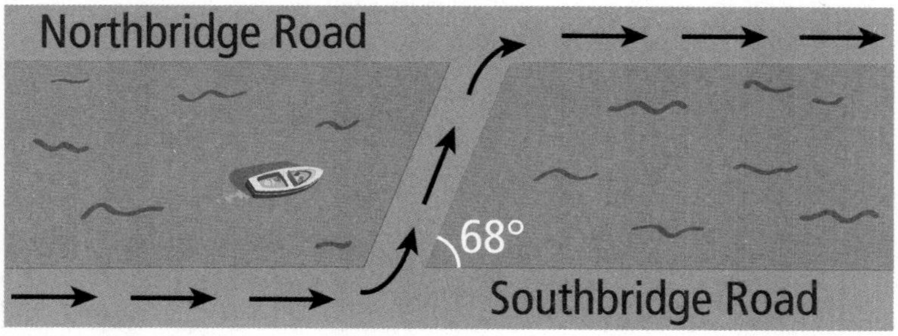

Use the diagram showing two parallel lines and a transversal to answer Problems 4–6.

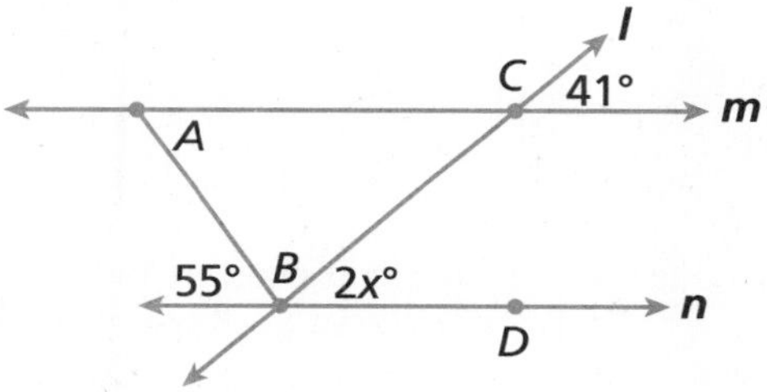

4. Which angle forms a pair of alternate interior angles with $\angle ACB$?

5. Which angle forms a pair of corresponding angles with the 41° angle?

6. Solve for x.

7. (MP) **Reason** The diagram shows two parallel lines cut by a transversal. Clarissa measured $\angle 1$ and $\angle 2$ with her protractor. She says the angles measure 43° and 142°, respectively. Is she correct? Explain.

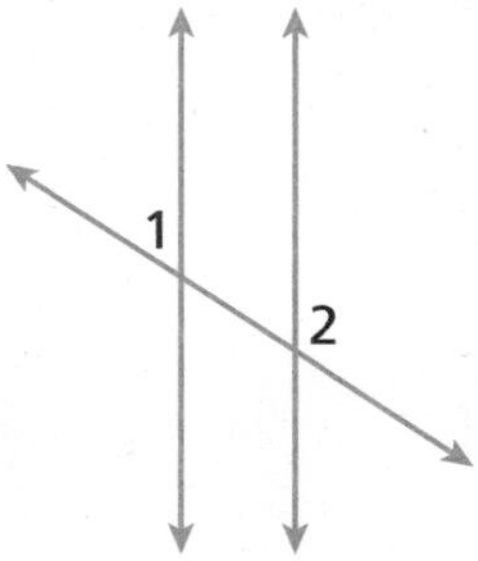

© Houghton Mifflin Harcourt Publishing Company

8. In the diagram, two parallel lines are cut by a transversal. Which of the numbered angles measures 152°?

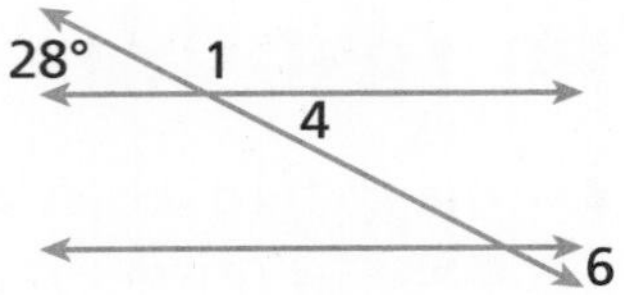

____

9. (MP) **Reason** You're not sure whether a pair of angles formed by two parallel lines and a transversal are same-side exterior angles or alternate exterior angles. Both angles measure 53°. Which of the two types must they be? Explain.

____

____

10. Which two angles have the same measure?

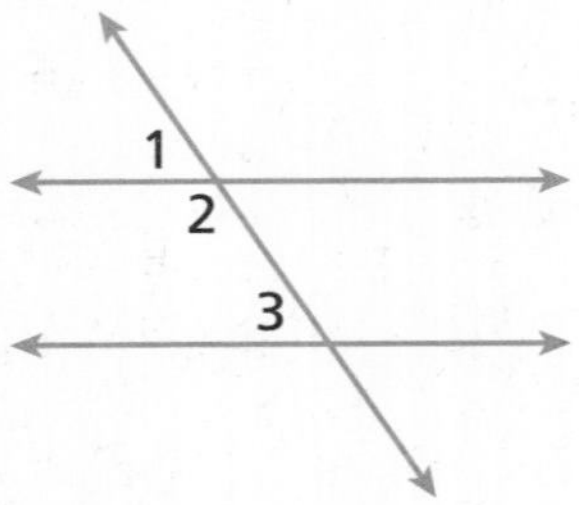

____

11. Lines *m* and *n* are parallel. Find the following angle pairs in the diagram. If you can't find any, write *none*.

alternate exterior ______________

corresponding angles ______________

same-side exterior ______________

alternate interior ______________

same-side interior ______________

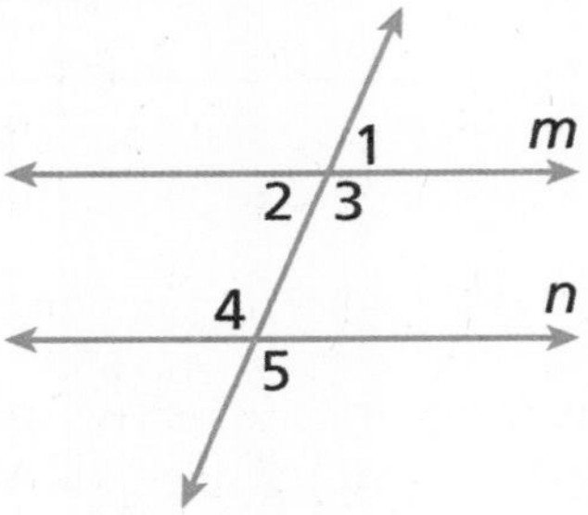

12. Two angles are same-side interior angles. The measures of the angles are represented by the expressions $10x + 9$ and $7x + 18$. What are the two angle measures?

____

I'm in a Learning Mindset!

What can I do to increase my understanding of how to find unknown angle measures when parallel lines are cut by a transversal?

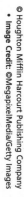

____

____

© Houghton Mifflin Harcourt Publishing Company • Image Credit: ©MegapixelMedia/Getty Images

Name ________________________________

LESSON 6.3
More Practice/ Homework

ONLINE
Video Tutorials and Interactive Examples

Explore Parallel Lines Cut by a Transversal

1. A room in an attic has a sloping wall that makes an angle of 55° with the floor, which is parallel to the ceiling. What is the measure of an angle that forms a pair of same-side interior angles with that angle?

____

2. **Math on the Spot** Line n is parallel to Line p. Find the measure of each angle.

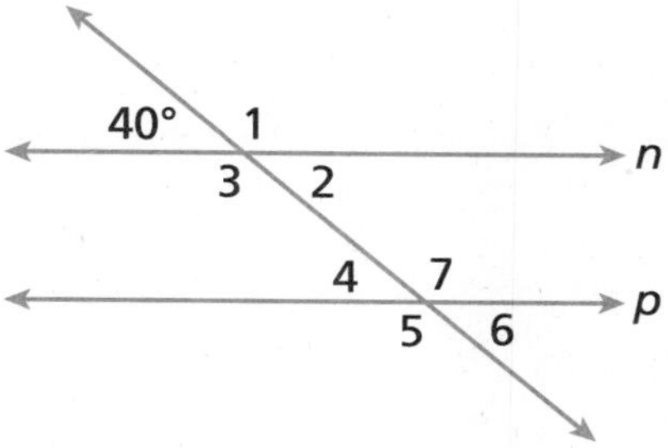

____

____

3. Oak Street runs parallel with Maple Street. The angle between North Main Street and West Oak Street where the turn is shown measures 65°. What is the measure of the angle between the roads at the turn shown from South Main Street onto West Maple Street? Explain.

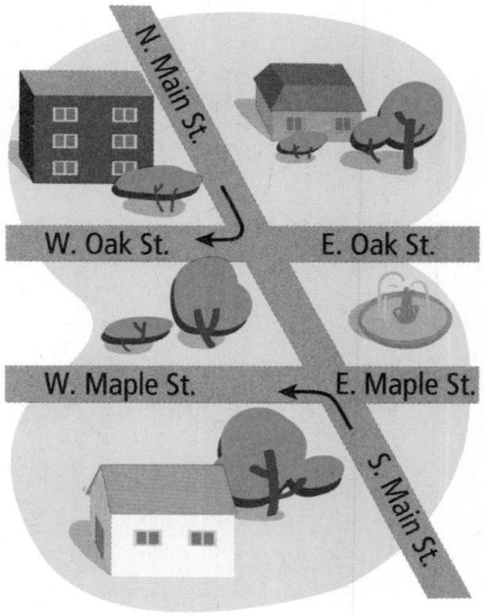

____

____

____

____

4. Two parallel lines are cut by a transversal and two of the same-side interior angles formed have measures of $(4x + 3)°$ and $(x + 2)°$.

A. How are the angles related?

____

B. Write and solve an equation to find the value of x.

____

C. What are the two angle measures?

____

5. (MP) **Reason** In the diagram, two parallel lines are cut by a transversal, and ∠1 and ∠6 do not form any of the kinds of angle pairs that you have learned. What is a way you can find the measure of ∠6 if you know that the measure of ∠1 is 132°? Explain.

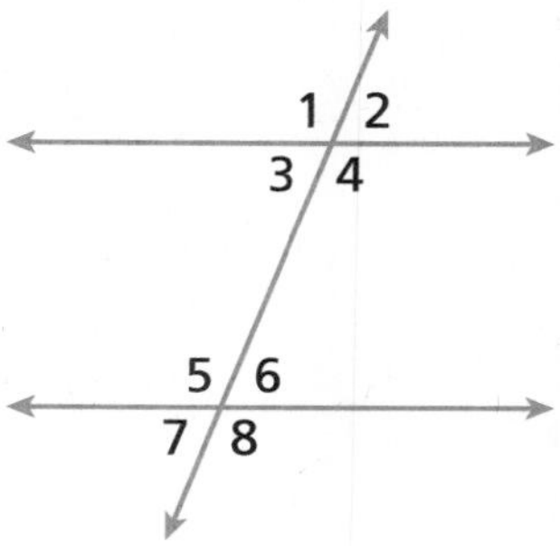

____

____

____

© Houghton Mifflin Harcourt Publishing Company

Test Prep

6. Two parallel lines are cut by a transversal. A pair of same-side interior angles formed have measures of $(2x - 11)°$ and $(9x + 6.75)°$. What is the measure of the smaller angle?

____

7. What are the values of x and y?

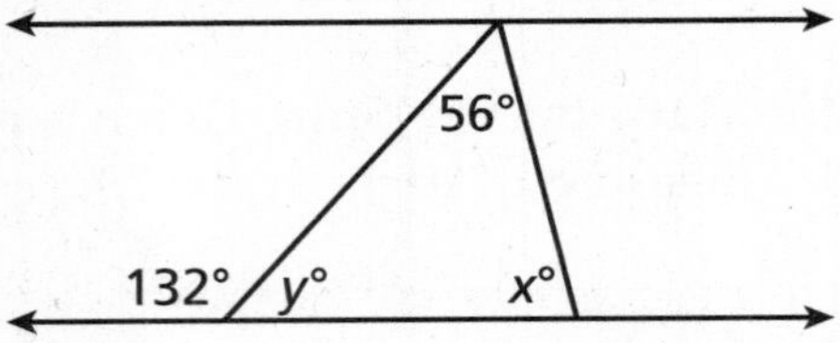

Ⓐ $x = 30$; $y = 76$

Ⓑ $x = 76$; $y = 48$

Ⓒ $x = 80$; $y = 54$

Ⓓ $x = 132$; $y = 48$

8. Two parallel lines are cut by a transversal. What kind of angle pair are Angles 1 and 2?

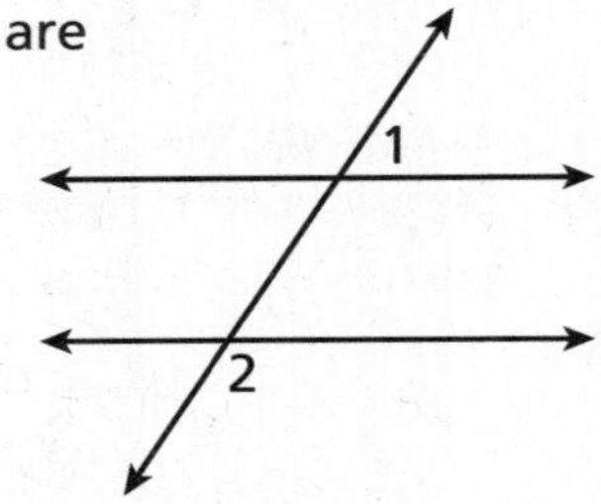

Ⓐ alternate interior angles

Ⓑ alternate exterior angles

Ⓒ same-side exterior angles

Ⓓ corresponding angles

Spiral Review

9. If a unit circle with a center at (–3, 4) is reflected across the x-axis, where will the center of the reflected image lie?

____

10. One triangle has angles that measure 45° and 83°. Another triangle has angles that measure 45° and 52°. Are the triangles similar? How do you know?

____

____

____

11. An office manager is planning to set up three computer workstations and a printer in a space that is 22 feet wide. The printer takes up 4 feet.

A. Write an equation that you could use to find the width w (in feet) of the space available for each computer workstation.

____

B. What is the width of the space available for each computer workstation?

____

© Houghton Mifflin Harcourt Publishing Company

Module 6

Name ____________________

Review

Vocabulary

In the diagram, Line *AF* is parallel to Line *BE*. Give one example of each type of figure in the diagram.

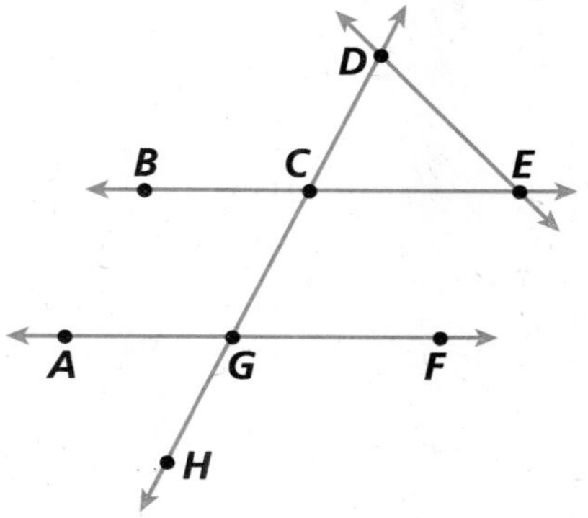

1. an exterior angle of a triangle ____________

2. a remote interior angle of the exterior angle you named in Problem 1 ____________

3. a transversal of a pair of parallel lines ____________

4. a pair of alternate interior angles formed by a pair of parallel lines and a transversal ____________

Concepts and Skills

5. If Triangle *ABC* is similar to Triangle *EDC*, which statements about the figures must be true?

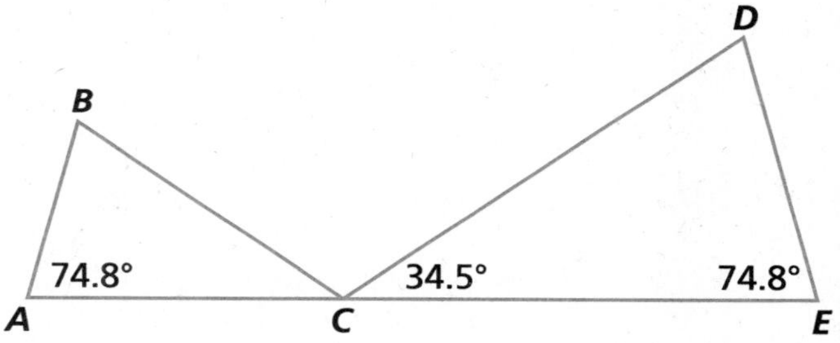

   Ⓐ Angle *B* measures 70.7°.

   Ⓑ Angle *ACB* measures 40.3°.

   Ⓒ Angle *A* is the largest interior angle of Triangle *ABC*.

   Ⓓ Triangle *EDC* can be produced from Triangle *ABC* by a dilation and a reflection.

   Ⓔ Triangle *EDC* can be produced from Triangle *ABC* by a rotation and a dilation.

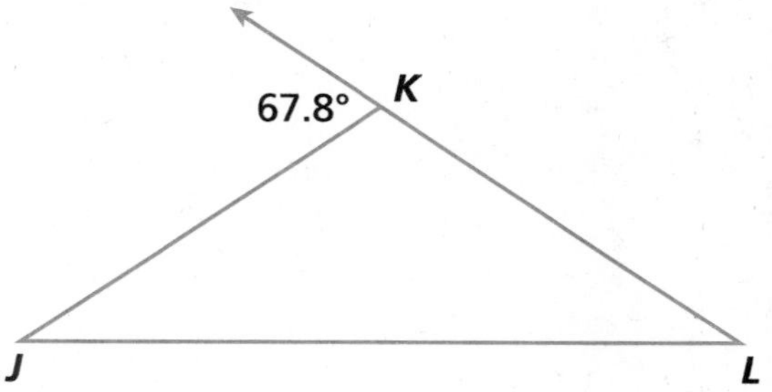

6. In Triangle *JKL*, ∠*J* is congruent to ∠*L*. What is the measure of ∠*L*? ____________

7. MP **Use Tools** A figure with parallel Lines *m* and *n* is shown. Find the measures of angles *A*, *B*, and *C*. State what strategy and tool you will use to answer the question, explain your choice, and then find the answer.

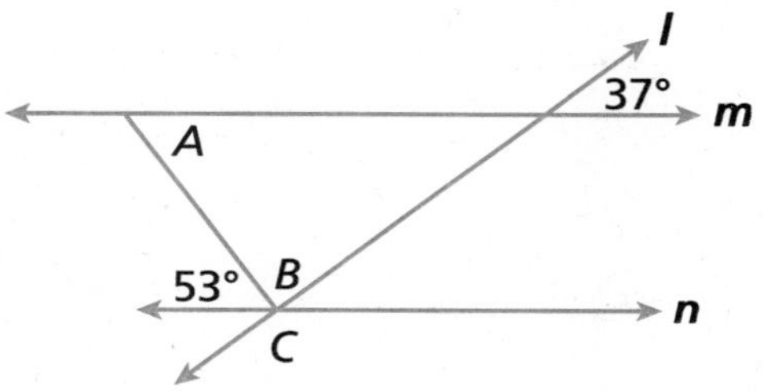

____

____

____

© Houghton Mifflin Harcourt Publishing Company

8. In the figure, Segments SV and RU intersect at Point T. Anna claims that Triangle RST is similar to Triangle UVT. Is Anna's claim correct? Explain your reasoning.

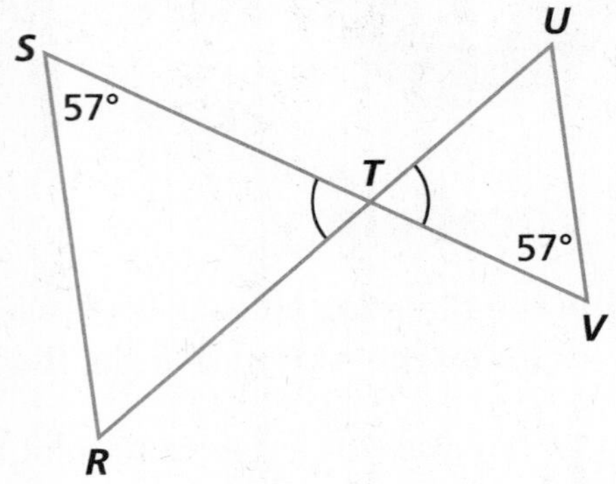

____

____

____

____

____

____

9. What is the value of x in the figure shown? ____________

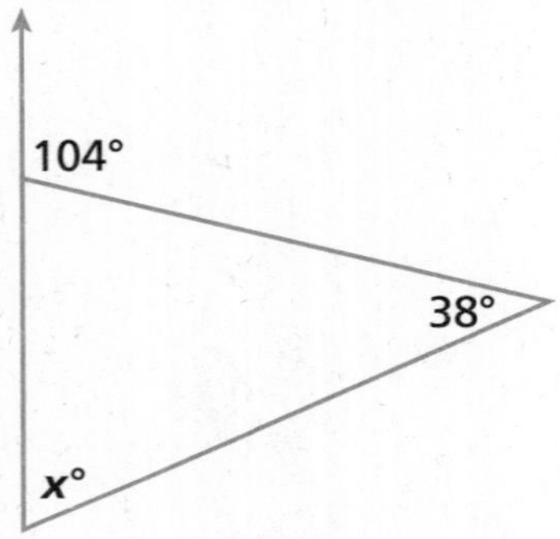

10. What is the value of z in the figure shown? ____________

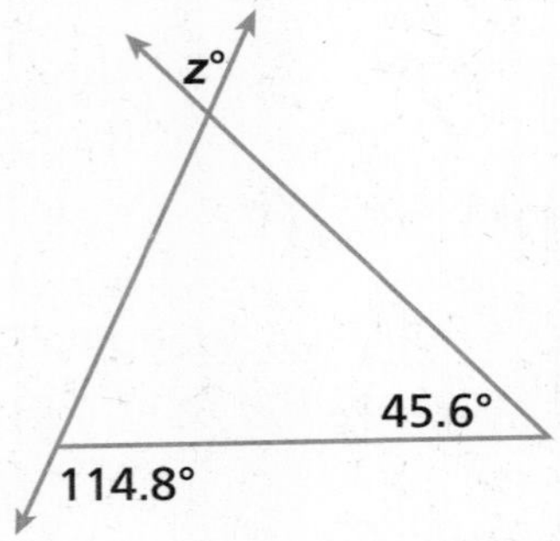

11. In the figure, Line a is parallel to Line b.

A. Which equation can be used to determine the value of x?

Ⓐ $3x = 2x + 20$

Ⓑ $90 - 3x = 2x + 20$

Ⓒ $3x = 180 - 2x + 20$

Ⓓ $3x + 2x + 20 = 180$

B. What are the values of x and y?

$x =$ ____________

$y =$ ____________

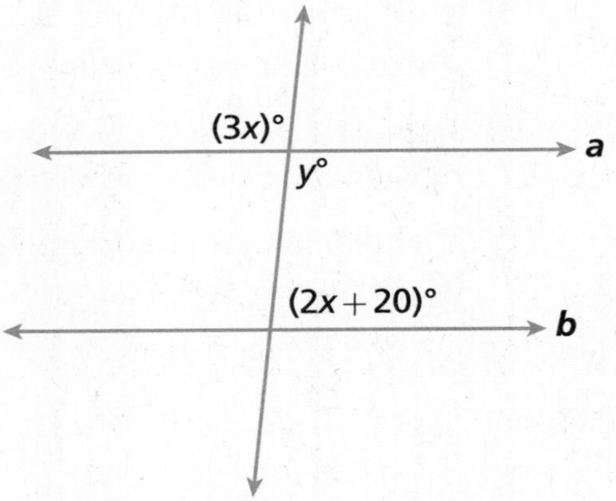

12. In the figure, Line ℓ is parallel to Line m. Select all true statements about the figure.

Ⓐ $g = 54$

Ⓑ $h = 126$

Ⓒ $f = g$

Ⓓ $g + h = 180$

Ⓔ $f = h$

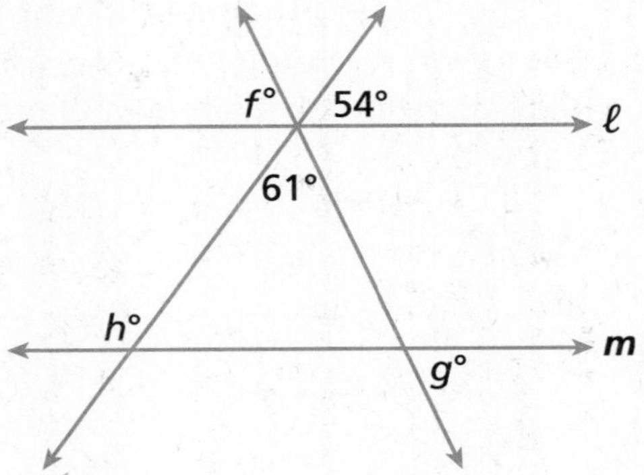

© Houghton Mifflin Harcourt Publishing Company

Module 7

Proportional Relationships

Proportional Smoothies

The owners of a smoothie shop want the price of each size of smoothie to be proportional to the amount of liquid it contains. A small smoothie will be 16 fluid ounces and sell for $3.52.

Complete the shop's price chart by deciding how many fluid ounces the other smoothie sizes will have and then determine the price of each smoothie.

Smoothies		
Size	**Fluid ounces**	**Price ($)**
Kid-size		
Small	16	3.52
Medium		
Large		

Turn and Talk

- Explain how you know that the prices of the smoothies are proportional to their volumes.

- The shop owners decide to charge $0.99 for each smoothie add-in. For smoothies with a single add-in, is the total price proportional to the fluid ounces? Explain.

© Houghton Mifflin Harcourt Publishing Company • Image Credit: ©Springfield Gallery/Adobe Stock

Are You Ready?

Complete these problems to review prior concepts and skills you will need for this module.

Tables and Graphs of Equivalent Ratios

Complete each table to represent the relationship.

1. Collette runs 6.5 kilometers each week. Let *d* represent the total distance, in kilometers, she runs in *w* weeks.

w	2		5
d		19.5	

2. A theater charges a service fee of $0.95 per ticket bought online. Let *t* represent the total fee paid for ordering *n* tickets.

n	1	3	
t			$5.70

Identify Proportional Relationships

Tell whether each relationship is proportional. Explain your reasoning.

3.

x	6	8	12	15
y	48	64	96	120

4.

x	9	15	18	36
y	18	24	27	45

Similar Triangles

Tell whether each pair of triangles is similar. Explain your reasoning.

5.

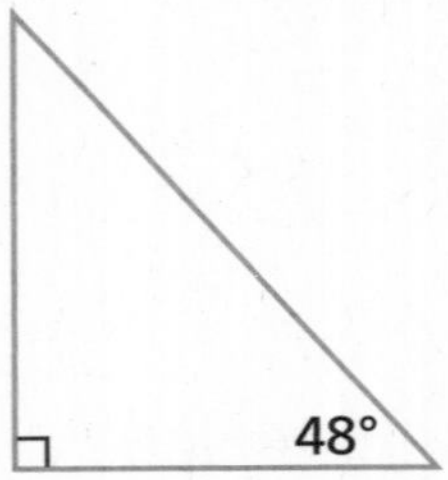

6.

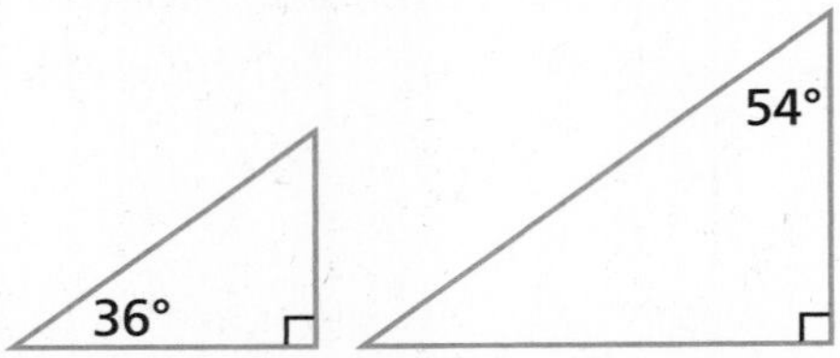

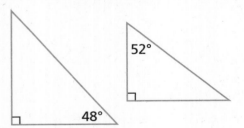

© Houghton Mifflin Harcourt Publishing Company

Name ______________________

Explain Slope with Similar Triangles

I Can determine the slope of a line and use it to find additional points on the line.

Spark Your Learning

PAIRS

A line passes through the origin. Two right triangles each have one side along the line and another side on the *x*-axis. How is $\triangle OAC$ related to $\triangle OBD$?

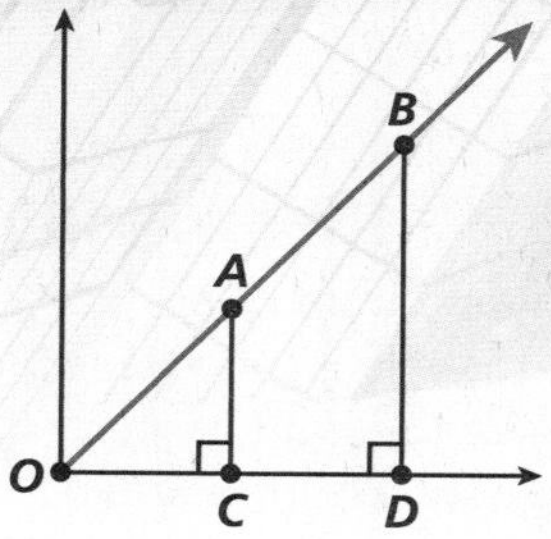

Turn and Talk Amie drew a different line through the origin and drew two new right triangles that have one side along the *x*-axis. How are her triangles different from the ones shown above? How are they the same?

© Houghton Mifflin Harcourt Publishing Company • Image Credit: ©Hendra Su/EyeEm/Getty Images

Build Understanding

1 Points on the line represent the vertical and horizontal distances a person would travel while climbing the path before steps were built to make the climb easier.

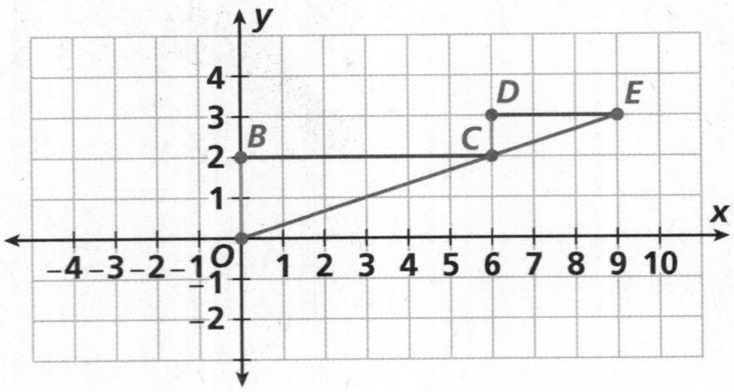

A. Write a sequence of transformations that maps one triangle onto the other to show that $\triangle OBC$ is similar to $\triangle CDE$.

____

____

____

Connect to Vocabulary

The **hypotenuse** of a right triangle is the side opposite the right angle. The **legs** of a right triangle are the sides adjacent to the right angle.

B. Complete the following based on $\triangle OBC$ and $\triangle CDE$.

$\dfrac{\text{length of } \overline{OB}}{\text{length of } \overline{CD}} = \dfrac{\text{length of } \overline{BC}}{\text{length of } \overline{DE}}$ Corresponding sides of similar triangles are proportional.

$\dfrac{\square}{1} = \dfrac{\square}{3}$ Substitute.

$\dfrac{\square}{1} \times \dfrac{1}{6} = \dfrac{\square}{3} \times \dfrac{1}{6}$ ____________________

$\dfrac{\square}{6} = \dfrac{\square}{3}$ ← rise ← run Multiply.

C. When moving from one point to another along a line, the change in the *y*-coordinates is the **rise** and the change in the *x*-coordinates is the **run**. The legs of $\triangle OBC$ and $\triangle CDE$ can help you visualize the rise and run. What does Part B show you about the rise-to-run ratios in $\triangle OBC$ and $\triangle CDE$?

____

© Houghton Mifflin Harcourt Publishing Company • Image Credit: ©Bob Ell/EyeEm/Getty Images

Name ______________________

Step It Out

2 A skateboard ramp is shown on a coordinate plane.

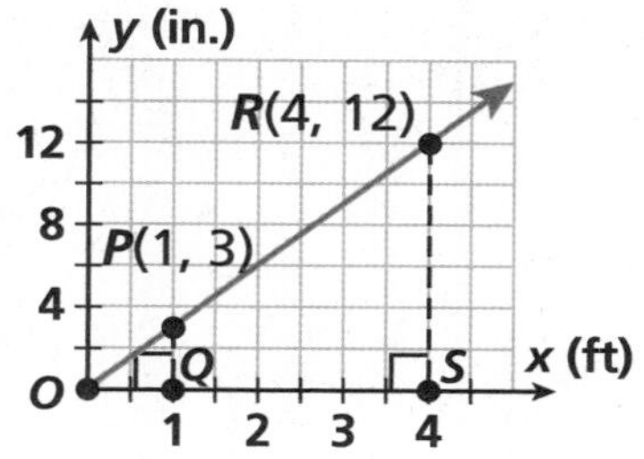

A. Line *OP* passes through the origin, Point *P*, and Point *R*. The coordinates of Point *Q* are (☐, ☐), and the coordinates of Point *S* are (☐, ☐).

B. Does this line represent a proportional relationship? Explain.

____

C. Since the run between the origin and Point *P* is 1, the unit rate is equal to the rise-over-run ratio. Find the unit rate of the relationship modeled by the line. Complete the equation using the coordinates of Point *P* and the origin.

$$\text{unit rate} = \frac{\text{rise}}{\text{run}} = \frac{\square - \square}{\square - \square} = \frac{\square}{\square} = \square \text{ in./ft}$$

Connect to Vocabulary

A rate is a comparison of two quantities that have different units. A **unit rate** is a rate with a denominator of one unit.

D. A vertical line segment from Point *R* to the *x*-axis forms a right triangle, $\triangle ORS$. Complete the statements to show $\triangle OPQ$ is similar to $\triangle ORS$.

m$\angle POQ$ is equal to m$\angle$ ☐. $\angle OQP$ and $\angle$ ☐ are right angles, so they are congruent / similar. By the AA Similarity Postulate, $\triangle OPQ$ is similar to $\triangle$ ☐.

E. Find the rise-over-run relationship modeled by the line, using the coordinates of Point *R* and the origin.

$$\frac{\text{rise}}{\text{run}} = \frac{\square - \square}{\square - \square} = \frac{\square}{\square} = \square \text{ in./ft}$$

F. Describe the slope of the line.

The rise-over-run ratio, or slope, between the origin and Point *P* is equal to / not equal to the rise-over-run ratio, or slope, between the origin and Point *R*. The slope of the line is constant /not constant.

Connect to Vocabulary

Slope is a measure of the steepness of a line and is described by the ratio of the line's rise to its run. A horizontal line has slope 0, and a vertical line's slope is undefined.

© Houghton Mifflin Harcourt Publishing Company • Image Credit: ©kongsky/Shutterstock

3 Points $M(2, 3)$ and $N(x, -6)$ lie on the same line. The line also passes through the origin. Find the value of x.

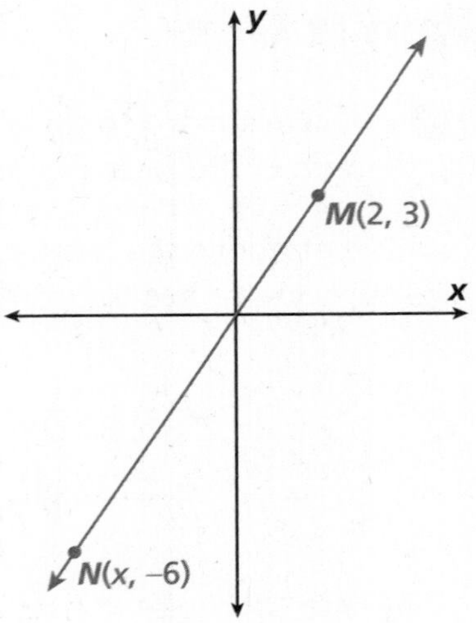

A. For a line passing through the origin, what do you notice about measuring rise over run from the origin to another point on the line?

____

____

B. Find the rise over run from the origin to Point M.

$$\frac{\text{rise}}{\text{run}} = \frac{\square - \square}{\square - \square} = \frac{\square}{\square}$$

C. The rise-over-run ratio, or slope, of any line is constant. Use this ratio to write an equation that can help you find the x-coordinate of Point N.

$$\frac{\square - 0}{x - 0} = \frac{\square}{\square}$$

D. Use proportional reasoning to solve for x.

$x = \square$

Turn and Talk Explain, using the rise and the run, why the slope of a horizontal line is 0.

Check Understanding

1. Explain how dilation scale factors can help you identify points on a line passing through the origin given one additional point.

____

____

____

____

2. A line passes through the origin and (5, 3). Identify two additional points on this line.

____

© Houghton Mifflin Harcourt Publishing Company

Name

On Your Own

3. A road sign is posted showing a road has a 10% grade, meaning the ratio of vertical to horizontal distance is 10%, or $\frac{1}{10}$. If a car driving on the road rises from an elevation of 543 feet above sea level to an elevation of 768 feet above sea level, how far has the car traveled horizontally?

____

4. (MP) **Attend to Precision** Line ℓ passes through the origin and the point (4, 5). Suppose point (x, y) also lies on Line ℓ.

A. The slope of Line ℓ from the origin to (4, 5) is ________.

B. Why is the slope of Line ℓ from the origin to (x, y) the same as the slope from the origin to (4, 5)?

____

____

____

____

5. Are Triangles *OPQ* and *ORS* similar? If so, give a sequence of transformations that maps $\triangle OPQ$ onto $\triangle ORS$.

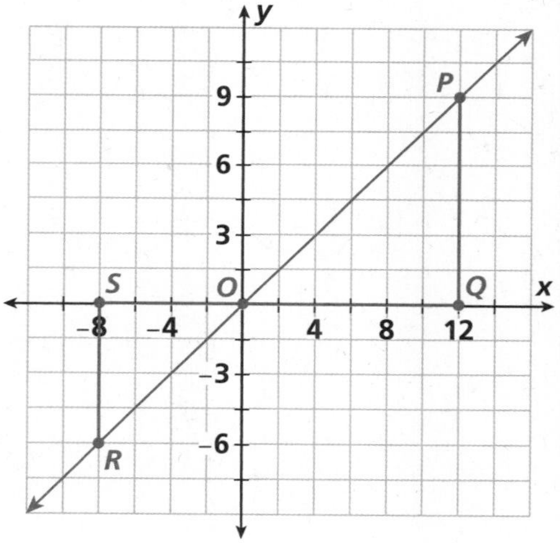

____

____

____

For Problems 6–9, find the value of *k* given that both points lie on a line passing through the origin.

6. (5, 10) and (−3, *k*)

____

7. (−12, −2) and (*k*, 8)

____

8. (*k*, 7) and (−81, −9)

____

9. (*k*, −24) and (5, 40)

____

10. At the bottom of a mountain, a ski lift starts four feet above the ground. At the top of the mountain, the lift is 1,356 feet higher. If the lift ascends one foot for every four feet it travels west, how far west of the starting position is the lift at the top of the mountain?

____

© Houghton Mifflin Harcourt Publishing Company • Image Credits: ©dowell/Moment/Getty Images; ©coberschneider/RooM/Getty Images

For Problems 11–13, use the given information.

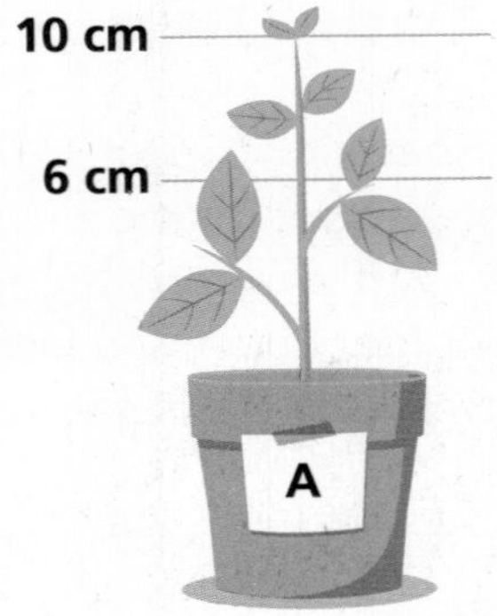

STEM Kylie is preparing for the science fair which will take place in six weeks. She has three plants that she has grown from seeds, which she considers to have height 0 centimeters, and she is measuring their heights as she applies different treatments to each.

11. The first plant is receiving Plant Food A. After 4 weeks, it is 10 centimeters tall, as shown. If it continues growing at this rate, how tall will it be after 6 weeks?

______

12. The second plant is receiving Plant Food B. After 3 weeks, it is 10 centimeters tall. If it continues growing at this rate, how tall will it be after 6 weeks?

______

13. The third plant is planted in the same soil as the others, but it receives only light and water. After 2 weeks, it is 6 centimeters tall. If it continues growing at this rate, how tall will it be after 6 weeks?

______

(MP) **Use Repeated Reasoning In Problems 14–16, a point is given that lies on a line passing through the origin. Identify four additional points that lie on the line. Include two points with positive coordinates and two points with negative coordinates.**

14. (17, 51) ______

15. (72, 18) ______

16. (−8, −5) ______

17. A line passes through (6, 3), (8, 4), and (n, −2). Find the value of n.

______

18. A line passes through (−2, 4), (−4, 8), and (n, −2). Find the value of n.

______

© Houghton Mifflin Harcourt Publishing Company

I'm in a Learning Mindset!

How was finding additional points that lie on a line an appropriate challenge for me?

______

______

Name

Explain Slope with Similar Triangles

Use the graph to answer Problems 1–4.

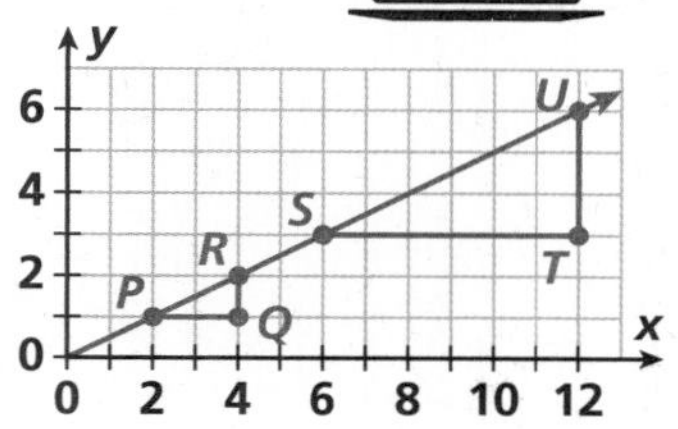

1. How is $\triangle PQR$ related to $\triangle STU$?

2. Describe a sequence of transformations that maps $\triangle PQR$ onto $\triangle STU$.

3. Identify one pair of corresponding angles and describe what you know about them.

4. What is the ratio of the length of the vertical side to the length of the horizontal side of each triangle? What is the slope of the line?

5. **Model with Mathematics** A person casts a shadow that aligns with the shadow of a tree. The person is 5.5 feet tall, and casts a shadow 8.25 feet long. The tree's shadow measures 22.5 feet long.

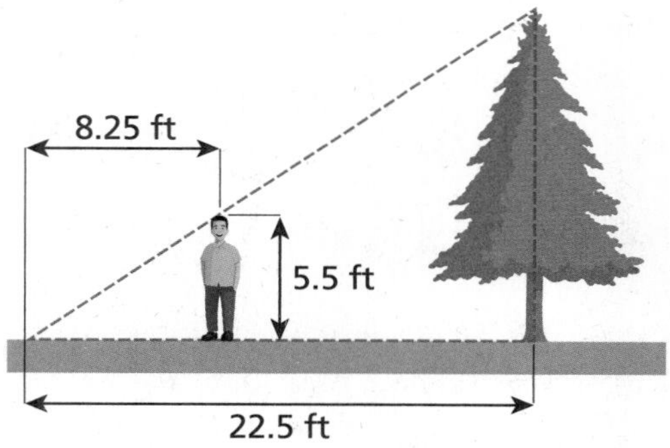

A. Write an equation you can use to find the tree's height.

B. How tall is the tree? How far is the person standing from the tree?

6. **Open Ended** Explain how it is possible to find the slope of a line given any two points on the line.

© Houghton Mifflin Harcourt Publishing Company

Test Prep

7. A line passes through the origin, (3, 5), and (−12, *b*). What is the value of *b*?

Ⓐ −20 Ⓒ −10

Ⓑ 20 Ⓓ −7

8. A line passes through the origin and (8, 2). Select the points that lie on this line.

Ⓐ (−8, −2) Ⓓ (−1, 1)

Ⓑ (−4, −1) Ⓔ (16, 4)

Ⓒ (−2, −8) Ⓕ (40, 10)

9. A line passes through (2, 3), (4, 6), and (−2, *n*). Find the value of *n*.

$n =$ ☐

Spiral Review

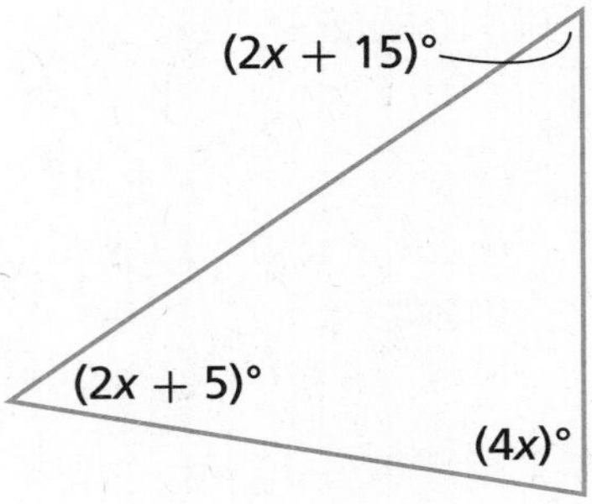

10. Find the value of *x*. Then find the measure of each angle.

____

11. Ben can buy 5 notebooks for $6.75 at Store A or 3 notebooks for $4.50 at Store B. Which store offers the better value?

____

12. Describe a transformation that maps *ABCD* onto *A′B′C′D′*.

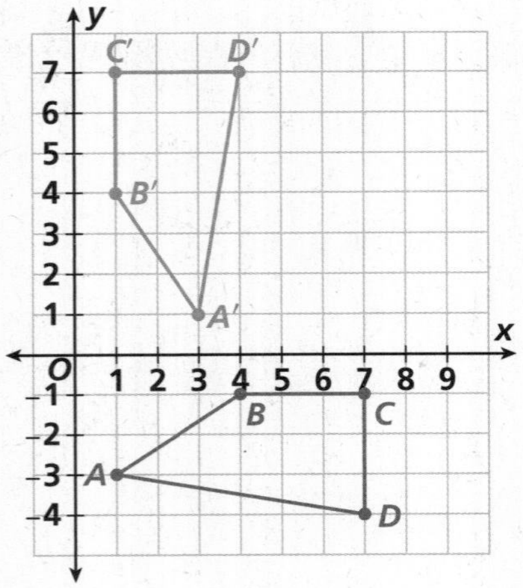

____

____

© Houghton Mifflin Harcourt Publishing Company

Name ____________________

Derive $y = mx$

I Can **write the equation of a line given a graph or a table of values.**

Spark Your Learning

PAIRS

Asiah's literature class is studying a new book. To complete the assigned reading on time, she has made a schedule. Asiah records her progress in a graph. What can you interpret from the graph?

Asiah's Reading Progress

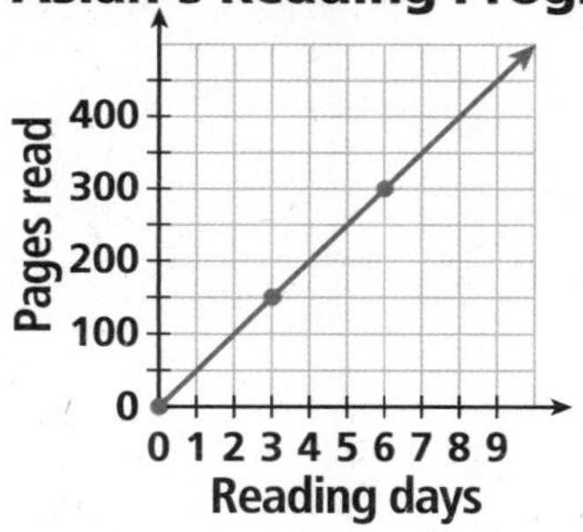

© Houghton Mifflin Harcourt Publishing Company • Image Credit: ©Chris Ryan/Caiaimage/Getty Images

Turn and Talk How would the graph look different if Asiah read more pages per day?

Build Understanding

1 Use the graph of Asiah's reading to answer the following questions.

A. The number of pages that Asiah has cumulatively read increases by

$\frac{\square \text{ pages}}{1 \text{ day}}$.

B. The graph shows the number of pages that Asiah has read at the end of each day. Complete the table, including a general expression for the number of pages Asiah will read in *x* days.

Asiah's Reading Progress	
Reading days	**Pages read**
1	
2	
4	
7	
x	

C. Use the variable *y* to stand for the number of pages that Asiah has read. Write an equation to model the number of pages read after *x* days.

D. From the point at 1 day to the point at 2 days, how much does the graph rise?

E. What is the slope, or rise over run, for Asiah's graph? Explain your reasoning.

F. How is the slope related to the unit rate of this proportional relationship?

G. Look at the equation from Part C. What do you notice about the equation when you compare it to the slope from Part E?

H. Asiah decides she wants to adjust her schedule so she will finish the book earlier than the due date. How will this change the slope? Explain your reasoning.

© Houghton Mifflin Harcourt Publishing Company • Image Credit: ©Tim Hall/Cultura/Getty Images

Step It Out

2 Don is a gifted wood carver, and he has started selling his wood carvings online. He tracks the total number of carvings sold.

Months in business	Carvings sold
2	5
6	15
8	20

A. Sketch a graph of the relationship between the number of months in business and the number of carvings sold.

B. Complete the explanation.

The graph of the relationship is / is not a straight line passing through the origin, so the relationship is / is not proportional.

C. Use the rise over the run to write the slope of the graph.

Slope = ______

D. Write an equation of the line in the form $y = mx$. ______

E. Use the linear equation to predict the number of carvings sold after being in business for 12 months. ______

Connect to Vocabulary

A **linear equation** is an equation whose solutions form a straight line on a coordinate plane.

Turn and Talk A line is modeled by the equation $y = mx$. Explain how the value of m affects the graph of the line.

Check Understanding

1. The Nguyen family is traveling cross-country, driving 300 miles each day. Let x represent the number of days in the trip and let y represent the total number of miles driven. Write an equation to model their trip.

______

2. Write an equation for the line passing through points (0, 0), (4, 5), and (8, 10).

______

© Houghton Mifflin Harcourt Publishing Company

On Your Own

3. (MP) **Reason** A clothing store is going out of business. To sell their remaining inventory, the managers drop the price of each item $5 each week until the item sells.

   A. A line is drawn to model the relationship between the number of weeks and the change in price. Is the slope of this line positive or negative? Explain.

   ____

   B. Write the equation of the line. ______________________________

For Problems 4–5, sketch the graph of the line represented by the equation. Plot and label three points on each line.

4. $y = \frac{5}{3}x$

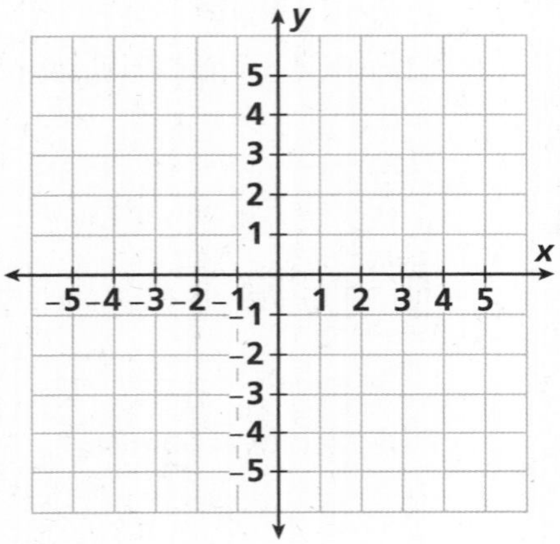

5. $y = -\frac{1}{4}x$

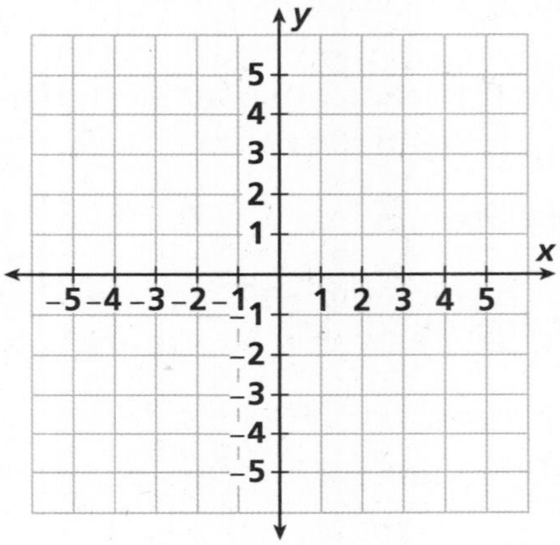

(MP) **Model with Mathematics For Problems 6–7, write an equation that models the relationship shown in the table.**

6.

x	y
−6	14
−3	7
3	−7
6	−14

____

7.

x	y
−8	−4
−4	−2
6	3
10	5

____

I'm in a Learning Mindset!

What challenges did I face writing an equation that modeled the relationship in the table for Problem 7?

____

____

© Houghton Mifflin Harcourt Publishing Company

Name ____________________

ONLINE
Video Tutorials and Interactive Examples

Derive $y = mx$

1. Sean tutors math students to earn extra money.

   A. How much would Sean earn from 4 hours of tutoring?

   ____

   B. Write an equation to model Sean's earnings, y, after x hours.

   ____

Sean charges $20 per hour.

2. (MP) **Attend to Precision** An inch is exactly 2.54 centimeters. Write an equation to convert the number of inches x to the corresponding length in centimeters.

   ____

3. Write an equation of the line passing through the points $(-5, -25)$, $(0, 0)$, and $(3, 15)$.

   ____

4. **Math on the Spot** The graph shows the distance Caleb runs over time.

   A. Identify four points on the line.

   ____

   ____

   B. Determine the slope of the line.

   ____

   C. Write an equation of the line.

   ____

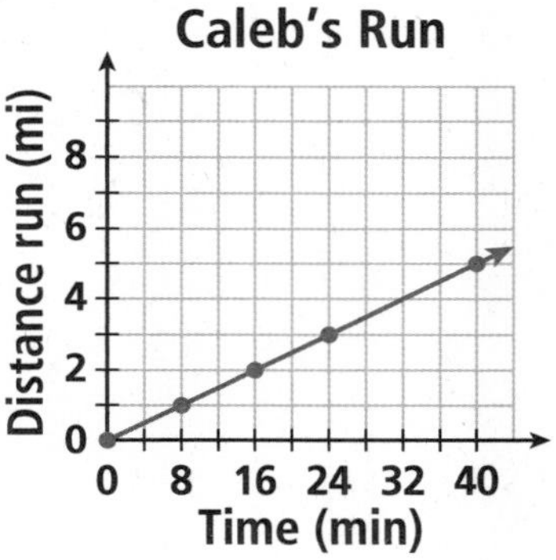

5. Sketch the graph of the line $y = 4x$.

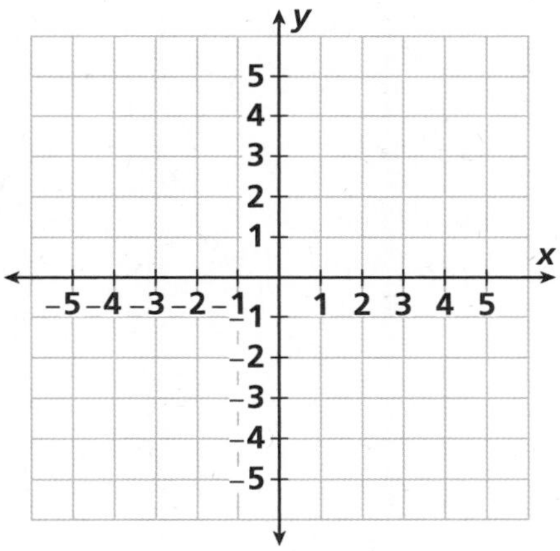

6. (MP) **Model with Mathematics** Write an equation that models the relationship shown in the table.

x	y
12	−9
8	−6
20	−15
32	−24

____

© Houghton Mifflin Harcourt Publishing Company • Image Credit: ©SpeedKingz/Shutterstock

Test Prep

7. What is the equation of the line passing through the points (−2, 5), (0, 0), and (4, −10)?

Ⓐ $y = -\frac{5}{2}x$

Ⓑ $y = -\frac{2}{5}x$

Ⓒ $y = \frac{2}{5}x$

Ⓓ $y = \frac{5}{2}x$

8. Write the equation of the line passing through the points (0, 0), (2, 1), and (−2,−1).

$y =$ ☐ x

9. The value of a house has been increasing by $5,000 each year. Write an equation to show how the value will have changed *x* years from now.

$y =$ ☐ x

10. Graph $y = \frac{2}{3}x$. Plot and label three points on the line.

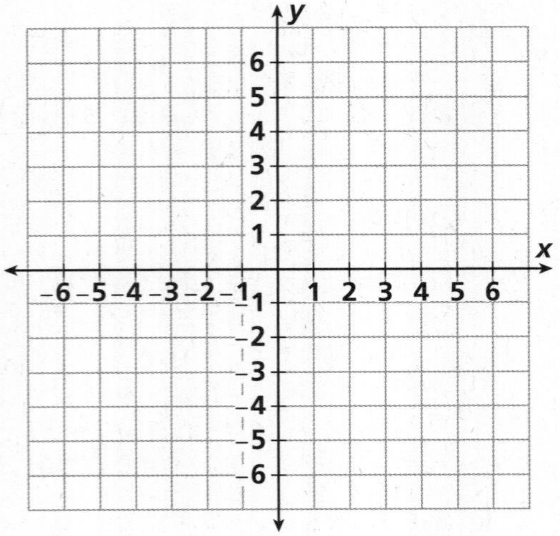

Spiral Review

11. Triangle *ABC* has vertices (1, 4), (5, 6), and (3, 10). It is reflected across the *y*-axis, making Triangle *A'B'C'*. What are the vertices of the new triangle?

____

12. Quadrilateral *ABCD* is dilated by a scale factor of 2, with the center of dilation at the origin. The vertices of *ABCD* are *A*(0, 0), *B*(5, 0), *C*(5, 3), and *D*(0, 3). What are the coordinates of the image of Vertex *C* under the dilation?

____

13. Solve the equation $3x - 2(x + 1) = 2x - 7$.

____

© Houghton Mifflin Harcourt Publishing Company

Name ______________________________

Graph, Interpret, and Compare Proportional Relationships

I Can graph proportional relationships and interpret the unit rate as the slope of the graph.

Spark Your Learning

PAIRS

An airplane is traveling toward its destination at a constant speed. The distance that the airplane has traveled at different points in time is shown in the table. How can you find the speed of the airplane?

Commercial Airplane	
Time (h)	**Distance (mi)**
0	0
1	400
2	800
3	1,200

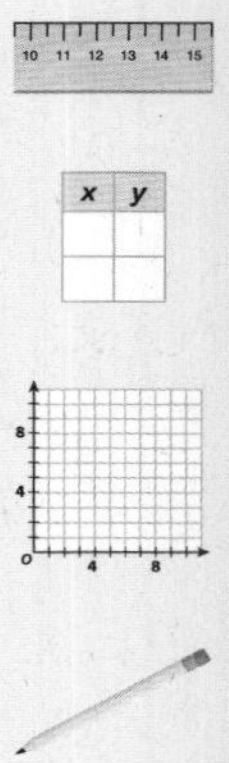

Turn and Talk Discuss how you found the speed of the airplane. How were the tools helpful?

© Houghton Mifflin Harcourt Publishing Company • Image Credit: ©Denis Belitsky/Shutterstock

Build Understanding

1 The Commercial Airplane table in Spark Your Learning shows data that can be graphed on a coordinate plane, where x is the time passed and y is the distance traveled.

A. One of the points is (3, 1,200). Describe what this point represents.

____

____

B. The airplane travels at a constant rate, so the relationship between distance and time is proportional. You already know that the unit rate of a proportional relationship can be calculated from any point on the graph of the relationship.

Use the point (3, 1,200) to calculate the number of miles that the airplane travels per hour. Show your work.

____

C. A second airplane starts from the same airport and is traveling at a different constant speed. After 4 hours the second airplane has flown 2,100 miles from the airport. Calculate the number of miles that the second airplane traveled per hour. Show your work.

____

D. Complete the table to show the distance that the second airplane has traveled at different points in time. Graph the points on the coordinate plane.

Second Airplane	
Time (h)	**Distance (mi)**
0	
1	
2	
3	

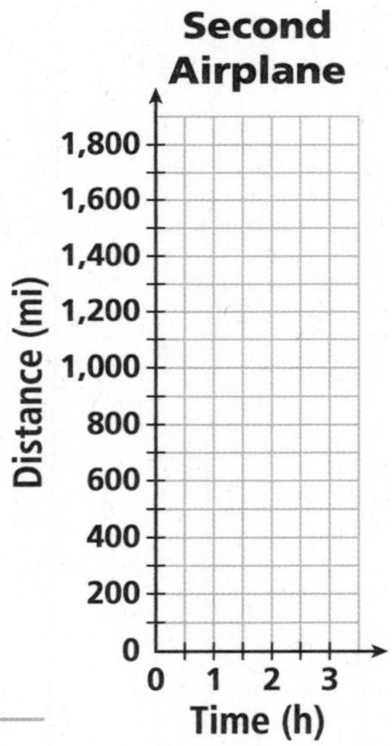

E. What can you conclude about the distance that the two airplanes will have traveled after 8 hours?

____

____

____

____

Turn and Talk Predict how the graph of the second airplane's travel will compare to the graph of the first airplane's travel. What will be the same and what will be different?

© Houghton Mifflin Harcourt Publishing Company • Image Credit: ©Xavier Gallego Morell/Shutterstock

Name ____________________

Step It Out

2 A fish tank is filling at a constant rate. The equation modeling the amount of water in the tank is $y = 5x$, where y represents the amount of water in gallons and x represents the amount of time passed in minutes. Use the equation to complete the table.

Time passed: 0 minutes

Time passed: 4 minutes

A. Substitute 1 for x in the equation to find the amount of water in the tank after 1 minute.

$y = 5(\square)$

$y = \square$

Enter your answer in the table.

B. Substitute the remaining values for x in the equation and complete the table.

C. Graph the points from the table.

Fish Tank	
Time (min)	**Water (gal)**
0	
1	
2	
4	

Fish Tank

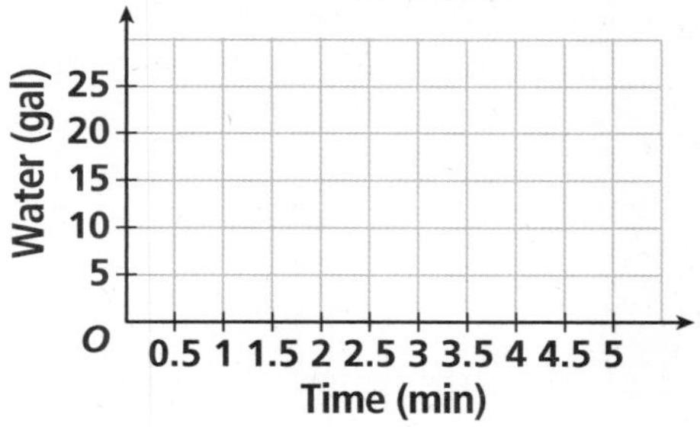

D. Describe what the point (4.5, 22.5) represents.

After ______ minutes, the tank contains ______ gallons.

You have used a continuous graph to graph a function, such as an equation for an airplane's distance. A **discrete graph** is a graph made of unconnected points. It represents data that only make sense at certain points.

> **Connect to Vocabulary**
>
> A **continuous graph** is a graph made up of connected points or curves.

3 The table shows how much a tailor charges to hem different numbers of shirts.

Tailor	
Number of shirts	**Cost ($)**
0	0
1	20
2	40
3	60

A. Would it make sense for the table to include the cost of hemming 2.5 shirts? Explain.

____

____

B. Graph the ordered pairs from the table. Decide whether or not to connect the points with a solid line. Should the graph be discrete or continuous? Why?

____

Tailor

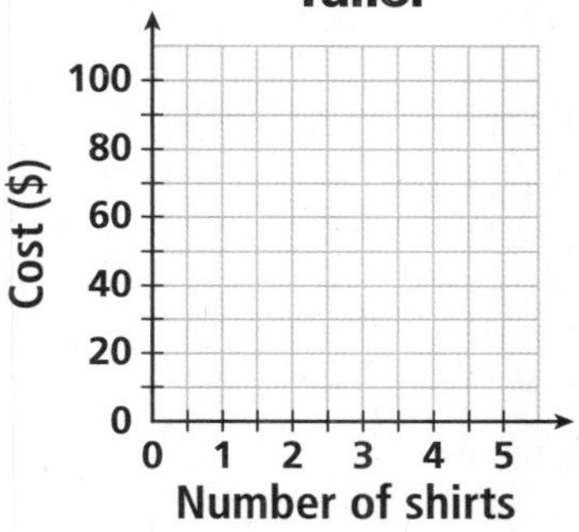

C. How many shirts can a customer have hemmed with $10? With $50?

____

© Houghton Mifflin Harcourt Publishing Company

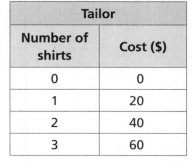

Step It Out

4 Three friends, Brooklyn, Lincoln, and Taylor, competed in a race over the weekend. Which runner ran the fastest?

Lincoln	
Time (h)	Distance (mi)
0	0
0.5	4.5
1	9

Brooklyn
Brooklyn's pace is represented by the equation $y = 7x$.

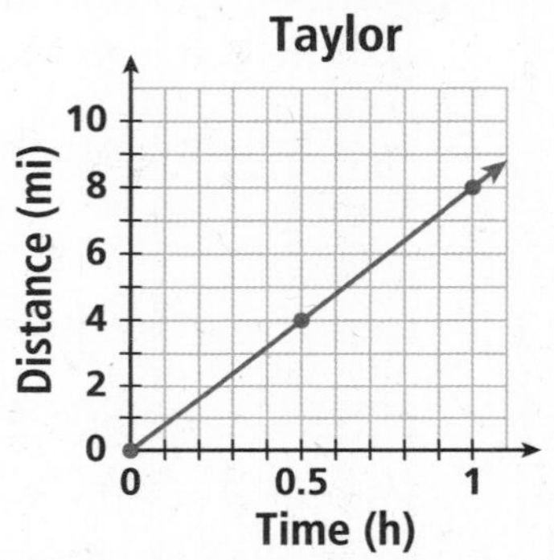

A. Taylor's pace is the same as the unit rate, which can be calculated by dividing the *y*-coordinate by the *x*-coordinate. Find a point on the graph and use it to calculate the pace, in miles per hour, at which Taylor ran.

____

____

B. Choose a point in the table and use it to calculate the pace, in miles per hour, at which Lincoln ran.

____

____

C. Determine Brooklyn's pace. Substitute 1 hour into the equation $y = 7x$ and solve for the distance traveled.

Brooklyn's unit rate is ______________ miles per hour.

D. The unit rates you found can now be compared. Which runner ran the fastest? Complete the following sentence.

______________ ran the fastest because his/her rate is the fastest at ______________ miles per hour.

Check Understanding

Use the information to answer Problems 1–2.

The height of a blimp over time is given by $y = 250x$, where y represents the height in feet and x represents the time in minutes. The height of a hot air balloon over time is given in the table.

Hot Air Balloon	
Time (min)	Height (ft)
0	0
1	600
2	1,200
3	1,800

1. Should the graph of the hot air balloon's travel be discrete or continuous? What about the blimp?

____

2. How fast is the hot air balloon rising? How fast is the blimp rising?

____

© Houghton Mifflin Harcourt Publishing Company • Image Credits: (tr) ©RyersonClark/iStockPhoto.com; (br) ©Ian Marsh/Design Pics/Corbis

Name

On Your Own

3. (MP) **Attend to Precision** A printer is printing pages at a constant rate. The table shows the time the printer takes to print different numbers of pages.

Printer	
Complete pages printed	Time (s)
0	0
1	2
2	4
3	6
4	8

A. Graph the ordered pairs from the table.

B. Did you represent the situation with a discrete graph or a continuous graph? Why?

C. Look at the point (3, 6) on the graph. Describe what this point represents.

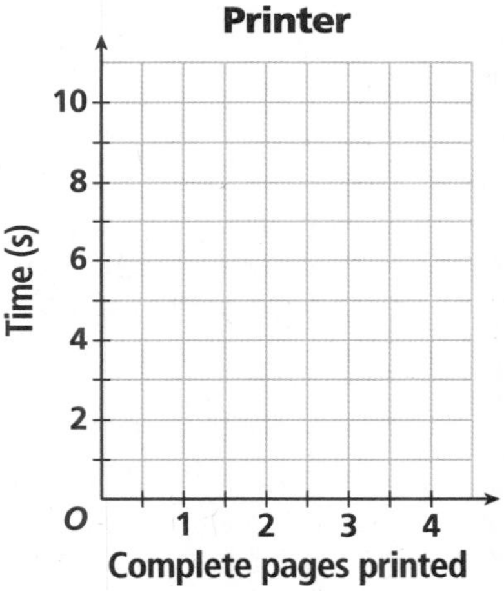

© Houghton Mifflin Harcourt Publishing Company • Image Credit: ©DarioEgidi/E+/Getty Images

(MP) **Construct Arguments** **For each relationship in Problems 4–6, decide whether you would represent it with a discrete graph or a continuous graph. Explain your reasoning.**

4. a graph of the cost of shipping different numbers of identical packages

5. a graph of the amount of fuel remaining in a car's gas tank while driving

6. a graph of the number of students that can be transported by different numbers of buses

7. (MP) **Reason** A rain barrel and a cistern are filling at constant rates. The amount of water in the rain barrel over time is shown in the graph. The amount of water in the cistern is given by $y = 200x$, where x is the time in hours and y is gallons of water.

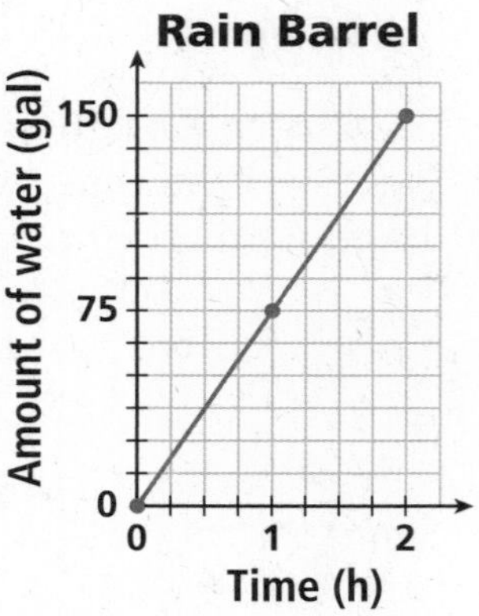

A. How fast is the rain barrel filling? How fast is the cistern filling?

____

____

B. If both the barrel and the cistern were empty at $t = 0$, which would completely fill first? Explain.

____

____

____

8. A video downloads at a constant rate given by $y = 5x$, where y represents the percent of the file downloaded and x represents the time in seconds. A game's download progress is shown in the table.

Game Progress	
Time (sec)	Percent downloaded
0	0%
2	40%
3	60%

A. At what rate are the game and the video each downloading? How long does it take to download the game and the video?

Game: __________ % per second; __________ seconds to download

Video: __________ % per second; __________ seconds to download

B. The size of a digital file can be measured in megabytes ("MB"). If the video is 200 MB and the game is 100 MB, what are the download speeds of the two files?

____

____

I'm in a Learning Mindset!

How can I maintain an appropriate level of challenge when I interpret and graph proportional relationships?

____

____

© Houghton Mifflin Harcourt Publishing Company • Image Credit: ©Garron Nicholls/Moment Select/Getty Images

Name ______________________________

ONLINE
Video Tutorials and
Interactive Examples

Graph, Interpret, and Compare Proportional Relationships

1. **STEM** The mass of a substance is equal to its density times its volume. The volume that a mass of water occupies is given in the table.

Water	
Mass (g)	Volume (cm^3)
0	0
1	1
2	2
3	3
4	4

Water

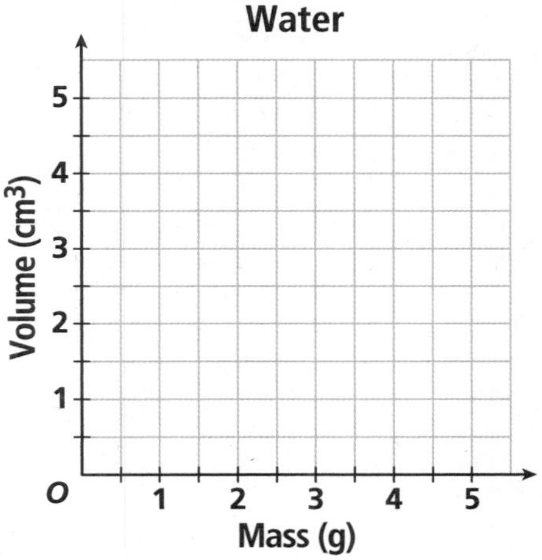

A. Graph the relationship.

B. Is your graph discrete or continuous? Explain.

____

____

2. **Financial Literacy** Hal's Hardware and Sal's Supermarket are both selling light bulbs.

Hal's Hardware	
Light bulbs	Cost ($)
1	
2	$2.08
3	

A. (MP) **Use Structure** Complete the table.

B. Calculate the unit price of light bulbs at Sal's Supermarket. What is the cost to purchase 6 light bulbs?

____

C. Compare the costs of 9 light bulbs from each store. Which store is selling light bulbs at a lower unit price? How much less does it cost to purchase 9 light bulbs from that store?

____

____

____

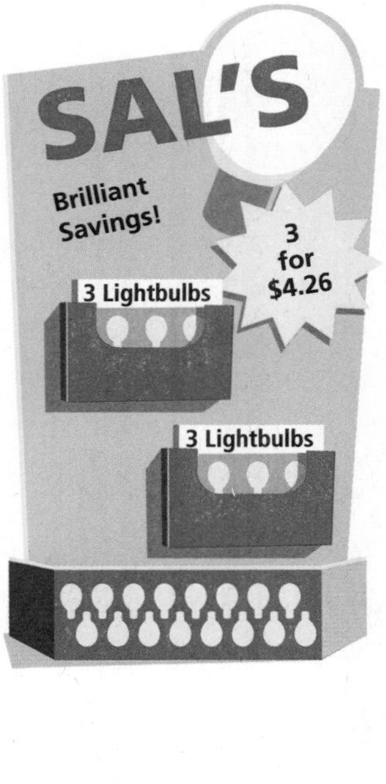

3. **Open Ended** Explain how the unit rate of a proportional relationship relates to the slope of its graph. Give a quantitative example.

____

____

____

© Houghton Mifflin Harcourt Publishing Company • Image Credit: ©Chuchawan/Shutterstock

Test Prep

4. The cost of gas, in dollars, on a particular day is given by the equation $y = 3x$, where x is the amount of gas purchased in gallons, and y represents the cost in dollars. Use the equation to complete the table and to graph the cost of gas.

Cost of Gas	
Gas (gallons)	**Cost ($)**
0	
1	
2	
3	
4	

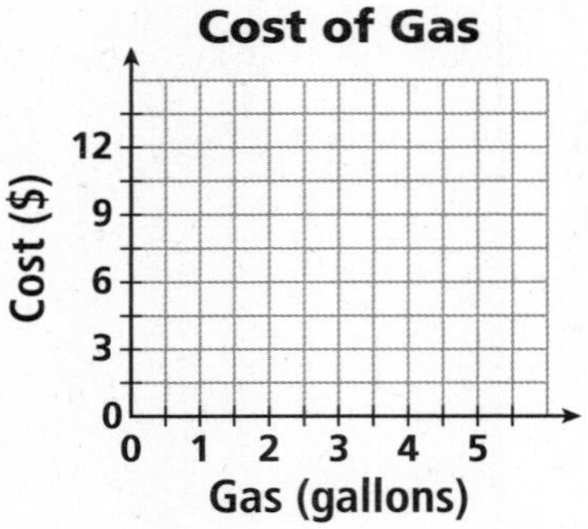

5. A graph showing the distance a person has walked over time is an example of a continuous / discrete graph.

6. A spider is crawling at a constant rate of 0.4 centimeters per second. The distance that a ladybug has walked over time is summarized in the table. The spider / ladybug is traveling at a faster rate.

Ladybug	
Time (s)	**Distance traveled (cm)**
2	1
3	1.5
4	2

7. The rate at which a mountain is eroding is given by $y = 0.5x$, where y represents the amount of erosion in millimeters and x represents the amount of time in years. A field is eroding at a rate of 2 millimeters per year. Is the field or the mountain eroding at a faster rate? By how much?

____

Spiral Review

8. Given the pair of lines shown, which two pairs of angles are alternate interior angles?

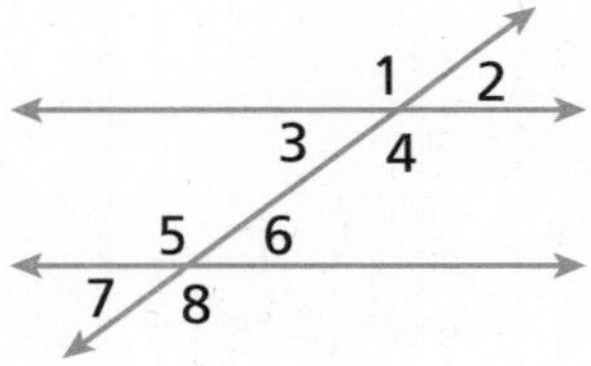

____

9. Write an equation and solve it to find the value of x in the triangle shown.

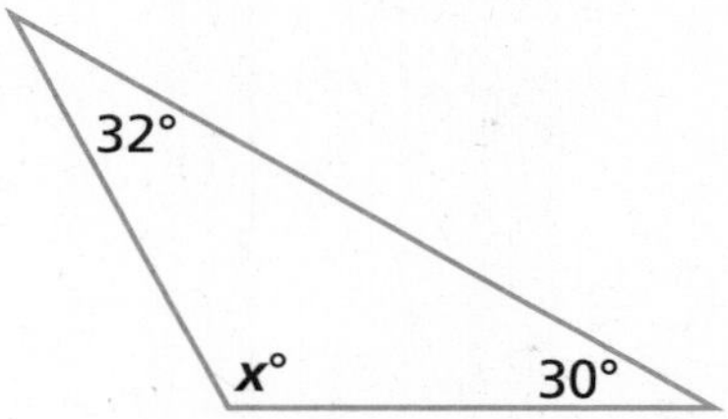

____

10. Solve $4(2 + x) = 6 + 6x$.

____

© Houghton Mifflin Harcourt Publishing Company

Module 7

Name ______________________

Review

Vocabulary

Choose the correct term from the box to complete each sentence.

Vocabulary
continuous discrete rise hypotenuse leg run

1. In a right triangle, the ______________ is the side opposite the right angle, and a ______________ is one of the sides that forms the right angle.

2. The slope of a non-vertical line is the ratio of the ______________ to the ______________ between any two points on the line.

3. The graph of the relationship between the time a train travels and the distance it travels at a constant speed would be a ______________ graph.

Concepts and Skills

4. Which of these can be used to show that the slope of a non-vertical line is the same anywhere along the line?

Ⓐ acute triangles

Ⓑ obtuse triangles

Ⓒ right triangles

Ⓓ any triangles

5. (MP) **Use Tools** The table and the equation each show a proportional relationship between time x, in seconds, and distance y, in meters. Who would finish a 100-meter race faster? How much faster? State what strategy and tool you will use to answer the question, explain your choice, and then find the answer.

Lauren's Run: $y = 8x$

Amani's Run	
Time (s)	**Distance (m)**
3	18
5	30
8	48

____

____

© Houghton Mifflin Harcourt Publishing Company

6. The graph shows right triangles *ABC* and *ADE*. The hypotenuse of each triangle lies on the same line.

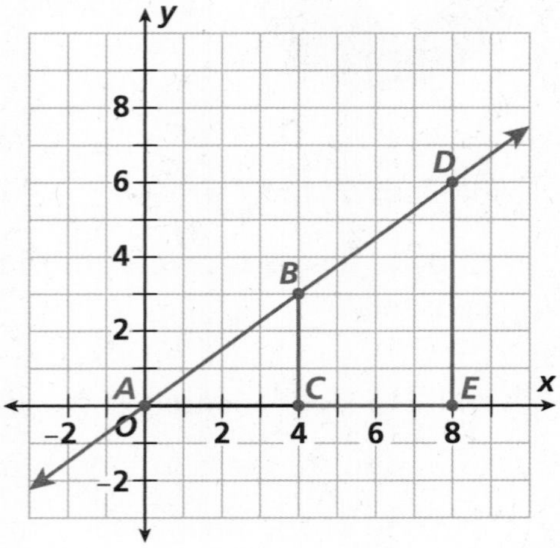

A. Explain how you know that the triangles are similar.

____

____

____

B. How does knowing the triangles are similar help you show that the slope of the line through the hypotenuses is constant?

____

____

____

____

7. The graph of a proportional relationship is shown.

A. What is the amount Kai earns per hour?

$ ________ per hour

B. Write an equation that relates Kai's earnings *y*, in dollars, to *x*, the number of hours he works.

____

8. The coordinates of two points are given in the table. Complete the table by giving the coordinates of a third point collinear with the first two points.

x	*y*
0	0
5	4

9. A fire hose sprays 2 gallons of water every 1.5 seconds.

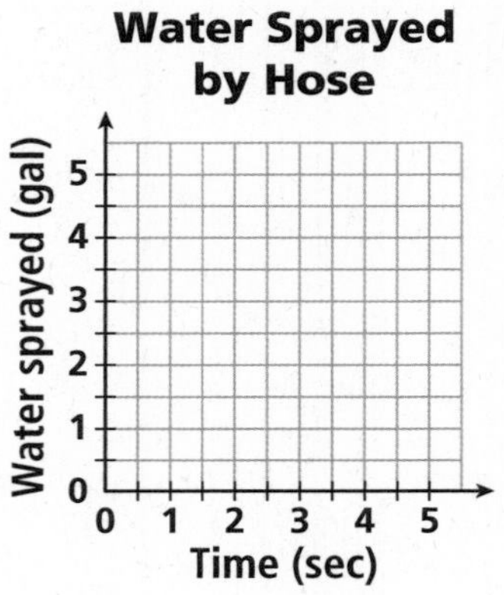

A. Draw a line on the graph to model the situation.

B. At what rate is the hose spraying water, in gallons per second? Use numbers from the box to show the rate in simplest form. Write a number in each box.

Rate: $\frac{\square}{\square}$

0 1 2 3 4 5 6 7 8 9

© Houghton Mifflin Harcourt Publishing Company

Module
8 Understand and Analyze Functions

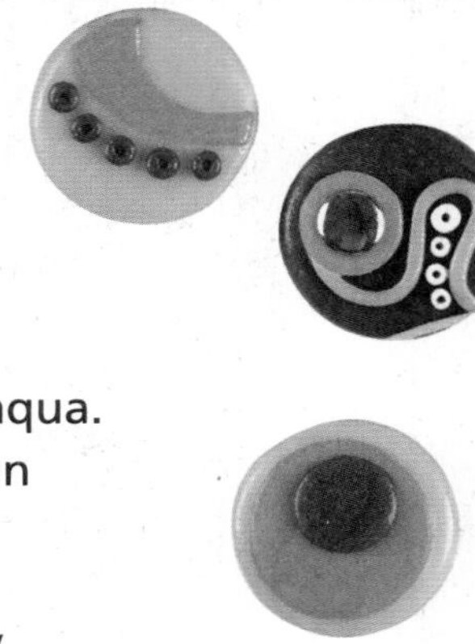

Bead or No Bead

A jeweler makes clay beads. To make the beads, different amounts of yellow clay and turquoise clay are mixed to make two new colors: lime and aqua. Lime has a greater ratio of yellow to turquoise than aqua does.

Fill in whether each mixture makes lime or aqua clay.

Mixture	Grams of yellow	Grams of turquoise	Color
A	16	12	
B	24	16	
C	30	20	
D	40	30	

For each color, write an equation that models the relationship between the amounts of yellow clay *y* and turquoise clay *t* used to make it.

Lime: ________ Aqua: ________

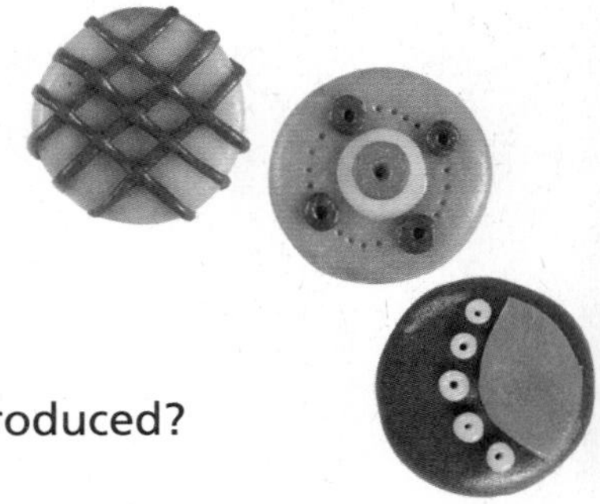

Turn and Talk

How did you know which color each mixture produced?

© Houghton Mifflin Harcourt Publishing Company • Image Credits: (t) ©Sergey Goruppa/Shutterstock; ©Steve Williams/Houghton Mifflin Harcourt

Are You Ready?

Complete these problems to review prior concepts and skills you will need for this module.

Represent Relationships with Variables

Identify the independent variable and the dependent variable for each situation.

1. the relationship between the amount of water *w* a household uses and the amount of the household's water bill *b*

independent: _____ dependent: _____

2. the relationship between the number of bags *b* of dog food a pet owner buys and the number of dogs *d* the pet owner has

independent: _____ dependent: _____

Model Proportional Relationships

Each table represents a proportional relationship. Write an equation to represent the relationship.

3.

Cups of flour, x	6	9	15
Loaves of bread, y	2	3	5

____

4.

Time (min), x	5	8	12
Distance (ft), y	75	120	180

____

Graph Proportional Relationships

Graph each proportional relationship.

5. $y = 4x$

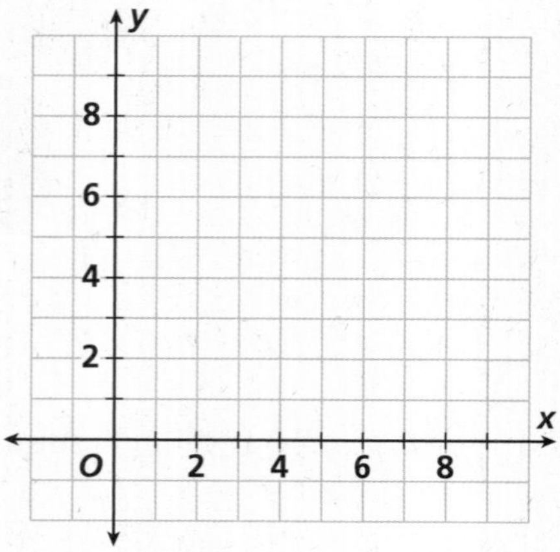

6. $y = \frac{2}{3}x$

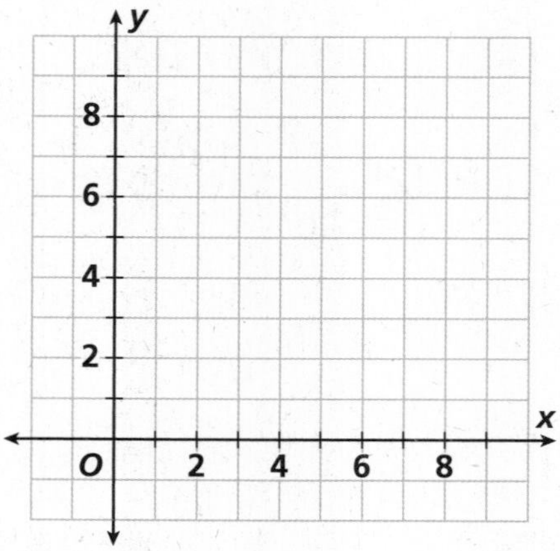

© Houghton Mifflin Harcourt Publishing Company

Name ____________________

Understand and Graph Functions

I Can form coordinate-pair tables from real-life scenarios, graph coordinate pairs from a table, and identify functions from both tables and graphs.

Spark Your Learning

PAIRS

Gina is researching purchasing a mobile device. The graph represents Gina's total cost of owning a device for the first year. What can you interpret about her costs from the graph?

Mobile Device Expense

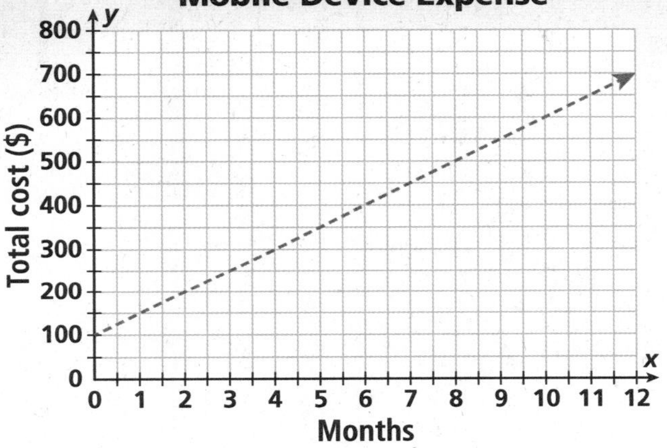

Turn and Talk The graph shows the cost for 12 months. How can you determine the cost for 13 or more months?

© Houghton Mifflin Harcourt Publishing Company • Image Credit: ©PaeJar/Shutterstock

Build Understanding

Connect to Vocabulary

A **relation** is any set of paired input and output values.

A **function** is a rule that assigns exactly one output to each input. Multiple inputs may have the same output value, but one input value may not have multiple output values.

The set of all possible **input** values of a function is known as the **domain**. The set of all possible **output** values of a function is known as the **range**.

1 A. Gina's cost, rounded to the nearest dollar, to operate a mobile device is a function. Gina's cost accumulates over the number of months she has the account, so months are the input for the function. Since the function's domain is defined by its input, what is the domain of this function? Why?

B. The total cost is the output of the function, which is the function's range. What is the range of the function? Why?

C. Gina's plan includes up to 50 free texts in the monthly fee. Does this table show a function? Explain.

Month	1	2	3	4	5	6
Texts used	41	26	32	35	37	43

D. A mistake was made in Gina's text usage and the number of texts for Month 5 was changed to be the same as for Month 4. Does the table show a function? Explain.

Month	1	2	3	4	5	6
Texts used	41	26	32	35	35	43

E. If the 2 in the Month row is accidentally changed to a 1, does the table show a function? Explain.

Month	1	1	3	4	5	6
Texts used	41	26	32	35	33	43

Turn and Talk Explain in your own words the difference between a function and a relation.

© Houghton Mifflin Harcourt Publishing Company • **Image Credit:** ©Daisy Daisy/Shutterstock

Name

Step It Out

2 Erin is taking a taxi to a destination no more than 10 miles away. The table shows what the cost of the taxi ride will be if it costs $6.00 to be picked up and an additional $2.00 per mile (prorated for partial miles).

Miles	0	2	4	6	8	10
Cost ($)	6	10	14	18	22	26

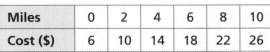

A. Describe the domain.

The domain is the number of miles

from ____ through ____.

B. Describe the range.

The minimum charge, for 0 miles, is ____ .

The cost for 10 miles is ____ .

The range is the numbers of dollars from ____ through ____.

C. The *x*-axis scale is based on the [domain / range] and should include values from ____ to ____. The *y*-axis scale is based on the [domain / range] and should include values from ____ to ____.

D. Plot the data in the table on the coordinate grid using the values in the table as ordered pairs, and draw a line through the plotted points. Miles are the input to the function and represented as *x*, and cost is the output of the function and represented by *y* in the ordered pairs.

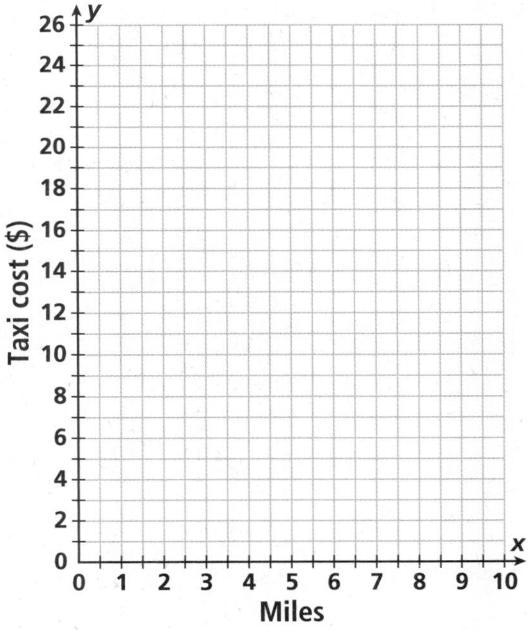

E. If Erin's taxi ride is 7 miles, how much will the taxi ride cost? Explain.

____

____

© Houghton Mifflin Harcourt Publishing Company • Image Credit: ©2shrimpS/Shutterstock

Turn and Talk If Erin paid $24, how many miles was her taxi ride? Explain.

The **vertical line test** can help determine whether a graph is a function or not by visually identifying where a single domain value is associated with more than one range value. If any vertical line can be drawn that passes through the graph more than once, the graph is not a function.

3 For each plot use the vertical line test to determine whether the plot shows a function. If the plot is not a function, draw a vertical line that intersects more than one point on the graph.

A.
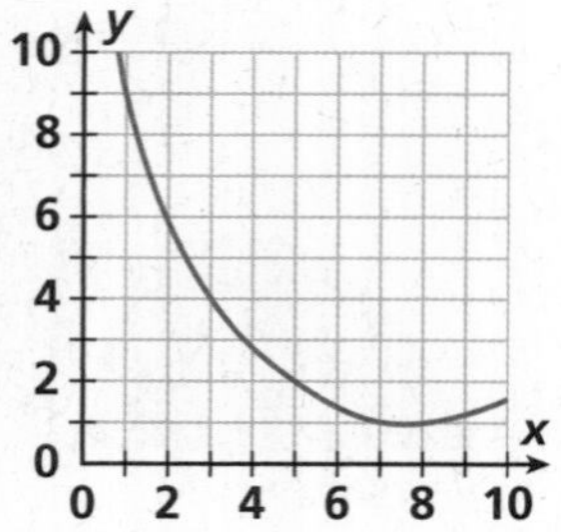

The graph | is / is not | a function.

B.
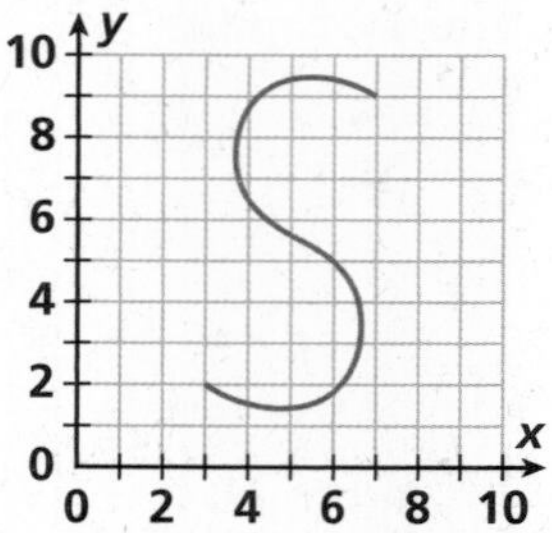

The graph | is / is not | a function.

C.
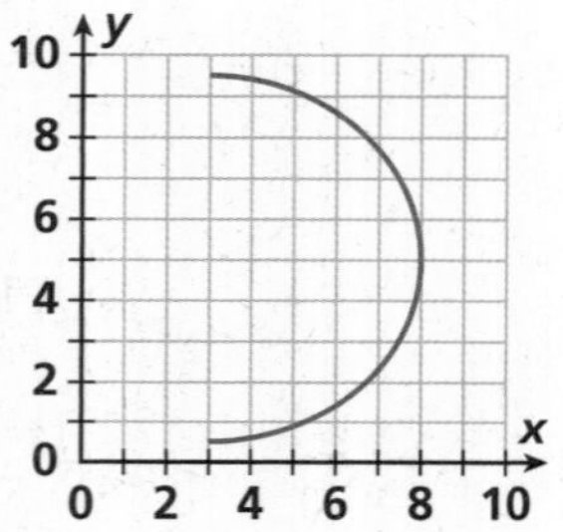

The graph | is / is not | a function.

D.
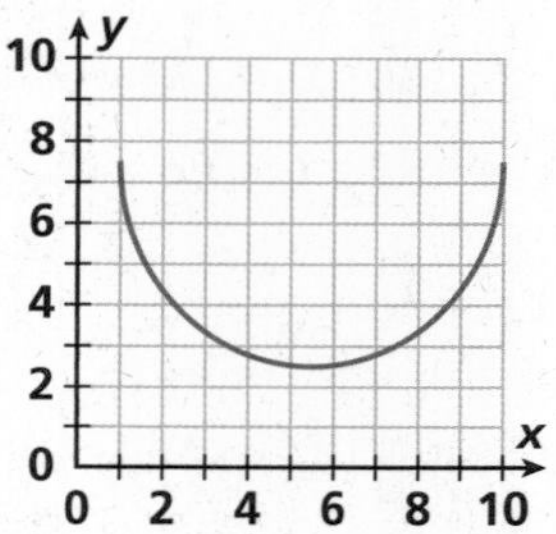

The graph | is / is not | a function.

Check Understanding

1. The function plotted represents the height of an arrow that is shot into the air and returns to the ground over time. From the graph, what are the domain, the range, and the plotted coordinates of the function?

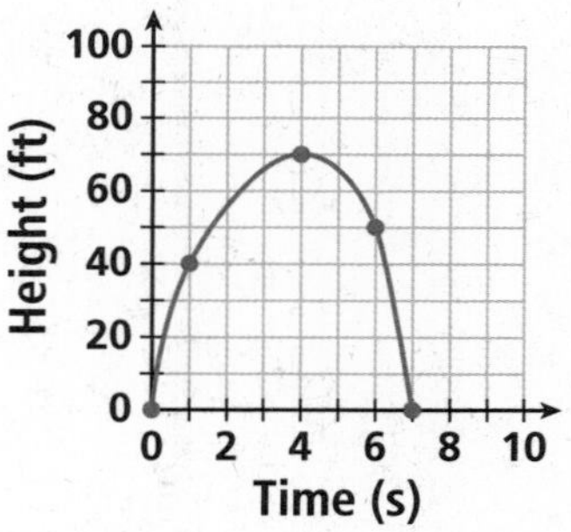

Domain: ______________________

Range: ______________________

Coordinates: ______________________

2. Does the oval graph represent a function? Explain.

____

____

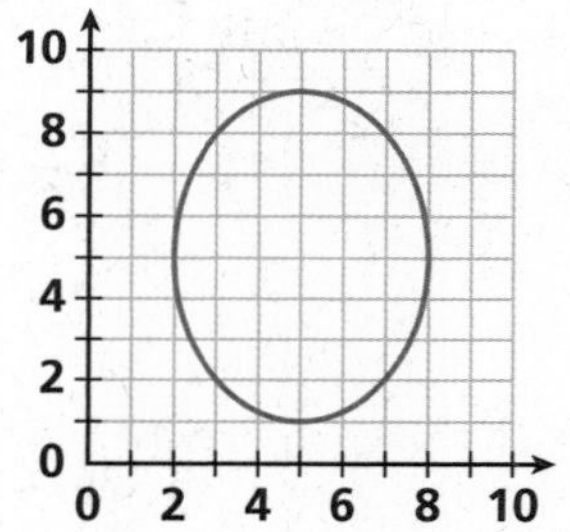

© Houghton Mifflin Harcourt Publishing Company

Name

On Your Own

3. Rico has a mobile device plan that charges only a \$4 monthly fee. He is also charged \$0.30 per minute for calls.

A. Fill in the table for the total cost per month for Rico to use his device for the given number of minutes.

Minutes	0	10	20	30	40	50	60
Total cost							

B. What is the domain of the function for Rico's mobile plan?

____

4. **STEM** An architect proposes a roof 36 feet wide that rises 1 foot for every 6 feet to its center, then sinks at the same rate to its end. The table shows the height of the roofline if its base is 12 feet high.

A. Complete the table.

Distance from left edge (ft)	0	6	12	18	24	30	36
Roof height from ground (ft)	12	13					12

B. Plot the graph of the roofline's height from the data in the table.

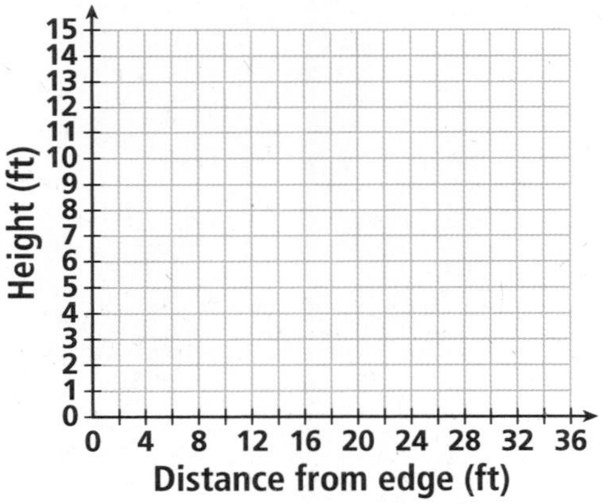

C. What is the range of the function representing the roofline?

____

D. What is the domain of the function representing the roofline?

____

5. (MP) **Use Structure** If the domain of the function $y = 4x + 1$ is $0 \leq x \leq 10$, what is the function's range? (Hint: Graph the line.)

____

© Houghton Mifflin Harcourt Publishing Company • Image Credit: ©John Burcham/Getty Images

MP Reason For Problems 6–7, determine whether the graph is a function and explain your reasoning.

6.

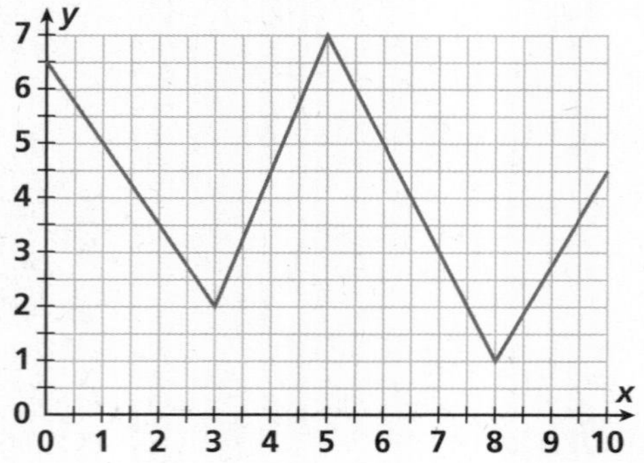

____

____

____

7.

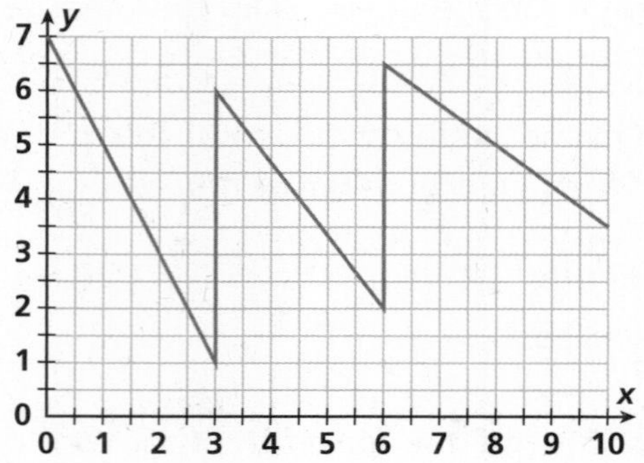

____

____

____

8. Emir is ordering movie tickets online for himself and up to three of his coworkers. The ordering fee is $4 and the cost per ticket is $8. Plot the function that represents the total cost of the tickets.

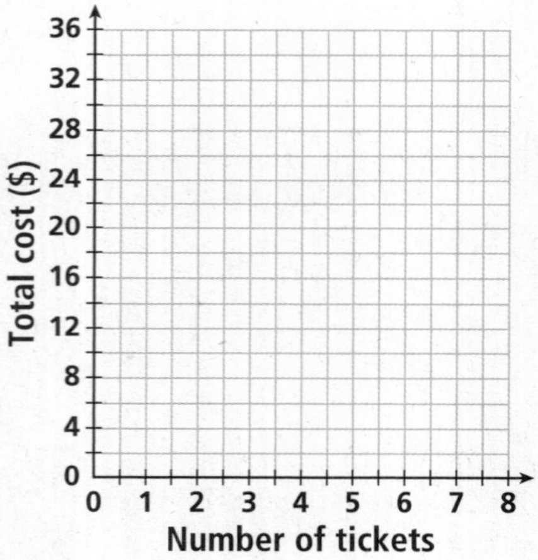

9. **Open Ended** Describe and graph a real-life situation that would represent a function.

____

____

I'm in a Learning Mindset!

How was identifying a function on a graph an appropriate challenge for me?

____

____

© Houghton Mifflin Harcourt Publishing Company • **Image Credit:** ©Rawpixel.com/Shutterstock

Name ______________________

LESSON 8.1
More Practice/ Homework

ONLINE
Video Tutorials and Interactive Examples

Understand and Graph Functions

Use the information to answer Problems 1–3.

Mrs. Aviles is planning a fruit-cup party for a class of 18 students and two teachers. She spends $10 for a package of snacks and also takes orders in advance for fruit cups that cost $3 each.

1. Describe the domain of the function both in words and numbers.

____

____

2. What is the range of the function?

____

3. Plot the data in the table on the coordinate plane. If the graph is continuous, draw a solid line through the plotted points.

Fruit Cup Orders	0	5	10	15	20
Cost ($)	10	25	40	55	70

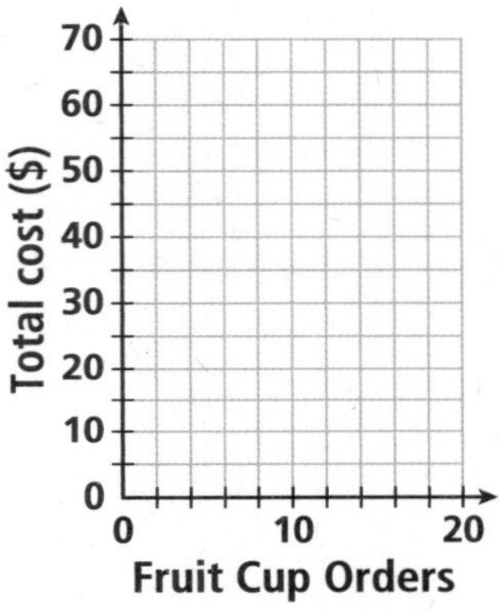

Use the graph to answer Problems 4 and 5.

4. (MP) **Construct Arguments** Does the graph represent a function? Explain.

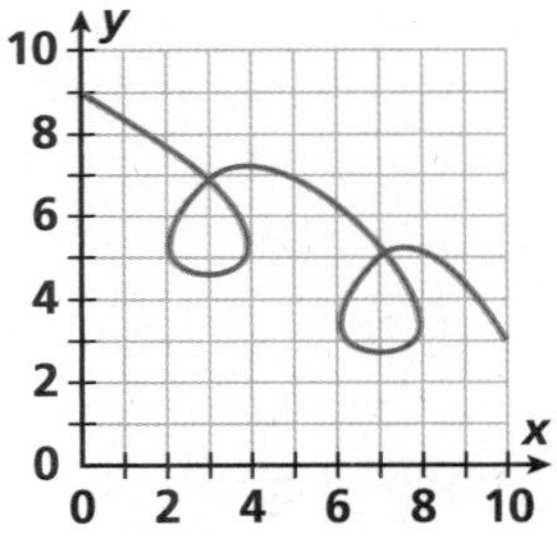

____

____

____

5. Name a section of the graph that, taken in isolation, is a function.

____

____

____

6. **Open Ended** Draw a graph that does not represent a function.

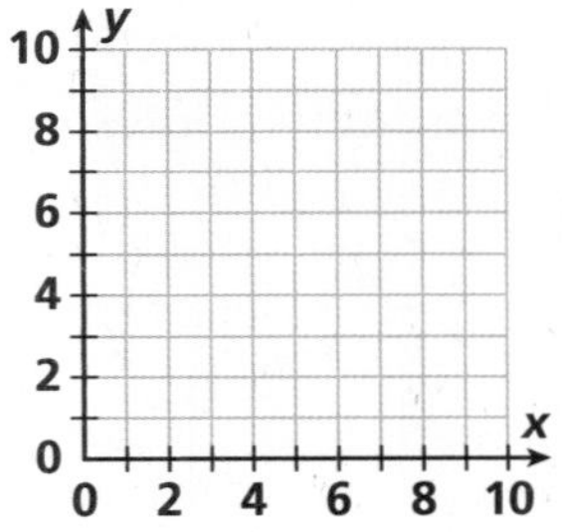

© Houghton Mifflin Harcourt Publishing Company • Image Credit: ©Oleksandra Naumenko/Shutterstock

Test Prep

7. Athar is buying hats for his baseball team. The shipping charge is $5, and each hat costs $8. There are ten people on his baseball team. The graph shows the total cost of the hats. Select all the true statements.

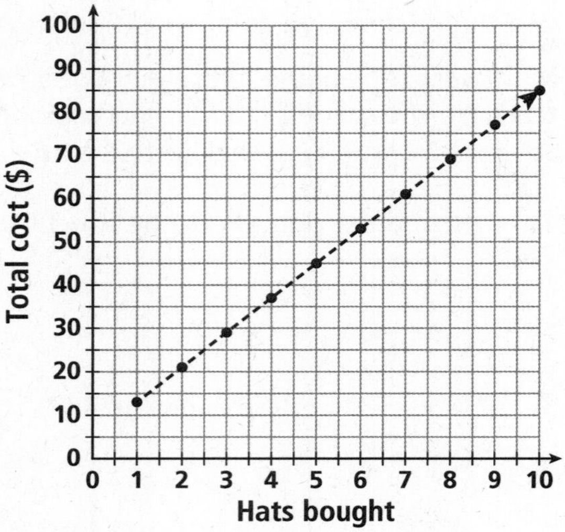

Ⓐ The ordered pair for 1 hat bought is (1, 8).

Ⓑ The domain is whole numbers of hats from 1 to 10.

Ⓒ The range is numbers of dollars from 0 to 100 in increments of 5.

Ⓓ The ordered pair for 5 hats bought is (5, 45).

Ⓔ The cost of ordering 10 hats is double the cost of ordering 5 hats.

8. An engineer is launching a rocket and is measuring its speed when launched. The table shows the speed for the first five seconds. Plot the data in the provided coordinate plane.

Time (s)	0	1	2	3	4	5
Speed (m/s)	0	4	8	12	16	20

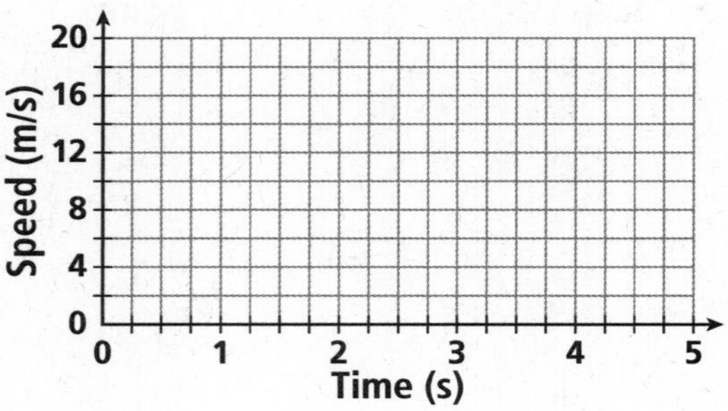

Spiral Review

9. What is the unit rate for the proportional relationship represented in the graph?

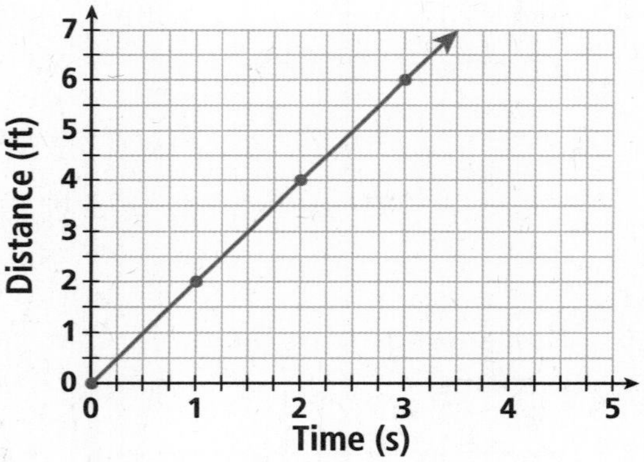

____

10. A painter has up to 16 hours to paint a living room and two bedrooms. He spends 7 hours painting the living room. Write and solve an inequality to find how much time he can spend on each bedroom if he splits his time equally.

____

____

11. Two complementary angles measure $(4x + 5)°$ and $(2x + 7)°$. What is the value of x? What are the measures of the angles?

____

____

© Houghton Mifflin Harcourt Publishing Company

Name ____________________

Derive and Interpret $y = mx + b$

I Can derive the equation for a line in the form $y = mx + b$ given the slope of the line and a point.

Spark Your Learning

PAIRS

Based on data from a science experiment, Sierra graphs Lines *A*, *B*, and *C*. Compare the lines. How are they the same? How are they different?

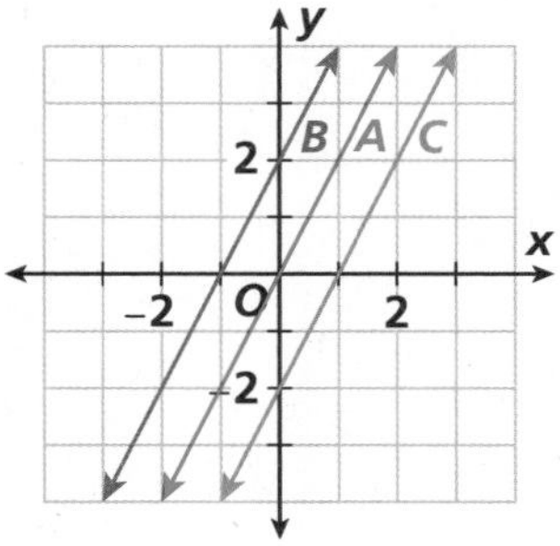

Turn and Talk What would be the equation of a line that passes through the origin and the point (1, −2)? Explain.

© Houghton Mifflin Harcourt Publishing Company • Image Credit: ©Nancy Honey/The Image Bank/Getty Images

Build Understanding

1 The ***y*-intercept** of a graph is the *y*-coordinate of the point where the graph crosses the *y*-axis, or the value of *y* when *x* equals 0. A line that passes through the origin can be represented by an equation of the form $y = mx$.

A. Consider a line with slope *m* and *y*-intercept *b*. Write the ordered pair that represents the *y*-intercept.

____

B. Recall that slope is rise over run, or the ratio of change in *y* to change in *x*. Complete the equation for the slope *m* of the line using the point from Part A and another point on the line (*x*, *y*).

$$m = \frac{y - \square}{\square - 0}$$

C. Solve the equation from Part B for *y*.

The $y = mx + b$ form of the equation of a line is called **slope-intercept form**.

D. Identify the slope and *y*-intercept of each graph.

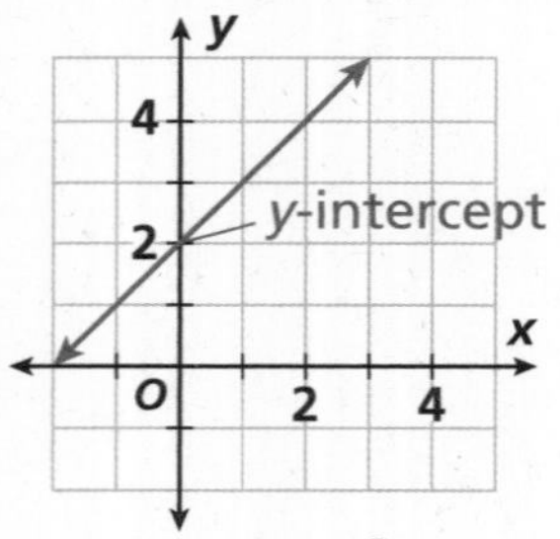

$y = x + 2$

slope: ______

y-intercept: ______

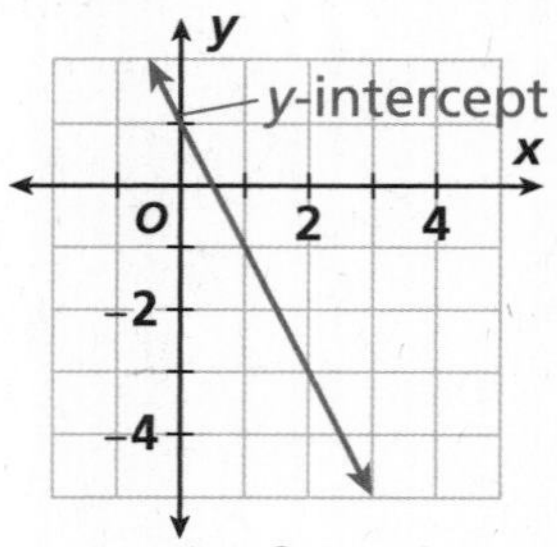

$y = -2x + 1$

slope: ______

y-intercept: ______

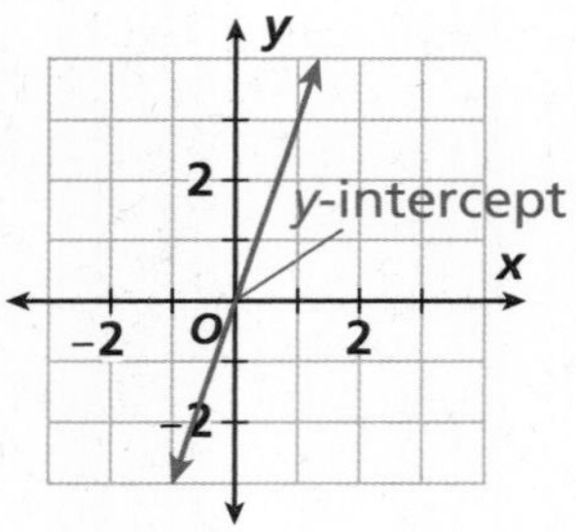

$y = 3x$

slope: ______

y-intercept: ______

E. How do the coefficient *m* of *x* and the constant *b* in each equation relate to the slope and *y*-intercept?

____

____

© Houghton Mifflin Harcourt Publishing Company

Step It Out

2 A. Is the slope of Line *A* positive or negative? Is the slope of Line *B* positive or negative?

____

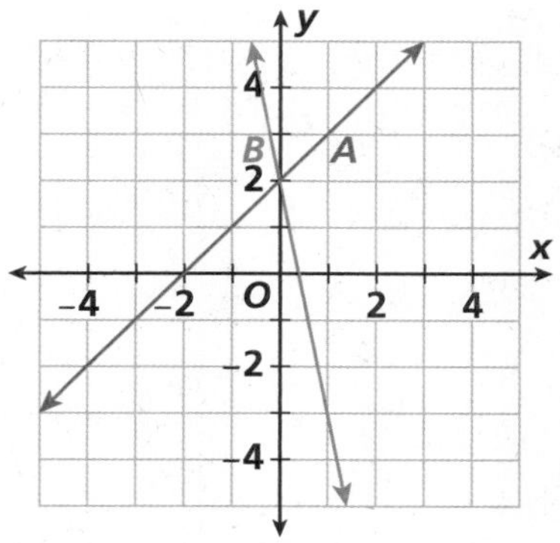

B. Find the slope of each line.

Line *A*: ☐ Line *B*: ☐

C. What are the y-intercepts of the lines?

____

D. Write the equation of Line *A* in slope-intercept form.

$y =$ ☐ $x +$ ☐

E. Write the equation of Line *B* in slope-intercept form.

$y =$ ☐ $x +$ ☐

3 A line has a slope $m = -1$. One point on the line is (2, 4). Substitute the x, y, and m values into the slope-intercept form of an equation to find the y-intercept. Then write the equation of the line in slope-intercept form.

$y =$ ☐, $m =$ ☐, and $x =$ ☐

$y = mx + b$

☐ $= -1$ (☐) $+ b$

☐ $=$ ☐ $+ b$

☐ $= b$

The y-intercept is ____.

The equation of the line is $y =$ ☐ $x +$ ☐.

Turn and Talk Does the graph of $y = 3x - 3$ pass through the origin? If so, how do you know? If not, what is the y-intercept?

© Houghton Mifflin Harcourt Publishing Company

Linear functions contain only points that lie on a straight line. Some examples of nonlinear functions are:

$yx = 5$ $\qquad y = \frac{2}{x}$ $\qquad y = x^2 + 2$

Connect to Vocabulary

The equation of any line can be written in the form $y = mx + b$. The graphs of functions whose equations cannot be put into this form are not straight lines. Such functions are called **nonlinear functions**.

4 Solve each equation for y. Then determine whether the function is linear or nonlinear.

A. $5y = 13x - 9$ ______________________

B. $\frac{y}{6} = 1$ ______________________

C. $xy = 25$ ______________________

$2y = 14x + 6$

divide both sides by 2

$y = 7x + 3$

LINEAR

$2xy = 36$

divide both sides by 2

$xy = 18$

divide both sides by x

$y = \frac{18}{x}$

NONLINEAR

Nonlinear functions contain points that do not lie on a straight line with the other points. For example, the formula for the area of a square, $A = s^2$, is nonlinear because it contains the points (1, 1), (3, 9), and (4, 16), which do not all lie on a straight line.

5 Graph three points for each equation on your own paper. Is the equation linear or nonlinear? List the three points you used.

A. $\frac{7}{2} = x - y$

____

B. $y = x^2 + x + 1$

____

C. $y - 3 = \frac{5x}{2}$

____

Check Understanding

1. The slope of a line is −3, and a point on the line is (4, −1). Can the equation of the line be expressed in slope-intercept form? If so, what is the equation? Does the line pass through the origin? How do you know?

____

____

2. Is the graph of $y = x^2 + 2$ a straight line? Explain.

____

____

© Houghton Mifflin Harcourt Publishing Company

Name

On Your Own

Use the information to answer Problems 3–4.

Abha is climbing a mountain. While covering 20 yards of horizontal distance, Abha's elevation increases by 40 yards. Consider Abha's climb as a linear function.

3. What is the slope of her climb?

4. When would the slope of Abha's climb be negative?

5. Does the line $54y = 13x$ pass through the origin? How do you know?

6. Daliyah is given one point on a line as (3, −1) and the slope of the line as −5.

A. What is the *y*-intercept of the line?

B. (MP) **Model with Mathematics** Write the equation of the line.

7. **Open Ended** Write one linear and one nonlinear equation.

For Problems 8–9, write the equation in slope-intercept form, identify the sign of the slope, and state whether the line passes through the origin.

8. $2y - 3x = 4$

9. $-5 = -y - 3x$

(MP) **Model with Mathematics** **For Problems 10–11, write the slope-intercept form of the line with the given slope and point.**

10. $m = 4$; (2, 3)

11. $m = -2$; (5, 1)

12. (MP) **Reason** Which graph is steeper: $y = -20x + 1$ or $y = 10x + 1$?

© Houghton Mifflin Harcourt Publishing Company

13. A. On the coordinate plane provided, plot the points (−2, −2), (−1, 1), and (1, 7), Connect the points with a straight line.

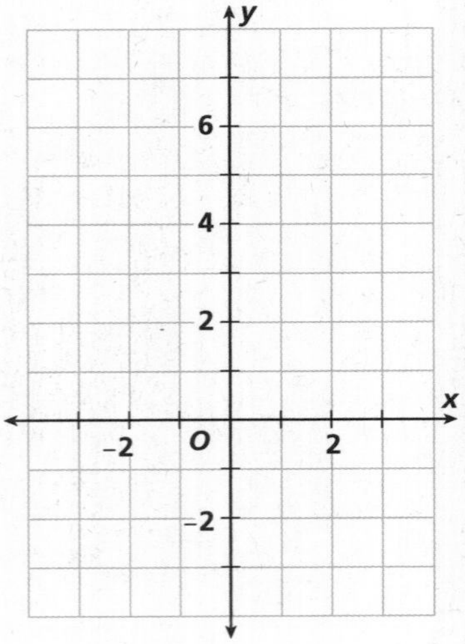

B. For each 1 unit increase in x, how much does y increase? What is the name for this value?

____

C. Does the line pass through the origin? What is the y-intercept?

____

D. (MP) **Model with Mathematics** What is the equation of the line in slope-intercept form?

____

E. Is the line with the equation $y = 3x + 1$ parallel to the line from Part A? Explain. (Hint: Graph the lines.)

____

14. Graph three points for the equation $x + (2y) - 1 = 9$ and determine if it is linear or nonlinear. List the points you used.

____

I'm in a Learning Mindset!

How does my understanding of equations in slope-intercept form impact my ability to find parallel lines?

____

____

© Houghton Mifflin Harcourt Publishing Company • Image Credit: ©genkur/iStock/Getty Images Plus/Getty Images

Name ______________________

LESSON 8.2
More Practice/ Homework

ONLINE
Video Tutorials and Interactive Examples

Derive and Interpret $y = mx + b$

1. **Attend to Precision** Tasha wants to graph a line that is parallel to the line with equation $y = 3x$. Give two examples of lines she could draw, one that is above the original line and one that is below the original line.

____

2. Shyann is trying to figure out if the line with equation $y = 5683x + 976$ will pass through the origin. Will the line pass through the origin? How do you know?

____

3. Paulo identifies one point on a line as (6, 3), and he knows that the slope is 2. How can he derive the equation of the line?

____

4. **Math on the Spot** An arcade deducts 3.5 points from a 50-point game card for each game played. The linear equation $y = -3.5x + 50$ represents the number of points y on a card after x games played. Graph the equation using the slope and y-intercept.

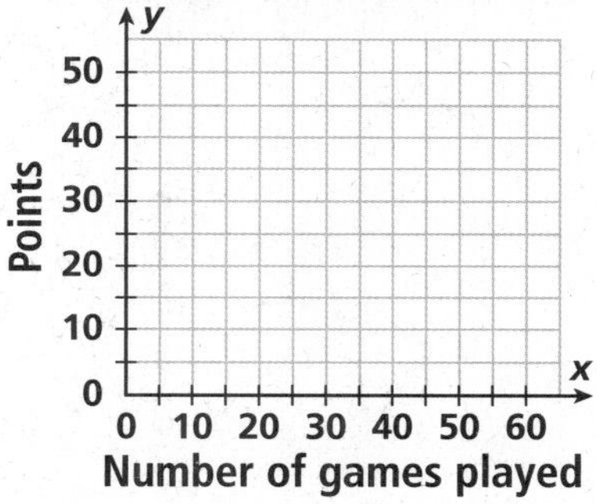

Write each equation in slope-intercept form and identify the y-intercept.

5. $5 = 10x - 5y$

6. $12x = -4y - 8$

Identify the slope and state whether the line rises or falls from left to right.

7. $y = 3x - 11$

8. $y = -\frac{1}{2}x + 2$

Identify the function as linear or nonlinear.

9. $y = \frac{3}{2}x + 9$

10. $y = \frac{3}{2x} + 9$

© Houghton Mifflin Harcourt Publishing Company • Image Credit: ©Bonnie Kamin/PhotoEdit

Test Prep

11. Find the equation of a line with slope −2 that contains the point (−3, 3).

$y = \square\, x - \square$

For Problems 12–14, complete each statement for the equation $y = \frac{1}{2}x - \frac{1}{2}$.

12. Is the equation linear or nonlinear? ______________

13. Is the equation a function? ______________

14. The graph crosses the *y*-axis at (0, ________).

15. Roscoe has a pie baking business. His profit is given by the equation $y = 15x - 5$. Sheena has a cake baking business. Her profit is given by an equation with a graph that is parallel to the graph of the equation for Roscoe's profit. Which equation could represent Sheena's profit?

Ⓐ $y = 15x + 10$

Ⓑ $y = 3x - 1$

Ⓒ $y = 5x - 5$

Ⓓ $y = -15x - 3$

16. Identify whether each equation is linear or nonlinear.

	Linear	Nonlinear
$xy = 4$	☐	☐
$4 = x - y$	☐	☐
$y = \frac{5}{4}x + \frac{1}{2}$	☐	☐
$y = x^2 + 1$	☐	☐

Spiral Review

17. Mr. Chin asked his class to solve for *y* in the equation $8(3y - 5) = 9(y - 5) - 1$. Explain how to solve for *y*. Then solve.

____

____

18. Claire wants to start a stamp collection. She spends \$15 on an album to hold her stamps and \$1.25 for each stamp. If she has \$40, what is the maximum number of stamps she can buy?

____

19. How many triangles can you construct with side lengths 5 inches, 8 inches, and 20 inches?

____

© Houghton Mifflin Harcourt Publishing Company

Name ______________________

Interpret Rate of Change and Initial Value

I Can **find and interpret initial value and rate of change of a function.**

Spark Your Learning

SMALL GROUPS

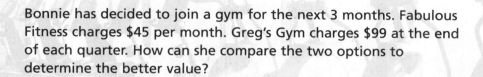

Bonnie has decided to join a gym for the next 3 months. Fabulous Fitness charges $45 per month. Greg's Gym charges $99 at the end of each quarter. How can she compare the two options to determine the better value?

Turn and Talk What is the rate of change per month for each membership and how do you know?

© Houghton Mifflin Harcourt Publishing Company • **Image Credit:** ©ER_09/Shutterstock

Build Understanding

Many real-world functional relationships have only nonnegative inputs and rates of change that are constant. You can use initial value and the rate of change to analyze such functions. Initial value is the value of a function when the input is zero. A constant rate of change describes the slope or steepness of a graph, or how quickly two quantities change.

1 Bonnie continues to research gym options and finds out that Fabulous Fitness charges no sign-up fee, while Greg's Gym charges \$50 for the initial sign-up. She makes the following table to help her compare the two options.

Costs	FABULOUS FITNESS	GREG'S GYM
Sign-up fee	\$0	\$50
Month 1	\$45	\$0
Month 2	\$45	\$0
Month 3	\$45	\$99

A. How much would Bonnie need to pay just to join each gym?

B. How much would Bonnie need to pay per month at each gym?

C. Use an equation to calculate the total cost for three months of each gym option. Show your work.

D. In the equation $y = mx + b$, the slope m represents the constant rate of change, or cost per month. What does the y-intercept b represent on the graph of the function?

Turn and Talk Why is it important to consider both initial value and rate of change when modeling functions in the real world?

© Houghton Mifflin Harcourt Publishing Company

Name

Step It Out

2 The owner of Fabulous Fitness wants to buy name tags for her staff. She writes the following linear function to represent the cost y for the quantity of name tags x from an online vendor.

$y = \$2.00x + \$7.00$

A. What is the rate of change?

____

B. What is the initial value and what could it represent?

____

____

C. The function representing the cost of the name tags purchased is shown in the graph. Complete the coordinates of the point shown on the graph.

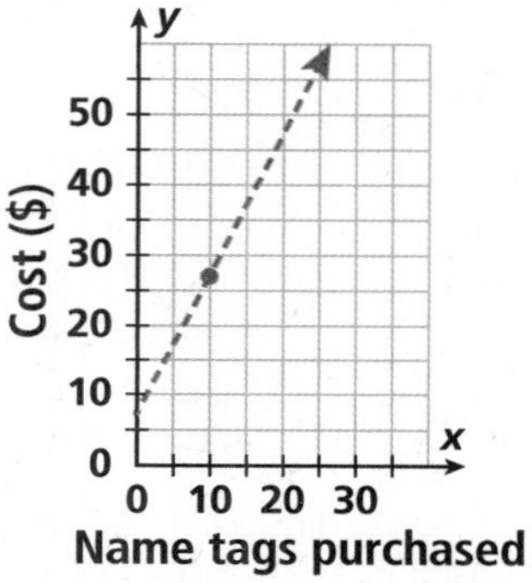

$(10, \square)$

D. Explain what the point means.

It will cost ________ for ________ name tags.

E. Substitute 25 for x in the equation and solve for y.

$y = 2x + 7$

$y = 2(\square) + 7$

$y = \square$

F. What point represents the values in Part E?

$(\square, \square)$

G. What is the meaning of the point?

It will cost ________ for ________ name tags.

H. How many name tags can the owner purchase for $93.00?

____

I. How did you determine the answer to Part H?

____

© Houghton Mifflin Harcourt Publishing Company

3 The following table shows how the value of a new car depreciates, or decreases, over time.

Time (yr)	0	1	2	3	4
Value ($)	24,000	20,000	18,000	17,000	15,000

A. What is the purchase price of the car? ______

B. Calculate the slope using these two points: (1, 20,000) and (3, 17,000).

$m =$ ☐

C. Calculate the slope using these two points: (3, 17,000) and (4, 15,000).

$m =$ ☐

D. Compare the two slopes. What do you notice?

They are / are not equal.

E. Explain whether or not the depreciation of the car is a linear function.

The rate of change is / is not constant, so the depreciation is / is not a linear function.

Check Understanding

1. Sam has $37 to spend at a festival. The price of admission is $10 and tickets to each attraction cost $0.75. How many tickets can he buy?

A. What is the initial value, and what does it represent?

______

______

B. What is the rate of change?

______

C. What is the maximum number of tickets Sam can purchase? Explain.

______

______

D. Complete the table for Sam's trip to the festival.

Number of tickets		5		15
Total cost	$10.75		$17.50	

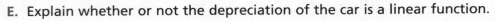

© Houghton Mifflin Harcourt Publishing Company • Image Credit: ©Robert Churchill/iStockphoto/Getty Images

Name

On Your Own

(MP) Reason **Use the following information to answer Problems 2–3.**

Jeffrey is shopping for a new mobile device. He needs a device as well as a data plan. He is deciding between the following two options:

	Option 1	Option 2
One-time phone cost	\$100	\$0
Data plan cost per month	\$100	\$150
Term	No commitment	One year

2. Which option has the lower initial value?

3. Which option has the lower rate of change?

4. (MP) Construct Arguments Toni is deciding whether to subscribe to app A or app B for streaming music. App A offers listeners a \$4 startup fee plus \$0.15 per song. App B offers listeners no startup fee and charges \$0.40 per song.

A. Which function has a greater initial value? Explain.

B. Which app has a greater rate of change? How can you tell?

C. Toni wants to listen to 20 songs per month. Which app should she choose? Why?

© Houghton Mifflin Harcourt Publishing Company • Image Credit: ©Gregory Costanzo/Getty Images

The graph shows the value of a comic book over time after a collector buys it. Use the graph for Problems 5–8.

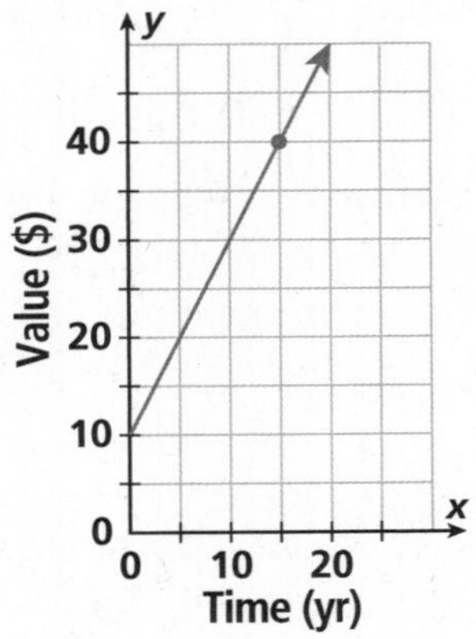

5. Is the rate of change positive or negative? What does this mean?

---

6. What does the point (15, 40) mean in the context of this linear function?

After ☐ years, the comic book is worth ☐ dollars.

7. **A.** Where do you find the initial value on this graph?

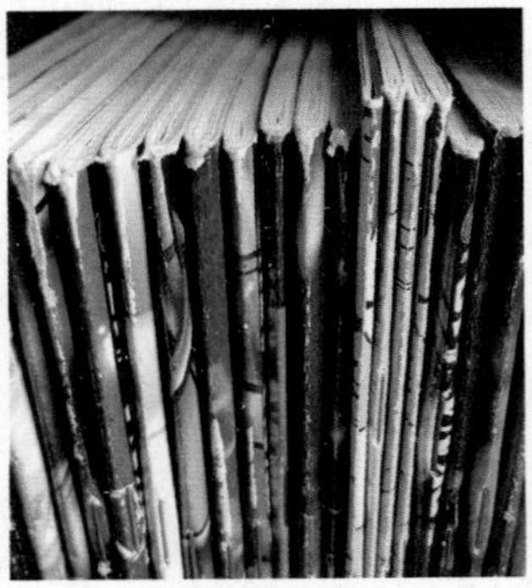

B. What is the initial value? What does it represent?

C. What is the slope of the line? What does it represent?

D. (MP) **Model with Mathematics** Write the equation of the line.

E. Use the linear equation to find the value of the comic book after 25 years.

---

8. **A.** If you extend the line, what is its x-intercept, the x-coordinate where the line crosses the x-axis?

B. Does the x-intercept make sense in the context of the problem? Explain.

I'm in a Learning Mindset!

What obstacles did I overcome to interpret the value of the comic book over time using the graph?

© Houghton Mifflin Harcourt Publishing Company • Image Credit: ©Studio Matitanera/Shutterstock

Name ______________________________

LESSON 8.3
More Practice/ Homework

ONLINE
Video Tutorials and Interactive Examples

Interpret Rate of Change and Initial Value

Use the information to answer Problems 1–3.

The following table shows the cost to order muffins to be delivered from a bakery.

Muffins	1	5	10	50	100
Cost ($)	17	25	35	115	215

1. What is the rate of change?

____

2. What is the initial value?

____

3. (MP) **Use Structure** Explain what the rate of change and initial value mean in this context.

____

____

____

Use the information to answer Problems 4–6.

The following linear function represents the cost of a home printer plus ink cartridges, where x represents the number of ink cartridges purchased and y represents the total cost.

$y = 25x + 115$

4. What is the rate of change, and what does it represent?

____

____

5. How much does the printer itself cost?

____

6. How much will the purchaser spend buying the printer and 6 ink cartridges?

____

7. **Open Ended** Write a scenario that can be modeled by the linear function $y = 25x + 40$.

____

____

© Houghton Mifflin Harcourt Publishing Company • Image Credit: (tr) ©David Hancock/Alamy; (br) ©Okssi68/iStock/Getty Images Plus/Getty Images

Test Prep

8. Jose starts a savings account with \$80. At the end of 6 months, the account has \$350. Assuming there is a constant rate, how much did Jose save per month?

Ⓐ \$270

Ⓑ \$72

Ⓒ \$60

Ⓓ \$45

9. Camille wants to set up a hot chocolate stand to raise money. She spends \$40 on hot chocolate and \$0.25 for each paper cup. She uses the equation $y = 0.25x + 40$ to keep track of her spending. If Camille has \$60 in donations to spend, what is the maximum number of paper cups she can buy?

Ⓐ 5 cups

Ⓑ 80 cups

Ⓒ 240 cups

Ⓓ 400 cups

10. Admission to a carnival costs \$15. Each game costs \$2 to play. Which statements about the function modeling the cost to attend the carnival are true? Select all that apply.

Ⓐ The slope is positive.

Ⓑ The initial value is \$15.

Ⓒ The rate of change is \$15.

Ⓓ The graph has a *y*-intercept of 2.

Ⓔ The graph passes through the origin.

Spiral Review

11. Solve $4x - 12 = -7x - 111$.

____

12. Calculate the slope of the line that passes through (3, 2) and (−7, 4).

____

13. The table shows a proportional relationship. Complete the table.

x	y
1	4
2	
3	12
5	20

© Houghton Mifflin Harcourt Publishing Company

Name ______________________________

Construct and Compare Functions

I Can **construct and compare functions represented in equations, tables, graphs, or verbal descriptions.**

Spark Your Learning

SMALL GROUPS

A scuba diver descends from the surface of the ocean at a constant rate of 5 feet per minute to a maximum depth of 130 feet. The diver's depth in feet y is a function of the number of minutes x since the diver began descending. What do you know about the function?

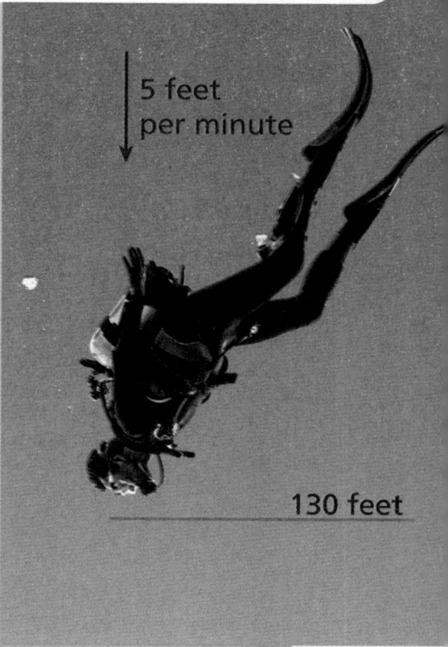

Turn and Talk Consider a function where x represents a number of people. Is this function discrete or continuous? What must be true of all x-values? Explain.

© Houghton Mifflin Harcourt Publishing Company • Image Credit: ©ostill/Shutterstock

Build Understanding

1 The parking lot near the scuba company opens for the day at 6:00 a.m. Between 7:00 a.m. and 11:00 a.m., cars park at a constant rate of 50 per hour. At 10:00 a.m., 165 cars are parked in the lot. Write an equation that represents the situation in the form $y = mx + b$.

A. What is a known point of the function, and what does each coordinate of the point represent?

B. What is the slope of the function? Use the slope and known point of the function to find the y-intercept and write the equation of the line.

C. Can time be a fractional number? Why or why not?

D. Can the number of cars be a fractional number? Explain.

E. Is this function discrete or continuous? Why?

F. What are the limits on what y can equal? How do you know?

G. What are the limits on what x can equal?

H. What does the y-intercept of the function represent in this equation?

© Houghton Mifflin Harcourt Publishing Company • Image Credit: ©Merla/Shutterstock

Name ______________________________

Step It Out

Choosing how to represent a linear function depends upon the situation and what you need to know. When linear functions are represented differently, finding the slope and y-intercept for each can help compare information.

2 Four friends researched companies to host a website with the results of their science fair project. The friends need to decide which company to use. Some of the companies charge a one-time fee for a domain name.

Peter found this table for Company A's costs.

Months	Cost ($)
5	20
6	22
7	24
8	26
9	28
10	30

Robyn found an ad for Company B.

Marley found this graph for Company C's costs.

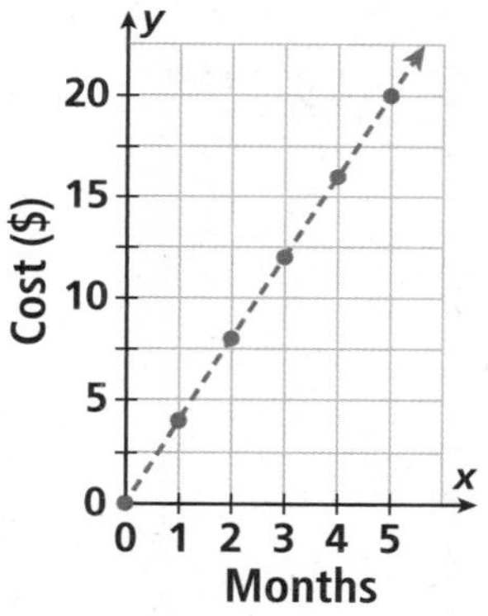

Claudia found this equation for Company D's costs.

$y = 3x + 5$

A. What are the slope and y-intercept for each representation?

Company A: slope = ☐ y-intercept: = ☐

Company B: slope = ☐ y-intercept: = ☐

Company C: slope = ☐ y-intercept: = ☐

Company D: slope = ☐ y-intercept: = ☐

B. What does the slope tell you about each company?

____

C. What does the y-intercept tell you about each company?

____

© Houghton Mifflin Harcourt Publishing Company • Image Credit: ©Wu Kailiang/Alamy

D. Peter says that Company C will always be the least expensive option because the domain name is free. Is Peter correct? Peter is / is not correct. Company _____ is the least expensive option for the first _____ months, but then starts to become more expensive than the other plans because the monthly charge / one-time fee is greater.

E. Marley says that Company A charges $2 per month. Is Marley correct? Marley is / is not correct. In the table, the cost increases by _____ for each additional month. This means the rate of change is / is not constant. The slope of the line is _____.

Turn and Talk Which representation do you prefer to use to decide which company offers the best plan long term? Explain your choice.

Check Understanding

Use the given information to answer Problems 1–3.

Lab Thinkers of Tomorrow has this table displayed on its website that shows its costs.

Months	Cost ($)
1	45
2	70
3	95
4	120
5	145

1. Roscoe wants to join a science club that sends him a new box of science experiments each month. Which club has the higher sign-up fee? Which has the higher monthly fee? Explain.

2. If Roscoe wanted to join a club for only six months, which club would be the better deal? Why?

3. Write equations for the total costs to join each club.

© Houghton Mifflin Harcourt Publishing Company • Image Credit: ©GlobalP/iStockphoto/Getty Images

Name

On Your Own

Use the graph and information to answer Problems 4–9.

Bridget has 13 gallons of gasoline to use for her lawn-mowing business. She uses gasoline in the lawn mower at a consistent rate. Let *x* represent the number of lawns mowed and *y* represent the amount of gasoline remaining. Look at the graph of this function. Construct the function for this scenario.

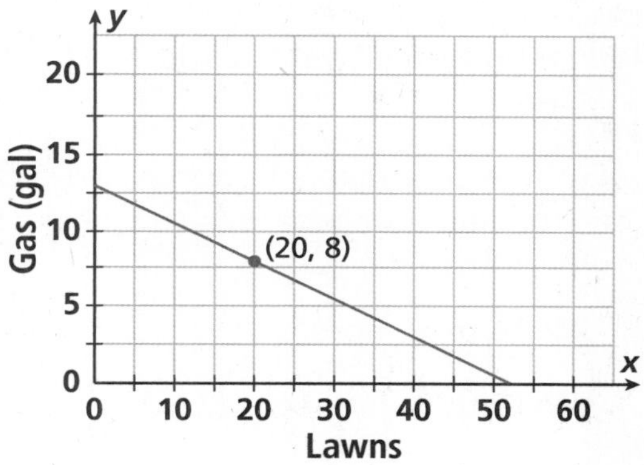

4. (MP) **Model with Mathematics** What is the equation of the line?

5. What is the initial value and what does it represent?

6. What is the slope and what does it mean?

7. (MP) **Reason** Is the graph discrete or continuous? Why?

8. (MP) **Attend to Precision** What is the domain? Explain any restrictions.

9. (MP) **Attend to Precision** What is the range? Explain any restrictions.

© Houghton Mifflin Harcourt Publishing Company • Image Credit: ©urbancow/iStock/Getty Images Plus/Getty Images

Use the information given to answer Problems 10–13.

Four aerial photographers need six batteries to operate their drones. Each found a different website that sells rechargeable batteries.

10. (MP) **Attend to Precision** Find the cost of 6 rechargeable batteries and a charger from each website. Which website has the best price?

Website A charges ________.

Website B charges ________.

Website C charges ________.

Website D charges ________.

Website ________ has the best price.

11. The fixed value represents

________________________.

The rate of change represents

________________________.

12. Determine the cost of the charger from Website C. ________

13. **Open Ended** Why might the photographers pick a battery that is not the cheapest?

____

____

____

____

Website A

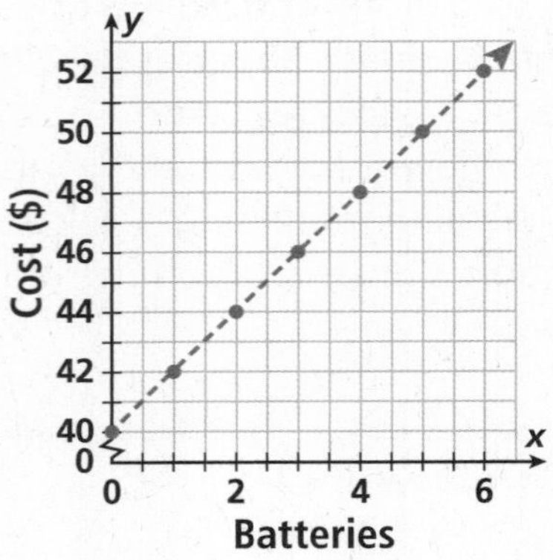

Website B

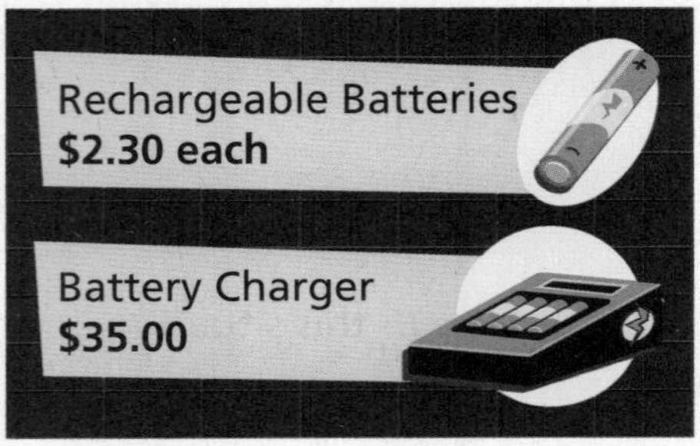

Website C

Batteries	Cost ($)
1	39.10
2	41.20
3	43.30
4	45.40
5	47.50
6	49.60

Website D

$y = 3.5x + 28$

© Houghton Mifflin Harcourt Publishing Company

I'm in a Learning Mindset!

Where do I fall within the growth-mindset spectrum when I write a linear function?

____

____

Name ______________________________

ONLINE
Ed
Video Tutorials and
Interactive Examples

Construct and Compare Functions

Use the information given to answer Problems 1–3.

To raise money to buy a microscope, four friends decide to start a dog-walking business.

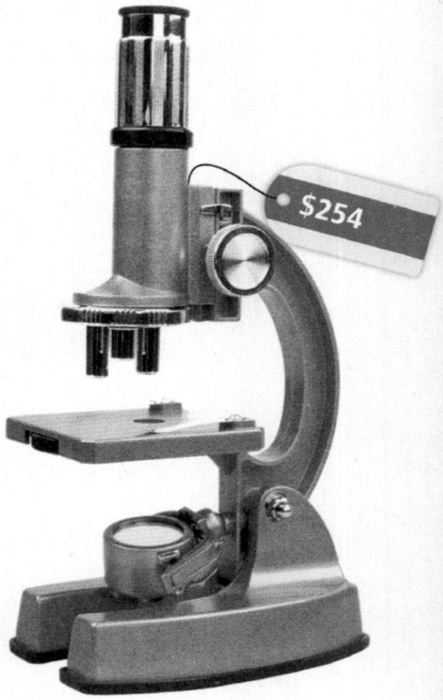

Dylan's Representation

Dogs walked	Profit ($)
8	19
9	22
10	25
11	28

Cliff's Representation

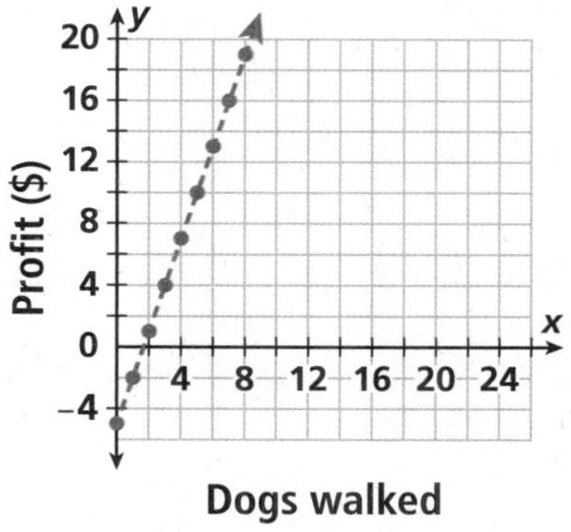

Tiana's Representation

In order to buy the microscope, we plan to walk dogs after school, charging $3 per dog. To reward the dogs, we will buy a box of treats for $5.

Andre's Representation

$y = 3x - 5$

1. What is the slope in this situation and what does it represent?

____

____

2. What is the *y*-intercept in this situation and what does it represent?

____

____

3. How many dogs do the friends need to walk in order to have enough money to buy the microscope? Which representation did you use to answer the question?

____

(MP) **Model with Mathematics** **For Problems 4 and 5, write a function with the given slope that passes through the point.**

4. slope $= -\frac{1}{4}$; passes through the point (4, 5)

____

5. slope $= 5$; contains the point (2, 1)

____

6. **Math on the Spot** Write the equation of the line that passes through $(-3, 1)$ and $(2, -1)$ in slope-intercept form.

____

© Houghton Mifflin Harcourt Publishing Company

Test Prep

Martha earns $15 per hour for babysitting. The parents always give her a $5 tip. Use the information to answer Problems 7–9.

7. What is the slope in this situation?

____

8. What is the y-intercept in this situation?

____

9. How many hours did Martha babysit if she made $65?

_______ hours

10. Two companies rent kayaks. Company A charges $10 per hour and a $7 flat fee for life jacket rental. Company B's charges are represented by the equation $y = 7x + 10$. Which company has a greater fixed cost for renting a kayak?

Ⓐ Company A

Ⓑ Company B

Ⓒ They have the same fixed cost.

Ⓓ Cannot be determined

11. A function has a slope of −6 and passes through the point (−3, 4). The graph of the function is a straight line. Choose all the statements that must be true.

Ⓐ The graph will pass through the point (1, 20).

Ⓑ The graph will pass through the point (−1, 8).

Ⓒ The graph is a discrete function.

Ⓓ The function has a y-intercept at (0, −14).

Ⓔ The rate of change is −6.

12. The cost c to rent a car for d days is shown in the table. Which equation represents this function?

Ⓐ $c = 75.3d$

Ⓑ $c = 72d - 40$

Ⓒ $c = 67d$

Ⓓ $c = 62d + 40$

Days, d	Cost, c
3	$226
4	$288
6	$412
8	$536

Spiral Review

13. Solve for x: $7x - 14 = 14 - 7x$.

____

14. Complete the table representing a linear function.

x	y
1	0
2	
5	40
	90

© Houghton Mifflin Harcourt Publishing Company

Name ______________________________

Describe and Sketch Nonlinear Functions

I Can **convert between a verbal description of a function and its graph, and between a graph and a verbal description of a function.**

Step It Out

ACTIVITY

1 Emanuel walks the North Trail at his local park. The graph shows his distance from the fountain at the center of the park as he walks along the trail. Use the graph to answer the questions.

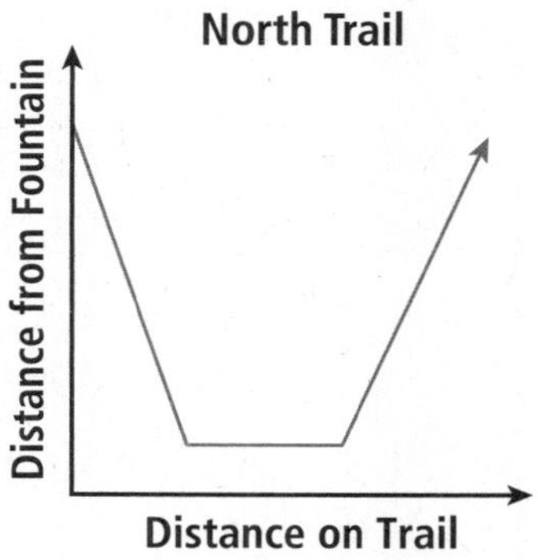

A. Each section of the graph is linear / nonlinear.

B. The slope for the first part of his walk is positive / negative, which means his distance from the fountain is increasing / decreasing at a constant rate.

C. The slope for the second part of his walk is ________.

What does that mean about his distance from the fountain?

____

D. The slope for the third part of his walk is positive / negative, which means his distance from the fountain is increasing / decreasing at a constant rate.

E. Emanuel returns to the park the next day and walks the South Trail.

The South Trail graph is linear / nonlinear.

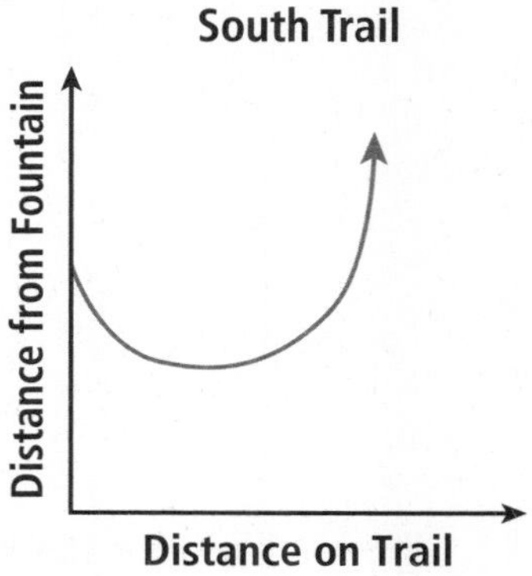

F. Early on, does his distance from the fountain decrease at a constant rate? ________

Near the end, does his distance from the fountain increase at a constant rate? ________

How do you know? ____________________

© Houghton Mifflin Harcourt Publishing Company • Image Credit: ©Malivan Iuliia/Shutterstock

Turn and Talk Describe potential scenarios for each path in relation to the fountain location.

2 When a state fair opened, the number of people attending the fair gradually increased at a constant rate in the morning. Then the number of people remained constant through the afternoon. In the evening, the attendance gradually decreased at a constant rate until near the end of the night, when the number of people decreased swiftly at a constant rate as they all left.

A. Where should the graph of the situation begin and why?

It starts at ____________ because there were __________ people there until the fair opened.

B. Describe what happens to the graph as the number of people gradually increased at a constant rate in the morning. Will the slope of this part of the graph be positive or negative? Will it be steep or gradual?

It will be [positive / negative] and [steep / gradual].

C. Describe what the graph looks like as the number of people remained constant through the afternoon.

This part of the graph will be ______________.

D. Describe what happens to the graph as the number of people gradually decreased at a constant rate. Will the slope of this part of the graph be positive or negative? Will it be steep or gradual?

It will be [positive / negative] and [steep / gradual].

E. Describe what happens to the graph near the end of the night, when the number of people decreased swiftly as they all left. Will the slope of this part of the graph be positive or negative? Will it be steep or gradual?

It will be [positive / negative] and [steep / gradual].

F. Use what you described to sketch the situation.

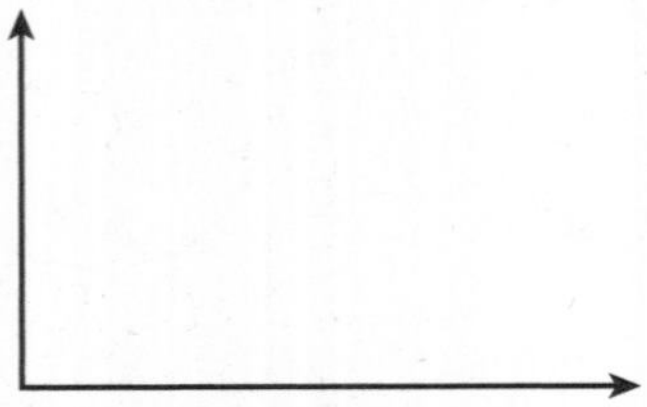

G. Suppose the number of people attending the fair continued to gradually increase at the same constant rate throughout the afternoon instead of remaining constant. Sketch a graph that represents this situation.

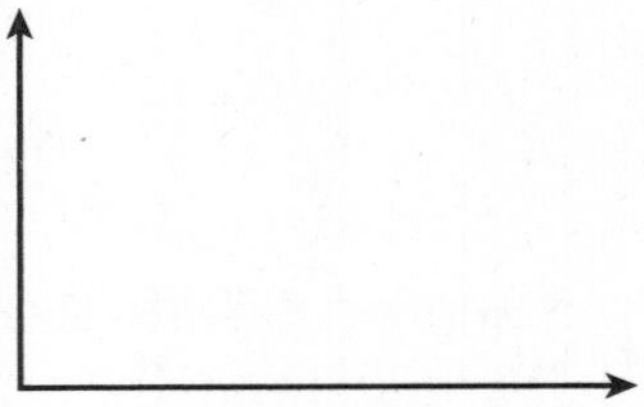

© Houghton Mifflin Harcourt Publishing Company • **Image Credit:** ©Granger Wootz/Blend Images/Getty Images

Name ___

3 Kevin says that this graph describes an airplane that takes off, climbs to cruising altitude, stays at the cruising altitude for the flight, and then descends for landing. Kate says that the graph better describes a model rocket that launches, rises to a maximum altitude, and then falls faster and faster until it reaches the ground.

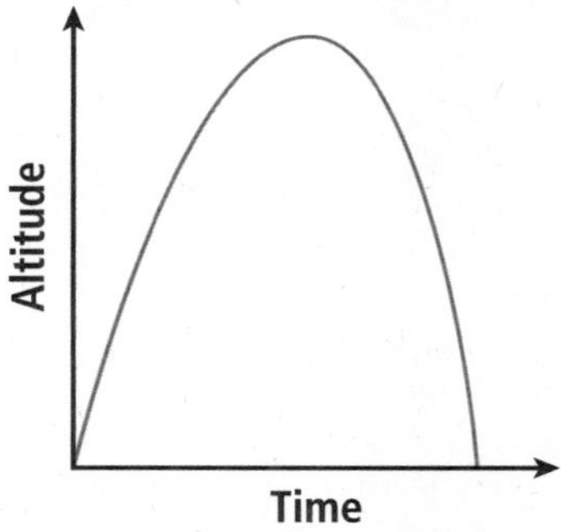

A. Is the graph linear, nonlinear, or a combination?

___

B. Is the graph increasing at a constant rate? Is the graph decreasing at a constant rate?

___

C. Is there a portion of the graph where the altitude is constant?

___

D. Whose description does the graph better represent, Kevin's or Kate's? Why?

___

___

___

Turn and Talk Sketch a graph to represent the airplane flight that Kevin suggested.

© Houghton Mifflin Harcourt Publishing Company • Image Credits: ©muratart/Shutterstock; ©Peter Barrett/Shutterstock

Check Understanding

1. Describe the temperature changes shown in the graph.

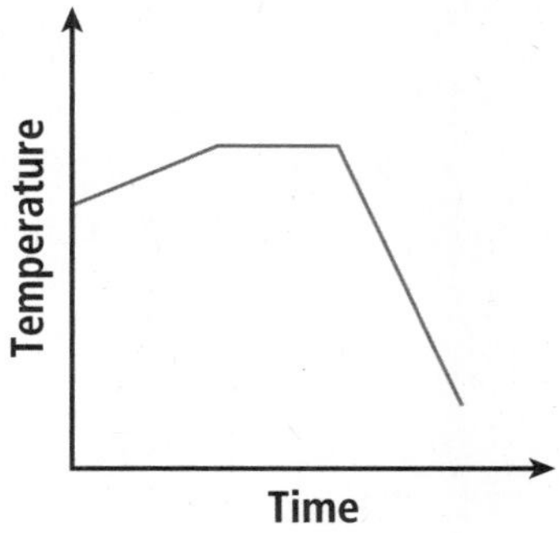

___

___

___

___

___

2. Selena hikes a trail. Her elevation decreases at a constant rate until she reaches a stream. Her elevation stays the same walking by the stream until she climbs a hill at a constant rate to reach the campground. Sketch a graph to represent the situation.

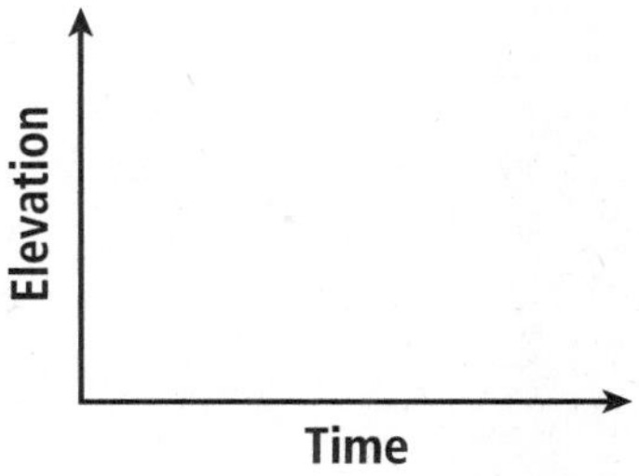

On Your Own

3. The graph represents the speed of a swimmer during a race. Describe the swimmer's speed during the course of the race.

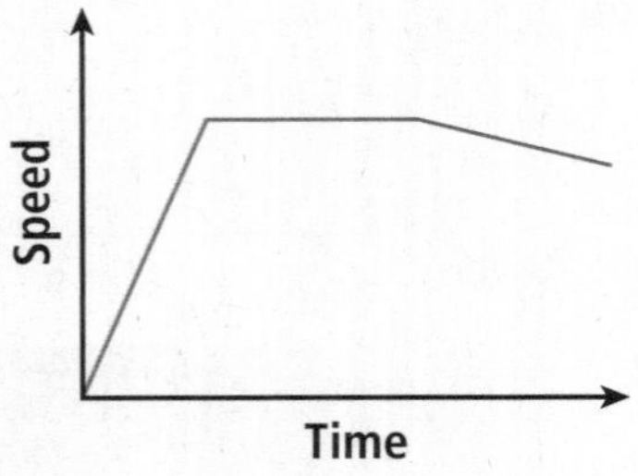

4. The value of a stock increases gradually at a constant rate at the beginning of the day. The value quickly decreases at a constant rate to below the original value during the middle of the day, and then stays the same for the rest of the day.

A. Sketch a graph that represents the situation.

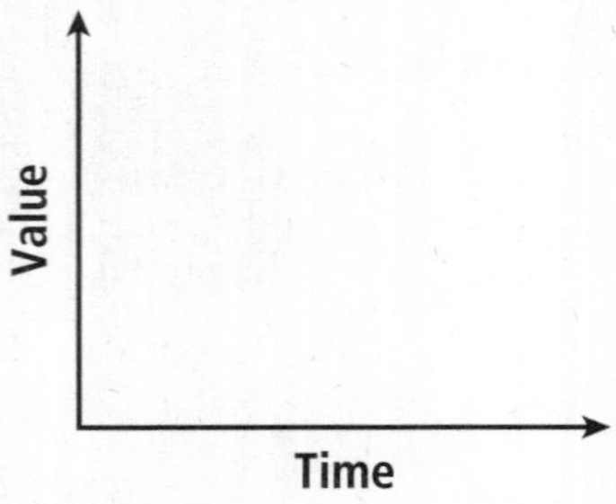

B. MP **Reason** How would the graph change if the stock gradually decreased during the middle of the day?

5. Sketch a graph that shows a value that starts increasing rapidly, then continues increasing but more gradually, then increases rapidly again.

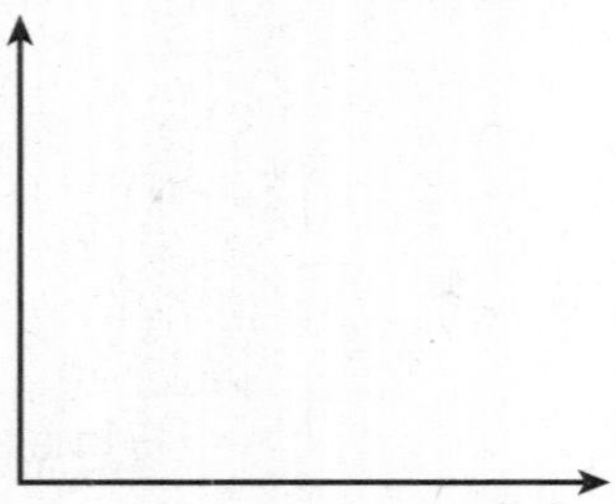

© Houghton Mifflin Harcourt Publishing Company • **Image Credit:** ©Bruno Rosa/Shutterstock

Name

For Problems 6–9, write a situation that the graph could represent.

6.

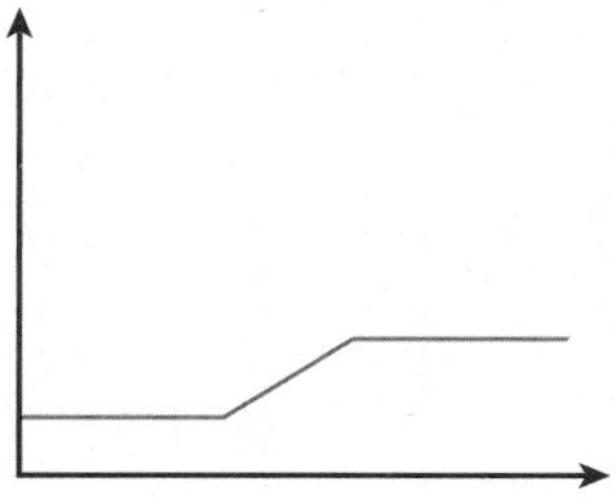

7.

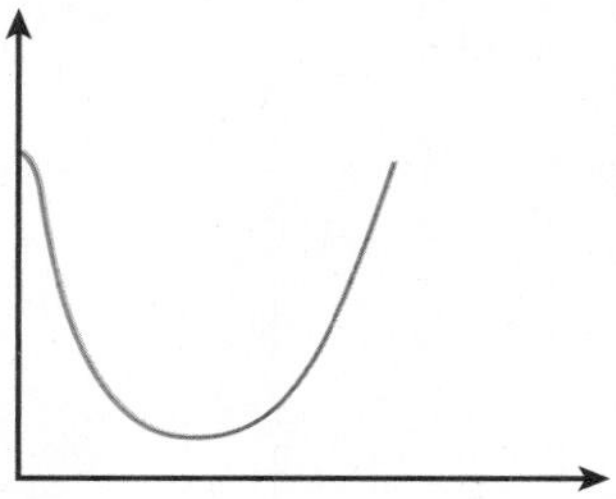

8.

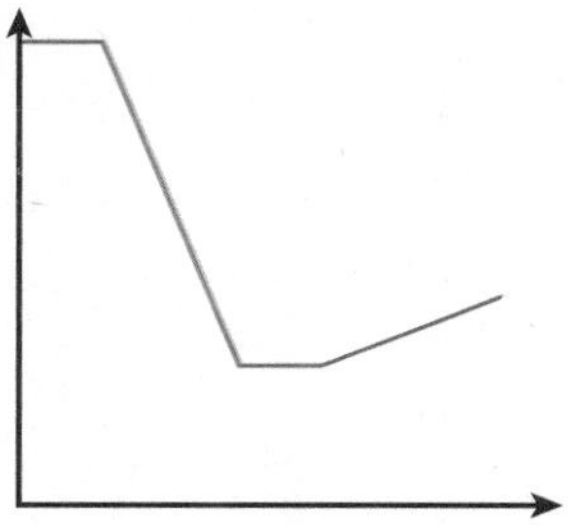

9.

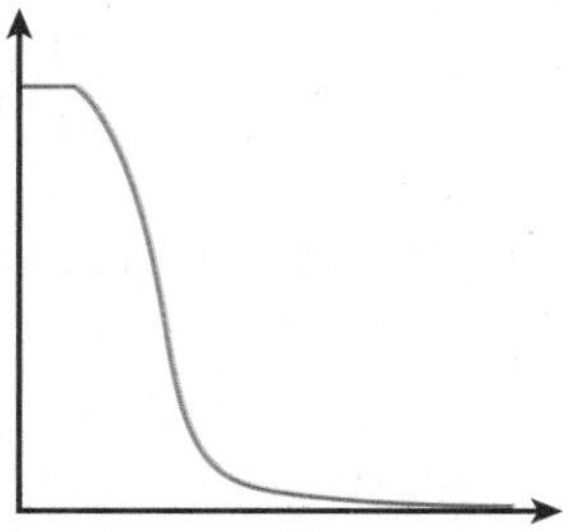

10. Manny completes a video game level. The elevation of his character is constant, then increases rapidly at a constant rate to a new constant elevation. The elevation then decreases rapidly at a constant rate to a new constant elevation to complete the level. Sketch a graph that represents the situation.

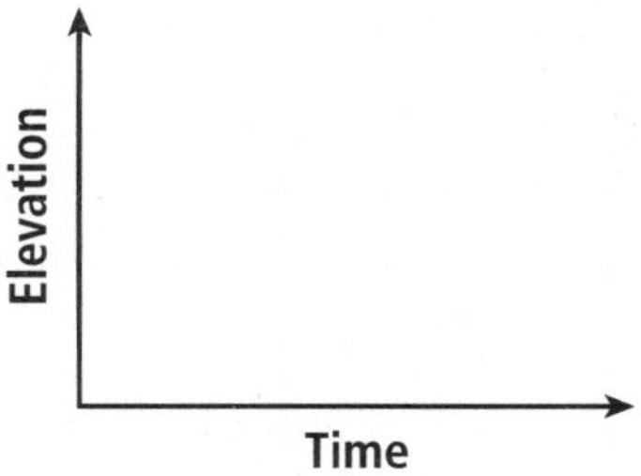

© Houghton Mifflin Harcourt Publishing Company • Image Credit: ©J Helgason/Shutterstock

The graph represents the height of a ball over time as the ball rolls across a ledge, then falls off. Use the graph to answer Problems 11–14.

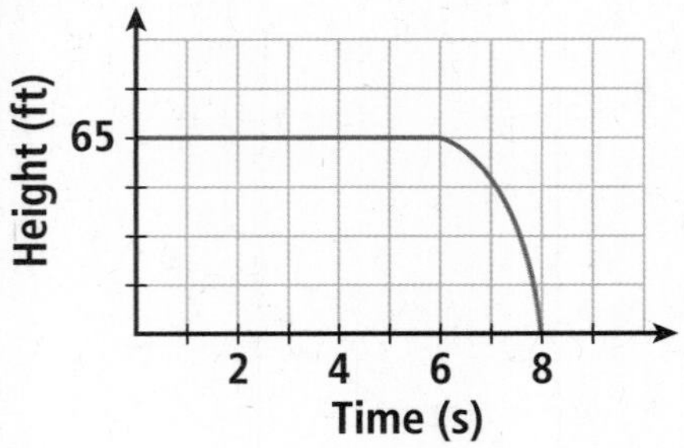

11. Starting at what time and ending at what time, when is the graph linear?

____

12. Starting at what time and ending at what time, when is the graph nonlinear?

____

13. What does the linear part of the graph describe?

____

____

14. STEM What does the nonlinear part of the graph describe? Why is it nonlinear?

____

____

____

____

____

____

Use the graph to answer Problems 15–16.

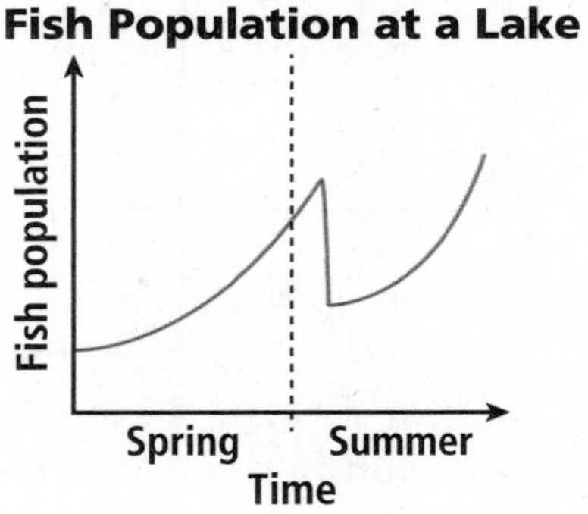

15. Social Studies What happens to the fish population in the spring? Use either the term *linear* or *nonlinear* in your response.

____

____

16. A fishing competition is held on the lake once a year.

A. Which part of the graph shows the result of the competition? In what season is the competition held?

____

B. Describe what happens to the fish population after the competition. Use either the term *linear* or *nonlinear* in your response.

____

© Houghton Mifflin Harcourt Publishing Company

Name ____________________

LESSON 8.5
More Practice/ Homework

ONLINE
Video Tutorials and Interactive Examples

Describe and Sketch Nonlinear Functions

1. **Open Ended** Write a situation that this graph could represent.

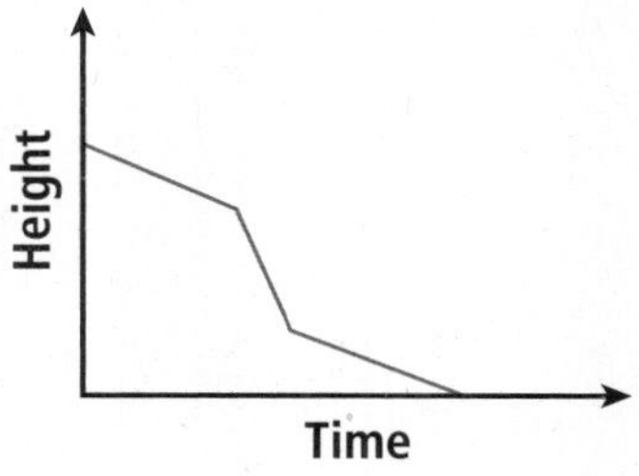

2. Darnell competes in an obstacle course. He climbs a ladder, runs across a bridge, then climbs down another ladder. Sketch a graph that represents his position above the ground as he completes the obstacle course.

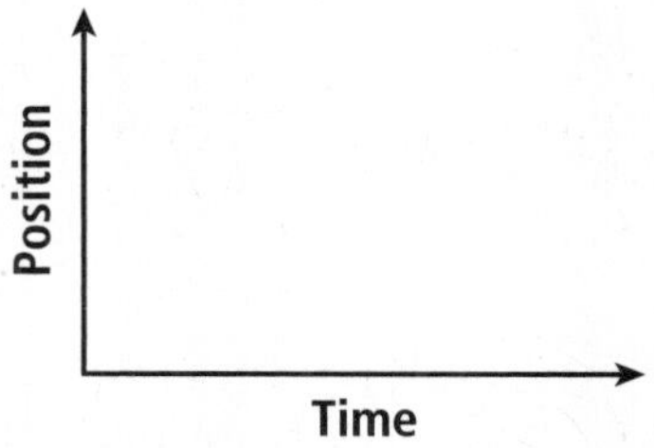

3. (MP) **Reason** The two graphs show the speeds of bicycles as they are coming to a stop. Describe how each of the bicycles comes to a stop.

Bicycle A

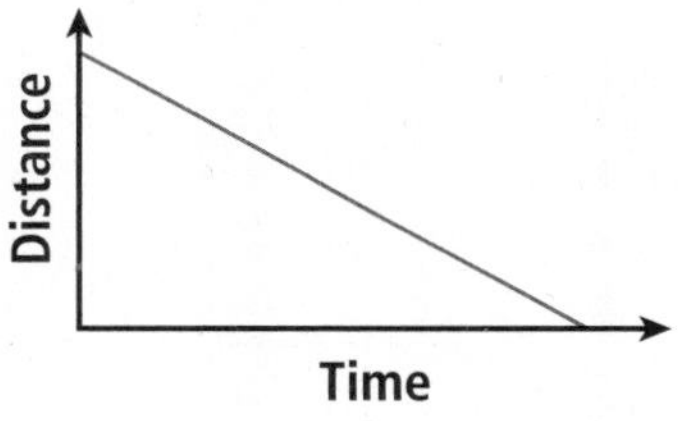

Bicycle B

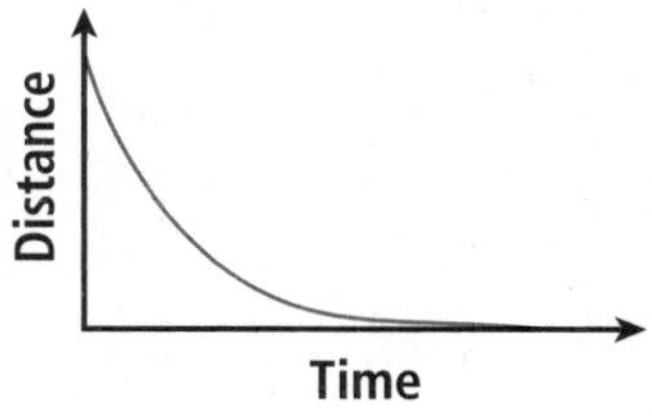

For Problems 4–5, sketch a graph that represents the given situation.

4. The number of points Sally earns in a video game increases at a constant rate, then stays constant, and then increases at a constant rate.

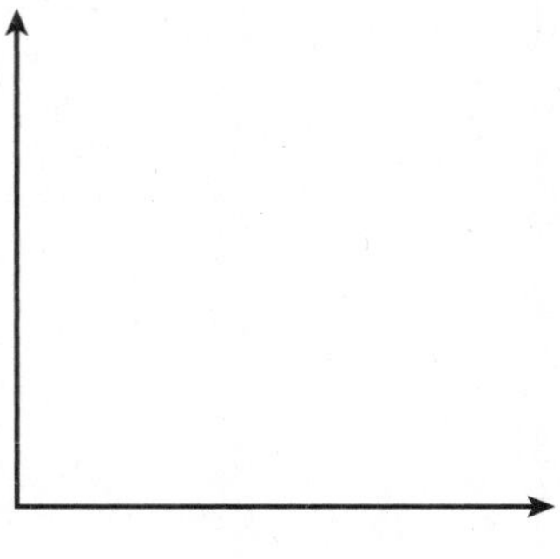

5. Rebecca drove at a constant speed on a street. She slowed at a constant rate to turn onto the highway, then sped up at a constant rate to drive at the speed limit.

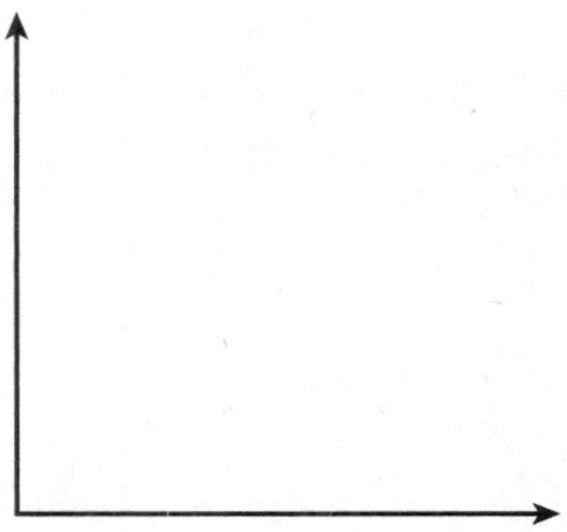

© Houghton Mifflin Harcourt Publishing Company

Test Prep

6. Which graph is a linear function decreasing at a constant rate?

Ⓐ

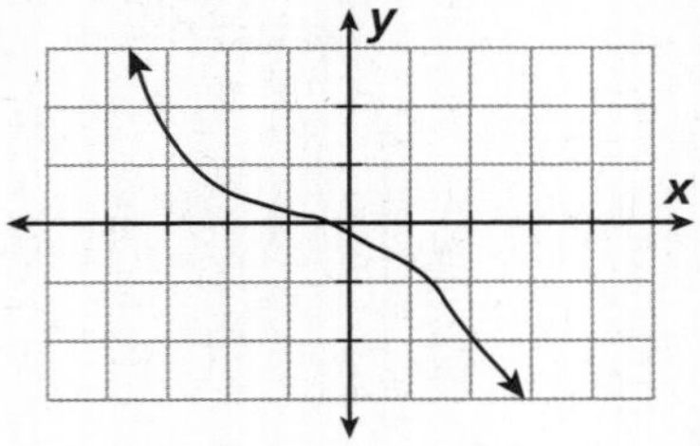

Ⓒ

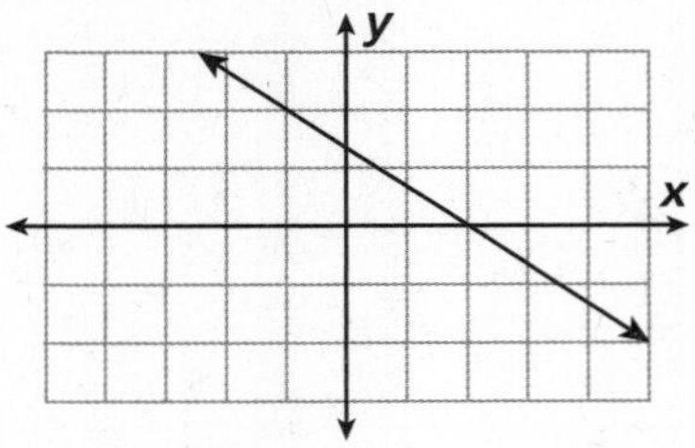

Ⓑ

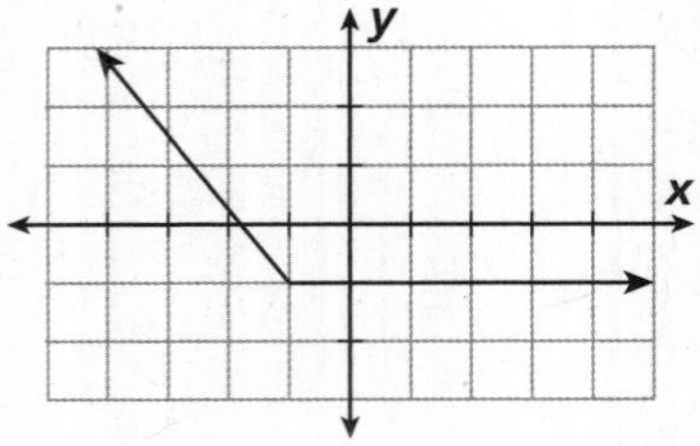

Ⓓ

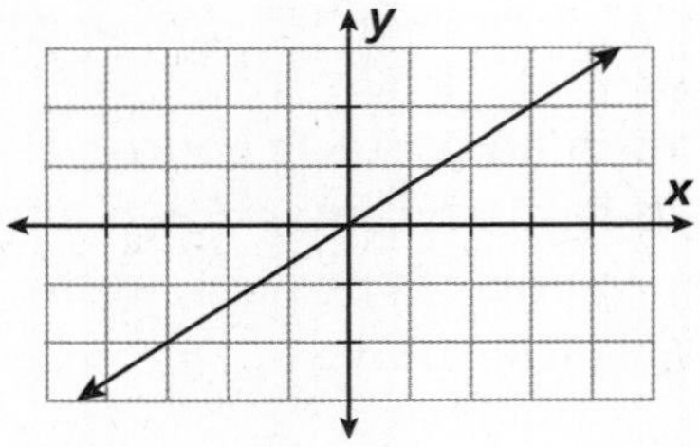

7. Select all statements that are true of the graph shown.

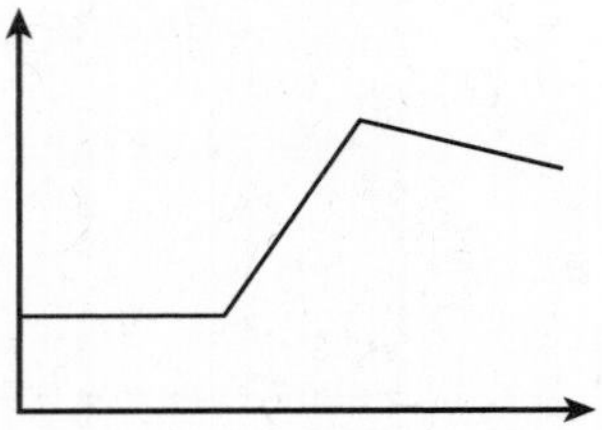

Ⓐ The rate of the increase is greater than the rate of the decrease.

Ⓑ The first segment of the graph is constant.

Ⓒ The second segment of the graph increases at a constant rate.

Ⓓ The rate of the decrease is greater than the rate of the increase.

Ⓔ The third segment of the graph is decreasing.

Spiral Review

8. Jamie starts a savings account with \$75. She deposits \$30 in her account weekly. Her friend Carmen's savings account balance is described by the equation $b = 25m + 100$, where b is the account balance and m is the number of months. Which account has a greater balance after 6 months?

____

9. Store A sells 2 sweatshirts for \$25 and 7 sweatshirts for \$87.50. Store B sells 3 sweatshirts for \$39 and 6 sweatshirts for \$78. Which store has a lower price for one sweatshirt?

____

© Houghton Mifflin Harcourt Publishing Company

Module 8

Name ______________________________

Review

Vocabulary

For Problems 1–6, choose the correct term from the Vocabulary box to complete each sentence.

Vocabulary
domain
function
linear
nonlinear
range
relation

1. A ____________ is any set of ordered pairs.
2. The ____________ of a function is the set of all possible input values.
3. A function whose graph is not a straight line is ____________.
4. The ____________ of a function is the set of all possible output values.
5. A ____________ is a relation with exactly one output for each input.
6. A function whose graph is a straight line is ____________.
7. What is $y = mx + b$, and what do m and b represent?

____

____

Concepts and Skills

8. (MP) **Use Tools** The graph shows how the temperature in a refrigerator changed over time, where x is the time in hours and y is the temperature in degrees Celsius. Write the equation of the line shown in the graph. State what strategy and tool you will use to answer the question, explain your choice, and then find the answer.

Refrigerator Temperature

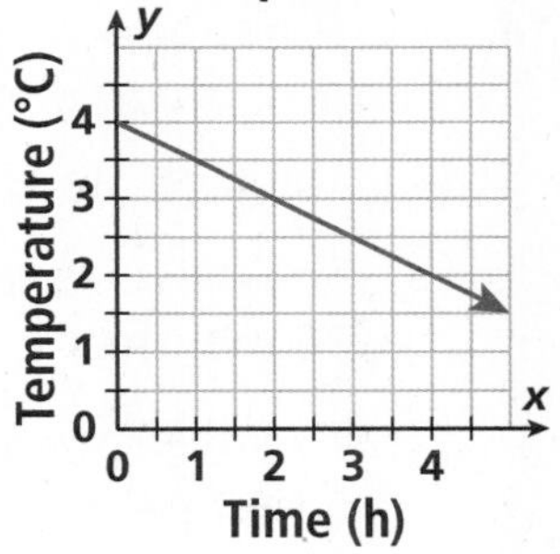

____

____

____

____

9. Which of these functions are linear? Select all that apply.

   (A) $y = \frac{4}{x}$
   (B) $y = -4x + 1$
   (C) $y = x^2 - 1$
   (D) $y = 2^x + 8$
   (E) $y = 4 - \frac{2}{3}x$
   (F) $y = 5(x - 0.6)$

10. On the coordinate plane, draw a linear function that increases at a constant rate.

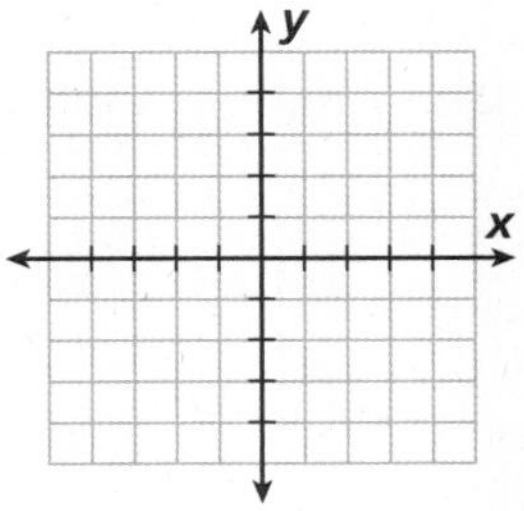

© Houghton Mifflin Harcourt Publishing Company

11. Is the relation shown in the graph a function? Explain.

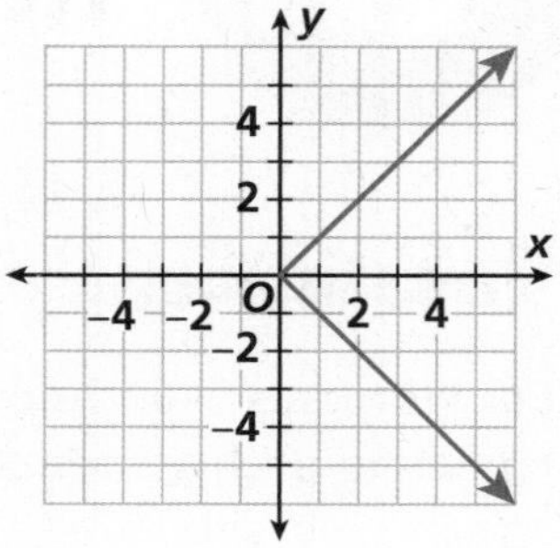

12. The table shows the total cost t of owning a smartphone for m months. Write an equation that represents this function.

Months, *m*	2	3	4	8
Total cost, *t* ($)	268	322	376	592

13. Which function has the greatest rate of change?

Ⓐ $y = 3x + 7$

Ⓑ

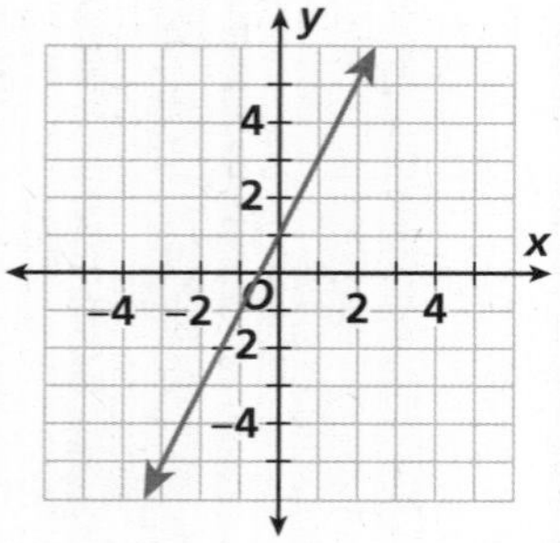

Ⓒ

x	1	2	4	5
y	7	12	22	27

Ⓓ You pay an initial fee of $10, then $1.00 per week for x weeks.

14. The equation $y = 5x - 30$ models a scuba diver's elevation in feet y after x minutes. Based on the equation, which statement is true?

Ⓐ The diver starts at sea level and reaches a depth of 30 feet after 5 minutes.

Ⓑ The diver starts at the ocean floor and reaches a depth of 5 feet after 30 minutes.

Ⓒ The diver starts 30 feet below sea level and ascends at a rate of 5 feet per minute.

Ⓓ The diver starts 5 feet above sea level and descends at a rate of 30 feet per minute.

15. It takes Zeke 45 minutes to walk 1.5 miles from his house to the library. He starts out walking fast, then stops for 10 minutes to talk to a friend. Then he continues on at a slower rate. Draw segments to complete a possible graph of Zeke's walk.

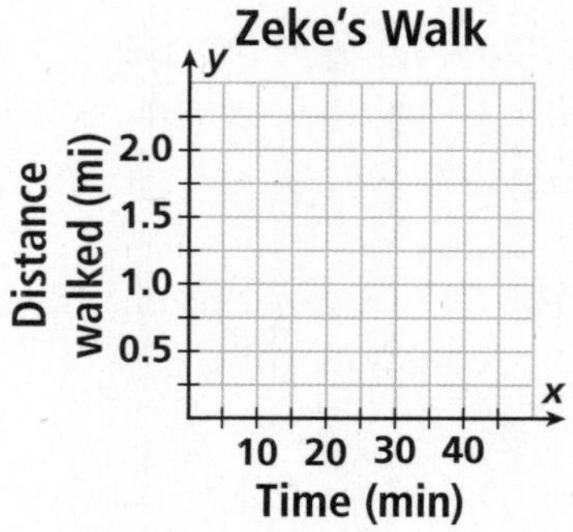

16. Complete the table to show a relation that is **not** a function.

x	−2		
y		5	

© Houghton Mifflin Harcourt Publishing Company

Systems of Linear Equations

Wags Per Mile

Nikki's
Dog Care
I take care of your pup while you're away!
Vacation Package:
$10 flat fee plus $15 per day
Each day includes two 30-minute visits.

Jaden's
Dog Sitting
Your dog won't even miss you!
Travel package:
$20 flat fee plus $13 per day
Each day includes 2 half-hour visits.

Write expressions showing the cost of using each service for *d* days.

A. Nikki's: ______________ B. Jaden's: ______________

Find when the dog services will cost the same.

C. The dog services cost the same on day ________.

Turn and Talk

Describe the steps you used to solve Part C.

© Houghton Mifflin Harcourt Publishing Company • Image Credit: ©Mark Taylor/naturepl.com

Are You Ready?

Complete these problems to review prior concepts and skills you will need for this module.

Identify Solutions of Equations

Use substitution to determine whether the given value of the variable is a solution of the equation.

1. $6x - 2x = 10$; $x = 2$

2. $4n + 4 = 14$; $n = 2.5$

3. $\frac{1}{3}a - 1 = \frac{1}{4}a$; $a = 12$

4. $\frac{3}{4}(t - 6) = 9$; $t = 20$

Solve Multi-Step Equations

Solve each equation.

5. $3b + 4 = 5b - 8$

6. $-2(x + 6) = 4x$

7. $\frac{1}{4}(s + 6) = -3$

8. $2m + 1.5 = 3m - 11.7$

Special Cases of Equations

Complete each equation by writing a number in the box so that the equation has the given number of solutions.

9. $\square\, x + 5 = 3(2x + 1)$; no solution

10. $-4n + 8 = 4n - 8n + \square$; infinitely many solutions

11. Saskia is solving an equation in one variable and gets the equivalent equation $3 = 3$. Assuming her work is correct, what can she conclude about the original equation? Explain.

© Houghton Mifflin Harcourt Publishing Company

Name ____________________

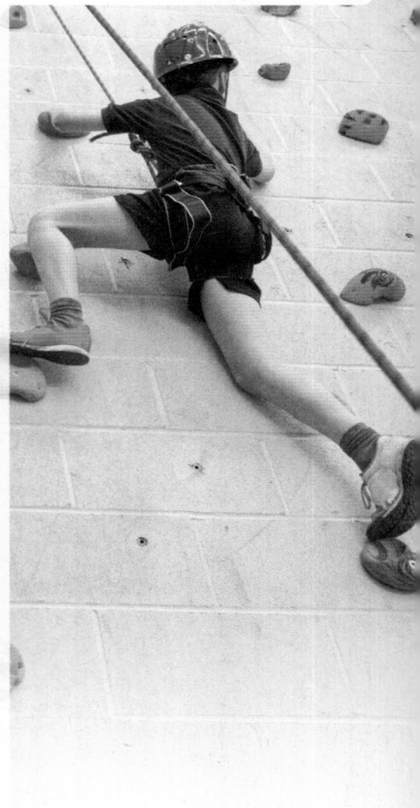

Represent Systems by Graphing

I Can **graph a pair of linear equations and draw a conclusion from the graph.**

Spark Your Learning

PAIRS

Natasha is comparing two rock climbing gyms in her town. Each gym charges a fixed fee for gear rental (shoes, harness, etc.) and an hourly fee for climbing. The graph shows the total cost at each gym based on the time spent climbing.

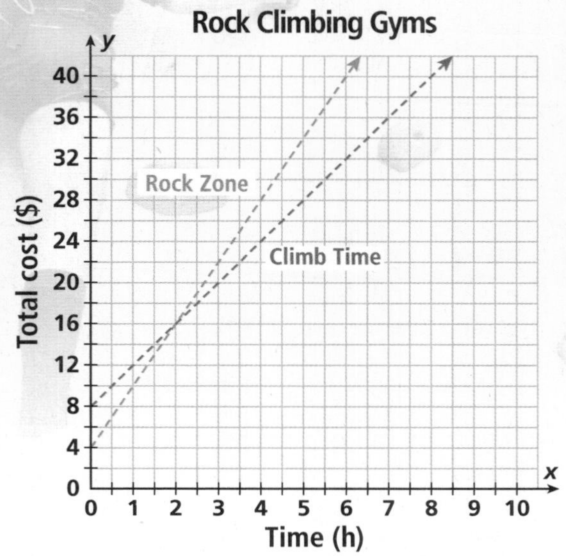

Natasha wants to choose the gym with the better deal. What recommendations can you make?

Turn and Talk What information do you get by comparing the *y*-intercepts of the lines? What information do you get by comparing the slopes of the lines?

© Houghton Mifflin Harcourt Publishing Companyy • Image Credit: ©Juice Images Limited/Shutterstock

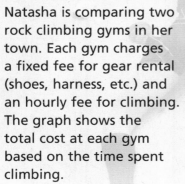

Build Understanding

1 Cody is comparing the total costs of two climbing gyms. Each gym charges a fixed fee for gear rental and an hourly fee for climbing. Cody graphs a pair of equations, as shown, to help him compare the costs.

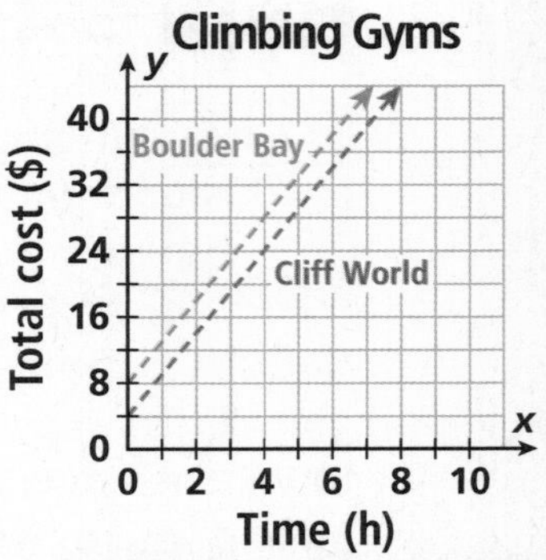

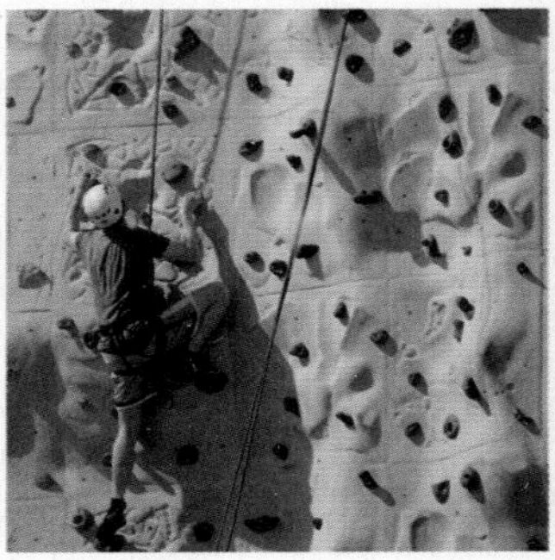

A. What does the slope represent in this context?

B. How do the slopes of the graphs compare? What does this tell you about the rock climbing gyms?

C. What does the y-intercept represent in this context?

D. What do the y-intercepts of the graphs tell you about the rock climbing gyms?

E. What does the difference in the y-intercepts mean in this context?

F. Which gym is a better deal if Cody plans to climb for 2 hours? if Cody plans to climb for 5 hours? How do you know?

G. Is there ever a situation in which Boulder Bay will cost less than Cliff World? Why or why not?

Turn and Talk Suppose Cliff World increases their gear rental fee to $6 but keeps their hourly rate the same. Does this change the answer to any of the Task 1 questions? Explain.

© Houghton Mifflin Harcourt Publishing Company • Image Credit: ©Darryl Brooks/Shutterstock

2 A mobile hotspot is a device that provides Wi-Fi. Both Cool Connect and Mobile Me offer mobile hotspots for a total monthly cost y which includes a fixed fee plus a charge x for the gigabytes (GBs) of data used.

A. Graph and label each equation on the coordinate plane.

B. What is the slope of each line? What do the slopes tell you?

Mobile Hotspot Rates	
Cool Connect	$y = 0.5x + 7$
Mobile Me	$y = 2x + 1$

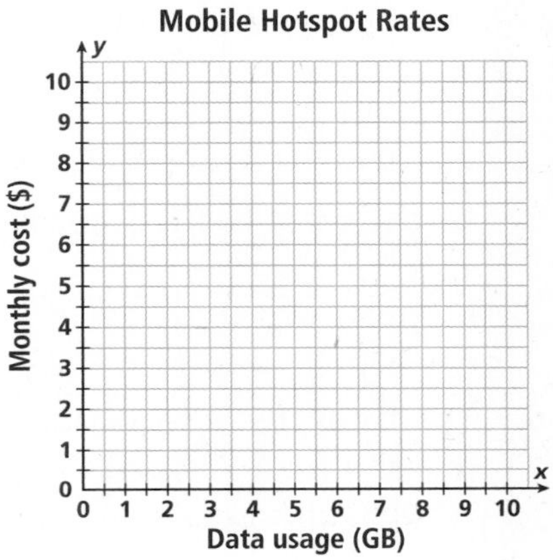

C. What is the y-intercept of each line? What do the y-intercepts tell you?

D. What does the point of intersection of the lines represent?

E. When does Cool Connect cost less than Mobile Me? Explain your thinking.

Turn and Talk If the two lines on the graph were the same line, what would that tell you about the two plans?

Check Understanding

Jovan is considering two job offers. Each company pays a fixed monthly salary plus a commission based on the amount of sales. The graph shows the income potential for each job. Use the graph to solve Problems 1–2.

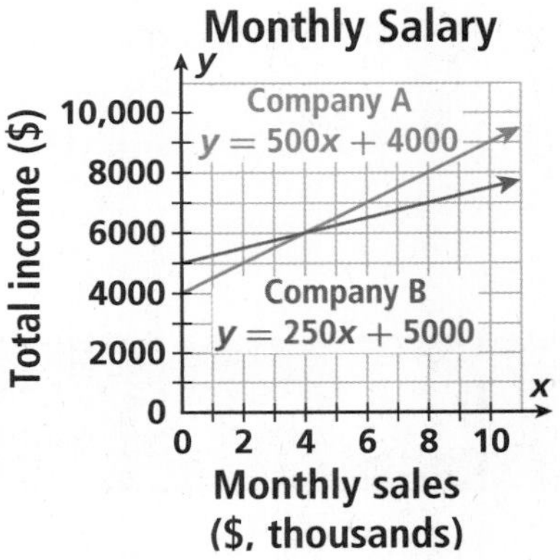

1. Which company pays a greater monthly salary? Explain.

2. Which company pays a greater commission? Explain.

© Houghton Mifflin Harcourt Publishing Company

On Your Own

Compare the cost of two ice skating rinks. Each rink charges a fixed fee for skate rentals and an hourly fee for skating. Use the graph to solve Problems 3–5.

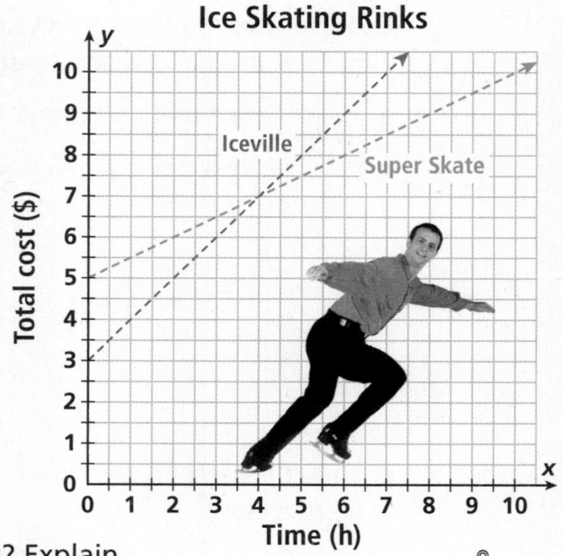

3. What do the slopes of the lines tell you in this context?

4. What do the *y*-intercepts tell you in this context?

5. Under what circumstances does Super Skate charge less? Explain.

6. The total cost *y* for a ride based on distance driven (in miles) *x* for XYZ Taxi is given by the equation $y = 0.5x + 4$ while Quick Ride is given in the table shown.

Quick Ride			
Distance, mi (*x*)	1	2	3
Total cost, $ (*y*)	5.50	6.00	6.50

A. Graph and label the equation representing XYZ Taxi. Graph the data from the table for Quick Ride on the coordinate plane and connect the points with a line.

B. Calculate, compare, and interpret the slopes and the *y*-intercepts.

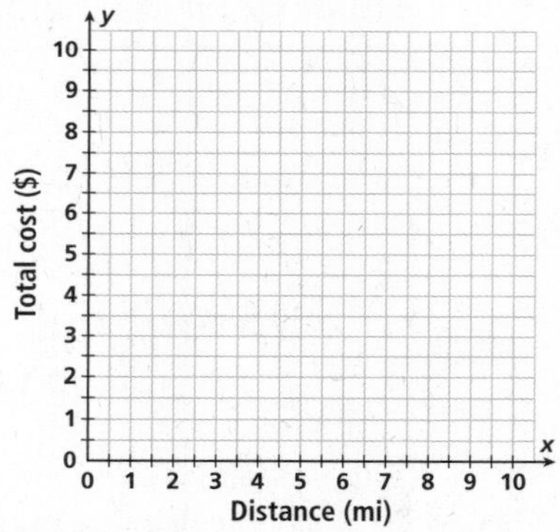

7. (MP) **Use Structure** The total cost in dollars *y* of a bus pass for *x* months in City A is given by $y = 30x + 5$. The total cost in City B is given by $y = 30x + 4.5$. After graphing both equations on your own paper, which bus pass is a better deal? How do you know?

I'm in a Learning Mindset!

How is representing multiple equations an appropriate challenge for me?

© Houghton Mifflin Harcourt Publishing Company • Image Credit: ©David Madison/Getty Images Sport/Getty Images

Name ______________________________

ONLINE
Video Tutorials and
Interactive Examples

Represent Systems by Graphing

Latrice is comparing the costs of two laundry services. Each service charges a fixed fee and a price per pound of laundry. Use the graph to solve Problems 1–3.

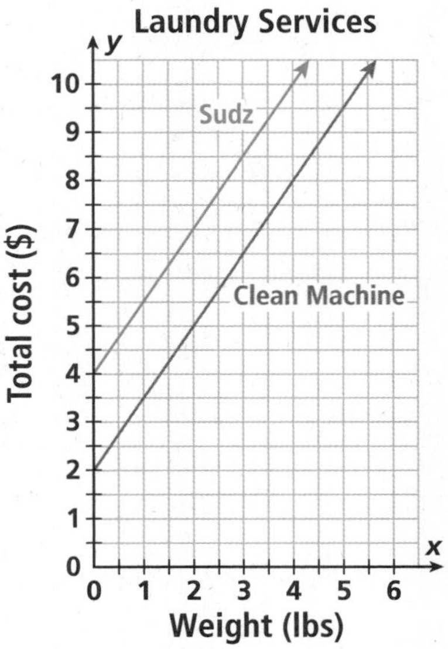

1. Compare the slopes. What does this tell you?

____

____

2. Compare the *y*-intercepts. What does this tell you?

____

____

____

3. Which service offers a lower price? Explain.

____

____

4. Compare the costs of two tablet computers. In addition to the cost of the tablet, there is a monthly data fee.

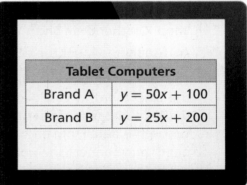

Tablet Computers	
Brand A	$y = 50x + 100$
Brand B	$y = 25x + 200$

A. Graph and label the equations on the coordinate plane.

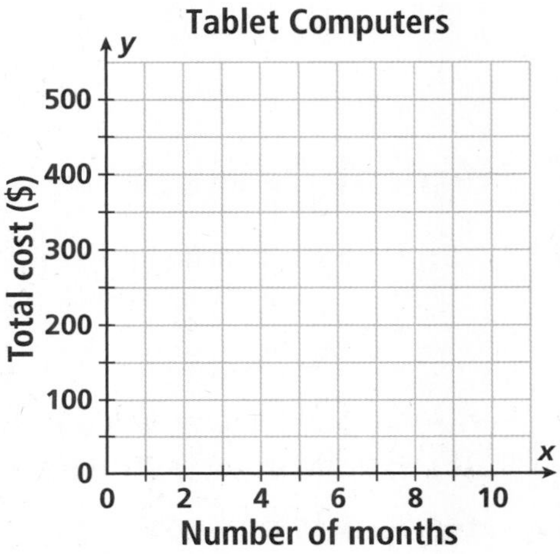

B. **Financial Literacy** Which tablet has a lower monthly data fee? Explain.

____

____

____

____

____

C. MP **Construct Arguments** Which tablet is a better deal? Explain.

____

____

____

____

____

© Houghton Mifflin Harcourt Publishing Company

Test Prep

Use the graph to solve Problems 5–8.

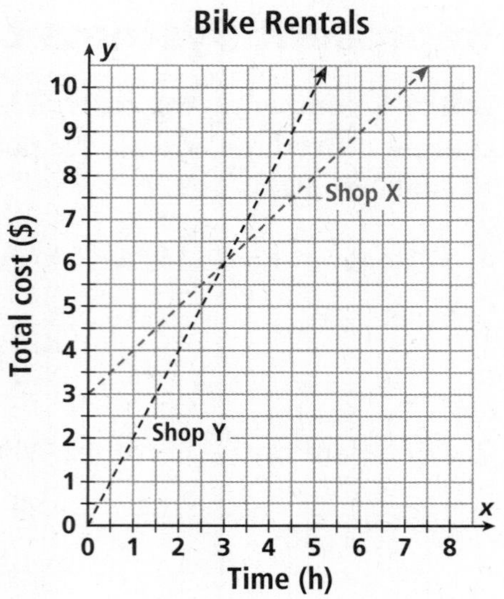

5. Based on the graph, which of the following is true?

Ⓐ For a 1-hour rental, Shop X is a better deal.

Ⓑ For a 6-hour rental, both shops have the same cost.

Ⓒ Shop Y is a better deal for any number of hours.

Ⓓ It costs \$6 to rent a bike for 3 hours at either shop.

6. What is the slope of each graph? What does this tell you about each shop?

Shop X slope: ☐ hourly rate: \$☐ per hour

Shop Y slope: ☐ hourly rate: \$☐ per hour

7. What is the *y*-intercept of each graph? What does this tell you about each shop?

Shop X *y*-intercept: ☐ fixed fee: \$☐

Shop Y *y*-intercept: ☐ fixed fee: \$☐

8. If you plan to rent a bike for 5 hours, how much do you save by choosing Shop X rather than Shop Y?

Ⓐ \$0.50 Ⓑ \$1.00 Ⓒ \$2.00 Ⓓ \$2.50

9. There are two dance studios. The tables show the total monthly cost *y* for each studio based on the number of classes taken that month. Graph the data from each table on your own paper and connect the points with a line. What can you conclude from your graph?

Dancer's World			
Number of Classes (x)	1	4	7
Total Monthly Cost, \$ (y)	35	65	95

Ultimate Dance			
Number of Classes (x)	2	3	8
Total Monthly Cost, \$ (y)	45	55	105

___

___

___

Spiral Review

10. $\angle P$ and $\angle Q$ are supplementary angles and $m\angle Q = 70°$. $\angle P$ and $\angle S$ are congruent. What are the measures of $\angle P$ and $\angle S$?

___

For Problems 11–12, tell whether each equation has one solution, no solution, or infinitely many solutions.

11. $3(x + 2) = x + 2x + 2$

___

12. $1.5y + y + 10 = 2.5(y + 4)$

___

© Houghton Mifflin Harcourt Publishing Company

Name ____________________

Solve Systems by Graphing

I Can solve a system of linear equations by graphing.

Spark Your Learning

PAIRS

Wes is laying out model train tracks along equations on a coordinate grid and wants to know if there is a place where the two trains might collide. Determine whether there are any such places, and explain your reasoning.

Model Train Tracks	
Section A	$y = 3x + 3$
Section B	$y = -\frac{1}{2}x - 4$

Turn and Talk How can you check that you correctly determined any possible places where the trains might collide? Explain.

© Houghton Mifflin Harcourt Publishing Companyy • Image Credit: ©AGF Srl/Alamy

Build Understanding

1 Gabriela is using a coordinate plane to design a race course for remote-controlled cars. She wants to use straight sections laid out according to the equations in the table. She needs to know where the cars might collide, if anywhere.

Model Race Course	
Section P	$y = -x + 2$
Section Q	$y = -2x - 4$

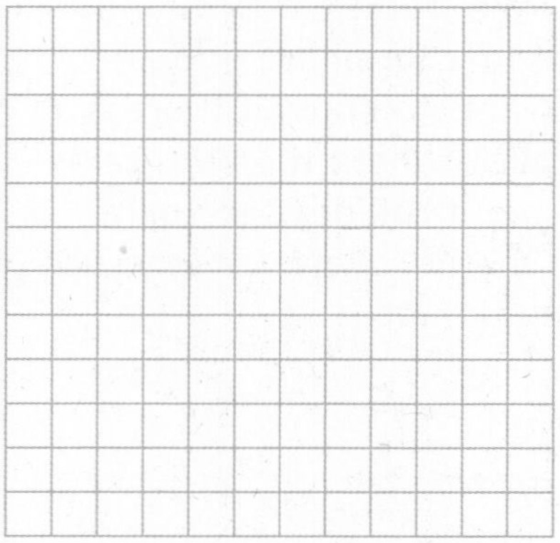

A. Graph the equations on the coordinate plane. Draw the *x*- and *y*-axis, and indicate the scale of your graph.

B. At what point might the cars collide? Why?

C. Compare your graph with those of other students. Did everyone make the same choices to see the point of intersection? Explain.

D. Is it possible that there is more than one point of intersection? Explain.

E. Show how you can use the coordinates of the intersection point and the given equations to check that you found the correct point.

Turn and Talk How can you tell just by looking at two given equations whether they must have a point of intersection?

© Houghton Mifflin Harcourt Publishing Company

Name

Step It Out

2 When you graph a system of linear equations, the point of intersection of the lines, if any, is the **solution of the system**.

A. Graph and label each equation on the coordinate plane. $\begin{cases} y = \frac{1}{3}x + 3 \\ y = -2x + 4 \end{cases}$

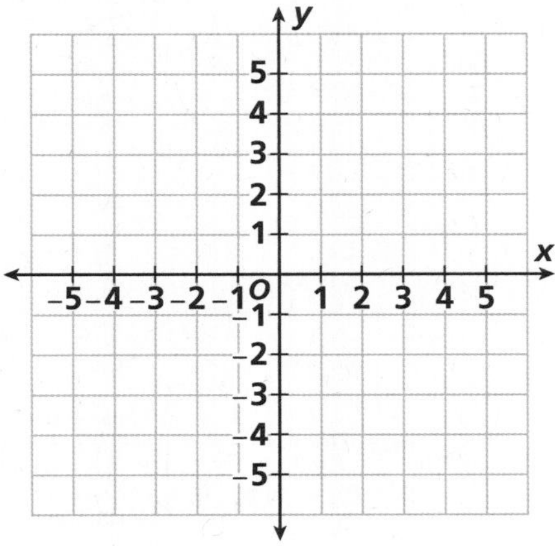

Connect to Vocabulary

A **system of equations** is two or more equations that contain two or more variables.

B. Estimate the solution to the system of equations.

____

C. Why is it difficult to determine the exact point of intersection from your graph directly?

____

D. A student claimed that the point of intersection of the lines is $\left(\frac{1}{4}, 3\frac{1}{2}\right)$. Is the student correct? How do you know?

____

____

Check Understanding

1. A city planner uses the equations $y = -3x - 2$ and $y = x - 10$ to represent two streets.

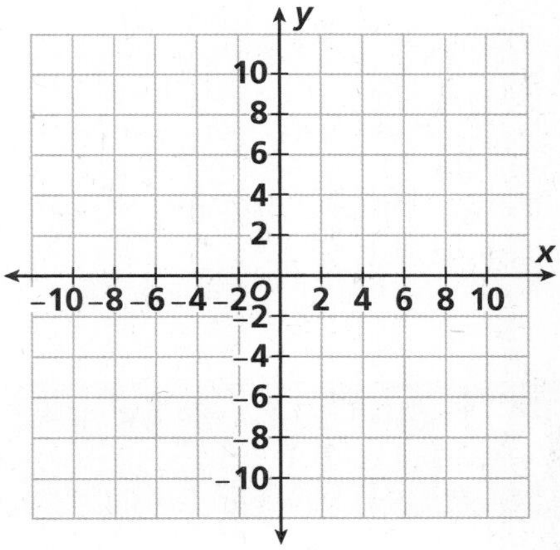

A. Graph and label the equations on the grid so that the point of intersection of the lines is shown.

B. What is the point of intersection of the lines? What does it represent?

____

C. Describe how you can check that you found the point of intersection correctly.

____

____

© Houghton Mifflin Harcourt Publishing Company

On Your Own

2. **STEM** A scientist uses two incubators to grow biological samples at different temperatures. In the equations, x represents the number of hours since the experiment started and y represents degrees Celsius.

Laboratory Incubators	
Incubator J	$y = x + 8$
Incubator K	$y = 0.5x + 10$

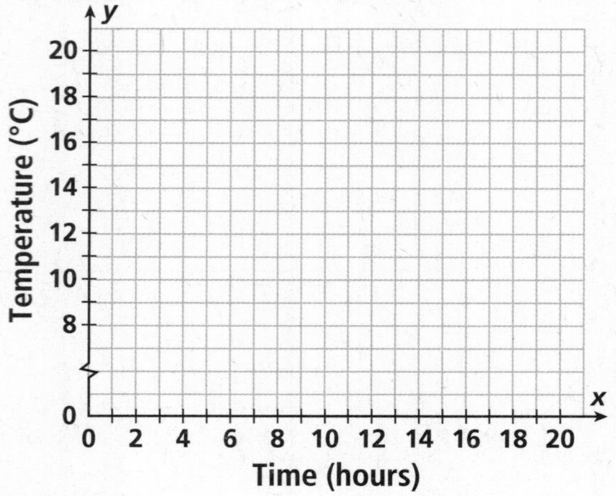

A. Graph and label the equations on the coordinate plane.

B. What is the intersection point of the lines? Explain what it represents.

____

____

3. **Open Ended** The graph shows a system of equations. Write a real-world problem, including a system of equations, that could be solved by drawing the graph shown.

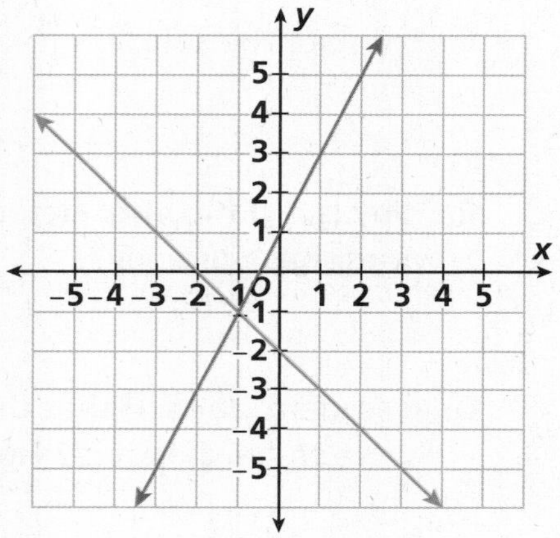

____

____

____

____

4. (MP) **Critique Reasoning** Brianna was asked to use graphing to solve the system of equations $y = 2x + 3.5$ and $y = 2.5x - 1$.

A. Brianna said the lines are parallel and do not intersect, so the system has no solution. Do you agree or disagree? Explain.

____

____

B. Another student says the solution is (9, 21.5). Is he correct? Explain.

____

© Houghton Mifflin Harcourt Publishing Company • Image Credit: ©Khamkhlai Thanet/Shutterstock

I'm in a Learning Mindset!

How was solving systems by graphing an appropriate challenge for me?

____

____

Name ______________________

Solve Systems by Graphing

1. Deshawn is using a coordinate plane to design a mural. Two of the straight lines on the mural are represented by the equations $y = 2x + 8$ and $y = \frac{1}{2}x - 4$.

A. Graph and label the equations on the grid so that the point of intersection of the lines is shown.

B. At what point do the lines intersect? ______________

C. (MP) **Reason** Show how you can check that the point of intersection is a solution.

____

____

____

2. The total cost y of renting a paddleboat for x hours is given by $y = 2x + 3$ at Lake Mitchell and by $y = \frac{1}{3}x + 7$ at Lake Sutro.

A. Graph and label each equation on the coordinate plane.

B. Estimate the solution of the system. What does the solution represent?

____

____

____

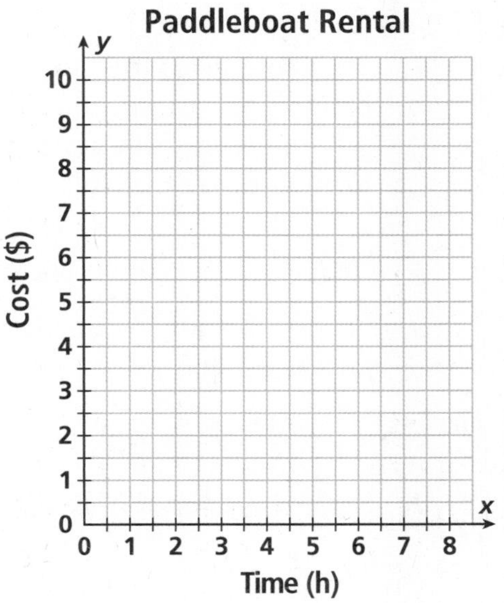

3. **Math on the Spot** Use a separate sheet of graph paper to solve each system by graphing. Check your answer.

A. $\begin{cases} y = x + 2 \\ y = -2x + 5 \end{cases}$ ______________

B. $\begin{cases} x - y = 2 \\ y = \frac{1}{2}x \end{cases}$ ______________

© Houghton Mifflin Harcourt Publishing Company • Image Credit: ©agsandrew/iStock/Getty Images

Test Prep

4. Which system of linear equations has a solution that is represented by a point in Quadrant II?

Ⓐ $\begin{cases} y = x \\ y = -x + 3 \end{cases}$

Ⓑ $\begin{cases} y = x \\ y = x + 3 \end{cases}$

Ⓒ $\begin{cases} y = -x \\ y = x + 3 \end{cases}$

Ⓓ $\begin{cases} y = -x \\ y = -x - 3 \end{cases}$

5. Alicia is using a coordinate plane to help her write a program for a video game. In the game, a rabbit moves along the line $y = -4x + 8$ and a fox moves along the line $y = -0.5x - 6$. Graph the two lines on the coordinate plane provided. Where do the lines intersect?

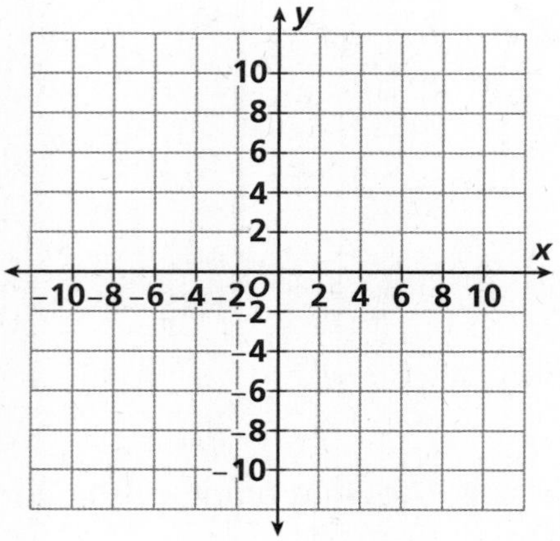

____

6. Which of the following is the solution to this system of equations? $\begin{cases} y = -3x - 5 \\ y = 5x \end{cases}$

Ⓐ $(-1, -3)$

Ⓑ $\left(-\frac{5}{8}, -\frac{25}{8}\right)$

Ⓒ $\left(-\frac{5}{2}, -\frac{25}{2}\right)$

Ⓓ $(-3, -5)$

Spiral Review

7. The table gives the altitude y, in meters, of a weather balloon at various times x, in minutes, since the balloon was released from a platform. Construct a function of the form $y = mx + b$ which describes the data.

Time (x)	Altitude (y)
3	170
4	220
5	270

____

8. Construct a linear function that has a slope of -3 and passes through the point $(-2, 3)$.

____

9. Solve the equation $3(x - 1) = 27 - 2x$. Check your solution.

____

© Houghton Mifflin Harcourt Publishing Company

Name ______________________

Solve Systems by Substitution

I Can solve systems of linear equations by substitution.

Spark Your Learning

SMALL GROUPS

A state fair offers two pricing plans. Each includes a flat fee for admission and a price per ride. The equations in the table show the total cost y, in dollars, to attend the fair and go on x rides. For how many rides do the two pricing plans cost the same? Solve this problem without graphing and explain your reasoning.

State Fair Pricing	
Super Saver	$y = 4x + 7$
Fun Pack	$y = 2x + 17$

Turn and Talk How can you check that you correctly found a solution to a system of linear equations?

© Houghton Mifflin Harcourt Publishing Company • Image Credit: ©kunchainub/iStock/Getty Images

Build Understanding

ACTIVITY

1 Solve the system $\begin{cases} y = -2x - 4 \\ y = 2x + 8 \end{cases}$.

A. Graph the system to estimate a solution.

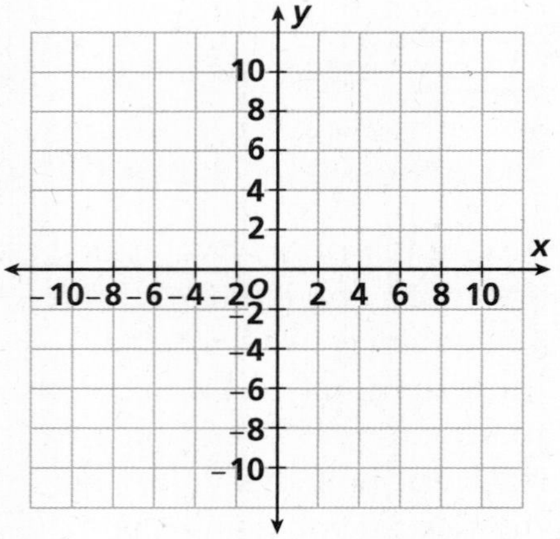

B. Since $y = -2x - 4$ and $y = 2x + 8$, what do you know about $-2x - 4$ and $2x + 8$ at the intersection point of the two lines?

C. Solve the equation $-2x - 4 = 2x + 8$.

D. What does the solution in part C represent?

E. How can you find the value of the other variable? What is the value?

F. What does the *y*-value tell you?

G. Check your solution by substituting *x* and *y* back into both original equations. Show your work.

H. What is the solution to the system of equations? ______

© Houghton Mifflin Harcourt Publishing Company

Name ______________________

Step It Out

2 Child tickets to a concert at the state fair, cost x dollars and adult tickets cost y dollars. Solve the system shown to find the price of each type of ticket.

$$\begin{cases} x + y = 10 \\ 4x + 8y = 64 \end{cases}$$

Connect to Vocabulary

You have already used substitution to evaluate expressions for specific values of a variable. To **substitute** is to replace a variable with a number or another expression in an algebraic expression.

A. Solve the system by first solving for x in the first equation.

Since $x + y = 10$, $x =$ ________.

Substitute into the other equation and solve for y.

$y =$ ____

B. Since $y =$ ____, $x = 10 -$ ____, and $x =$ ____.

Each child ticket is ____, and each adult ticket is ____.

Turn and Talk How would the solution process change if you substituted into the first equation rather than the second equation? What would remain the same?

3 Use substitution to solve the system.

$$\begin{cases} 4x - 3y = -5 \\ -8x + 2y = 2 \end{cases}$$

A. Solve for one of the variables in the first equation.

$x =$ ____________ or $y = \frac{4}{3}x + \frac{5}{3}$

B. Make a substitution in the other equation and then solve for the remaining variable. Then substitute the value you found into either equation to solve for the value of the other variable.

The solution is ______.

Check Understanding

Use the system of equations for Problems 1–2.

$$\begin{cases} x - y = 3 \\ 2x - 0.5y = 0 \end{cases}$$

1. Describe the steps for solving the system by substitution. Explain how to check the solution.

____

____

____

____

____

2. What is the solution to the system? ________

© Houghton Mifflin Harcourt Publishing Company • Image Credit: ©WilliamSherman/iStock Unreleased/Getty Images Plus/Getty Images

On Your Own

3. STEM Scientists use drones with digital cameras to help them identify plants, predict flooding, and construct 3-D maps of different landscapes. A team of scientists are using two drones to map a region. The heights of the drones are represented by the equations given, where x is the number of minutes since the drones were released from the scientists and y is the height in meters.

A. Solve the system of equations.

____

B. What does your solution tell you about the drones?

____

____

4. Consider the system of equations $\begin{cases} 2x + 5y = 18 \\ 3x + 1.5y = 9 \end{cases}$.

A. Graph to estimate the solution of the system.

Estimated solution: ____________

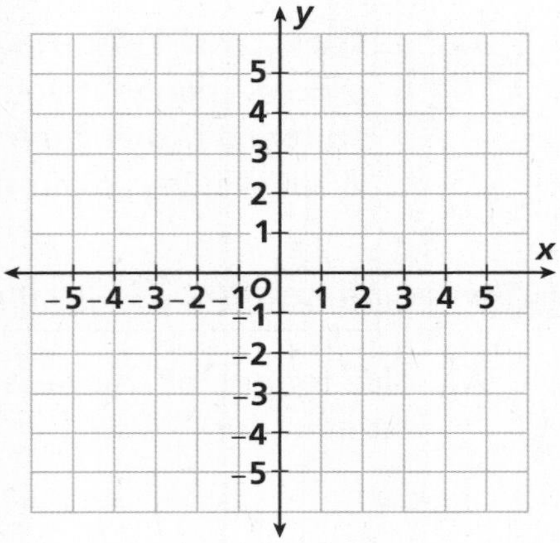

B. Solve the system by substitution.

____

5. MP **Reason** Complete the system of two linear equations so it has the solution $(-1, 7)$. Check by using substitution to solve the system.

$$\begin{cases} x + y = \square \\ \square x - y = \square \end{cases}$$

For Problems 6–9, solve the system of equations.

6. $\begin{cases} 3x - y = 15 \\ x + y = 1 \end{cases}$

____

7. $\begin{cases} -2x + y = 8 \\ y = 6 \end{cases}$

____

8. $\begin{cases} 4y = 20 \\ x - y = 7 \end{cases}$

____

9. $\begin{cases} 3x - 6y = 5 \\ 2x + y = 0 \end{cases}$

____

I'm in a Learning Mindset!

How can I modify my process for solving systems by substitution to maintain an appropriate level of challenge?

____

© Houghton Mifflin Harcourt Publishing Company • Image Credit: ©Volodymyr Goinyk/Shutterstock

Name ______________________________

ONLINE
Ed Video Tutorials and Interactive Examples

Solve Systems by Substitution

1. There are x trumpet players and y saxophone players in a school's jazz band. The equations in the system shown here relate x and y. Solve the system by substitution. What does the solution mean?

$$\begin{cases} 2x + 3y = 23 \\ y = 3x - 7 \end{cases}$$

____

____

2. Jars of baking soda cost x dollars each, and bottles of vinegar cost y dollars each. The system shown relates the prices of these items.

$$\begin{cases} 5x + 3y = 17 \\ x + y = 4 \end{cases}$$

A. Graph to estimate the solution of the system.

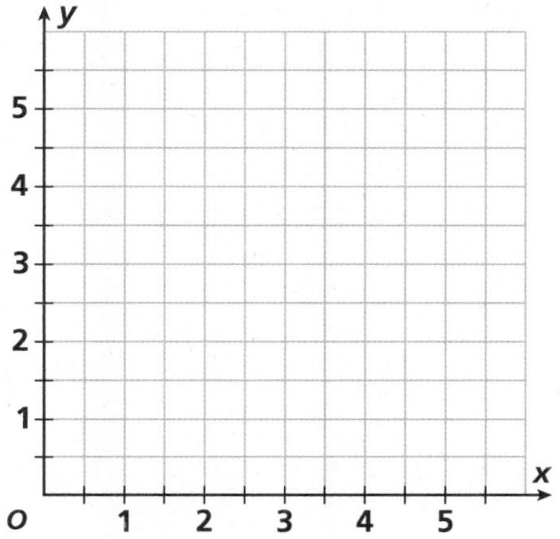

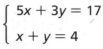

Estimated solution: ______________________________

B. (MP) **Attend to Precision** Solve the system. What does the solution represent?

____

____

3. In this system, both linear equations are given in standard form.

$$\begin{cases} 3x - 2y = -10 \\ -4x + 3y = 13 \end{cases}$$

A. Solve one of the equations for either variable.

____

B. Use substitution to find the solution of the system. ______________

4. **Math on the Spot** Solve each system by substitution.

A. $\begin{cases} y = 3x \\ y = x + 4 \end{cases}$ __________

B. $\begin{cases} x - y = 4 \\ x + 2y = 4 \end{cases}$ __________

For Problems 5–6, solve the system by substitution.

5. $\begin{cases} 2x + y = -3 \\ 3x + 2y = -2 \end{cases}$ __________

6. $\begin{cases} 4x + 3y = -7 \\ -2x + 2y = -7 \end{cases}$ __________

© Houghton Mifflin Harcourt Publishing Company • Image Credit: ©focal point/Shutterstock

Test Prep

7. Which is a correct step in solving this system of equations by substitution? $\begin{cases} x + y = 3 \\ 3x - 4y = -5 \end{cases}$

   (A) Substitute $x + 3$ for x in the equation $3x - 4y = -5$.

   (B) Substitute $x + 3$ for y in the equation $3x - 4y = -5$.

   (C) Substitute $-x + 3$ for x in the equation $3x - 4y = -5$.

   (D) Substitute $-x + 3$ for y in the equation $3x - 4y = -5$.

8. Brodie is using a coordinate plane to design two straight paths in a community garden. The paths are represented by the lines $2x + 3y = 6$ and $-3x - 2y = 1$. At what point, if any, do the two paths intersect?

   ______

9. Celia used substitution correctly to solve one of the systems of equations shown here. As part of her solution process, she solved the equation $-2x + 3(-2x + 4) = -3$. Which system did Celia solve?

   (A) $\begin{cases} -2x + y = 4 \\ -2x + 3y = -3 \end{cases}$

   (B) $\begin{cases} 2x - y = 4 \\ -2x + 3y = -3 \end{cases}$

   (C) $\begin{cases} 2x + y = 4 \\ -2x + 3y = -3 \end{cases}$

   (D) $\begin{cases} -2x - y = 4 \\ -2x + 3y = -3 \end{cases}$

10. Which is a true statement about the solution of this system of equations? $\begin{cases} 6x - 2y = -3 \\ 4x + 6y = 9 \end{cases}$

   (A) The values of both x and y are integers.

   (B) The values of x and y are equal.

   (C) The solution lies in Quadrant III of the coordinate plane.

   (D) The solution lies on one of the axes of the coordinate plane.

11. Solve the system. $\begin{cases} 2x + 3y = -9 \\ -x + 4y = 10 \end{cases}$ ______

Spiral Review

In the figure, Line *m* is parallel to Line *n*. Use the figure to solve Problems 12 and 13.

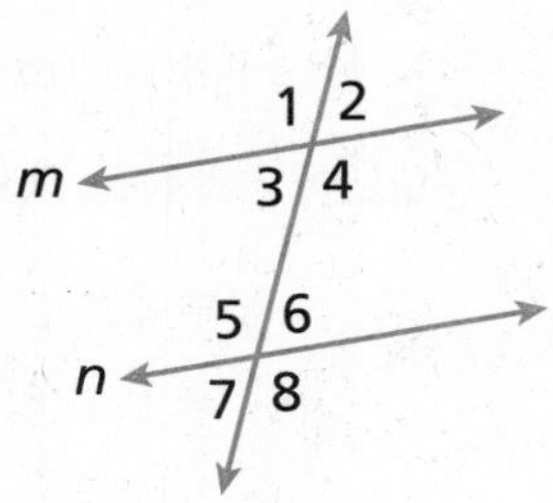

12. Name all of the pairs of corresponding angles in the figure.

   ______

13. The measure of $\angle 3$ is $(4x + 1)°$ and the measure of $\angle 6$ is $(6x - 29)°$. Find the value of x and the measures of $\angle 3$ and $\angle 6$.

   ______

14. Solve the equation $4(x + 3) + 3 = 5(x + 4)$. ______

© Houghton Mifflin Harcourt Publishing Company

Name ______________________

Solve Systems by Elimination

I Can solve a system of linear equations by elimination.

Spark Your Learning

SMALL GROUPS

A football team is selling pennants and shirts. One fan bought 6 shirts and 2 pennants for \$114.00. Later the fan returned 4 shirts and 2 pennants for \$84.00.

How could you use an operation with equations to determine the price for each shirt and each pennant?

Turn and Talk If the fan only returned 1 shirt and 1 pennant, would you still be able to determine the price for each shirt and each pennant using the same method? Explain.

© Houghton Mifflin Harcourt Publishing Company

Build Understanding

You previously learned how to solve a system of equations by replacing a variable through substitution with an **equivalent expression**. **Elimination** is the algebraic process of eliminating a variable in a system of equations by adding the equations together to eliminate one of the variables.

$$\begin{array}{r} x + 2y = 16 \\ \underline{2x - 2y = -4} \\ 3x + 0y = 12 \end{array}$$

1 Solve the system of equations shown using elimination.

$$\begin{cases} 3x + 2y = 24 \\ 7x - 2y = 36 \end{cases}$$

A. Which variable has coefficients that sum to zero? ________

B. If you add the x terms together, what is the result? ________

C. If you add the constant terms together, what is the result? ________

D. Add the two equations, then solve the resulting equation.

$$\begin{array}{r} 3x + \quad 2y = 24 \\ \underline{7x - \quad 2y = 36} \\ \square\, x + \square\, y = \square \end{array}$$

$x =$ ________

E. Substitute the value of x into either original equation to solve for y.

F. Write the solution as an ordered pair. ________

G. Check your solution by substituting the values into both original equations.

© Houghton Mifflin Harcourt Publishing Company • **Image Credit:** ©Castleski/Shutterstock

Name ______________________________

Step It Out

2 Solve the system of equations.

$$\begin{cases} x + y = 7 \\ 2x + 4y = 18 \end{cases}$$

A. Graph the system and estimate the solution.

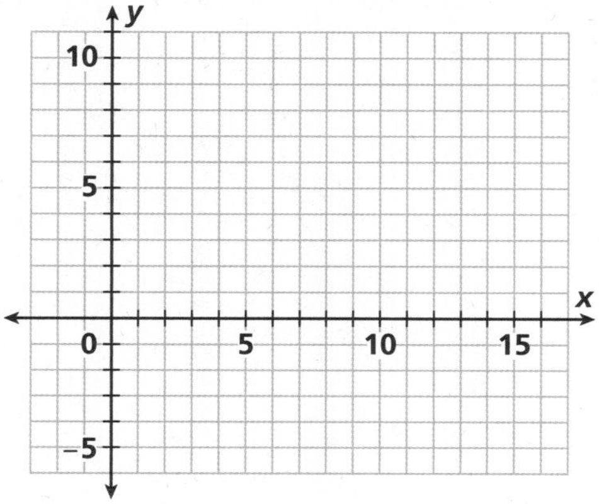

I estimate the solution is (☐ , ☐).

B. Multiply the first equation by a number so that the coefficient of the x-term is opposite of the coefficient of the x-term in the second equation.

☐ $x +$ ☐ $y =$ ☐

$2x + \quad 4y = 18$

C. Add the equations, and solve for y.

☐ $y =$ ☐ $\qquad y =$ ☐

D. Use the value of y to solve for x in either original equation.

$x +$ ☐ $= 7$ $\qquad$ or $\qquad 2x + 4$ ☐ $= 18$

$x =$ ☐ $\qquad\qquad\qquad\qquad 2x +$ ☐ $= 18$

$2x =$ ☐

$x =$ ☐

E. Check that the values of x and y make both equations true:

☐ $+$ ☐ $\stackrel{?}{=} 7$ $\qquad 2$ ☐ $+ 4$ ☐ $\stackrel{?}{=} 18$

☐ $= 7$ $\qquad\qquad$ ☐ $+$ ☐ $\stackrel{?}{=} 18$

☐ $= 18$

F. The solution is (☐ , ☐).

Turn and Talk How would you choose which variable to eliminate first when solving a system of equations?

© Houghton Mifflin Harcourt Publishing Company • Image Credit: ©Yury Stroykin/Shutterstock

3 A store sells two blends of snack mix. The situation is represented by the system of equations shown.

$$\begin{cases} 2c + 3p = 34 \\ 3c - 5p = 55 \end{cases}$$

	Packs of cranberries	Packs of pecans	Cost of mix ($)
Blend 1	2	3	34
Blend 2	3	5	55

A. Is one coefficient of c a multiple of the other? ____________

Is one coefficient of p a multiple of the other? ____________

B. Eliminate c by multiplying the first equation by −3 and the second equation by 2:

$-3(2c) + -3(3p) = -3(34) \rightarrow$ ____ $c +$ ____ $p =$ ____

$2(3c) + 2(5p) = 2(55) \rightarrow$ ____ $c +$ ____ $p =$ ____

C. Add the equations and solve.

$p =$ ____

D. Use the value of p to solve for c in either equation.

$2c + 3$ ____ $= 34$

$2c +$ ____ $= 34$

$2c =$ ____

$c =$ ____

The pecans cost ____________ per pack and the cranberries cost ____________ per pack.

Check Understanding

1. The system of equations shown represents the length and width in centimeters of a rectangle. What are the length and width?

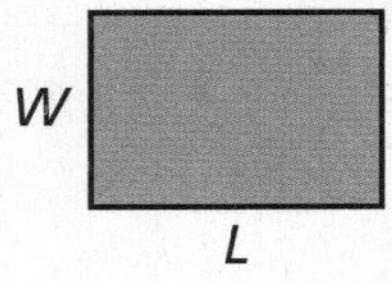

$$\begin{cases} 2L + 2W = 52 \\ L - W = 2 \end{cases}$$

____

2. What is the solution to the given system of equations?

$$\begin{cases} 3x - y = 2 \\ 3x - 2y = 10 \end{cases}$$ ____________

© Houghton Mifflin Harcourt Publishing Company • Image Credit: ©Steve Williams/Houghton Mifflin Harcourt

Name

On Your Own

3. Gareth has 15 total quarters and dimes with a total value of \$2.10. The system of equations shown can be used to solve for the number of each type of coin Gareth has.

$$\begin{cases} Q + D = 15 \\ 25Q + 10D = 210 \end{cases}$$

Complete the table to show the quantities and values of the coins Gareth has.

	Quarters	Dimes
Quantity		
Total value		

4. Liliana spends \$4.00 on 2 boxes of popcorn and 2 drinks. Nadette spends \$5.25 on 2 boxes of popcorn and 3 drinks. The prices of the popcorn and drinks can be determined by solving the system of equations shown.

$$\begin{cases} 2p + 2d = 4.00 \\ 2p + 3d = 5.25 \end{cases}$$

A. What variable will you eliminate first? How?

B. What is the solution to the system?

C. What is the price of a box of popcorn? a drink?

5. (MP) **Construct Arguments** Consider the system of equations $\begin{cases} x + y = 6 \\ x - y = 12 \end{cases}$.

A. To solve by elimination, which variable would you eliminate and why?

B. Will the solution be different if substitution is used instead of elimination? Explain.

6. What is the solution to the system? $\begin{cases} 3x + 2y = 37 \\ 7x - 6y = 1 \end{cases}$

© Houghton Mifflin Harcourt Publishing Company • Image Credit: ©Khairil Azhar Junos/Shutterstock

For Problems 7–10, solve the system of equations using elimination.

7. $\begin{cases} 3x - 2y = 5 \\ x + 2y = 3 \end{cases}$

8. $\begin{cases} 4x + 3y = 3 \\ 4x - 2y = 18 \end{cases}$

9. $\begin{cases} x - y = 3 \\ 2x + 2y = 50 \end{cases}$

10. $\begin{cases} 3x + 5y = 22.5 \\ 5x + 3y = 17.5 \end{cases}$

11. STEM A chemist uses the system of equations shown to find the amounts of pure water and salt water needed to make a new solution.

$\begin{cases} x + y = 80 \\ x + 0.25y = 32 \end{cases}$

A. Graph the system and estimate the solution.

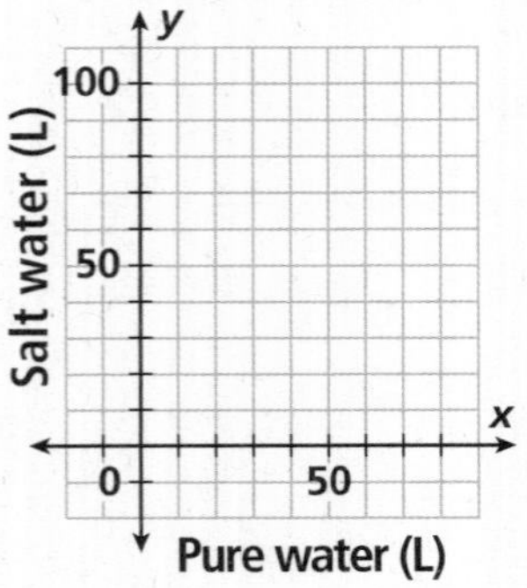

B. Solve the system for the precise answer. How many liters of pure water did the chemist use? How many liters of salt water?

12. Open Ended Complete the system of equations so that it has a solution of (4, 7).

$\begin{cases} 5x + \square\, y = 34 \\ 2x - \square\, y = \square \end{cases}$

I'm in a Learning Mindset!

How was solving systems by elimination a challenge for me? Is it still a challenge?

© Houghton Mifflin Harcourt Publishing Company • Image Credit: (t) ©Buriy/iStock / Getty Images Plus/Getty Images; (b) ©Houghton Mifflin Harcourt

Name ______________________________

LESSON 9.4
More Practice/ Homework

ONLINE Ed Video Tutorials and Interactive Examples

Solve Systems by Elimination

1. A rectangular box has a perimeter of 76 inches. If two of the boxes are placed next to each other on the long side, the new box is a rectangular shape with a perimeter of 112 inches.

The system represents the perimeters of the boxes:

$$\begin{cases} 2L + 2W = 76 \\ 2L + 4W = 112 \end{cases}$$

What are the dimensions of the original box.

____

2. **Math on the Spot** Solve the system by eliminiation.

$$\begin{cases} 2x + 5y = 4 \\ 2x - y = -8 \end{cases}$$

A. Which variable would you eliminate to solve the system using elimination? Explain.

____

____

B. What is the solution to the system? ______________________________

3. (MP) **Critique Reasoning** Carsen incorrectly solved a system of equations. His first step is shown.

$6x + 5y = 36 \rightarrow 6x + 5y = 36$

$3x - 2y = -9 \rightarrow -6x - 4y = 18$

What was Carsen's error? What is the correct solution to the system?

____

____

For Problems 4–7, solve the system of equations by elimination.

4. $\begin{cases} 2x - 3y = 2 \\ -2x - y = -26 \end{cases}$

____

5. $\begin{cases} 4x + y = -16 \\ 2x - 3y = -8 \end{cases}$

____

6. $\begin{cases} 7x + 2y = 28 \\ 3x + 2y = 20 \end{cases}$

____

7. $\begin{cases} 3x + 4y = 1 \\ 5x + 3y = -2 \end{cases}$

____

© Houghton Mifflin Harcourt Publishing Company • Image Credit: ©Juan Ci/Shutterstock

Test Prep

8. Bailey and Miranda sell ads for the school yearbook. Their first month's sales totals are represented by the system shown, where x is the price of a small ad and y is the price of a full-page ad. What are the prices of small ads and full page ads?

$$\begin{cases} 14x + 5y = 975 \\ 10x + 4y = 750 \end{cases}$$

small ad: $ ______ full page ad: $ ______

9. What is the y-coordinate of the solution to the system of equations shown?

$$\begin{cases} 2x + 3y = 5 \\ 3x - 2y = -12 \end{cases}$$

Ⓐ −3

Ⓑ −2

Ⓒ 2

Ⓓ 3

10. A triangle has two congruent angles and one unique angle. The solution to the system of equations shown represents the relationship between the angle measures. What are the measures of the angles in the triangle?

$$\begin{cases} 2x + y = 180 \\ x - y = 30 \end{cases}$$

____

Spiral Review

11. Explain how similar triangles can be used to prove the slope of the line is the same through Points $A(0, 3)$ and $B(2, 8)$ as through $B(2, 8)$ and $C(6, 18)$.

____

____

____

____

12. What is the equation of the line through the points (4, 6), (8, 12), and (10, 15)?

____

13. What is the domain of the function with points (–2, 4), (–1, 1), (0, 0), (1, 1), and (2, 4)?

____

© Houghton Mifflin Harcourt Publishing Company

Name

Examine Special Systems

I Can identify the number of solutions to a system of linear equations in any form.

Spark Your Learning

SMALL GROUPS

What values would give you no solutions to the system of equations. How do you know?

$$\begin{cases} y = 2x + 5 \\ y = \square x + \square \end{cases}$$

Turn and Talk What values would make the system of equations have an infinite number of solutions?

© Houghton Mifflin Harcourt Publishing Company • Image Credit: ©Pavel L Photo and Video/Shutterstock

Build Understanding

Just as when solving a linear equation, the solution set for a system of two linear equations can have one solution, no solution, or infinitely many solutions.

A system of two linear equations has no solution if the graphs of the two lines never intersect because the lines are parallel.

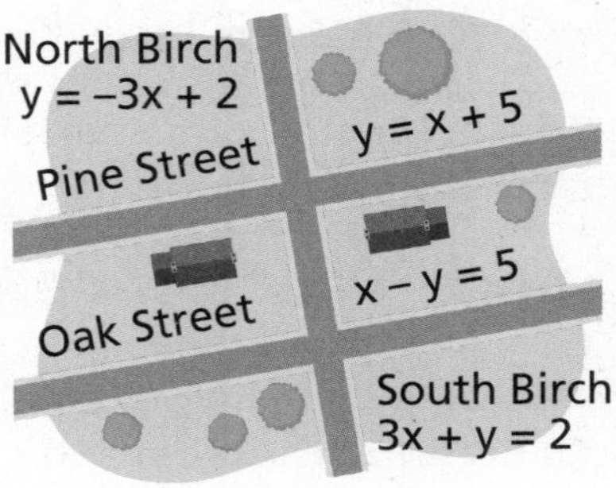

1 On a map, a street that runs in a straight line can be represented by a linear equation.

A. Solve the system of equations represented by Oak Street and Pine Street.

B. What was the result? What does it tell you about the number of solutions to the system?

C. What are the slopes of the two streets? the *y*-intercepts?

A system of two linear equations has infinitely many solutions if the graphs of the two lines are concurrent and therefore intersect at infinitely many points.

D. Solve the system of equations represented by South Birch and North Birch.

E. What was the result? What does this tell you about the number of solutions to the system?

F. What are the slopes of the two streets? the *y*-intercepts?

Turn and Talk Compare the answers for Parts C and F. Explain the similarities and differences between a system with no solutions and infinitely many solutions.

© Houghton Mifflin Harcourt Publishing Company

Name ____________________

Step It Out

2 The system $\begin{cases} x + 2y = 6 \\ 2x + 4y = 12 \end{cases}$ has infinitely many solutions.

A. Graph the system on your own paper. What do you notice about the graphs and the equations?

____

____

B. Fill in the blanks to use elimination to solve the system:

$\square\,(x + 2y = 6) \rightarrow \square\, x + (\square)\, y = \square$

$2x + 4y = 12 \rightarrow \quad 2x + \quad 4y = \quad 12$

$\square = \square$

C. How does the final equation relate to the system having infinitely many solutions?

____

____

____

3 The system $\begin{cases} 2x + y = 3 \\ 4x + 2y = 8 \end{cases}$ has no solution.

A. Graph the system on your own paper. What do you notice about the graphs and the equations?

____

____

____

B. Solve the system by substitution:

$2x + y = 3 \rightarrow y = \square\, x + \square$

$4x + 2(\square) = 8$

$4x + \square\, x + \square = 8$

$\square = 8$

C. How does the final equation relate to the system having no solutions?

____

____

Turn and Talk If you solve the equations in Task 3 for y, what equations do you get? How is that related to the graph of the two lines?

© Houghton Mifflin Harcourt Publishing Company • Image Credits: (tr) ©ikurdyumov/Shutterstock

4 How many solutions does each system of equations have? Explain.

A. $\begin{cases} 6x + 8y = 20 \\ 9x + 12y = 30 \end{cases}$

$6x + 8y = 20$ can be simplified, resulting in the equation ________.

$9x + 12y = 30$ can be simplified, resulting in the equation ________.

The equations are equivalent / unique. Therefore the system has

________ solution(s).

B. $\begin{cases} 5x + 2y = 7 \\ 15x + 6y = 24 \end{cases}$

All terms in $15x + 6y = 24$ can be divided by __, resulting in the

equation ________.

The expression $5x + 2y$ can / cannot equal both 7 and __. Therefore

the system has ________ solution(s).

Check Understanding

1. Rory bought a pencil and a folder for \$0.35. Emily bought 3 pencils and 3 folders for \$1.05. The system of equations shown represents this.

$\begin{cases} x + y = 35 \\ 3x + 3y = 105 \end{cases}$

Could each of them have paid the same price for pencils and for folders?

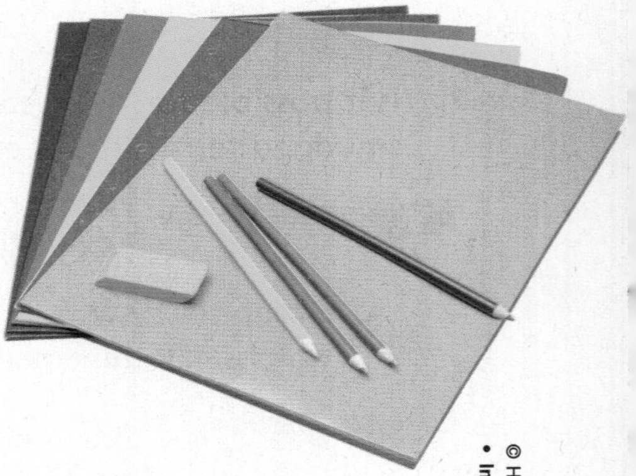

____

____

Use the information to answer Problems 2–4.

Consider the system of equations $\begin{cases} 6x + 4y = 14 \\ 9x + 6y = C \end{cases}$.

2. Which value(s) of C represent a system with infinitely many solutions?

____

3. Which value(s) of C represent a system with no solution?

____

4. Is there any value of C that would result in the system having one solution? Why or why not?

____

____

© Houghton Mifflin Harcourt Publishing Company • Image Credit: ©jldeines/iStock/Getty Images Plus/Getty Images

Name

On Your Own

5. Stacy and Bridget are wrapping presents. Their times are represented by the system shown, where x is the wrapping rate in minutes per box and y is the packing rate in minutes per bag.

$$\begin{cases} 6x + 3y = 36 \\ 2x + y = 12 \end{cases}$$

How many solutions does the system have? Explain.

Use the information to answer Problems 6–7.

A system of two equations includes the equation $2x + 6y = 8$. The other equation in the system was smudged but shows $3x + \blacksquare = 12$.

6. Is it possible for the system to have infinitely many solutions? If so, what could be the smudged term? If not, explain your reasoning.

7. Is it possible for the system to have no solutions? If so, what could be the smudged term? If not, explain your reasoning.

8. **Open Ended** Provide an equation that, when combined with the equation $7x - y = 5$ could form a system with the given number of solutions.

   A. infinitely many solutions

   B. no solutions

For Problems 9–12, state the number of solutions to the system: one, none, or infinitely many.

9. $\begin{cases} 3x + 4y = 7 \\ 3x + 4y = 9 \end{cases}$

10. $\begin{cases} x + y = 2 \\ y - x = 12 \end{cases}$

11. $\begin{cases} y = 3x - 5 \\ y = -3x - 5 \end{cases}$

12. $\begin{cases} y = 5 + 2x \\ y = 2x + 5 \end{cases}$

© Houghton Mifflin Harcourt Publishing Company • Image Credit: ©Weronica Ankarörn/Houghton Mifflin Harcourt

13. Rosie spends 2 hours building each model plane x and 6 hours building each model boat y. She has a total of 40 hours to spend each week. Yuri spends 1 hour building each model plane and 3 hours building each model boat but has only 20 hours to spend each week. The system shown represents their total work times.

$$\begin{cases} 2x + 6y = 40 \\ x + 3y = 20 \end{cases}$$

How many solutions does the system have? Explain.

____

____

14. (MP) **Reason** Devante and Jim each draw a rectangle. The perimeter of Devante's rectangle is 60 centimeters. The sum of the length and width of Jim's rectangle is 15 centimeters. The system shown represents the dimensions of their rectangles.

$$\begin{cases} 2L + 2W = 60 \\ L + W = 15 \end{cases}$$

Do the rectangles have the same dimensions? Explain.

____

For Problems 15–20, solve each system of equations.

15. $\begin{cases} x + 2y = 7 \\ 4x + 8y = 28 \end{cases}$

____

16. $\begin{cases} 5x - 2y = 19 \\ 5x + 2y = 11 \end{cases}$

____

17. $\begin{cases} 6x - 4y = 2 \\ -9x + 6y = 3 \end{cases}$

____

18. $\begin{cases} -4x + 2y = 12 \\ y = 2x + 6 \end{cases}$

____

19. $\begin{cases} 12x - 18y = 9 \\ 2x - 3y = 1 \end{cases}$

____

20. $\begin{cases} x = 2y - 10 \\ 4y = x + 12 \end{cases}$

____

I'm in a Learning Mindset!

Which special systems were the most challenging for me? Why?

____

____

© Houghton Mifflin Harcourt Publishing Company • Image Credit: ©akihiro1963/iStock/Getty Images Plus/Getty Images

Name ______________________________

ONLINE
Video Tutorials and
Interactive Examples

Examine Special Systems

1. Gabe bought 6 singles and 9 albums from an online music store. Jenny bought 4 singles and 6 albums at a different online music store. The system shown represents their totals for singles that cost *x* dollars each and albums that cost *y* dollars each.

$$\begin{cases} 6x + 9y = 96 \\ 4x + 6y = 38 \end{cases}$$

A. Solve the system. What does the solution mean?

____

B. Is it possible to know if Gabe and Jenny purchased the singles and albums for the same prices? Explain.

____

For Problems 2–4, use the system of equations shown.

$$\begin{cases} 3x + 5y = 4 \\ 6x + 10y = 4 \end{cases}$$

2. Does the system have a solution? Explain.

____

____

3. (MP) **Critique Reasoning** Manuel says that he can change the 4 in the second equation to any number and the system will have no solution. Is Manuel correct? Explain.

____

____

4. How can one number in the second equation be changed so the system has only one solution? Explain.

____

____

For Problems 5–10, solve the system of equations.

5. $\begin{cases} x + y = 3 \\ x - y = -3 \end{cases}$ ______________

6. $\begin{cases} 5x + y = 7 \\ 10x + 2y = 16 \end{cases}$ ______________

7. $\begin{cases} 3x + 4y = 9 \\ 12x + 16y = 36 \end{cases}$ ______________

8. $\begin{cases} 4x + 3y = 11 \\ 3x + 4y = 17 \end{cases}$ ______________

9. $\begin{cases} 3x + 12y = 9 \\ 5x + 20y = 15 \end{cases}$ ______________

10. $\begin{cases} 4x - 2y = 16 \\ -14x + 7y = -49 \end{cases}$ ______________

© Houghton Mifflin Harcourt Publishing Company • Image Credit: ©ymgerman/Shutterstock

Test Prep

11. The system of equations $\begin{cases} ax - 4y = 10 \\ -9x + 6y = -15 \end{cases}$ has infinitely many solutions.

What is the value of a?

Ⓐ 5

Ⓑ 6

Ⓒ 7

Ⓓ 8

12. Consider the system of equations $\begin{cases} y = -\frac{3}{2}x + 4 \\ y = -\frac{3}{2}x - 4 \end{cases}$.

The system has [no / one / infinitely many] solution(s).

13. Mark whether each system has infinitely many solutions, no solution or one solution.

	Infinitely many solutions	No solution	One solution
$\begin{cases} x + 3y = 6 \\ 6x + 18y = 36 \end{cases}$	☐	☐	☐
$\begin{cases} 2x - 3y = -3 \\ 4x + 6y = 18 \end{cases}$	☐	☐	☐
$\begin{cases} 3x + 2y = 6 \\ 6x + 4y = 24 \end{cases}$	☐	☐	☐
$\begin{cases} 8x - 10y = 6 \\ -4x + 5y = 3 \end{cases}$	☐	☐	☐
$\begin{cases} 4x + 10y = 16 \\ 10x + 25y = 40 \end{cases}$	☐	☐	☐

Spiral Review

Use the information to answer Problems 14–15.

The height in inches of a candle that has been burning for x hours is represented by the equation $h = 16 - 2x$.

14. What is the meaning of the slope in the context of the burning candle?

____

15. What is the meaning of the y-intercept in the context of the burning candle?

____

16. What is the solution of the system of equations $\begin{cases} x = 2y - 5 \\ 2x + y = 20 \end{cases}$?

____

© Houghton Mifflin Harcourt Publishing Company

Name ______________________________

Apply Systems of Equations

I Can write and solve a system of equations to solve a real-world problem.

Step It Out

ACTIVITY

1 There are 12 people in an adventure club going to an adventure park. An adult's pass is \$55, a child's pass is \$42, and they spend a total of \$569. How many adults and how many children go together to the park?

A. What equation can you write to represent the number of adults a and children c that are in the group?

$\square + \square = 12$

B. How much is an adult's pass? How much is a child's pass? What was the total spent on day passes?

____

What equation can you write to represent the total amount spent by the group?

$\square a + \square c = \square$

C. You can use the two equations from Parts A and B to write a system of equations to solve the problem. Write the system of equations.

$\square + \square = 12$

$\square a + \square c = \square$

D. Solve the system of equations using elimination.

$a = \square$

$c = \square$

E. How many adults and how many children go together to the park?

____

Turn and Talk Is there another way to solve the system of equations? Explain.

© Houghton Mifflin Harcourt Publishing Company • Image Credit: ©Francesco Gustincich/Alamy

2 Kailee is holding an event at a ballroom with tables that seat 6 people and tables that seat 4 people. Kailee orders a total of 12 tables for the 57 people coming to the event. How many tables of each kind should she order?

A. Let x represent the number of tables that seat 6 people and y represent the number of tables that seat 4 people. Complete the two equations shown, one of which represents the number of tables, and the other which represents the number of seats.

$\square + \square = \square$

$\square x + \square y = 57$

B. These two equations comprise the system of equations that represent the problem. Begin solving the system of equations by first solving one equation for y.

$x + y = 12 \quad \rightarrow \quad y = \square$

Substitute the resulting expression for y into the second equation and solve for x.

$6x + 4y = 57$

$6x + 4(\square) = 57$

$6x + \square - \square = 57$

$\square + \square = 57$

$\square = \square$

$x = \square$

C. Does the value for x make sense for this problem? Why or why not?

____

D. Round the value for x up to the nearest whole number, and use that value to solve for y.

$\square + y = 12$

$y = \square$

She should order ________ tables that seat 6 people and ________ tables that seat 4 people.

E. Substitute x and y into the second equation. If Kailee orders these tables, will she have enough seats for all the attendees? Explain.

$6(\square) + 4(\square) = \square$

____

Turn and Talk If a value doesn't make sense for the solution to a problem, do you always round the value up? Explain.

© Houghton Mifflin Harcourt Publishing Company • Image Credit: ©Trinette Reed/age fotostock

Name

3 Line A passes through points (0, 1) and (2, 5). Line B passes through points (1, 1) and (4, 10).

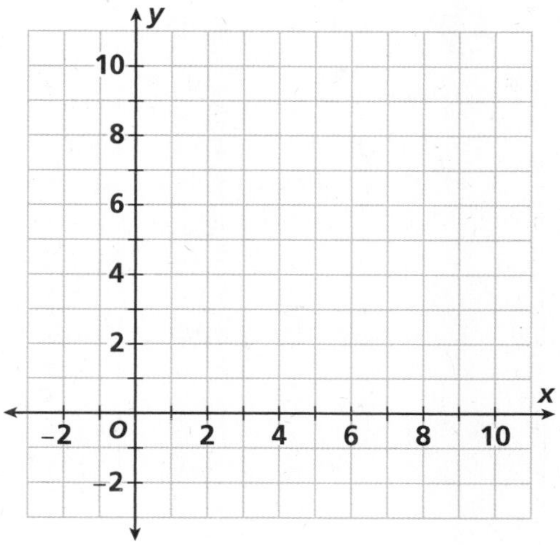

A. Plot the points for Line A and draw a line through them.

B. Plot the points for Line B and draw a line through them.

C. Do the lines intersect? ________

D. Use the graph to estimate the point of intersection.

____

E. How could you find the exact point of intersection?

____

Check Understanding

Write and solve a system of equations to solve Problems 1–3.

1. The Spartan basketball team scored 108 points in last night's game. They scored 48 baskets in all, making a combination of two-point and three-point baskets. There were no points due to free throws. How many three-point baskets did the Spartans make?

____

____

2. Mr. Chen buys 5 tomato plants and 3 cucumber plants for $33.00. His neighbor buys 4 tomato plants and 2 cucumber plants of the same varieties for $24.90 at the same nursery. What is the cost of each type of plant?

____

____

____

Tomato plant

Cucumber plant

3. One line passes through (0, 1) and (4, −7). A second line passes through (−1, −1) and (1, −5). Do the two lines intersect? If so, where? Show your work.

____

____

____

____

© Houghton Mifflin Harcourt Publishing Company • Image Credits: (tr) ©vkbhat/E+/Getty Images; (br) ©Madlen/Shutterstock

On Your Own

4. (MP) **Model with Mathematics** A museum charges different rates for adults and students. Mrs. Lopez's class went to the museum last week and spent $232.50 on 25 tickets. How many students and how many adults went to the museum?

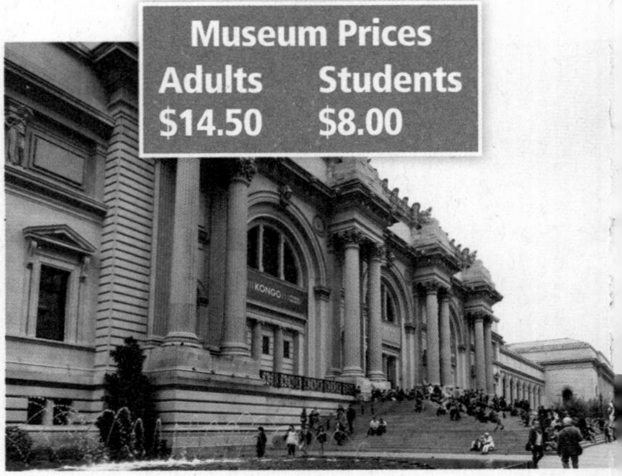

   A. Write a system of equations to model the problem.

   ____

   B. Find the solution using any method.

   ____

   C. What is the meaning of the solution in the context of the problem?

   ____

5. Tony is hiking at a rate of 4 feet per second when he sees his friend Nathan 30 feet ahead hiking 2 feet per second.

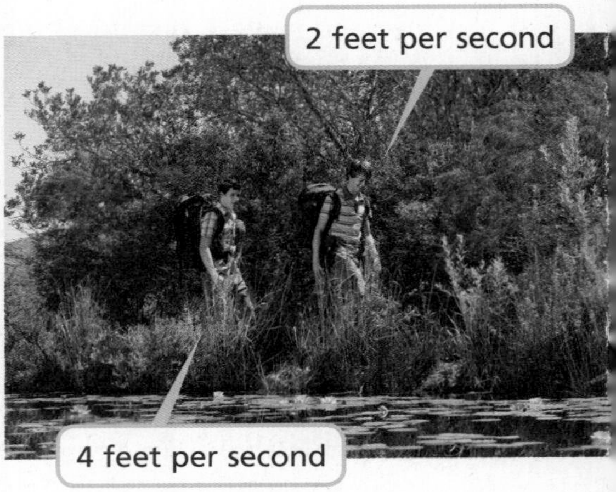

   A. Graph a system of equations to model the situation.

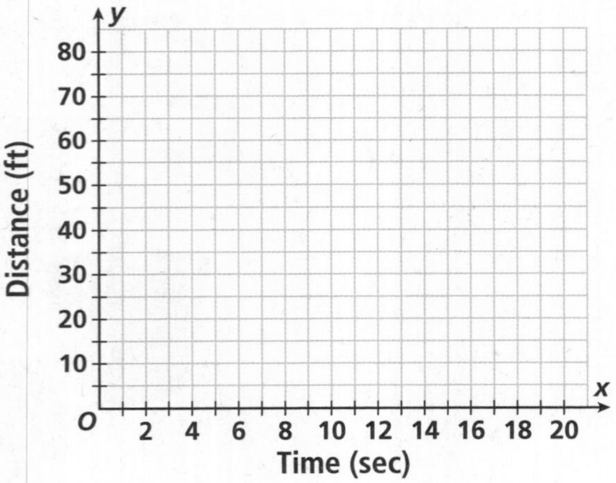

   B. Will Tony catch up to Nathan? Explain.

   ____

   ____

6. The sum of two numbers is 18. The sum of the greater number and twice the lesser number is 25.

   A. Let x represent the greater number and y represent the lesser number. Write a system of equations to find the numbers.

   ____

   B. Solve the system. What are the two numbers? ______________

© Houghton Mifflin Harcourt Publishing Company • Image Credits: (tr) ©Siempreverde22/iStock Editorial/ Getty Images Plus/Getty Images;(br) ©Moodboard/Alamy

Name

7. Two angles are complementary if the sum of their measures is equal to 90°. Georgia draws two complementary angles. One of the angles measures 15° more than 2 times the other angle's measure.

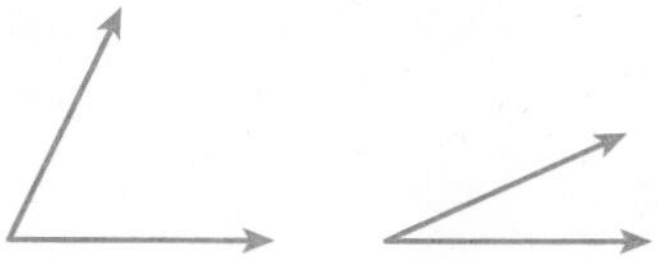

A. Write a system of equations to represent the situation.

____

B. What are the measures of the two angles? ____________

8. **Open Ended** Write a problem that could be solved using the graph shown. Explain what happens and how it relates to the solution.

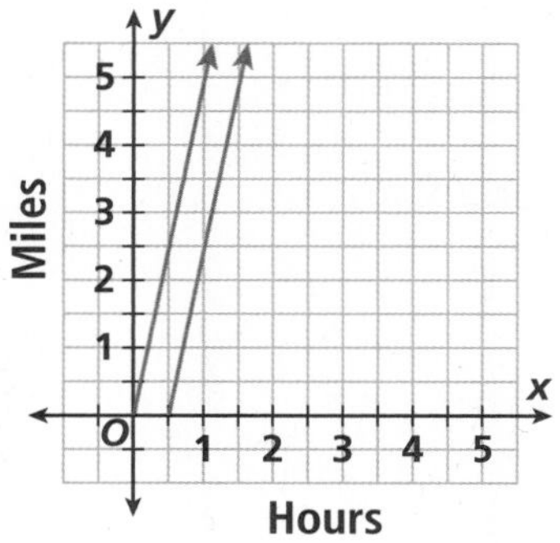

____

____

____

____

____

9. (MP) **Reason** Mrs. Bennett gives her math class a test worth 145 points. Some of the questions are worth two points and some are worth five points. Is there enough information to determine how many five-point questions are on the test? If so, how many? If not, what additional information is needed?

____

____

10. The Fairplay sporting goods store sells two different models of a popular fitness tracker. In one month the store sold 42 trackers for a total of $6,574.

Fitness Trackers	
Model A	Model B
$127	$189

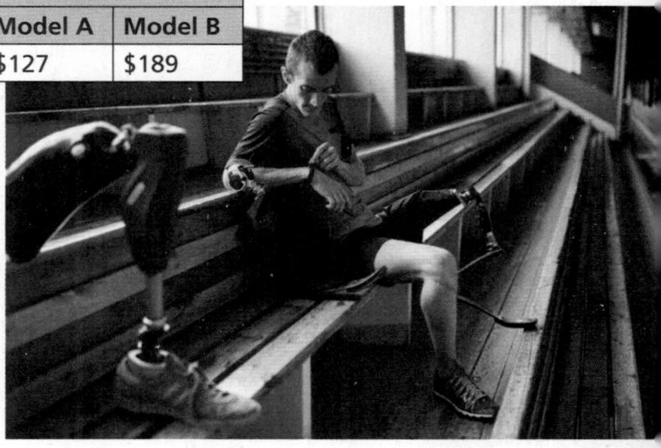

A. Write a system of equations that represents the situation.

____

B. How many of each type of tracker were sold?

____

© Houghton Mifflin Harcourt Publishing Company • Image Credits: ©Konstantin Pelikh/Alamy

11. Bowling costs \$6 per game and virtual golf costs \$0.50 per hole. Bowling takes 30 minutes per game and virtual golf takes 7.5 minutes per hole. Maya spends 1 hour and \$8 between the two activities.

A. (MP) **Model with Mathematics** Write a system of equations relating b, the number of games of bowling played, to g, the number of holes of virtual golf played.

B. Solve the system you wrote and interpret your solution

---

12. The table shows two options provided by an internet service provider.

	Setup fee	Monthly fee
Option 1	\$100	\$55
Option 2	\$30	\$75

A. Write a system of equations modeling this situation, where c represents the total cost for m months of service.

B. After how many monthly payments will the cost of the two options be the same? Explain.

C. Which option would you recommend for someone who is only going to stay in town for 5 months? Why?

---

13. Alicia bought 4 sandwiches and 5 bowls of soup, spending \$38.50. Adam spent \$47.25 to buy three sandwiches and nine bowls of soup. Write and solve a system of equations to find out the cost of each sandwich and each bowl of soup.

© Houghton Mifflin Harcourt Publishing Company • Image Credit: ©bonchan/iStockphoto/Getty Images

Name ____________________

ONLINE
Video Tutorials and Interactive Examples

Apply Systems of Equations

1. A builder is developing a neighborhood of one-bedroom and two-bedroom houses. The builder wants to build 12 houses and has 88 windows. The one-bedroom houses need 6 windows and the two-bedroom houses need 9 windows.

A. Write and solve a system of equations to represent the situation.

____

B. How many of each type of house should the builder build?

____

2. Math on the Spot Doug has 45 coins worth $9.00. The coins are all quarters or dimes. How many of each type of coin does Doug have?

____

3. A young horse, Alex, is chasing an older horse, Champ. Alex is 60 meters behind Champ. Graph a system of equations to solve the problem. Will Alex catch up to Champ? If so, when? If not, why not?

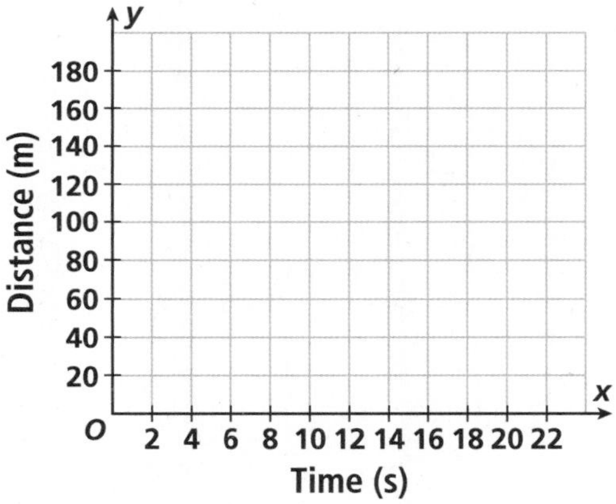

____

4. (MP) **Reason** A family owns two cars. One car gets 35 miles per gallon and the other car gets 27 miles per gallon. In one week the family drove a total of 480 miles and used 16 gallons of gas. Can you determine the number of miles the family drove each car? Explain.

____

____

____

____

© Houghton Mifflin Harcourt Publishing Company • Image Credits: (tr) ©photovs/iStock/Getty Images Plus/Getty Images; (br) ©Anja Ehgartner/EyeEm/Getty Images

Test Prep

5. The Greenery landscaping company puts in an order for 2 pine trees and 5 hydrangea bushes for a neighborhood project. The order costs $150. They put in a second order for 3 pine trees and 4 hydrangea bushes that cost $144.50. What is the cost for one pine tree?

$ ________

6. Sonia is older than her brother Eddie. The sum of their ages is 38. The difference is 14. How many years old are Sonia and Eddie?

Sonia: ☐ years old   Eddie: ☐ years old

7. The Chenery School sold a total of 78 tickets for the spring concert. Advance tickets sold for $5.00 and tickets purchased the night of the concert cost $10.50. If the total revenue for the night was $533, how many advance tickets were sold?

___ tickets

8. Two angles are supplementary. This means that the sum of the two angles is equal to 180°. One of the angles measures 20 degrees more than three times the other angle. What is the measure of the larger angle?

Ⓐ 40°
Ⓑ 120°
Ⓒ 200°
Ⓓ 140°

Spiral Review

9. Which two triangles are similar? How do you know?

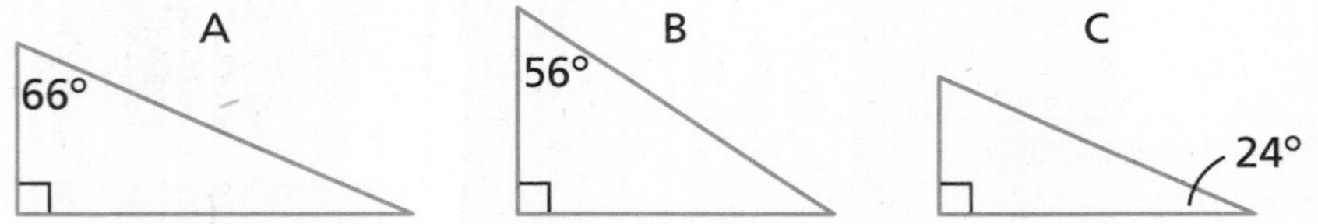

____

10. A line passes through the origin and (4, 6). What are two other points on this line?

____

11. What is an equation of the line with slope –3 through the point (3, 5)?

____

© Houghton Mifflin Harcourt Publishing Company

Module 9

Name ________________

Review

Vocabulary

Choose the correct term from the Vocabulary box.

Vocabulary
elimination
equivalent expressions
substitution
system of equations

1. A ________________ is two or more equations that contain two or more variables.

2. A method of solving a system of equations that involves adding equations to remove a variable is called ________________.

3. ________________ are expressions with the same total value.

Concepts and Skills

4. North Shore Kayak and South Shore Kayak each charge a flat fee plus an hourly rate. The graph shows *y*, the cost in dollars, for renting a kayak from each company for *x* hours. Which statement about the companies is true?

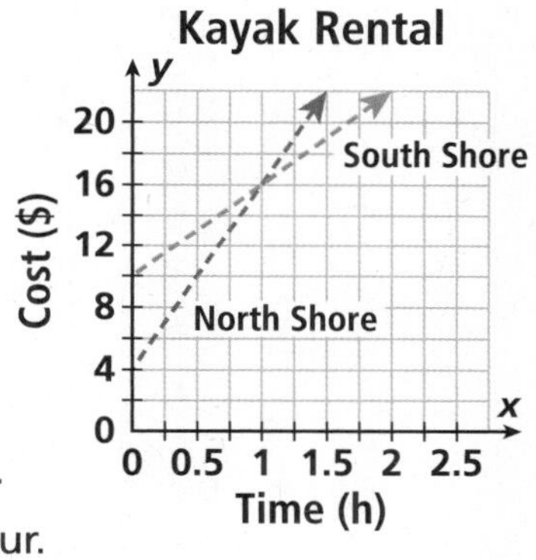

Ⓐ The companies have the same hourly rate.

Ⓑ South Shore costs more when renting a kayak for 2 hours.

Ⓒ The flat fee is higher for North Shore than for South Shore.

Ⓓ The companies cost the same when renting a kayak for 1 hour.

5. A graph of a system of two equations is shown. What is the solution of the system? Write the ordered pair.

(________, ________)

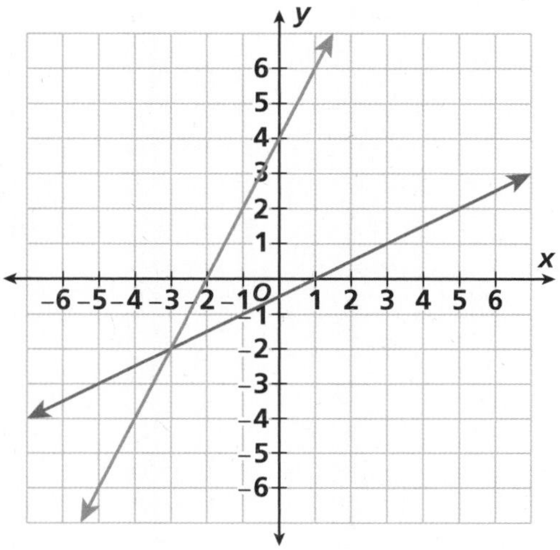

6. (MP) **Use Tools** Determine the solution of the system of equations shown. State what strategy and tool you will use to answer the question, explain your choice, and then find the answer.

$$\begin{cases} y = x + 1 \\ y = -2x + 4 \end{cases}$$

____

____

____

© Houghton Mifflin Harcourt Publishing Company

Determine the solution of each system of equations.

7. $\begin{cases} y = -6x + 4 \\ y = 2x + 12 \end{cases}$ (_______, _______)

8. $\begin{cases} 3x + 2y = 9 \\ 4x - y = 34 \end{cases}$ (_______, _______)

9. A system of equations is shown. Which method could be used to eliminate a variable from the system?

$\begin{cases} 5x + 6y = 28 \\ 4x + 2y = 14 \end{cases}$

Ⓐ Multiply the first equation by −4, and then add the equations.

Ⓑ Multiply the first equation by −2, and then add the equations.

Ⓒ Multiply the second equation by −3, and then add the equations.

Ⓓ Multiply the second equation by −2, and then add the equations.

10. Select the number of solutions for each system of two linear equations.

	No solution	One solution	Infinitely many solutions
$\begin{cases} 3x + 5y = 10 \\ 2x + 5y = 10 \end{cases}$	☐	☐	☐
$\begin{cases} x - 3y = 4 \\ 2x - 6y = 8 \end{cases}$	☐	☐	☐
$\begin{cases} 4x - 2y = 6 \\ 4x - 2y = 8 \end{cases}$	☐	☐	☐

11. Tickets for a high school basketball game cost $4 for adults and $3 for students. The school sells 120 tickets and makes $412 in ticket sales. The system of equations shown can be used to determine the number of adult tickets *a* and the number of student tickets *s* the school sold. How many adult tickets and how many student tickets did the school sell?

$\begin{cases} a + s = 120 \\ 4a + 3s = 412 \end{cases}$

_________ adult tickets _________ student tickets

12. Corinne's pumpkin weighs 28 ounces and is growing at a rate of 5 ounces per week. Ron's pumpkin weighs 10 ounces and is growing at a rate of 13 ounces per week. Let *t* represent time in weeks and *w* represent weight in ounces. Which system of equations can be used to determine when the weights of the two pumpkins will be equal?

Ⓐ $\begin{cases} w = 5 + 28t \\ w = 13 + 10t \end{cases}$

Ⓑ $\begin{cases} w = 5(t + 28) \\ w = 13(t + 10) \end{cases}$

Ⓒ $\begin{cases} w = 5t - 28 \\ w = 13t - 10 \end{cases}$

Ⓓ $\begin{cases} w = 5t + 28 \\ w = 13t + 10 \end{cases}$

© Houghton Mifflin Harcourt Publishing Company

Unit 4

Data Analysis and Sampling

Research Assistant

A research assistant collects or verifies information in a laboratory setting, or even in an office for a field such as law or media. Responsibilities of a research assistant may include conducting surveys, analyzing data, providing quality control, managing information storage, and preparing results for presentation or publication. Research assistants often use computers to help them perform these tasks.

STEM Task:

Work as a class to record the birth month of each class member. Assign the number 1 to represent January, the number 2 to represent February, and so on. Use the class data to make a dot plot. What observations and conclusions can you make by looking at the dot plot? What questions do the data raise? Explain your thinking.

© Houghton Mifflin Harcourt Publishing Company • Image Credits: (t) ©Hero Images/Getty Images; (b) ©NAN728/Shutterstock

Learning Mindset

Resilience Manages the Learning Process

Resilience is the ability to move forward when obstacles arise. Developing resilience allows you to identify a barrier, learn from it, and overcome the challenges it presents. Here are some ways you can increase your resilience.

- Consider where you are within the learning process. Do you think you may encounter barriers to completing a task? If so, try to identify them.
- Review the steps you are taking to direct your learning. Monitor your feelings, motivation, and interest level to keep yourself on task.
- If necessary, modify learning situations and activities so that they lead to successful conclusions.

© Houghton Mifflin Harcourt Publishing Company • Image Credit: ©Jason Butcher/Cultura/Getty Images

Reflect

Q **What strategies did you use to overcome barriers you encountered during the STEM Task?**

Q **What steps can you take to direct your learning and better understand how to collect and analyze data?**

Module 10 Scatter Plots

TAKEN for a RIDE

Use the graphs to answer the questions.

A. The graph shows the cost y of using Company A's ride-sharing service for a trip of x miles. Find the rate of change in the graph. What does it represent?

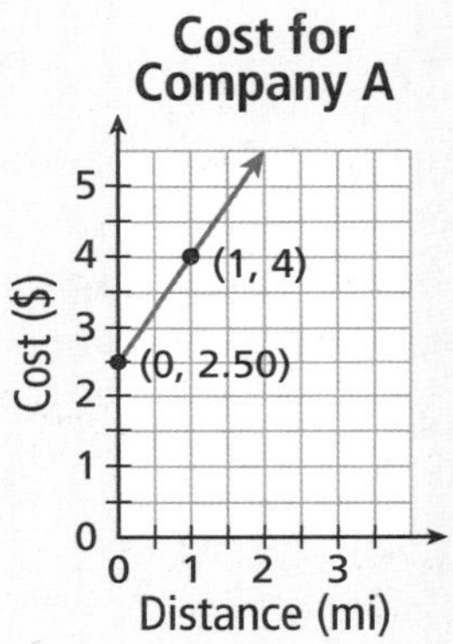

B. Company B wants to compete with Company A. It will have the same initial fee as Company A, but a lower price per mile.

Write an equation of a function that could represent the total cost y of using Company B's ride-sharing service for a trip of x miles. Then graph your equation.

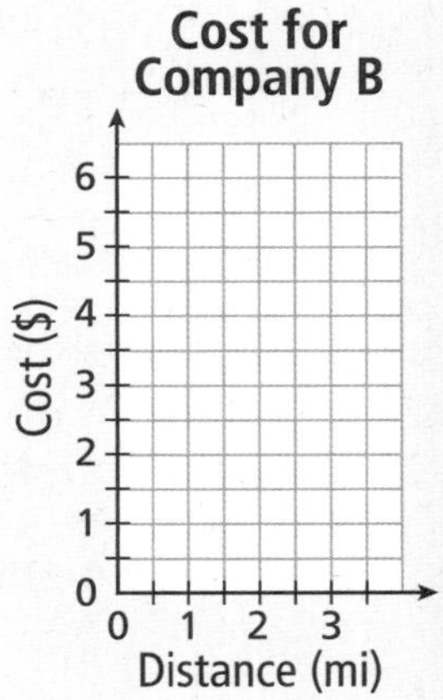

Turn and Talk

How does the equation you wrote for Company B indicate the initial fee and the rate of change?

© Houghton Mifflin Harcourt Publishing Company • Image Credit: ©Michael Shake/Shutterstock

Are You Ready?

Complete these problems to review prior concepts and skills you will need for this module.

Dot Plots

1. Marie recorded the number of ducks seen at a pond each day for 12 days. The data set is listed.

8, 10, 12, 14, 13, 15, 13, 15, 14, 15, 16, 16

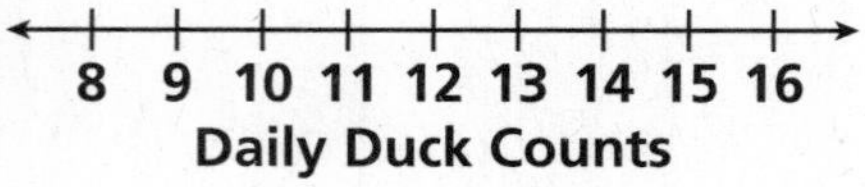

A. Display Marie's data in the dot plot.

B. Describe the center, spread, and overall shape.

____

____

A phone company tested the battery life of a random sample of 20 of its newest model phones. The dot plot shows the company's results. Use the dot plot to answer Problems 2–3.

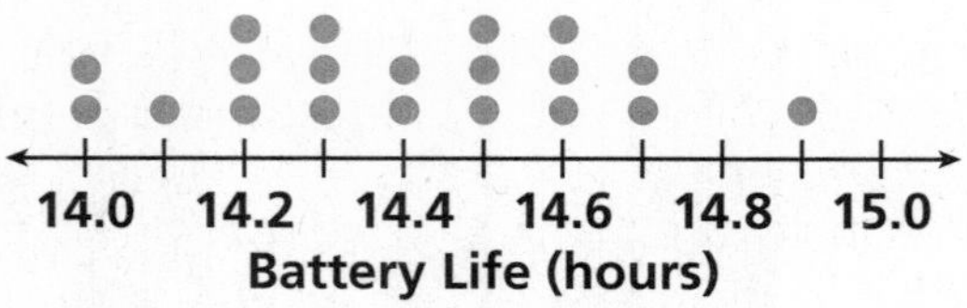

2. Calculate the mean battery life of the phones in the sample.

____

3. Based on the sample, how many of the newest phone model in a shipment of 2,000 phones can be expected to have a battery life of less than 14.2 hours?

____

Interpret Linear Functions

The graph shows the linear relationship between the number of hours a candle burns and the weight in ounces of the candle. Use the graph to answer Problems 4–6.

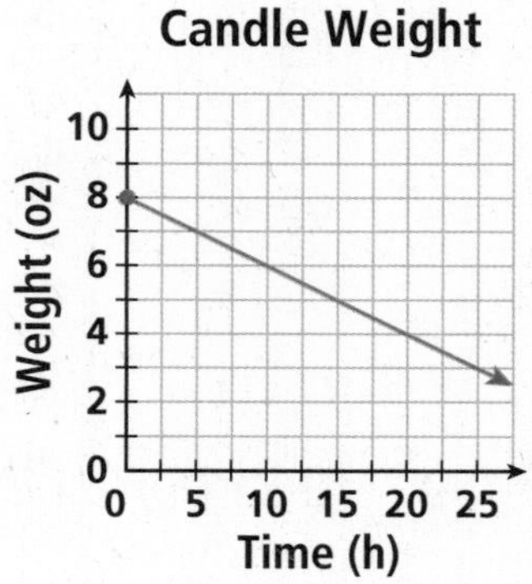

4. What is the initial value in this situation, and what does it represent?

____

5. What is the rate of change in this situation, and what does it represent?

____

6. Write the equation of the function.

____

© Houghton Mifflin Harcourt Publishing Company

Name ______________________

Construct Scatter Plots and Examine Association

(I Can) construct a scatter plot, determining whether an association is positive or negative, strong or weak, and nonlinear or linear. I can recognize outliers and clusters.

Spark Your Learning

PAIRS

Mrs. Tenney gave her students a test. The students had 3 weeks to study for the test, and Mrs. Tenney tracked the number of hours that each student studied and the scores they got on the test. Graph the data in the table. Describe the graph.

Study time (h)	Test score
19	97
12	81
16	89
20	98
10	75
12	99
15	90
15	88
19	100
16	91
8	72
10	78
15	72
18	95
21	98

Turn and Talk Why do you think there is not a constant rate of change for the number of hours studied and the test scores?

© Houghton Mifflin Harcourt Publishing Company • Image Credit: ©Monkey Business Images/Shutterstock

Build Understanding

An **association** is the description of the relationship between two **data sets**. Two data sets have a **positive association** when their data values increase together or decrease together.

Connect to Vocabulary

A **scatter plot** is a graph with points plotted to show a possible relationship between two sets of data.

1 The graph of the data from Mrs. Tenney's class is shown in a scatter plot.

A. Describe the change that you see in the graph.
As the ______________ increases, the ______________ increases.

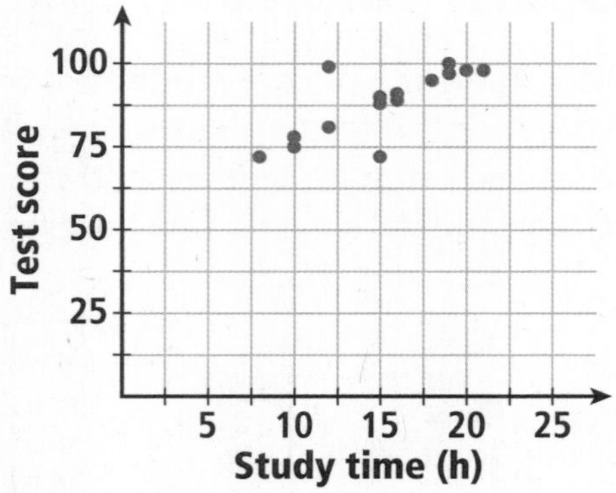

B. When data points lie roughly along a line, the data set displays a **linear association**. When the data seem to follow a pattern resembling anything other than a line, the data set displays either a **nonlinear association** or no association at all. Do you think the relation between test scores and study time appears linear? Explain.

____

____

Two data sets have a **negative association** if one set of data values increases while the other decreases.

Mrs. Tenney also tracked the number of hours students spent on social media sites and the scores they got on the test. The data are shown in the scatter plot.

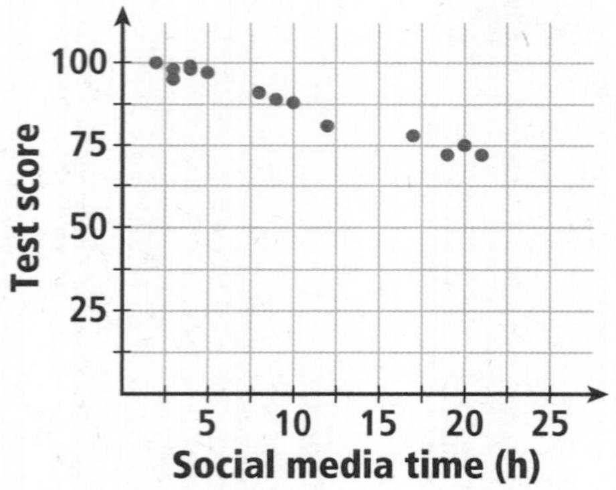

C. Describe the change that you see in the graph.
As the ______________ increases, the ______________ decreases.

D. Do you think the relation between test scores and social media time appears linear? Explain.

____

____

© Houghton Mifflin Harcourt Publishing Company • Image Credit: (br) ©Monkey Business Images/Shutterstock

Name ______________________

Two data sets have **no association** when there is no relationship between their data values.

Mrs. Tenney wanted to see if there was any relationship between the number of siblings that a student has and their score on the test. The data are shown in the scatter plot.

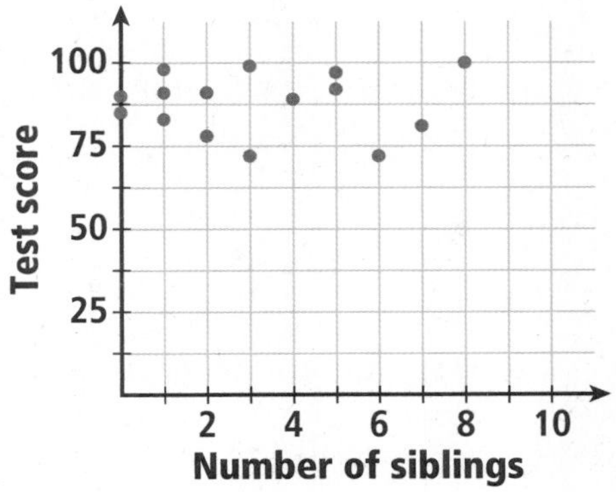

E. Describe the change in test scores that you see in the graph.

____

____

____

F. Do you think the relation between test scores and number of siblings appears linear? Explain.

____

____

Connect to Vocabulary

An **outlier** for a data set of ordered pairs is a point that does not follow the overall pattern on a graph of the data set.

Step It Out

ACTIVITY

2 If a scatter plot has an association, that association can also be strong or weak. For linear data, the association is stronger the closer the points are to making a line.

A

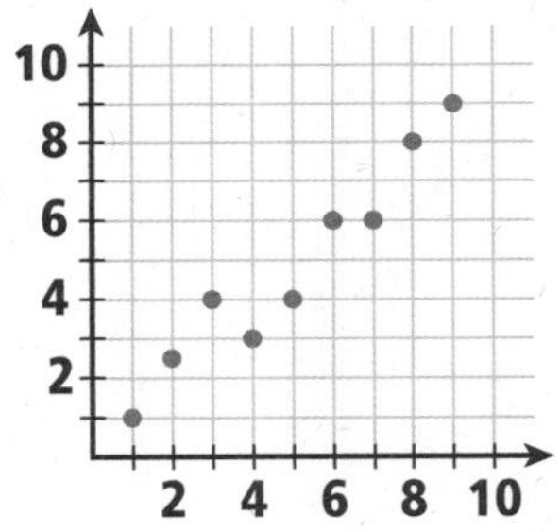

B

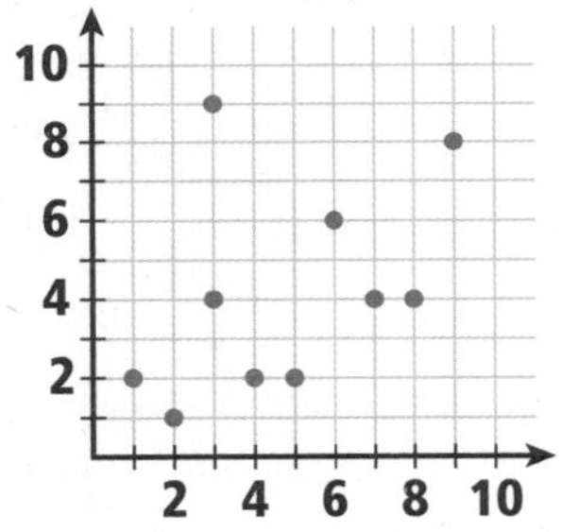

C

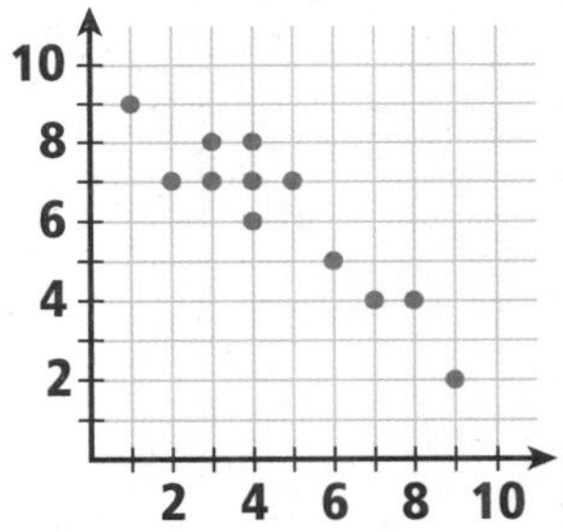

D

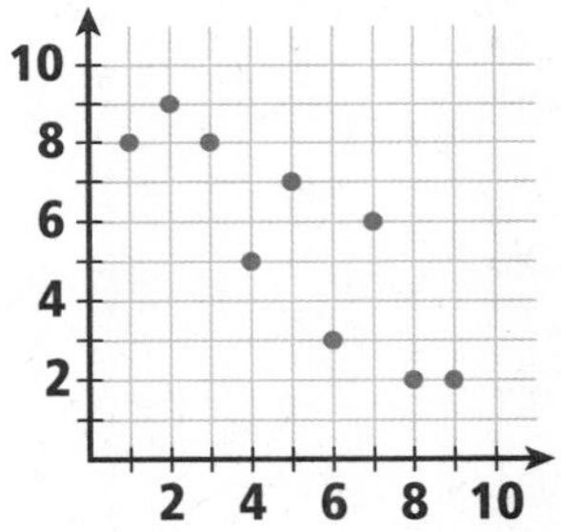

A. Which scatter plot(s) have a positive association? Is the association of each strong positive or weak positive?

____

B. Which graph or graphs appear to have outliers? ______________________

C. A **cluster** is a set of closely grouped data. Which graph or graphs appear to have a cluster? ______________________

Turn and Talk Which scatter plot(s) have a negative association? Is the association of each strong negative or weak negative? How do you know?

© Houghton Mifflin Harcourt Publishing Company

3 Jack earned $60 doing odd jobs for his neighbor. Each week he spends some of the money and records the amount of money left.

Week	1	2	3	4	5	6	7
Money remaining	$57.00	$53.00	$49.00	$48.00	$47.00	$44.00	$19.00

A. Graph the data.

Jack's Savings

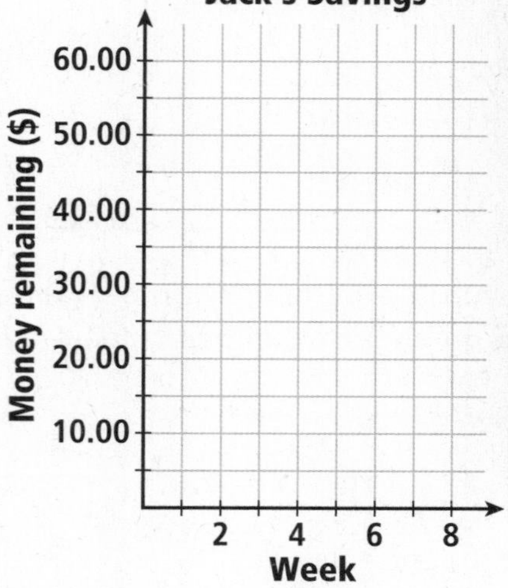

B. Does the scatter plot have a negative or positive association?

C. Describe and interpret the shape of the graph.

D. Are there any clusters or outliers? If so, what might explain the cluster or outliers?

E. Is the association strong or weak?

Check Understanding

1. The table shows the amount of money Anna spends each week.

Items	1	2	3	4	5	5	6	6
Spending	$1.90	$3.50	$4.25	$6.00	$6.25	$6.50	$6.20	$5.90

A. Graph the relationship in the scatter plot.

B. Describe the relationship, including any outliers or clusters.

Thrift Store Purchases

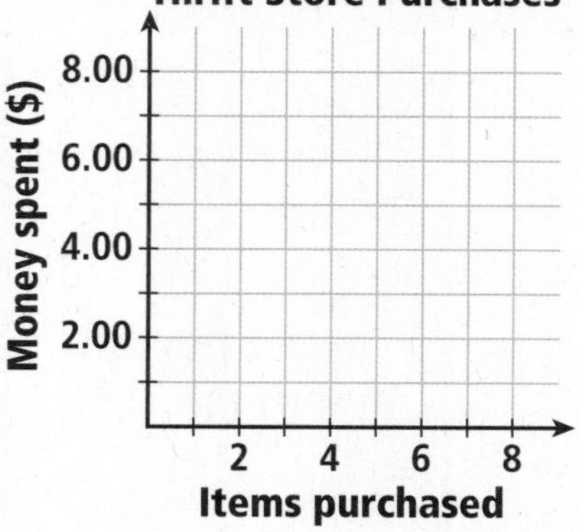

© Houghton Mifflin Harcourt Publishing Company • Image Credit: ©plastique/Shutterstock

Name ______________________________

On Your Own

2. (MP) **Use Structure** The Pep Club is selling bracelets to raise money for a pet shelter. The club members staff the booth for a total of 11 hours selling bracelets. The table records the amount of money they earned each hour.

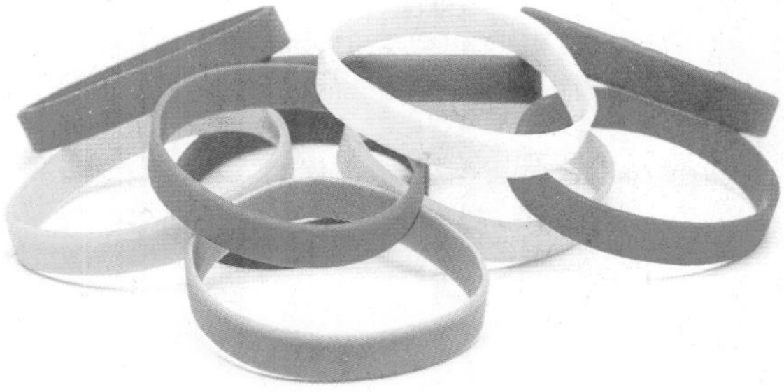

A. Graph the data in the table.

Hour	Money earned ($)
1	$17
2	$22
3	$18
4	$16
5	$40
6	$28
7	$25
8	$23
9	$31
10	$27
11	$21

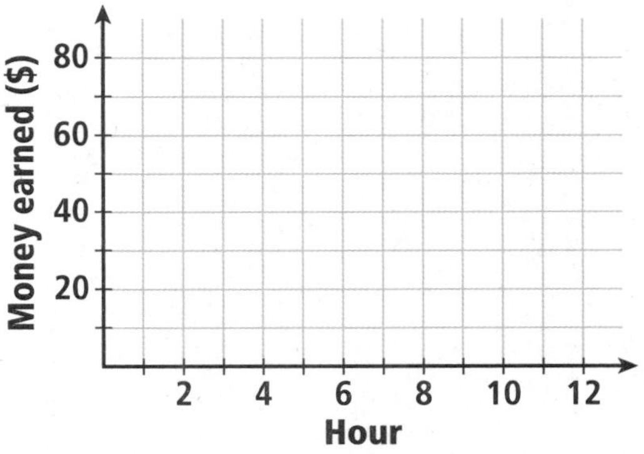

B. Describe in detail the association of the graph. Include whether it is linear or nonlinear, whether it is positive or negative, whether it is strong or weak, and whether it has any clusters or outliers.

____

____

____

____

3. Bob works at a movie theater collecting tickets. He tracked how many people came to each showing one day. Which showtime is an outlier?

Showtime	Attendance
11:00 a.m.	16
2:00 p.m.	17
4:00 p.m.	15
6:30 p.m.	115
9:00 p.m.	20

____

© Houghton Mifflin Harcourt Publishing Company • Image Credit: (tr) ©FilosofArtFoto/Shutterstock; (br) ©Tyler Olson/Shutterstock

4. (MP) **Critique Reasoning** Chantelle says that the scatter plot has a strong positive association because the numbers at the bottom of the graph are increasing and the shape of the graph is linear. Is she correct? Explain.

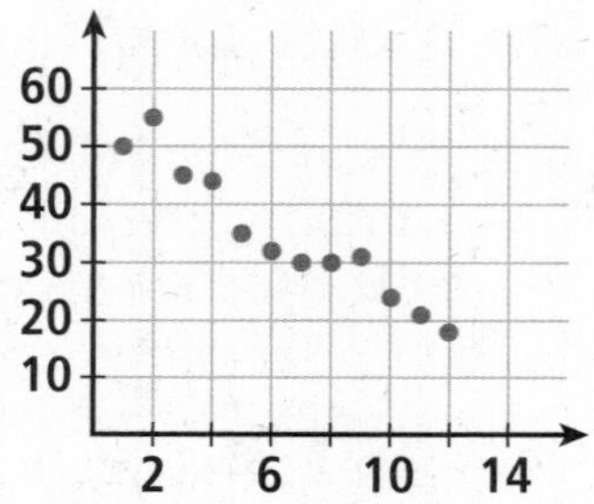

5. **Open Ended** Ellianna made a scatter plot that showed a positive association and had one outlier. Write a possible scenario for Ellianna's scatter plot.

© Houghton Mifflin Harcourt Publishing Company • Image Credit: ©Tanate Raktaengan/Shutterstock

Use the graph to answer Problems 6–8.

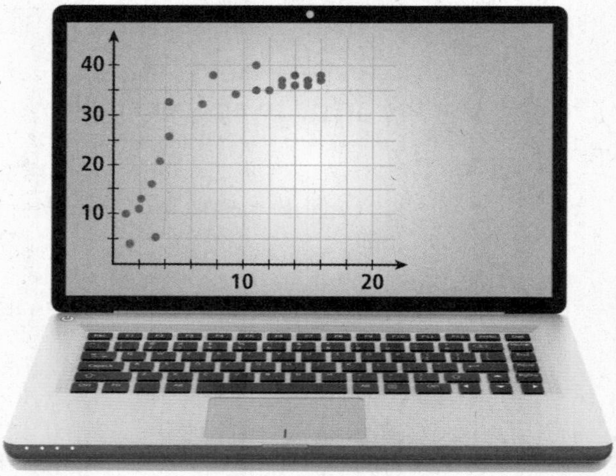

6. Is there any association to the data? If so, which type?

7. Is the scatter plot linear or nonlinear?

8. Are there any outliers or clusters in the graph?

9. **Open Ended** Give an example of a scenario for a scatter plot that would show no association.

I'm in a Learning Mindset!

What steps am I taking to direct my own learning about scatter plots?

Name

Construct Scatter Plots and Examine Association

ONLINE
Ed
Video Tutorials and Interactive Examples

1. The table shows the number of fundraiser items each person in the band sold and how much money each raised.

Items sold	Money raised
6	\$34
2	\$12
7	\$52
8	\$66
6	\$32
6	\$30
21	\$98
5	\$28

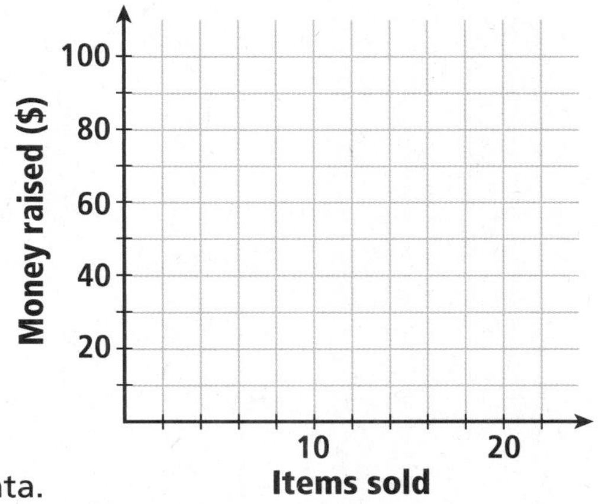

A. Construct a scatter plot for the data.

B. Describe the association and any features of the scatter plot.

© Houghton Mifflin Harcourt Publishing Company

Use the graph to answer Problems 2–4.

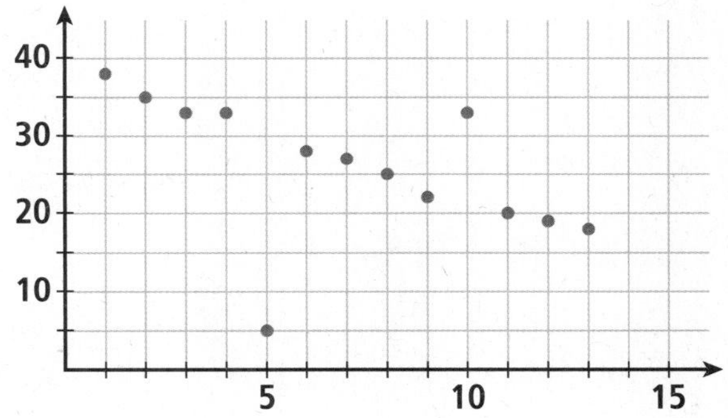

2. Describe the association, if there is one.

3. (MP) **Use Structure** Does the scatter plot appear linear or nonlinear?

4. (MP) **Use Structure** Are there any outliers or clusters in the scatter plot?

5. **Math on the Spot** The table shows the number of runs scored by a softball team in their first 7 games of the year. Use the given data to make a scatter plot. Describe the association.

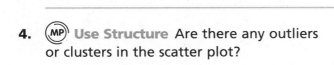

Game	1	2	3	4	5	6	7
Runs scored	3	1	5	9	12	10	12

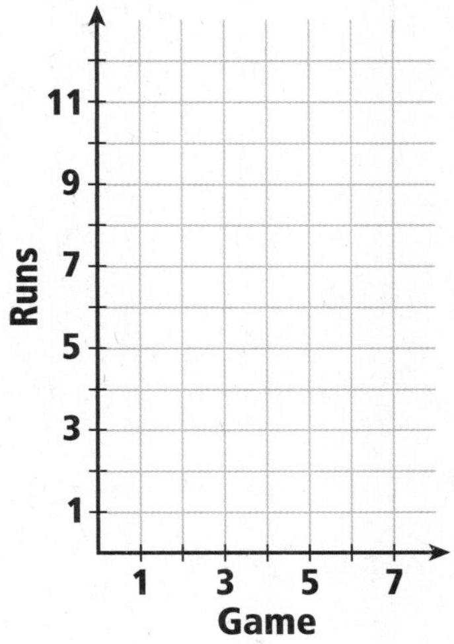

Test Prep

6. Choose all the sentences that describe this scatter plot.

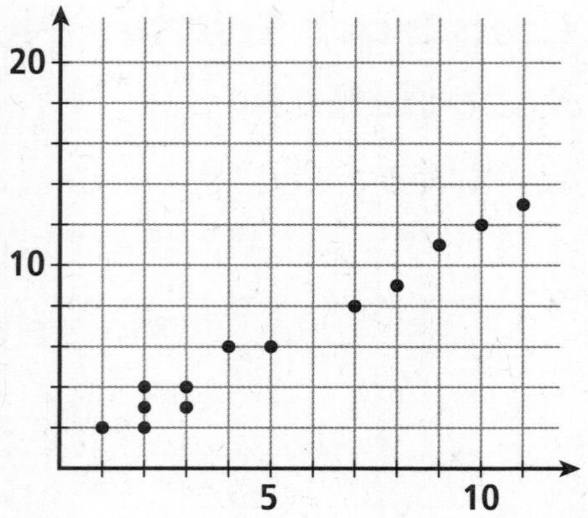

Ⓐ It shows a positive association.

Ⓑ It shows a negative association.

Ⓒ It shows no association.

Ⓓ It has at least one outlier.

Ⓔ It shows a cluster.

7. Describe each scatter plot as having positive linear, negative linear, positive nonlinear, negative nonlinear, or no association.

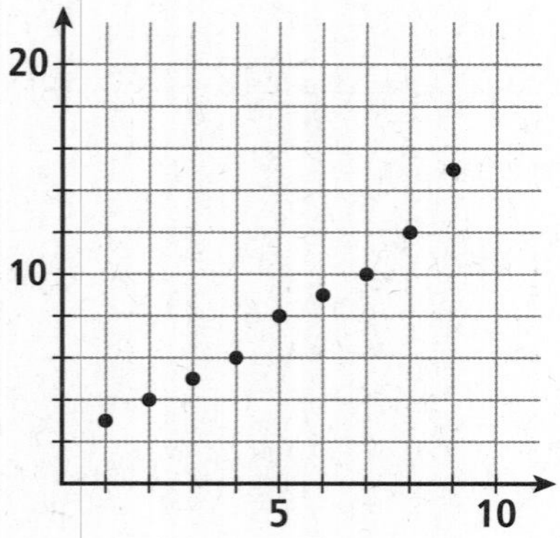

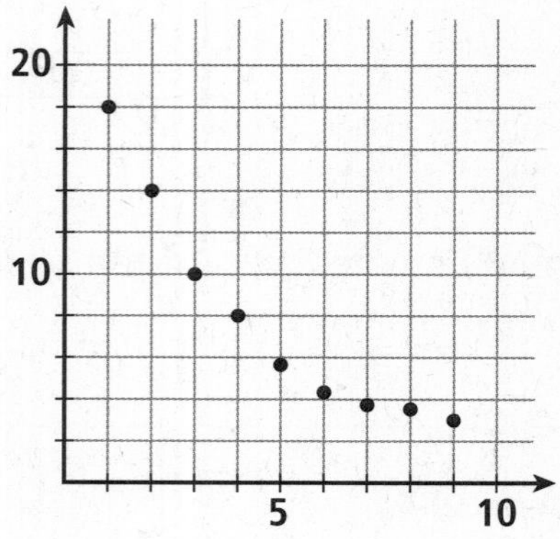

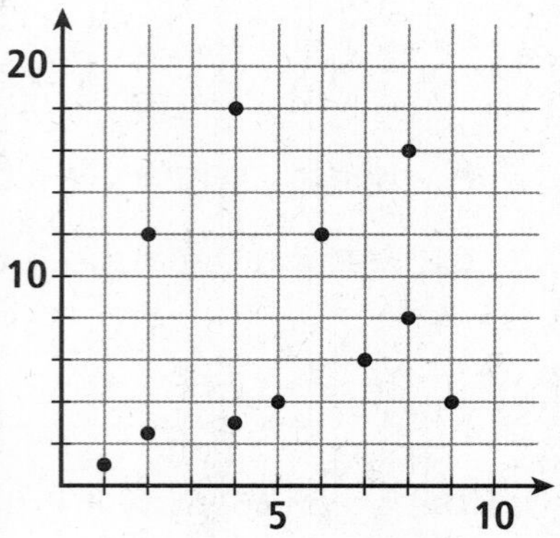

Spiral Review

8. Breck has 22 dimes and nickels. The total value of the coins is $1.45. How many dimes and how many nickels does Breck have?

9. Solve this system of linear equations.

$$\begin{cases} 4x + 4y = 12 \\ 6x - 4y = -32 \end{cases}$$

10. Find an equation of the line with a slope of –7 that passes through the point (–3, 12).

© Houghton Mifflin Harcourt Publishing Company

Name ______________________________

Draw and Analyze Trend Lines

I Can determine a trend line and informally assess it by judging the closeness of the data points to the line. I can write an equation that describes a trend line.

Spark Your Learning

PAIRS

Skyler collected data from several different types of cars. The scatter plot displays the relationship between the weight of each car and the average number of miles it can travel in the city on a single gallon of gas. What conclusions can you draw from the data?

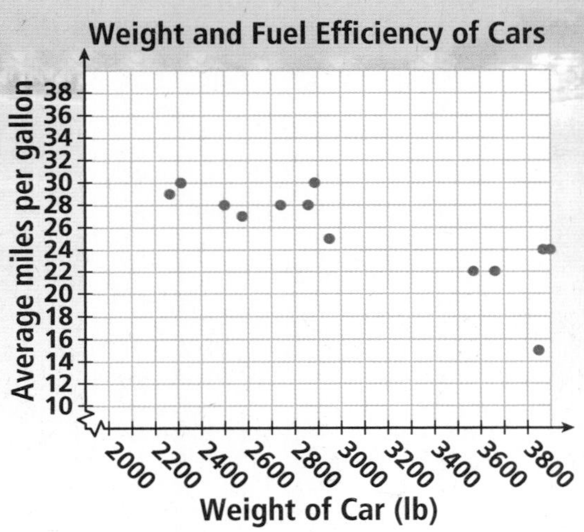

Turn and Talk Estimate the average miles per gallon for a car weighing 3400 pounds. How did you determine your estimate?

© Houghton Mifflin Harcourt Publishing Company • Image Credit: ©Kwangmoozaa/Shutterstock

Build Understanding

1 A class draws four different models, or trend lines, for the same data set. To evaluate each trend line, consider the following questions.

How many points lie above the trend line? How many points lie below? How many points does the trend line touch or pass through? What is the greatest vertical distance between any point and the trend line?

Model A

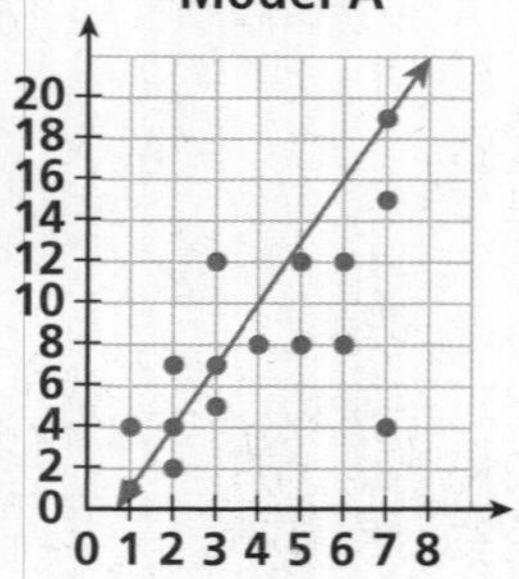

Model B

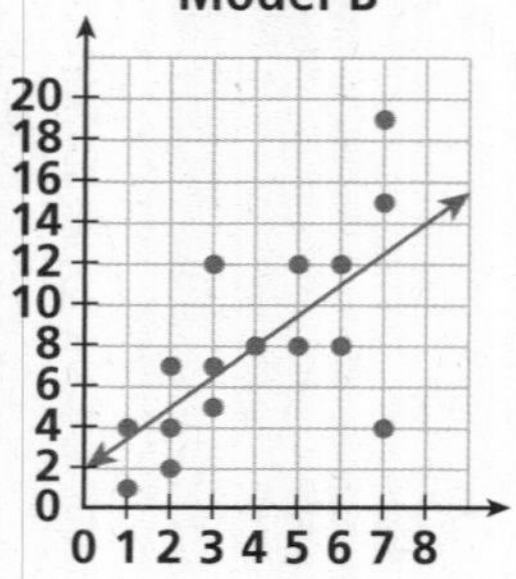

Model C

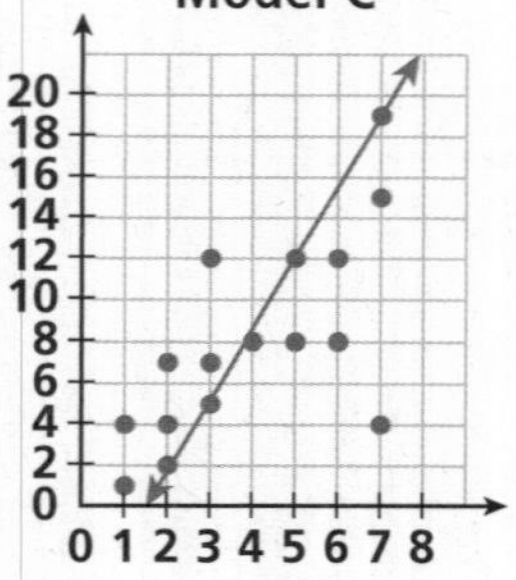

Model D

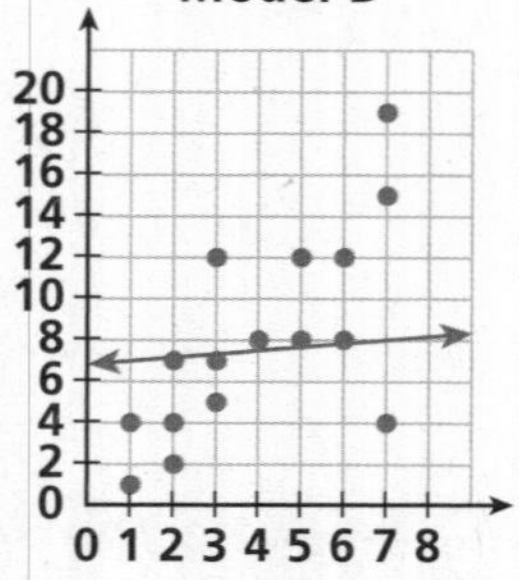

Connect to Vocabulary

A **trend line** models the behavior of data displayed in a scatter plot. When a scatter plot shows a positive association, the trend line will have a positive slope. The trend line for data with a negative association will have a negative slope.

Turn and Talk Which trend line is the best model of the relationship? Explain.

© Houghton Mifflin Harcourt Publishing Company • **Image Credit:** ©Yuri Arcurs/Digital Vision/Getty Images

Name

Step It Out

2 The scatter plot shows a negative linear association.

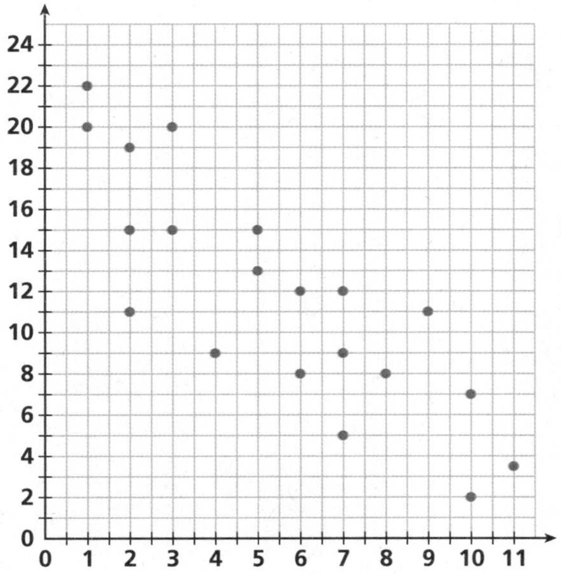

A. How many points are there in the data set? About how many points would an ideal trend line have above and below it?

B. Use a ruler to sketch a trend line to model the association shown.

C. How many points does your trend line touch or pass through?

D. How many points lie above your trend line? How many lie below your trend line?

E. How many points have a vertical distance from the trend line of more than 3 units?

F. What is the greatest vertical distance between any point and the trend line?

© Houghton Mifflin Harcourt Publishing Company • Image Credit: ©Sebastian Julian/E+/Getty Images

Turn and Talk Describe a real-world situation that could be modeled by this data.

3 A. Analyze the scatter plots, and sketch a trend line for each.

Data Set A

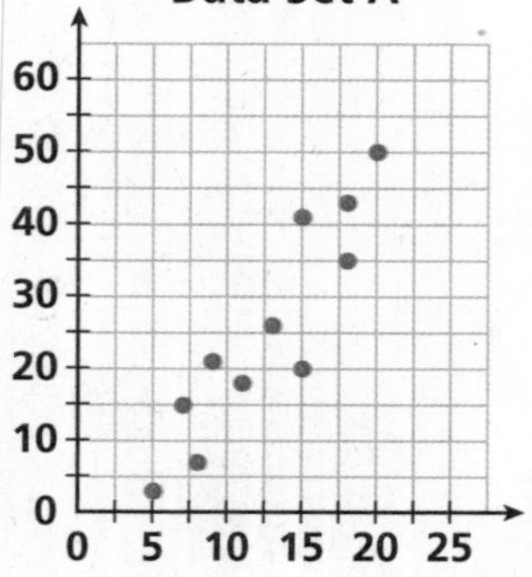

Data Set B

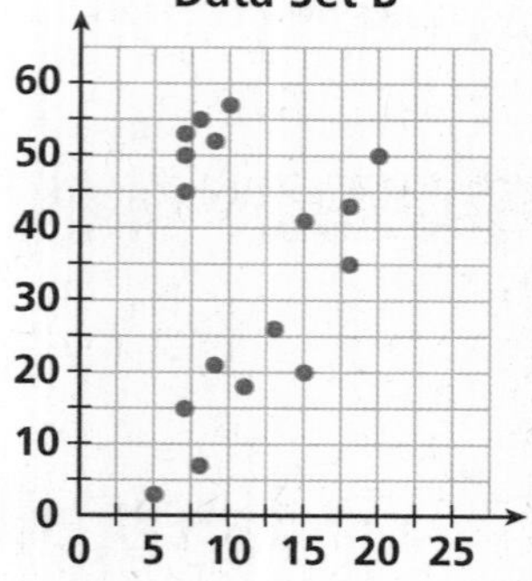

Data Set C

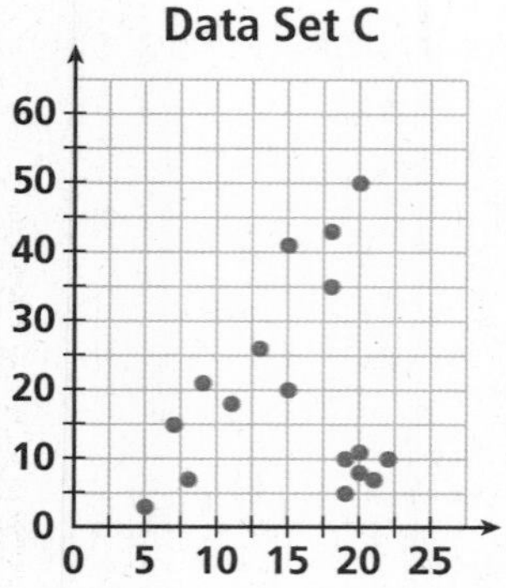

B. Compare the trend lines for data sets A, B, and C. How do outliers influence the trend lines?

Turn and Talk Should outliers be ignored when drawing a trend line? Why or why not?

Check Understanding

1. What are key characteristics of a reasonable trend line for a scatter plot?

2. Harold and Chloe each drew a trend line for the given data set.

A. Whose trend line is a closer fit? Why?

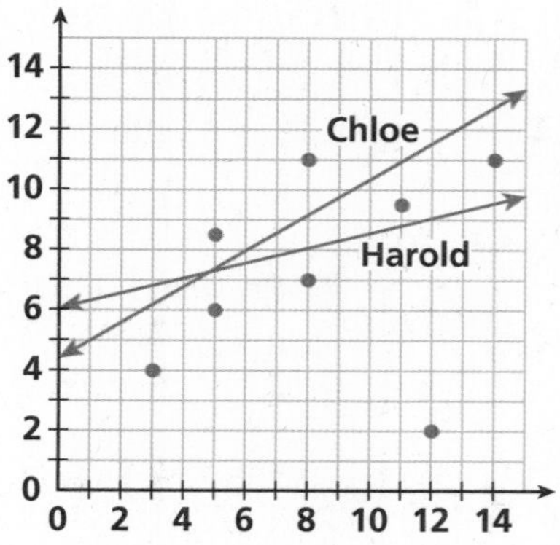

B. For the other line, analyze what mistake might have been made.

© Houghton Mifflin Harcourt Publishing Company • Image Credit: ©VladyslavDanilin/Shutterstock

Name

On Your Own

3. MP **Reason** The Flan family enjoys making cat videos and posting them on social media sites. They construct the scatter plot shown.

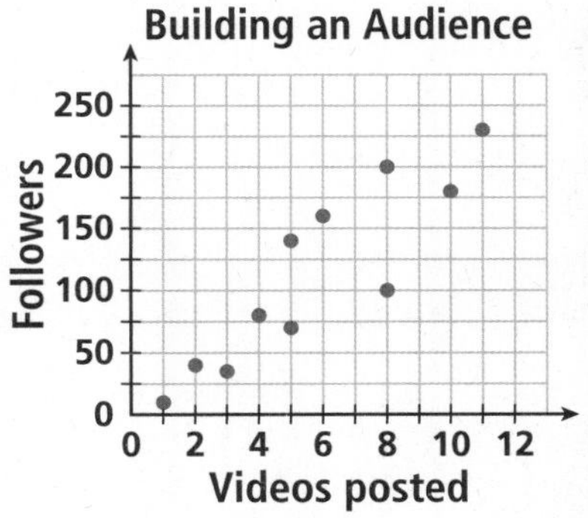

A. Is a trend line an appropriate way to model these data? Explain.

B. Sketch a reasonable trend line for this data and justify your choice.

C. Estimate the number of followers that the Flan family might expect when they have posted 20 videos.

D. How did you make your estimate? What might cause your estimate to be incorrect?

4. When is it *not* appropriate to model the relationship in a scatter plot with a trend line?

© Houghton Mifflin Harcourt Publishing Company • **Image Credit:** (inset) ©lopurice/E+/Getty Images; (border) ©Sitade/iStockphoto.com/Getty Images

5. **Open Ended** The trend line of a data set is shown. Plot a data set with at least 5 points on the graph that could result in the trend line shown.

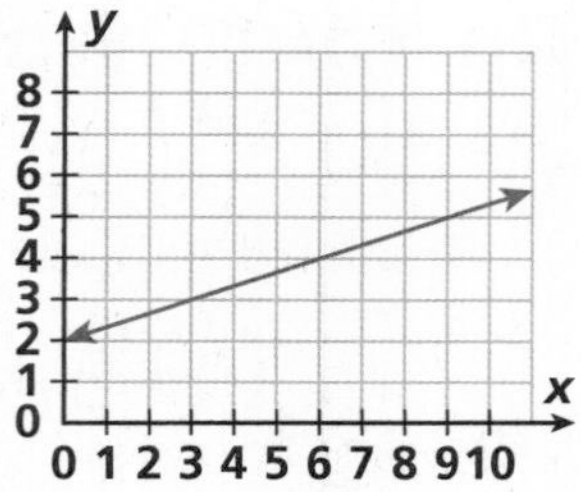

6. **STEM** The average length of an animal's life is related to the average length of pregnancy for that type of animal. The scatter plot shows data for several different animals.

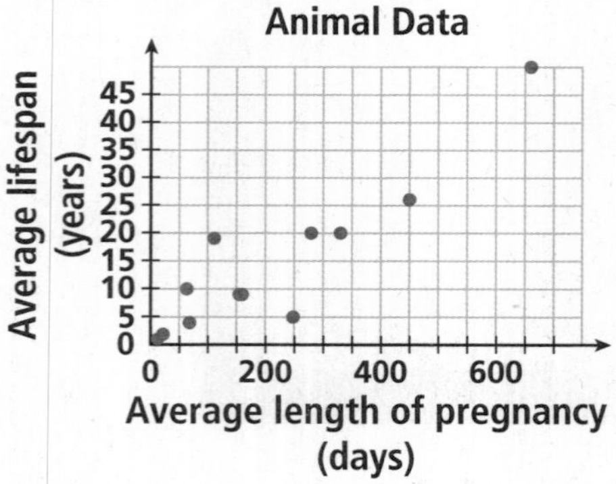

A. Sketch a trend line to model the data. Circle the outlier and explain how it influences your choice for the trend line.

B. How would the trend line change if the outlier were removed?

C. The average length of pregnancy for a polar bear is 240 days. Use the trend line to estimate the average length of a polar bear's life.

© Houghton Mifflin Harcourt Publishing Company • Image Credit: ©Bryan Hall/Shutterstock

I'm in a Learning Mindset!

How do I keep myself motivated to draw and analyze trend lines?

Name ______________________

LESSON 10.2
More Practice/ Homework

ONLINE
Video Tutorials and Interactive Examples

Draw and Analyze Trend Lines

1. **A.** (MP) **Construct Arguments** Is the trend line shown on the scatter plot a good fit for the data? Explain. If the line is not a good fit, sketch a more appropriate trend line.

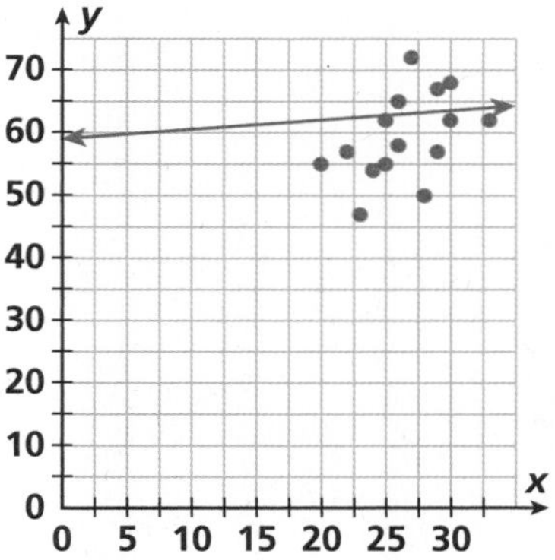

____

____

____

B. The point (25, 20) is added to the data set. How will its addition influence the trend line?

____

____

____

____

2. **Open Ended** Plot at least five points to display a data set that has the trend line $y = \frac{1}{2}x$. Include the graph of the trend line in your sketch.

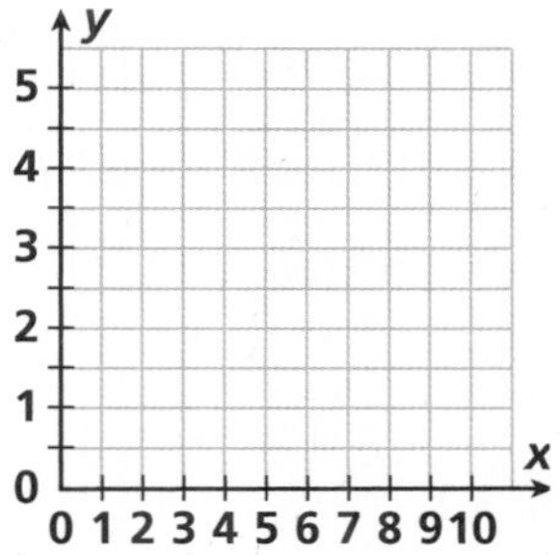

3. (MP) **Critique Reasoning** Mateo sketches a trend line to model a data set. Eight points lie above the trend line and three points lie below. Did Mateo make a mistake? Explain your reasoning.

____

____

____

© Houghton Mifflin Harcourt Publishing Company • Image Credit: ©WDnet Creation/Shutterstock

Test Prep

4. Which of the following is NOT a reason the displayed trend line is a good fit?

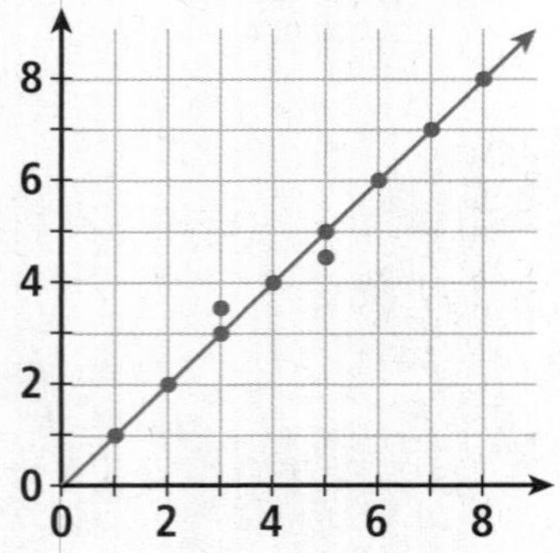

Ⓐ There are equal numbers of points above the trend line and below it.

Ⓑ The data set shows positive linear association.

Ⓒ The greatest vertical distance of any data point from the trend line is less than 1.

Ⓓ The trend line touches most of the points in the data set.

5. Explain how adding outliers to a data set might not influence the data set.

____

____

6. Calhoun sketched a scatter plot comparing the numbers of hours studied to test scores for his class's latest test. He found a trend line that was a good fit for the data. Which would you expect to be true? Select all that apply.

Ⓐ There are data points above and below the trend line.

Ⓑ The data have a linear association.

Ⓒ The data points on the graph line up in a perfectly straight line.

Ⓓ The slope of the trend line is positive.

Ⓔ There are more data points that are outliers than data points that are not outliers.

Spiral Review

7. Solve the equation $3(x - 7) = 2(x - 5)$. ____________

8. What is the solution to the system of equations?

$$\begin{cases} 2x - 6y = 10 \\ -5x + 15y = 30 \end{cases}$$

____

9. Write an equation of a linear function with slope -2 that passes through the point $(4, -5)$.

____

© Houghton Mifflin Harcourt Publishing Company

Name ______________________________

Interpret Linear Data in Context

I Can use the equation of a line to solve problems in the context of bivariate measurement data, interpreting the slope and intercept.

Step It Out

ACTIVITY

1 Janelle is making a graph that compares the salaries and ages of the members of the planning department. She lists the salaries in tens of thousands of dollars and the ages in years.

Age (years)	Salary ($10,000's)
25	4.5
31	2.9
31	6.0
35	5.5
35	6.2
37	7.2
38	6.8
43	8.3
46	12.1
50	11.9

A. Use the graph provided to make a scatter plot of the data in the table.

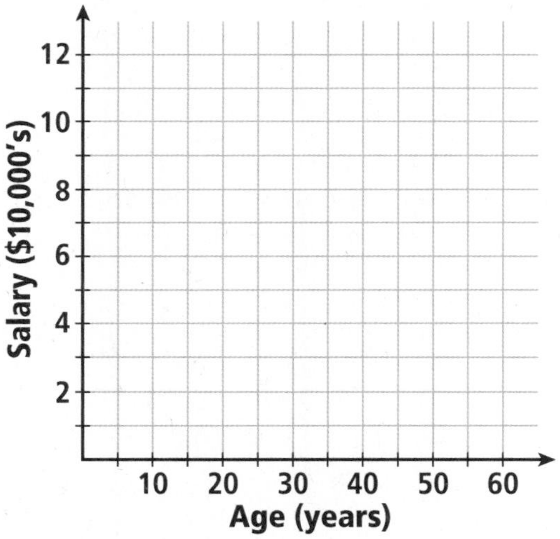

B. The line $y = 0.36x - 6.1$ is a trend line for the scatter plot. Add the trend line to the graph.

C. Complete the interpretation of the slope of the trend line.

The slope is ______. This means that for every 1 year increase in age, there is a salary increase of ______ of $10,000. For every one year increase in age, there is a salary increase of $______.

Turn and Talk Does every older worker make more money than any particular younger worker? Explain.

© Houghton Mifflin Harcourt Publishing Company • Image Credit: ©wavebreakmedia/Shutterstock

2 An educator decided to investigate the relationship between the amount of time a group of students spent reading and the amount of time they spent watching television in one week. She graphed her result as shown.

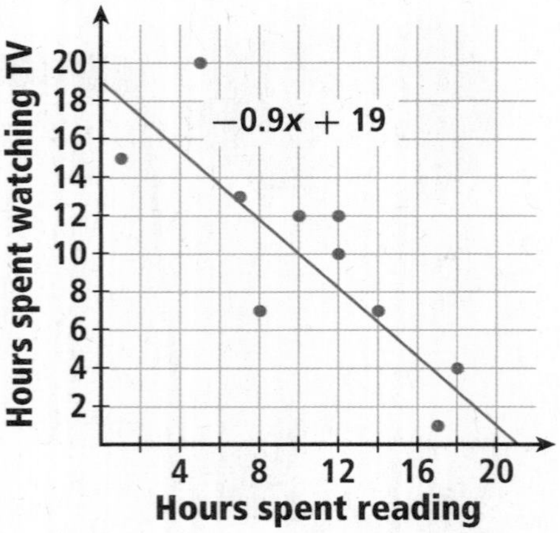

A person reads about 4 hours per week. If he or she also watched television about 4 hours per week, would you consider that data point to be an outlier? Explain.

Turn and Talk Why might predictions made from a trend line not always be accurate?

Check Understanding

1. For the graph in Task 2, what does the trend line show?

2. For the data set given in the table, estimate the rate of change of a trend line with good fit.

Time (minutes)	4.3	5.8	24.0	2.3	1.7	105.0	19.0
Boxes assembled	2	3	15	1	1	50	11

© Houghton Mifflin Harcourt Publishing Company • Image Credits: (tr) ©Juice Images Limited/Shutterstock; (cr) ©Rawpixel.com/Shutterstock

Name ______________________________

On Your Own

3. Health and Fitness The coach of a basketball team compared the heights of the players and their average numbers of rebounds per game.

Height (ft)	Average rebounds per game
5.3	2.5
5.6	1.2
5.8	2
5.9	3.7
5.9	2.9
6.0	4
6.0	3.4
6.2	6.3
6.3	4
6.4	7.1

A. Graph the data and the trend line $y = 4.4x - 22$.

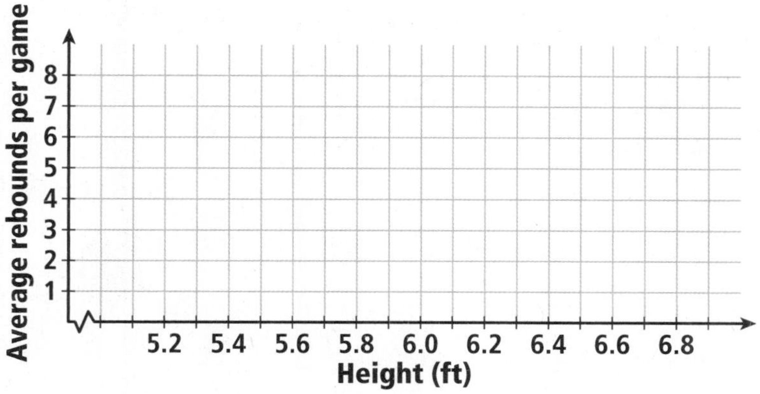

B. What is the y-intercept of the trend line?

____

C. What does the y-intercept mean in this situation? Is it useful? Explain.

____

____

D. The scatter plot shows that as players get taller they tend to get more rebounds. Does that mean that the tallest player would get the most rebounds? Explain.

____

____

____

____

E. The coach also made this scatter plot of the average numbers of points made by the five top-scoring players, compared to their heights. Compare the general trends from each scatter plot.

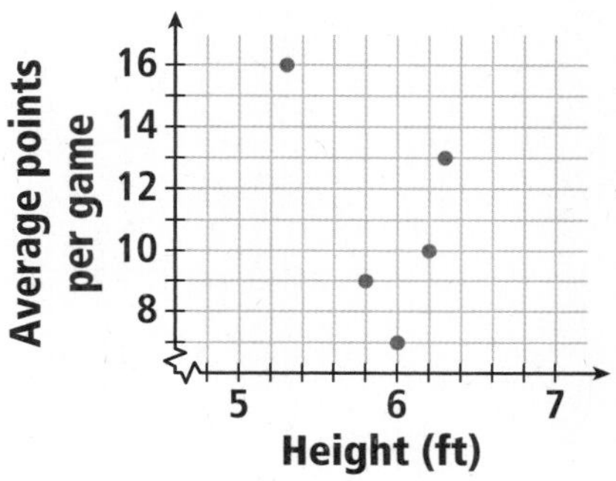

____

____

____

____

____

© Houghton Mifflin Harcourt Publishing Company • **Image Credit:** ©Photodisc/Getty Images

Use the information to answer Problems 4–6.

Mr. Peabody asked his class to keep track of how many hours they spent studying for the midterm math exam. Then he made the scatter plot shown. A 10 was the best a person could do on the test.

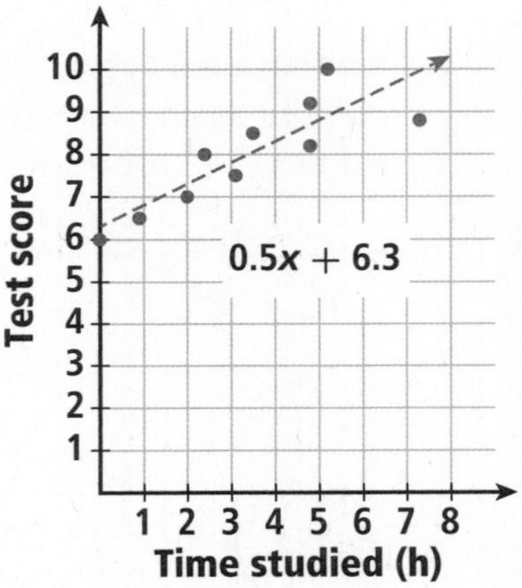

4. MP **Critique Reasoning** Mr. Peabody said the scatter plot and trend line show that people who studied more got higher scores on the test. Would you agree? Explain.

5. According to the equation of the trend line, each additional hour spent studying raises test scores by how much? How do you know?

6. MP **Model with Mathematics** Mr. Peabody wanted to see if there was a relationship between students' grades in math and in music. Nine of his students who studied both math and music agreed to share their grades in each subject.

A. Make a scatter plot of the data. Draw a trend line.

Math grade, x	Music grade, y
75	80
80	70
80	85
87	97
90	100
92	75
95	90
97	85
100	95

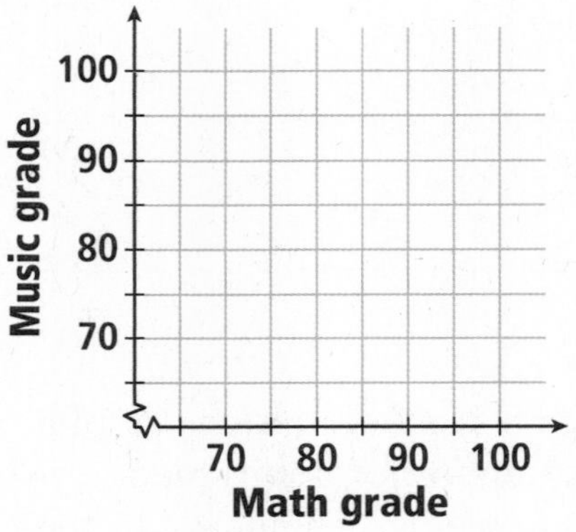

B. How would you describe the association, if any? Explain.

© Houghton Mifflin Harcourt Publishing Company • **Image Credit:** ©GaudiLab/Shutterstock

Name ______________________________

ONLINE
Ed
Video Tutorials and
Interactive Examples

Interpret Linear Data in Context

1. A group of people aged 15 to 30 were asked to rate a movie they had just seen from 1 to 5 stars. The managers of the theater looked at the scatter plot of the data to see what they could learn about the movie. The provided trend line is $y = -\frac{x}{8} + 6\frac{1}{8}$.

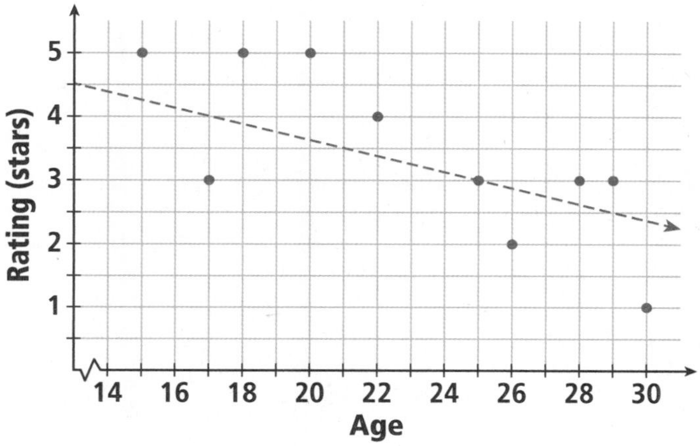

What does the direction of the trend line tell you about the popularity of the movie with older audiences? Explain.

____

____

2. A sports watch company conducted a trial of its new watch with eight people. The watches tracked the distance each person walked per day.

Age, x	Miles walked, y
20	3.2
21	8.7
23	6.3
25	4.2
26	9.4
27	5.2
27	8.4
28	7.4

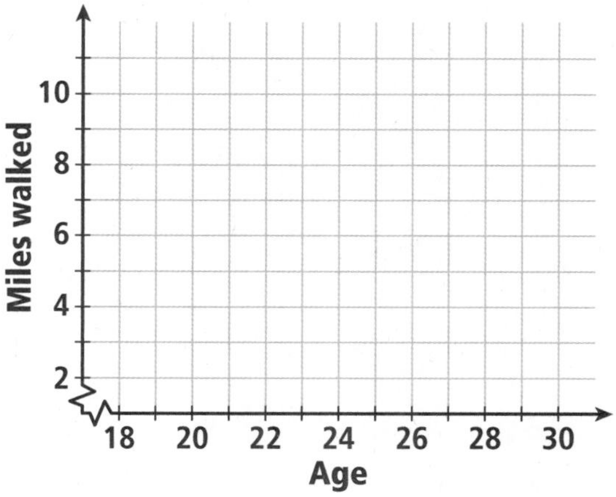

A. Make a scatter plot of the data.

B. **Open Ended** What type of association between the variables does the scatter plot show? Can you draw a good trend line? If so, give its equation.

____

____

© Houghton Mifflin Harcourt Publishing Company • Image Credit: ©martinedoucet/E+/Getty Images

Test Prep

3. Diners were surveyed after eating at a restaurant. Their ages were associated with their rating of the food. A good trend line for the scatter plot was $y = 0.002x + 4$. What does the slope tell you about this information?

Ⓐ The older the diner, the better chance they liked the food.

Ⓑ The younger the diner, the better chance they liked the food.

Ⓒ No one liked the food.

Ⓓ Both young and old diners liked the food about the same.

4. A scatter plot is made comparing x, the number of hours since midnight, with y, the number of lights turned on in a house. What would a point at (7, 8) on the scatter plot mean?

When the time was ______________, there were ________ lights on.

Use the graph to answer Problems 5–7. The slope of the trend line (not shown) is about 12.5.

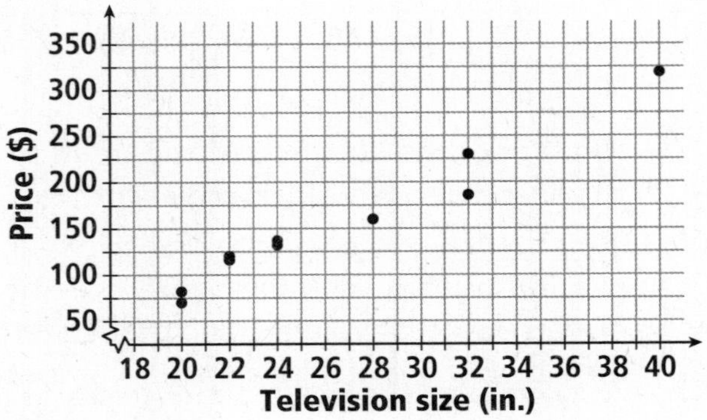

5. An increase of 5 inches in television size is associated with an increase of ________.

Ⓐ $5.00 Ⓒ $25.00

Ⓑ $12.50 Ⓓ $62.50

6. According to the trend, if Jesse finds a 26-inch television for $75, is that a good deal? Explain.

____

____

7. A 38-inch television is on sale for $250. Raphaela considers this an outlier to the trend shown in the graph because it is not near any of the other data points. Correct her mistake.

____

____

Spiral Review

8. Solve the system of equations: $\begin{cases} y = 8x + 14 \\ y = 4x + 14 \end{cases}$ ______________

9. A sprinter runs 100 yards in 10 seconds. A long-distance runner runs a mile in 4 minutes. Find the time it takes each of them to run 10 yards. How much less time does the sprinter take to run the 10-yard distance?

____

____

© Houghton Mifflin Harcourt Publishing Company

Module 10

Name ____________________

Review

Vocabulary

Choose the correct term from the Vocabulary box.

Vocabulary
outlier
cluster
trend line
association
scatter plot
domain

1. A(n) ____________ is a set of closely grouped data points.
2. A(n) ____________ is a data point that is far from the other points on the graph of a set of paired data.
3. A(n) ____________ is a description of the relationship between two data sets.
4. A(n) ____________ is a line on a scatter plot that helps show a linear association.
5. A(n) ____________ is a graph that uses points to show how two data sets are related.

Concepts and Skills

6. (MP) **Use Tools** The scatter plot shows the relationship between the numbers of hours players spent playing a video game and their high scores. Draw a trend line for the scatter plot. State what strategy and tool you will use to answer the question, explain your choice, and then find the answer.

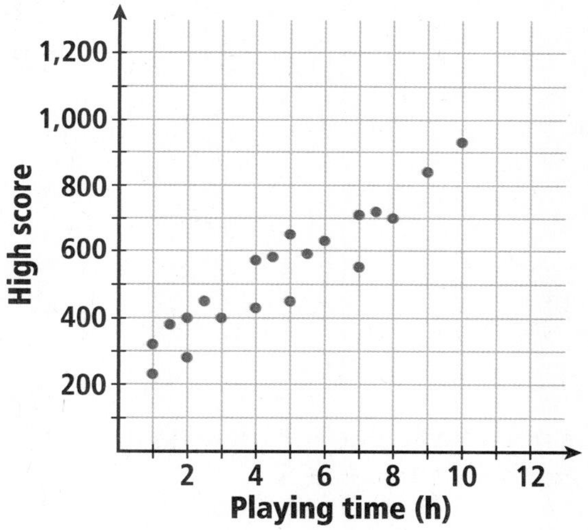

____

____

____

____

7. The scatter plot shows the ages of the used cars at a car dealership and the numbers of miles the cars have been driven. Select all statements that correctly interpret the scatter plot.

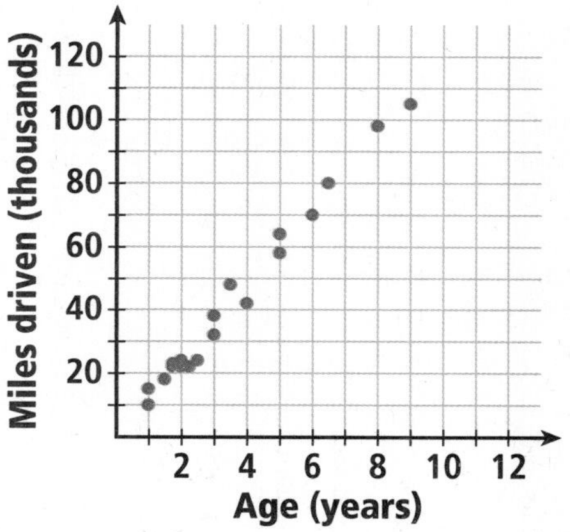

Ⓐ The data show a positive association.

Ⓑ The data point at (9, 105) is an outlier.

Ⓒ The data show a negative association.

Ⓓ The data show a nonlinear association.

Ⓔ There is a cluster of data points near (2, 23).

© Houghton Mifflin Harcourt Publishing Company

8. The scatter plot shows data for students in Brenna's class. A trend line for the data is $y = 0.054x - 0.099$.

Use the trend line to predict how long, to the nearest minute, it would take a student in Brenna's class to walk 5 miles.

________ minutes

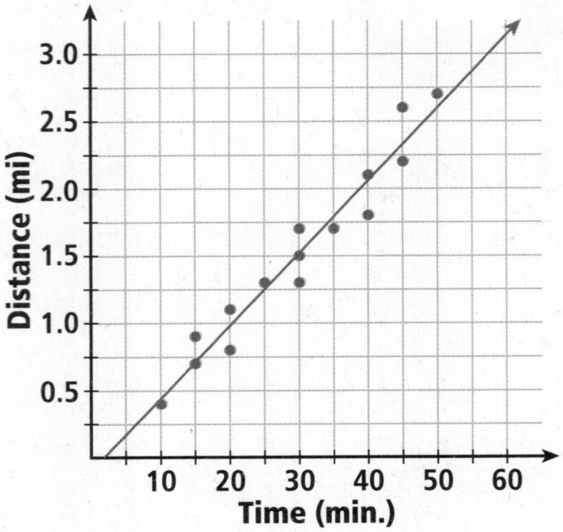

9. Calista surveyed eight classmates about the numbers of texts they sent and received in the past 3 hours. The table shows her results. Use the data set from the table to complete the scatter plot.

Name	Texts sent	Texts received
Daniel	5	10
Ahmed	6	7
Rosa	10	10
Lea	7	8
Malory	3	8
Nico	7	6
Cameron	3	9
Keri	1	4

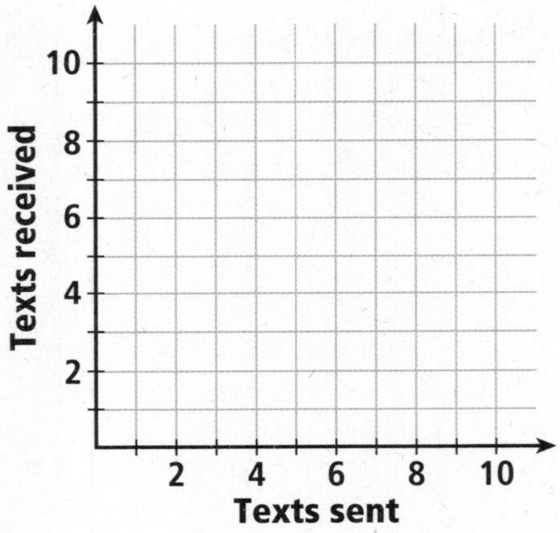

A good trend line for the data in the table is $y = -0.0036x + 70.64$. Use this trend line for Problems 10 and 11.

Elevation (ft), x	Average annual temperature (°F), y
4,852	53.7
4,856	52.6
5,285	50.2
6,178	49.0
7,233	45.5
7,530	44.0
8,054	42.1
8,645	37.8

10. What does the number -0.0036 in the trend line represent in this situation?

____

____

____

11. What does the number 70.64 in the trend line represent?

____

____

____

© Houghton Mifflin Harcourt Publishing Company

Module 11 Proportional Reasoning with Samples

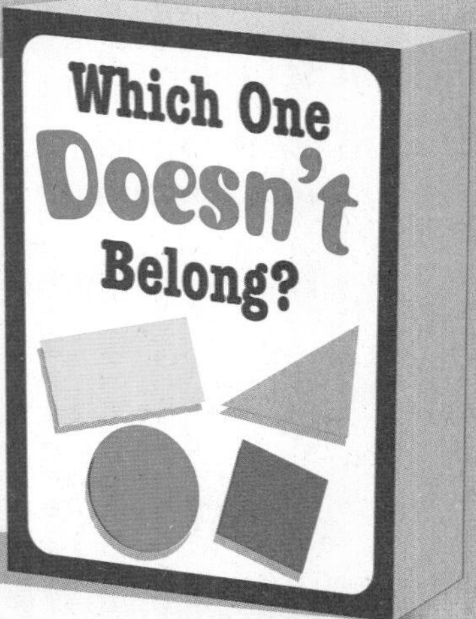

WHICH FRACTION DOES NOT BELONG?

Each diagram represents a fraction. All but one of the fractions can be matched with a partner, but not based on the shapes of the models.

Write the fraction that each model represents.

A.

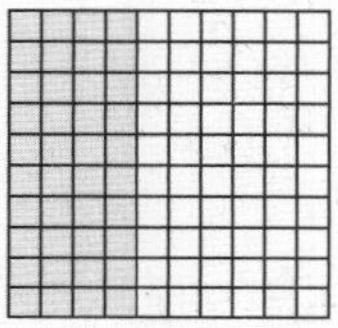

B.

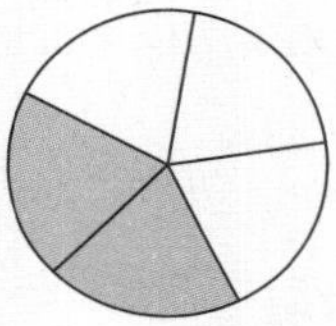

C.

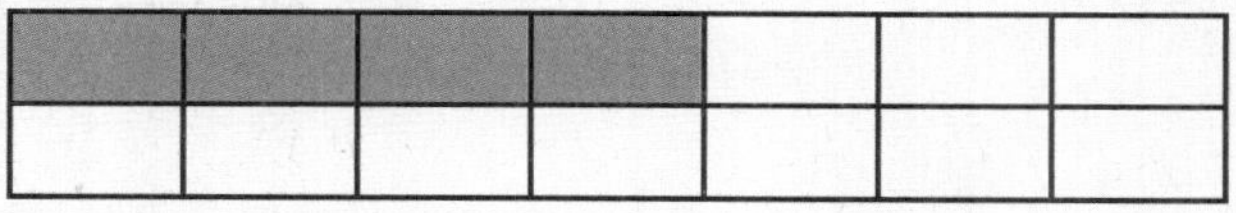

D.

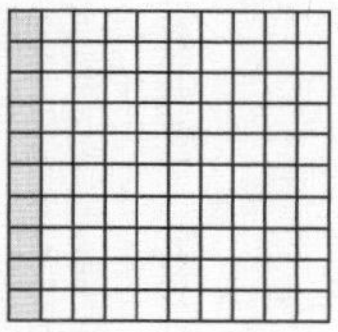

E.

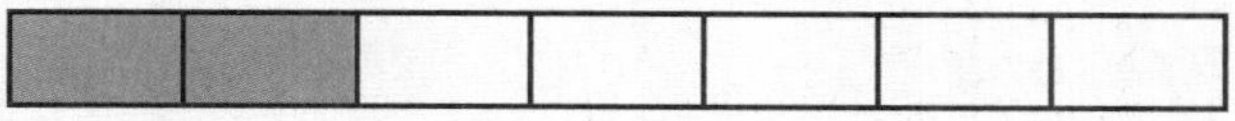

Turn and Talk

How can you pair up the fractions? Which is the fraction that does not belong? Explain your answers.

© Houghton Mifflin Harcourt Publishing Company

Are You Ready?

Complete these problems to review prior concepts and skills you will need for this module.

Statistical Data Collection

For Problems 1–2, tell whether the question is a statistical question. Explain your reasoning.

1. How many days are in the month of March?

____

____

2. How tall are the giraffes at the zoo?

____

3. Write a statistical question about your school.

____

Representing Equivalent Ratios

Complete the table of equivalent ratios.

4.

Size (oz)	Price ($)
4	1.00
	2.00
10	
12	

5.

Time (h)	Distance (mi)
	84
3	126
5	
	336

Use Ratio and Rate Reasoning

Write an equation to model each proportional relationship. Then solve the problem.

6. The ratio of tables, x, to chairs, y, in a restaurant is 2 to 7. The restaurant has a total of 12 tables. How many chairs does it have?

Equation: ______________ Solution: ________ chairs

7. Let x represent the number of batteries and y represent the cost of the batteries. A package of 8 rechargeable batteries costs $12. At this rate, how much would a package of 20 rechargeable batteries cost?

Equation: ______________ Solution: $________

© Houghton Mifflin Harcourt Publishing Company

Name ______________________________

Understand Representative Samples

I Can identify the population and sample for a given survey scenario and say whether a sample is random. I can determine whether a sample is likely to be representative of the population.

Spark Your Learning

SMALL GROUPS

In the fall, the residents of a large city will be voting on whether to use state funding to build a new football stadium. A research analyst wants to know the opinion of all the registered voters of the city in order to predict the outcome of the upcoming vote. Without polling all the residents, how can the research analyst be sure that the poll represents the opinion of the registered voters?

Turn and Talk Is it reasonable for the research analyst to poll every registered voter of the city about using state funding to build a new stadium? Explain.

© Houghton Mifflin Harcourt Publishing Company • Image Credit: ©sArhange1/iStock/Getty Images Plus/Getty Images

Build Understanding

1 A chain restaurant is thinking of entering a city for the first time. The owners want to determine if the teenagers in the city like the kind of food served by the restaurant.

A. In this case, what is the population the restaurant needs to survey? Is it reasonable for them to survey the entire population? Why or why not?

____

____

____

> **Connect to Vocabulary**
>
> When information is being gathered about a group, the entire group of objects or individuals considered for a survey is the **population.**

When a population is too large to survey, a subset of the population, or a sample, is used to represent the population. If the sample is representative, it can be used to infer data about the population. The restaurant owners made a list of possible samples.

> **Connect to Vocabulary**
>
> A **sample** is part of the population that is chosen to represent the entire group.
> A **representative sample** is a sample that has the same characteristics as the population.
> When a sample does not accurately represent the population, it has **bias**.

List of potential samples of the population:

1. Survey every 10th person coming out of a competitor's restaurant.
2. Call every 100th person in the local phonebook.
3. Survey 10% of the students at the city's middle schools and high schools.
4. Survey teenagers leaving a fast-food restaurant.

B. Which of the potential samples are more likely to be representative of the population? Why?

____

C. Of the representative samples of the population, which is most representative of the entire population? Explain.

____

____

D. Which of the potential samples are biased? Explain.

____

____

____

© Houghton Mifflin Harcourt Publishing Company

Name ______________________

A sample in which every member of the population has an equal chance of being selected is a **random sample**.

SURVEY
What is your favorite genre of music?
?

2 Aiden asks the survey question shown to determine what genre of music to play at an employee event.

A. He asks every tenth employee on a list of all employees. Is this sample random? Explain.

____

B. Is the sample in Part A representative of the population? Explain.

____

____

C. On Thursday, he asks every third employee that gets off the elevator on the fifth floor the survey question. Is this sample biased? Explain.

____

____

D. Is the sample in Part C a random sample? Explain.

____

Turn and Talk Does a random sample always generate a representative sample? Explain.

Check Understanding

1. Isabella wants to know the favorite sport of the students in her school. She randomly asks every fifth person entering the football game Friday night. Is this sample biased? Explain.

____

____

2. Noah assigned a number to each of the 200 students in seventh grade. He put the numbers in a bag. Noah randomly chose 30 numbers and surveyed those students. Identify the population and sample.

____

____

3. Wyatt wants to poll the opinion of a neighborhood about safety. Give an example of a biased sample. Justify your answer.

____

____

____

© Houghton Mifflin Harcourt Publishing Company

On Your Own

For Problems 4–5, use this survey information: Every hundredth resident of voting age listed on the county census was surveyed about building a library.

4. Identify the population and sample.

A. Population: ______________________________

B. Sample: ______________________________

5. (MP) **Reason** Is the sample random? Is the sample representative of the population? Explain.

____

____

For Problems 6–7, identify the population and sample. Determine whether each sample is random and whether it is biased. Explain your reasoning.

6. Juanita surveys 50 adults at a local swimming pool during the summer to determine the favorite month of adults in her city.

A. Population: ______________________________

B. Sample: ______________________________

C. Random? ______________________________

D. Representative? ______________________________

7. Cameron surveys every tenth student who walks into school to determine the favorite type of movie of students in his school.

A. Population: ______________________________

B. Sample: ______________________________

C. Random? ______________________________

D. Representative? ______________________________

8. (MP) **Construct Arguments** Addison surveys every 25th customer who leaves a grocery store to determine whether students at her school prefer to pack a lunch or purchase a lunch. Is her sample biased? Explain.

____

____

I'm in a Learning Mindset!

What barriers are there to my understanding of representative samples?

____

____

© Houghton Mifflin Harcourt Publishing Company

Name

ONLINE
Ed Video Tutorials and Interactive Examples

Understand Representative Samples

1. The president of a national soccer fan club, Abdul, wants to determine if the club's 10,000 members are in favor of using club dues to make a new online video to support their team in the upcoming championship. He assigns a number to each member and uses a random number generator to choose 250 members to survey.

A. Identify the population and sample.

B. Is the sample representative of the entire population? Explain.

C. Suppose 212 of the 250 members in a random sample are in favor of using club dues to make a new video for their team. What can Abdul conclude about the results of the survey? Explain.

2. **Math on the Spot** Determine whether the sample is representative or biased. Explain.

A. A teacher chooses the grades of 50 students at random from his classes to calculate the average grade earned in his class.

B. Seventy-five people exiting a bookstore are surveyed to find out the average amount of time spent reading each day by people in the area.

3. **Open Ended** A random sample of 10 students and a random sample of 200 students are chosen from a student population of 1,200 students. Which sample do you think is more likely to be representative of the population? Explain.

© Houghton Mifflin Harcourt Publishing Company

Test Prep

4. Jayla wants to know the favorite sports team of the adults in her city. Which survey method is representative of the population?

   Ⓐ Randomly survey 1,000 adults as they leave a professional basketball game.

   Ⓑ Randomly survey 2,000 adults in one neighborhood.

   Ⓒ Survey every 100th adult customer who enters the local grocery store.

   Ⓓ Survey every 20th student who enters the high school.

For Problems 5–6, determine whether each situation *does* or *does not* show bias.

5. Haley wants to know if people use the store's bags or bring their own reusable bags. She surveys every tenth person who leaves a grocery store.

   This situation | does / does not | show bias.

6. Josiah wants to know the favorite pet of adults in his city. Josiah assigned a number to each of the 200 people on the list to adopt a dog from a dog shelter. He puts the numbers in a hat. Josiah randomly chose 40 numbers and surveyed those people.

   This situation | does / does not | show bias.

7. Fayard wants to know the favorite instrument of students in his school. He puts the names of all the students in a jar, draws 5 names, and surveys those students. Suppose Julia conducts the same survey in the same way, but she draws 15 names. Which method is more representative? Explain.

   ____

   ____

   ____

Spiral Review

8. The drawing is a scale drawing of a house. If the scale is 2 inches = 4.5 feet, what is the actual height of the house? Round to the nearest hundredth.

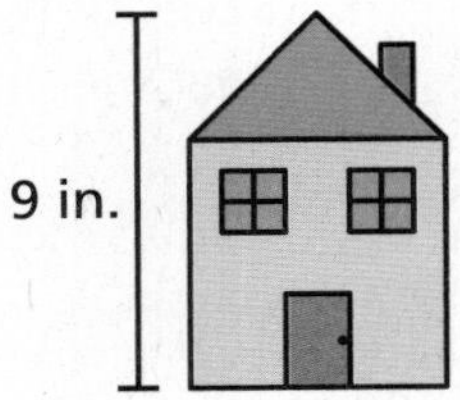

   ____

9. A gardener is building a rectangular planter for vegetables. The length of the planter is 2 times its width and the perimeter is 42 feet. What is the width of the planter?

   ____

© Houghton Mifflin Harcourt Publishing Company

Name ____________________

Make Inferences from a Random Sample

I Can use proportional reasoning to make inferences about populations based on the results of a random sample.

Spark Your Learning

PAIRS

At a grocery store, a bin is filled with trail mix made by mixing raisins with a large 30-pound bag of nuts. Zane buys a small bag of a trail mix that contains $1\frac{1}{2}$ pounds of nuts and $\frac{1}{2}$ pound of raisins. If the nuts and raisins in Zane's bag are proportional to the nuts and raisins in the bin of trail mix, how many pounds of raisins do you think the store used to make the entire bin of trail mix?

© Houghton Mifflin Harcourt Publishing Company • Image Credit: ©ewastudio/iStock/Getty Images Plus/Getty Images

Turn and Talk How is the connection between the sample (small bag) and population (large bin) of trail mix similar to the sample and population of a survey?

Build Understanding

1 To estimate the number of pets that students in your school have, conduct a survey of ten randomly selected students in your class.

A. Plot the results of your survey on the grid provided.

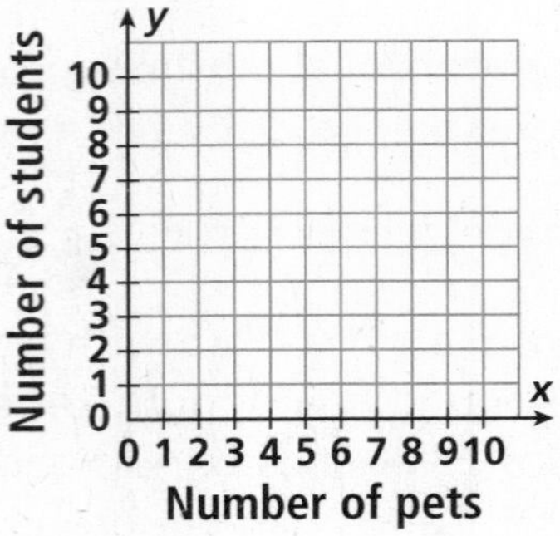

B. According to my survey, most students in my school have ________ pets.

C. According to my survey, about ________% of the students in my school have more than two pets.

D. According to my survey, about ________% of the students in my school have zero pets.

Conduct the same survey again using a second set of ten randomly selected students in your class.

E. Plot the results of your survey on the grid provided.

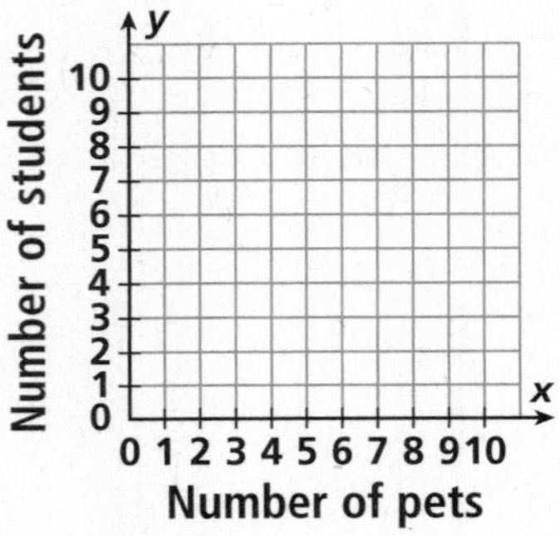

F. According to my survey, most students in my school have ________ pets.

G. According to my survey, about ________% of the students in my school have more than two pets.

H. According to my survey, about ________% of the students in my school have zero pets.

I. Compare the results from both of your samples.

- Are the results from the two samples exactly the same?

  ____

- Will a different sample give a different estimate?

  ____

A sample ratio can be used to estimate a population ratio. However, because different samples will likely vary, a sample ratio must be considered as only an estimate of the population ratio.

Turn and Talk Discuss how samples from random surveys can be improved to obtain better estimates about a population.

© Houghton Mifflin Harcourt Publishing Company

Name ______________________

Step It Out

To make inferences about a population based on a random representative sample, you can use proportional reasoning.

2 Javier randomly selects 12 cartons of eggs from the grocery store. He finds that 2 cartons have at least one broken egg.

Suppose there are 144 cartons of eggs at the grocery store. What is an estimate of the total number of those 144 cartons that have at least one broken egg?

A. Identify the sample.

____

B. Identify the population.

____

C. Write the ratio of cartons with at least one broken egg to the total number of cartons in the sample.

$\frac{\square}{\square}$

D. Use the sample ratio to write an equation for the proportional relationship.

$y = \frac{\square}{\square} \cdot 144$

E. Use your equation in Part D to estimate the number of cartons in the population that have at least one broken egg.

____

____

____

Turn and Talk Discuss how to write an equation for the proportional relationship using a decimal or a percent for the sample ratio.

© Houghton Mifflin Harcourt Publishing Company • Image Credits: (t) ©Stolk/iStock/Getty Images Plus/Getty Images; (b) ©grey_and/Shutterstock

3 A worker randomly selects one out of every 7 sets from the 3,500 sets of headphones produced. The results are shown.

A. The [population / sample] is the total of 3,500 sets of headphones produced. The 500 selected for testing is the [population / sample].

B. Write the ratio of defective headphones to total headphones in the sample. Then write the ratio as a decimal and as a percent.

$\frac{\square}{\square} = \square = \square\%$

C. Write and solve an equation to find the number of headphones in the population that can be estimated to be defective.

$y = \frac{\square}{\square} \cdot 3{,}500$

There would be about ☐ defective headphones.

Check Understanding

1. William conducted a random survey of the students in his school regarding the number of hours of sleep they got last night. The box plot shows the results of his survey. Make an inference about the entire population.

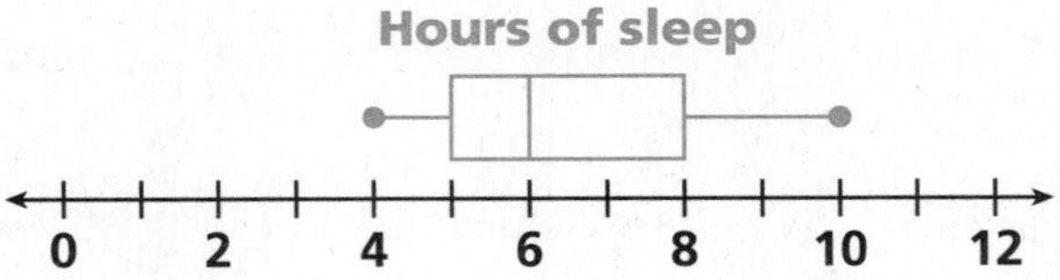

____

____

2. Hazel assigned a number to each of the 100 students in the band and put the numbers in a bag. She randomly chose 20 numbers and found that 3 students did not complete their homework for today. Make an inference about the number of students in the band that did not do their homework. If Hazel randomly chose 20 more numbers, what results would you expect? Explain.

____

____

____

© Houghton Mifflin Harcourt Publishing Company • Image Credit: ©Marynchenko Oleksandr/Shutterstock

Name ____________________

On Your Own

For Problems 3–5, make an inference about the ages of all drama club students at a theater conference using the dot plot showing the ages of students in a random sample of conference attendees.

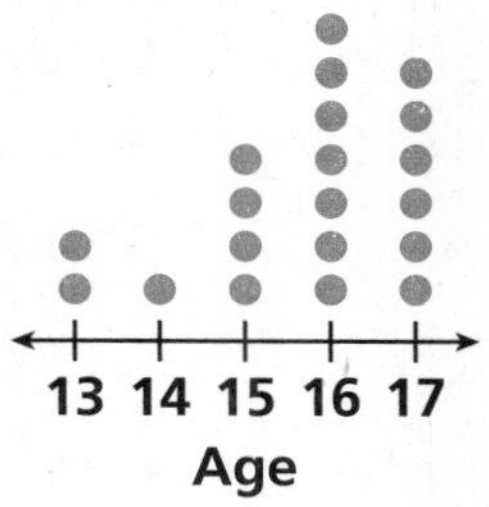

3. Most drama club students at the conference are __________ 15 years old.

4. About _____% of the students at the conference are 16 years old or older.

5. (MP) **Construct Arguments** Would you think that it is likely for the number of 16-year-old students and the number of 17-year-old students to be almost equal in another random sample of conference attendees? Explain.

____

____

6. A manager randomly selects 1,500 ink pens produced today and finds 12 of them defective. There were 12,000 ink pens produced today. Make an inference about the number of ink pens produced today that are defective.

The sample ratio of defective pens is $\frac{\square}{\square}$ or $\square$%.

Inference: In the 12,000 population, the number of defective pens is estimated to be $\square \cdot 12{,}000 = \square$.

7. Gabby assigned a number to each of the 120 athletes at her school and put the numbers in a box. She randomly chose 25 numbers and found that 10 athletes were female. Use this sample to make an inference about how many athletes at Gabby's school are female.

____

8. A random sample of dry-erase board markers at Juan's school shows that 9 of the 60 dry-erase board markers do not work. There are 200 dry-erase board markers at Juan's school. Make an inference about the number of dry-erase board markers at Juan's school that do not work.

____

9. A mail carrier randomly inspects every 20th letter being mailed. Out of 600 letters in the sample, 3 were open. There were 18,000 letters being mailed. Make an inference about the number of all the letters being mailed that were open.

____

© Houghton Mifflin Harcourt Publishing Company

For Problems 10–13, use the box plot, which shows the results of a survey of the number of minutes that people at a variety of randomly selected gyms exercise. Make an inference about the number of minutes that people at gyms exercise according to this survey.

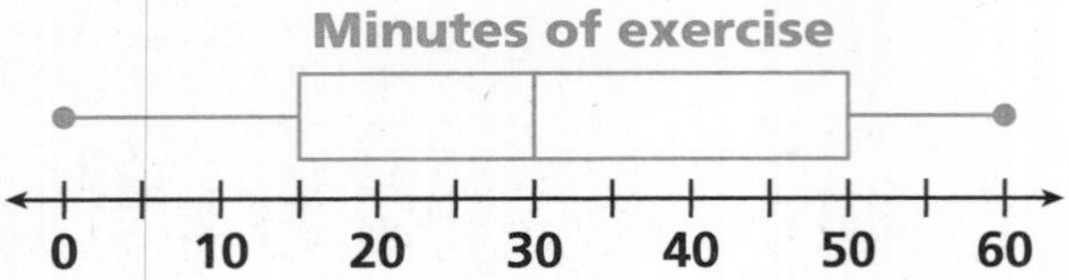

10. According to the survey, 75% of people at gyms exercise for ________ minutes or longer.

11. According to the survey, 25% of people at gyms exercise for more than ________ minutes.

12. According to the survey, ________% of people at gyms exercise from 15 to 50 minutes.

13. According to the survey, ________% of people at gyms exercise from 15 to 30 minutes.

14. **Health and Fitness** Would the owners of another gym be able to use data from a survey like the one in Problems 10–13 to make inferences about the number of minutes people exercise at their gym? Explain your reasoning.

15. A wildlife park manager is working on a request to expand the park. In a random selection during one week, 3 of every 5 cars have more than 3 people inside. If about 5,000 cars come to the park in a month, estimate how many cars that month would have more than 3 people inside. Show your work.

I'm in a Learning Mindset!

How is making inferences from random samples similar to the way I make decisions when I am learning something new?

© Houghton Mifflin Harcourt Publishing Company • **Image Credit:** ©CrackerClips/iStock/Getty Images Plus/Getty Images

Name ____________________

ONLINE
Video Tutorials and Interactive Examples

Make Inferences from a Random Sample

1. Xavier surveyed a random sample of the grade levels of the Spanish Club members in the county. The bar graph shows the results of his survey.

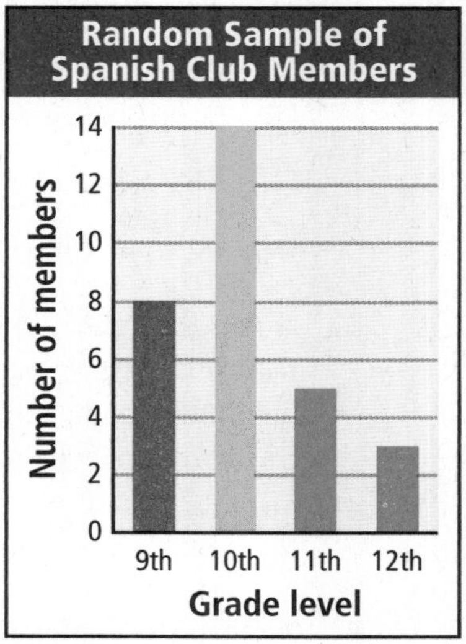

A. The largest number of students in the Spanish Club are in ________ grade.

B. The same number of students in the Spanish Club are in the ________ grade as are in the 11th and 12th grades combined.

C. If there are 300 students in the Spanish Club in the county, predict how many are 10th graders.

____

D. Of the 300 students, predict about how many are 9th graders.

____

E. Xavier conducted another random survey of the grade levels of the Spanish Club members in the county. In what grade would you expect to find the most students in Spanish Club? Explain.

____

____

____

2. A manager at a factory finds that in a random sample of 200 clocks, 15 are defective.

A. What percent of the clocks are defective?

____

B. Of the 10,000 clocks from which the sample was chosen, about how many clocks are probably not defective?

____

C. The next day the manager finds only 8 of the 200 randomly selected clocks are defective. About how many clocks out of the 10,000 produced that day are probably defective?

____

3. (MP) **Use Structure** Based on a sample survey, a tutoring company claims that 90% of their students pass their classes. Out of 300 students, how many would you predict will pass?

____

© Houghton Mifflin Harcourt Publishing Company

Test Prep

4. Ronnie surveyed a random selection of real-estate agents in his town about the numbers of bedrooms in the houses for sale that week. The dot plot shows the results. Which inference is correct?

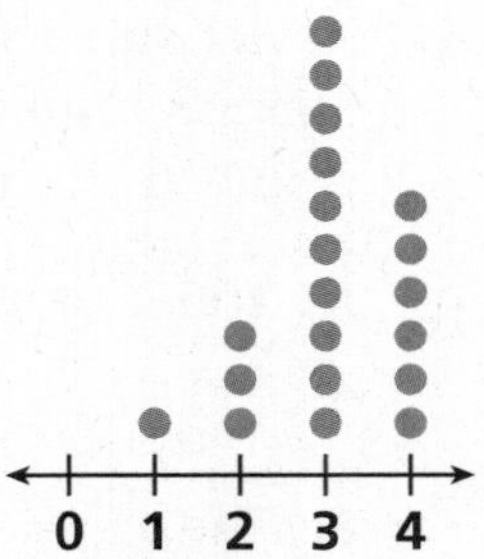

Ⓐ Most of the houses have fewer than 3 bedrooms.

Ⓑ Some houses have 0 bedrooms.

Ⓒ More than 50% of the houses have exactly 3 bedrooms.

Ⓓ 80% of the houses have 3 or 4 bedrooms.

5. A random sample of laptop computers at an electronics store shows that 1 of the 25 sampled laptop computers has a malfunction. There are 300 laptop computers at the electronics store. Estimate the number of laptop computers at the electronics store that have malfunctions.

____

6. Jaylen used the seat number for each of the 6,500 fans' seats in the stands at a college football game and put the numbers in a computer program. He randomly chose 200 numbers and found that 36 of those people had also purchased a parking voucher. Estimate the number of fans in the stands at a sold-out football game that purchased a parking voucher. Explain.

____

____

____

____

Spiral Review

7. Ricardo jogged up 864 steps in $13\frac{1}{2}$ minutes. What is Ricardo's average number of steps per minute?

____

____

8. Imani wants to know the favorite day of the week of adults in the town where she lives. Imani surveys every tenth adult that enters a convenience store between 4:00 p.m. and 8:00 p.m. Identify the population and sample.

____

____

____

____

© Houghton Mifflin Harcourt Publishing Company

Name ______________________________

Make Inferences from Repeated Random Samples

I Can use multiple random samples of the same size from a population to make inferences about a survey result.

Step It Out

1 The results of a school-wide survey of all students at a middle school about renaming the school mascot from Grizzlies to Bears are shown at the right. Since all students in the school were surveyed, these ratios are the population ratios. The students in a math class had an assignment to collect random samples of 20 students in the school and compare the sample ratio to the population ratio. The results are shown below. Find each sample ratio for those who prefer "Bears," and write it as a percent.

A. Sample 1: 13 students prefer "Bears"

Sample ratio of those who prefer "Bears": $\frac{\square}{20} = \square\%$

B. Sample 2: 16 students prefer "Bears"

Sample ratio of those who prefer "Bears": $\frac{\square}{20} = \square\%$

C. Sample 3: 15 students prefer "Bears"

Sample ratio of those who prefer "Bears": $\frac{\square}{20} = \square\%$

D. Do these sample ratios support the finding that 70% of the entire school population prefer the mascot name "Bears"? Explain.

____

____

____

____

Turn and Talk Why are the sample ratios different from the population ratio?

© Houghton Mifflin Harcourt Publishing Company • Image Credit: ©Jozef Polc/Alamy

2 A bagel shop offering regular or toasted bagels makes the claim shown. Use each method to explore how much variation can be expected from a sample.

A. Construct a mock population by placing 60 red slips of paper (for toasted) and 40 blue slips of paper (for not toasted) in a bag.

B. Randomly select 10 slips of paper from the bag and record the results in the column for Sample 1. Be sure to return each slip of paper to the bag before you draw another.

C. Repeat Step B nine more times, recording your results in the table.

	Samples									
	1	2	3	4	5	6	7	8	9	10
Toasted bagels (red)										
Untoasted bagels (blue)										
Sample ratio of toasted bagels										

D. Plot the results in the dot plot.

E. How do the sample ratios compare with the population ratio?

____

____

____

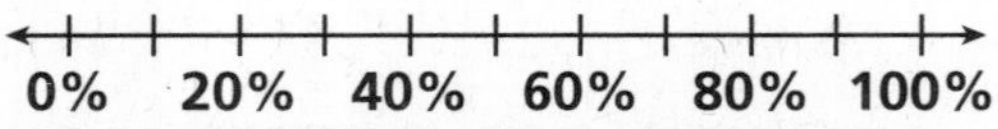

Sample Ratios of Toasted Bagels

Turn and Talk How can repeated random samples of the same size from a population help you to understand the variation in the sample ratios?

Check Understanding

A company claims that 75% of employees prefer day shifts to night shifts.

1. The manager took a random sample of 20 employees and found that 16 employees prefer the day shift. Does the sample ratio support the company's claim about the population ratio? Explain.

____

2. With repeated samples, is the average of sample ratios more likely to approximate the population ratio than a single sample?

____

© Houghton Mifflin Harcourt Publishing Company • Image Credit: ©sergeyskleznev/iStock/Getty Images Plus/Getty Images

On Your Own

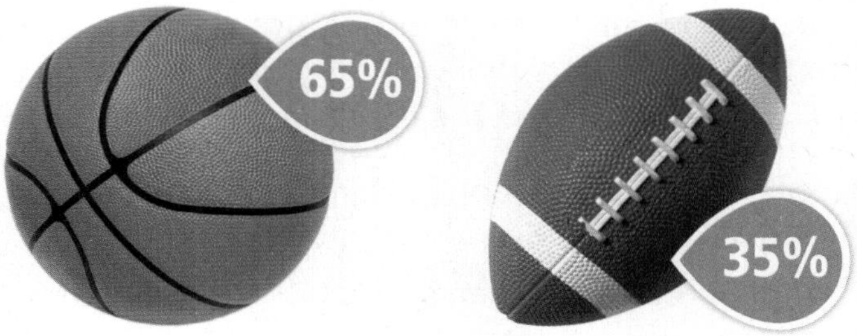

3. Health and Fitness The results of a survey about whether students at a middle school prefer to participate in basketball or football are shown.

Bella used a random number generator to generate 10 samples of the population.

Numbers 1–65: basketball
Numbers 66–100: football

Sample 1	62	1	73	53	85	31	79	68	8	14	13	29	30	25	61	28	26	67	24	80
Sample 2	48	66	65	59	58	21	85	92	34	56	67	76	82	26	28	18	93	39	73	97
Sample 3	99	12	92	45	13	2	62	40	96	64	100	69	35	70	93	14	78	48	67	15
Sample 4	85	32	25	37	8	49	28	24	60	31	43	61	94	16	58	63	59	12	52	1
Sample 5	28	36	3	78	46	6	54	52	99	59	39	65	84	80	81	98	75	14	53	79
Sample 6	60	66	53	40	18	55	72	38	44	69	49	51	93	17	34	67	64	89	91	13
Sample 7	28	56	93	7	84	29	57	11	35	74	87	65	78	80	27	85	99	41	91	40
Sample 8	58	46	82	56	24	26	12	67	73	61	6	52	68	29	48	21	43	85	49	2
Sample 9	3	43	98	76	17	88	44	13	65	23	87	2	18	93	49	60	58	57	86	29
Sample 10	57	11	8	3	68	98	1	67	97	29	23	99	59	56	65	72	60	79	89	30

A. Use the random numbers from each sample to complete the table.

	Samples									
	1	**2**	**3**	**4**	**5**	**6**	**7**	**8**	**9**	**10**
Numbers 1–65										
Numbers 66–100										
Sample ratio of numbers 1–65										

B. Plot the results from the table in the dot plot.

C. How does the Sample 9 ratio compare to the population ratio?

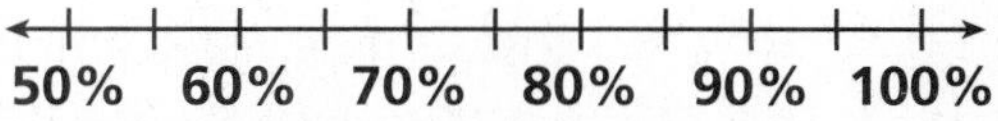

Sample Ratios of Numbers 1–65

D. MP **Use Structure** How do the sample ratios compare to the population ratio?

© Houghton Mifflin Harcourt Publishing Company • **Image Credits:** (tl) ©Davies and Starr/Getty Images; (tr) ©Houghton Mifflin Harcourt

4. A factory owner surveyed employees about whether they prefer working 5 regular workdays or 4 longer workdays. The results are shown.

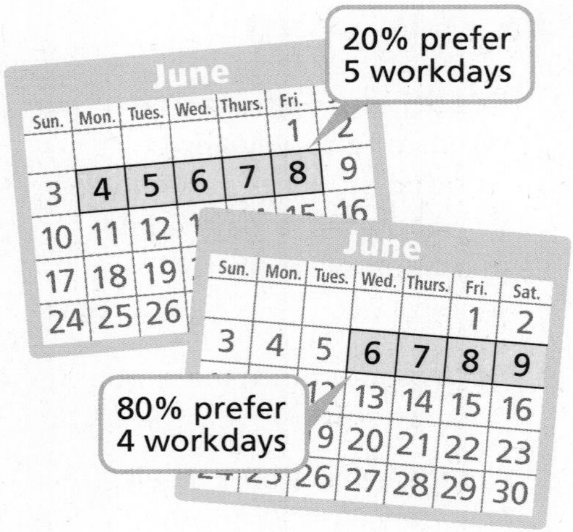

A. Construct a mock population using blue and green slips of paper.

Blue: prefer 5 regular workdays
Green: prefer 4 longer workdays.

- Place 10 blue slips and 40 green slips in a hat.
- Randomly select a sample of 10 slips of paper from the hat, and record the ratio.
- Replace the slips, and repeat for 10 samples.

	Samples									
	1	**2**	**3**	**4**	**5**	**6**	**7**	**8**	**9**	**10**
5 workdays (blue)										
4 workdays (green)										
Sample ratio of 5 workdays										
Sample ratio of 4 workdays										

B. Plot the ratios of those who prefer 5 workdays in the dot plot.

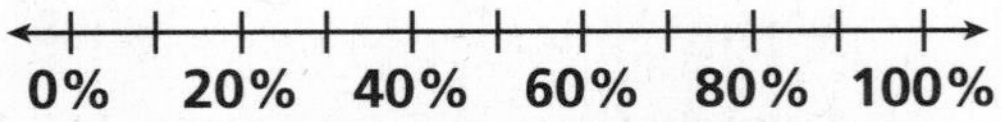

Sample Ratios of 5 Workdays

C. How do the sample ratios of those who prefer 5 workdays compare to the population ratio?

____

____

D. (MP) **Attend to Precision** Plot the ratios of those who prefer 4 workdays in the dot plot.

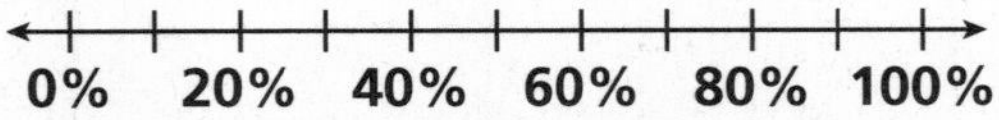

Sample Ratios of 4 Workdays

E. How do the sample ratios of those who prefer 4 workdays compare to the population ratio?

____

____

© Houghton Mifflin Harcourt Publishing Company

Name ______________________________

ONLINE
Video Tutorials and Interactive Examples

Make Inferences from Repeated Random Samples

1. A poll was conducted among all students at a middle school about whether they prefer blue or red. The resulting population ratios are shown.

A. Glen used a random number generator to generate the sample ratios shown in the chart.

Numbers 1–55: students who prefer blue
Numbers 56–100: students who prefer red

	Samples									
	1	**2**	**3**	**4**	**5**	**6**	**7**	**8**	**9**	**10**
Blue preference	12	11	13	8	11	12	10	9	10	9
Red preference	8	9	7	12	9	8	10	11	10	11
Sample ratio of blue preference	60%	55%	65%	40%	55%	60%	50%	45%	50%	45%

The sample ratio for blue preference in Sample 1 is [above / below] the population ratio.

The sample ratio for blue preference in Sample 8 is [above / below] the population ratio.

B. Plot the results for blue preference from the table on the dot plot.

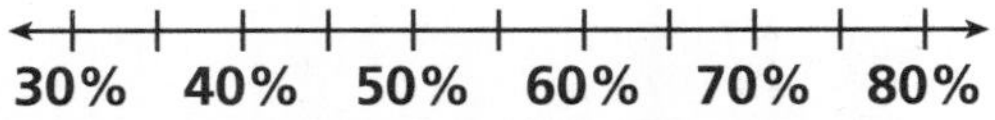

Sample Ratios of Blue Preference

C. **Open Ended** How do the sample ratios Glen generated compare to the population ratio?

____

____

____

D. (MP) **Reason** Predict what would happen to the sample ratios in the dot plot as more samples are taken.

____

____

____

© Houghton Mifflin Harcourt Publishing Company • Image Credits: ©Mizkit/Shutterstock

Test Prep

2. Abner researched and found that 60% of students in his school ride the bus to school. Abner took a random sample of 50 students and found that 38 ride the bus to school. Which statement correctly describes the sample ratio?

Ⓐ The sample ratio is 38%, which is below the population ratio.

Ⓑ The sample ratio is 38%, which is above the population ratio.

Ⓒ The sample ratio is 76%, which is below the population ratio.

Ⓓ The sample ratio is 76%, which is above the population ratio.

3. The population ratio of male employees in a large office is 55%. Random samples of 20 employees are taken. Select how the sample ratio varies in relation to the actual ratio of the population.

	5% Above	10% Above	5% Below	10% Below
45% of employees are male.	☐	☐	☐	☐
10 out of 20 employees are male.	☐	☐	☐	☐
60% of employees are male.	☐	☐	☐	☐
13 out of 20 employees are male.	☐	☐	☐	☐

4. Research claims that 30% of dental customers have had braces. Julie used a random number generator to generate samples, where numbers 1–3 represent having braces and numbers 4–10 represent not having braces. One sample is shown. How does the sample compare to the population?

Sample 5: 2, 1, 7, 5, 8, 3, 9, 6, 8, 4, 3, 2, 3, 5, 6, 8, 6, 7, 2, 8

____

____

____

Spiral Review

5. The results of a random survey about the number of siblings of students are shown in the box plot. Make an inference about the larger student population.

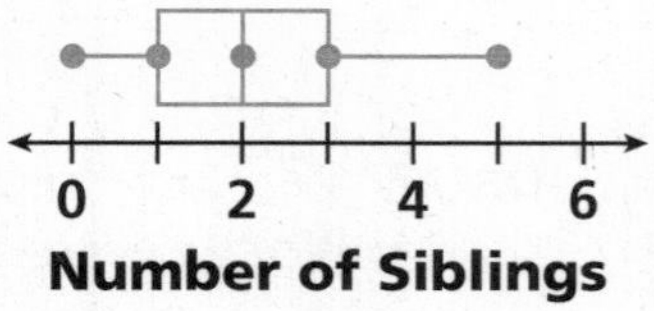

____

____

6. Libby bought 224 ounces of flour. If each bag contains 32 ounces of flour, how many bags of flour did Libby buy?

____

© Houghton Mifflin Harcourt Publishing Company

Module 11

Name

Review

Vocabulary

Dana wants to know how many students at her school watch sports on television. She selects 40 students from her school to survey. Use this information to answer each question.

1. What is the population in this situation?

2. What is the sample?

3. What is the difference between a representative sample and a biased sample in this situation?

Concepts and Skills

4. A theater owner wants to survey the audience about the types of plays they want to see. At a sold-out show, there are 100 people in VIP seats, 700 on the main floor, and 400 in the balcony. Which sample can best help the owner see the preferences of all the audience members?

(A) 5 people in VIP seats, 20 on the main floor, and 35 in the balcony

(B) 5 people in VIP seats, 35 on the main floor, and 20 in the balcony

(C) 20 people in VIP seats, 20 on the main floor, and 20 in the balcony

(D) 10 people in VIP seats, 7 on the main floor, and 4 in the balcony

5. (MP) **Use Tools** There are 580 students at Alejandro's school. He surveys a random sample of 60 students and finds that 21 of them regularly bring their lunch. Based on these results, estimate how many students at Alejandro's school regularly bring their lunch. State what strategy and tool you will use to answer the question, explain your choice, and then find the answer.

© Houghton Mifflin Harcourt Publishing Company

6. A city librarian wants to see if visitors want to add a cafe to the library. On a Monday morning, the librarian surveys every fourth visitor to the library. Is this sample likely to be representative of all library visitors? Explain.

____

____

____

7. A factory produces a batch of 4,800 pens. The company dictates that if a random sample of the batch shows that more than 2% of the pens are defective, the batch needs additional testing. A worker checks a random sample of 60 pens from the batch and finds that 2 are defective. Based on this information, which statement(s) about the sample are true? Select all that apply.

Ⓐ It indicates the batch needs additional testing.

Ⓑ It indicates probably about 96 pens in the batch are defective.

Ⓒ It indicates there are probably about 160 defective pens in the batch.

Ⓓ It indicates probably about 4,580 pens in the batch have no defects.

Ⓔ It indicates that about 1.25% of the pens in the batch are defective.

8. A company makes short-sleeved and long-sleeved T-shirts. The company checks a random sample of 60 T-shirts of each type. It finds that 4 short-sleeved shirts have problems and 1 long-sleeved shirt has problems. How many T-shirts should the company predict have problems in a shipment of 3,000 shirts of each type?

________ total T-shirts

9. An inspector takes 20 different random samples of 25 apples each from a shipment of 2,000 apples. Based on the data, which is the most reasonable prediction of the number of apples in the shipment that weigh more than 7 ounces?

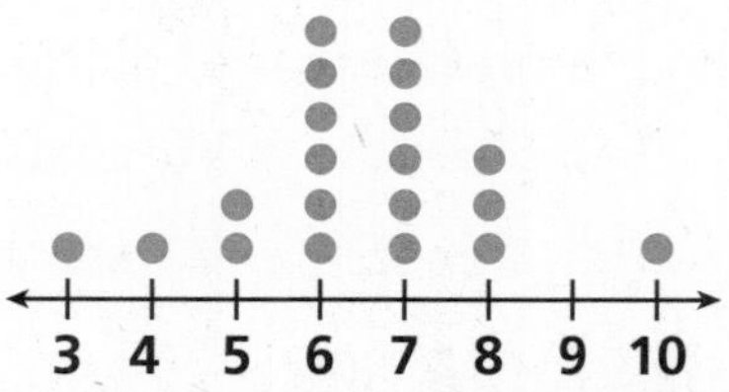

Number of Apples Weighing More Than 7 Ounces

Ⓐ about 200 apples

Ⓑ about 320 apples

Ⓒ about 520 apples

Ⓓ about 560 apples

10. Karen and Zeb each use a computer program to randomly select 50 students from the school directory. They ask the students about the school rules. They find that 68% from Karen's sample and 72% from Zeb's sample say the rules are fair. Explain why Karen and Zeb got different results, even though they used the same sampling method.

____

____

____

© Houghton Mifflin Harcourt Publishing Company

Module

12 Use Statistics and Graphs to Compare Data

And the Best Player Is...

Three friends have a tournament to see who is best at playing a popular game on their phones. They each play the game 9 times. Their scores are shown.

Find the mean, median, range, and interquartile range for each player. Who is the best player?

A.

Arianna's Scores		
68	88	89
90	77	75
67	41	98

Mean: ________

Median: ________

Range: ________

Interquartile range: ________

B.

Deshauna's Scores		
98	79	41
93	24	93
91	31	35

Mean: ________

Median: ________

Range: ________

Interquartile range: ________

C.

Mayumi's Scores		
90	65	78
10	67	71
97	81	80

Mean: ________

Median: ________

Range: ________

Interquartile range: ________

Turn and Talk

Which player do you think is the best player? Justify your answer.

© Houghton Mifflin Harcourt Publishing Company • Image Credit: ©Iakov Filimonov/Shutterstock

Are You Ready?

Complete these problems to review prior concepts and skills you will need for this module.

Mean

Find the mean of each set of data.

1. The table lists the weights of a random sample of 11 tents from an outdoor store. What is the mean weight?

____

Tent Weights (ounces)		
79	73	77
81	76	50
64	56	47
59	75	

2. 17, 25, 22, 18, 18, 20 ________

3. 48, 12, 35, 57, 42, 15, 74, 29 ________

4. 24, 27, 29, 31, 8, 16, 24, 19, 11 ________

Dot Plots

Rosa is growing pea plants for a science experiment. The dot plot shows the heights of her 11 plants. Use the dot plot to determine each measure of center or variability.

5. Mean ________

6. Median ________

7. Range ________

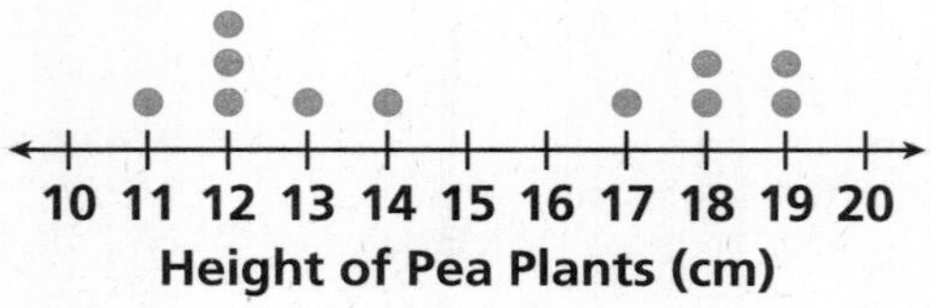

Box Plots

A karate studio offers 10 classes per week for middle school students. The numbers of students in the classes are listed.

13, 15, 14, 10, 12, 10, 13, 16, 15, 13

8. Use the number line to make a box plot of the data set. Be sure to give the box plot a title.

9. Median ________

10. Range ________

11. Interquartile range ________

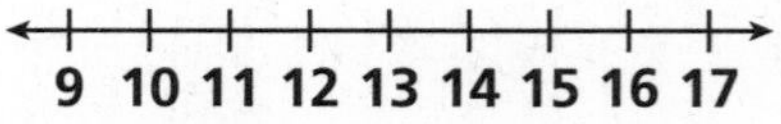

© Houghton Mifflin Harcourt Publishing Company

Name ______________________________

Compare Center and Spread of Data Displayed in Dot Plots

I Can compare two data sets displayed in dot plots and make inferences about two populations.

Step It Out

1 At the end of the first week of school, Mr. Parrish asked 15 freshman students how much time they spent studying that week. He also surveyed 15 sophomore students to investigate whether their habits were different.

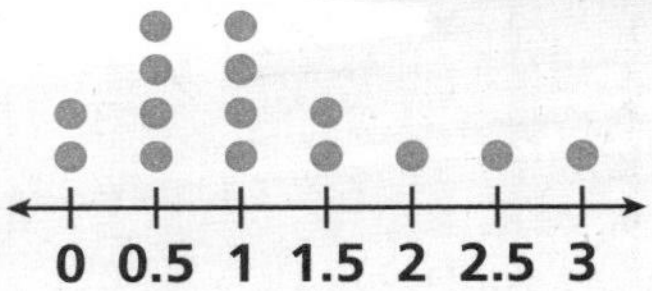

Freshman Study Time (h)

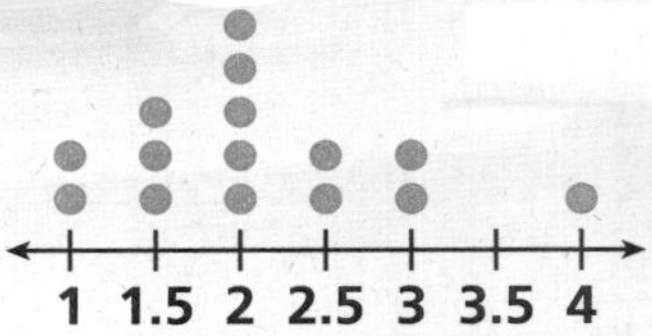

Sophomore Study Time (h)

A. Compare the shapes of the dot plots by describing where the values are clustered in each plot.

____

____

____

B. Find the **median** and **mean** of each data set.

Freshman: median = ______ Sophomore: median = ______

Freshman: mean = ______ Sophomore: mean = ______

C. Find the **range** for each data set.

Freshman range: 3 − ______ = ______ hours

Sophomore range: 4 − ______ = ______ hours

Both data sets have a range of ______ hours.

D. What do the data tell you about study habits?

____

____

Turn and Talk How does a dot plot help you look at trends in data?

© Houghton Mifflin Harcourt Publishing Company • Image Credit: ©Blend Images - Moxie Productions/Brand X Pictures/Getty Images

2 Bill grows oranges and Carla grows apples. Each selected 13 trees at random and counted the pieces of fruit they produced to the nearest hundred.

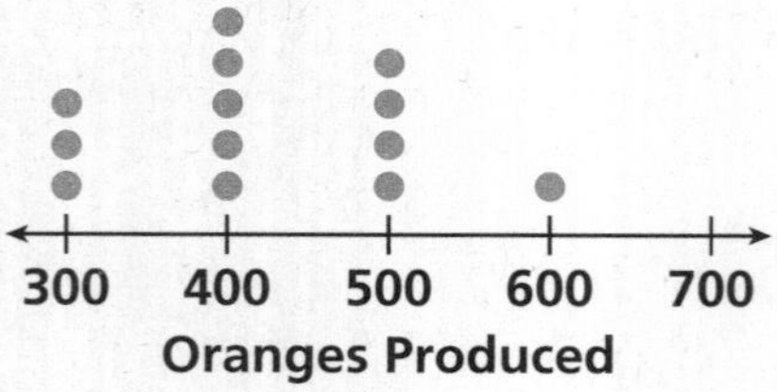

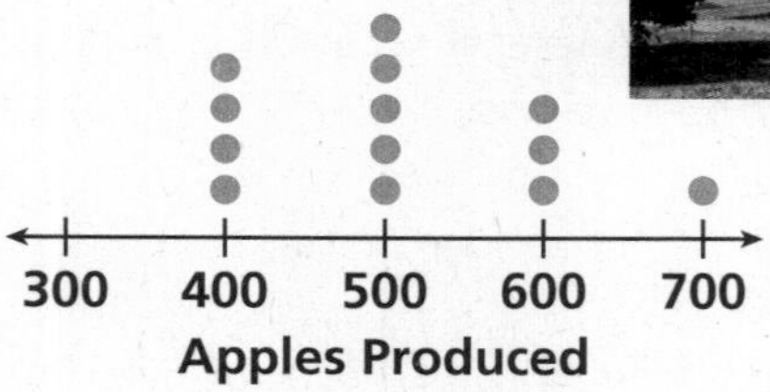

A. How are the shapes of the dot plots alike in terms of their peaks?

B. What is the median of each data set? Compare the centers of the plots.

C. Use the dot plots to compare the ranges of the data.

Check Understanding

The members of two book clubs kept track of how many hours they spent reading over one weekend. Use the dot plots for Problems 1–3.

1. Compare the means of the data sets and draw one conclusion.

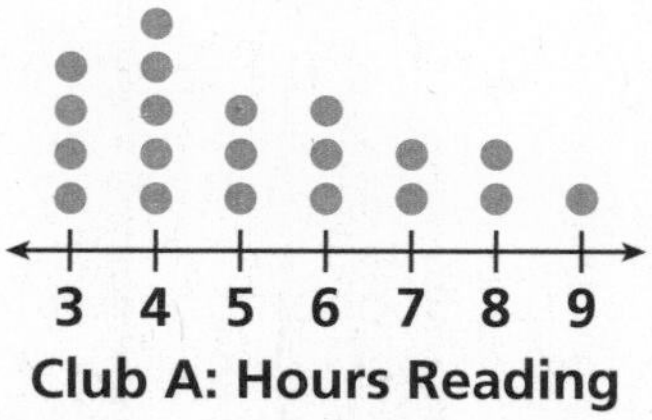

2. Compare the ranges of the data sets and draw one conclusion.

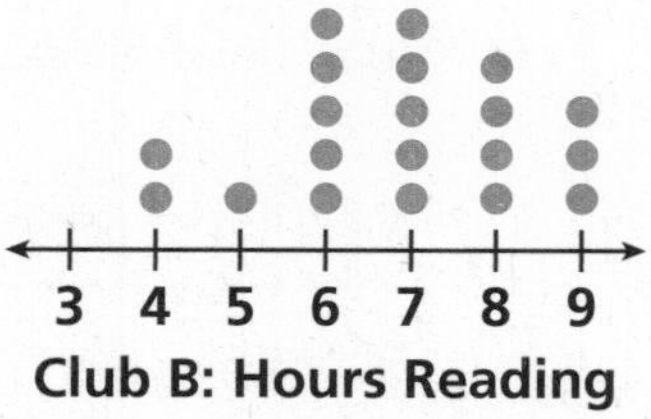

3. Draw one conclusion from the shape of the data distribution.

© Houghton Mifflin Harcourt Publishing Company • **Image Credit:** ©ChrisBoswell/iStock/Getty Images Plus/Getty Images

Name

On Your Own

4. The dot plots show recorded wait times for two food trucks.

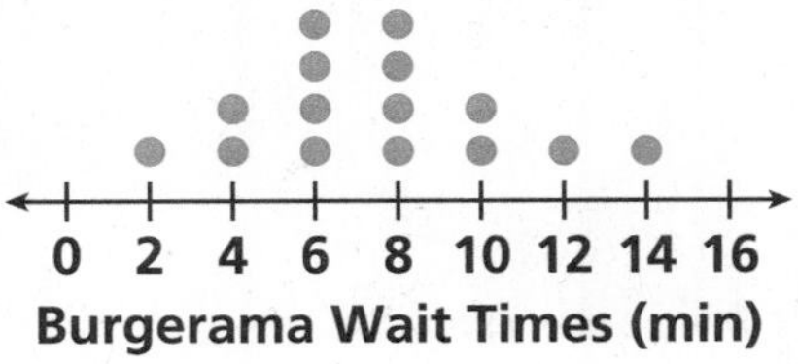

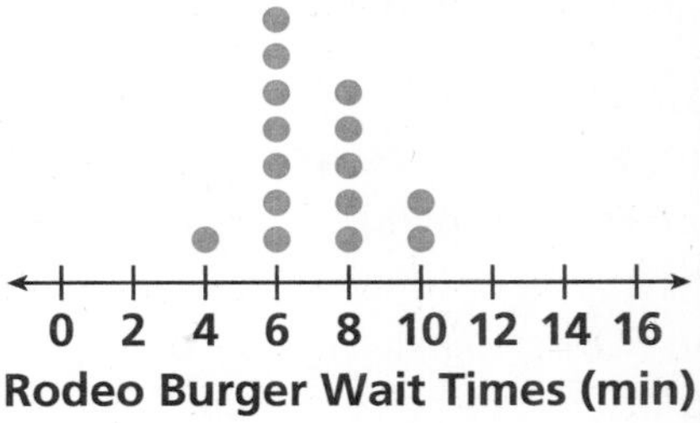

A. (MP) **Use Structure** Visually compare the spreads of the data sets.

____

____

B. (MP) **Use Structure** Visually compare the centers of the data sets.

____

C. Complete the table to verify your visual assessments.

	Burgerama	Rodeo Burger
Number of observations		
Median		
Range		

D. Do you expect the means to be about the same or to be different for each data set? Explain your visual assessment.

____

____

____

____

E. Find the mean to the nearest tenth to check your visual assessment.

Burgerama mean: __________ Rodeo Burger mean: __________

F. (MP) **Construct Arguments** Based on the data, which restaurant would have more predictable wait times? Explain.

____

____

____

© Houghton Mifflin Harcourt Publishing Company • Image Credit: ©Blulz60/Shutterstock

5. Fabulous Fashions selected employees at random to review salary distribution for the company.

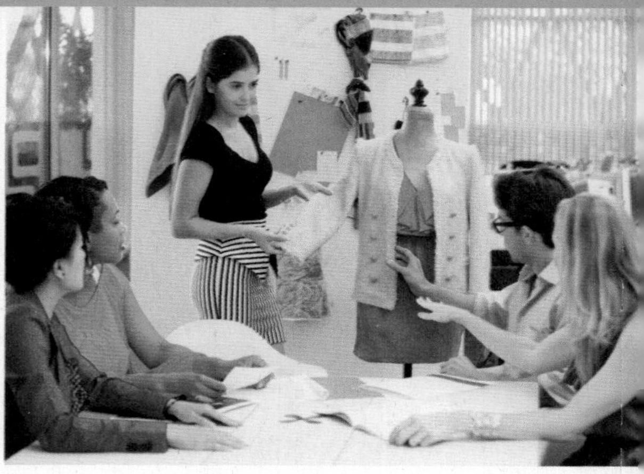

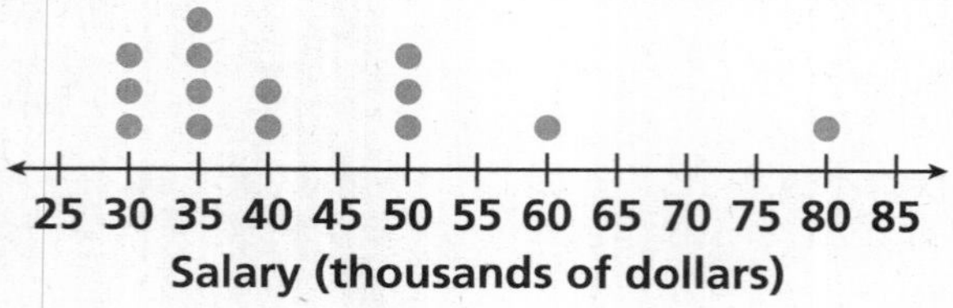

A. What is the median? Describe the shape of the data, including any clusters.

____

____

B. What is the range of the data? ______________________

C. (MP) **Use Structure** What do the data in the dot plot tell you about what most employees earn?

____

____

6. The dot plots show the ages in years of the players for both the Wolves and the Jets basketball teams.

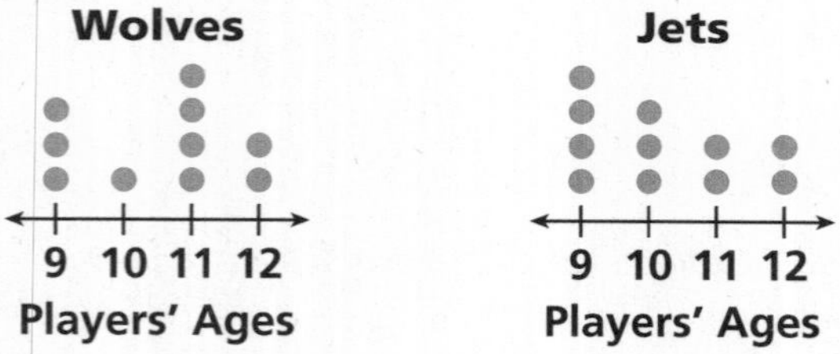

A. Compare the shapes of the dot plots.

____

____

B. Compare the modes and medians of the data sets.

____

____

C. What is the range of each data set?

____

D. (MP) **Use Structure** What do the dot plots tell you about the ages of the players on the two teams?

____

____

© Houghton Mifflin Harcourt Publishing Company • Image Credit: ©Monkey Business Images/Shutterstock

Name ____________________

ONLINE
Ed
Video Tutorials and
Interactive Examples

Compare Center and Spread of Data Displayed in Dot Plots

Tallahassee and Key West are at opposite ends of the state of Florida. The dot plots show high temperatures recorded in each city in May of one year. Use this information for Problems 1–7.

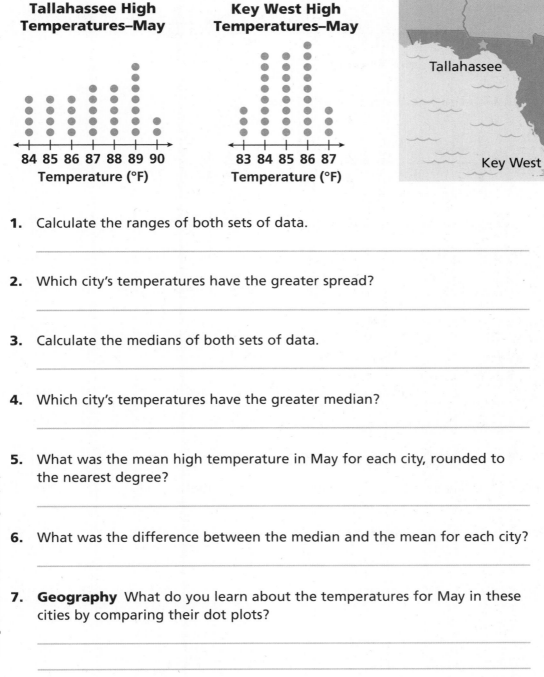

Tallahassee High Temperatures–May

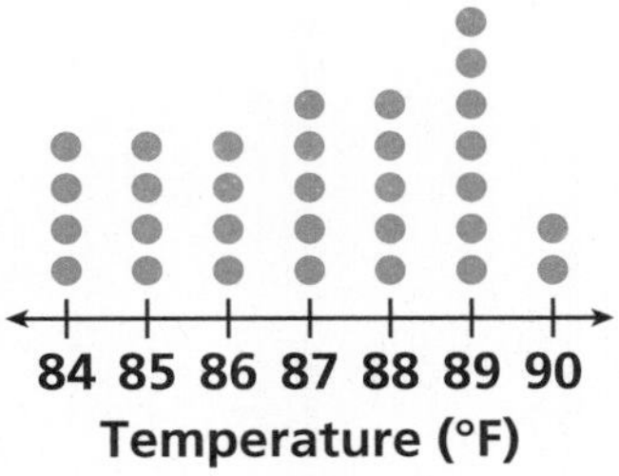

Key West High Temperatures–May

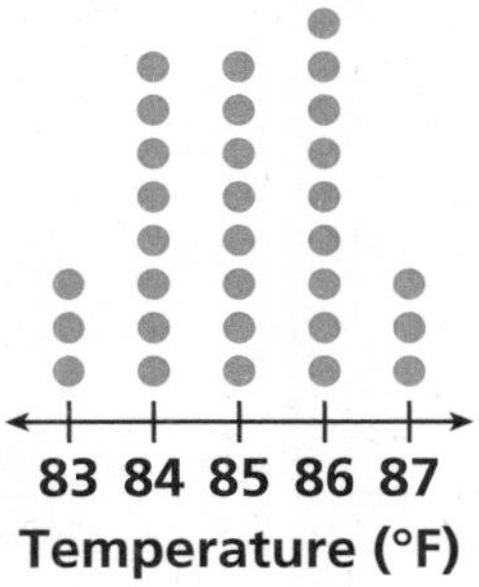

1. Calculate the ranges of both sets of data.

____

2. Which city's temperatures have the greater spread?

____

3. Calculate the medians of both sets of data.

____

4. Which city's temperatures have the greater median?

____

5. What was the mean high temperature in May for each city, rounded to the nearest degree?

____

6. What was the difference between the median and the mean for each city?

____

7. **Geography** What do you learn about the temperatures for May in these cities by comparing their dot plots?

____

____

____

____

© Houghton Mifflin Harcourt Publishing Company

Test Prep

Use the dot plots for Problems 8–11.

Social Media Accounts in Middle School

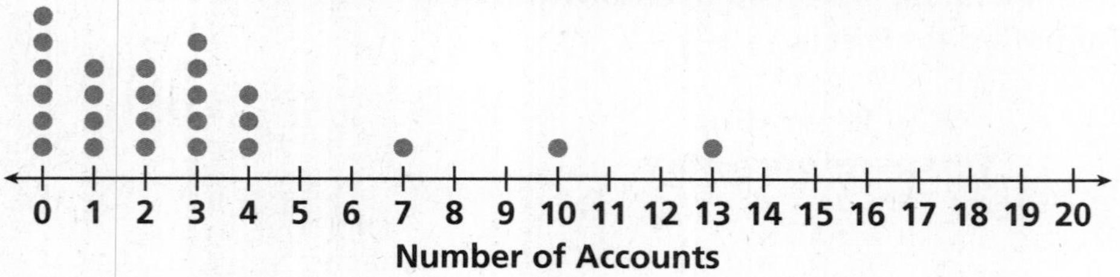

Social Media Accounts in High School

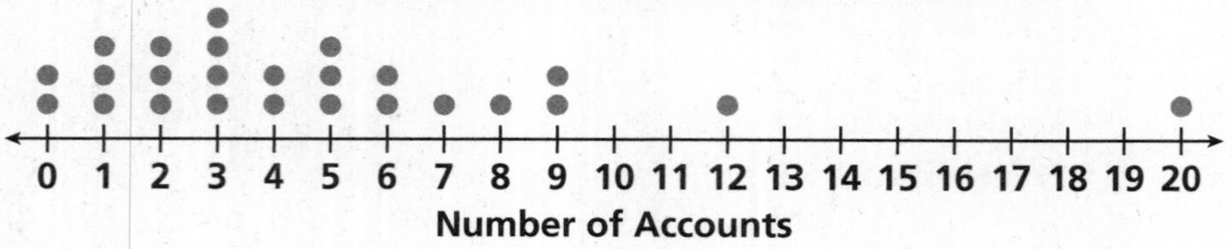

8. What is the median for the middle school data?

Ⓐ 0 Ⓑ 1 Ⓒ 2 Ⓓ 3

9. What is the median for the high school data?

Ⓐ 3 Ⓑ 4 Ⓒ 5 Ⓓ 6

10. Which of the following best describes the shape of the data in the middle school dot plot?

Ⓐ Most of the data points are less than 2.

Ⓑ Most of the data points are 5 or more.

Ⓒ Most of the data points are 4 or less.

Ⓓ There are no outliers.

11. What can you conclude about the variations among populations represented in this survey?

____

____

Spiral Review

12. What is the solution of the equation $2w - 3 = 11$? ______________

13. If the slope of a line is 3 and the y-intercept is 0, what is an equation that represents the line?

____

© Houghton Mifflin Harcourt Publishing Company

Name ____________________

Compare Center and Spread of Data Displayed in Box Plots

I Can **compare two data sets displayed in box plots and make inferences about two populations.**

Step It Out

1 The sixth- and seventh-grade students are having a reading contest. Their progress is shown in the **box plots**.

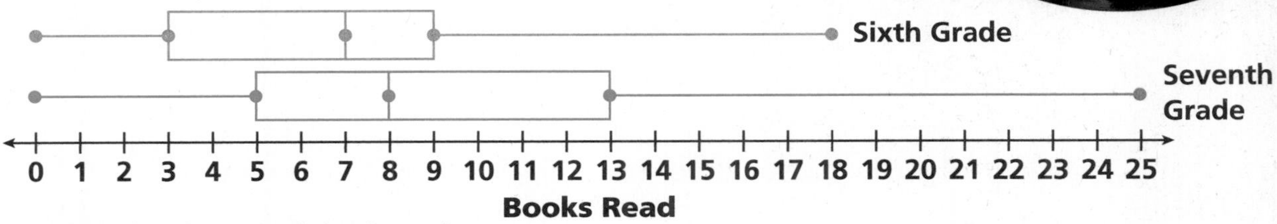

A. Describe the shapes of the box plots.

B. Compare the *centers* of the box plots by comparing their medians.

C. Find the ranges and the **interquartile ranges**. Complete the table.

	Sixth grade	Seventh grade
Range		
Interquartile range		

D. Why would the data sets appear to have similar spreads using interquartile range and very different spreads using the range?

E. Explain what the left whiskers of the box plots tell you about the data sets.

Turn and Talk Can you project the winner of the contest based on this data? Explain.

© Houghton Mifflin Harcourt Publishing Company • Image Credit: ©Andersen Ross/Blend Images/Getty Images

2 The times in minutes for students to complete a test on paper and the same test on a computer are shown.

Paper: 42, 48, 52, 54, 59, 61, 61, 64, 65, 67, 68, 70, 72, 75, 80	Computer: 46, 47, 48, 50, 52, 55, 58, 60, 62, 64, 64, 64, 69, 73, 74

A. Find the five key values that describe the test scores collected from pencil-and-paper exams.

The least value, the minimum, is ________ minutes.

The greatest value, the maximum, is ________ minutes.

The median, or middle value, is ________ minutes.

The **lower quartile** is the median of only the values less than the median, so $Q_1 =$ ________ minutes.

The **upper quartile** is the median of the top half of the data, so $Q_3 =$ ________ minutes.

B. Identify the five key values for the sample of computer exam scores.

Minimum: ________ Median: ________ Maximum: ________

Q_1: ________ Q_3: ________

C. Sketch box plots to represent each sample.

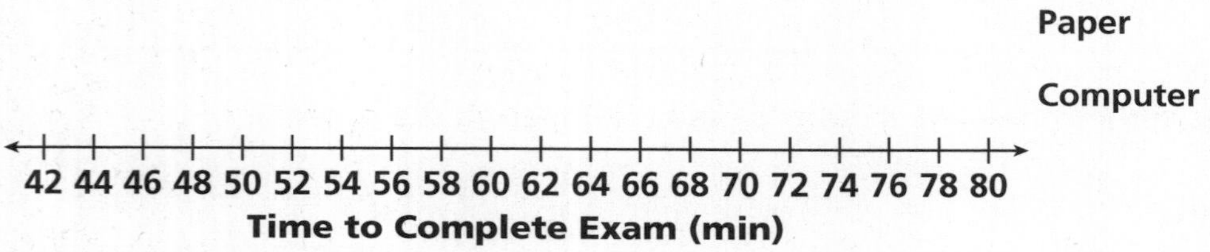

D. Compare the centers and spreads of the box plots. Which testing format takes students longer to complete?

____

____

Check Understanding

1. Two groups of 8 violin students kept track of the hours they practiced in a week. The results are:

A: 0, 1, 3, 5, 5, 6, 6, 8

B: 2, 3, 3, 3, 5, 6, 9, 10

Sketch box plots representing each data set. Draw one conclusion based on the plots.

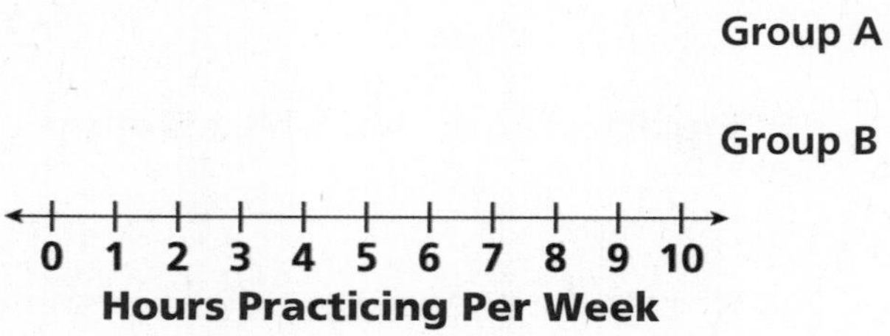

____

2. About how many data points fall below the median of a data set?

____

© Houghton Mifflin Harcourt Publishing Company • Image Credit: ©FatCamera/Getty Images

Name ______________________________

On Your Own

3. The box plots show the distribution of ages for players on two football teams.

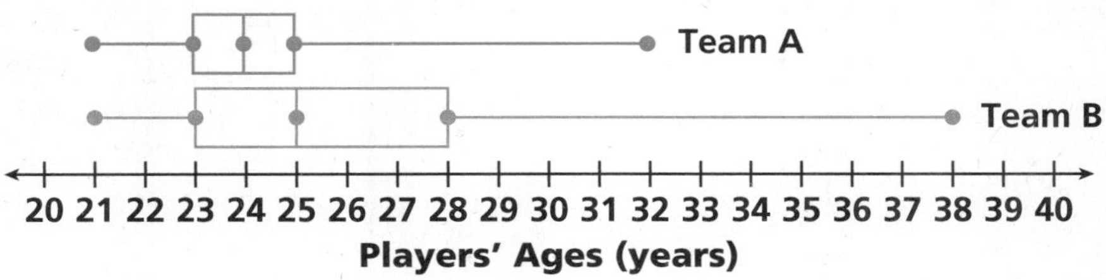

A. (MP) **Use Structure** How are the distributions alike?

____

____

B. Which measure of spread would you choose to describe these data sets? Use it to compare the spread of the data in these sets.

____

____

____

____

C. Use the box plots to complete the table.

D. Compare the centers of the box plots.

____

____

____

____

	Team A	Team B
Minimum		
Lower quartile		
Median		
Upper quartile		
Maximum		

E. Explain the significance of the age 25 years in each box plot.

____

____

____

F. (MP) **Reason** Where is the greatest difference in the box plots? Justify your choice.

____

____

____

© Houghton Mifflin Harcourt Publishing Company • Image Credit: ©skynesher/E+/Getty Images

4. Each year the Academy Awards honor excellence in film, including awards for Best Actor and Best Actress. The data sets shown are random samples of the ages in years at which these awards have been won.

A. Find the five key values for each data set.

B. Sketch box plots to represent each sample.

Best Actor

Best Actress

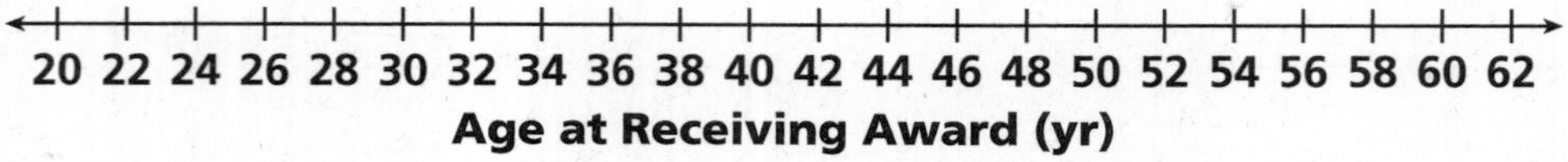

C. Compare the centers and spreads of the box plots.

D. (MP) **Critique Reasoning** After looking at the box plots, Tomás expresses surprise that most award-winning actresses are under the age of 41. Martha disagrees, pointing out that the right whisker is the longest part of the Best Actress box plot. Therefore, she argues, there are more winners from ages 41 to 62 than in the other intervals. Determine which friend is correct, and explain why.

E. What do the box plots for the samples tell you about the populations?

F. **Open Ended** Add two more possible ages to the data set for Best Actress winners so that the median of the data set does not change. Do not use the median age of 33 years.

© Houghton Mifflin Harcourt Publishing Company

Name ______________________________

ONLINE
Ed
Video Tutorials and
Interactive Examples

Compare Center and Spread of Data Displayed in Box Plots

Ms. Horvat is investigating prices of laptop computers at her local stores. She visits two different stores and selects a random sample of computers, recording their prices.

1. The box plot representing the data from Store A is shown.

The five key values for the data from Store B are:

minimum = \$300, Q_1 = \$500, median = \$800, Q_3 = \$1,000, maximum = \$1,500

A. Use the key values to sketch the box plot for Store B.

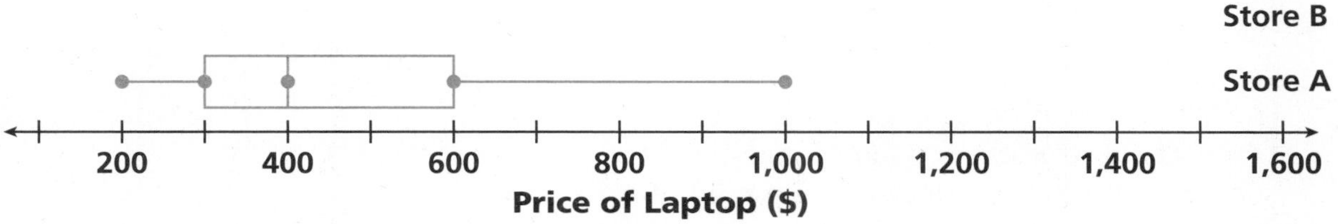

B. Compare the centers and shapes of the box plots.

____

____

C. Compare the spreads of the box plots.

____

____

____

____

D. (MP) **Use Structure** The price \$1,000 is a key value for each box plot. Explain the significance of this price for each store's data.

____

____

____

E. For each store, compare the spread of the lower half of the data with the spread of the upper half of the data.

____

____

____

____

© Houghton Mifflin Harcourt Publishing Company • Image Credit: ©Maskot/Getty Images

Test Prep

2. Which measures are used to make a box plot? Select all that apply.

Ⓐ maximum
Ⓑ mean
Ⓒ median
Ⓓ minimum
Ⓔ mode

3. When comparing two sets of data represented by box plots, compare the shape, ________, and ________.

4. Which is the preferred measure of spread for a data set with outliers?

Ⓐ interquartile range
Ⓑ mean
Ⓒ median
Ⓓ range

5. Moesha and Justin are competing in an online game to see who can solve puzzles in less time. The dot plots show the distribution of their times. Compare the centers and shapes of the box plots.

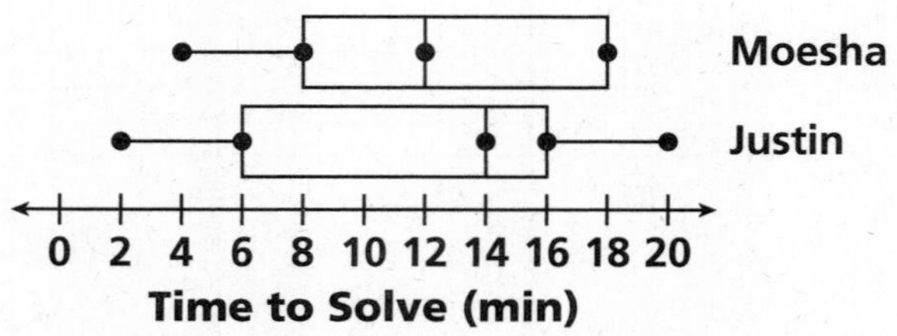

____

____

____

____

Spiral Review

6. Gretchen is delivering boxes of cookies to her neighbors. Her wagon weighs 12 pounds and will hold up to 9 boxes. Each box of cookies weighs 1 pound. What is the range of the function whose input is the number of boxes in the wagon and whose output is the combined weight of the wagon and boxes?

____

7. Luna knows that a line crosses the y-axis at $(0, -1)$. She also knows that the point $(3, 2)$ is on the line. What is the slope of this line?

____

8. How many triangles can you construct with side lengths 5 inches, 8 inches, and 20 inches?

____

© Houghton Mifflin Harcourt Publishing Company

Name ____________________

Compare Means Using Mean Absolute Deviation and Repeated Sampling

I Can **use the means and MADs to assess the amount of visual overlap of two numerical data distributions.**

Step It Out

1 Elia collected data from 10 randomly selected eighth-graders about the number of text messages they sent in one day. Results are shown in the table.

104	92	107	83	96
98	70	91	119	90

Recall that the **mean absolute deviation** (MAD) is the average distance from the data points to the mean. It is a measure of the spread of data because it describes the variation of data values from the mean.

A. What is the range of the data? What is the mean number of messages sent in this sample?

____

B. Complete the table to show each data point's absolute deviation or distance from the mean.

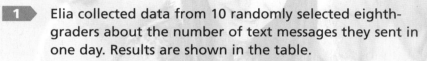

$\lvert 104 - 95 \rvert = 9$	$\lvert 92 - 95 \rvert = 3$	$\lvert 107 - 95 \rvert =$ ____	$\lvert 83 - 95 \rvert =$ ____	$\lvert 96 - 95 \rvert =$ ____
$\lvert 98 - 95 \rvert =$ ____	$\lvert 70 - 95 \rvert =$ ____	$\lvert 91 - 95 \rvert =$ ____	$\lvert 119 - 95 \rvert =$ ____	$\lvert 90 - 95 \rvert =$ ____

C. Find the sum of the absolute deviations. ____________

D. Find the mean absolute deviation (MAD) by finding the mean of the absolute deviations.

The mean absolute deviation is ________ messages.

E. Which data points have a distance from the mean that is less than or equal to the MAD? These data points are said to be *within* the MAD.

____

Turn and Talk How does the mean absolute deviation describe data differently than the mean of the data?

© Houghton Mifflin Harcourt Publishing Company • Image Credit: ©aldomurillo/Getty Images

2 Quentin collected data about the numbers of minutes students spent completing a math puzzle at the beginning of the year and at the end of the year.

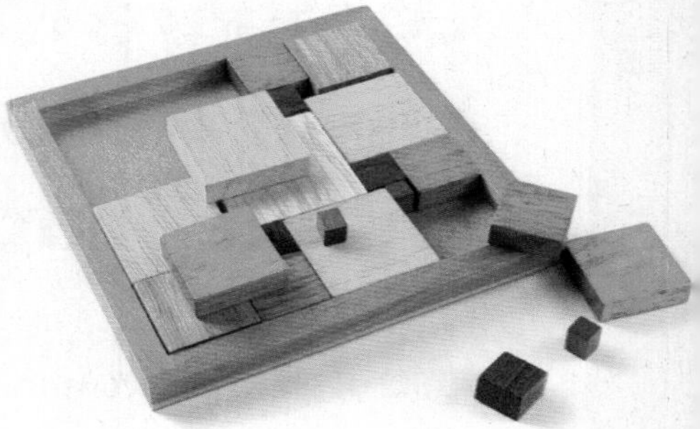

Beginning of Year				
12	18	20	16	11
14	16	22	17	14

End of Year				
12	6	3	4	9
4	5	8	9	10

A. Complete the table.

	Begining of Year	End of Year
Mean		
MAD		

B. The MADs for these data sets happen to be the same. Compare the difference of the means to the MAD. Round to the nearest tenth.

$\frac{\text{difference of means}}{\text{MAD}} = \frac{\square}{\square} =$ ______

The difference of the means is ______ times the MAD.

C. When two data sets are displayed in dot plots, the points might overlap a lot, a little, or not at all. The centers might be close or far apart. The ratios of the difference of the means to the MADs can help you describe how much separation there will be between the two distributions. The greater the ratio, the greater the separation. When the MADs of the data sets are similar, these ratios will be similar.

These plots show the puzzle-solving data. The yellow shading shows values within the mean absolute deviation.

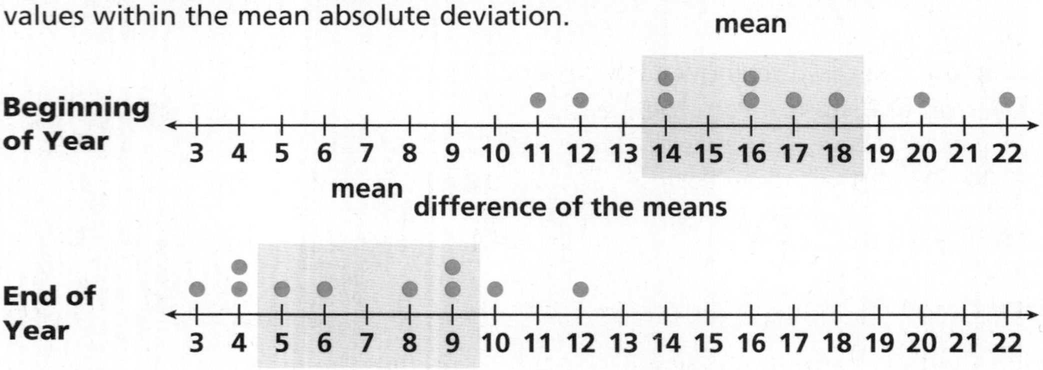

What does the ratio you calculated in Part B tell you about the separation between the two distributions?

The distance between the means is ______, which is ______ times the MAD, which indicates that there is a (large / small) separation between the centers of the data and (a lot of / not much) overlap in the two distributions.

Turn and Talk Why is it important to compare the difference of the means to the MADs?

© Houghton Mifflin Harcourt Publishing Company • **Image Credit:** ©Tutiun/iStock/Getty Images Plus/Getty Images

Name ______________________________

3 Two random samples are shown. The first random sample shows the heights in inches of students in the orchestra when they were in sixth grade. The second shows their heights when they were in eighth grade.

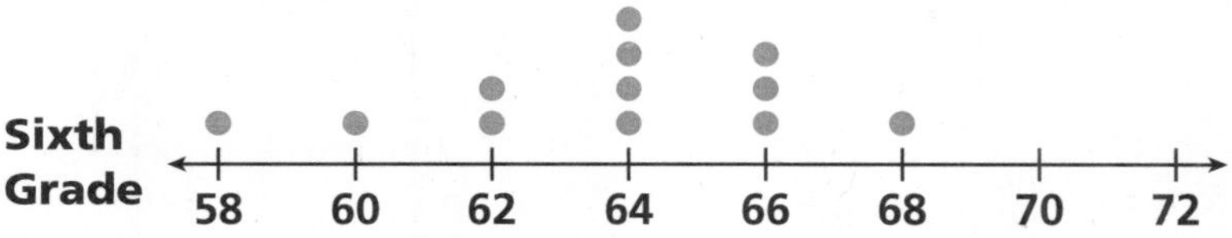

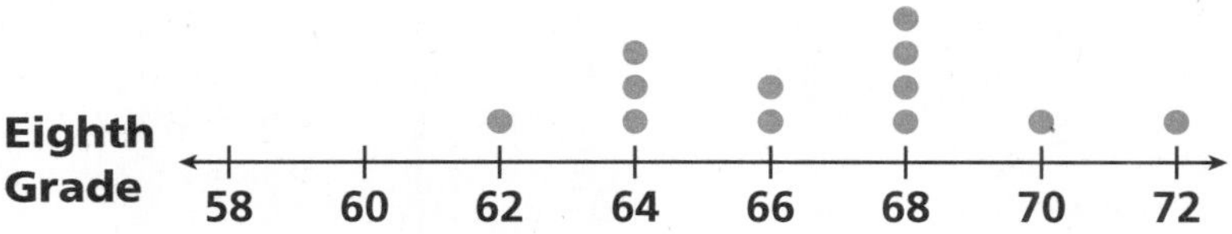

A. Complete the table. Round to the nearest tenth.

	Sixth Grade	Eighth Grade
Mean		
MAD		

B. For each plot, draw a dashed vertical segment to show the mean. Then, shade the region that shows the values that are within the MAD.

C. Find the ratio of the difference of the means to the MAD for each data set.

Grade 6: $\frac{\text{difference of means}}{\text{MAD}} =$ ________ Grade 8: $\frac{\text{difference of means}}{\text{MAD}} =$ ________

D. What do the ratios you calculated in Part C tell you about the visual separation between the two distributions?

____

____

____

Check Understanding

1. The difference of the means of two data sets is 0.5. Both data sets have a MAD of 1. How does the difference of the means compare to the MADs? If the data were displayed in dot plots, how much overlap would you expect to see? Explain.

____

____

2. A survey of adults and teens recorded the daily time in minutes each person spent messaging on a cell phone. These are the results:

Adults: 5, 10, 20, 15, 10 Teens: 50, 60, 40, 10, 80

The MAD for ________ is more than ________ times the MAD for ________, so the variation for ________ is much greater than for ________.

© Houghton Mifflin Harcourt Publishing Company • Image Credit: ©Monkey Business Images/Getty Images

On Your Own

3. A video game company is developing two games. One group is writing computer code for "Find the Gem." The other group is writing code for "Cross the Ocean." The plots show how long each programmer spent writing code for that game.

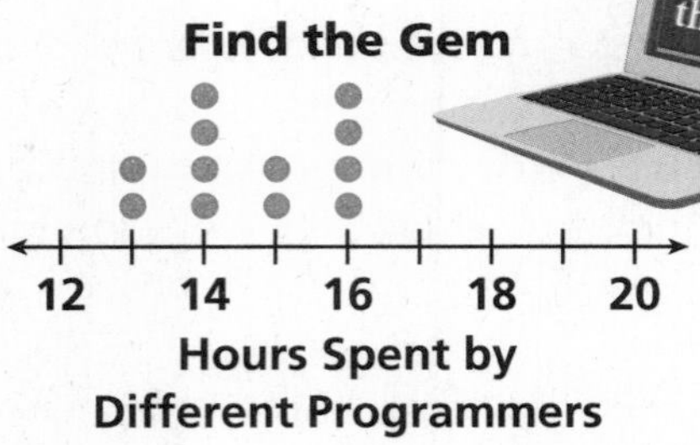

A. To the nearest tenth, what is the mean of each sample data set?

Find the Gem: ________

Cross the Ocean: ________

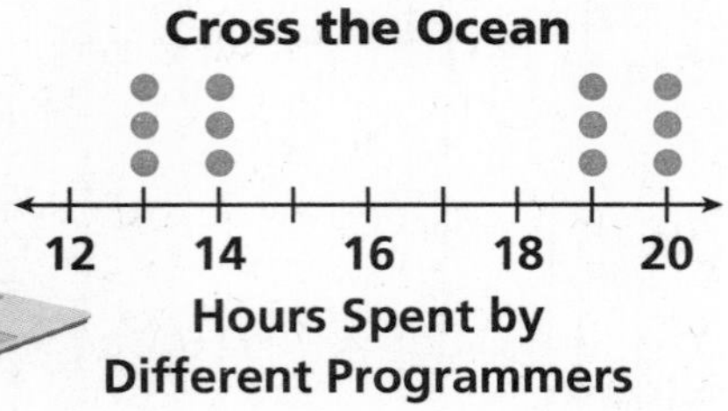

B. Which distribution do you predict will have the greater MAD? Why?

____

C. What is the MAD of each data set?

MAD of "Find the Gem" ________ MAD of "Cross the Ocean" ________

D. (MP) **Attend to Precision** Complete the statement.

The MAD for "Cross the Ocean" is ________ times the MAD for "Find the Gem."

For Problems 4–7, write the approximate ratio of the difference of the means to the MADs for the given data sets. Then tell how much overlap you would expect to see in dot plots of the sample data.

4.

	Sample A	Sample B
Mean	45	48
MAD	1.5	1.5

____

5.

	Sample A	Sample B
Mean	112	107
MAD	4.8	5.2

____

6.

	Sample A	Sample B
Mean	36	43
MAD	14	14

____

7.

	Sample A	Sample B
Mean	27.5	27.2
MAD	0.09	0.09

____

© Houghton Mifflin Harcourt Publishing Company

Name

8. (MP) **Reason** Randomly selected high school students with summer jobs and adult workers were surveyed about their hourly wages in dollars. The data are shown.

Hourly Wage of Students ($)				
15.00	15.00	15.00	15.00	15.00
15.25	15.25	15.50	15.50	15.50
15.75	16.00	18.00	19.00	20.00

Hourly Wage of Adults ($)				
15.00	15.00	16.00	17.50	18.00
19.00	21.00	22.00	24.00	25.00
27.00	28.00	28.00	31.50	32.00

A. What are the mean and MAD of each sample data set rounded to the nearest hundredth?

High school students:

The mean is ________.

The MAD is ________.

Adults:

The mean is ________. The MAD is approximately ________.

B. Complete the statement.

The MAD for adults is about ________ times the MAD for the students. This means the variation in the wages for adults is much ________ than the variation in the wages for the students.

C. **Open Ended** Suggest a change to one hourly wage in the student table so that the MAD will be less than before.

____

____

9. Two lab groups are each given a bag of identically shaped beads with letters. The groups are instructed to select 20 beads randomly and then record the number of vowels in the sample. They each perform the process 8 times, and their data are shown.

Group A	3	1	0	2	3	4	1	2
Group B	3	0	4	4	2	1	4	2

A. What are the mean and MAD, rounded to the nearest hundredth, of each data set?

Group A:

The mean is ________ vowel(s).

The MAD is ________ vowel(s).

Group B:

The mean is ________ vowel(s).

The MAD is ________ vowel(s).

© Houghton Mifflin Harcourt Publishing Company • Image Credit: ©SeventyFour/Shutterstock; ©Fotos593/Shutterstock

B. MP **Construct Arguments** If the data for the two groups were displayed in dot plots, how much separation would you expect to see in the distributions? Explain. Support your answer by finding the difference of the means and comparing it to the MADs.

____

____

____

10. Randomly selected seventh-graders in two classes are each asked to measure the entire length of their pointer finger and its length from the tip to the middle joint. The ratio of the lengths is recorded. The data are then organized for each class.

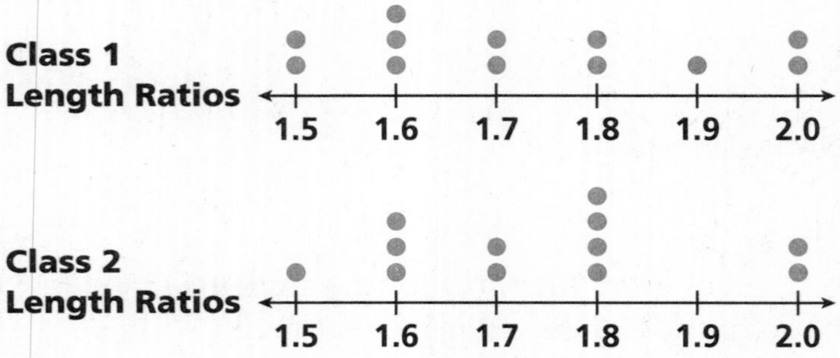

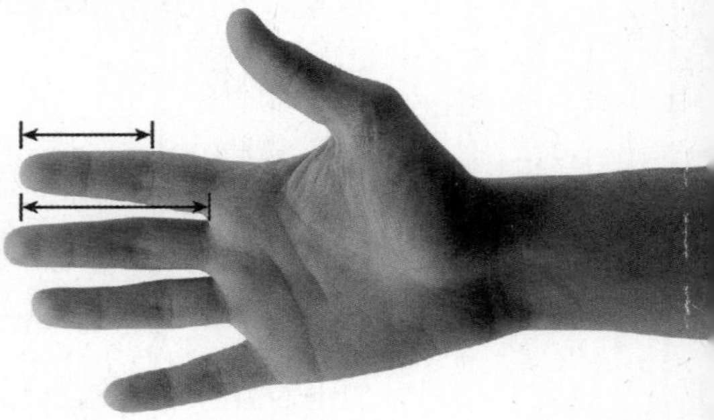

A. Do the two data sets overlap a lot, a little, or not at all?

____

B. What is the mean of each data set to the nearest hundredth?

Class 1: ________ Class 2: ________

C. What is the MAD of each data set to the nearest thousandth?

Class 1: ________ Class 2: ________

D. Use the means and MADs above to approximate the ratio of the difference of the means to the MADs for each data set. Round your ratios to the nearest hundredth.

Class 1: ________ Class 2: ________

E. Do your answers to Part D support your answer to Part A? Explain.

____

____

F. Are there meaningful differences in the two data sets? Explain.

____

____

____

© Houghton Mifflin Harcourt Publishing Company • Image Credit: ©dem10/Getty Images/iStockphoto.com

Name ______________________________

ONLINE
Video Tutorials and Interactive Examples

Compare Means Using Mean Absolute Deviation and Repeated Sampling

1. STEM Akuchi is experimenting with the effect of using plant food on the growth of sunflowers. The dot plots show the heights in inches of randomly selected sunflowers.

A. What are the means of each sample data set?

The mean height of sunflowers that grew with no food is ________ inches.

The mean height of sunflowers that grew with food is ________ inches.

B. What are the mean absolute deviations of the sample data?

The MAD for the sunflowers that grew with no food is ________ inches.

The MAD for the sunflowers that grew with food is ________ inches.

C. Are the data distributions visually separate? Explain why you would or would not expect them to be.

____

____

2. Math on the Spot The tables show the number of minutes per day students spend outside of school reading and doing their math homework.

Minutes spent outside of school reading
15, 15, 15, 20, 30, 30, 30, 30, 45, 60
Minutes spent outside of school doing math homework
25, 30, 30, 30, 30, 40, 45, 45, 55, 60

What is the difference of the means as a multiple of the approximate mean absolute deviations?

____

© Houghton Mifflin Harcourt Publishing Company • Image Credit: ©Corbis

Test Prep

Use this information for Problems 3 and 4.

Aubree records the duration in minutes of randomly selected hit songs from 2015. Her data are represented in the dot plot.

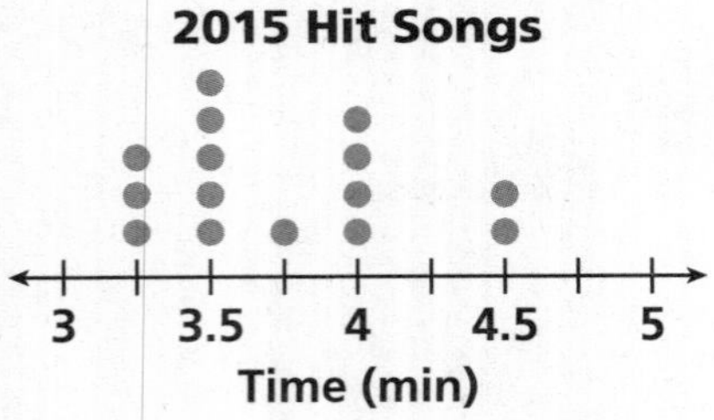

3. What is the mean, rounded to the nearest hundredth, for 2015 hit songs?

Ⓐ 3.55 minutes
Ⓑ 3.63 minutes
Ⓒ 3.73 minutes
Ⓓ 4.10 minutes

4. What is the MAD, rounded to the nearest thousandth, for 2015 hit songs?

Ⓐ 0.250 minute
Ⓑ 0.315 minute
Ⓒ 0.333 minute
Ⓓ 0.349 minute

Spiral Review

5. The box plots represent data for the daily temperatures in one month for two cities in Colorado at different altitudes.

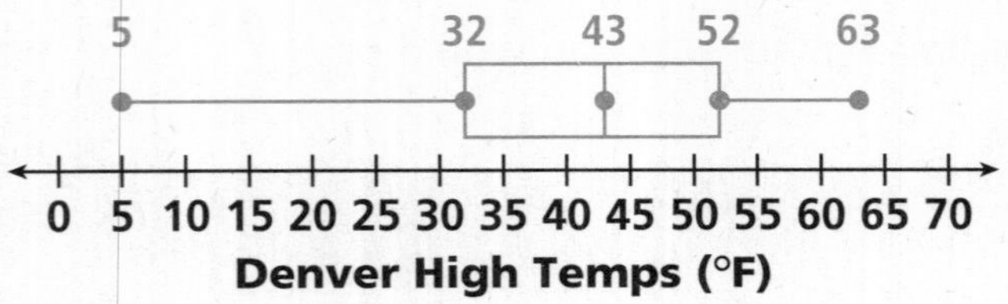

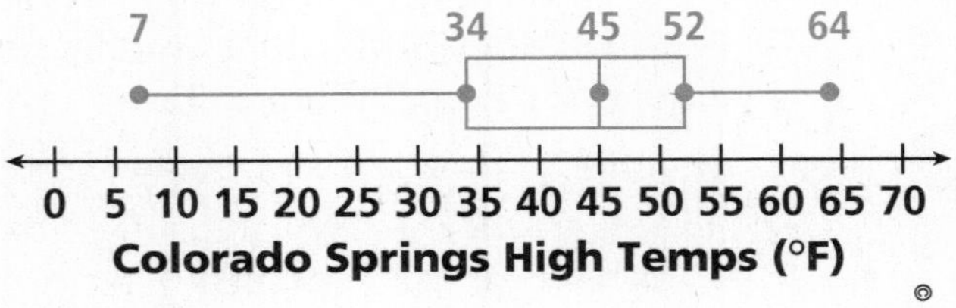

How do the medians compare?

____

____

6. The slope of a line is 3. Point (1, 4) is on the line. Name another point on this line.

____

7. Solve $3x - 1 = 5$.

____

© Houghton Mifflin Harcourt Publishing Company

Module 12

Name ______________________

Review

Vocabulary

1. How is a dot plot similar to a box plot? How are they different?

____

____

2. How are the median and upper quartile of a data set related?

____

____

____

Concepts and Skills

3. Cheri skated 10 laps on a skating rink, and Kristen skated 9 laps. The dot plots show the time it took them to skate each lap. Plot a dot on Kristen's dot plot to show a time she must get on her tenth lap so that her median time is equal to Cheri's median time.

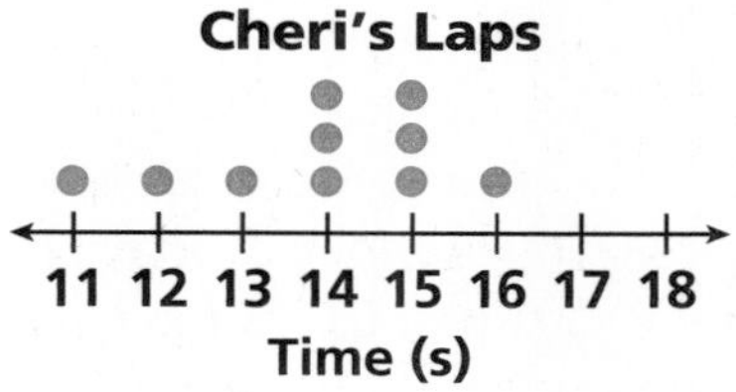

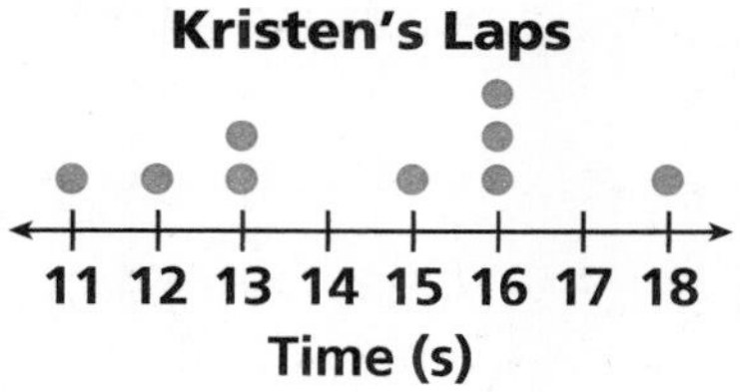

4. (MP) **Use Tools** A shipment includes 500 boxes of wheat cereal and 500 boxes of corn cereal. The dot plots show the masses of a random sample of 20 boxes of each type. Which cereal has a greater median mass? How much greater? State what strategy and tool you will use to answer the question, explain your choice, and then find the answer.

____

____

____

____

____

____

____

____

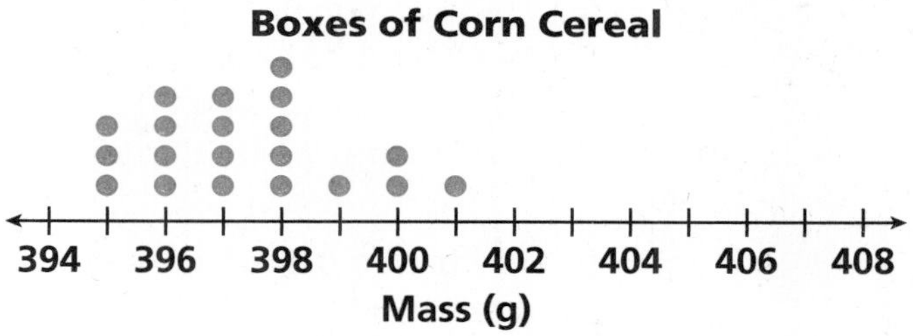

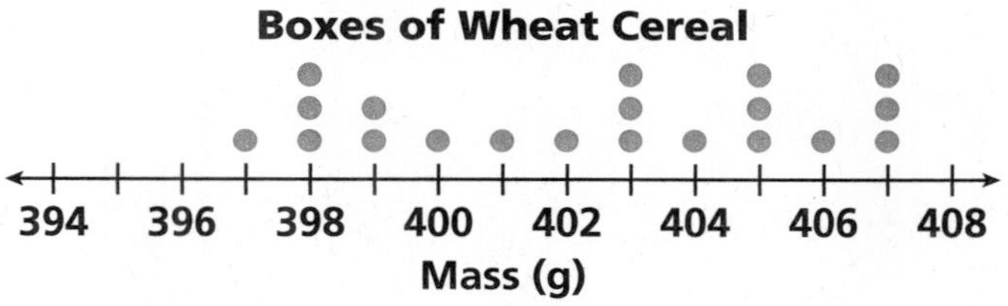

© Houghton Mifflin Harcourt Publishing Company

5. The box plot shows the numbers of students in a random sample of 30 classes at Lincoln Middle School and a random sample of 30 classes at Fairview Middle School. Which statements about the classes at the two schools are supported by the random samples? Select all that apply.

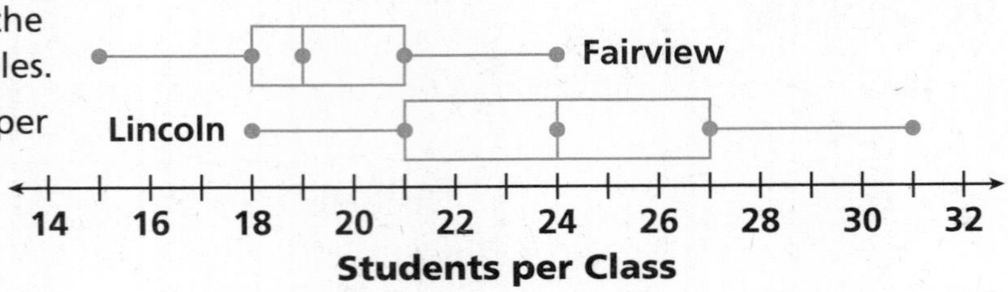

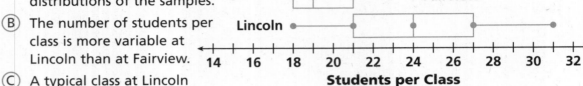

Ⓐ There is little overlap in the distributions of the samples.

Ⓑ The number of students per class is more variable at Lincoln than at Fairview.

Ⓒ A typical class at Lincoln has about 10 more students than a typical class at Fairview.

Ⓓ About half the sampled classes at Lincoln have more students than the largest sampled class at Fairview.

Ⓔ The interquartile range for the number of students per class at Fairview is about 3 times the interquartile range at Lincoln.

6. Ignacio surveyed a random sample of students at his school about the number of math problems they had for homework on Monday and on Friday. The box plot shows his results. What is the difference in the ranges of the two data sets? ________ problems

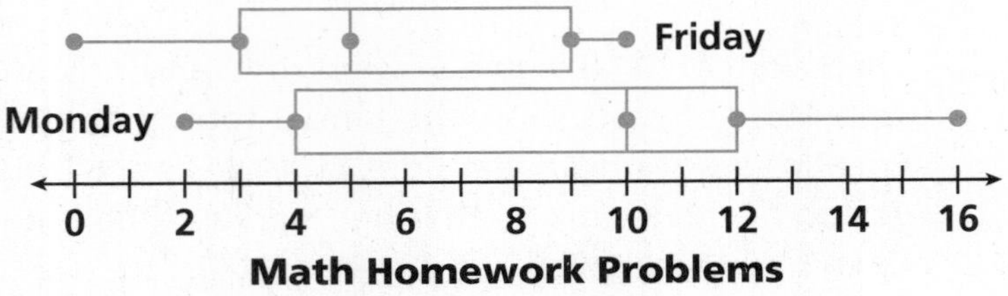

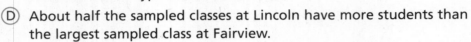

7. The dot plots show the weights of a random sample of 20 two-week-old male kittens and 20 two-week-old female kittens at a shelter. The mean weight of the males is 11.75 ounces, and the mean weight of the females is 11 ounces. The difference in the mean weights is about 0.6 times the mean average deviation of either sample. Which statement is best supported by the random samples?

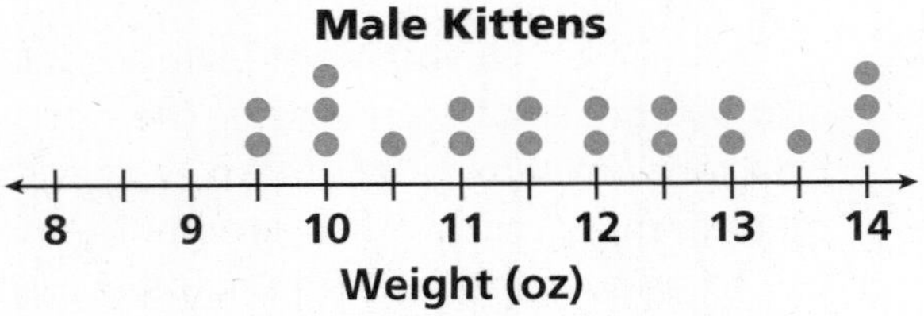

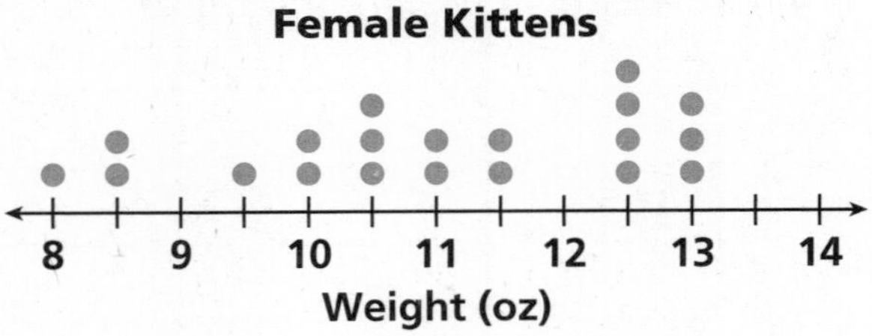

Ⓐ There is a lot of overlap between the two samples; the samples are similar.

Ⓑ There is very little overlap between the two samples; the samples are very different.

Ⓒ On average, all two-week-old male kittens at the shelter weigh more than all two-week-old female kittens.

Ⓔ There is more variation in the weights of all two-week-old male kittens at the shelter than in the weights of all two-week-old female kittens.

© Houghton Mifflin Harcourt Publishing Company

Module

13 Two-Way Tables

Build a Deck

A new card game will have a deck of 100 cards. Each card will have a number and a color. The deck needs to follow these rules: When selecting a card from the deck at random, drawing …

- a pink card is as likely as unlikely.
- a purple card is unlikely.
- a blue card is impossible.
- a number less than 10 is likely.
- a number less than or equal to 20 is certain.

Design a deck of cards that follows the rules. Tell how many cards of each color will be in the deck and how the cards of each color will be numbered.

Turn and Talk

Explain how you know that the deck needs to include at least 3 colors of cards.

© Houghton Mifflin Harcourt Publishing Company

Are You Ready?

Complete these problems to review prior concepts and skills you will need for this module.

Fractions, Decimals, and Percents

Write the percent as a decimal and as a fraction in simplest form. Then calculate the percent of the quantity.

1. There are 30 students in Jacob's class and 40% ride a bus to school.

______

2. In a bag of 220 marbles, 65% of the marbles are red.

______

3. The sales tax rate in Suki's town is 8%. She buys a table that costs $154.

______

Add and Subtract Rational Numbers

Add or subtract. Write your answer in simplest form.

4. $-\frac{3}{8} + \frac{1}{8} =$ ______ **5.** $-1\frac{1}{2} - 2\frac{1}{2} =$ ______ **6.** $\frac{2}{5} - \left(-\frac{4}{5}\right) =$ ______

7. The temperature in a freezer changes by $-2.3°$ in the morning and $+1.4°$ in the afternoon. What is the overall change in the temperature?

______

Multiply and Divide Rational Numbers

Multiply or divide. Write your answer in simplest form.

8. $-35 \div \left(-\frac{1}{2}\right) =$ ______ **9.** $\frac{3}{4} \times \left(-\frac{8}{9}\right) =$ ______ **10.** $-\frac{2}{15} \div 5 =$ ______

11. The elevation of a hot-air balloon changes by -85.5 feet over a period of 3 minutes. If the elevation changes at a constant rate, what is the change in elevation each minute?

______

© Houghton Mifflin Harcourt Publishing Company

Name ____________________

Construct and Interpret Two-Way Frequency Tables

I Can construct a two-way table summarizing data, complete a table given partial data, and interpret data to determine whether there is an association between two variables.

Spark Your Learning

PAIRS

A technology company conducts a survey to find out how many people have a selfie stick and how many have a photo-editing app on their phone. The table shows the results of the survey.

What can you determine from the data in the table?

	Has selfie stick	No selfie stick
Has app	51	26
No app	31	42

© Houghton Mifflin Harcourt Publishing Company • Image Credit: ©Syda Productions/Shutterstock

Turn and Talk Does there seem to be any relationship between owning a selfie stick and having a photo editing app? Explain.

Build Understanding

1 A software company gives its employees the choice of using a treadmill desk or a regular desk. Employees can also choose a laptop computer or a tablet computer. The two-way table shows the results from a survey of 200 company employees.

Connect to Vocabulary

You have already used tables to look for patterns in data. A **two-way table** is a table that displays two-variable data by organizing it into rows and columns.

	Treadmill desk	Regular desk	TOTAL
Laptop		79	
Tablet	20		
TOTAL	34		200

A. Explain how you can fill in the missing value in the bottom row of the table. Then fill in the value.

B. Explain how you can fill in the missing values in the "Treadmill desk" column and "Regular desk" column. Then fill in the values.

Treadmill Desk

C. Explain how you can fill in the missing values in the "TOTAL" column on the right side of the table. Then fill in the values.

D. Explain how you can check that the values you wrote in the "TOTAL" column are correct.

Turn and Talk Is there a different sequence of steps you can use to fill in the two-way table? Explain.

© Houghton Mifflin Harcourt Publishing Company • Image Credit: ©Richard Sennott/Minneapolis Star Tribune/MCT/Alamy

Name

Step It Out

2 A survey asked 80 adults about gym memberships and exercise apps. Of those without a gym membership, 16 had an exercise app on their phone. Construct a two-way table to display the data.

36 adults have a gym membership and an exercise app.
48 adults have a gym membership.

A. Fill in the given information: the TOTAL number of adults in the bottom right cell, the 48 TOTAL adults with a membership, the 16 adults without a membership and with an exercise app, and the 36 adults with both a membership and an exercise app.

	Has app	No app	TOTAL
Has membership			
No membership			
TOTAL			

B. Complete the TOTAL column: you know that 48 of the 80 adults surveyed have a gym membership. The rest, 32, do not.

C. Now fill in the top row. Use the fact that 36 of those with a gym membership have an exercise app on their phone. The remaining adults with a membership, 12, do not have an app.

D. Next, fill in the second row. Use the fact that 16 of the adults without a membership have an exercise app on their phone.

E. Finally, in each column, add the values in the two interior cells to get the value for the TOTAL cell in the bottom row.

F. What percentage of the adults surveyed have an exercise app?

$$\frac{\text{Total number of adults with app}}{\text{Total number of adults surveyed}} = \frac{\square}{80} = \square = \square\%$$

G. What percentage of the adults surveyed who have a gym membership have an exercise app?

$$\frac{\text{Number of adults with gym membership and app}}{\text{Total number with gym membership}} = \frac{\square}{48} = \square = \square\%$$

H. Is there an association between having a gym membership and having an exercise app? Explain.

____

____

____

© Houghton Mifflin Harcourt Publishing Company • Image Credit: ©Peter Muller/age fotostock

3 At a school, 120 students were asked whether they take the subway to school. They were also asked whether they arrived late to school in the past week. The two-way table shows the results. Is there an association between taking the subway and arriving late to school?

	Takes subway	Does not take subway	TOTAL
Late	12	6	18
Not late	18	84	102
TOTAL	30	90	120

A. Find the percentage of all students who arrived late at school.

$$\frac{\text{Total number of students who arrived late}}{\text{Total number of students surveyed}} = \frac{\square}{120} = \square = \square\%$$

B. Find the percentage of students who arrived late among those who took the subway.

$$\frac{\text{Number of students who took subway and arrived late}}{\text{Total number of students who took subway}} = \frac{\square}{\square} = \square = \square\%$$

C. Students who took the subway to school were [more / less] likely to arrive late than the general population of students. There [is / is not] an association between taking the subway and arriving late.

Check Understanding

1. Customers at a sporting goods store were surveyed.

A. Complete the table.

B. How many customers were surveyed?

____

C. Is there an association between watching and playing soccer? Explain.

	Plays soccer	Does not play soccer	TOTAL
Watches soccer		216	
Does not watch soccer		84	140
TOTAL	200		

____

____

____

____

© Houghton Mifflin Harcourt Publishing Company • Image Credit: ©Tim Macpherson/The Image Bank/Getty Images

Name ______________________________

On Your Own

2. In a survey of 160 people who have reptiles as pets, 40% have a pet snake. Of those with a pet snake, 25% also have a pet lizard. Of those who do not have a pet snake, 75% have a pet lizard.

A. Construct a two-way frequency table to display the data.

	Has lizard	No lizard	TOTAL
Has snake			
No snake			
TOTAL			

B. What percentage of those surveyed have a pet lizard?

____

C. What percentage of those surveyed have both a snake and a lizard?

____

3. (MP) **Reason** A park ranger surveyed 300 visitors to a national park as they arrived. She asked the visitors whether they planned to camp in the park and whether they planned to hike in the park. The two-way table shows the results.

	Camping	No camping	TOTAL
Hiking	135	30	165
No hiking	45	90	135
TOTAL	180	120	300

Is there an association between camping in the park and hiking in the park? Explain.

____

____

____

____

____

© Houghton Mifflin Harcourt Publishing Company • Image Credit: (rt) ©amwu/iStock / Getty Images Plus/Getty Images; (rb) ©Rolf_52/Alamy

4. **STEM** Scientists often use two-way frequency tables to determine the effectiveness of a treatment. Suppose scientists want to know whether a new herbal tea helps reduce headaches. They may ask a group of people to drink the tea for a week and record whether or not they get a headache.

	Headache	No headache	TOTAL
Tea	156	84	240
No tea	234	126	360
TOTAL	390	210	600

Based on the results in the two-way frequency table, can the scientists conclude that the herbal tea helps reduce headaches? Explain.

5. **Open Ended** Conduct a survey of students in your class. Each student that you survey should be asked whether or not he or she has a curfew on school nights and whether or not the student has assigned chores at home. Record your survey data in the table.

	Curfew	No curfew	TOTAL
Chores			
No chores			
TOTAL			

Is there evidence of an association between having a curfew on school nights and having chores? Explain.

© Houghton Mifflin Harcourt Publishing Company • Image Credit: ©Syda Productions/Shutterstock

I'm in a Learning Mindset!

What steps am I taking to direct my own learning of ways to construct and interpret two-way frequency tables?

Name

ONLINE
Video Tutorials and
Interactive Examples

Construct and Interpret Two-Way Frequency Tables

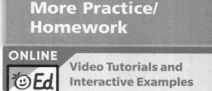

1. In a survey of 200 people who visited China, 85% visited the Great Wall. Of those who visited the Great Wall, 30% also visited the Chengdu Panda Center. Of those who did not visit the Great Wall, 80% visited the Panda Center. Complete the two-way frequency table.

	Visited Great Wall	Did not visit Great Wall	TOTAL
Visited Chengdu Panda Center			
Did not visit Chengdu Panda Center			
TOTAL			

2. **Math on the Spot** Determine whether there is an association between the events.

A. Thirty-two students were polled about whether they have a phone plan with texting and whether they have had an accident. Find the percentages of those having an accident for both the general population of students and for students who have a phone with texting. Is there an association between having a phone with texting and having an accident?

	Accident	No accident	TOTAL
Phone plan with texting	12	8	20
Phone plan without texting	4	8	12
TOTAL	16	16	32

B. Middle school and high school students were polled about whether they had visited a new amusement park. Find the percentages of those having visited an amusement park for both the general population of students and for high school students. Is there an association between being a high school student and visiting an amusement park?

	Visited	Did not visit	TOTAL
Middle school student	20	5	25
High school student	60	15	75
TOTAL	80	20	100

© Houghton Mifflin Harcourt Publishing Company • Image Credit: Digital Vision / Getty Images

Test Prep

3. Keysha surveyed adults in her city. The results are shown in the table. Which of the following is a true statement?

	Bike	No bike	TOTAL
Car	27	41	68
No car	38	4	42
TOTAL	65	45	110

Ⓐ More people own a bike than own a car.

Ⓑ A total of 68 people surveyed own a bike.

Ⓒ Of the people with a bike, 27 also have a car.

Ⓓ There are 42 bike owners who do not own a car.

4. A gardener tried a new spray on some plants to see if the spray prevents aphids. The table shows the results, but some values are missing. What is the value of x?

	Spray	No spray	TOTAL
Aphids	6		13
No aphids		x	
TOTAL	24		41

Ⓐ 7

Ⓑ 10

Ⓒ 18

Ⓓ 28

5. Students at a local community college can study Spanish or French. They also have a choice of band or chorus for their music classes. The table shows the results of surveying 100 students. Which is a correct statement about this situation?

	Spanish	French	TOTAL
Band	16	9	25
Chorus	48	27	75
TOTAL	64	36	100

Ⓐ There is no association because students who study Spanish are no more or less likely than other students to choose band.

Ⓑ There is no association because students who study Spanish are less likely than other students to choose band.

Ⓒ There is an association because students who study Spanish are more likely than other students to choose band.

Ⓓ There is an association because students who study Spanish are less likely than other students to choose band.

Spiral Review

6. A chili cook-off has adult tickets a and child tickets c. A group of visitors buys 3 adult tickets and 2 child tickets and pays a total of $26. Another group buys 5 adult tickets and 3 child tickets and pays $42. Write and solve a system of equations to find the price of each type of ticket.

____

7. Without graphing, find the point of intersection of the lines $-x + 2y = -4$ and $2x + y = 3$. ________

8. The graph of a proportional relationship passes through the point (6, 21). What is the equation for the relationship? ________

© Houghton Mifflin Harcourt Publishing Company

Name ____________________

Analyze and Interpret Two-Way Relative Frequency Tables

I Can **construct two-way frequency tables, find relative frequencies, and use them to determine if there is an association between two variables.**

Step It Out

1 Lamar surveyed 200 people who visited Everglades National Park in Florida. He asked them to name their favorite activity in the park. He made this two-way frequency table and used it to construct a **two-way relative frequency table**, which is a two-way table that displays relative frequencies.

	Airboat tour	Gator farm	Other	TOTAL
Children	44	12	16	72
Adults	50	48	30	128
TOTAL	94	60	46	200

A. Divide each value in the frequency table by the total number of data values. Write each quotient as a decimal, rounding to the nearest hundredth if necessary.

	Airboat tour	Gator farm	Other	TOTAL
Children				
Adults				
TOTAL				

Connect to Vocabulary

A **frequency** is the number of times a data value occurs. A **relative frequency** is the frequency of a specific data value divided by the total number of data values in the set. It shows how common a data value is, relative to its data set.

B. A **joint relative frequency** is the frequency in a particular category divided by the total number of data values.

Identify the joint relative frequency of children whose favorite activity was the airboat tour. ________

C. A **marginal relative frequency** is the sum of the joint relative frequencies in a row or column of a two-way table.

What is the marginal relative frequency of visitors who were children? What percentage of visitors were children?

____

Turn and Talk What is the relationship between the joint relative frequencies and the marginal relative frequencies?

© Houghton Mifflin Harcourt Publishing Company • Image Credits: (t) ©H. Mark Weidman Photography/Alamy; (b) ©Dennis MacDonald/Alamy

Step It Out

2 A landscaper uses a new fertilizer on some orchid plants, and keeps track of whether or not the orchid plants produce flowers. The landscaper wants to know if there is an association between an orchid plant receiving the fertilizer and producing flowers.

Connect to Vocabulary

An **event** is an outcome or set of outcomes of an experiment or situation.

A **conditional relative frequency** is the ratio of a joint relative frequency to a related marginal relative frequency. A conditional relative frequency is used to find the likelihood of an event assuming another event also occurred.

A. Complete the two-way relative frequency table.

	Fertilizer	No fertilizer	TOTAL
Flowers		0.18	
No flowers	0.33		0.55
TOTAL	0.6	0.4	

B. What is the marginal relative frequency that an orchid plant produced flowers? What is the marginal relative frequency that an orchid plant received fertilizer?

____

C. What is the conditional relative frequency that an orchid plant produced flowers given that the orchid plant was fertilized?

$\frac{\square}{0.6} = \square$

D. Were the orchid plants that received the fertilizer more, less, or equally likely to produce flowers than the overall population?

____

E. What is the marginal relative frequency that an orchid plant did not produce flowers? What is the marginal relative frequency that an orchid plant did not receive fertilizer?

____

F. What is the conditional relative frequency that an orchid plant did not produce flowers given that the orchid plant did not receive fertilizer?

$\frac{\square}{0.4} = \square$

Turn and Talk Based on the information in the task, is there an association between an orchid plant receiving fertilizer and producing flowers? Should the landscaper continue to spend the money to fertilize the orchid plants? Why or why not?

© Houghton Mifflin Harcourt Publishing Company • Image Credit: ©Elena Blokhina/Shutterstock

Name

3 The table shows the results of a survey of people who went bird watching. Is there an association between using binoculars and seeing finches?

	Binoculars	No binoculars	TOTAL
Saw finches	0.21	0.04	0.25
No finches	0.49	0.26	0.75
TOTAL	0.7	0.3	1

Zebra Finches

A. What is the marginal relative frequency that a person who was surveyed saw finches?

____

B. What is the conditional relative frequency that a surveyed person saw finches, given he or she used binoculars? $\frac{\square}{\square} = \square$

C. Is there an association between using binoculars and seeing finches?

____

D. What is the marginal relative frequency that a person who was surveyed did not see finches? ______________

E. What is the conditional relative frequency that a surveyed person did not see finches, given that the person did not use binoculars? Round to the nearest hundredth. $\frac{\square}{\square} \approx \square$

F. Is there an association between not using binoculars and not seeing finches? ______________

Check Understanding

1. The relative frequency table shows the results of a survey of 7th and 8th graders.

	Bikes	Does not bike	TOTAL
7th grader		0.21	
8th grader	0.16		0.51
TOTAL		0.56	

A. Complete the table.

B. List the joint relative frequencies.

____

C. List the marginal relative frequencies.

____

D. Find the conditional relative frequency that a student who was surveyed bikes, given that the student is a 7th grader. Give your answer as a percent.

____

E. Is there an association between biking and being a 7th grader? Explain.

____

© Houghton Mifflin Harcourt Publishing Company • Image Credit: ©Wang LiQiang/Shutterstock

On Your Own

2. A company that organizes whale watching tours keeps track of the time of day the boats leave and whether or not any whales were spotted. A frequency table is made to show the results.

	Morning	Afternoon	TOTAL
Whales	35	3	38
No whales	4	8	12
TOTAL	39	11	50

A. Convert the table to show the relative frequencies.

	Morning	Afternoon	TOTAL
Whales			
No whales			
TOTAL			

B. What is the joint relative frequency of morning trips that saw whales? What percentage of trips took place in the morning and spotted whales?

____

C. What is the marginal relative frequency of not seeing whales? What percentage of trips did not see whales?

____

Use the information for Problems 3–4.

(MP) **Use Structure** Boba tea is a drink made from tea and tapioca "pearls" (or "bubbles"). A boba tea shop offers two flavors and two sizes. The owner of the shop keeps track of sales and makes a relative frequency table.

Strawberry Mango

	Strawberry	Mango	TOTAL
Small	a	b	c
Large	d	e	f
TOTAL	g	h	1

3. Write an equation that relates the quantities a, b, and c.

____

4. Write an equation solved for c in terms of f.

____

© Houghton Mifflin Harcourt Publishing Company • **Image Credits:** (t) ©Schilde Bill/Perspectives/Getty Images; (b) ©stockcreations/Shutterstock;

Name

5. **STEM** A doctor participated in a study of a new allergy treatment. The doctor kept track of whether or not her patients got a rash or a headache as a side effect of the treatment. The two-way relative frequency table shows the results.

Did you get a rash or a headache?

	Rash	No rash	TOTAL
Headache	0.03	0.04	0.07
No headache	0.02	0.91	0.93
TOTAL	0.05	0.95	1

What percentage of patients got a headache but not a rash? If the doctor tried the treatment on 300 patients, how many got a headache but not a rash?

Use the information to solve Problems 6–8.

Moira grows pumpkins to sell at a farmers' market. She sorts the pumpkins by color and size and then makes this frequency table to display the data.

	Small	Medium	Large	TOTAL
Green	3	15	12	30
Orange	22	17	21	60
TOTAL	25	32	33	90

6. Find the conditional relative frequency that a pumpkin is orange, given that it is a small pumpkin. Express your answer as a fraction, decimal, and percent.

7. Find the conditional relative frequency that a pumpkin is a medium pumpkin, given that it is green. Express your answer as a fraction, decimal, and percent.

8. How likely is it that a pumpkin is a small pumpkin, given that it is green? Use a conditional relative frequency to justify your answer.

© Houghton Mifflin Harcourt Publishing Company • Image Credits: (t) ©Stuart Jenner/Shutterstock; (b) ©Ramon Espelt Gorgozo/Alamy

9. A restaurant offers a choice of two soups and two sandwiches. The manager keeps track of the orders and makes this relative frequency table.

	Chicken soup	Tomato soup	TOTAL
Ham sandwich	0.06	0.34	0.4
Turkey sandwich	0.09	0.51	0.6
TOTAL	0.15	0.85	1

A. What is the conditional relative frequency that a customer orders tomato soup, given that he or she orders a turkey sandwich?

____

B. MP **Construct Arguments** Is there an association between the type of sandwich a customer orders and the type of soup he or she orders? Why or why not?

____

____

____

____

____

10. Open Ended The two-way relative frequency table shows data about the sea stars at an aquarium.

	Orange	Purple	TOTAL
Has 5 legs	0.59	0.2	0.79
Has more than 5 legs	0.09	0.12	0.21
TOTAL	0.68	0.32	1

Write a question about the data that can be answered using a conditional relative frequency. Provide the answer to the question.

____

____

____

____

© Houghton Mifflin Harcourt Publishing Company • Image Credit: ©Amanda Nicholls/Shutterstock

Name

© Houghton Mifflin Harcourt Publishing Company • Image Credits: (b) ©B Moose Peterson/ardea.com; (t) ©Susan Beatty/Animals Animals/Earth Scenes

Analyze and Interpret Two-Way Relative Frequency Tables

1. **STEM** An optometrist surveys some patients to find out whether they mostly wear glasses or contacts and whether or not they sometimes need eye drops during the day to help with dry eyes. The optometrist records the data in a table.

	Eye drops	No eye drops	TOTAL
Glasses		0.07	0.37
Contacts	0.51		
TOTAL			

A. Complete the two-way relative frequency table.

B. What is the joint relative frequency of patients who wear glasses and use eye drops?

C. What is the marginal relative frequency of patients who wear contacts?

2. **STEM** Rock pocket mice live in the deserts of the southwestern United States. The mice have dark fur or light fur depending on the color of the rocks or sand where they live. The relative frequency table shows data about a biologist's sample of rock pocket mice.

	Male	Female	TOTAL
Dark fur	0.42	0.33	0.75
Light fur	0.14	0.11	0.25
TOTAL	0.56	0.44	1

Is there an association between the mouse being male or female and the color of the fur for the sample? Explain.

Test Prep

Use the information and table to solve Problems 3–4.

The students at Harriet Tubman Middle School are choosing a new school mascot and new school color. This relative frequency table shows their preferences.

	Eagles	Jaguars	TOTAL
Green	0.24	0.08	0.32
Yellow	0.46	0.22	0.68
TOTAL	0.7	0.3	1

3. What percentage of students surveyed prefer Eagles as the school mascot?

Ⓐ 7%　Ⓑ 24%　Ⓒ 46%　Ⓓ 70%

4. What is the marginal relative frequency of students who prefer Jaguars as the school mascot?

Ⓐ 0.22　Ⓑ 0.3　Ⓒ 0.32　Ⓓ 0.7

Use the information and table to solve Problems 5–6.

A manager at a gas company collects data on a sample of 200 customers to find out whether they paid their last bill by mail or online and whether they paid late or on time. This two-way table shows the results.

	Paid by mail	Paid online	TOTAL
Paid on time	66	101	167
Paid late	20	13	33
TOTAL	86	114	200

5. To the nearest hundredth, what is the conditional relative frequency that a customer paid his or her bill on time, given that he or she paid online?

Ⓐ 0.57　Ⓑ 0.60　Ⓒ 0.84　Ⓓ 0.89

6. To the nearest hundredth, what is the conditional relative frequency that a customer paid by mail, given that the customer paid late?

Ⓐ 0.23　Ⓑ 0.33　Ⓒ 0.61　Ⓓ 0.86

Spiral Review

7. Bucket A is filled with water according to the equation $y = 2.5x$, where x is the time in minutes and y is the volume in fluid ounces. Bucket B is filled with water according to the data in the table. Which bucket is filled at a faster rate?

Time (min)	Volume (fl oz)
3	12.6
4	16.8
5	21.0
6	25.2

____

8. Solve for x: $4(x + 1.5) = 3x + 9.2$.

____

© Houghton Mifflin Harcourt Publishing Company

Module

13 Review

Name ______________________________

Vocabulary

For Problems 1–3, tell whether each description represents a *joint, marginal*, or *conditional relative frequency* for the two-way table.

	Preferred Frozen Yogurt Flavor		
	Strawberry	**Mango**	**TOTAL**
Adults	20	32	52
Children	36	28	64
TOTAL	56	60	116

1. The ratio of the number of people who chose mango to the total number of people surveyed

____

2. The ratio of the number of children who chose strawberry to the total number of people who chose strawberry

____

3. The ratio of the number of adults who chose strawberry to the total number of people surveyed

____

4. What does it mean when a two-way table shows an association between two data sets?

____

Concepts and Skills

5. Two hundred twenty students were surveyed about whether a mural should be painted on a wall of the cafeteria. Complete the two-way table showing the results of the survey.

	Agree	**Disagree**	**TOTAL**
7th graders		20	
8th graders	94		
TOTAL		38	220

6. (MP) **Use Tools** Three hundred people at a movie theater were asked whether they bought popcorn or a drink at the theater. How many more people surveyed did NOT buy popcorn than did buy popcorn? State what strategy and tool you will use to answer the question, explain your choice, and then find the answer.

	Drink	**No drink**	**TOTAL**
Popcorn	76	5	
No popcorn	58	161	
TOTAL			

____

____

© Houghton Mifflin Harcourt Publishing Company

7. Three hundred students were surveyed about whether they are right- or left-handed. Complete the two-way relative frequency table.

	Right-handed	Left-handed	TOTAL
7th graders		0.05	
8th graders			0.49
TOTAL	0.89		1.00

8. Five hundred randomly selected voters were surveyed about whether they support a new park. The two-way table shows the results of the survey. Which statement is **best** supported by the survey results?

	For park	Against park	TOTAL
Under 40	144	48	192
40 or older	182	126	308
TOTAL	326	174	500

Ⓐ A voter's age appears to be unrelated to his or her opinion about the park.

Ⓑ Voters aged 40 or older are more likely to be for the park than voters under age 40.

Ⓒ Voters against the park are more likely to be under age 40 than voters for the park.

Ⓓ Voters under age 40 are more likely to be for the park than voters aged 40 or older.

9. A random sample of 200 students at a school were surveyed about whether they prefer red or blue as a new school color. Complete the relative frequency table. Based on the table, select all the true statements.

	Red	Blue	TOTAL
7th graders	0.25	0.20	
8th graders	0.27	0.28	
TOTAL			

Ⓐ More 8th graders were surveyed than 7th graders.

Ⓑ More of the surveyed students prefer red than prefer blue.

Ⓒ 8th graders at the school are more likely to prefer red than 7th graders are.

Ⓓ A randomly selected 7th grader at the school is more likely to prefer red than blue.

Ⓔ Students at the school who prefer blue are more likely to be in 7th grade than 8th grade.

10. The table shows data for a random sample of flights for a particular airline. Complete the table. Based on the table, what is the conditional relative frequency that a flight will be on time given that it is a morning flight? ____________

	On time	Delayed	TOTAL
Morning	528	132	
Afternoon	251	89	
TOTAL			

© Houghton Mifflin Harcourt Publishing Company

Unit 5

Applications of Real Numbers and Exponents

Historian

We know that the pyramids of Egypt were built about 5,000 years ago and that the people who built them used math to do so. But *how* do we know? Our knowledge is largely due to historians, who study the people, events, and ideas of the past and their influence on today's world. Historians use the information they gather to develop theories and draw conclusions about their subjects.

STEM Task:

An ancient Egyptian multiplication method based on doubling is used below to find 11×19. Use the method to find 13×24.

$11 \times 19 = 209$

(1)	19	19
(2)	38	38
4	76	
(8)	152	+152
16	304	
		209

© Houghton Mifflin Harcourt Publishing Company • Image Credits: (t) ©WitR/Shutterstock; (b) ©Fedor Selivanov/Shutterstock

Learning Mindset

Resilience Manages the Learning Process

Resilience is the ability to "bounce back" after experiencing a disappointment or a defeat. When you encounter difficulty or setbacks, watch out for a fixed-mindset voice in your head telling you to give up. Here are some statements you can tell yourself to activate your growth–mindset voice and strengthen your resilience. Can you think of others?

- Mistakes and challenges are opportunities to learn.
- If this were easy, I would not learn anything from it.
- I have overcome challenges in the past, so I know I can do it again.
- When I solve this problem, I can be proud because it is not easy.
- I may be struggling, but I am still making progress.

Reflect

Q **As you worked on the STEM Task, did anything trigger a fixed-mindset voice in your head? If so, what?**

Q **In the past, what situations have caused a fixed-mindset response in your head? What is your plan for activating your growth mindset when you encounter similar situations in the future?**

© Houghton Mifflin Harcourt Publishing Company • Image Credit: ©saiko3p/Shutterstock

Real Numbers

Track the Distance

A group of five friends went running at the school track. They ran the distances shown.

Use the clues to determine which friend ran each distance.

- Ara and Tyrone ran the same distance.
- Morgan's distance written as a decimal has 3 nonzero digits.
- Shane's distance in miles is equal to a repeating decimal.
- Julius ran the greatest distance.
- Tyrone's distance in miles is given as a fraction in simplest form.

Ara ran ________ mile. Morgan ran ________ mile.

Shane ran ________ mile. Julius ran ________ mile.

Tyrone ran ________ mile.

Turn and Talk

Another friend, Knox, ran farther than Shane but not as far as Tyrone. What possible distance could Knox have run? Explain.

© Houghton Mifflin Harcourt Publishing Company • Image Credit: ©Sergey Novikov/Shutterstock

Are You Ready?

Complete these problems to review prior concepts and skills you will need for this module.

Solve One-Step Equations

Solve each equation.

1. $x + 5 = 25$ ________

2. $x + 4 = 7$ ________

3. $x - 3 = 7$ ________

4. $x - 2 = 6$ ________

5. $19x = 76$ ________

6. $5x = 70$ ________

7. $\frac{x}{4} = 12$ ________

8. $\frac{x}{3} = 8$ ________

Rational Numbers on a Number Line

Plot each rational number on the number line.

9. 0.75

10. $-\frac{5}{8}$

11. -1.5

12. $1\frac{1}{8}$

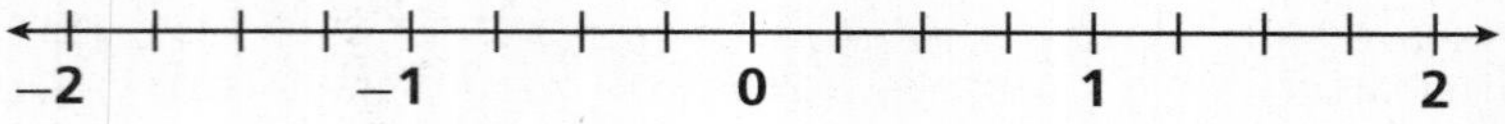

Convert Fractions to Decimals

13. How can you convert a fraction to a decimal?

____

____

Write each fraction as a decimal.

14. $\frac{4}{5}$ ________

15. $\frac{3}{8}$ ________

16. $\frac{11}{20}$ ________

17. $\frac{3}{4}$ ________

18. $\frac{1}{16}$ ________

19. $\frac{13}{25}$ ________

© Houghton Mifflin Harcourt Publishing Company

Name

Understand Rational and Irrational Numbers

I Can determine whether a number is rational and write a given rational number as a fraction.

Spark Your Learning

SMALL GROUPS

In softball, a player's batting average is the number of hits divided by the number of at-bats. Write each player's batting average as a decimal.

What do you notice?

Player	Hits	At-bats
Jamilla	2	5
Callie	1	8
Mayumi	4	9
Elena	37	99
Kaycee	7	36

© Houghton Mifflin Harcourt Publishing Company • Image Credit: ©Hero Images/Getty Images

Turn and Talk Do you think all fractions have decimal representations that either end or have digits that repeat? Try some additional fractions and discuss your conjecture.

Build Understanding

A **rational number** is any number that can be written as a ratio in the form $\frac{a}{b}$, where a and b are integers and b is not 0. Every rational number can be written as a **terminating decimal** or a **repeating decimal**. Examples of rational numbers are shown:

$\frac{3}{8} = 0.375$ $\quad$ $7 = \frac{7}{1}$

$0.2 = \frac{1}{5}$ $\quad$ $0.11111... = \frac{1}{9}$

Connect to Vocabulary

An **irrational number** is a number that cannot be written in the form $\frac{a}{b}$, where a and b are integers and b is not 0.

1 Is every number rational?

A. Consider the decimal 1.345345634567... .

Does the decimal appear to have a repeating pattern? Explain.

____

Do you think 1.345345634567... is a rational number? Why or why not?

____

B. You have learned that pi (π) is the ratio of the circumference of any circle to its diameter. The decimal value of pi is shown.

$\pi = 3.1415926535897932...$

Pi is an irrational number, but it can be written as a ratio. How can this be?

____

____

____

____

____

There are two ways to write a repeating decimal.
You can use an ellipsis (three dots) to show that the repeating pattern continues:

0.111... , 0.235235235... , and 0.244444444...

Or, you can write an overbar over the part of the decimal that repeats:

$0.\overline{1}$, $0.\overline{235}$, and $0.2\overline{4}$

Turn and Talk Convert $\frac{1}{36}$ to a decimal. Write the decimal using an ellipsis and using an overbar. Explain the process you used.

© Houghton Mifflin Harcourt Publishing Company • Image Credit: ©koss13/Adobe Stock

Name ______________________________

Step It Out

2 A basketball player's free throw percentage is 82.5%, or 0.825. Write this as a fraction.

A. Identify the place value of the last digit in the terminating decimal. Use this to determine the denominator of the fraction. The digits to the right of the decimal point are the numerator of the fraction.

$$0.825 = \frac{825}{\square}$$

B. Write the fraction in lowest terms. Identify the greatest common factor (GCF) of the numerator and denominator. Divide the numerator and denominator by the GCF.

$$0.825 = \frac{825}{\square} = \frac{825 \div \square}{\square \div \square} = \frac{\square}{\square}$$

3 You can also convert a repeating decimal to a fraction.

Write $0.\overline{18}$ as a fraction. Let x be the given decimal.

A. Write the first few repeating digits. $x = 0.1818...$

B. Multiply both sides of the equation by 100 so that the two repeating digits appear just to the *left* of the decimal point. $100x =$ ______

C. Subtract an expression equal to x from both sides.

$100x =$ ______

$-x \quad -0.1818...$

$99x =$ ____

D. Solve for x. Then simplify the fraction. $x = \frac{\square}{\square} = \frac{\square}{\square}$

Check Understanding

1. Convert $\frac{1}{18}$ to a decimal.

A. Write the decimal form. ______________________________

B. Is this number rational? Explain.

____

For Problems 2–4, write the rational number as a simplified fraction or as a mixed number in simplest form.

2. 1.905 ______

3. 0.828282... ______

4. $0.4\overline{3}$ ______

© Houghton Mifflin Harcourt Publishing Company • Image Credit: ©Stephen Dunn/Getty Images Sport/Getty Images

On Your Own

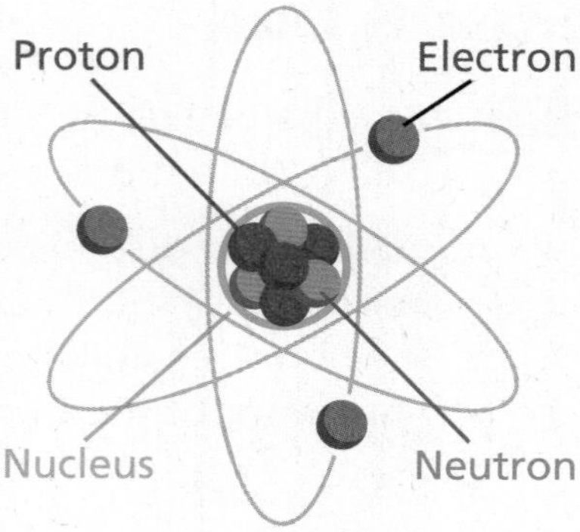

5. **STEM** The atomic weight of an element is the total mass of the protons, neutrons, and electrons. The ratio of the mass of the protons in radon to the atomic mass of radon is 0.387387387... . Write the decimal as a fraction.

____

6. Convert $\frac{1}{15}$ to a decimal. Write the decimal using an ellipsis, then write the decimal using an overbar.

____

7. (MP) **Critique Reasoning** Mitchell was asked to write 0.616161... as a fraction. His work is shown. Do you agree with his answer? If not, explain the error and correct it.

Let $x = 0.616161...$
Then $10x = 6.16161...$
Subtract: $10x = 6.16161...$
$-x \quad -0.616161...$
$9x = 6$
$x = \frac{6}{9} = \frac{2}{3}$

____

For Problems 8–13, write the number as a fraction or mixed number in simplest form.

8. 4.024   **9.** $-1.111...$ **10.** $-0.\overline{39}$

11. $0.61\overline{4}$ **12.** 2.484848...   **13.** 0.7222...

© Houghton Mifflin Harcourt Publishing Company

I'm in a Learning Mindset!

How am I using feedback to solve problems about rational numbers?

____

Name ______________________________

LESSON 14.1
More Practice/ Homework

ONLINE
Video Tutorials and Interactive Examples

Understand Rational and Irrational Numbers

1. Kara and Nathan participated in a 60-minute maze race.

A. Use ratio notation and decimal notation to describe the relationship between Kara's time and the total time of the race.

____

B. Is the relationship in Part A rational or irrational? Justify your answer.

____

____

2. **Math on the Spot** Write the decimal $0.\overline{63}$ as a fraction in simplest form.

____

3. The average number of hourly visitors to an art exhibit is $45.1\overline{3}$. Write the average number of hourly visitors as a mixed number in simplest form.

____

4. (MP) **Critique Reasoning** Katrina said the number 0.101100111000... is a rational number because it consists only of the digits 0 and 1, and these digits repeat. Do you agree or disagree? Explain.

____

____

____

5. Convert $\frac{1}{27}$ to a decimal. Write the decimal using an ellipsis, then write the decimal using an overbar.

____

Write the rational number as a fraction or mixed number in simplest form.

6. 0.0606060... ______

7. -8.725 ______

8. 0.424242... ______

9. 1.52888... ______

10. $-10.\overline{7}$ ______

11. $0.\overline{57}$ ______

© Houghton Mifflin Harcourt Publishing Company • Image Credits: (t) ©Monty Rakusen/Alamy; (b) ©Kiev.Victor/Shutterstock

Test Prep

12. Midori wrote a ratio of two integers. Which of the following must be true about the number Midori wrote?

Ⓐ The decimal form of the number is a terminating decimal.

Ⓑ The decimal form of the number is a repeating decimal.

Ⓒ The number is rational.

Ⓓ The number is irrational.

13. Which of the following is $0.\overline{15}$ written as a fraction in simplest form?

Ⓐ $\frac{1}{15}$ Ⓒ $\frac{3}{20}$

Ⓑ $\frac{1}{9}$ Ⓓ $\frac{5}{33}$

14. Paolo keeps track of his favorite baseball player's batting average, and notices the average is 0.4727272... . If his player has 55 at bats, what is the number of hits?

____ hits

Spiral Review

15. In a survey of 120 people who visited a lake, 20% went fishing. Of those who went fishing, 75% also went swimming. Of those who did not go fishing, 50% went swimming.

A. Construct a two-way frequency table to display the data.

	Fishing	No fishing	TOTAL
Swimming			
No swimming			
TOTAL			

B. What percent of those surveyed did not go swimming?

____

16. In the figure, line p is parallel to line q. Write an equation you can use to find the value of y, and explain why you can use it. Then solve the equation and use your result to help you find the measure of $\angle 1$.

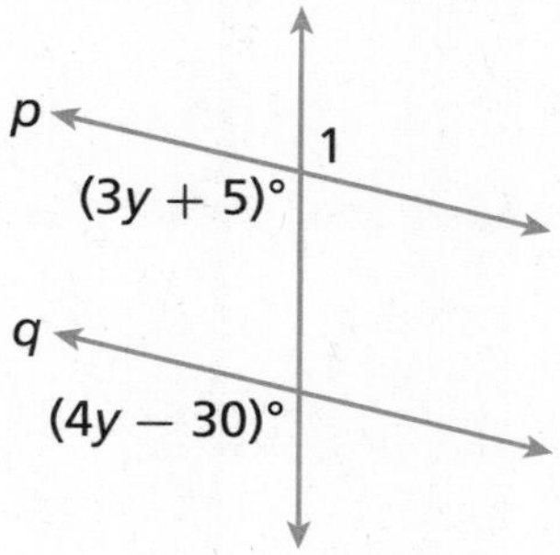

____

____

____

© Houghton Mifflin Harcourt Publishing Company

Name ____________________

Investigate Roots

I Can evaluate square roots and cube roots.

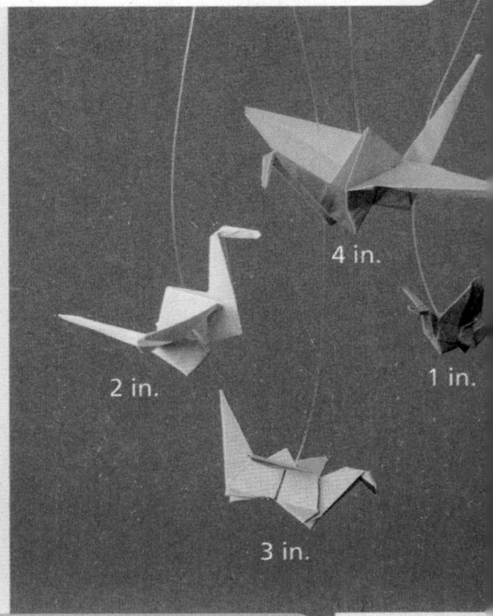

Spark Your Learning

SMALL GROUPS

Aaron plans to make origami cranes, which can be folded from a square piece of paper. He starts by drawing small squares with side lengths 1 inch, 2 inches, 3 inches, and 4 inches.

Find the area of each square. What do you notice about the relationship between the side lengths and the area of each square?

Turn and Talk Consider a square with an area of 23 square inches. Explain how you would determine the length of each side for such a square.

© Houghton Mifflin Harcourt Publishing Company • Image Credit: ©Betsy Hansen/Houghton Mifflin Harcourt

Build Understanding

1 Aaron is also planning to make origami **cubes** of different sizes. The edge lengths of the cubes are 1 inch, 2 inches, 3 inches, and 4 inches.

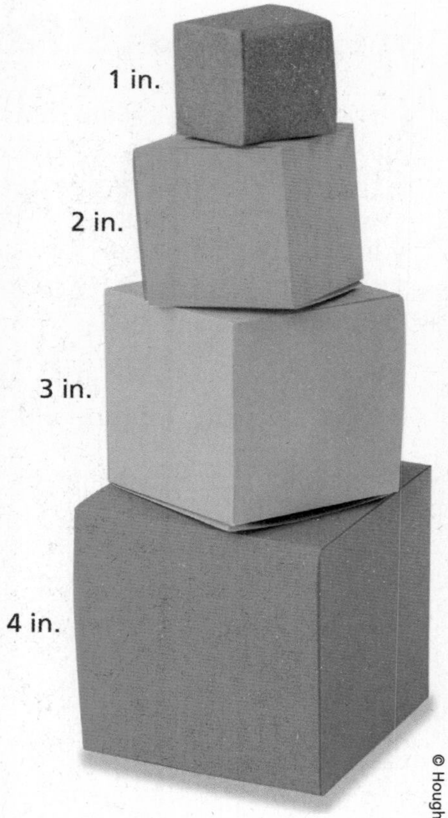

A. Talk to a partner, then write down a formula to determine the volume of a cube.

____

____

B. Find the volume of each of the cubes. Complete the table and look for patterns.

Edge length (in.)	Volume (in^3)
1	
2	
3	
4	

C. What do you notice about how the volumes change as the edge length increases?

____

____

D. If you are given the volume of a cube, how can you find the edge length?

____

____

E. What is the edge length of a cube with a volume of 125 cubic inches? Why is it difficult to express the edge length of a cube with a volume of 10 cubic inches?

____

____

____

Turn and Talk A student completed the table in Part B and claimed it is impossible for a cube to have a volume of exactly 50 cubic centimeters since this number will not appear in the "Volume" column. Do you agree? Why or why not?

© Houghton Mifflin Harcourt Publishing Company • Image Credit: ©Betsy Hansen/Houghton Mifflin Harcourt

Step It Out

The **square root** of a positive number p is x when $x^2 = p$. Note that every positive number has two square roots. For example, $3^2 = 9$ and $(-3)^2 = 9$, so the two square roots of 9 are 3 and -3. These are sometimes written together as ± 3, and read as "plus or minus three."

A **perfect square** is a whole number whose square roots are integers. For example, 16 is a perfect square since its square roots are the integers 4 and -4. The square root of any number that isn't a perfect square is another example of an irrational number.

The symbol $\sqrt{}$ (**radical symbol**) is used to indicate the positive square root, or **principal square root**, of a number. So, $\sqrt{16} = 4$.

2 Use the information about roots to evaluate each expression.

A. Find the square roots of 81.

$\square^2 = 81$ and $\square^2 = 81$.

So, the square roots of 81 are ____ and ____ .

B. Find $\sqrt{\frac{4}{9}}$.

Both $\left(\frac{\square}{\square}\right)^2 = \frac{4}{9}$ and $\left(-\frac{\square}{\square}\right)^2 = \frac{4}{9}$.

The square root symbol indicates the principal square root.

So, $\sqrt{\frac{4}{9}} = \frac{\square}{\square}$.

Suppose Aaron wants a square piece of origami paper with an area of 2 square centimeters.

C. What is the length of one side of the piece of paper? Use a square root symbol in your answer.

____ centimeters

D. Is 2 a perfect square? Why or why not?

yes / no; There is / is not an integer whose square is 2.

E. Is the square root of 2 rational or irrational?

rational / irrational; $\sqrt{2}$ can / cannot be written as a ratio of two integers.

© Houghton Mifflin Harcourt Publishing Company • Image Credit: Houghton Mifflin Harcourt

The **cube root** of a positive number p is x when $x^3 = p$. Every positive number has one cube root. For example, $4^3 = 64$, so the cube root of 64 is 4. The symbol for a cube root is similar to the symbol for square root and written as $\sqrt[3]{\ }$. $\sqrt[3]{64} = 4$ is read out loud as, "The cube root of 64 equals 4."

A **perfect cube** is a whole number whose cube root is an integer. For example, 64 is a perfect cube, since its cube root is an integer, 4.

3 Find the cube root of $\frac{8}{27}$.

$\square^3 = 8$ and $\square^3 = 27$, so $\left(\frac{\square}{\square}\right)^3 = \frac{8}{27}$.

So, the cube root of $\frac{8}{27}$ is $\left(\frac{\square}{\square}\right)$. You also can write $\sqrt[3]{\frac{8}{27}} = \frac{\square}{\square}$.

4 Solve each problem.

A. What is the side length of the square picture frame shown?

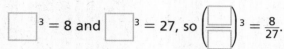

$x^2 = 100$	Write the equation.
$x = \pm\sqrt{100}$	Apply the definition of square root.
$x = \pm$ ______	Find integers that equal 100 when squared.

The side length of the picture frame is ______ inches.

Note that the square root −10 is not used since it is not a possible length for a real-world object.

B. Solve for y: $y^3 = \frac{1}{14}$.

$y = \sqrt[3]{\frac{1}{14}}$	Apply the definition of cube root.

Since no rational number when cubed equals $\frac{1}{14}$, ______ represents the solution to $y^3 = \frac{1}{14}$.

Check Understanding

1. Solve each equation.

A. $x^2 = 7$ $x =$ ______

B. $x^3 = \frac{1}{64}$ $x =$ ______

For Problems 2–4, find the indicated root.

2. $\sqrt{121}$ ______

3. $\sqrt{\frac{16}{25}}$ ______

4. $\sqrt[3]{125}$ ______

© Houghton Mifflin Harcourt Publishing Company • Image Credit: ©LiliGraphie/Shutterstock

Name

On Your Own

5. A band stores its equipment in a large cube. The cube has sound-dampening foam designed to allow the drummer to play inside the cube when the band is practicing.

125 cubic feet

A. Is 125 a perfect cube? Why or why not?

B. What is the edge length of the band's cube? Explain.

6. Find the square roots of 400.

7. Find the cube root of $\frac{8}{125}$. Show how you can check that you found the cube root correctly.

8. (MP) **Reason** A student claimed 7 and −7 are the two cube roots of 343. Do you agree or disagree? Explain.

9. Solve the equation $x^2 = 196$. Show your work and explain your steps.

10. Solve the equation $z^3 = \frac{125}{216}$. Show your work and explain your steps.

© Houghton Mifflin Harcourt Publishing Company • Image Credit: ©Gary Lee/Photoshot/NewsCom

11. Open Ended A square tile has an area of less than 1 square foot. The area and length are rational numbers. What is a possible area for the tile in square feet? What is the corresponding edge length?

____

12. (MP) **Use Repeated Reasoning** What do perfect squares have in common?

A. Complete the table of squares.

x	1	2	3	4	5	6	7	8	9	10	11	12
x^2												

B. What do you notice about the ones digit in each of the perfect squares in your table?

____

C. Suppose you extend the table and continue to find perfect squares. Do you think the number 10,402 will eventually appear in the x^2 row? Explain.

____

____

____

13. Does the square root of 0 exist? What about the cube root of 0? Explain your answers.

____

For Problems 14–16, find each root.

14. $\sqrt{225}$

15. $\sqrt[3]{729}$

16. $\sqrt[3]{\frac{64}{343}}$

For Problems 17–19, solve each equation.

17. $x^2 = \frac{1}{49}$

18. $n^3 = 19$

19. $y^3 = \frac{27}{125}$

I'm in a Learning Mindset!

How did I model constructive feedback when solving Problem 12B?

____

____

© Houghton Mifflin Harcourt Publishing Company • Image Credit: ©Lesinka372/Shutterstock

Name

ONLINE
Ed Video Tutorials and Interactive Examples

Investigate Roots

1. A puzzle maker built the cube puzzle shown.

A. What is the edge length of the cube puzzle? Explain.

B. Suppose the puzzle maker wants to build a larger cube puzzle and wants the volume to be a perfect cube when measured in cubic inches. If the volume must be less than 1000 cubic inches, what are some volumes the puzzle maker could use? Explain.

2. Find the square roots of 169. Then find $\sqrt{169}$. Explain why the answers are not exactly the same.

3. Solve the equation $y^3 = \frac{64}{729}$. Show your work and explain your steps.

4. **Math on the Spot** Solve each equation for x.

A. $x^2 = 81$

B. $x^2 = \frac{25}{144}$

For Problems 5–7, find each root.

5. $\sqrt{289}$

6. $\sqrt[3]{512}$

7. $\sqrt[3]{\frac{1}{1,000}}$

For Problems 8–10, solve each equation.

8. $z^2 = \frac{81}{121}$

9. $x^3 = 343$

10. $y^3 = \frac{8}{729}$

© Houghton Mifflin Harcourt Publishing Company • Image Credit: ©prill/iStock / Getty Images Plus/Getty Images

Test Prep

11. Which of the following is NOT a perfect cube?

Ⓐ 1 Ⓑ 8 Ⓒ 9 Ⓓ 27

12. Iris wrote a square root of 144 on a piece of paper. Which one of the following must be true about the number she wrote?

Ⓐ The number is 12.

Ⓑ The number is −12.

Ⓒ The number multiplied by itself equals 144.

Ⓓ None of the above is true.

13. Which of the following is an irrational number?

Ⓐ $\sqrt[3]{1}$ Ⓑ $\sqrt{2}$ Ⓒ $\sqrt[3]{27}$ Ⓓ $\sqrt{25}$

14. Which number when squared makes 26?

Ⓐ 52 Ⓑ 13 Ⓒ 5.5 Ⓓ $\sqrt{26}$

15. A square flower bed has an area of $\frac{169}{36}$ square yards. What is the perimeter of the flower bed?

☐ $\frac{☐}{☐}$ yards

Spiral Review

Use the information and graph to solve Problems 16–17.

Ava is comparing the pricing at two different parking lots in the downtown area of her city. Both lots charge a fixed fee as well as an hourly rate. Ava makes the graph shown to compare the lots.

16. Which parking lot charges a greater hourly rate? Explain.

____

____

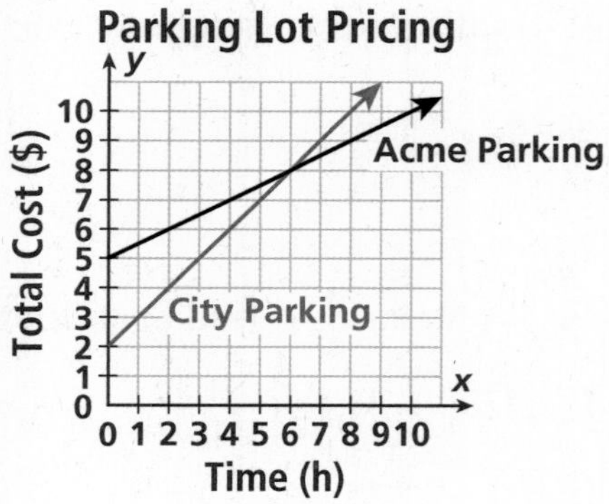

17. Which parking lot charges a greater fixed fee? Explain.

____

____

18. Is the number 0.575757... rational or irrational? If it is rational, express it as a fraction in simplest form. If it is irrational, explain why.

____

© Houghton Mifflin Harcourt Publishing Company

Name ____________________

Order Real Numbers

(I Can) accurately order a list of real numbers containing fractions, decimals, and irrational numbers.

Step It Out

ACTIVITY

All **real numbers** correspond to a position on a number line. Real numbers include rational and irrational numbers.

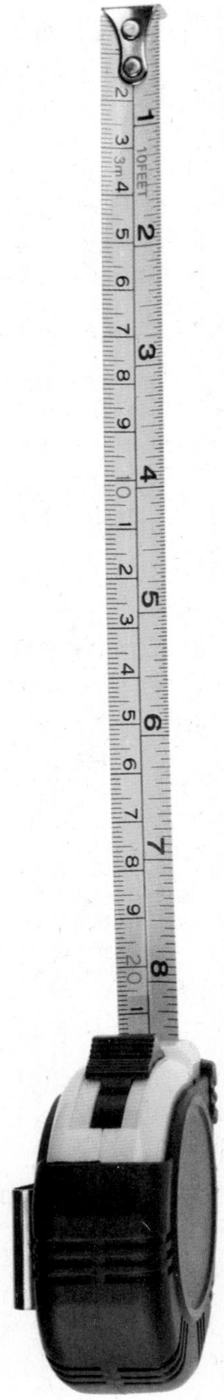

1 Estimate $\sqrt{50}$ to the nearest tenth.

A. Find the two perfect squares closest to 50, one greater than 50 and one less than 50.

________ and ________

B. What are the square roots of the two perfect squares?

________ and ________

C. The whole number that most closely estimates $\sqrt{50}$ is ________.

D. Refine your estimate of $\sqrt{50}$. Circle the true statement. Then underline the value closer to 50.

$7.0^2 < 50 < 7.1^2$ $\quad$ $7.2^2 < 50 < 7.3^2$ $\quad$ $7.4^2 < 50 < 7.5^2$

$7.1^2 < 50 < 7.2^2$ $\quad$ $7.3^2 < 50 < 7.4^2$ $\quad$ $7.5^2 < 50 < 7.6^2$

2 Estimate $\sqrt[3]{100}$ to the nearest hundredth.

A. Find the two perfect cubes closest to 100, one greater than 100 and one less than 100.

________ and ________

B. What are the cube roots of the two perfect cubes?

________ and ________

C. Circle the pair of cubes $\sqrt[3]{100}$ lies between.

4.5^3 $\quad$ 4.6^3 $\quad$ 4.7^3 $\quad$ 4.8^3 $\quad$ 4.9^3 $\quad$ 5.0^3

D. Within your interval, test cubes of values expressed in hundredths. Which cube is closest to 100? "Approximately equal to" is represented by the $\approx$ symbol.

________ is closest to 100, so $\sqrt[3]{100} \approx$ ________.

Turn and Talk What is your strategy for estimating a square root or a cube root to the nearest hundredth?

© Houghton Mifflin Harcourt Publishing Company • Image Credit: ©STILLFX/Shutterstock

3 You can use estimates of square roots to help you estimate and compare numerical expressions involving square roots.

A. Compare the values below. Write $<$ or $>$ to complete each statement.

2 ◯ 6, so $\sqrt{3} + 2$ ◯ $\sqrt{3} + 6$.

-1 ◯ -3, so $\sqrt{7} - 1$ ◯ $\sqrt{7} - 3$.

6 ◯ 7, so $2\sqrt{6}$ ◯ $2\sqrt{7}$.

B. Complete the statement with consecutive square integers.

8 is between the perfect squares ________ and ________,

so the value of $\sqrt{8}$ is between the integers ________

and ________.

Use this information to complete the inequality with integer values.

________ $< \sqrt{8} + 3 <$ ________

C. Compare the values given. Write $<$ or $>$ to complete each statement.

$\sqrt{7}$ ◯ $\sqrt{3}$, so $2\sqrt{7}$ ◯ $2\sqrt{3}$.

$\sqrt{11}$ ◯ $\sqrt{21}$, so $5\sqrt{11}$ ◯ $5\sqrt{21}$.

Complete the statements with integers.

5 is between the perfect squares ________ and ________,

so the value of $\sqrt{5}$ is between the consecutive integers ________

and ________.

Use this information to complete the inequality with integer values.

________ $< 3\sqrt{5} <$ ________

D. Complete the inequalities using consecutive integers.

________ $< \sqrt{13} - 1 <$ ________

________ $< \sqrt[3]{40} + 1 <$ ________

________ $< \sqrt[3]{25} + 2 <$ ________

________ $< \sqrt{111} - 4 <$ ________

© Houghton Mifflin Harcourt Publishing Compan • Image Credit: ©Rubberball/age fotostock

Turn and Talk Explain the strategy you used to complete Part D.

4 **A.** Identify the integers between which each number is located.

______ $< \frac{3}{2} <$ ______

______ $< \pi <$ ______

______ $< \sqrt{5} <$ ______

______ $< 0.\overline{3} <$ ______

Use the comparisons to plot and label the points on the number line.

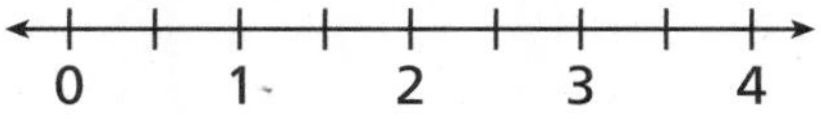

B. Identify the consecutive integers between which each number is located.

______ $< -\sqrt{12} <$ ______

______ $< -4.75 <$ ______

______ $< \sqrt{3} - 8 <$ ______

______ $< -\frac{17}{3} <$ ______

Use the comparisons to plot and label the points on the number line.

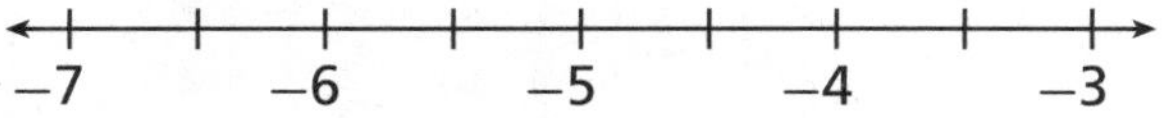

Check Understanding

For Problems 1–3, use $<$ or $>$ to compare the expressions.

1. $\sqrt{6}$ ◯ $\sqrt{7}$ **2.** $\sqrt{10}$ ◯ $\sqrt[3]{25}$ **3.** $\sqrt{5}+4$ ◯ $\sqrt{50}+1$

Use the information to solve Problems 4–5.

Marc and Amber are producing a design for a side table. They want the top of the table to have a length of $\sqrt{7}$ feet and the side of the table to have a length of $\sqrt{3}$ feet. Estimate each length to the nearest tenth, then label the points on the number line.

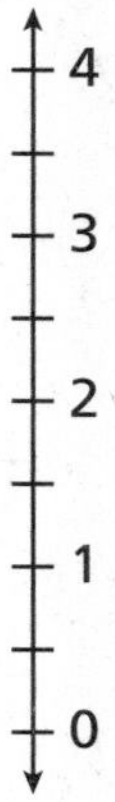

4. $\sqrt{3}$ feet ______

5. $\sqrt{7}$ feet ______

© Houghton Mifflin Harcourt Publishing Company • Image Credits: (t) ©anon_tae/Shutterstock;

On Your Own

6. Answer the questions and complete the statements in Parts A–C. Then complete the statement in Part D.

A. Is $\sqrt{14}$ between 3.0 and 3.5 or 3.5 and 4.0? ____________

To the nearest integer, $\sqrt{14} \approx$ ______.

B. Is $\sqrt{35}$ between 5.75 and 5.85 or 5.85 and 5.95? ____________

To the nearest tenth, $\sqrt{35} \approx$ ______.

C. Is $\sqrt{75}$ between 8.655 and 8.665 or 8.665 and 8.675? ____________

To the nearest hundredth, $\sqrt{75} \approx$ ______.

D. (MP) **Reason** How do the intervals selected in Parts A–C help you estimate the value of the square root?

____

____

____

7. Estimate $\sqrt{84}$

A. to the nearest integer. $\sqrt{84} \approx$ ______

B. to the nearest tenth. $\sqrt{84} \approx$ ______

8. Estimate $\sqrt[3]{60}$

A. to the nearest integer. $\sqrt[3]{60} \approx$ ______

B. to the nearest tenth. $\sqrt[3]{60} \approx$ ______

9. **History** The Spiral of Theodorus was used to prove the irrationality of several square roots. Estimate $\sqrt{2}$ to the nearest hundredth. Show your work.

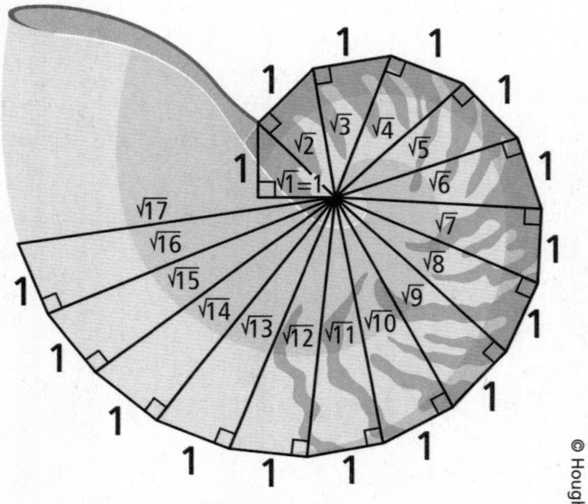

Spiral of Theodorus

© Houghton Mifflin Harcourt Publishing Company

Name ____________________

For Problems 10–13, Write $<$ or $>$ to complete each statement.

10. $\sqrt{15} - 4$ ◯ $\sqrt{15} - 7$

11. $2\sqrt{18}$ ◯ $2\sqrt{21}$

12. $-\sqrt[3]{30}$ ◯ -3

13. $\sqrt{8} + 1$ ◯ $\sqrt{17} - 2$

For Problems 14–17, complete each inequality using the greatest possible integer for comparison.

14. $\sqrt{42} >$ ______

15. $\sqrt{150} >$ ______

16. $\sqrt{245} >$ ______

17. $\sqrt{398} >$ ______

For Problems 18–21, circle the lesser of the two numbers.

18. $\sqrt{30} + 4$ $\quad$ 8

19. $\sqrt{11}$ $\quad$ $\sqrt{20} - 2$

20. $\sqrt{7}$ $\quad$ $\sqrt[3]{40}$

21. $15 - \sqrt{2}$ $\quad$ $\sqrt{125}$

For Problems 22–28, complete each inequality using a pair of consecutive integers.

22. ______ $< \sqrt{10} + 4 <$ ______

23. ______ $< \sqrt{19} + 8 <$ ______

24. ______ $< \sqrt{61} - 5 <$ ______

25. ______ $< \sqrt{92} - 11 <$ ______

26. ______ $< \sqrt[3]{50} - 1 <$ ______

27. ______ $< \sqrt[3]{100} + 2 <$ ______

28. ______ $< \sqrt[3]{17} + 5 <$ ______

29. (MP) **Reason** Is there a limit to the number of decimal places to which you can approximate an irrational number? Explain.

____

____

____

© Houghton Mifflin Harcourt Publishing Company

For Problems 30–32, plot the expressions on the number line.

30. $\sqrt{10}$, $\frac{7}{4}$, $2.\overline{2}$, $(\sqrt{13} - 1)$

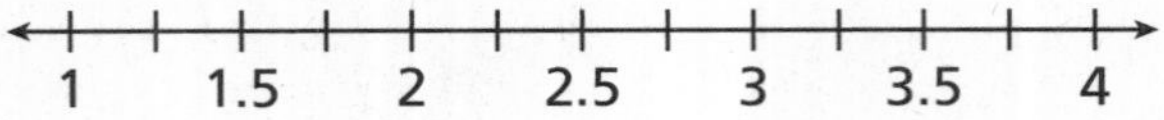

31. $-\sqrt{15}$, $-\frac{5}{3}$, $-\sqrt[3]{27}$, $(\sqrt{12} - 6)$

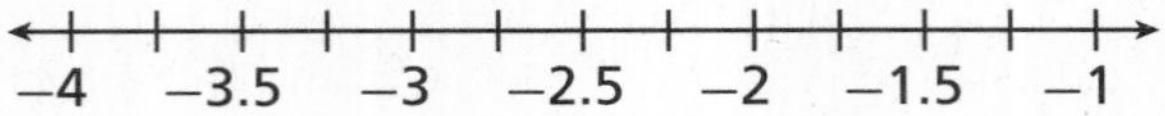

32. $(\sqrt{24} - 5)$, $(\sqrt{48} - 8)$, $(\sqrt{60} - 5)$, $\sqrt{17}$

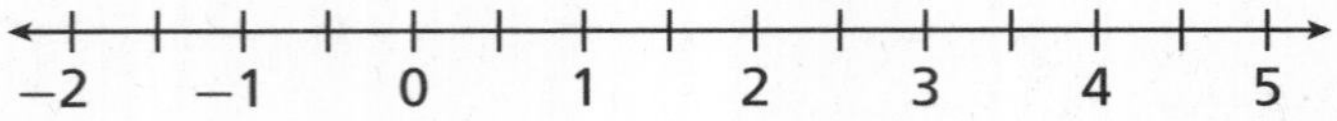

For Problems 33–34, order the expressions from greatest to least.

33. $\sqrt{27}$, $\frac{17}{6}$, $\sqrt[3]{70}$, π, 1.8

____

34. $\frac{2}{3}$, $\sqrt{2}$, $\frac{2}{9}$, $(\sqrt{3} - 1)$, $\frac{10}{9}$

____

For Problems 35–36, order the expressions from least to greatest.

35. $0.\overline{7}$, $2\sqrt{3}$, $(\sqrt{32} - 8)$, $(-2 + \sqrt{19})$, $\left(4 - \frac{21}{4}\right)$

____

36. $-\frac{12}{5}$, $(-6 + \sqrt{30})$, $(\sqrt{15} - 7)$, $\left(3 - \frac{30}{7}\right)$, $-3\sqrt{2}$

____

37. Which number is the best approximation for π^2: 9, 9.3, 9.6, or 9.9?

____

38. Which number is the best approximation for $\frac{\pi}{3}$: 1, 1.03, 1.05, or 1.07?

____

© Houghton Mifflin Harcourt Publishing Company • **Image Credit:** ©Douglas Sacha/Moment/Getty Images

Name ______________________________

ONLINE
Video Tutorials and
Interactive Examples

Order Real Numbers

1. (MP) **Attend to Precision** Through calculations, Jack and Kelsey estimated the diameter of the fountain in the park. If the actual length is 15 feet, which student's estimate is more accurate? Explain your reasoning.

____

____

2. Complete the inequality with consecutive integers.

$\_\_\_\_\_ < \sqrt{357} < \_\_\_\_\_$

3. **Math on the Spot** Compare the expressions. Write $<$, $>$, or $=$.

$\sqrt{6} + 3$ ◯ $6 + \sqrt{3}$

4. Estimate $\sqrt{74}$ and $\sqrt[3]{74}$ to the nearest tenth.

____

5. **Open Ended** Identify two rational numbers and one irrational number between $\sqrt{2}$ and $\sqrt{3}$. Show how you know they are in this range.

____

____

For Problems 6–7, plot the expressions on the number line.

6. $\sqrt{17}$, $\frac{\pi}{2}$, π, $\frac{11}{4}$

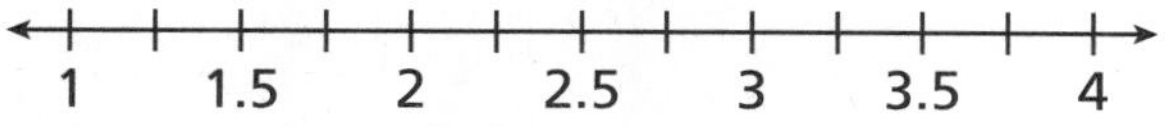

7. $\sqrt{15}$, $(\sqrt{22} - 6)$, $\frac{16}{5}$, $(-5 + \sqrt{25})$

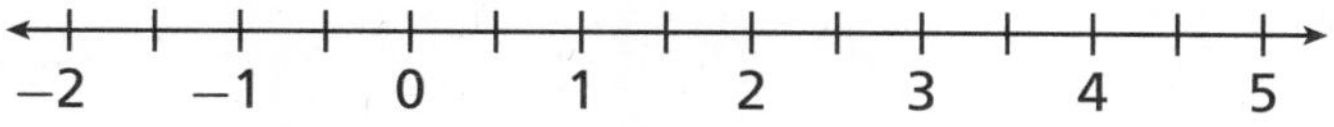

8. Order the expressions from least to greatest.

$\sqrt{31}$, $\frac{29}{9}$, $(\sqrt{24} + 2)$, $\sqrt[3]{90}$

____

9. Order the expressions from greatest to least.

$(\sqrt[3]{99} - 5)$, $(-\sqrt{45} + 9)$, $(\sqrt{71} - 8)$, $\frac{12}{7}$, $-\frac{8}{5}$

____

© Houghton Mifflin Harcourt Publishing Company

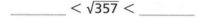

Test Prep

10. Which numbers make the inequality true? Select all that apply.

$7 < \square < 8$

Ⓐ $\sqrt{56}$

Ⓑ $\sqrt{99} - 1$

Ⓒ $\sqrt{38} + 1$

Ⓓ $3\sqrt{3} + 2$

Ⓔ $2\sqrt{2} + 3$

11. Which is the best estimate of $\sqrt{200}$?

Ⓐ 14.0

Ⓑ 14.1

Ⓒ 14.2

Ⓓ 14.3

12. Which is the best estimate of $\sqrt[3]{84}$?

Ⓐ 4.38

Ⓑ 4.39

Ⓒ 4.40

Ⓓ 4.41

13. Order the numerical expressions from least to greatest.

$-\frac{52}{5}$ $\quad -\sqrt{130} \quad$ $-3 - \sqrt{47}$

____

Spiral Review

14. Would the number of hours traveled and the remaining distance to a destination likely have a strong negative or a strong positive association? Why?

____

____

15. Does your music preference influence your choices for pet ownership? Keisha conducted a study of 41 students at her middle school. The results are displayed in the table to the right. Compare relative frequencies to determine whether there is a strong association between music choices and owning pets.

	Favorite Type of Music		
	Country	**Hip-hop**	**Pop**
Pet	4	5	6
No pet	7	8	11

____

____

____

16. Solve the equation $5x - 7 = 2(x + 8)$.

____

© Houghton Mifflin Harcourt Publishing Company

Module 14

Name ____________________

Review

Vocabulary

For Problems 1–4, give two examples of each type of number.

1. rational number

2. irrational number

3. terminating decimal

4. repeating decimal

5. Explain how the terms *perfect square* and *square root* are related.

Concepts and Skills

6. Select all numbers that are irrational.

(A) $-\frac{5}{12}$
(B) $\frac{\pi}{2}$
(C) $0.\overline{15}$
(D) $\sqrt{5}$
(E) $\frac{1}{6}$
(F) $\sqrt{25}$

7. Determine whether each number is rational or irrational.

	Rational	Irrational
$\sqrt{49}$	☐	☐
$\sqrt{90}$	☐	☐
$\sqrt{125}$	☐	☐
$\sqrt{169}$	☐	☐

8. (MP) **Use Tools** Write a fraction equivalent to $0.\overline{24}$. State what strategy and tool you will use to answer the question, explain your choice, and then find the answer.

© Houghton Mifflin Harcourt Publishing Company

For Problems 9–10, write each repeating decimal as a fraction.

9. $0.\overline{18}$ ______ **10.** $0.3\overline{6}$ ______

11. Do you see a pattern in the number 0.31311311131111...? Is it rational or irrational? Explain your reasoning.

______

______

______

______

For Problems 12–13, find all solutions of the equation.

12. $x^3 = 11$

$x =$ ______

13. $n^2 = 0.16$

$n =$ ______

14. A cube has a volume of 216 cubic inches. What is the edge length of the cube?

Ⓐ 6 inches
Ⓑ 15 inches
Ⓒ 18 inches
Ⓓ 36 inches

15. Explain why the equation $x^2 = 64$ has two solutions, but the equation $x^3 = 64$ has only one solution.

______

______

______

______

For Problems 16–17, estimate the value of the root to the nearest whole number.

16. $\sqrt{53}$ ______ **17.** $\sqrt[3]{118}$ ______

18. Select all values that are greater than 4.

Ⓐ $\sqrt[3]{8}$
Ⓑ $\sqrt{9}$
Ⓒ $\sqrt{10}$
Ⓓ $\sqrt[3]{12} + 2$
Ⓔ $\sqrt{27}$
Ⓕ 2π

For Problems 19–20, plot the set of numbers at their approximate locations on the number line.

19. $\sqrt[3]{6}$, $\sqrt[3]{39}$, and $\sqrt[3]{150}$

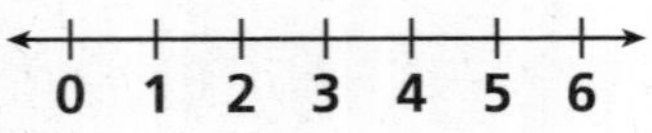

20. $\sqrt{2}$ and $\sqrt{8}$

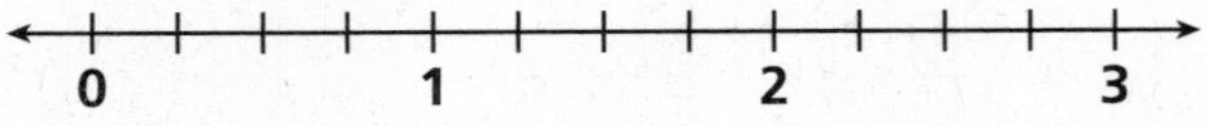

© Houghton Mifflin Harcourt Publishing Company

Module
15 The Pythagorean Theorem

Try Your Angle

A worker is making wooden triangles to use as obstacles for minigolf. The sides of the triangles can have any of the lengths shown. A triangle can be isosceles, but none of the triangles can be equilateral.

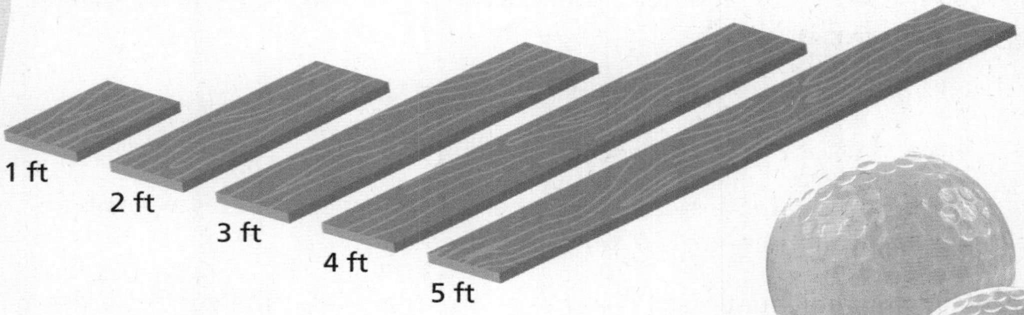

Name the side lengths of four different triangles to be used as obstacles. No two triangles should have the same set of lengths.

Triangle 1: ________, ________, and ________

Triangle 2: ________, ________, and ________

Triangle 3: ________, ________, and ________

Triangle 4: ________, ________, and ________

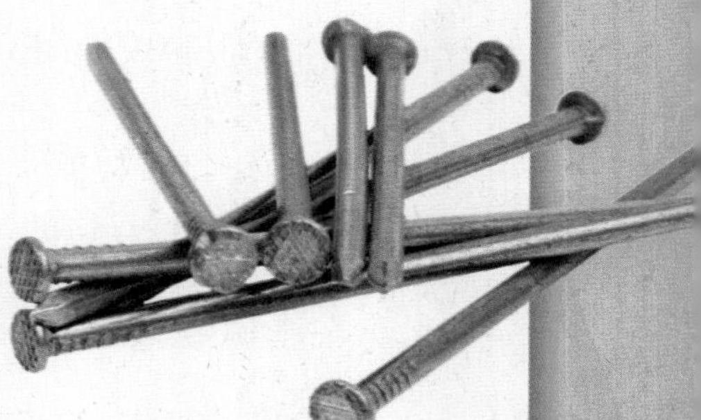

Turn and Talk

How do you know that each set of lengths can form a triangle?

© Houghton Mifflin Harcourt Publishing Company • Image Credits: (tr) ©iStock / Getty Images Plus/Getty Images, (b) ©Mykola Velychko/Shutterstock

Are You Ready?

Complete these problems to review prior concepts and skills you will need for this module.

Order of Operations

Determine the value of each expression.

1. $18 + 7^2 - 24$ ________ **2.** $2(10 - 4)^2 + 8$ ________

3. $8^2 + 5^2$ ________ **4.** $20^2 - 12^2$ ________

Draw Shapes with Given Conditions

For Problems 5–6, state whether a triangle can be formed from the set of side lengths. Write *yes* or *no*.

5. 1 centimeter, 2 centimeters, and 4 centimeters ________

6. 2 centimeters, 2 centimeters, and 3 centimeters ________

7. Two sides of a triangle measure 6 inches and 8 inches. What is a possible length of the third side? Explain your reasoning.

____

____

____

Use Roots to Solve Equations

For Problems 8–11, solve the equation.

8. $a^2 = 100$ **9.** $c^2 = 35$

________ ________

10. $b^2 = 144$ **11.** $x^2 = 225$

________ ________

12. A square park has an area of 8100 square meters.

A. Write an equation that can be used to determine the side length s, in meters, of the park.

____

B. Solve your equation, and interpret the solution.

____

____

© Houghton Mifflin Harcourt Publishing Company

Name

Prove the Pythagorean Theorem and Its Converse

I Can **prove the Pythagorean Theorem and its converse, use the Pythagorean Theorem to find unknown side lengths of right triangles, and identify a Pythagorean triple.**

Spark Your Learning

PAIRS

The given squares form a right triangle. Find the side lengths and areas of each. What patterns do you notice about the squares and side lengths?

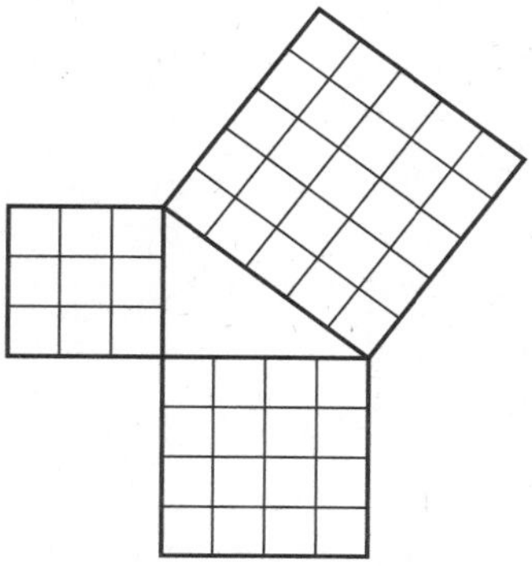

Turn and Talk What types of objects in the real world are in the shape of a right triangle? Can you find some right triangles in the classroom?

© Houghton Mifflin Harcourt Publishing Company • Image Credit: ©OmaPhoto/Shutterstock

Build Understanding

The **Pythagorean Theorem** states that in a right triangle, the square of the length of the hypotenuse is equal to the sum of the squares of the lengths of the legs.

If a and b are the lengths of the legs and c is the length of the hypotenuse, then $a^2 + b^2 = c^2$. If a, b, and c are all integers, they are called a **Pythagorean triple**.

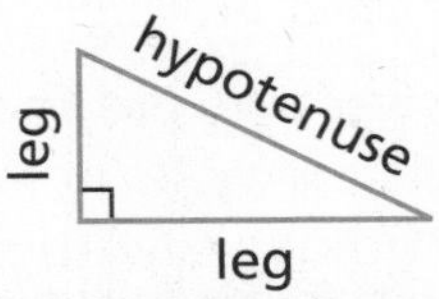

1 Pythagoras was a Greek philosopher and mathematician who is credited with being the first to prove the Pythagorean Theorem. You can use what you know about similar triangles to prove the Pythagorean Theorem.

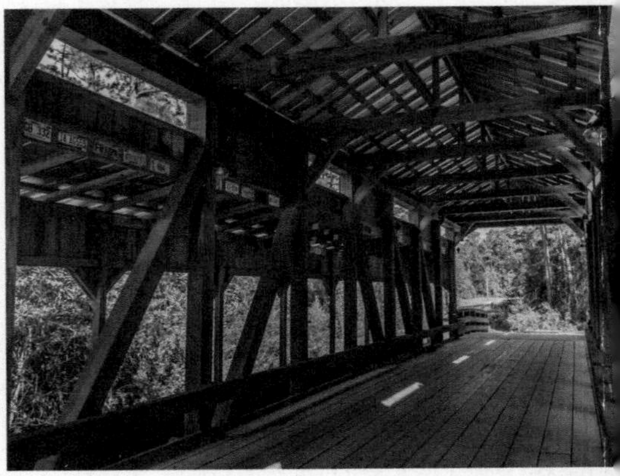

A. Using $\triangle ABC$, draw a line from Point C perpendicular to the hypotenuse. Label the point where this line intersects the hypotenuse as Point D. This breaks the length c into two parts and forms two smaller triangles. Label $\overline{AD}$ as length e, and label $\overline{DB}$ as length f. Repeat the labels in the two smaller triangles.

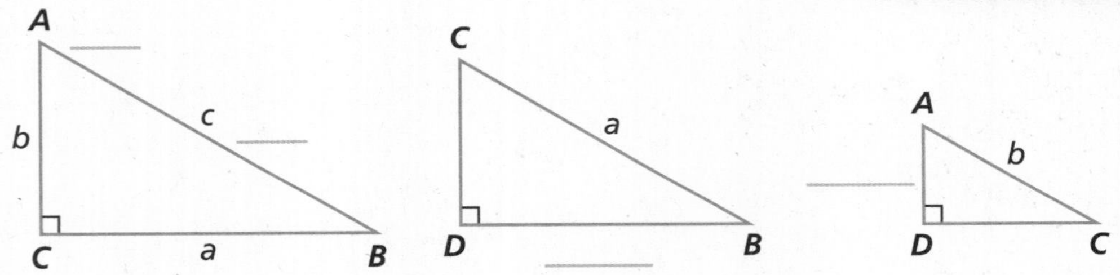

B. Because of Angle-Angle Similarity, $\triangle ABC$ is similar to $\triangle CBD$ and $\triangle ACD$. What do you know about the corresponding sides of similar triangles?

____

C. Use similar triangles to compare corresponding hypotenuses and corresponding longer legs in $\triangle CBD$ and $\triangle ABC$. $\frac{a}{c} = \frac{f}{\square}$

Use similar triangles to compare corresponding hypotenuses and corresponding shorter legs in $\triangle ABC$ and $\triangle ACD$. $\frac{c}{b} = \frac{b}{\square}$

D. Use the Multiplication Property of Equality to rewrite the equations. $cf =$ ______ and $b^2 =$ ______

E. Use addition to write $a^2 + b^2$ in terms of c, e, and f. Then simplify to complete the proof.

© Houghton Mifflin Harcourt Publishing Company • **Image Credit:** ©RSBPhoto/Alamy

Name

Consider this statement: *If I am in this class, then I am in the 7th grade*. The converse of this statement is: *If I am in the 7th grade, then I am in this class.* The converse of a theorem reverses the hypothesis and the conclusion.

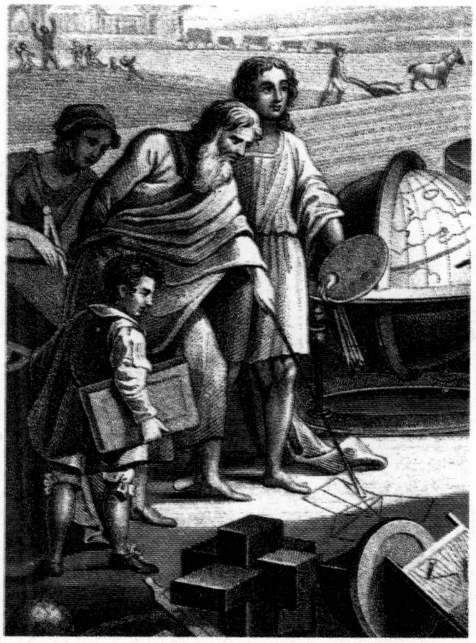

The Pythagorean Theorem states:
If a triangle is a right triangle, then the sum of the squares of the shorter sides is equal to the square of the longest side.

The converse of that statement is:
If the sum of the squares of the two shorter sides of a triangle is equal to the square of the longest side, then the triangle is a right triangle.

2 Show that, given a triangle *ABC* with side lengths a, b, and c, if $a^2 + b^2 = c^2$, then the triangle is a right triangle with a right angle at *C*.

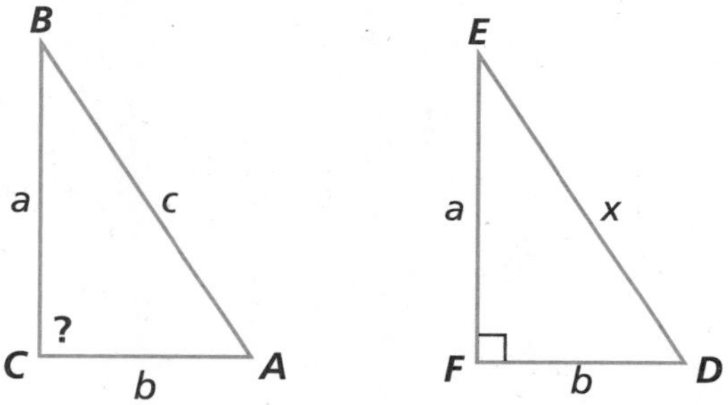

A. Let Triangle *DEF* be a triangle such that $EF = a$, $DF = b$, $DE = x$, and F is a right angle. We need to show that Triangles *ABC* and *DEF* are congruent.

B. Can we apply the Pythagorean Theorem to Triangle *DEF*? Why or why not? If so, what can we conclude?

C. How can we relate x to c?

D. What can you conclude about the measure of Angle *C*? Explain, and include the classification for Triangle *ABC*.

© Houghton Mifflin Harcourt Publishing Company • Image Credit: ©World History Archive/Alamy

Step It Out

3 Use the Pythagorean Theorem to find the length of the set of stairs.

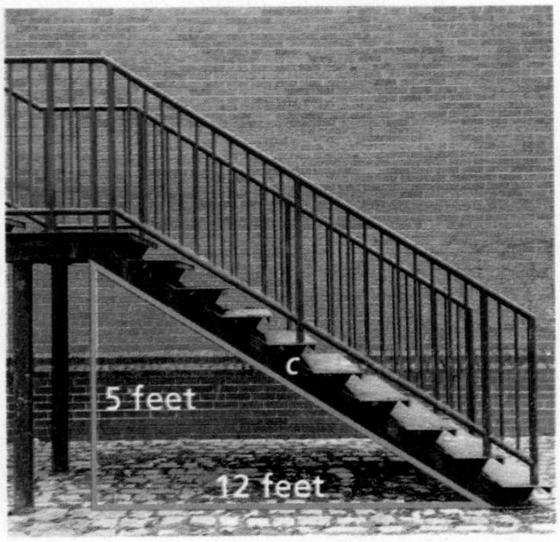

A. Use the equation $a^2 + b^2 = c^2$. Substitute the leg lengths into the equation and simplify.

$$a^2 + b^2 = c^2$$

$$\square^2 + \square^2 = c^2$$

$$\square + \square = c^2$$

$$\square = c^2$$

B. Take the square root of both sides to solve for c, the hypotenuse.

$\sqrt{\square} = \sqrt{c^2}$ $\quad c = \square$ feet

4 Side a measures $\sqrt{3}$ inches.
Side b measures $\sqrt{4}$ inches.
Side c measures $\sqrt{7}$ inches.

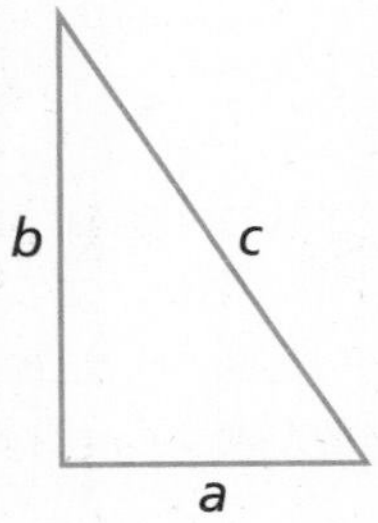

Are all the side lengths integers? ________

Does $a^2 + b^2 = c^2$? ________

Is the triangle a right triangle? ________

This is / is not a Pythagorean triple.

Check Understanding

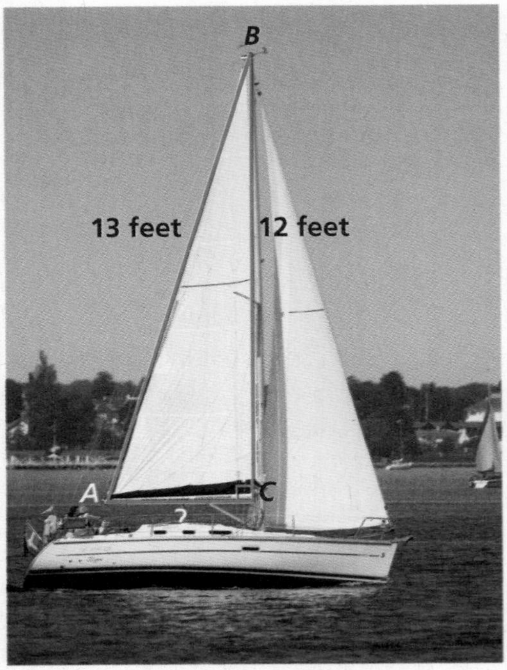

1. **A.** A sail shaped like a right triangle is shown. Find the unknown side length.

   ____

   B. Do these lengths form a Pythagorean triple? ________

2. Side a measures $\sqrt{100}$ inches.

   Side b measures 24 inches.

   Side c measures 26 inches.

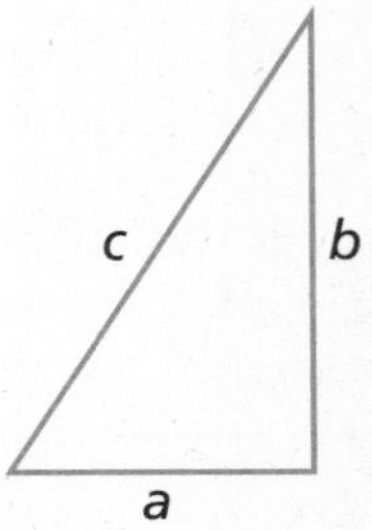

Are all the side lengths integers? ________

Does $a^2 + b^2 = c^2$? ________

Is the triangle a right triangle? ________

Is the triple a Pythagorean triple? ________

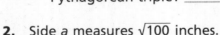

© Houghton Mifflin Harcourt Publishing Company • Image Credits: (t) ©Luis Alvarenga/EyeEm/Getty Images; (b) ©Niels-DK/Alamy

Name ______________________

On Your Own

3. In your own words, describe the Pythagorean Theorem and how you can use it.

____

____

____

4. Find the unknown length.

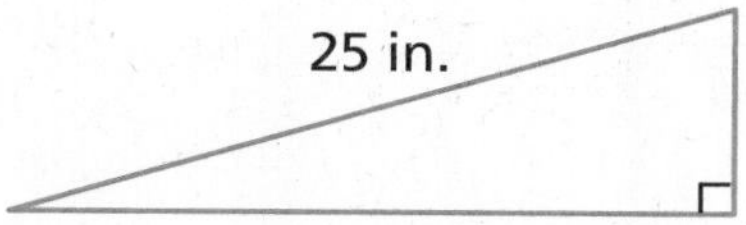

____

For Problems 5–6, determine whether each set of three side lengths forms a right triangle.

5. 12, 35, and 37

____

6. 8, 11, and 13

____

7. (MP) **Reason** Rafael found the unknown side length of the given triangle using the Pythagorean Theorem. Is he correct? Explain.

$$5^2 + 13^2 = c^2$$
$$25 + 169 = c^2$$
$$194 = c^2$$
$$14 \approx c$$

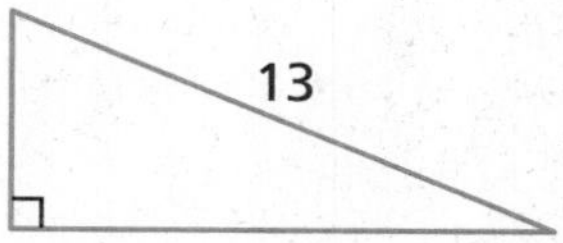

____

____

____

____

8. A right triangle has a leg length of 10 meters and a hypotenuse of length 26 meters. What is the length of the other leg?

____

9. **Open Ended** What is a Pythagorean triple? Give one example.

____

____

____

© Houghton Mifflin Harcourt Publishing Company

10. STEM A high school is converting an entry staircase into a ramp to increase accessibility. The entrance door is 7 feet off the ground. By law, a ramp this height needs to start 24 feet away from the building. If the length of the ramp is 25 feet, will the ramp form a right triangle with the building?

A. Fill in the measurements on the illustration shown.

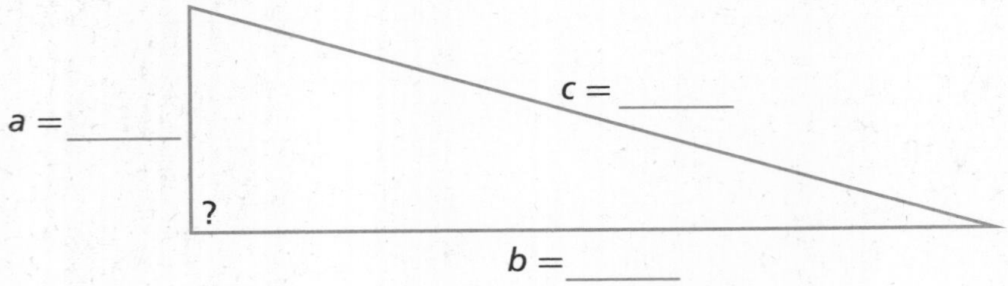

B. Determine whether the ramp forms a right triangle.

Does $\square^2 + \square^2 = \square^2$?

Does $\square + \square = \square$?

Does the 25-foot ramp form a right triangle? ______

11. A sculpture is shaped like a pair of right triangles. The leg lengths for each triangle are 8 feet and 15 feet. What is the length of each hypotenuse? ______

12. (MP) **Critique Reasoning** Ashley claims she found the unknown side length of the triangle. Is she correct? Explain.

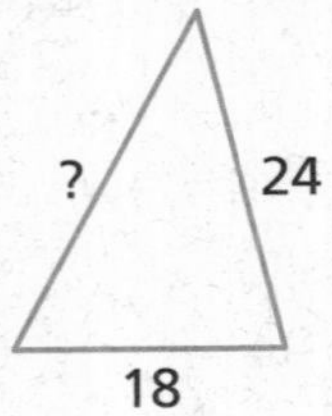

$$18^2 + 24^2 = c^2$$
$$324 + 576 = c^2$$
$$900 = c^2$$
$$30 = c$$

______

______

______

______

I'm in a Learning Mindset!

How did I apply the feedback I was given about the Pythagorean Theorem to my understanding of the converse of the Pythagorean Theorem?

______

______

© Houghton Mifflin Harcourt Publishing Company • Image Credit: ©Leslie Garland Picture Library/Alamy

Name ____________________

ONLINE
Video Tutorials and Interactive Examples

Prove the Pythagorean Theorem and Its Converse

© Houghton Mifflin Harcourt Publishing Company • Image Credits: (t) ©TK Images/Alamy

1. **Open Ended** Draw a right triangle on graph paper. Measure the length of each leg and the hypotenuse. Write an equation using your triangle's side lengths to show the Pythagorean Theorem holds true for your triangle.

2. A window shaped like a right triangle has the measurements shown. What is the length of the other leg?

3. Determine whether the set of measurements is a Pythagorean triple.
Side *a* measures 5 feet.
Side *b* measures 16 feet.
Side *c* measures 20 feet.

$\square^2 + \square^2 \stackrel{?}{=} \square^2$

$\square + \square \stackrel{?}{=} \square$

Is this a Pythagorean triple? ______

4. **Math on the Spot** Lynnette is buying a triangular parcel of land. If the lengths of the three sides are 300 yards, 400 yards, and 500 yards, will the parcel of land have a right angle? Explain.

5. **A.** Find the unknown side length of a right triangle with leg length 5 yards and hypotenuse 13 yards.

B. Find the unknown side length of a right triangle with leg length 50 yards and hypotenuse 130 yards.

C. (MP) **Use Structure** How are the lengths of the leg and hypotenuse in Part A related to the lengths of the leg and hypotenuse in Part B?

Test Prep

6. Identify in the table whether the measurements could be the side lengths of a right triangle.

	Right triangle	Not a right triangle
6, 8, and 14	☐	☐
3, 4, and 5	☐	☐
9, 12, and 15	☐	☐
5, 6, and 7	☐	☐

7. Which are examples of Pythagorean triples? Select all that apply.

Ⓐ 6, 8, 10

Ⓑ 8, 10, 12

Ⓒ 10, 16, 15

Ⓓ 12, 16, 20

Ⓔ 14, 18, 20

8. A right triangle has leg lengths of 12 inches and 9 inches. What is the length of the hypotenuse?

______ inches

9. Amber claims that a triangle with sides measuring 3 inches, 6 inches, and 9 inches is a right triangle because $3 + 6 = 9$. Explain her error.

____

____

____

Spiral Review

10. Solve the system of equations by graphing. Check your solution.

$$\begin{cases} y = 1 - x \\ y = 5 - 2x \end{cases}$$

____

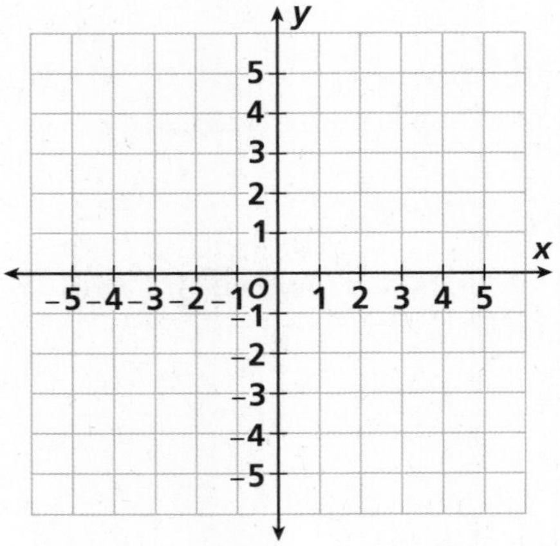

11. Order the numbers from least to greatest.

$\frac{10}{4}$, -3, $\sqrt{8}$, 2.7

____

© Houghton Mifflin Harcourt Publishing Company

Name ______________________________

Apply the Pythagorean Theorem

I Can apply the Pythagorean Theorem to solve real-life problems involving the legs and hypotenuse of a right triangle, including problems in three dimensions.

Step It Out

1 The red team and blue team are playing Capture the Flag. Each team places their flag at opposite corners of the field. The red team sends two players, Alfredo and Angelina, from the red flag to capture the blue flag.

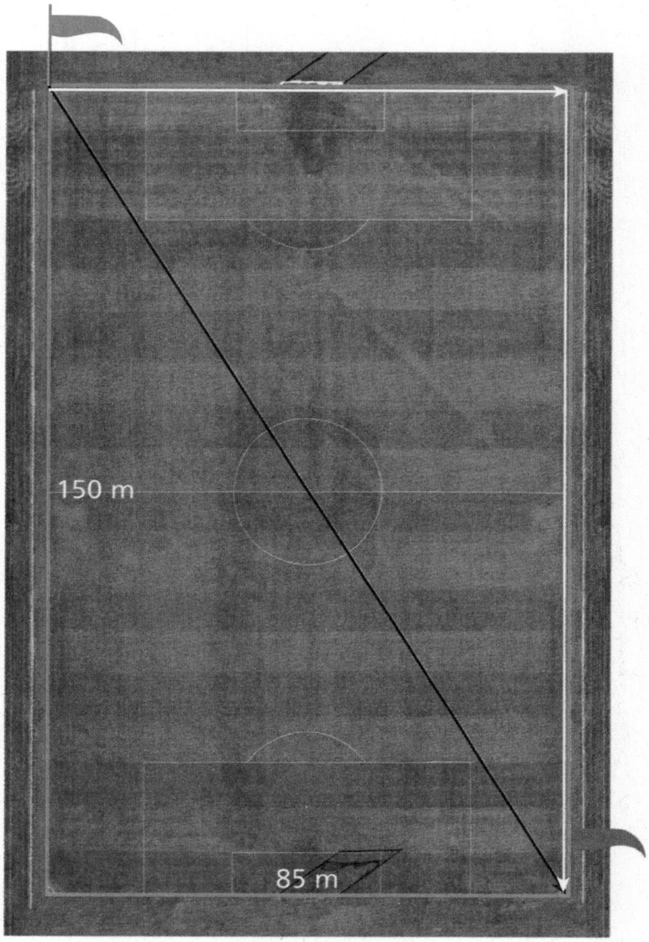

A. Alfredo must follow the white arrows to the flag. How far does he run?

[ ] + [ ] = [ ]

Alfredo runs ________ meters.

B. Angelina must follow the black arrow to the flag. Use the Pythagorean Theorem to determine how far she runs. Round to the nearest tenth.

$$a^2 + b^2 = c^2$$

$$[\ \ ]^2 + [\ \ ]^2 = c^2$$

$$[\ \ ] = c^2$$

$$\sqrt{[\ \ ]} = c$$

$$[\ \ ] \approx c$$

Angelina runs ________ meters.

C. How much farther does Alfredo run than Angelina?

[ ] − [ ] = [ ]

Alfredo runs ________ meters farther than Angelina.

Turn and Talk Will the direct route between two points always be shorter than a route with a right angle? Why or why not?

© Houghton Mifflin Harcourt Publishing Company • Image Credit: ©Anthony Brown/Alamy

The Pythagorean Theorem can be used to find lengths inside a three-dimensional object by finding right triangle relationships inside the object.

2 Jada wants to ship a 3-foot curtain rod to a customer. The biggest box at the post office is shown. Jada wants to know if the box is large enough to ship the curtain rod.

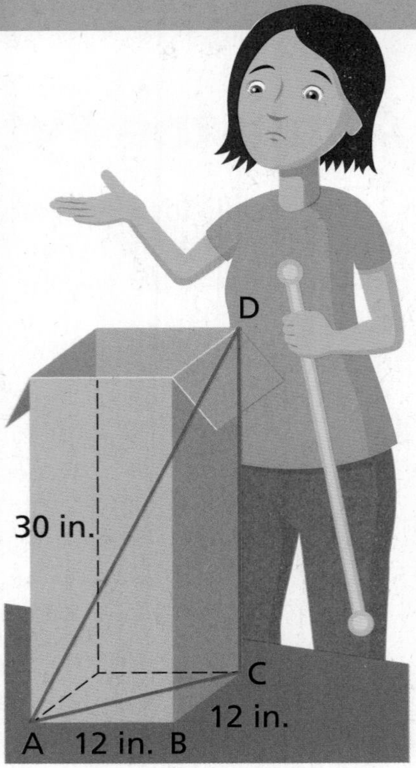

A. The longest distance in the box is the diagonal *AD* between opposite corners.

It forms the hypotenuse of $\triangle ACD$.

What is the length of $\overline{DC}$? ________ inches

B. To find the length of $\overline{AD}$ we must know the length of $\overline{AC}$. Look at the bottom of the box. $\overline{AC}$ is the hypotenuse of another right triangle, $\triangle ABC$. Use the Pythagorean Theorem to find the length of $\overline{AC}$. Round to the nearest tenth if necessary.

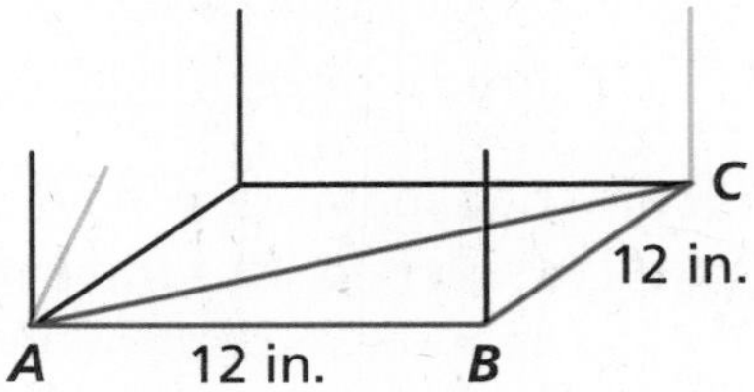

$$a^2 + b^2 = c^2$$

$$\square^2 + \square^2 = c^2$$

$$\square = c^2$$

$$c = \sqrt{\square} \approx \square$$

The length of $\overline{AC}$ is about ____ inches.

C. Use the length of $\overline{AC}$ to find the length of $\overline{AD}$. Round to the nearest tenth of an inch.

$$AC^2 + CD^2 = AD^2$$

$$\square^2 + \square^2 = c^2$$

$$\square = c^2$$

$$c = \sqrt{\square} \approx \square$$

The length of $\overline{AD}$ is about ________ inches.

D. About how long is the longest rod that could fit in the box?

________ inches

E. Can the curtain rod fit in the box?

____

© Houghton Mifflin Harcourt Publishing Company

Name

3 Cara measured the radius and outside length of an ice cream **cone**. Identify the right triangle in the cone, then use Cara's measurements to find the height of the cone. Round your final answer to the nearest hundredth.

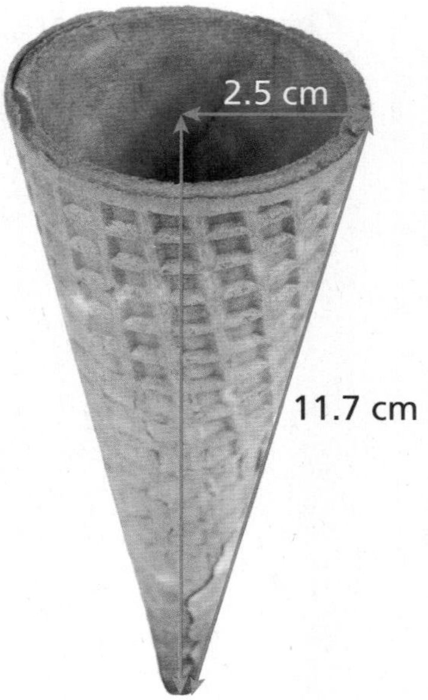

$\square^2 + b^2 = \square^2$

$\square + b^2 = \square$

$b^2 = \square - \square$

$b = \sqrt{\square}$

$b \approx \square$

The height of the cone is about ________ centimeters.

Turn and Talk Cara has another ice cream cone. The radius and the height of the second cone is known. Explain how to use these dimensions to find the outside length of the cone.

Check Understanding

1. Computer monitors are measured diagonally, from corner to corner. If the rectangular screen of a 40-inch monitor is 35 inches wide, what is the height of the monitor? Round to the nearest tenth.

____

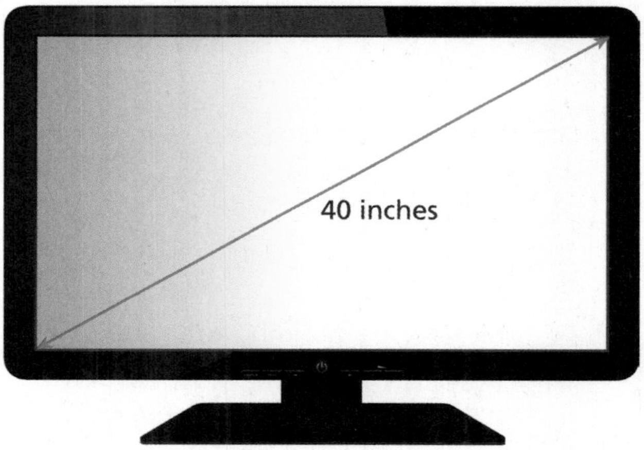

2. A 20-inch rod fits perfectly in a box 15 inches tall. What is the measurement of x in the diagram? Round to the nearest tenth.

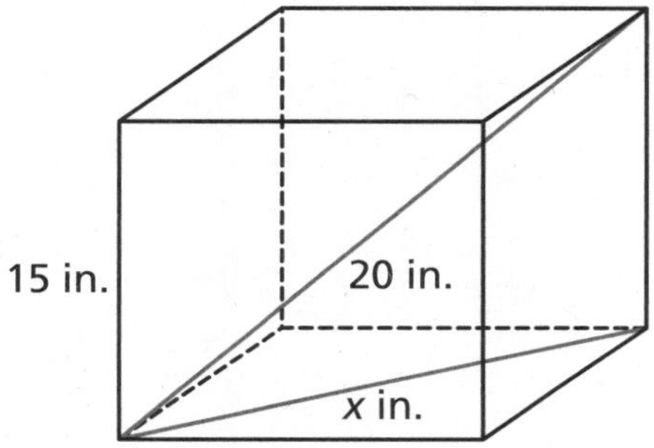

____

© Houghton Mifflin Harcourt Publishing Company • Image Credits: (t) ©Anatoly Vartanov/Alamy; (b) ©Diseñador/Fotolia

On Your Own

3. Alexa can follow the sidewalk from the library to the school or she can travel across the grass directly.

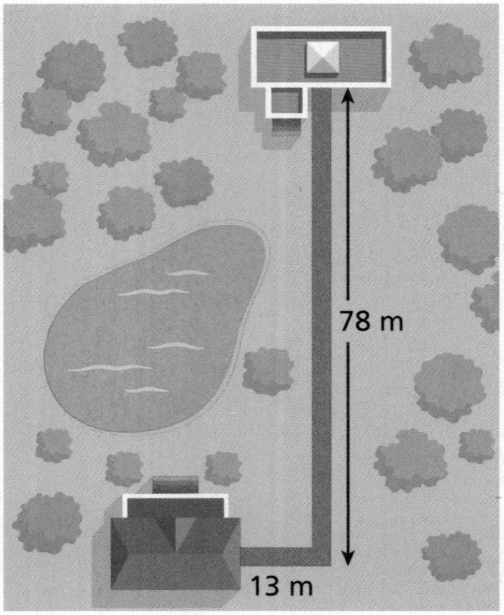

A. Which route is longer?

____

B. What is the difference between the lengths of the two routes?

____

4. Adam's closet measures 36 inches by 24 inches by 96 inches. What is the longest distance between corners inside his closet? Round to the nearest tenth.

____

5. The top of a building is a cone 10 meters tall with a radius of 4 meters at the base. What is the measurement of x in the diagram? Round to the nearest hundredth.

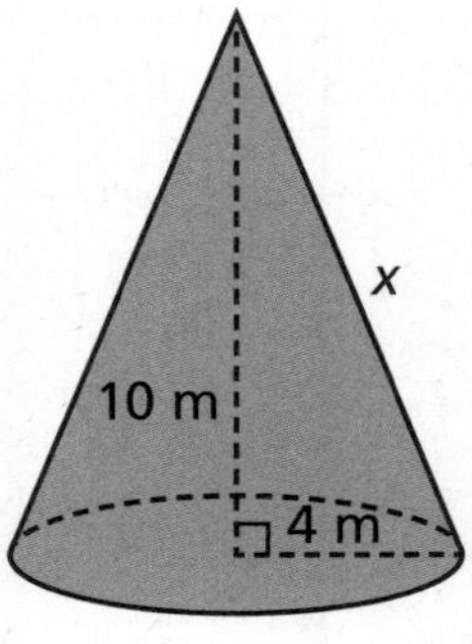

____

6. **Open Ended** Brianne purchased a box with a base diagonal length that is 45 centimeters long. What are two possible pairs of dimensions for the length and width of the box? Round to the nearest tenth.

____

____

© Houghton Mifflin Harcourt Publishing Company

For Problems 7–9, find the value for the unknown measurement in each rectangular prism or right cone. Round to the nearest tenth.

7.

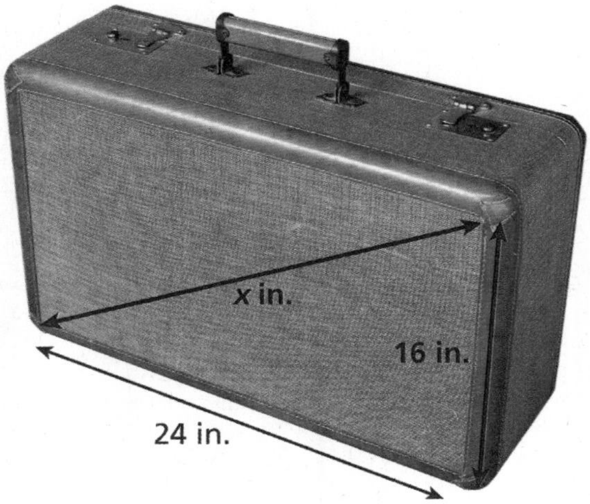

8.

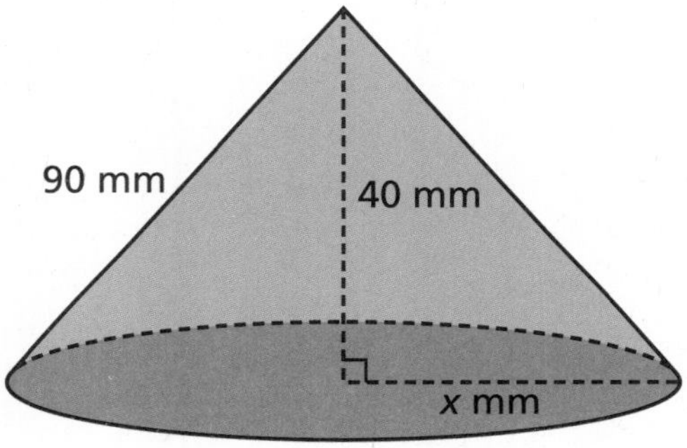

9.

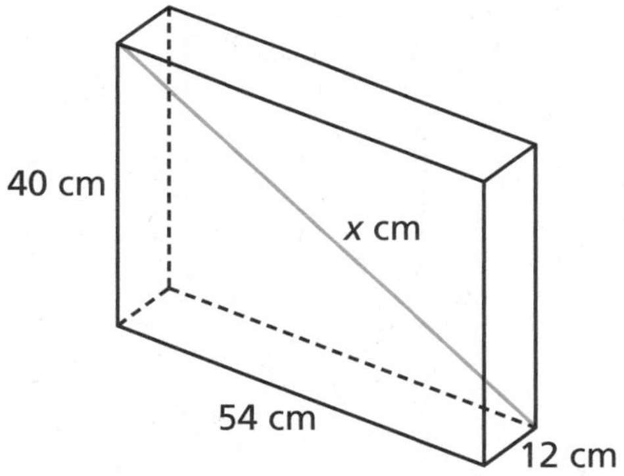

10. (MP) **Use Structure** The Maron Luggage Company claims they have a suitcase large enough to fit a 34-inch baseball bat inside. If the suitcase has height and depth 17 inches by 11 inches, what must its whole-number length be, at minimum?

© Houghton Mifflin Harcourt Publishing Company • Image Credit: ©Corbis

11. A. Which is taller, Cone *A* or Cone *B*?

	x	*y*
Cone *A*	10 cm	17 cm
Cone *B*	12 cm	18 cm

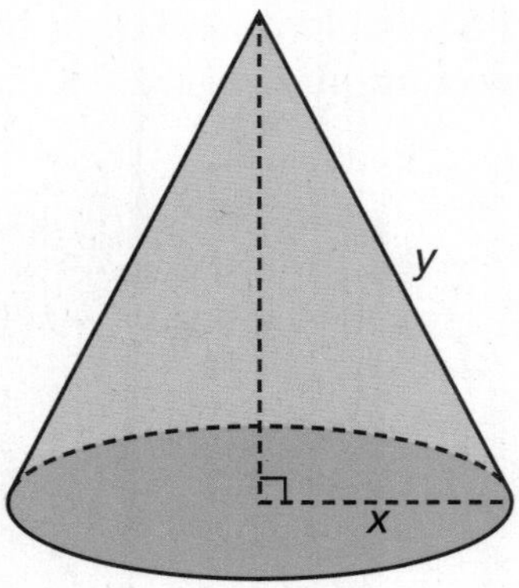

B. By how much? Round to the nearest hundredth.

12. Find the value of *x* in the diagram to the nearest tenth.

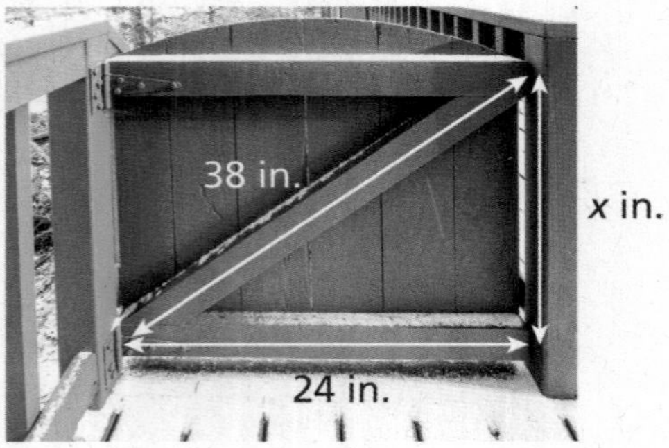

13. (MP) **Reason** What is the length of the longest rod that can fit inside this cube? Round to the nearest hundredth, and show your work.

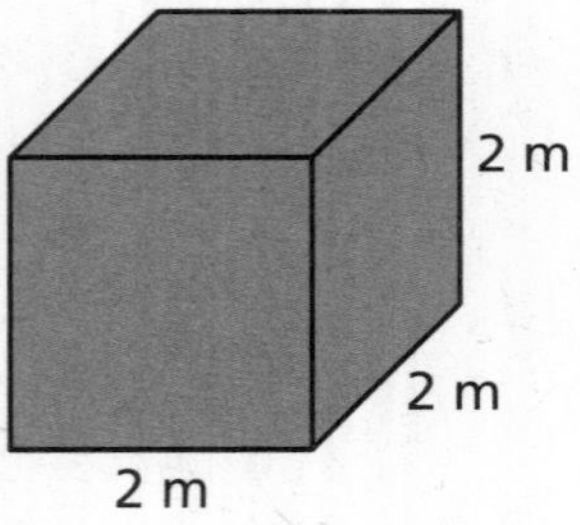

© Houghton Mifflin Harcourt Publishing Company • **Image Credit:** ©Julie Diebolt-Price/Alamy

Name

ONLINE
Video Tutorials and Interactive Examples

Apply the Pythagorean Theorem

1. The distances between Centerville, Springfield, and Capital City form a right triangle. The distance between Centerville and Springfield is 913 kilometers and the distance between Springfield and Capital City is 976 kilometers.

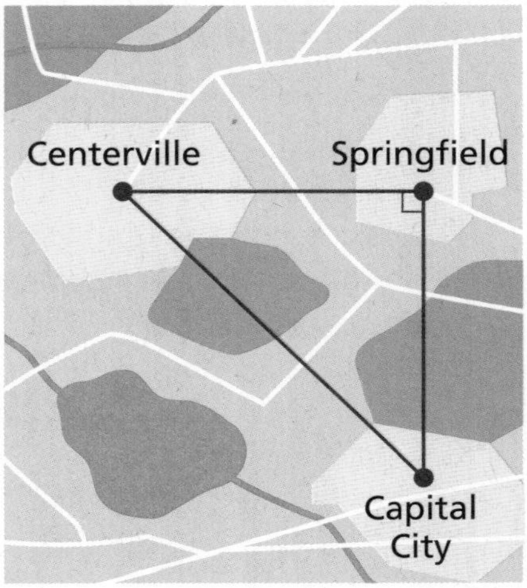

A. What is the direct distance between Centerville and Capital City? Round to the nearest kilometer.

____

B. Anwell travels from Centerville to Springfield, then on to Capital City. Yue travels directly from Centerville to Capital City. How much farther does Anwell travel than Yue? Round to the nearest kilometer.

____

2. **Math on the Spot** A child has an empty box that measures 4 inches by 6 inches by 3 inches. What is the length of the longest pencil that will fit into the box, given that the length of the pencil must be a whole number of inches? Do not round until your final answer.

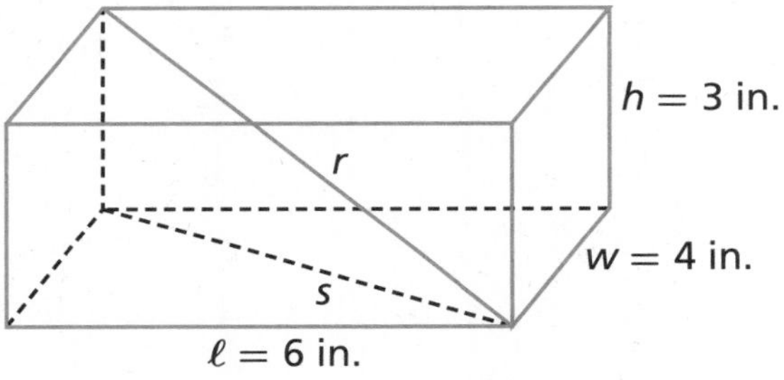

____

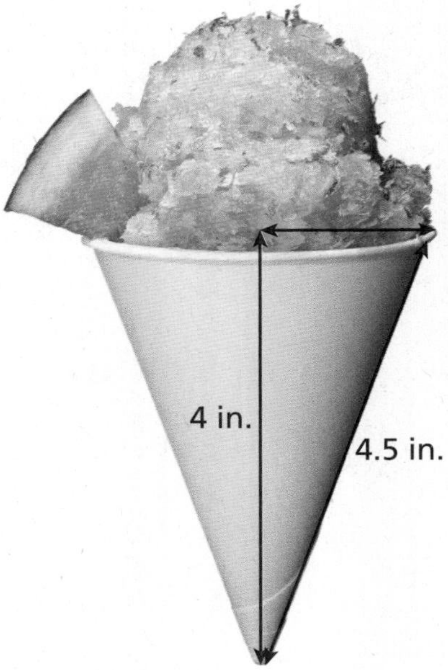

3. (MP) **Attend to Precision** Find the radius of the ice cup shown. Round to the nearest tenth.

____

4. Mr. Johnston supports a young tree by using a stake and a rope forming a right angle with the ground. What is the length of the rope? Round to the nearest tenth.

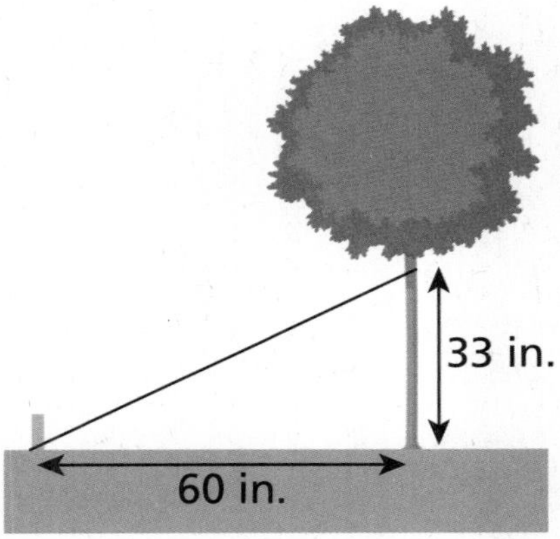

____

© Houghton Mifflin Harcourt Publishing Company • Image Credit: ©Ralph Smith/The Image Bank/Getty Images

Test Prep

5. The state of Wyoming is almost rectangular, with an approximate width of 365 miles and an approximate height of 276 miles. If you fly across the state from opposite corners, what is the best approximation of the distance you travel?

Ⓐ 448 miles
Ⓑ 450 miles
Ⓒ 458 miles
Ⓓ 462 miles

6. Calculate the length of the longest rod that can fit in a box measuring 100 centimeters by 130 centimeters by 400 centimeters. Round to the nearest tenth.

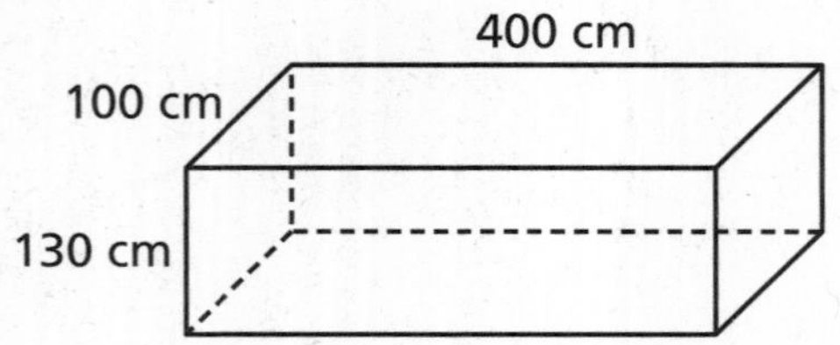

________ centimeters

7. Which set of measurements could possibly fit the given cone diagram?

Ⓐ $x = 3$, $y = 4$, $z = 5$
Ⓑ $x = 9$, $y = 6$, $z = 10$
Ⓒ $x = 3$, $y = 8$, $z = 5$
Ⓓ $x = 6$, $y = 10$, $z = 8$

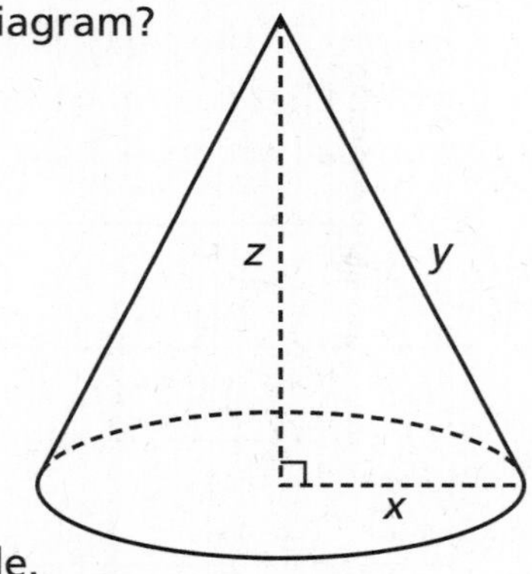

Spiral Review

8. A fun park charges $10 for admission and then $2 for every ride. Write a function that determines the amount of money spent, y, based on the number of rides ridden, x.

____

9. Reflect the triangle across the y-axis and draw the image.

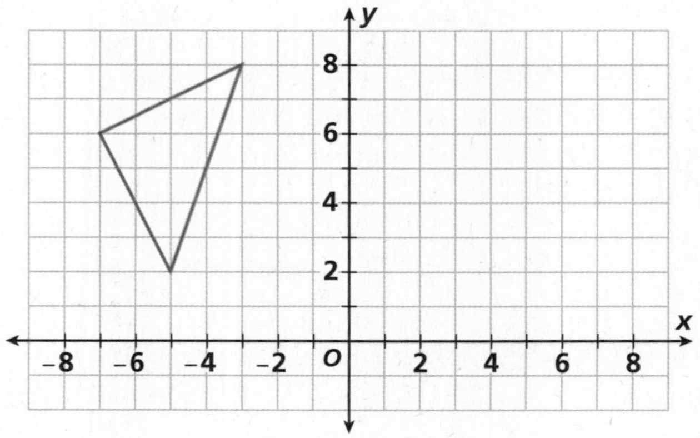

© Houghton Mifflin Harcourt Publishing Company

Name ______________________________

Apply the Pythagorean Theorem in the Coordinate Plane

I Can apply the Pythagorean Theorem to find the lengths of line segments on the coordinate plane, including line segments that are part of a composite figure.

Step It Out

ACTIVITY

1 To find the distance between two points in a coordinate system (on a coordinate plane), draw a right triangle using the horizontal and vertical lines of the grid, with the given points as endpoints of the hypotenuse. Use the Pythagorean Theorem to find the distance between the points.

A. Plot the Points $P(9, 8)$ and $Q(2, 4)$, then use a straightedge to draw a line segment between the points.

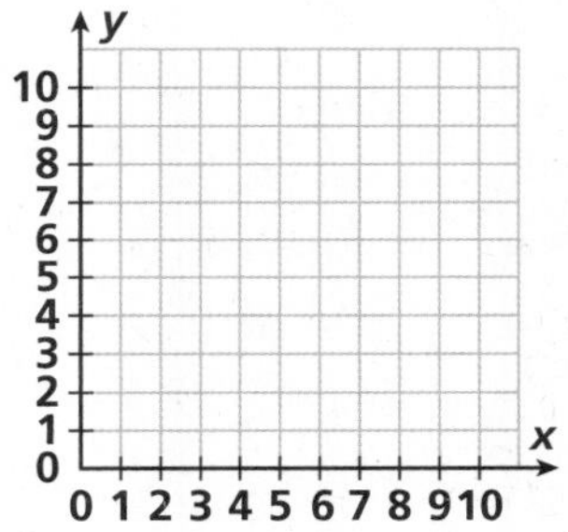

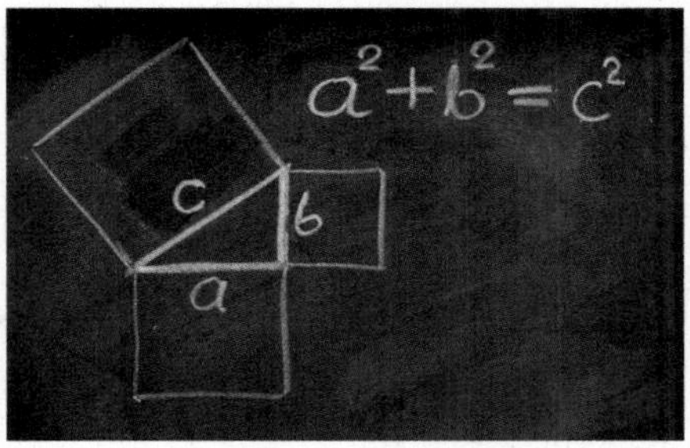

B. Use the horizontal and vertical lines of the coordinate system to draw the legs of a right triangle with Point P and Point Q as vertices.

C. Determine the lengths of the horizontal and vertical legs, then use the Pythagorean Theorem to determine the length of $\overline{PQ}$. Round to the nearest tenth.

$$a^2 + b^2 = c^2$$

$$\square^2 + \square^2 = c^2$$

$$\square + \square = c^2$$

$$\square = c^2$$

$$c = \sqrt{\square} \approx \square$$

The distance between Points P and Q is approximately ________ units.

Turn and Talk How many right triangles can you draw using a given pair of points as endpoints of the hypotenuse? Justify your reasoning.

© Houghton Mifflin Harcourt Publishing Company • Image Credit: ©marekuliasz/Shutterstock

2 The Purple Movers drew their logo on graph paper. They want to know the perimeter of the design.

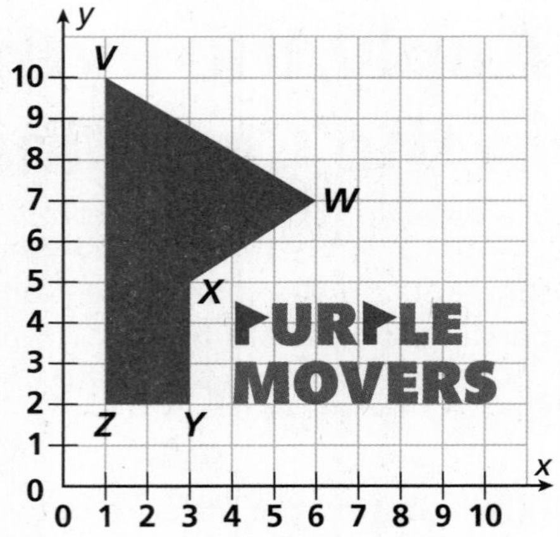

A. Complete the table with the coordinates.

Point	Coordinates
V	(1, 10)
W	
X	
Y	
Z	

B. Draw horizontal and vertical grid lines to draw the legs of a right triangle with $\overline{VW}$ as the hypotenuse. Use the Pythagorean Theorem to calculate the length of $\overline{VW}$. Round to the nearest tenth.

________ units

C. Use the same method to determine the length of $\overline{WX}$. Round to the nearest tenth.

________ units

D. What is the perimeter of the Purple Movers logo? Round to the nearest tenth.

________ units

Check Understanding

1. On the graph provided, draw a right triangle with Points *G* and *H* as endpoints of the hypotenuse. Find the distance between Points *G* and *H*. Round to the nearest tenth.

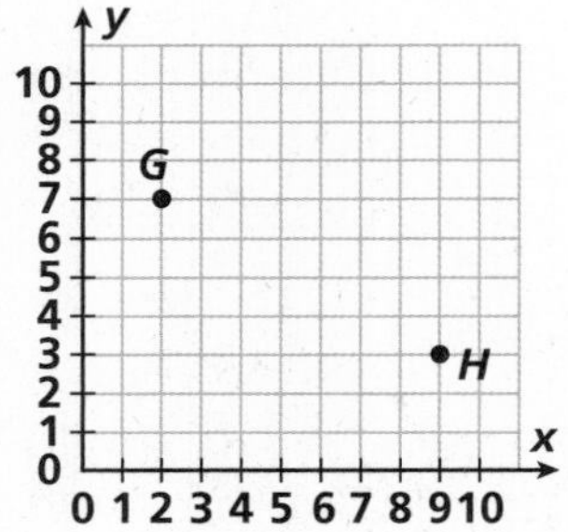

____

2. A. On your own paper, plot the points (−2, 6) and (5, −5). Find the distance between these two points. Round to the nearest tenth.

____

B. What is the perimeter of a triangle that has (−2, 6) and (5, −5) as the end points of its hypotenuse? Round to the nearest tenth.

____

3. On your own paper, plot the points (3, 60) and (−5, 45). Find the distance between these two points. Round to the nearest tenth if necessary.

____

© Houghton Mifflin Harcourt Publishing Company

Name ______

On Your Own

4. (MP) **Use Structure** The town halls of Havertville and Northtown are shown on the map. If the distance between grid lines represents 1 mile, what is the distance between the two town halls? Round your answer to the nearest tenth.

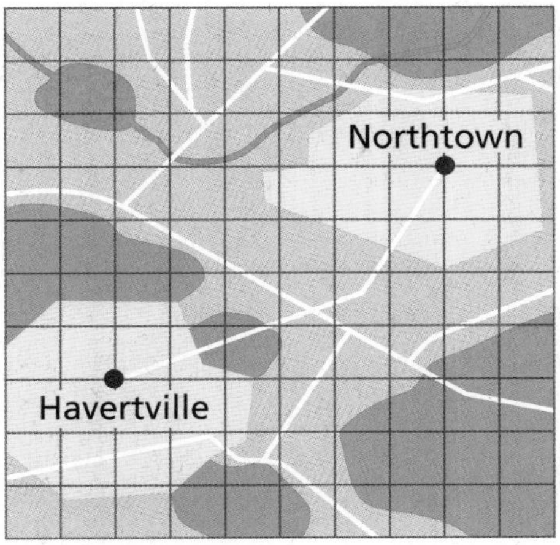

______

Use the graph to answer Problems 5–6.

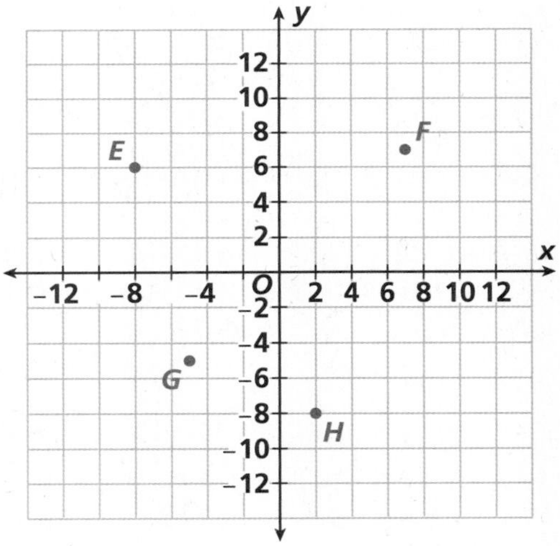

5. (MP) **Attend to Precision** Which point is exactly 10 units from (0, 0)?

______

6. What is the distance between Points *E* and *H*? Round to the nearest tenth.

______ units

7. On your own paper, graph the points (−5, 4) and (4, 2). Use the grid lines to draw a right triangle with the given points as endpoints of the hypotenuse.

A. Give two possible coordinate pairs for the third vertex.

______

B. Find the distance between the given points. Round to the nearest tenth of a unit.

______

C. Find the perimeter of the triangle to the nearest tenth of a unit.

______

© Houghton Mifflin Harcourt Publishing Company

8. (MP) **Critique Reasoning** Elena plots the points (1, −1), (1, 2), and (5, 2). She says that the length of the hypotenuse of the right triangle formed by these points, rounded to the nearest tenth, is equal to 2.6 units, and the perimeter of the triangle is 9.6 units. Is Elena correct? How do you know?

____

____

____

____

____

____

9. Georgia placed a grid over the map of the post office and the local library. The distance between grid lines is 0.5 mile.

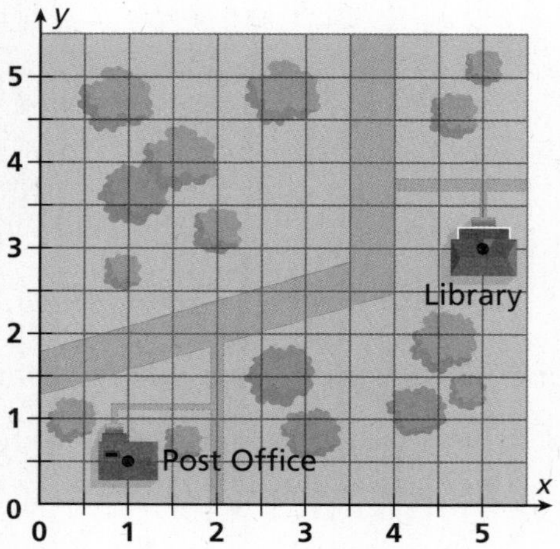

A. Give the coordinates of the post office and the library.

____

B. Find the distance between the two buildings. Round to the nearest hundredth.

____

10. Ali drew the 3-pointed star shown on the graph.

A. What is the perimeter of this 3-pointed star? Round to the nearest tenth.

____

B. Explain how you used right triangles to find the perimeter.

____

____

____

____

____

____

____

____

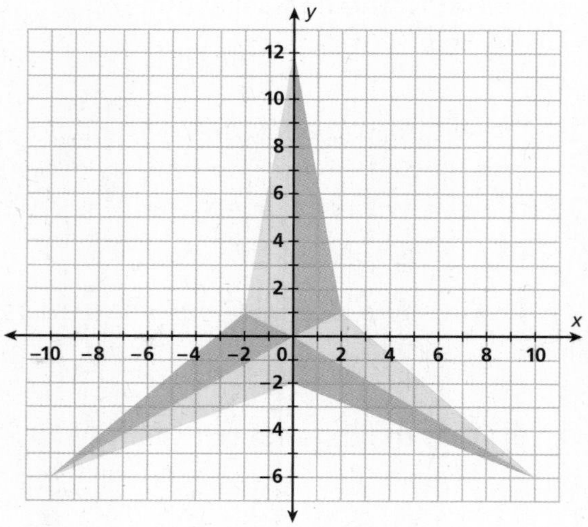

© Houghton Mifflin Harcourt Publishing Company

Name

Apply the Pythagorean Theorem in the Coordinate Plane

1. Renee takes a boat directly from the lodge to the campsite. If the distance between grid lines represents 500 feet, how far does Renee travel? Round to the nearest 10 feet.

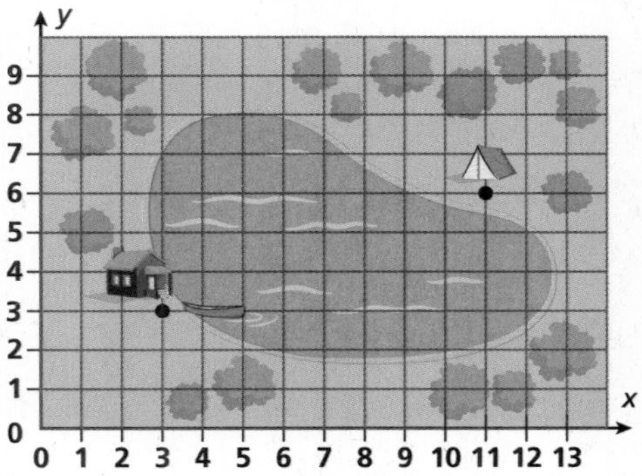

scale: 1 unit = 500 ft

2. (MP) **Use Tools** On your own paper, plot the Points $E(-2, 2)$ and $F(8, 10)$. Use the vertical and horizontal grid lines to draw a right triangle with these two points as endpoints of the hypotenuse.

A. Label the third vertex of your right triangle Point *G*. Identify two possible coordinate pairs for Point *G*.

B. What is the distance between Points *E* and *F*? Round to the nearest tenth of a unit.

C. What is the perimeter of $\triangle EFG$? Round to the nearest tenth of a unit.

3. (MP) **Use Tools** On your own paper, graph the points $(-2, -4)$ and $(4, -1)$. Use the grid lines to draw a right triangle with the given points as endpoints of the hypotenuse.

A. Give a possible coordinate pair for the third vertex.

B. What is the vertical distance between the points? What is the horizontal distance between the points?

C. Find the distance between the given points. Round to the nearest tenth of a unit.

D. What is the perimeter of the triangle you drew? Round to the nearest tenth of a unit.

© Houghton Mifflin Harcourt Publishing Company

Test Prep

4. What is the distance between Point *A* and Point *C* on Parallelogram *ABCD*?

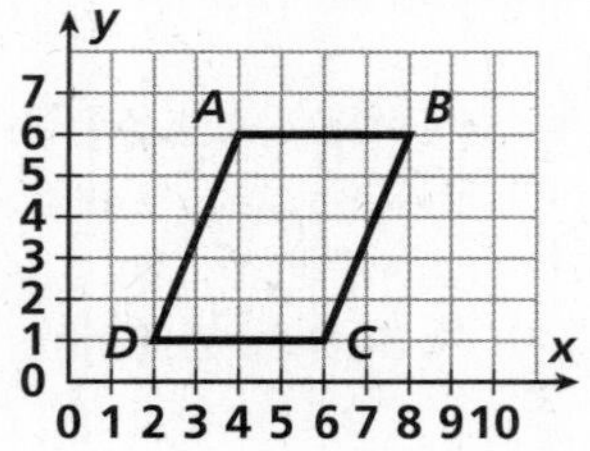

Ⓐ 4.8 units　　Ⓒ 5.2 units

Ⓑ 5 units　　Ⓓ 5.4 units

Use the graph for Problems 5–7.

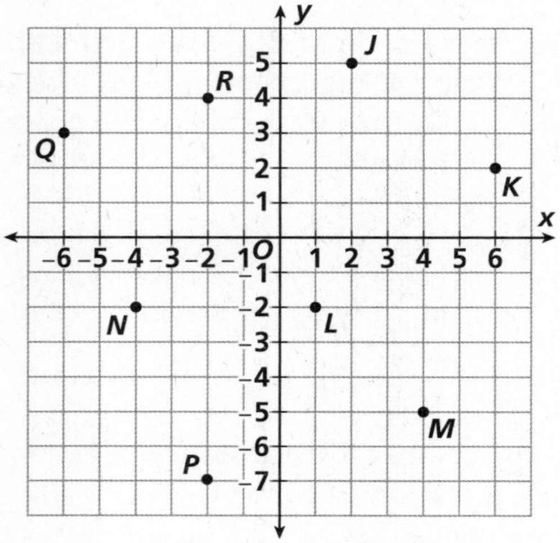

5. Which two points are exactly 5 units apart?

Ⓐ *J* and *K*　　Ⓒ *N* and *P*

Ⓑ *L* and *M*　　Ⓓ *Q* and *R*

6. How far apart are *L* and *M*?

Ⓐ 6 units　　Ⓒ $\sqrt{12}$ units

Ⓑ $\sqrt{9}$ units　　Ⓓ $\sqrt{18}$ units

7. Which two points are $\sqrt{29}$ units apart?

Ⓐ *J* and *L*　　Ⓒ *N* and *P*

Ⓑ *P* and *M*　　Ⓓ *Q* and *R*

8. What is the perimeter of Trapezoid *EFGH*?

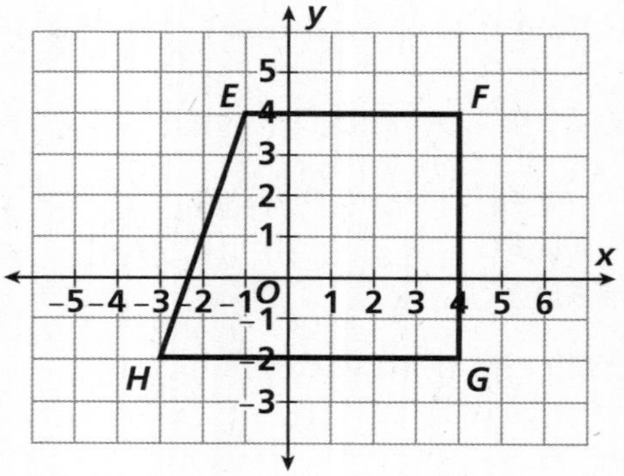

Ⓐ 24 units　　Ⓒ 25 units

Ⓑ 24.3 units　　Ⓓ 25.3 units

Spiral Review

9. Find the value of *x* that makes the equation true.
$12x = 4(x + 2) + 20$

____

10. A line has a slope of 8 and crosses the *y*-axis at (0, 12). Write an equation of the line in slope-intercept form.

____

© Houghton Mifflin Harcourt Publishing Company

Module

15 Review

Name ______________________________

Vocabulary

For Problems 1–3, choose the correct term from the Vocabulary box to complete each sentence.

Vocabulary
hypotenuse
leg
Pythagorean Theorem
Pythagorean triple

1. The ____________________ describes the relationship among the lengths of the sides of any right triangle.
2. A ____________________ of a right triangle is one of the sides that forms the right angle.
3. A ____________________ is a set of three whole numbers that could be the side lengths of a right triangle.
4. Write the converse of this statement: *If a triangle has a right angle, then it is a right triangle.*

____

Concepts and Skills

5. Which set of side lengths could form a right triangle?

   (A) 5 cm, 5 cm, and 10 cm
   (B) 6 cm, 7 cm, and 8 cm
   (C) 8 cm, 15 cm, and 17 cm
   (D) 9 cm, 12 cm, and 16 cm

6. (MP) **Use Tools** The diagram represents a set of beams that form part of a bridge support. Label $\overline{AB}$ and $\overline{BD}$ with their lengths, rounded to the nearest foot. State what strategy and tool you will use to answer the question, explain your choice, and then find the answer.

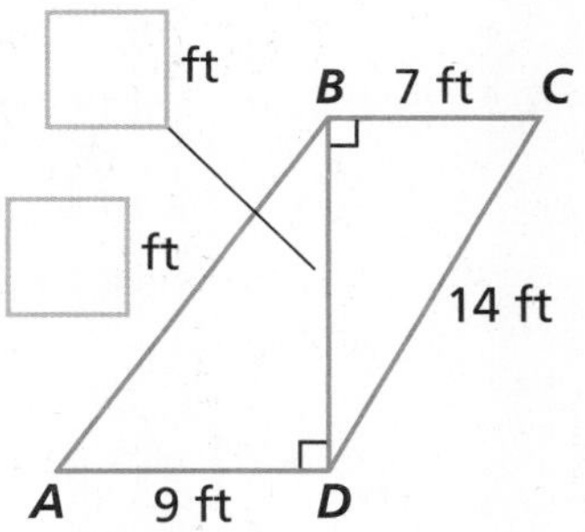

____

____

For Problems 7 and 8, determine the unknown side length of each right triangle to the nearest hundredth.

7. What is the length of $\overline{JL}$?

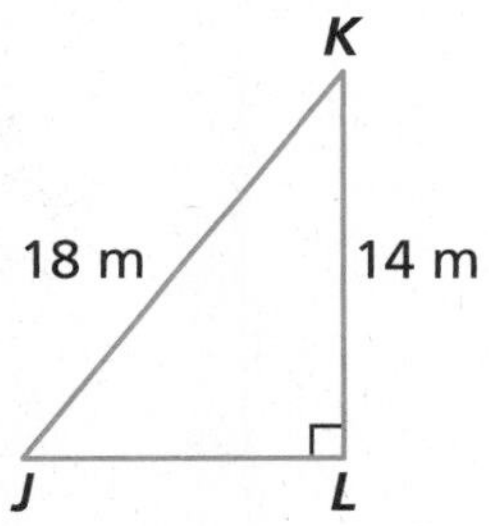

____________________ meters

8. What is the length of $\overline{ST}$?

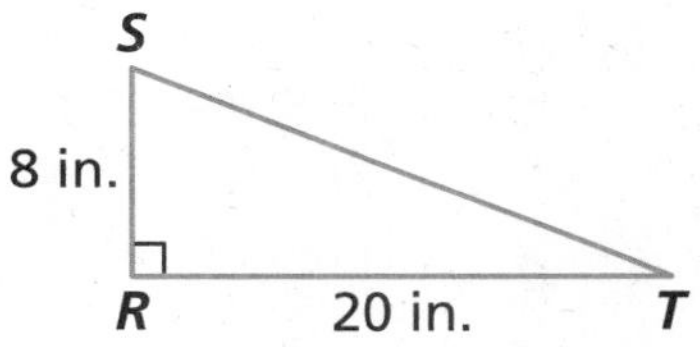

____________________ inches

© Houghton Mifflin Harcourt Publishing Company

9. The steps shown can be used to prove the Pythagorean Theorem.

Step 1: Draw a figure using two squares.

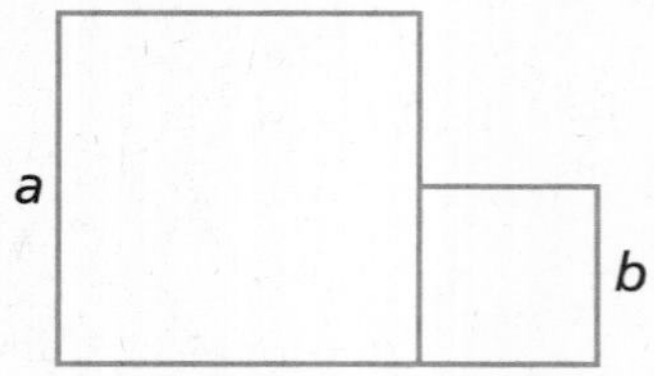

Step 2: Draw two congruent right triangles inside the figure.

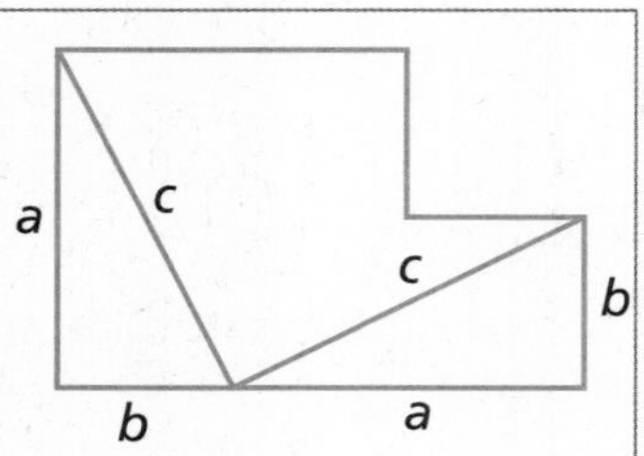

Step 3: Rotate the two triangles.

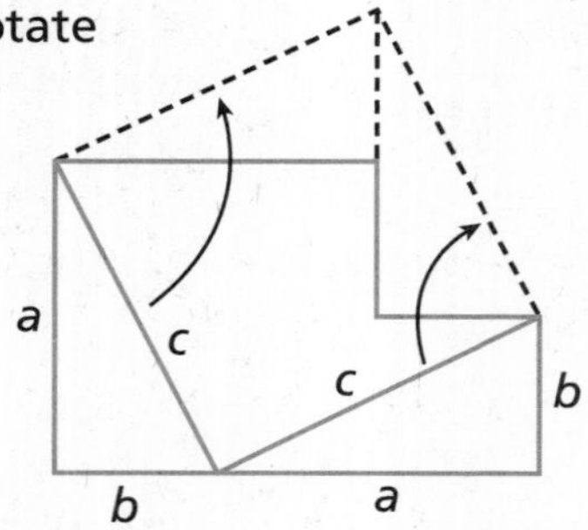

Step 4: The resulting figure is a square of side length *c*.

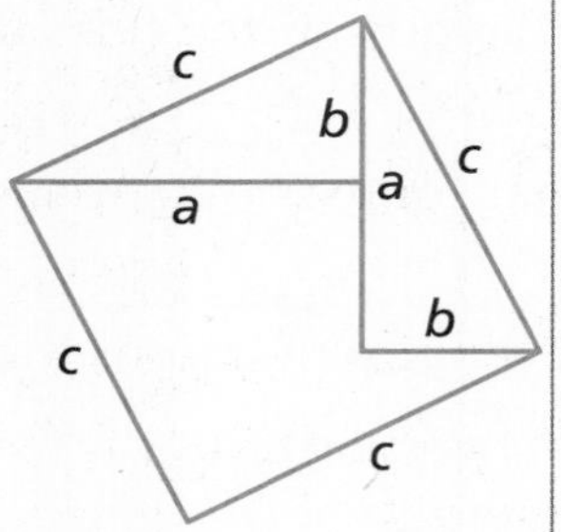

Explain how the steps prove the Pythagorean Theorem. *Hint:* Write expressions for the total area of the figures in Step 1 and in Step 4.

____

____

____

____

10. Which set of side lengths form a right triangle?

Ⓐ 3 ft, 5 ft, 12 ft

Ⓑ 5 ft, 12 ft, 13 ft

Ⓒ 12 ft, 13 ft, 16 ft

Ⓓ 13 ft, 16 ft, 24 ft

11. Meg is making a scale model of an Egyptian pyramid. The model is a right square pyramid as shown. To the nearest centimeter, what is the base length *b* of the model?

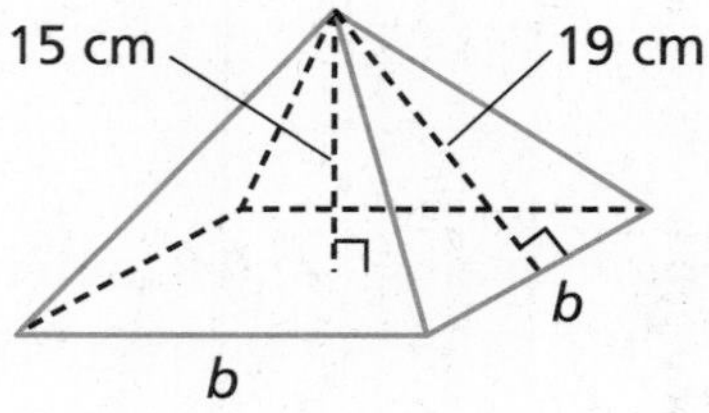

Ⓐ 12 cm

Ⓑ 16 cm

Ⓒ 23 cm

Ⓓ 48 cm

For Problems 12–14, determine the distance between the pair of points to the nearest hundredth of a unit.

12. $A(-2, 1)$ and $B(3, 5)$ ________________ units

13. $C(-5, -2)$ and $D(0, -4)$ ________________ units

14. $E(7, 3)$ and $F(-2, 6)$ ________________ units

© Houghton Mifflin Harcourt Publishing Company

Module

16 Exponents and Scientific Notation

A-Mazing Expressions

Find a path through the maze by evaluating each of the expressions shown. You can move from one space to the next only if the value of the expression in the space you are in is less than the value of the expression in the space you are moving to. You can move left, right, up, or down, but not diagonally.

START

$(4 + 2) \div 5^2$ ________	$(8 \div 10^2) + 2.3$ ________	$1.5 \times 6 - 4 \times 2$ ________
$1.8 \div 10^2$ ________	$12 - 3.8 + 4.7$ ________	$15 + (7 - 5)^3$ ________
$5 \times 71 - 340$ ________	$0.8^2 + 4^3$ ________	$(1.4 \times 10^2) \div 5$ ________
$(10 + 2)^2 - 1$ ________	2.46×10^2 ________	6.74×10^3 ________

FINISH

Turn and Talk

Explain how to determine whether you can move from 2.46×10^2 to 6.74×10^3 without performing any operations.

© Houghton Mifflin Harcourt Publishing Company

Are You Ready?

Complete these problems to review prior concepts and skills you will need for this module.

Order of Operations

For Problems 1–8, determine the value of each expression.

1. 36×10^5 ______________

2. 1.24×10^4 ______________

3. $179 \div 10^3$ ______________

4. $1.5 \div 10^2$ ______________

5. $(3.5 \times 10^3) + (4.27 \times 10^3)$ ______________

6. $(6.7 \times 10^4) - (5.82 \times 10^2)$ ______________

7. $(8.3 \times 10^3) \times (9.71 \times 10^2)$ ______________

8. $(5.52 \times 10^2) \div (4.6 \times 10^3)$ ______________

Solve Multi-Step Problems

9. At a grocery store, sliced turkey from the deli counter costs $7.92 per pound. A customer purchases 0.625 pound of sliced turkey. Excluding tax, how much change will she receive if she pays with a $20 bill?

$ ______________

10. It takes Steven 12.25 minutes to run 1.4 miles. At this rate, how long will it take him to run 2.6 miles?

______________ minutes

11. An account with $600 earns 4% simple interest per year. The next year all the money is put into a new account that earns 4.5% simple interest per year. How much money does the account have at the end of the second year? Explain.

____

____

____

12. Anthony has two cube-shaped pots with an interior edge length of 8 inches and two cube-shaped pots with an interior edge length of 6.5 inches. He wants to fill each pot full of potting soil. His bag of potting soil is one cubic foot. How much soil will he have left after he fills each pot full of soil?

____

© Houghton Mifflin Harcourt Publishing Company

Name ____________________

Know and Apply Properties of Exponents

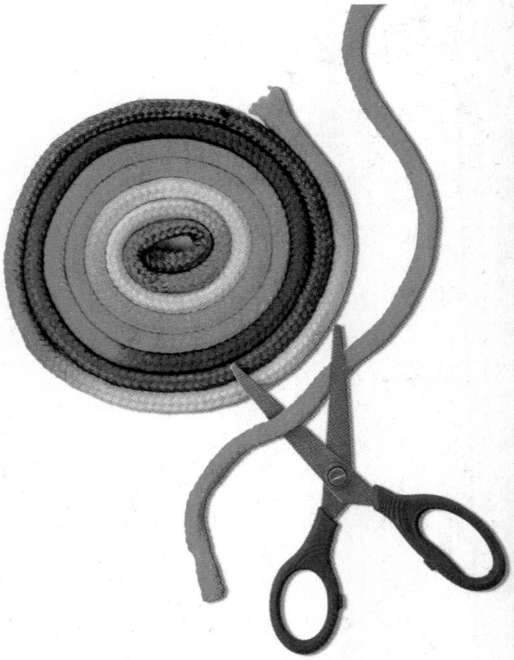

I Can **use properties of integer exponents to simplify expressions.**

Spark Your Learning

SMALL GROUPS

Alex has a rope that is 2^4, or 16 feet long. He folds the rope in half and cuts it, so he now has two pieces of rope that are each 2^3, or 8 feet long. Alex then folds each of the new pieces in half and cuts them, so he now has four pieces of rope that are each 2^2, or 4 feet long. Alex repeats this process until his pieces of rope are each 1 foot long. What would happen if Alex took each 1-foot section of rope and continued this process? What pattern do you notice?

© Houghton Mifflin Harcourt Publishing Company • Image Credit: ©Betsy Hansen/Houghton Mifflin Harcourt

Turn and Talk Look for patterns in how these pairs are related: 2^{-3} and 2^3, 2^{-2} and 2^2, 2^{-1} and 2^1. What generalization can you make about a^{-b}, where a and b are natural numbers (1, 2, 3,...)?

Build Understanding

1 The patterns in the Spark Your Learning lead to the following two properties of exponents.

If $a \neq 0$ and b is an integer, then $a^{-b} = \frac{1}{a^b}$.

If $a \neq 0$, then $a^0 = 1$.

Connect to Vocabulary

In the **power** 2^4, 2 is the **base** and 4 is the **exponent**.
The **properties of exponents** are rules for operations with exponents.

A. You can look for patterns to develop the product of powers property for multiplying powers with the same base. Complete the table.

Product of powers	Factors	Single power
$3^2 \cdot 3^4$	$(3 \cdot 3) \cdot (3 \cdot 3 \cdot 3 \cdot 3)$	3^6
$7^3 \cdot 7^2$		
$2^4 \cdot 2^3$		

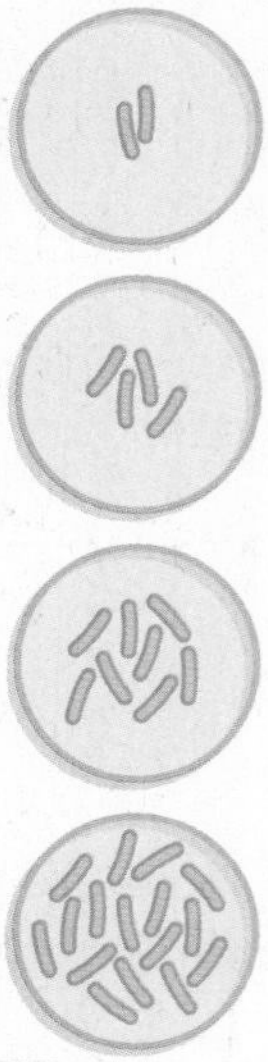

$2^1 = 2$

$2^2 = 4$

$2^3 = 8$

$2^4 = 16$

B. How are the exponents in the left column and the exponent in the right column related?

____

____

C. You also can look for patterns to develop the quotient of powers property for dividing powers with the same base. Complete the table.

Quotient of powers	Factors	Single power
$\frac{2^7}{2^4}$	$\frac{\cancel{2} \cdot \cancel{2} \cdot \cancel{2} \cdot \cancel{2} \cdot 2 \cdot 2 \cdot 2}{\cancel{2} \cdot \cancel{2} \cdot \cancel{2} \cdot \cancel{2}}$	2^3
$\frac{6^5}{6^3}$		
$\frac{5^8}{5^2}$		

D. How are the exponents in the left column and the exponent in the right column related?

____

____

E. Make a conjecture about two additional properties of exponents based on your findings.

____

____

Turn and Talk Can you use the properties of exponents you discovered to simplify $5^2 \cdot 2^5$? If so, how? If not, why not?

© Houghton Mifflin Harcourt Publishing Company

Name ______________________

Step It Out

2 In 2002, a high school student broke the record for folding a sheet of paper in half multiple times. When the paper was opened, the number of regions formed was $(2^4)^3$. How many times did the student fold the paper? To answer, you can develop the power of a power property.

A. First look for patterns using specific examples of a power of a power. Complete the table.

Power of powers	Expanded form	Factors	Single power
$(5^2)^3$	$5^2 \cdot 5^2 \cdot 5^2$	$(5 \cdot 5) \cdot (5 \cdot 5) \cdot (5 \cdot 5)$	5^6
$(7^4)^2$			
$(8^3)^2$			
$(4^3)^3$			

B. How are the exponents in the far-left column and the exponent in the far-right column related?

The ______________ of the exponents in the far-left column equals the ______________ in the far-right column.

C. Complete the conjecture about a property of exponents based on your findings:

If $a \neq 0$, then $\left(a^{\square}\right)^{\square} = a^{\square}$.

D. The number of regions formed by the high school student's folded paper was $(2^4)^3$. Use a single exponent to write this expression.

$(2^4)^3 = 2^{\square}$

E. How many times did the student fold the paper in half?

The student folded the paper _____ times. This is because 1 fold results in $2^{\square}$ regions, 2 folds results in $2^{\square}$ regions, and so on.

Continuing the pattern shows that _____ folds results in $\square^{12}$ regions.

Turn and Talk Does the property of exponents you discovered apply to negative powers? For example, can you use it to simplify $(7^{-2})^2$? Explain.

© Houghton Mifflin Harcourt Publishing Company • Image Credit: ©nacroba/Shutterstock

3 Simplify each expression.

A. $2^4 \cdot 2^9$

$= 2^{\square + \square}$ Apply the product of powers property.

$= 2^{\square}$ Add the exponents.

$=$ ______ Simplify.

B. $3^3 \cdot 3^{-5}$

$= 3^{\square + \square}$ Apply the product of powers property.

$= 3^{\square}$ Add the exponents.

$= \dfrac{\square}{\square}$ Write the power without a negative exponent.

$=$ ______ Simplify.

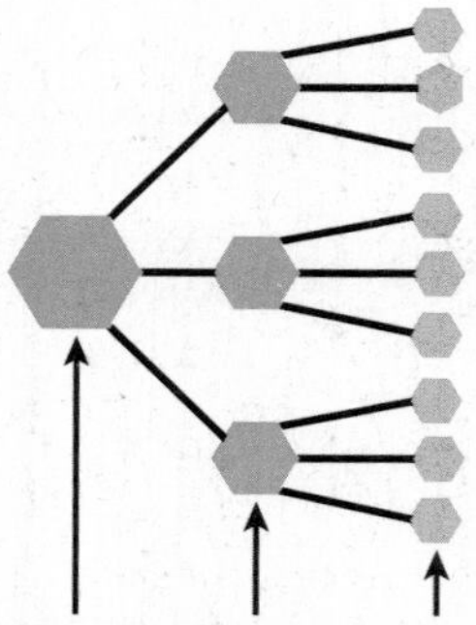

C. $(4 + 8)^0$

$= \square^{0}$ Simplify within parentheses.

$=$ ______ Simplify.

D. $\dfrac{(5^2)^5}{5^6}$

$= \dfrac{\square}{\square}$ Apply the power of powers property in the numerator.

$= \square^{\square}$ Apply the quotient of powers property.

$=$ ______ Simplify.

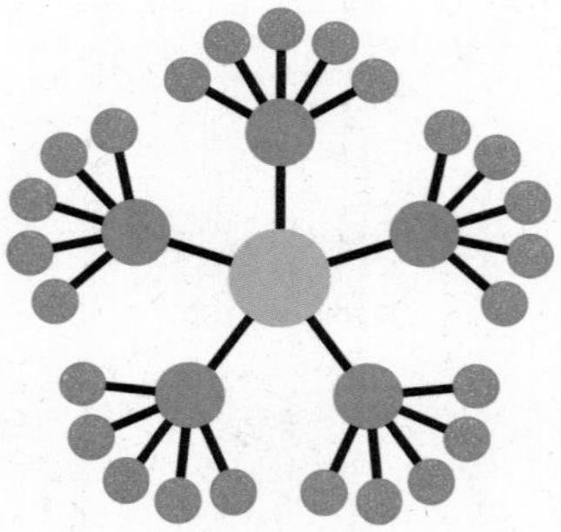
Powers of 5

Check Understanding

1. If $a \neq 0$, what is the value of $a^m \cdot a^{-m}$? How do you know?

____

2. Simplify $3^0 - 3^4 \cdot 3^{-5}$. Show your work and write the result as a fraction.

____

© Houghton Mifflin Harcourt Publishing Company

Name

On Your Own

3. **STEM** According to one estimate, the number of stars in the Milky Way Galaxy is about $10^2 \cdot 10^3 \cdot 10^6$.

A. Write the number of stars in the Milky Way Galaxy as a single power. Which property of exponents did you use?

____

B. Write the estimated number of stars in the Milky Way Galaxy without using exponents.

____

4. The formula for the volume V of a cube with edge length s is $V = s^3$. The formula for the surface area A of the cube is $A = 6s^2$.

A. A cube has edges of length 2 centimeters. Write expressions using exponents for the volume of the cube (in cubic centimeters) and for the surface area of the cube (in square centimeters).

____

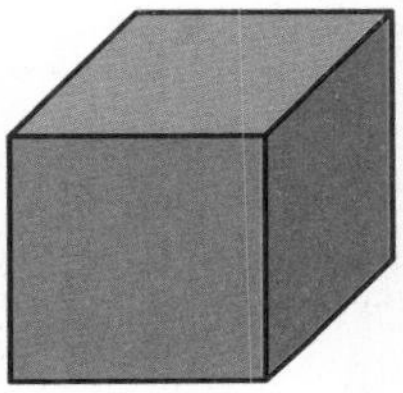

s

B. (MP) **Reason** What is the ratio of the cube's volume to its surface area? Use the expressions you wrote in Part A and show how to simplify the ratio. Show your work and name any properties of exponents you use.

For Problems 5–7, use the table shown.

Description	Distance (m)
Distance from the Sun to Saturn	$(10^2)^6$
Diameter of the Solar System	$10^5 \cdot 10^8$
Diameter of Saturn	$((10^2)^2)^2$
Diameter of the disc of the Milky Way	$\frac{10^{23}}{10^2}$

5. What is the greatest distance shown? Write it as a power of 10 with a single exponent.

____

6. What is the least distance shown? Write it as a power of 10 with a single exponent.

____

7. The distance from Earth to the star Vega is approximately 10^{17} meters. Which of the distances in the table, if any, are less than this?

____

____

© Houghton Mifflin Harcourt Publishing Company • Image Credit: ©Alex Mit/Shutterstock

8. **Open Ended** Write an expression involving two or more operations and three or more powers of 5 that can be simplified to $\frac{1}{5}$.

9. (MP) **Use Repeated Reasoning** You can look for patterns to develop the power of a product property.

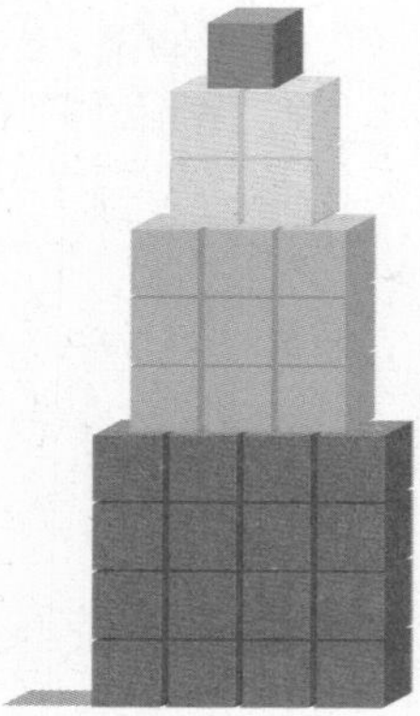

A. Complete the table.

Power of product	Factors	Product of powers
$(4 \cdot 3)^2$	$(4 \cdot 3) \cdot (4 \cdot 3) = (4 \cdot 4) \cdot (3 \cdot 3)$	$4^2 \cdot 3^2$
$(2 \cdot 9)^2$		
$(5 \cdot 8)^3$		

B. Look for patterns in the table. State a property of exponents based on what you observe.

C. Show two different ways to simplify the expression $(3 \cdot 2)^5$.

For Problems 10–13, simplify each expression. Write your answer without using exponents.

10. $3^2 \cdot 3^0 \cdot 3^4$

11. $\frac{4^6 \cdot 4^{-2}}{4^5}$

12. $\frac{2^5}{(2^2)^5}$

13. $8^0 + 8^6 \cdot 8^{-4}$

© Houghton Mifflin Harcourt Publishing Company

I'm in a Learning Mindset!

What is challenging about solving a problem involving exponents? Can I work through it on my own, or do I need help?

Name

LESSON 16.1
More Practice/
Homework

ONLINE
Video Tutorials and Interactive Examples

Know and Apply Properties of Exponents

Problems 1–2 involve crayon production.

1. According to one crayon manufacturer, the average number of crayons produced in its factories each day is greater than $\frac{10^4 \cdot 10^6}{10^3}$.

   A. Write the number of crayons as a single power of 10. Which property or properties of exponents did you use?

   B. Write the number of crayons without using exponents.

2. One of the boxes produced by the crayon manufacturer contains $2^2 \cdot 2^0 \cdot 2^4$ crayons. How many crayons are in the box?

3. Katie and Lawrence collect guitar picks. Katie has $(2^2)^4$ guitar picks in her collection. Lawrence has $(3^2)^2$ guitar picks in his collection. Who has more guitar picks? How many more?

4. (MP) **Reason** Simplify $3^0 + 3^4 \cdot 3^{-6}$. Show your work and explain your steps.

For Problems 5–8, simplify each expression.

5. $8^{-1} \cdot 8^{-5} \cdot 8^3$

6. $4^3 \cdot 4^{-4} \cdot 4^2$

7. $\frac{9^{-2} \cdot 9^7}{9^3}$

8. $\frac{[6^3]^5}{6^{18}}$

© Houghton Mifflin Harcourt Publishing Company • Image Credit: ©William Thomas Cain/Stringer/Getty Images

Test Prep

9. Which expression is equivalent to $3^2 \cdot 3^{-8} \cdot 3^0$?

(A) $\frac{1}{3^6}$

(B) $\frac{1}{3^{-6}}$

(C) 3^6

(D) 3^0

10. Draw a line to match each expression to its value.

$\frac{4^2 \cdot 4^{-4}}{4^3}$	$\frac{1}{1,024}$
$4^2 \cdot 4^8 \cdot 4^{-7}$	$\frac{1}{256}$
$\frac{4^6}{4 \cdot 4^3}$	1
$4^{-2} \cdot 4^2 \cdot 4^{-4}$	16
$\frac{4^3 \cdot 4^0}{4^2 \cdot 4}$	64

11. What is the value of the expression $(-2 + 9)^5 \cdot (4 + 3)^{-3} + 7^0$?

(A) $\frac{1}{343}$

(B) $1\frac{1}{49}$

(C) 49

(D) 50

Spiral Review

12. Miguel keeps track of whether or not he brought an umbrella with him to work and whether or not it actually rained that day. He collects the data and makes the two-way relative frequency table shown.

	Rain	No rain	TOTAL
Umbrella	0.2		
No umbrella		0.47	
TOTAL	0.35		

A. Complete the two-way relative frequency table.

B. On what percent of the days did Miguel bring an umbrella? Which value in the table gives you this information?

13. If the domain of the function $y = 2x - 6$ is $2 < x < 8$, what is the function's range?

© Houghton Mifflin Harcourt Publishing Company

Name ______________________________

Understand Scientific Notation

I Can use scientific notation to describe very large or very small quantities and to compare quantities.

Step It Out

1 What does one trillion dollars look like? If you could stack one trillion one-dollar bills, the stack would be about 68,000 miles tall. This is more than one-fourth the distance from the Earth to the moon!

The **standard,** or **decimal, form** of a number is one way to write numbers. It uses the base-ten system to show all of a number's digits. For example, the way to write one trillion in standard form is 1,000,000,000,000.

There is a shorthand way, called **scientific notation**, to write large numbers without so many zeros. 1,000,000,000,000 in scientific notation is 1×10^{12}.

A. To write 68,000 miles in scientific notation, first move the decimal point to the left to get a number that is greater than or equal to 1 but less than 10.

68,000.

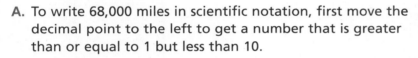

The decimal point moves ________ places to the left.

Remove the extra zeros to get the first factor for scientific notation: ________.

B. Use this factor and a power of 10 to write the number in scientific notation.

$68{,}000 =$ ________ $\times 10^{\square}$

When you write a number in scientific notation, its value does not change.

C. Write one billion, 1,000,000,000, in scientific notation.

$1{,}000{,}000{,}000 =$ ________ $\times 10^{\square}$

Connect to Vocabulary

Scientific notation is a method of writing very large or very small numbers by using powers of 10. In scientific notation, a number is written as the product of two factors. The first factor is greater than or equal to 1 but less than 10, and the second factor is a power of 10.

Turn and Talk Is the number 16×10^7 written in scientific notation? Why or why not?

© Houghton Mifflin Harcourt Publishing Company • Image Credit: ©Alamy

2 You can also use scientific notation for very small numbers. The thickness of a dollar bill is about 0.0043 inches. Write this quantity in scientific notation.

A. First move the decimal point to the right to get a number that is greater than or equal to 1 but less than 10.

0.0043 The decimal point moves _______ places to the right.

Remove the extra zeros to get the first factor: _______.

B. Since 0.0043 is less than 1, you moved the decimal point to the right, so the exponent in the power of 10 will be negative.

$0.0043 =$ _______ $\times 10^{\square}$

3 In 2016, the United States Mint produced about 9.1×10^9 pennies. Write this quantity in standard form.

A. Use the power of 10 to determine how many places you will need to move the decimal point.

Move the decimal point _______ places.

B. Write the number with placeholder zeros. Then move the decimal point to the right the appropriate number of places.

9.100000000 So, $9.1 \times 10^9 =$ _______________.

4 Scientific notation makes it easy to compare quantities.

2016 Half-Dollar Production	
Denver Mint	2.1×10^6
All U.S. mints	4.2×10^6

A. The table shows the number of half-dollar coins produced in 2016. Use a ratio to compare these quantities.

$\frac{4.2 \times 10^6}{2.1 \times 10^6}$

The powers of 10 are the same: $\frac{10^6}{10^6} = 10^0$ or _______.

Compare the first factors: $\frac{\square}{2.1} =$ _______.

So, the total number of half-dollar coins minted is about $\square \cdot \square =$ _______ times the number of half-dollar coins minted in Denver.

Turn and Talk Why is scientific notation a good way to express very large or very small numbers that you are estimating?

© Houghton Mifflin Harcourt Publishing Company • Image Credits: (t) ©Stephen Hilger/Bloomberg/Getty Images; (b) ©Getty Images

Name ____________________

B. Use the ratio $\frac{3.45 \times 10^{-8}}{3.45 \times 10^{-11}}$ to compare 3.45×10^{-8} and 3.45×10^{-11}.

First compare the powers of 10.

$\frac{\square}{10^{-11}} = 10^{\square} =$ ______

Compare the first factors: $\frac{\square}{3.45} =$ ______.

So, 3.45×10^{-8} is $\square \cdot \square =$ ______ times as great as 3.45×10^{-11}.

C. Use a ratio to compare 4.8×10^{9} and 12,000,000.

Write 12,000,000 in scientific notation. 12,000,000 = ______

Compare the powers of 10. Compare the greater power to the lesser power.

$\frac{10^{9}}{\square} = 10^{\square} =$ ______

Compare the first factors: $\frac{4.8}{\square} =$ ______.

So, 4.8×10^{9} is ______ $\times$ ______ $=$ ______ times as great as 12,000,000.

D. Use a ratio to compare 0.00222 and 66,600.

In scientific notation, 0.00222 = ______.

In scientific notation, 66,600 = ______.

66,600 is ______ $\times$ ______ $=$ ______ times as great as 0.00222.

Check Understanding

1. Which number is greater: 8.9×10^{5} or 2.1×10^{7}? How can you tell without writing the numbers in standard notation?

______

2. Write 0.000501 in scientific notation.

______

3. Write 5.31×10^{3} in standard form.

______

© Houghton Mifflin Harcourt Publishing Company • Image Credit: ©LAMB/Alamy

On Your Own

4. The photo shows a road sign in western Australia.

A. Write the distance to Rome in scientific notation.

____

B. Write the distance to Sydney in scientific notation.

____

C. (MP) **Reason** Explain how you can use the scientific notation version of the distances to determine whether it is farther to Rome or to Sydney.

____

____

5. **STEM** The diameter of a carbon atom is approximately 0.000000017 centimeter.

A. When the diameter is expressed in scientific notation, will the exponent be positive or negative? How do you know?

____

B. Write the diameter in scientific notation. Show your work and explain your steps.

For Problems 6–7, use the table which shows the number of miles on the odometers of several cars.

Car	Miles
A	7.51×10^4
B	6.03×10^3
C	1.1×10^5
D	4×10^4
E	8.9×10^3

6. Write the number of miles on Car A's odometer in standard form.

____

7. (MP) **Attend to Precision** Nicole wants to buy a used car with fewer than 50,000 miles on the odometer. Which of the cars shown should Nicole consider? Explain.

____

____

© Houghton Mifflin Harcourt Publishing Company • Image Credit: ©ENP/Alamy

Name

For Problems 8–9, use the table of bridge lengths shown.

Bridge	Length (ft)
Atchafalaya Basin	9.6×10^4
General W.K. Wilson Jr.	3.2×10^4
Manchac Swamp	1.2×10^5
Frank Davins Memorial	2.9×10^4

8. Which of the bridges shown is the longest? How do you know?

9. How many times as long as General W.K. Wilson Jr. Bridge is Atchafalaya Basin Bridge? Explain.

10. STEM A geologist is comparing two rock samples. Sample A has a mass of 0.0015 gram. Sample B has the mass shown on the scale.

A. Write the masses in scientific notation.

B. How many times as great as the mass of Sample A is the mass of Sample B? Show your work.

11. MP **Use Tools** Most calculators display scientific notation when a result is longer than the number of digits the screen can display.

A. To find out how your calculator displays scientific notation, enter 2^{40} and press the ENTER key. What does the calculator display? What number in scientific notation does it represent?

B. Write the value of 2^{40} rounded to the nearest trillion.

© Houghton Mifflin Harcourt Publishing Company • Image Credits: ©Fedorov Ivan Sergeevich/Shutterstock; ©Guy Jarvis/Houghton Mifflin Harcourt

12. (MP) **Reason** What must be true about the exponent when you write a whole number between 1 and 10 in scientific notation? Why? Give an example.

For Problems 13–16, write each number in scientific notation.

13. 47,100,000

14. 6,004

15. 0.0000000009

16. 0.00053

For Problems 17–20, write each number in standard form.

17. 3.2×10^8

18. 5.111×10^2

19. 1.06×10^{-3}

20. 7.7×10^{-9}

For Problems 21–24, determine which number is greater and tell how many times as great.

21. 2×10^5 and 8×10^9

22. 3.9×10^4 and 1.3×10^{-1}

23. 24,000,000 and 2.4×10^{10}

24. 1.5×10^{-6} and 0.0063

25. Social Studies The Smithsonian Institution in Washington, D.C., is the world's largest museum, with approximately 15.4×10^7 artifacts. Explain why this number is not written in scientific notation and show how to write it correctly.

© Houghton Mifflin Harcourt Publishing Company • **Image Credit:** ©Andriy Kravchenko/Alamy

Name ______________________

LESSON 16.2
More Practice/ Homework

ONLINE
Video Tutorials and Interactive Examples

Understand Scientific Notation

1. A group of researchers in Hawaii estimated that the number of grains of sand on Earth is 7,500,000,000,000,000,000. Write this number using scientific notation.

____

2. A snail moves across a table at a rate of 0.00093 mile per hour. Write this rate in scientific notation.

____

3. Math on the Spot The approximate population of Brazil in 2008 is shown. Write this number in standard form.

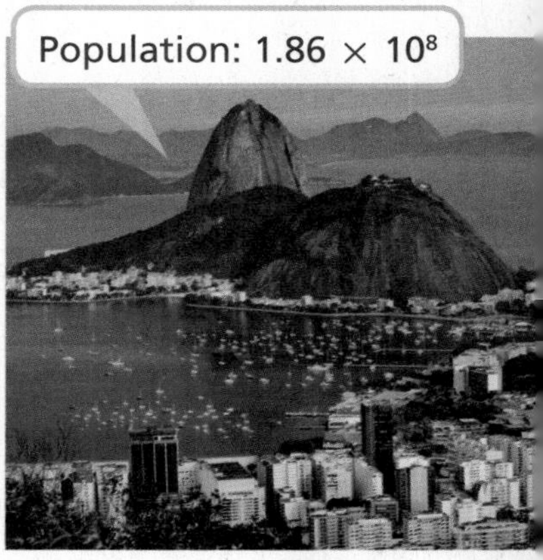

____

For Problems 4–7, write each number in scientific notation.

4. 239,000,000,000

5. 405

6. 0.0000101

7. 0.00000000000006

For Problems 8–11, write each number in standard form.

8. 5.5×10^5

9. 6.07×10^7

10. 2.04×10^{-4}

11. 4×10^{-6}

For Problems 12–14, determine which number is greater and tell how many times as great.

12. 7×10^{12} and 3.5×10^9

____

13. 1.4×10^{-5} and 2.8×10^{-4}

____

14. 16,000 and 1.6×10^8

____

15. Open Ended Write two numbers in scientific notation so that the second number is 10 times as great as the first number.

____

© Houghton Mifflin Harcourt Publishing Company • Image Credit: ©Adam G. Gregor/Alamy

Test Prep

16. Kendrick wants to write the number 0.000065 in scientific notation. What exponent should he use for the power of 10?

Ⓐ −5
Ⓑ −4
Ⓒ 4
Ⓓ 5

17. Jenna collected data about the number of annual visitors to two sports blogs. The table shows the data. The number of visitors to Sports Space is ______ times the number of visitors to Team Zone.

Blog	Annual visitors
Sports Space	4.8×10^5
Team Zone	12,000

Ⓐ 4
Ⓑ 40
Ⓒ 400
Ⓓ 4,000

18. What is 5.003×10^3 written in standard form?

Ⓐ 0.0005003
Ⓑ 0.005003
Ⓒ 5,003
Ⓓ 5,003,000

19. Which of the following numbers is greatest?

Ⓐ 6.1×10^7
Ⓑ 8.9×10^6
Ⓒ 55,000,000
Ⓓ 9,070,000

Spiral Review

20. The figure shows the dimensions of a rectangular city park. A member of the parks commission is considering a new diagonal path that would cut through the park from *A* to *C*. If the path is built, how much shorter would it be to walk along the path from *A* to *C* rather than walking along the edge of the park from *A* to *C*? Explain.

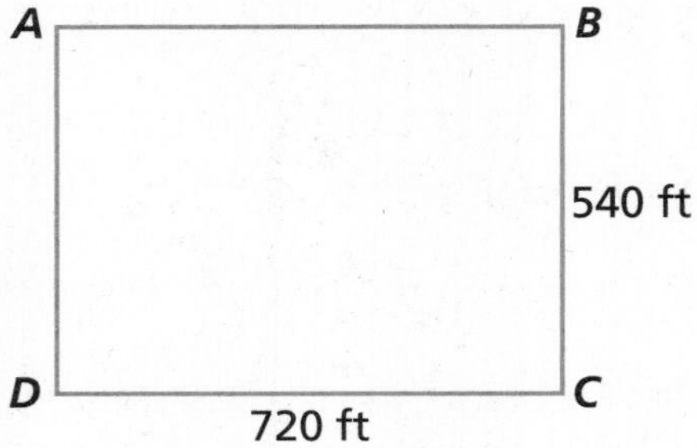

____

____

____

21. What is the height of the cone shown? Round to the nearest tenth of a centimeter.

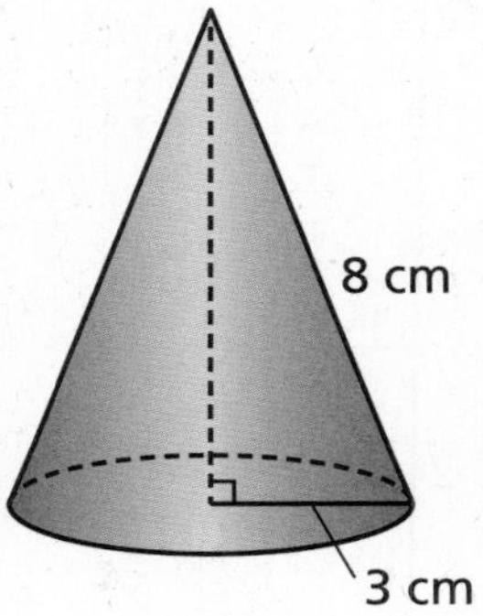

____

22. Simplify the expression $7^0 + \frac{7^2}{(7^3)^2}$.

____

© Houghton Mifflin Harcourt Publishing Company

Name ______________________________

Compute with Scientific Notation

I Can **compute with numbers in scientific notation and choose appropriate units for very large or small quantities.**

Step It Out

1 You can add and subtract with scientific notation to analyze the data in the table.

National Park Visitors, 2016	
Park	**Visitors**
Great Smoky Mountains	1.13×10^7
Grand Canyon	5.97×10^6
Yellowstone	4.26×10^6

A. How many more people visited Grand Canyon National Park than Yellowstone National Park?

To add or subtract with scientific notation, first express the quantities with the same power of 10. These data have the same power of 10.

Use the Distributive Property:
$5.97 \times 10^6 - 4.26 \times 10^6 = (5.97 - 4.26) \times 10^6$

Subtract the first factors: 5.97 − ______ = ______.

Express the difference with the same power of 10.

______ $\times 10^6$ more people, or ________ more people, visited Grand Canyon National Park than Yellowstone National Park.

B. What was the total number of visitors to Great Smoky Mountains National Park and Grand Canyon National Park?

Since the numbers are written with different powers of 10, we need to rewrite one so they have the same power of 10. To do this, multiply the first factor by 10 and divide the power of 10 by 10.

$1.13 \times 10^7 = (1.13 \times 10) \times (10^7 \div 10) =$ ______ × ______

Now add the first factors: ______ + ______ = ______.

Express the sum with the same power of 10: ______ $\times 10^6$.

To write your answer in scientific notation, determine how to write the first factor as a number between 1 and 10. In this case, divide 17.27 by 10. To keep the value the same, multiply 10^6 by 10 to get 10^7.

______ $\times 10^6 =$ ______ $\times 10^7$

Turn and Talk How could you solve the problem in Part B by rewriting the quantity for the Grand Canyon rather than the Great Smoky Mountains?

© Houghton Mifflin Harcourt Publishing Company • Image Credit: ©Leonid Serebrennikov/Alamy

2 You can multiply or divide numbers in scientific notation by multiplying or dividing the first factors and multiplying or dividing the powers of 10.

A. Find $(3.3 \times 10^{-4}) \times 500$. Write your answer in scientific notation.

$$(3.3 \times 10^{-4}) \times 500 = (3.3 \times 10^{-4}) \times \left(5 \times 10^{\square}\right)$$

$$= (3.3 \times 5) \times \left(10^{-4} \times 10^{\square}\right)$$

$$= \_\_\_\_\_\_ \times 10^{\square}$$

Rewrite the product in scientific notation.

$$16.5 \times 10^{-2} = \_\_\_\_\_\_ \times 10^{\square}$$

B. Find $(8.864 \times 10^{15}) \div (1.6 \times 10^{4})$. Write your answer in scientific notation.

$$(8.864 \times 10^{15}) \div (1.6 \times 10^{4}) =$$

$$(8.864 \div \_\_\_\_\_\_) \times \left(10^{15} \div 10^{\square}\right)$$

$$= \_\_\_\_\_\_ \times 10^{\square}$$

C. Many calculators have a key labeled EE that allows you to enter values in scientific notation. The display may look like scientific notation with the "$\times$ 10" replaced. For example, 4.1×10^{9} may appear as 4.1E9.

Use a calculator to check your answer to Part B. Write the quotient as it appears on your calculator. Then write it in scientific notation.

____

Turn and Talk How could you find the product in Part A of Task 2 without first writing 500 in scientific notation?

Check Understanding

Add or subtract. Express your answer in scientific notation.

1. $(5.7 \times 10^{8}) + (3.2 \times 10^{6})$

____

2. $(1.3 \times 10^{-4}) - (7.5 \times 10^{-5})$

____

Multiply or divide. Express your answer in scientific notation.

3. $(2.8 \times 10^{7}) \times (3.5 \times 10^{-3})$

____

4. $(7.2 \times 10^{12}) \div (3 \times 10^{5})$

____

© Houghton Mifflin Harcourt Publishing Company • Image Credit: ©Betsy Hansen/Houghton Mifflin Harcourt

Name

On Your Own

For Problems 5–7, use the data shown about the average number of vehicles per day crossing each bridge. Express your answers in scientific notation.

Golden Gate Bridge

San Francisco-Oakland Bay Bridge

5. Find the total average number of vehicles per day crossing the bridges.

6. How many more vehicles cross the San Francisco-Oakland Bay Bridge each day than the Golden Gate Bridge, on average?

7. (MP) **Use Structure** What is the average number of vehicles that cross each bridge in one year?

8. **STEM** A typical *Escherichia coli* (or *E. coli*) bacterial cell is about 7.9×10^{-5} inch long. Suppose you could line up *E. coli* cells, end to end, across a Petri dish with a diameter of 2 inches. About how many cells would fit across the dish? Explain your method.

For Problems 9–10, a ream of paper contains 500 sheets. A case of paper contains 10 reams.

9. An office supply store gets a delivery of 400 cases. How many sheets of paper are in the delivery? Express your answer in scientific notation.

10. A ream of paper is 4.5×10^{-2} meter thick.

A. (MP) **Use Tools** Use a calculator to find the thickness of a single sheet of paper. Write your answer in scientific notation.

B. Express the answer to Part A using a more appropriate unit of length.

© Houghton Mifflin Harcourt Publishing Company • Image Credits: (t) ©Ian Dagnall/Alamy Images; (b) ©Markus Mainka/Alamy

11. About how many sesame seeds are in one gram of sesame seeds?

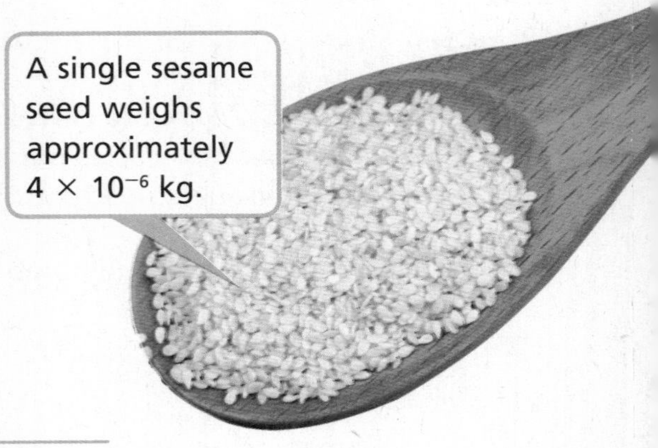
A single sesame seed weighs approximately 4×10^{-6} kg.

____

12. **Open Ended** Write two numbers in scientific notation so that all of the following are true.
- Both numbers are greater than 1×10^2.
- Both numbers are less than 1×10^6.
- The product of the two numbers is 5×10^6.

____

13. (MP) **Reason** New Zealand consists of hundreds of islands. Most of the population lives on the North Island, which has an area of 1.14×10^5 square kilometers, and the South Island, which has an area of 151,000 square kilometers. The North Island and South Island make up almost all of New Zealand's area.

A. Which island has a greater area? How many square kilometers greater is it? Express your answer in scientific notation.

____

B. The combined population of the North and South islands is about 4.8×10^6. Find the approximate combined population density in people per square kilometer, rounded to the nearest unit. Explain your steps.

____

____

____

____

14. (MP) **Critique Reasoning** Tim was asked to find the difference of 5.9×10^7 and 2.4×10^7. His work is shown here. Did he find the difference correctly? If so, name the mathematical properties he used. If not, explain his error and find the correct difference.

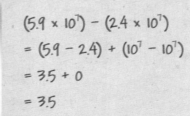

$(5.9 \times 10^7) - (2.4 \times 10^7)$
$= (5.9 - 2.4) + (10^7 - 10^7)$
$= 3.5 + 0$
$= 3.5$

____

____

____

____

15. The top speed at which a Galapagos tortoise can travel is 3×10^{-1} km/h. At its top speed, how far does the tortoise travel in one minute? Use an appropriate unit of length for your answer.

____

© Houghton Mifflin Harcourt Publishing Company • Image Credit: ©Stepan Popov/Alamy

Name

ONLINE
Video Tutorials and Interactive Examples

Compute with Scientific Notation

1. School District A has 5.6×10^5 students. School District B has 2.5×10^5 students. What is the total number of students in the two school districts?

The mass of a typical aphid is shown in the photo. The mass of a typical worker ant is 3×10^{-6} kilogram. Use this information to answer Problems 2–3. Use a calculator to verify your answers.

Aphid mass: 2×10^{-7} kg

2. What is the combined mass of an aphid and a worker ant?

3. How much greater is the mass of a worker ant than the mass of an aphid?

4. (MP) **Attend to Precision** A factory produces boxes of paper clips that each contain 2.5×10^2 paper clips. Every hour, the factory produces 8,000 boxes. Assuming the factory operates 24 hours per day, how many paper clips are produced in one week? Express your answer in scientific notation.

5. **Math on the Spot** The table shows the approximate surface areas for three oceans given in square meters. What is the total surface area of these three oceans? Write the answer in scientific notation using more appropriate units.

Ocean	Atlantic	Indian	Arctic
Surface area (m^2)	7.68×10^{13}	6.86×10^{13}	1.41×10^{13}

Add or subtract. Express your answer in scientific notation.

6. $(7.7 \times 10^6) - (2.5 \times 10^6)$

7. $(3.9 \times 10^4) + (7.5 \times 10^5)$

8. $(5.22 \times 10^{-2}) + (3.85 \times 10^{-3})$

9. $(1.4 \times 10^{-7}) - (4.4 \times 10^{-8})$

Multiply or divide. Express your answer in scientific notation.

10. $(7.2 \times 10^4) \times (1.8 \times 10^3)$

11. $(8.4 \times 10^{-5}) \div (4.2 \times 10^{-6})$

12. $(4.1 \times 10^{12}) \times (3.5 \times 10^{-7})$

13. $(5.2 \times 10^{-3}) \div (4 \times 10^6)$

© Houghton Mifflin Harcourt Publishing Company • Image Credit: ©Design Pics Inc./Alamy

Test Prep

14. Draw a line to match each expression with its correct value.

$(2 \times 10^4) + (2 \times 10^3)$ •	• 1×10^1
$(2 \times 10^4) - (2 \times 10^3)$ •	• 2.2×10^4
$(2 \times 10^4) \times (2 \times 10^3)$ •	• 4×10^7
$(2 \times 10^4) \div (2 \times 10^3)$ •	• 1.8×10^4

The table shows the total seasonal attendance for four soccer teams. Use the table to answer Problems 15–17.

Team	Seasonal attendance
Aviators	2.3×10^4
Wranglers	16,000
Barracudas	8.9×10^3
Manatees	20,200

15. What was the combined seasonal attendance for the Aviators and the Wranglers?

Ⓐ 2.46×10^4 attendees

Ⓑ 3.9×10^4 attendees

Ⓒ 3.68×10^8 attendees

Ⓓ 3.9×10^8 attendees

16. How much greater was the Wranglers' seasonal attendance than the Barracudas' seasonal attendance? Write your answer in scientific notation.

____

17. The Aviators' season consisted of 8 games. What was the average attendance per game? Express your answer in scientific notation and in standard form.

____

Spiral Review

18. Ava wants to use $\triangle PQR$ to prove the Pythagorean Theorem. She draws $\overline{QT}$ as shown. She starts her proof by identifying three similar triangles in the figure and writing proportions based on their side lengths. Complete the proportions.

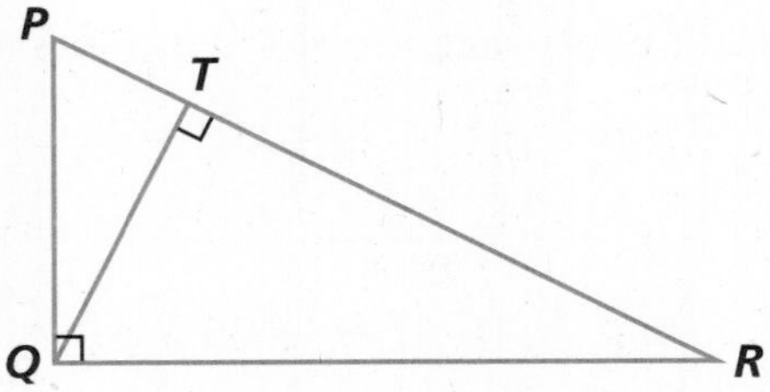

$\frac{QR}{TR} = \frac{PR}{\square}$ $\frac{QP}{TP} = \frac{PR}{\square}$

19. Use the Pythagorean Theorem to find the distance between the points (2, 3) and (−1, −2). Round to the nearest tenth.

____

20. Order the values from least to greatest: $(3 + \sqrt{5})$, π, $\frac{5}{2}$, $(6 + \sqrt{2})$, $-\sqrt{16}$.

____

© Houghton Mifflin Harcourt Publishing Company

Module 16

Name ______________________

Review

Vocabulary

In Problems 1–3, complete each sentence with the correct operation to explain the properties of exponents.

1. To raise a power to a power, keep the base the same and ______________ the exponents.

2. To divide two powers with the same base, keep the base the same and ______________ the exponents.

3. To multiply two powers with the same base, keep the base the same and ______________ the exponents.

4. What is the difference between the standard form of a number and the number written in scientific notation?

____

____

____

____

Concepts and Skills

5. (MP) **Use Tools** Write an expression with a single exponent that is equivalent to $8^{-4} \cdot (8^2)^4$. State what strategy and tool you will use to answer the equation, explain your choice, and then find the answer.

____

____

6. Compare each expression to 6^6.

	Less than 6^6	Greater than 6^6	Equal to 6^6
$(6^{-1} \cdot 6^4)^2$	☐	☐	☐
$\frac{6^8}{(6^2)^2}$	☐	☐	☐
$\left(\frac{6^2}{6^0}\right)^4$	☐	☐	☐

7. Select all the expressions equivalent to $\frac{9^3 \cdot 9^5}{9^2}$.

Ⓐ 3^8

Ⓑ 3^{12}

Ⓒ 9^6

Ⓓ 9^4

Ⓔ 27^2

Ⓕ 27^4

© Houghton Mifflin Harcourt Publishing Company

8. What are possible values for a and b in the equation $\frac{4^a}{4^b} = 4^{-1}$? What must be true about the values of a and b?

$a =$ ________ $b =$ ________

____

9. The diameter of Earth is about 1×10^4 kilometers, and the diameter of a basketball is about 2×10^{-4} kilometer. About how many times as great is the diameter of Earth as the diameter of a basketball?

Ⓐ 5,000 times as great
Ⓑ 50,000 times as great
Ⓒ 50,000,000 times as great
Ⓓ 500,000,000 times as great

10. A bee hummingbird has a mass of 0.0023 kilogram. What is the mass of a bee hummingbird written in scientific notation?

________ kilogram

11. Naomi says that 9.8×10^5 is greater than 3.2×10^6. Is Naomi correct? Explain your reasoning.

____

____

____

____

12. Which expression is equivalent to $\frac{(8 \times 10^3) + (4 \times 10^3)}{(3 \times 10^{-2})}$?

Ⓐ 4×10^1
Ⓑ 4×10^4
Ⓒ 4×10^5
Ⓓ 4×10^8

13. What is the difference between 8.5×10^{-4} and 2.8×10^{-4}, written in standard form?

____

14. Mount Everest is growing at a rate of about 1.1×10^{-5} meter per day. Express this rate using units of a more appropriate size, and explain why the units you chose are more appropriate.

____

____

____

____

15. An elephant has a mass of 4,500 kilograms. How many mice, with a mass of 2×10^{-2} kilogram each, would it take to equal the mass of the elephant?

Write your answer in standard form. ________ mice

© Houghton Mifflin Harcourt Publishing Company

Unit 6

Area and Volume

Data Analyst

STEM POWERING INGENUITY

A data analyst helps companies make good business decisions by collecting, analyzing, and storing data. The data may be related to sales, market research, costs, errors, or just about anything. A data analyst looks for patterns and trends in the data and then presents the results in a meaningful way.

STEM Task:

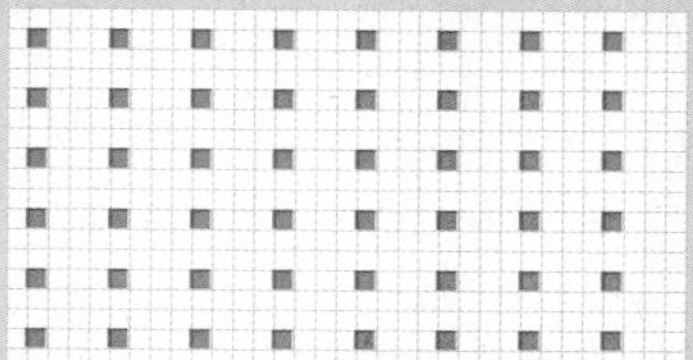

A rectangular electronic game board is 16.5 inches by 12 inches. It includes a grid with 8 rows of 8 squares, each 0.5 inch on a side. When you aim a laser at any of the red squares, data are collected on the accuracy of the hits. What are the ratios of (a) the area of one square to the area of the board, and (b) the combined area of the squares to the area of the board? Explain.

© Houghton Mifflin Harcourt Publishing Company • Image Credit: ©triloks/Getty Images

Learning Mindset

Perseverance Learns Effectively

Perseverance is the ability to stick with a task until it is complete. But it can be difficult to persevere when a task seems too big or complicated. If you feel overwhelmed by a task, try dividing it into smaller, easier steps. Here's how:

- Identify the end goal of the task. Then work backward. What do you need to do before you can reach the end goal? What do you need to do before that? And before that?
- Alternatively, start by identifying just the first step. Sometimes completing the first step will help you see the second step.
- Each step should be specific and small enough to feel achievable. If a step feels overwhelming, break it down into even smaller steps.

Reflect

Q **What steps were involved in completing the STEM Task?**

Q **Can you compute a ratio from the STEM Task more efficiently by refining how you used an area formula? Explain.**

© Houghton Mifflin Harcourt Publishing Company • Image Credit: ©PeopleImages/iStock/Getty Images Plus/Getty Images

Module

17 Analyze Figures to Find Circumference and Area

What Comes Next in the Pattern?

The figures shown are squares, non-square rectangles, and triangles.

Find the area of each figure in square centimeters. Look for patterns.

A.

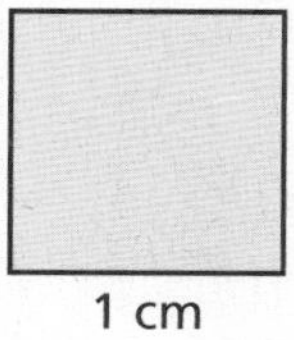

_______ cm^2

B.

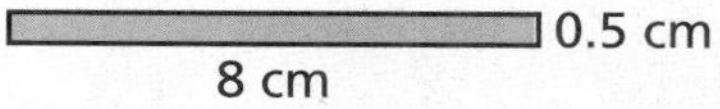

_______ cm^2

C.

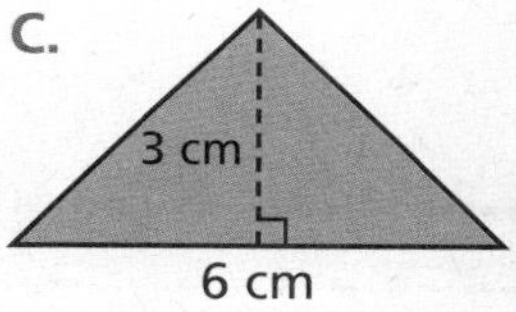

_______ cm^2

D.

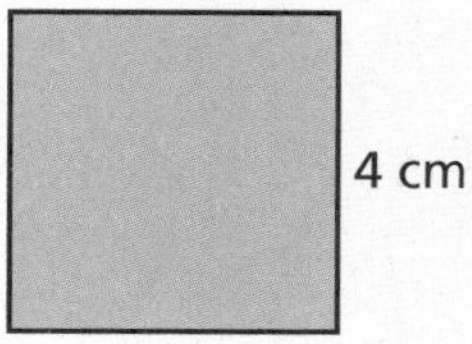

_______ cm^2

E.

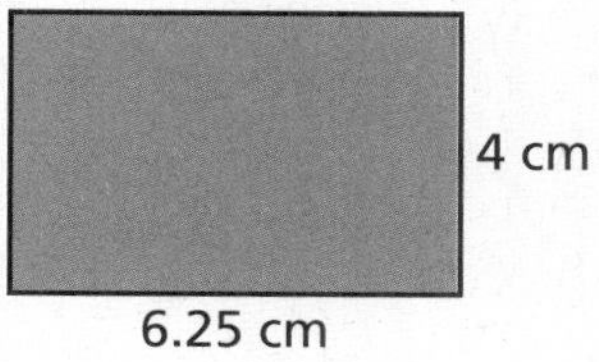

_______ cm^2

F.

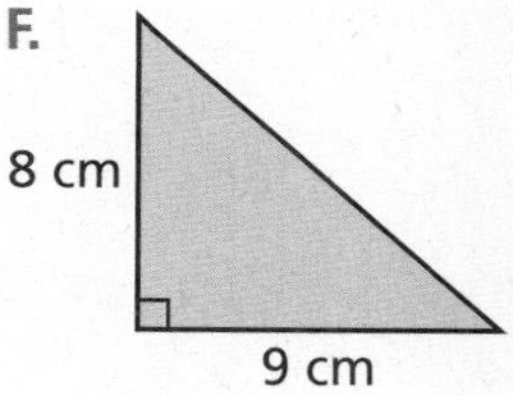

_______ cm^2

Turn and Talk

If the pattern continues, what three figures will appear in the next row? What will the areas of the figures be? Explain.

© Houghton Mifflin Harcourt Publishing Company • Image Credit: ©Nenov/iStock/Getty Images Plus/Getty Images

Are You Ready?

Complete these problems to review prior concepts and skills you will need for this module.

Solve One-Step Equations

Solve the equation.

1. $\frac{x}{2} = 5$ for x ________ **2.** $2w = \frac{10}{3}$ for w ________ **3.** $\frac{h}{20} = \frac{5}{4}$ for h ________

Evaluate Algebraic Expressions

Evaluate each given expression for $n = -3$.

4. $4n + n$ ________ **5.** $-n + n^2$ ________ **6.** $3 - n^2$ ________

Area of Quadrilaterals and Triangles

7. What is the area of a rectangle that has a base of 5 centimeters and a height of 2 centimeters?

____

8. What is the area of a square with a side length of 2.5 feet?

____

9. What is the area of the triangle shown?

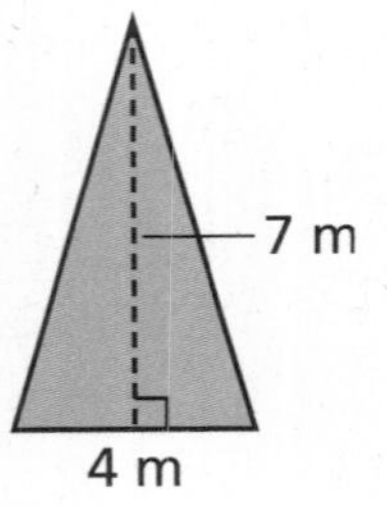

____

10. What is the area of the parallelogram shown?

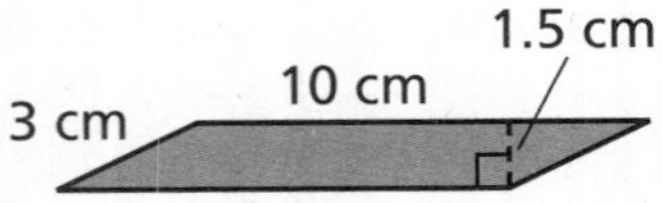

____

© Houghton Mifflin Harcourt Publishing Company

Name ______________________________

Derive and Apply Formulas for Circumference

I Can **find the circumference of a circle when I know either the radius or the diameter.**

Spark Your Learning

PAIRS

A woodworker has twelve spokes. To make the wheel's rim, there are two pieces of wood that can be curved using steam. They are 6 feet and 8 feet long.

The measure along the spokes from the center to the inside of the rim is shown. Is the 6-foot piece of wood long enough to curve around for the wheel's rim? Is the 8-foot piece of wood long enough? Use measuring tools, large paper, and string to help solve.

Turn and Talk Did this experiment give you an idea of how much longer a string that makes up the rim of a wheel must be than one of the spokes? Explain.

© Houghton Mifflin Harcourt Publishing Company • Image Credit: ©vicspacewalker/Shutterstock

Build Understanding

1 Find circular objects or objects that have a circular face. For each object, follow the steps to complete the table.

A. List the name of the object in the table.

B. Measure and record the circumference of the circular face.

C. Measure and record the diameter of the circular face.

D. Calculate the ratio of the circumference to the diameter. Write the ratio as a decimal in the table.

Connect to Vocabulary

The **circumference** of a circle is like the perimeter of a rectangle; it is the distance around the figure.

Object	Circumference, C	Diameter, d	Ratio, $\frac{C}{d}$
small bowl	about 16 in.	5 in.	

Turn and Talk Describe what you notice about the ratio $\frac{C}{d}$ in your table. Does the relationship between the circumference and diameter of a circle appear to be proportional? Explain.

2 Pi, represented by the symbol π, is the ratio of a circle's circumference to its diameter. You can use this relationship to find a formula for circumference.

A. Write an equation for π using C for circumference and d for diameter.

$$\pi = \frac{\square}{\square}$$

Connect to Vocabulary

The ratio of circumference to diameter, $\frac{C}{d}$, is the same for all circles and is called π or **pi**. The value of π can be approximated by 3.14 or by $\frac{22}{7}$.

B. How can you rewrite the equation as a formula for circumference C?

$C = \square \cdot \square$

C. How are diameter and radius related?

The diameter is equal to ________ times the radius.

D. Rewrite your equation for C in terms of the radius r.

$C = \square \cdot 2 \square$

© Houghton Mifflin Harcourt Publishing Company • Image Credit: ©fotoyarsk/Shutterstock

Step It Out

3 Juanita wants to put a circular fence around the edge of the circular garden shown. How much fencing will she need to the nearest foot? Use 3.14 for π.

$C = \pi d$

$C \approx 3.14 \cdot$ ☐

$C \approx$ ☐

Juanita will need about ______ feet of fencing.

4 The circumference of a men's adult basketball hoop is about 56.52 inches. The diameter of a basketball is about 9.55 inches. Show that the ball can fit through the hoop. Use 3.14 for π.

Find the diameter of the hoop using $C = \pi d$.

$C = \pi d$

☐ $\approx$ ☐ $\cdot d$

$\frac{☐}{☐} \approx d$

☐ $\approx d$

The diameter of the hoop is about ______ inches, which is / is not greater than the diameter of the basketball.

Check Understanding

1. At a park, the jogging trail is a circle with a radius of 200 meters. How far is it around the trail? Use 3.14 for π. Show your work.

2. A contractor is installing a semicircular window with a radius of 3.5 feet. Find the distance around the window. Use $\frac{22}{7}$ for π. Explain your answer.

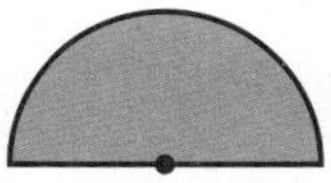

© Houghton Mifflin Harcourt Publishing Company • Image Credit: ©bblitz/Shutterstock

On Your Own

3. Toni rides the Ferris wheel shown for 15 revolutions.

A. How far does Toni travel in one revolution? Use $\frac{22}{7}$ for π.

____

B. How far does Toni travel for the entire ride?

____

4. (MP) **Reason** Paul is making a ball toss game for his club booth at the fair. He wants to make the circumference of the holes at least 3 inches greater but not more than 4 inches greater than the circumference of the ball. One person suggests that Paul make the diameter of the hole 1 inch greater than that of the ball. Another suggests the diameter should be 2 inches greater. Which suggestion should Paul choose? Explain.

____

5. **Health and Fitness** Juan runs a total of 11,775 feet around a circular track, burning 12 calories each lap. The track's diameter is 150 feet. How many calories does Juan burn? Round your answer to the nearest whole number. Use 3.14 for π.

____

For Problems 6–7, find the circumference. Round your answer to the nearest hundredth. Use 3.14 for π.

6.

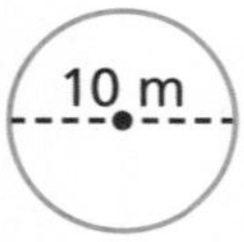

____

7.

____

© Houghton Mifflin Harcourt Publishing Company • Image Credit: ©Vitaliy/Shutterstock

I'm in a Learning Mindset!

Did my strategy for deriving and applying circumferences work? How did I adjust my strategy when I got stuck?

____

Name ______________________________

LESSON 17.1
More Practice/ Homework

ONLINE Ed — Video Tutorials and Interactive Examples

Derive and Apply Formulas for Circumference

1. **Math on the Spot** A counter recorded 254 revolutions of the bicycle wheel shown. How far did the bicycle travel? Use $\frac{22}{7}$ for π.

   A. How far does the wheel roll for one tire revolution?

   ____

   B. What is the total distance recorded?

   ____

2. (MP) **Use Structure** Hans opens a circular window that is 3.5 feet across at its widest point. What is the circumference of the window to the nearest whole number? Use 3.14 for π.

   ____

3. **STEM** Forest rangers estimate the age of trees by dividing a tree's radius by its average ring width, which represents a year's worth of growth. If an oak tree has a circumference of 151 inches and an average ring width of $\frac{1}{2}$ inch, approximately how old is the tree to the nearest whole year? Use 3.14 for π.

   ____

For Problems 4–9, find the circumference. Round your answer to the nearest hundredth. Use 3.14 for π.

4. 

   ____

5. 

   ____

6. 

   ____

7. 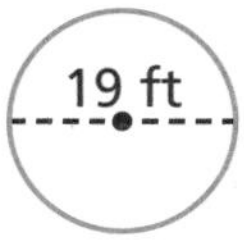

   ____

8. 

   ____

9. 

   ____

© Houghton Mifflin Harcourt Publishing Company • Image Credit: ©Todd Gipstein/Corbis Documentary/Getty Images

Test Prep

10. What is the circumference of the circle to the nearest hundredth? Use 3.14 for π.

Ⓐ 26.69 in.

Ⓑ 53.38 in.

Ⓒ 106.76 in.

Ⓓ 907.46 in.

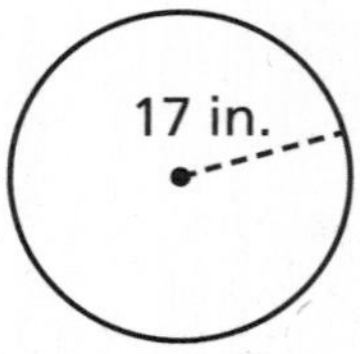

11. Randy is designing a circular garden that is 18 feet in diameter. He is buying plastic edging that costs $1.50 per foot. He can only buy edging in whole-foot amounts. How much does it cost Randy to buy edging for his garden? Use 3.14 for π.

____

For Problems 12 and 13, find the circumference of each circle to the nearest hundredth. Use 3.14 for π.

12.

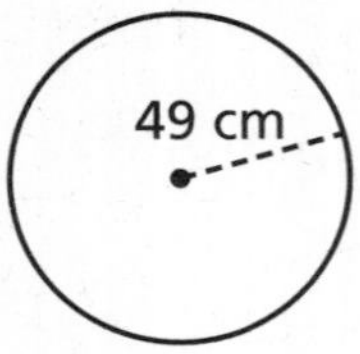

____

13.

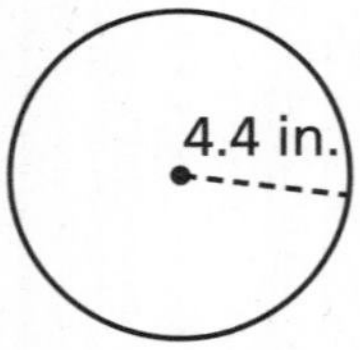

____

Spiral Review

14. Nada is making square coasters with sides of 3 inches. On each coaster is a circular design. What is the radius of the largest circle that fits on one of the coasters?

____

15. In the circle in the diagram, $\overline{AC}$ is the diameter and $\overline{BD}$ is the radius that splits the upper semicircle in half. What is the measure of $\angle ABD$?

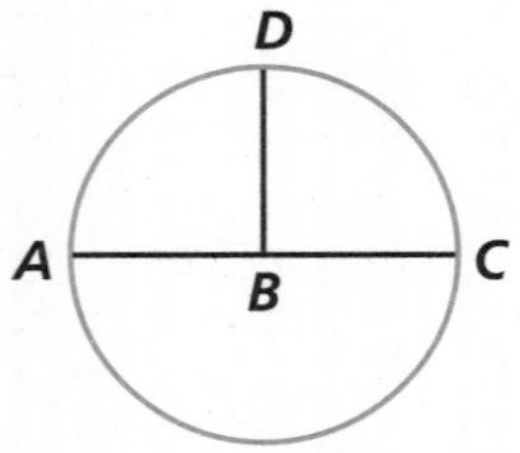

____

© Houghton Mifflin Harcourt Publishing Company

Name ______________________________

Derive and Apply a Formula for the Area of a Circle

I Can use formulas for the area and circumference of a circle to solve problems and informally derive the relationship between the circumference and the area.

Spark Your Learning

SMALL GROUPS

A designer plans for a circular rug in a 9-foot by 9-foot square bedroom. What is the largest area of a rug that can fit in the bedroom?

Turn and Talk How close do you think your estimate of the rug's area was? Explain.

© Houghton Mifflin Harcourt Publishing Company • Image Credit: ©Photographee.eu/Shutterstock

Build Understanding

1 Use a parallelogram to find the area of a circle.

A. Use a compass to draw a circle on a piece of paper. Cut out the circle. Fold the circle in half three times as shown to get wedges of equal size.

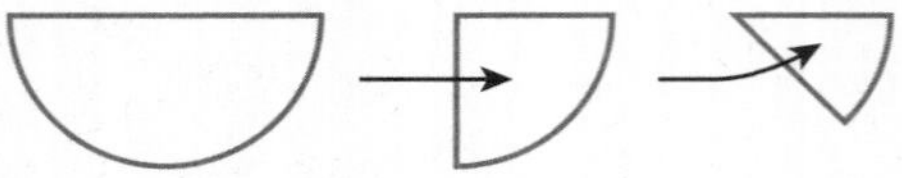

B. Cut the circle along the fold lines to separate the circle into eight equal wedges.

C. Arrange the wedges to form a figure resembling a parallelogram. Label the base of the parallelogram in terms of the circumference C. Label the height of the parallelogram in terms of the radius r.

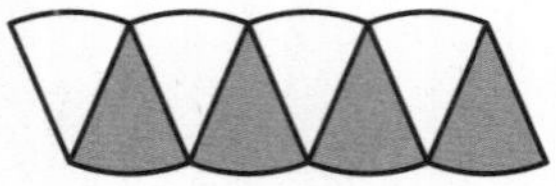

D. Use the labels on your parallelogram of wedges to substitute for b and h in the formula for area of a parallelogram.

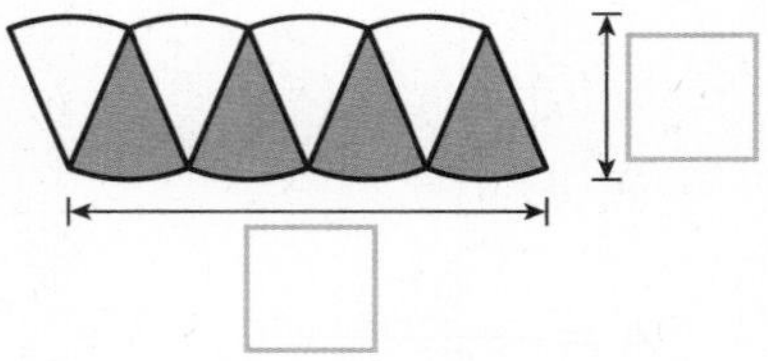

$A = b \cdot h$

$A = \square \cdot \square$

E. The formula for the circumference of a circle is $C = \pi \square$.

So half of the circumference can be written in terms of the radius as:

$\frac{1}{2}C = \pi \square$

F. Finally, complete the formula for the area of your parallelogram of wedges.

$A = \frac{1}{2}C \cdot r$

$A = \square \cdot r$ Substitute for $\frac{1}{2}C$.

$A = \square$ Write using an exponent.

G. The parallelogram of wedges is made from a circle, so the formula for the area of a circle is:

$A = \square$

Turn and Talk How could you make your parallelogram of wedges look more like a parallelogram with straight edges?

© Houghton Mifflin Harcourt Publishing Company

Name ______

Step It Out

2 The formula for the area of a circle is $A = \pi r^2$. This formula allows you to find the area of a circle if you know the radius or diameter. How can you find the area if you know only the circumference?

A. Write the formula for circumference using r. Then solve for r.

$$C = \pi d$$

$$C = \square$$

$$\frac{C}{\square} = r$$

B. Substitute the expression for r into the formula for area of a circle and simplify.

$$A = \pi r^2$$

$$A = \pi \left(\frac{\square}{\square}\right)^2 \quad \text{Substitute for } r.$$

$$A = \frac{\square}{\square \cdot \square} \quad \text{Simplify.}$$

C. Use your formula to find the area, to the nearest square meter, of the pen shown. Use 3.14 for π.

$$A = \frac{\square}{\square}$$

$$A = \frac{\square^2}{4\pi} \approx \square \text{ square meters}$$

Check Understanding

1. The new circular community swimming pool has a diameter of 64 feet.

   A. What is the radius of the community pool?

   ______

   B. What is the area of the surface of the pool? Use 3.14 for π.

   ______

2. To the nearest square centimeter, what is the area of a circle with a circumference of 75.36 centimeters? Use 3.14 for π.

   ______

© Houghton Mifflin Harcourt Publishing Company • Image Credit: ©Inu/Shutterstock

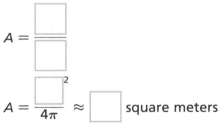

On Your Own

3. A circular mirror has the radius shown.

A. To the nearest hundredth, what is the area of the mirror? Use 3.14 for π.

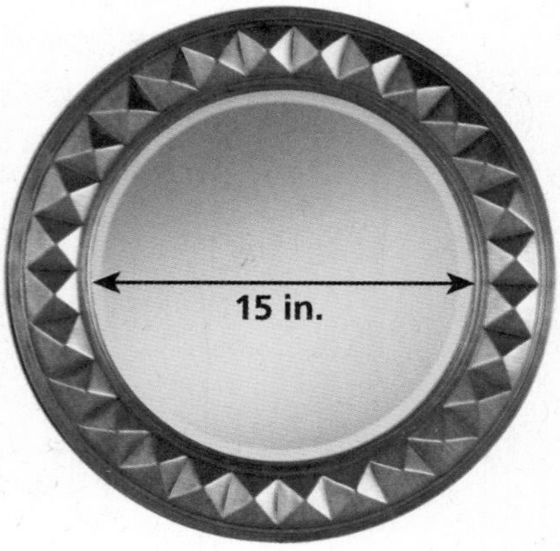

B. The mirror has a frame. The radius of the mirror with the frame is 11 inches. To the nearest hundredth, what is the area of the mirror with the frame?

C. (MP) **Reason** To the nearest hundredth, what is the area of the frame?

4. A disk is shaped like a flat circular plate. Its circumference is 26.69 inches. To the nearest hundredth, what is the area of the disk? Use 3.14 for π.

5. (MP) **Critique Reasoning** A classmate states that if the radius of a circle is doubled, then its area is doubled. Do you agree or disagree? If you disagree, how much larger do you think the area will be? Explain.

For Problems 6–7, find the area to the nearest hundredth. Use 3.14 for π.

6.

7.

I'm in a Learning Mindset!

How effective were the strategies I used to find the area of a circle using the circumference of the circle?

© Houghton Mifflin Harcourt Publishing Company • Image Credit: ©Room27/Shutterstock

Name

ONLINE
Video Tutorials and
Interactive Examples

Derive and Apply a Formula for the Area of a Circle

1. To make grape juice, water is added to a large cylindrical vat of grapes. If the diameter of the vat is 16 feet, what is the area of the base of the vat? Use 3.14 for π.

2. **Math on the Spot** A group of historians is building a tepee to display at a local multicultural fair. The tepee has a height of 7 feet 4 inches at its center, and it has a circular floor of radius 14 feet. What is the area of the floor of the tepee to the nearest square foot? Use $\frac{22}{7}$ for π.

3. The face of a clock has a circumference of 14π inches. What is its area? Use 3.14 for π.

4. A carpenter cuts a circle out of a piece of wood. The radius of the circle is about 23 inches. The carpenter cuts the circle into two semicircles. What is the area of one semicircle? Use 3.14 for π.

5. MP **Use Structure** Four identical circles are lined up in a row with no gaps between them such that the diameters form a segment that is 68 centimeters long. What is the combined area of all the circles to the nearest hundredth? Use 3.14 for π.

6. Ms. Flynn's class is painting a circular canvas. Its diameter is 5 feet. What is the area of the canvas to the nearest whole number? Use 3.14 for π.

For Problems 7–12, find the area of each circle described. Use 3.14 for π.

7. Radius of 10 centimeters

8. Diameter of 2 feet

9. Circumference of 62.8 inches

10. Diameter of 8 inches

11. Circumference of 18.84 miles

12. Radius of 99 millimeters

© Houghton Mifflin Harcourt Publishing Company • Image Credit: ©Stefano Buttafoco/Shutterstock

Test Prep

13. Larry drew a circle with a circumference of 40.82 centimeters. What is the approximate area of the circle? Use 3.14 for π.

____

14. Safeta put a circular placemat on a table. The radius of the placemat is 7.5 inches. What is the area of the placemat? Use 3.14 for π.

____

15. The length of the curved part of a semicircle is 25.12 inches. What is the approximate area of the semicircle? Use 3.14 for π.

(A) 25.12 in^2

(B) 50.24 in^2

(C) 100.48 in^2

(D) 200.96 in^2

16. On a middle school basketball court, there is a large circle painted on the floor. The diameter of the circle is 12 feet. What is the area of the circle? Use 3.14 for π.

(A) 18.84 ft^2

(B) 113.04 ft^2

(C) 452.16 ft^2

(D) 1,808.64 ft^2

17. Find the area of a circle with a radius of 33 millimeters. Use 3.14 for π.

____

Spiral Review

18. Carlos drew a figure on the smartboard and said it was a triangle with angles of 100°, 35°, and 55°. Nate said that was impossible. Who is correct? Explain.

____

____

19. The diameter of a wheel is 3 feet. What is the circumference? Use 3.14 for π.

____

© Houghton Mifflin Harcourt Publishing Company

Name ____________________

Areas of Composite Figures

I Can break a composite figure into simple shapes and use area formulas to find its area.

Step It Out

ACTIVITY

1 Rahim drew an outline of the front of a house on grid paper. He wants to find the area of his model.

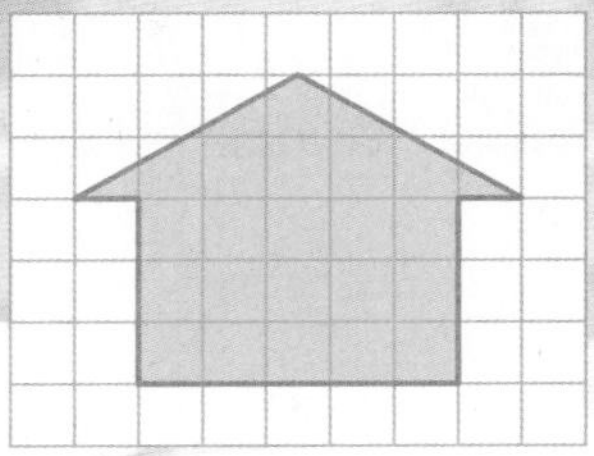

A. Separate the **composite figure** into simple geometric figures. What simple geometric figures are used to form the outline?

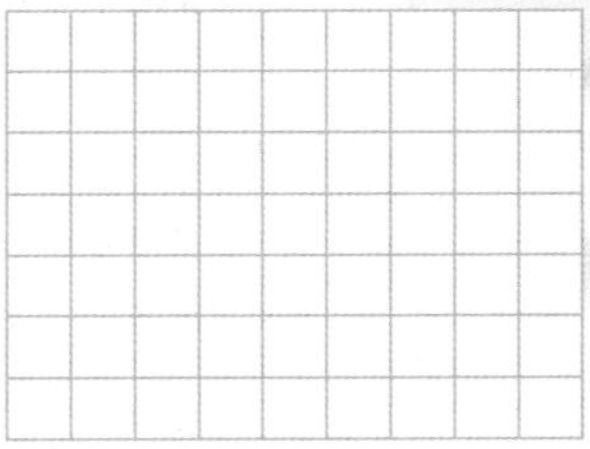

____

B. Determine the dimensions and then find the area of each of the simple geometric figures.

____

____

____

C. Find the area of the composite figure.

____

____

____

Turn and Talk Can you separate the composite figure into different simple geometric figures? Explain.

© Houghton Mifflin Harcourt Publishing Company • Image Credit: ©George Rudy/age fotostock

2 A section of a basketball court is shown.

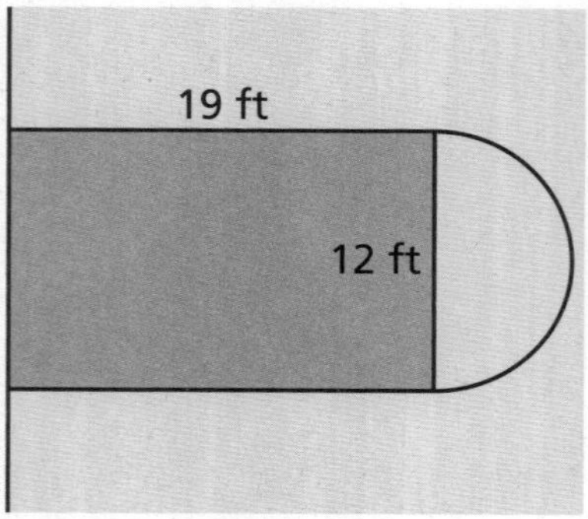

A. Determine the simple geometric figures that are used in the composite figure.

____

____

B. Find the dimensions of the simple geometric figures.

____

____

C. How is the area of a semicircle related to the area of a circle with the same radius?

____

____

____

D. Find the area of the simple geometric figures to the nearest square foot. Use 3.14 for π.

____

____

E. Find the area of the composite figure.

____

____

Turn and Talk Describe the method you would use to determine the simple geometric figures of a composite figure.

© Houghton Mifflin Harcourt Publishing Company • **Image Credit:** ©Jim West/PhotoEdit

Name ___

3 The manager of a hotel wants to put new carpet in the lobby. The dimensions of the lobby are shown. There is a statue with a circular base in the lobby that does not need to have carpet under it.

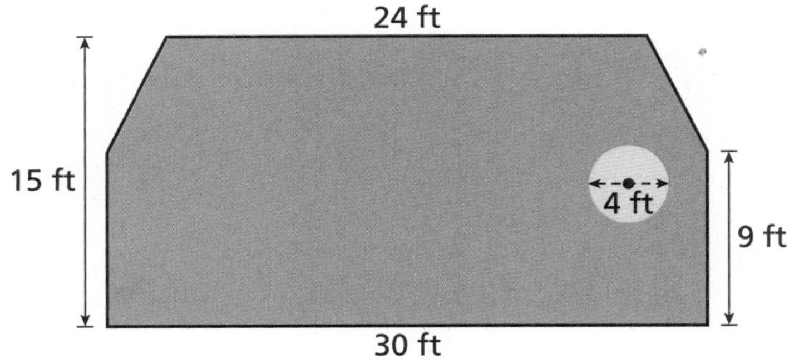

A. Determine the simple geometric figures that are in the composite figure. Find the dimensions of the simple geometric figures.

B. Find the areas of the simple geometric figures. Use 3.14 for π.

C. Find the area of the lobby that needs carpet. Explain how you found the area.

Check Understanding

1. Find the area of the composite figure.

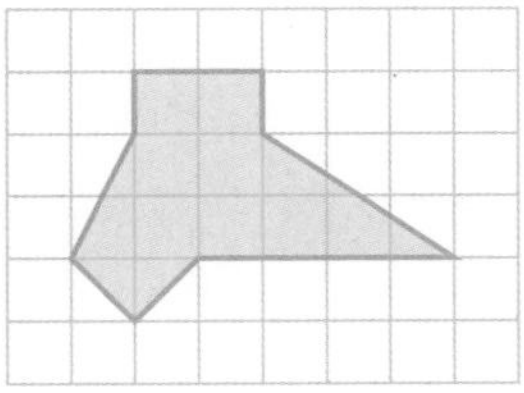

2. Farrah has a piece of paper that is 11 inches long and 8 inches wide. She cuts a semicircle with a radius of 4 inches out of the piece of paper. What is the area of the piece of paper she has left after the cut to the nearest hundredth? Use 3.14 for π.

© Houghton Mifflin Harcourt Publishing Company

On Your Own

3. Greg designed a trophy using grid paper. What is the area of the drawing of the trophy shown?

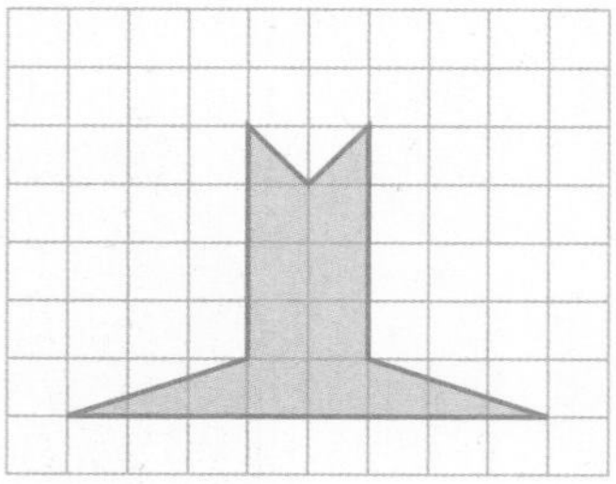

____

4. (MP) **Attend to Precision** Clara is making a pennant. She attaches a rectangle that is 1 inch wide and 6 inches long to a triangle that has a base of 6 inches and a height of 28 inches. What is the area of the pennant?

____

5. **Financial Literacy** Mary is installing carpet in a closet for a customer. A floor plan of the closet is shown. Mary charges $5.60 per square foot of carpet, plus a $150 installation fee.

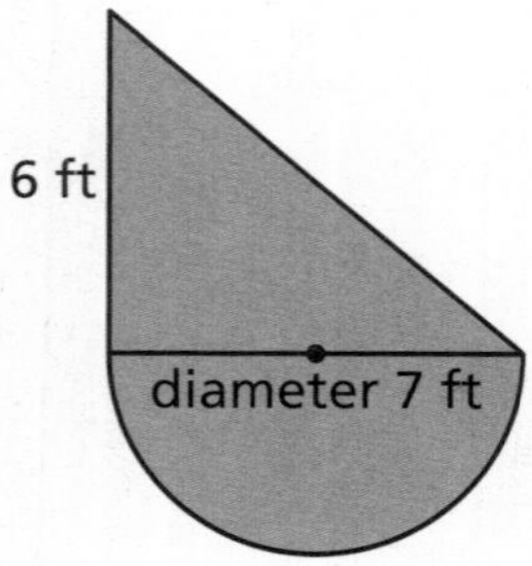

How much should Mary charge the customer to the nearest cent? Use 3.14 for π.

____

For Problems 6–9, find the area of the composite figure shown to the nearest half unit. Use 3.14 for π.

6. 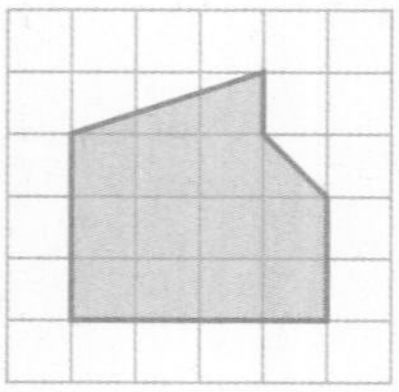

____

7. 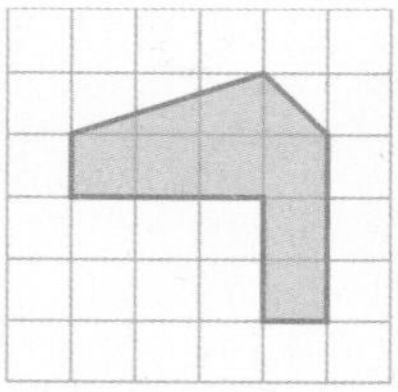

____

8. 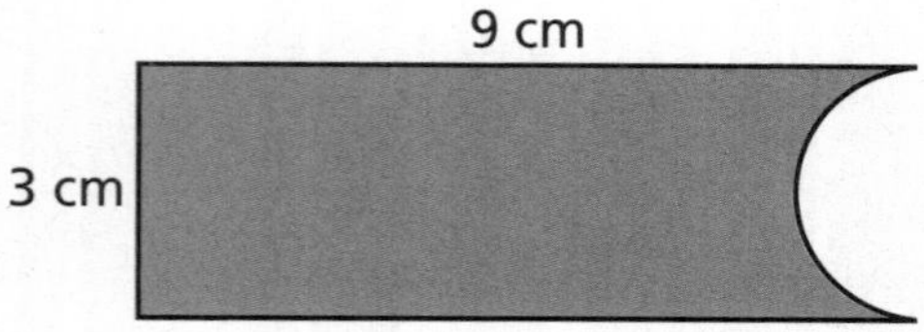

____

9. 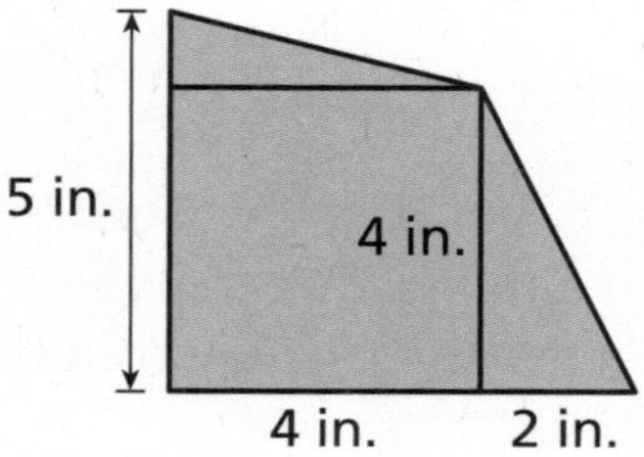

____

© Houghton Mifflin Harcourt Publishing Company

Name

ONLINE
Video Tutorials and Interactive Examples

Areas of Composite Figures

1. A driveway consists of two rectangles. One rectangle is 80 feet long and 15 feet wide. The other is 30 feet long and 30 feet wide. What is the area of the driveway?

2. (MP) **Use Tools** A patio is made of two sections. One is shaped like a trapezoid, and the other like a semicircle. The bases of the trapezoid are 12 feet and 8 feet. The height of the trapezoid is 4 feet. The diameter of the semicircle is the same as the trapezoid's shorter base. Use geometry software or another tool to draw a model of the patio. Find the patio's area. Use 3.14 for π.

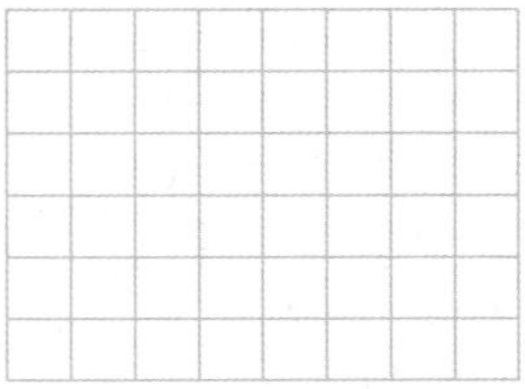

3. **Open Ended** Juanita is making a ribbon as shown.

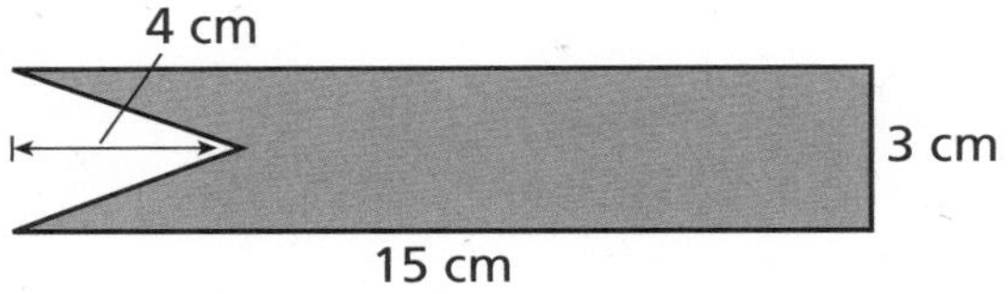

Explain two different ways you can find the area of the ribbon. Then find the area of the ribbon.

For Problems 4–5, find the area of the composite figure. Use 3.14 for π.

4.

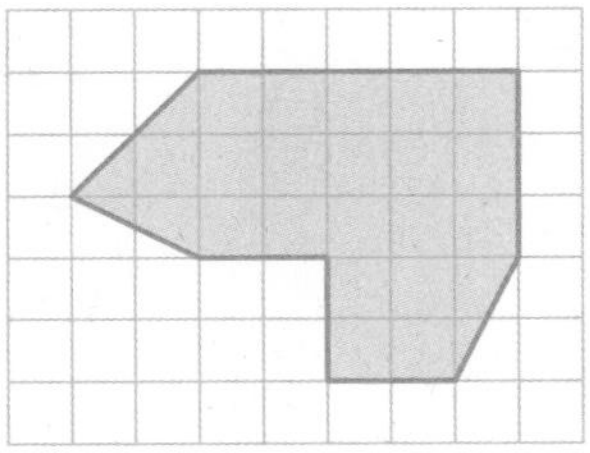

5.

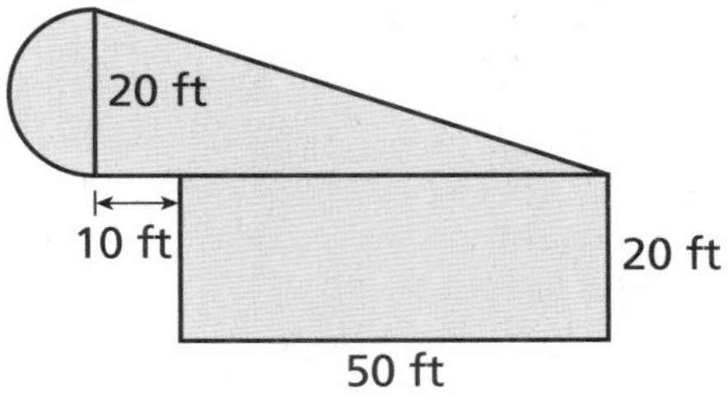

© Houghton Mifflin Harcourt Publishing Company • Image Credit: ©haveseen/iStock/Getty Images Plus/Getty Images

Test Prep

6. A model of a plot of grass behind a building is shown. What is the area of the plot of grass?

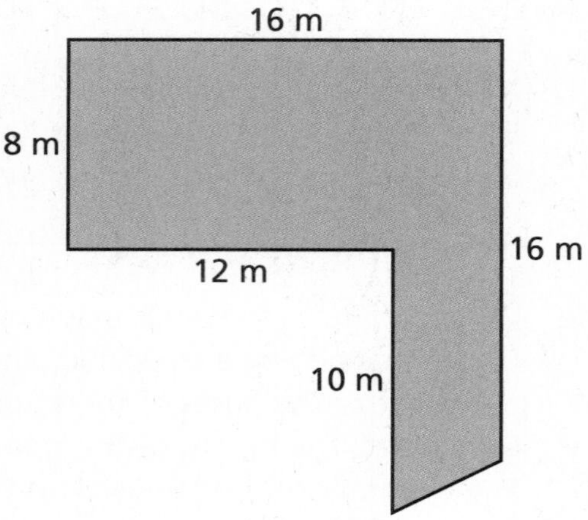

____

7. Eric is designing a logo for a company. The logo consists of two identical parallelograms joined at their longest sides. One of the parallelograms has a base of 2.5 centimeters and a height of 1.25 centimeters. What is the area of the logo?

____

8. Find the approximate area of the composite figure. Use 3.14 for π.

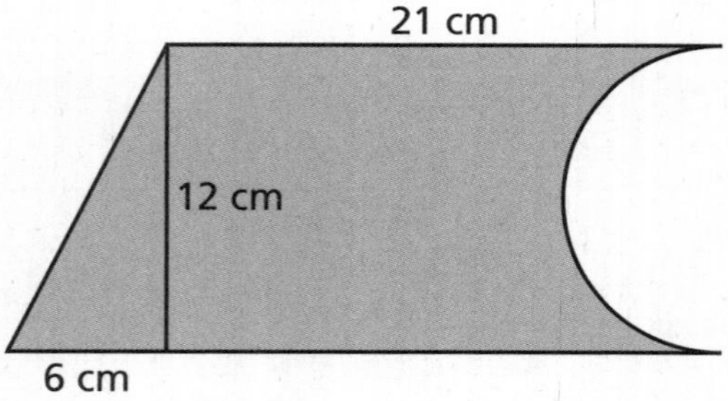

Ⓐ 159.48 cm^2

Ⓑ 231.48 cm^2

Ⓒ 288 cm^2

Ⓓ 344.52 cm^2

Spiral Review

9. Find the area of a circle of radius 6 cm. Use 3.14 for π.

____

10. If the domain of the function $y = 2x - 6$ is $2 < x < 8$, what is the function's range?

____

11. A circle has area 712 square inches. What is the diameter of the circle? Use 3.14 for π.

____

© Houghton Mifflin Harcourt Publishing Company

Module 17

Name ______________________________

Review

Vocabulary

Choose the correct term from the Vocabulary box.

Vocabulary
circumference
composite figure
pi

1. The distance around a circle

____

2. A figure made up of simple geometric figures

____

3. The ratio of the distance around a circle to the distance across the circle

____

Concepts and Skills

Use the circle for Problems 4–5.

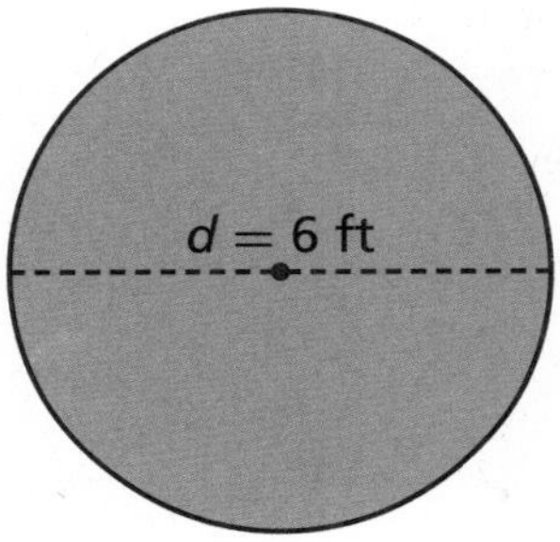

4. Calculate the circumference of the circle in terms of π.

____

5. What is the area of the circle in terms of π?

____

6. Given that $\pi \approx 3.14$, which values are reasonable for the area of a circle with radius 5 inches? Select all that apply.

Ⓐ 10π in^2

Ⓑ 15.7 in^2

Ⓒ 25π in^2

Ⓓ 31.4 in^2

Ⓔ 78.5 in^2

7. (MP) **Use Tools** Given that the circumference of a circle is 8π centimeters, calculate the area of the circle in terms of π. State what strategy and tool you will use to answer the question, explain your choice, and then find the answer.

____

____

© Houghton Mifflin Harcourt Publishing Company

8. To the nearest square inch, what is the area of a circle with a circumference of 15.8 inches? Use 3.14 for π.

9. A circular garden has a diameter of 24 feet. What is the area of the garden to the nearest hundredth? Use 3.14 for π.

10. A parking lot is a composite figure consisting of two rectangles. One part of the parking lot is 160 feet long and 80 feet wide. The other part is 70 feet long and 45 feet wide. What is the area of the parking lot?

For Problems 11–12, calculate the area of the given figure.

11.

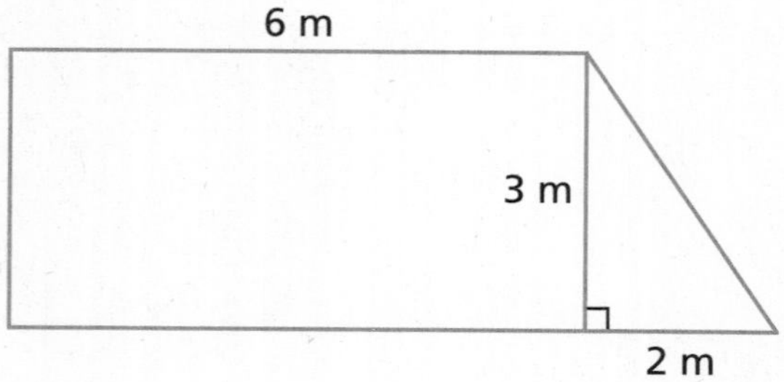

(A) 48 m^2

(B) 34 m^2

(C) 21 m^2

(D) 24 m^2

12.

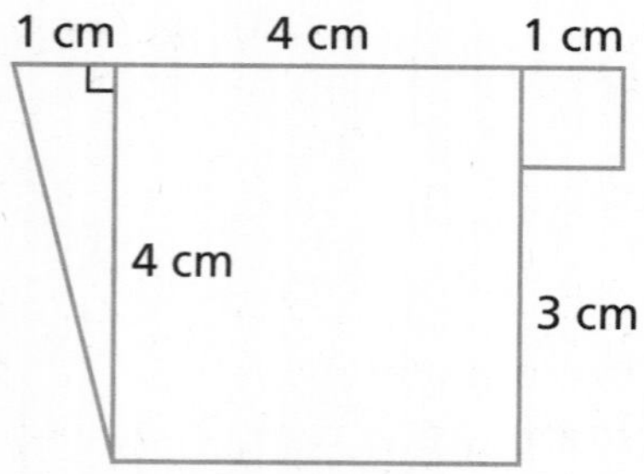

13. The new circular community water fountain has a diameter of 192 feet. What is the area of the surface of the circular community water fountain? Use 3.14 for π. Round to the nearest square foot.

© Houghton Mifflin Harcourt Publishing Company

Module

18 Cross Sections, Surface Area, and Volume

The Prism Family

Each of the rectangular prisms shown is made from cubes with an edge length of 1 centimeter. All of the prisms in this family have something in common.

Investigate by finding the dimensions, surface area, and volume of each prism. How are they all related?

A.

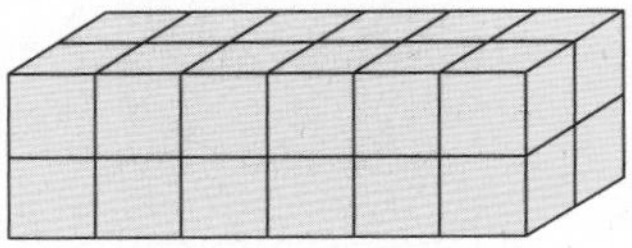

Dimensions:

________, ________, ________

Surface area: ________

Volume: ________

B.

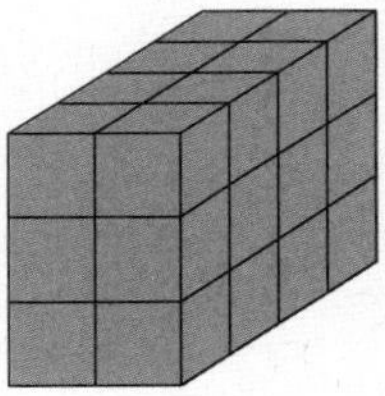

Dimensions:

________, ________, ________

Surface area: ________

Volume: ________

C.

Dimensions:

________, ________, ________

Surface area: ________

Volume: ________

Turn and Talk

Describe the family of rectangular prisms.

© Houghton Mifflin Harcourt Publishing Company

Are You Ready?

Complete these problems to review prior concepts and skills you will need for this module.

Explore Volume

Each rectangular prism is composed of cubes with an edge length of 1 inch. Determine the volume of each prism.

1. 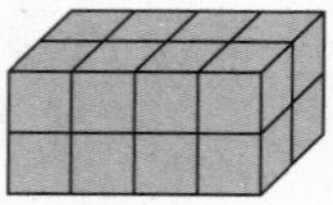 ________ in^3

2.  ________ in^3

Nets and Surface Area

For Problems 3–4, draw a net of each prism. Then use the net to determine the surface area of the prism.

3.

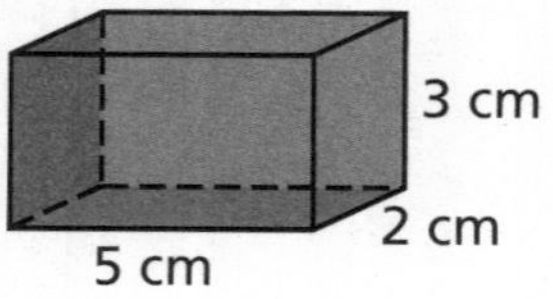

________ cm^2

4.

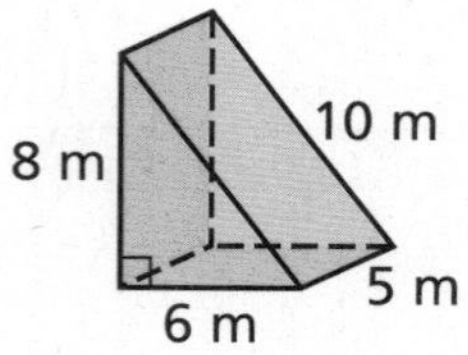

________ m^2

Area of Circles

For Problems 5–6, determine the area of each circle. Use 3.14 for π. Round each answer to the nearest hundredth.

5.

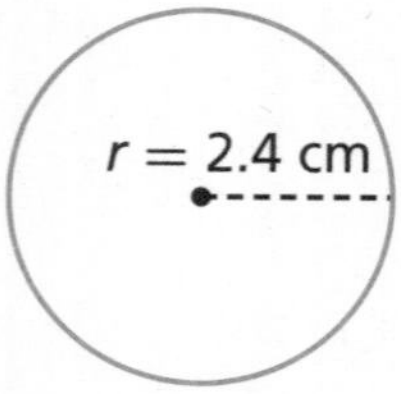

________ cm^2

6.

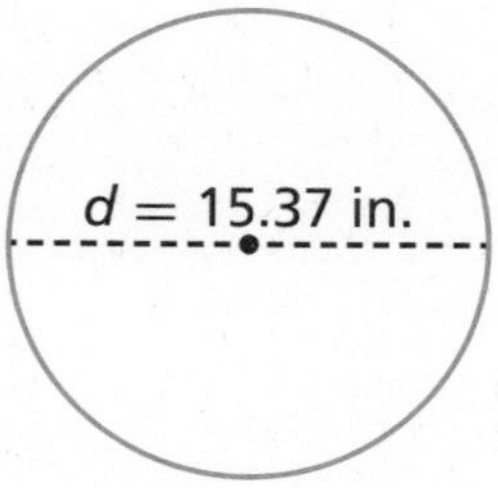

________ in^2

7. On the ice of a hockey rink, there is one circle with a 12-inch diameter, and one with a 24-inch diameter. How much more area does the larger circle have than the smaller? Explain how you know. Use 3.14 for π.

____

____

© Houghton Mifflin Harcourt Publishing Company

Name ____________________

Describe and Analyze Cross Sections of Solids

I Can identify the shapes of cross sections of solids and solve problems involving the areas of cross sections.

Spark Your Learning

PAIRS

Cassie and Amanda are making a cylindrical layer cake with four different-flavored layers. Amanda wants a circular piece of cake with only one flavor. Cassie wants a piece of cake with a rectangular face and all four flavors. Show how each girl could make a single cut to the cake to get the piece she wants. Can both girls get the piece of cake they want from the same cake? Explain.

Turn and Talk For each type of cut, does the location where the cake is cut change the shape of the piece of cake? Explain.

© Houghton Mifflin Harcourt Publishing Company • Image Credits: (tr) ©Julia Kuznetsova/Shutterstock; (tl) ©kali9/E+/Getty Images

Build Understanding

A **cross section** is an inside view made by making a cut or slice. In this lesson, only cuts made parallel or perpendicular to the base will be shown.

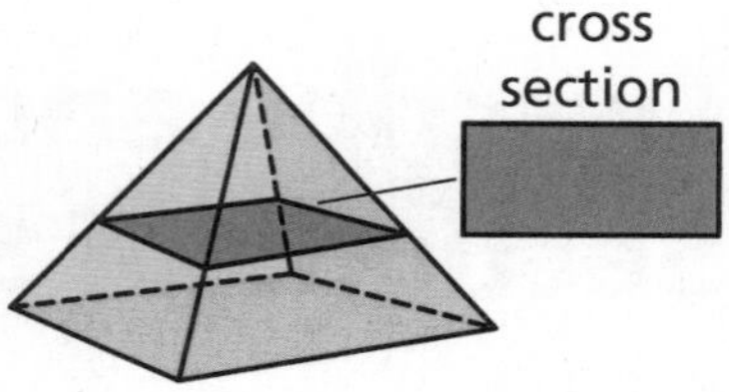

1 Analyze the shipping box shown, which is in the shape of a **rectangular prism** with two square faces. What are the figures formed when slicing the box from different directions?

A. The box is a prism. What polygon describes the two-dimensional bases of this prism? What polygon describes the other faces?

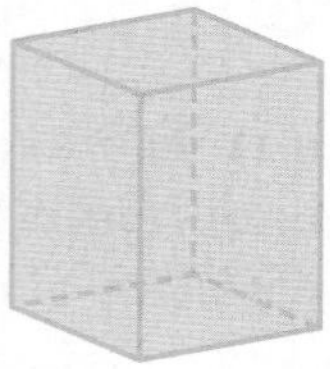

____

____

B. Suppose you slice the prism parallel to its base as shown. What two-dimensional figure is the cross section?

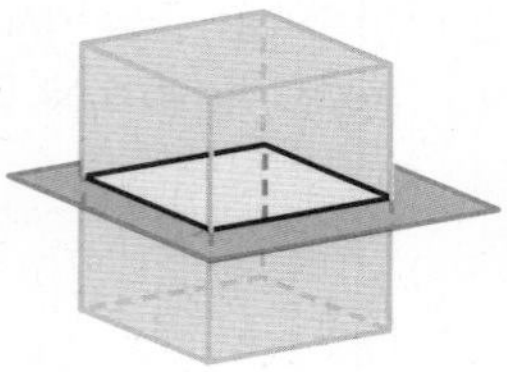

____

C. Suppose you slice the prism perpendicular to its base as shown. What two-dimensional figure is the cross section?

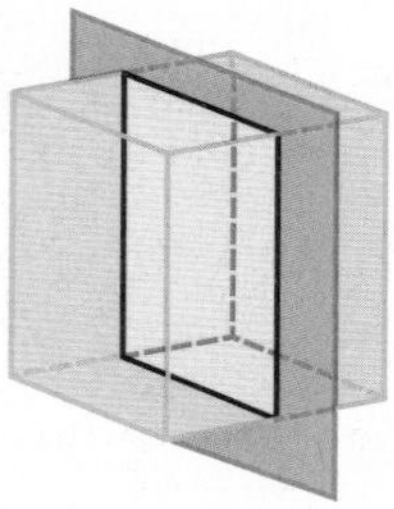

____

D. Consider the **pyramid** shown. Identify the two-dimensional base and faces. What is the name of this pyramid?

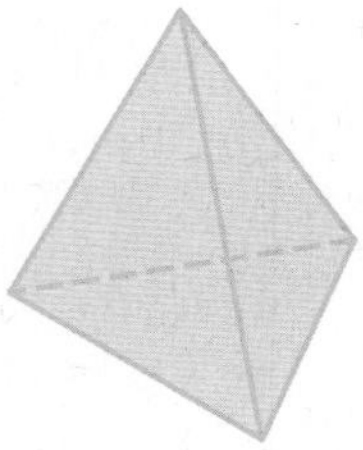

____

____

____

E. Suppose you slice the pyramid parallel to its base. What two-dimensional figure is the cross section?

____

F. Suppose you slice the pyramid perpendicular to its base, through the vertex. What two-dimensional figure is the cross section?

____

© Houghton Mifflin Harcourt Publishing Company • Image Credit: ©realperson/Shutterstock

Name ______

Step It Out

2 Rajesh is doing a research project on the Pentagon, which is located near Washington, D.C. Rajesh sketched a pentagonal prism to help him model the Pentagon.

A. When Rajesh slices the pentagonal prism parallel to the bases, the result is a plane figure that has the same shape as the [bases / faces connecting the bases]. So the figure is a ______.

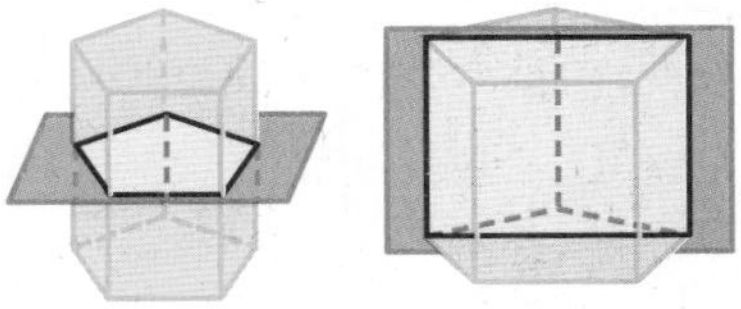

B. When you slice the pentagonal prism perpendicular to the bases, the result is a figure of the same type as [the bases / the faces connecting the bases]. So the figure of this cross section is a ______.

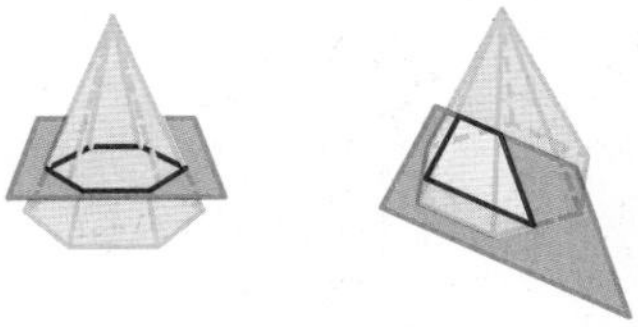

C. Now consider a hexagonal pyramid. The two-dimensional figure that results from slicing the hexagonal pyramid parallel to the base is a ______.

D. The two-dimensional figure that results from slicing the hexagonal pyramid perpendicular to the base, but not through the vertex, is a ______.

Turn and Talk How are the following related: the shape of a base and the cross section of a slice parallel to the base of a prism or pyramid? The shape of the faces and the cross section of a slice perpendicular to the base?

Check Understanding

1. A triangular prism is sliced parallel to its base. What two-dimensional figure is the cross section? Use a sketch to support your answer.

2. What cross section is made when a hexagonal pyramid like the one in Task 2 is sliced perpendicular to its base through its vertex?

______

3. Suppose the box of cereal shown is sliced parallel to its base. What is the resulting cross section?

______

4. Compare the cross sections made from slicing the cereal box parallel to its base and slicing it perpendicular to its base.

______

______

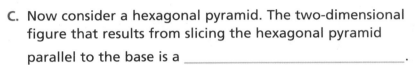

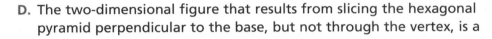

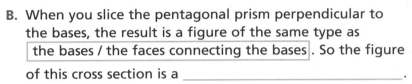

© Houghton Mifflin Harcourt Publishing Company • Image Credit: Digital Vision/Getty Images

On Your Own

For Problems 5 and 6, use the picture of the hotel with a roof in the shape of a regular pentagonal pyramid.

5. **Use Structure** Describe how the roof can be sliced to make a cross section in the shape of a pentagon.

____

6. **Use Structure** Describe how the roof can be sliced to make a cross section in the shape of a triangle.

____

7. **Reason** The diameter of a sphere is 8 inches. What are the circumference and area of the cross section formed by a plane slicing through the sphere's center? Round to the nearest hundredth. Use 3.14 for π.

____

For Problems 8–13, identify the shape of the two-dimensional cross section shown.

8. perpendicular to base of a rectangular prism

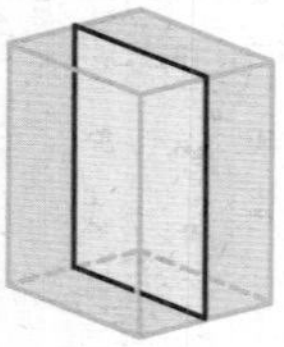

____

9. perpendicular to base, not through vertex of a rectangular pyramid

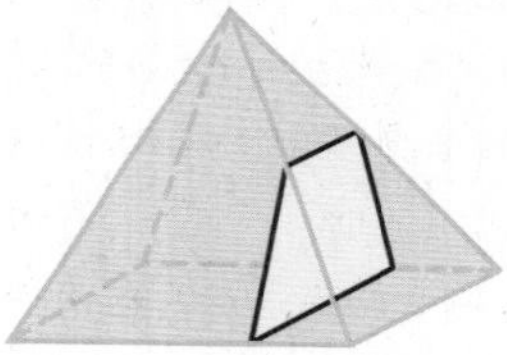

____

10. perpendicular to base and through vertex of a square pyramid

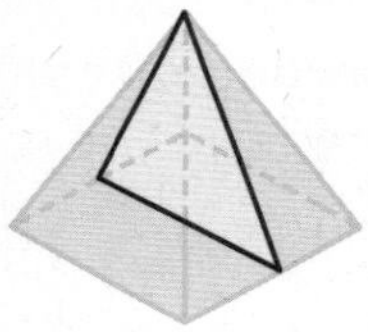

____

11. parallel to base of a pentagonal prism

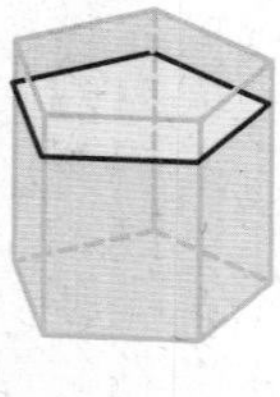

____

12. parallel to base of a hexagonal prism

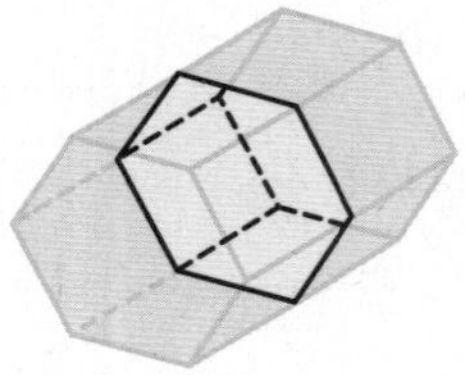

____

13. parallel to base of a square pyramid

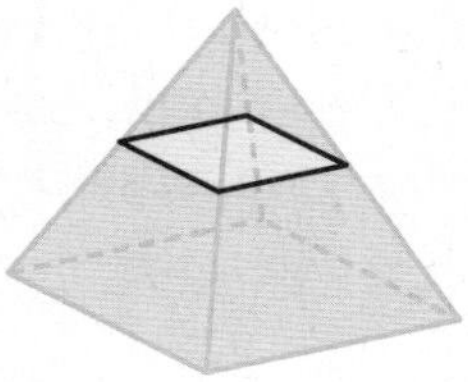

____

© Houghton Mifflin Harcourt Publishing Company

I'm in a Learning Mindset!

What methods are most effective for analyzing cross sections of solids?

____

Name ______________________________

LESSON 18.1
More Practice/ Homework

ONLINE
Video Tutorials and Interactive Examples

Describe and Analyze Cross Sections of Solids

For Problems 1–2, describe the two-dimensional figure that results from slicing the given three-dimensional figure.

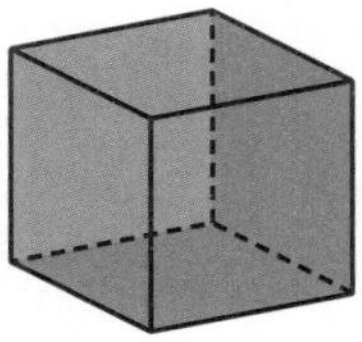

1. Slice parallel to the base

____

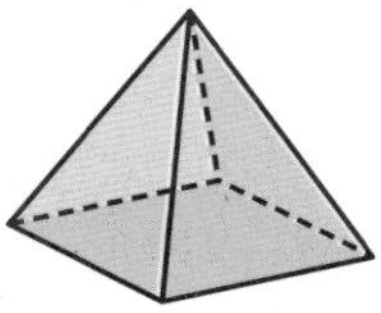

2. Slice perpendicular to the base, not through the vertex

____

____

For Problems 3–5, tell whether the slice must be parallel or perpendicular to the base to make the given cross section.

3. A slice of a pentagonal pyramid results in a pentagon.

____

4. A slice of a triangular prism results in a triangle.

____

5. A slice of a hexagonal pyramid results in a triangle.

____

6. (MP) **Use Repeated Reasoning** A sphere has a radius of 12 inches.

A. Describe the cross section formed by slicing through the sphere's center.

____

B. Describe the cross sections formed by slicing the sphere many times, each time farther from the center of the sphere.

____

____

____

7. (MP) **Use Structure** What cross sections might you see when slicing a cone that you would not see when slicing a pyramid or a prism?

____

© Houghton Mifflin Harcourt Publishing Company

Test Prep

8. Two chefs are working on cylindrical cakes. David wants to make a stripe of frosting in his cake, and he makes a cut that shows a rectangle. Terri wants to put a layer of frosting in the middle of her cake, so she makes a cut that shows a circle. How was Terri's cut different from David's?

____

9. Select all of the following three-dimensional figures that could have a cross section of a triangle when sliced parallel to the base, perpendicular to the base through the vertex, or perpendicular to the base *not* through the vertex.

Ⓐ cone
Ⓑ triangular prism
Ⓒ rectangular prism
Ⓓ triangular pyramid
Ⓔ sphere

10. Match each description of slicing a three-dimensional figure with the resulting two-dimensional figure shown.

Slice a square pyramid parallel to base • •

Slice a non-square rectangular prism parallel to base • •

Slice a square pyramid perpendicular to base through the vertex • •

Slice a pentagonal prism parallel to base • •

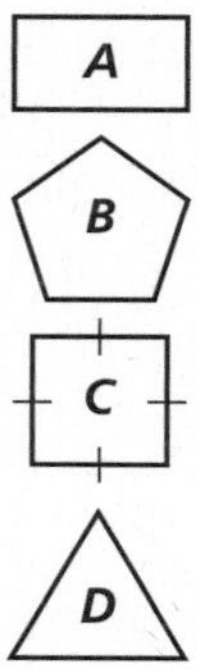

Spiral Review

11. Find the area of the composite figure.

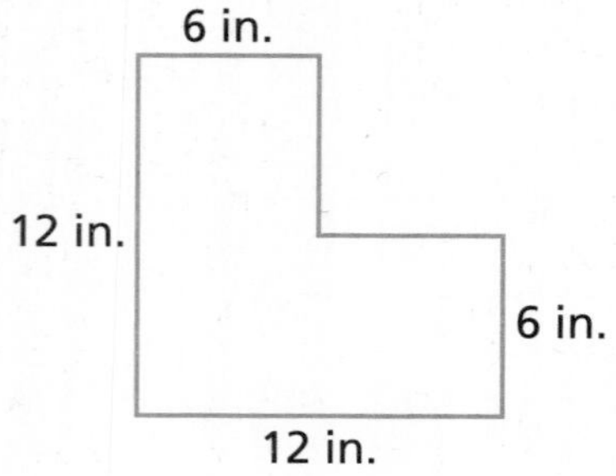

____

12. How many unique triangles can be made with the angle measures 48°, 64°, and 68°: none, one, or infinitely many?

____

© Houghton Mifflin Harcourt Publishing Company

Name ____________________

Derive and Apply Formulas for Surface Areas of Cubes and Right Prisms

I Can derive and apply the formulas for surface area of any right prism.

Spark Your Learning

SMALL GROUPS

Sara is wrapping a gift box with dimensions 10 inches by 14 inches by 5 inches with wrapping paper. What is the least amount of wrapping paper she will need to cover the gift box without any overlap?

Turn and Talk What is the difference between area and surface area?

© Houghton Mifflin Harcourt Publishing Company • Image Credit: ©JGI/Jamie Grill/Blend Images/Getty Images

Build Understanding

1 A wooden toy box is represented by the net shown with it.

A. How many faces make up the toy box? How does the net show these faces?

____

____

B. Are any of the faces congruent? If so, which ones?

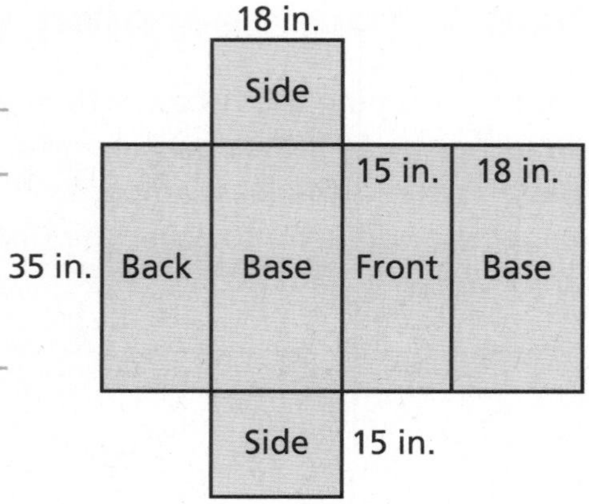

____

____

C. What is the shape of the two bases? What is their combined area?

____

D. What is the combined area of the front and back faces?

____

E. What is the combined area of the left and right faces?

____

F. How can you find the total **surface area** of the box? What is this value?

____

G. Use the net to derive a formula for surface area of a box with length ℓ, width w, and height h:

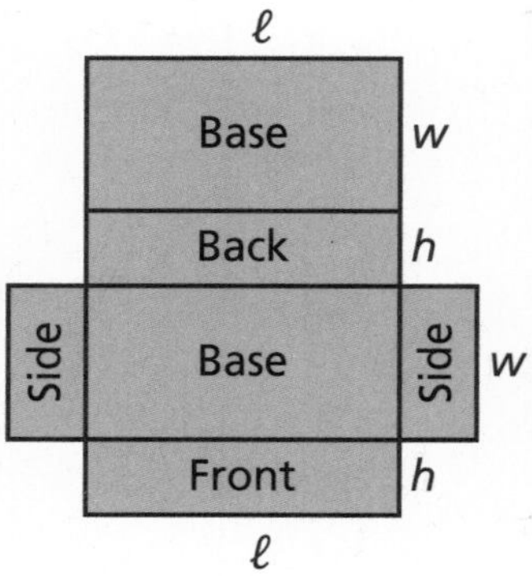

Surface area $= 2\ell w +$ ☐ $+$ ☐

Since ℓw is the area of a [base / front or back / side], replace ℓw with B: $2B + 2\ell h + 2wh$.

Both parts of the expression $2\ell h + 2wh$ contain an h, so factor it out: $2B + h($☐ $+$ ☐$)$.

Since $2\ell + 2w$ represents the [area / perimeter] of the base, replace $2\ell + 2w$ with P:

Surface Area $= 2B +$ ☐ h

Turn and Talk How could you change the surface area formula for a cube to make it simpler?

© Houghton Mifflin Harcourt Publishing Company • Image Credit: ©Six Dun/Shutterstock

Name ____________________

Step It Out

The surface area of a right prism is $S = 2B + Ph$, where B is the base area, P is the base perimeter, and h is the height of the prism.

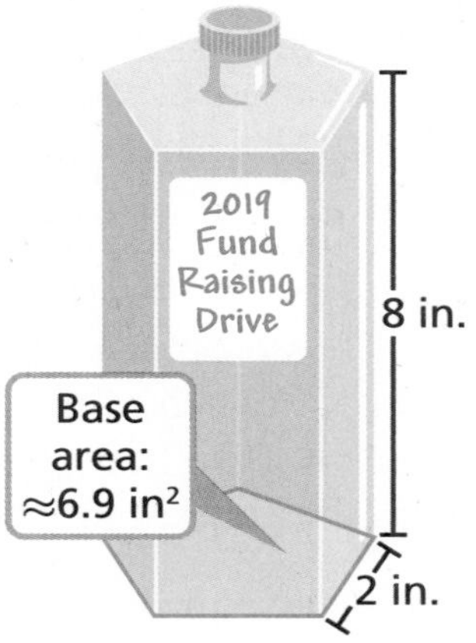

2 A foundation has the water bottle shown as giveaways for its annual fundraiser. What is the approximate surface area of the water bottle, treating the top surface as flat and ignoring the spout?

A. From the picture, the area of the base is approximately $\square$ square inches and the height is $\square$ inches.

The perimeter of the base is $\square \times \square = \square$ inches.

B. Find the approximate surface area. Treat the top surface as flat. Ignore the spout.

$S = 2B + Ph$

$S \approx 2\square + \square(\square)$

$S \approx \square + \square$

$S \approx \square$

The surface area of the water bottle is approximately $\square$ square inches.

Check Understanding

1. A couch cushion needs to be covered with fabric. The dimensions of the cushion are 1.5 feet long by 1.5 feet wide by 0.5 foot high. What is the least amount of fabric needed to cover the couch cushion?

____

2. Bobby is sanding a five-sided storage chest with the dimensions shown. The base is a regular pentagon. If he sands only the outside of the chest, approximately how much area must he sand?

____

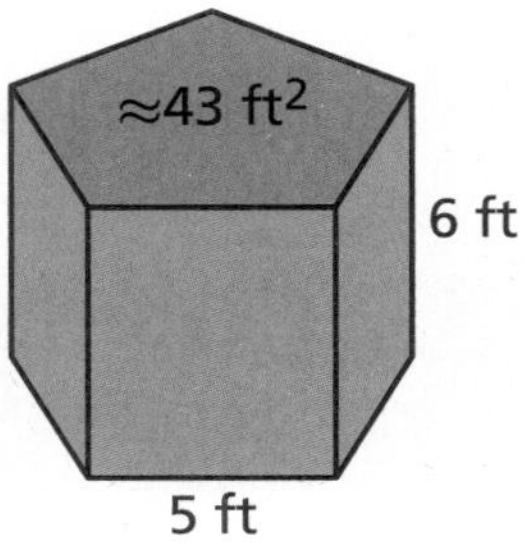

3. A photographer's darkroom needs a new coat of black paint on all surfaces of the room, including the ceiling and the floor. The room is a cube with edge length 11 feet. How much surface area must be painted? _______________

© Houghton Mifflin Harcourt Publishing Company

On Your Own

4. Lily is using paper to cover a box with dimensions 7 centimeters by 10 centimeters by 5 centimeters. What is the least amount of paper Lily will need to cover the box? ______________________

5. (MP) **Use Structure** Gavin is making a scale replica of a tent for his social studies project. The replica is in the shape of a triangular prism. It has an isosceles triangle base with side lengths 6 inches, 5 inches, and 5 inches. The height of the triangle is 4 inches, and the depth of the tent is 7 inches. How much fabric will Gavin need to make the outside of the replica, including the "floor"? ______________

6. Blake made a storage bin out of poles in the shape of a regular hexagonal prism, as shown. He wants to cover the surface area of the prism, including the floor, with a tarp to protect his things from the weather. What is the approximate surface area that the tarp will cover? Explain.

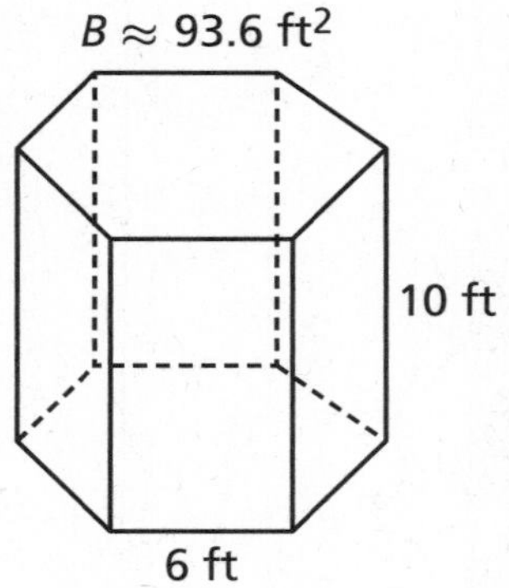

____

____

____

Find the surface area of each prism.

7.

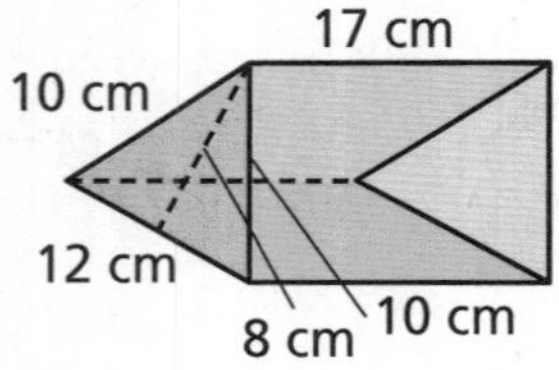

____

8.

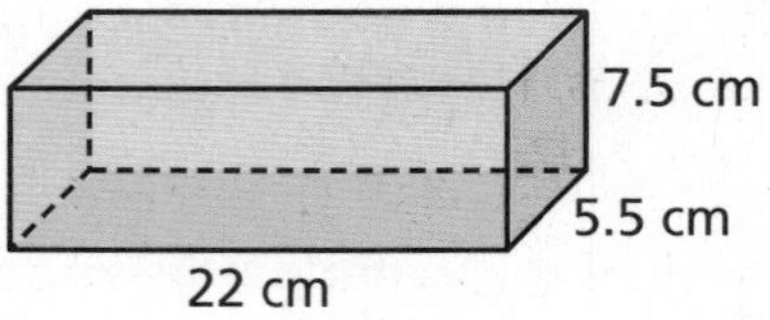

____

9.

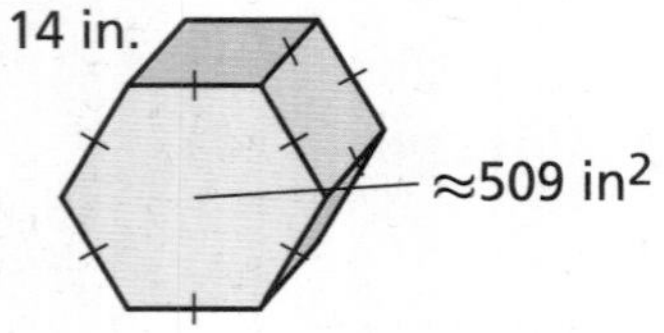

____

10.

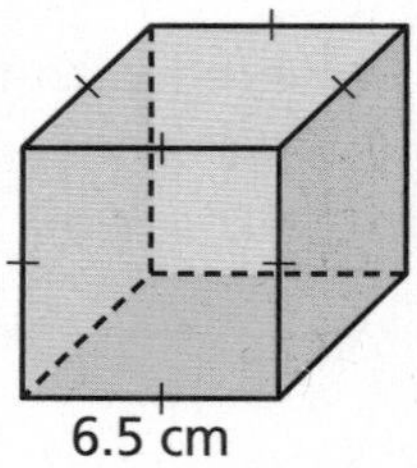

____

© Houghton Mifflin Harcourt Publishing Company

I'm in a Learning Mindset!

How does using the formulas for surface area of right prisms help me find surface area more efficiently?

____

____

Name ______________________________

LESSON 18.2
More Practice/ Homework

ONLINE
Video Tutorials and Interactive Examples

Derive and Apply Formulas for Surface Areas of Cubes and Right Prisms

1. (MP) **Use Structure** Melissa baked a cake. The box for the cake is in the shape of a cube with edges 9 inches in length. Draw a supporting picture and find how many square centimeters of cardboard are needed to make the box.

2. Sue is upholstering a rectangular ottoman that measures 21 centimeters by 18 centimeters by 15 centimeters. What will be the total square centimeters of fabric that Sue must use to cover all faces of the ottoman?

____

3. A drawing of the attic in a house is shown. It needs insulation on all sides. How many square feet of insulation are needed?

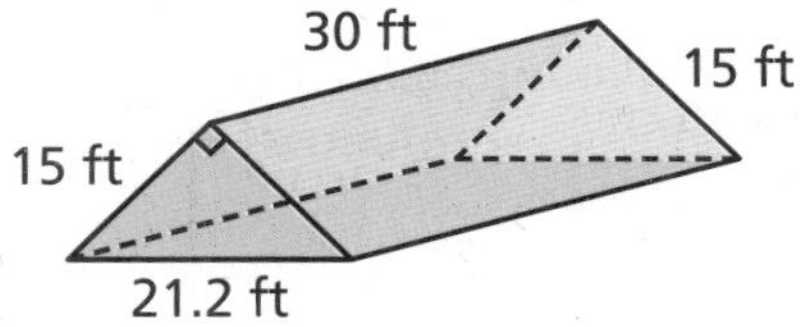

____

Find the surface area of each prism.

4. **Math on the Spot**

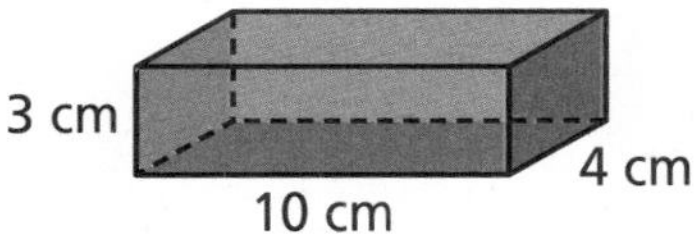

____

5.

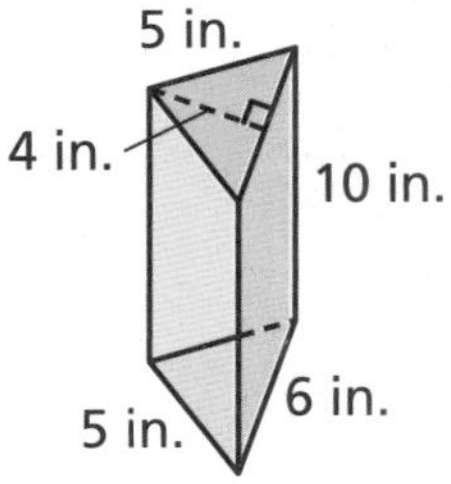

____

Find the surface area. Round to the nearest tenth if necessary.

6. Regular pentagon base

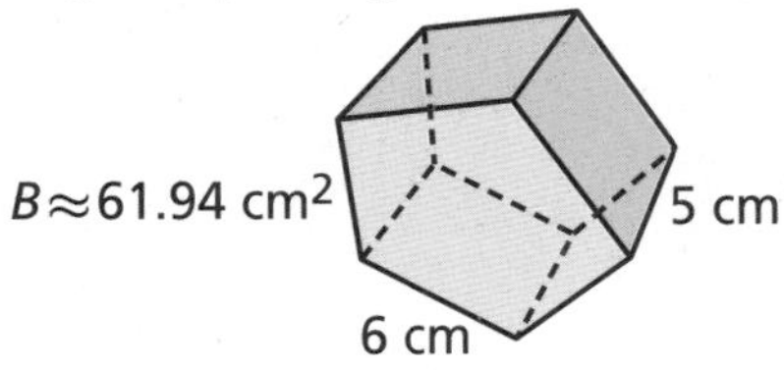

____

7.

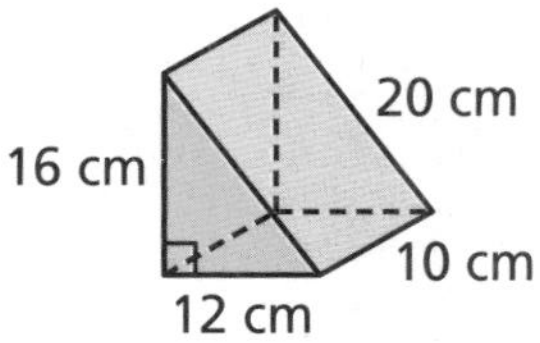

____

© Houghton Mifflin Harcourt Publishing Company • Image Credit: ©leezsnow/iStock/Getty Images Plus

Test Prep

8. Find the surface area of the figure.

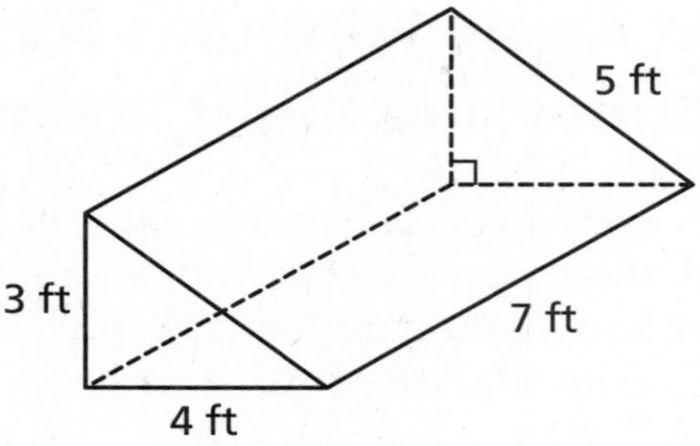

Ⓐ 41 ft^2

Ⓑ 69 ft^2

Ⓒ 75 ft^2

Ⓓ 96 ft^2

9. Mark bought a jewelry box in the shape of a cube. The jewelry box has edge lengths of 6 inches. What is the total surface area of the jewelry box?

Ⓐ 36 in^2

Ⓑ 108 in^2

Ⓒ 216 in^2

Ⓓ 1,296 in^2

10. Find the surface area of a rectangular prism with length of 4.7 inches, width of 6.4 inches, and height of 8.2 inches. Round to the nearest tenth.

____

11. Find the surface area of a regular hexagonal prism with side length 4.2 millimeters, height 3.9 millimeters, and base area of approximately 45.8 square millimeters. Round to the nearest tenth.

____

Spiral Review

12. Identify the two-dimensional figure that results from slicing a cylinder parallel to its base.

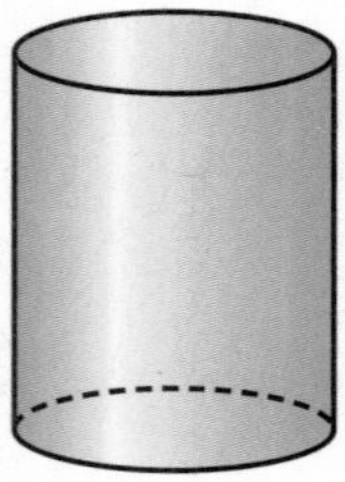

____

13. Find the area of the composite figure.

____

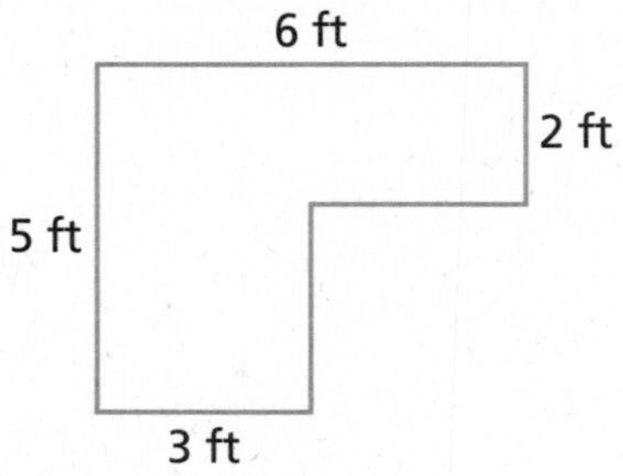

© Houghton Mifflin Harcourt Publishing Company

Name ____________________

Derive and Apply a Formula for the Volume of a Right Prism

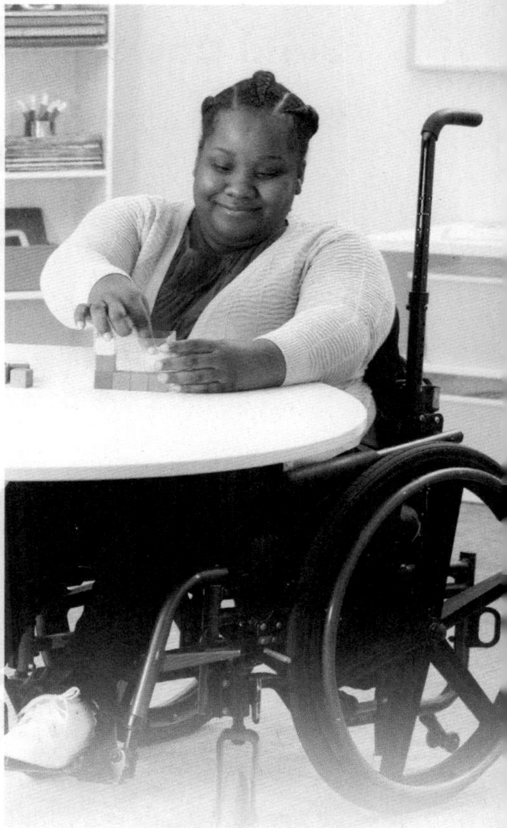

I Can **accurately apply the formula to find the volume of right prisms.**

Spark Your Learning

PAIRS

Use unit cubes or graph paper to find how many 1-inch cubes could fit into a rectangular prism with edge lengths shown. Describe how you found your answer.

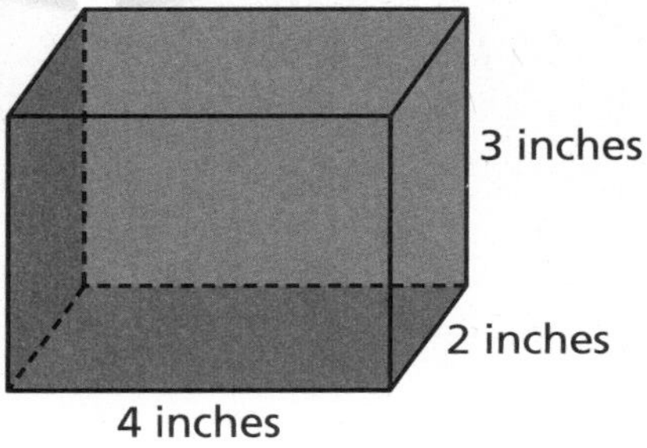

© Houghton Mifflin Harcourt Publishing Company • Image Credit: ©Houghton Mifflin Harcourt

Turn and Talk How are the dimensions of the box related to the number of unit cubes required to fill it?

Build Understanding

1 To derive the formula for volume of any right prism, imagine filling a right rectangular prism with 1-inch cubes.

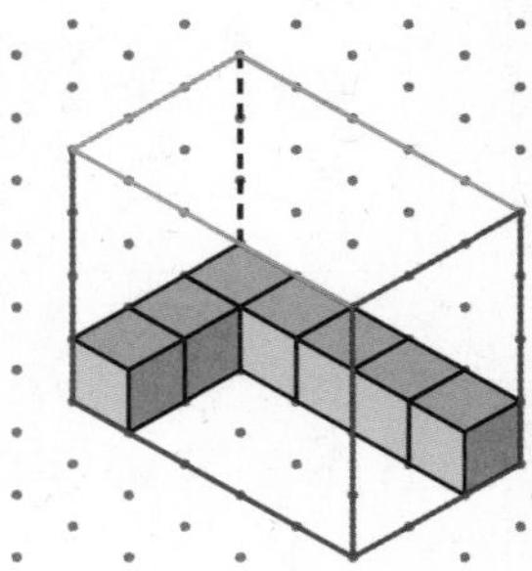

A. How many 1-inch cubes can be placed along the length of the prism shown here? The width of the prism?

______

B. How many cubes are needed to make one horizontal layer in the prism? Explain how you found your answer.

______

______

C. How is completing the first layer like finding the area of the base or a cross section of the prism? How is it different?

______

______

______

D. How will the number of cubes needed to make the first layer compare to the number of cubes needed to complete any other layer?

______

E. How many layers will it take to fill the prism shown? How did you find your answer?

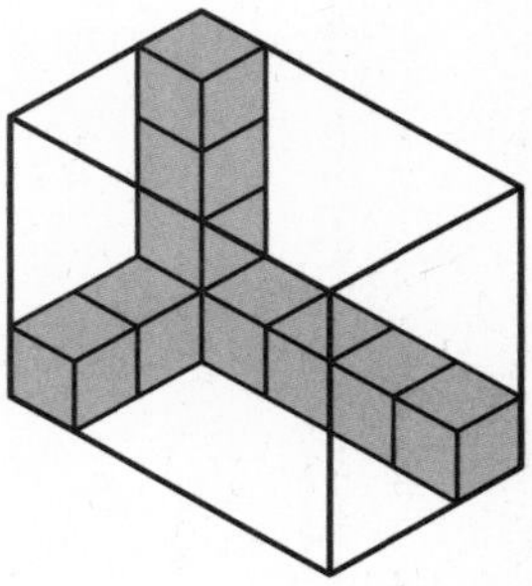

______

______

F. Using the concept of "layers," how can you determine the number of cubes it will take to fill up the entire volume of the prism? What is the volume of the prism?

______

______

G. Using Parts A through F, complete the statements to derive the formula for the volume V of a right prism.

V = (length × ______) × ______

V = area of the ______ × ______

© Houghton Mifflin Harcourt Publishing Company

Turn and Talk Using what you know about the formulas for area of triangles and trapezoids, will this same formula work for other types of prisms?

Name

Step It Out

The formula for volume, $V = Bh$, is the area of the base (B) of a prism multiplied by its height (h).

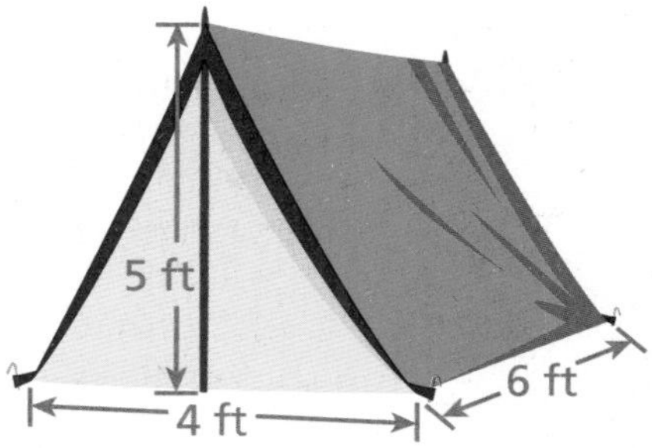

2 Find the volume of the tent shown.

A. Since the tent is shaped like a prism, the base of the prism is a triangle / rectangle.

B. Write an expression for the area of the base of the prism.

$B = (\square)(\square)(\square)$

C. The length of the tent is $\square$ feet. This represents the base / height of the prism.

D. Use the formula.

$V = Bh$

$V = (\square \cdot \square \cdot \square)\square = \square$ ft³

3 A hexagonal prism has a volume of 60 cubic centimeters. The hexagonal base has an area of 12 square centimeters. Find the height of the prism.

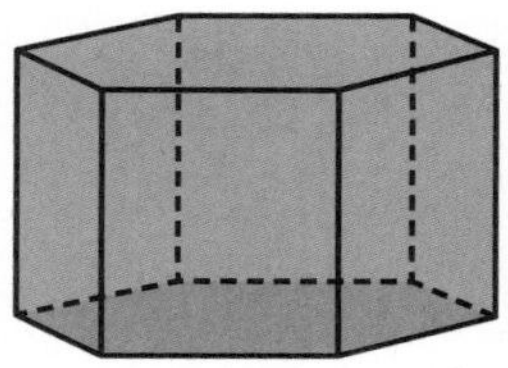

A. The base of this prism is a hexagon / rectangle.

B. Use the formula.

$V = Bh$

$\square = \square h$

$\square = h$; So, the height of the hexagonal prism is $\square$ centimeters.

Check Understanding

1. A rectangular sandbox measures 4 feet by 7 feet by 2 feet. How many cubic feet of sand can the sandbox hold? ______

2. A triangular prism has a base length of 1.5 centimeters, a base height of 3 centimeters, and a height of 12 centimeters.

A. Find the volume of the prism. ______

B. A pentagonal prism has the same volume as the triangular prism in Part A. Its base has an area of $4\frac{1}{2}$ square centimeters. Find its height.

______

© Houghton Mifflin Harcourt Publishing Company

On Your Own

3. Leah is filling a cube-shaped box with packing material and gift items. Each edge length of the box is 20 inches. What is the greatest possible volume of all the presents inside the box?

4. (MP) Use Structure A lantern is represented by the pentagonal prism shown. What is the area of the base of the lantern? Explain your reasoning. Round to the nearest tenth.

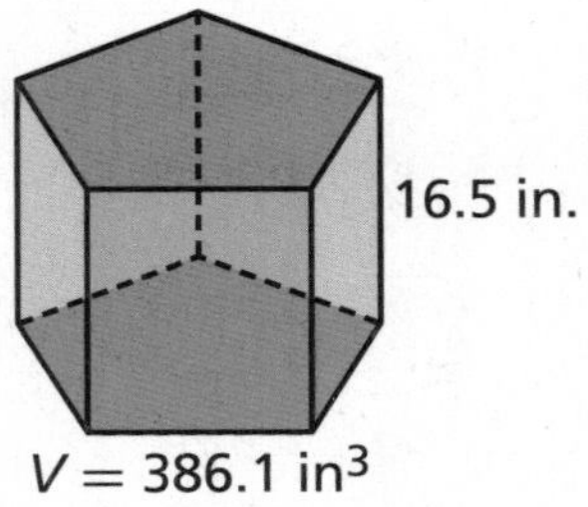

5. A rectangular water tank can hold 142.5 cubic meters of water. Its base is 9.5 meters by 5 meters. What is the height?

6. A triangular prism has the dimensions shown. What is the length x if its volume is 72 cubic feet?

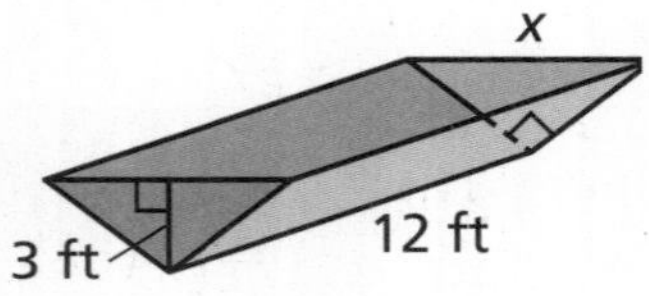

For Problems 7–8, find the volume of the figure.

7.

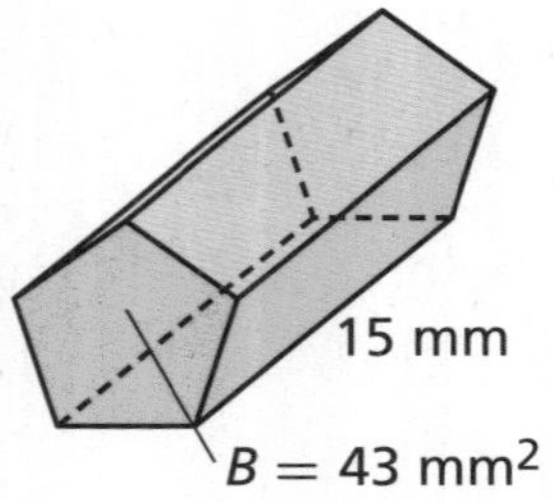

8.

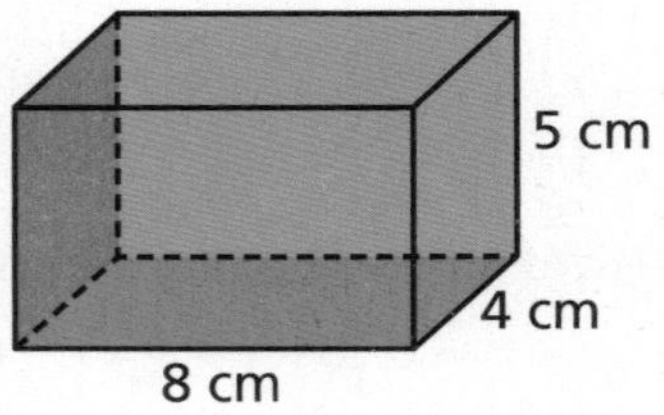

© Houghton Mifflin Harcourt Publishing Company

I'm in a Learning Mindset!

Did I manage my time well when I applied the formulas for volumes of right prisms? What can I do to manage my time better?

Name ______________________________

LESSON 18.3
More Practice/ Homework

ONLINE
Video Tutorials and Interactive Examples

Derive and Apply a Formula for the Volume of a Right Prism

1. The Truit family rented a cabin in the shape of a triangular prism. The cabin is 30 feet deep. What is the volume of the cabin?

2. A piece of copper tubing is in the shape of a hexagonal prism. The area of the base of the prism is 3 square centimeters. The volume of the prism is 51 cubic centimeters. What is the length of the tubing?

3. **Open Ended** A restaurant's walk-in commercial refrigerator has a capacity of 120 cubic feet. It is a rectangular prism 6 feet tall. Using graph paper, model the possible dimensions of the length and width of the refrigerator's footprint. (Hint: Have each square on the graph paper represent one square foot.) Are your answers reasonable? Explain.

4. **Math on the Spot** Find the volume of the triangular prism.

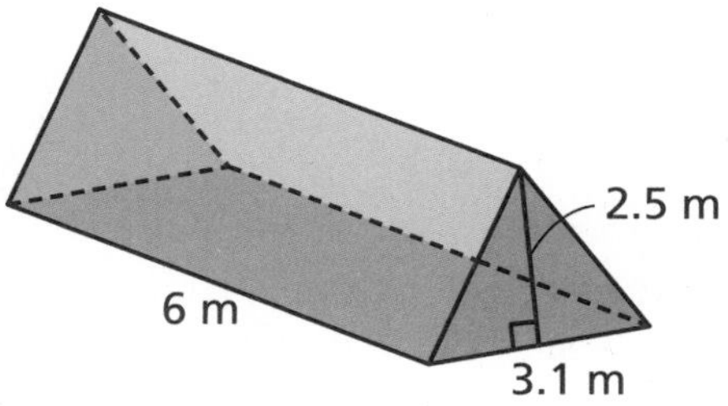

For Problems 5–6, find the volume of each figure.

5.

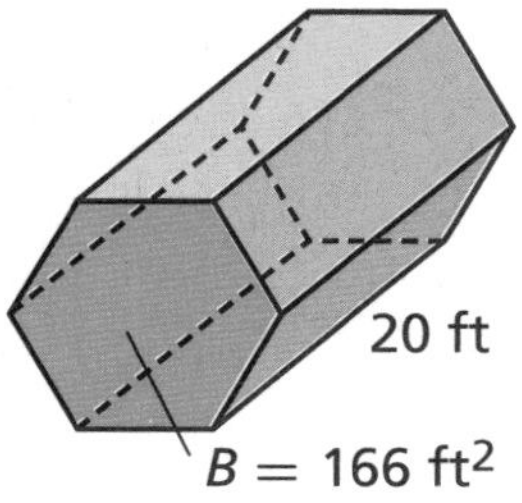

6.

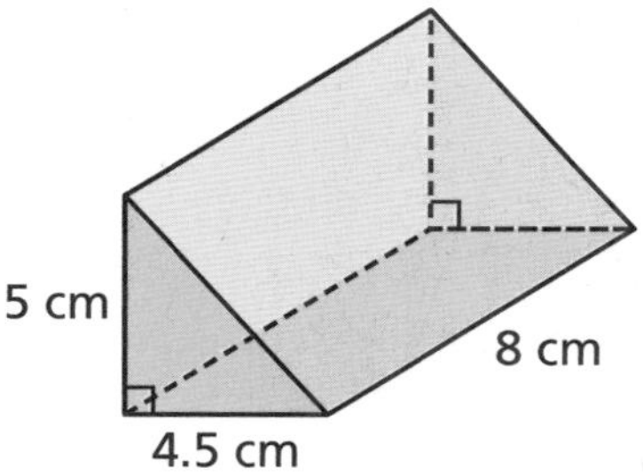

© Houghton Mifflin Harcourt Publishing Company • Image Credit: ©asbe/E+/Getty Images

Test Prep

7. Jerome bought an aquarium that measured 12 inches by 18 inches by 24 inches. Lim bought an aquarium that was 12 inches by 30 inches by 12 inches. Both aquariums are rectangular prisms. How much more volume does Jerome's aquarium have than Lim's?

____

8. An attic for a dollhouse is represented by a triangular prism with the dimensions shown. What is the volume of the attic?

Ⓐ 11.5 in^3 Ⓒ 44 in^3

Ⓑ 22 in^3 Ⓓ 88 in^3

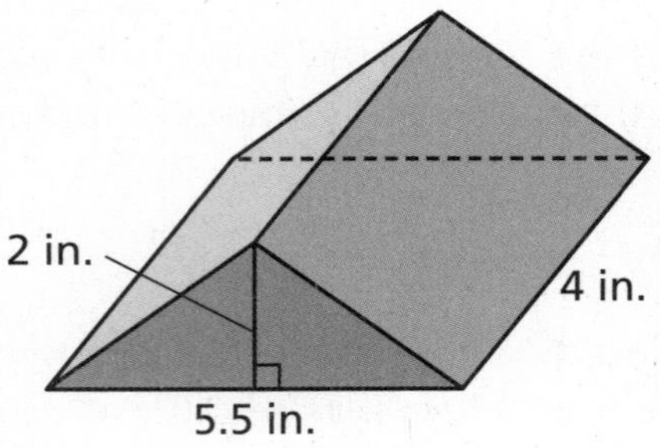

9. The volume of an octagonal prism is 1,260 cubic meters. The base has an area of 28 square meters. Write and solve an equation to find the height of the prism.

____

10. A rectangular prism has a volume of 98 cubic feet, a width of 2 feet, and a length of 7 feet. Find the height of the rectangular prism.

____

Spiral Review

11. Use geometry software to draw a quadrilateral with two pairs of parallel sides and four right angles. What is the quadrilateral?

____

12. Find the surface area of the right triangular prism.

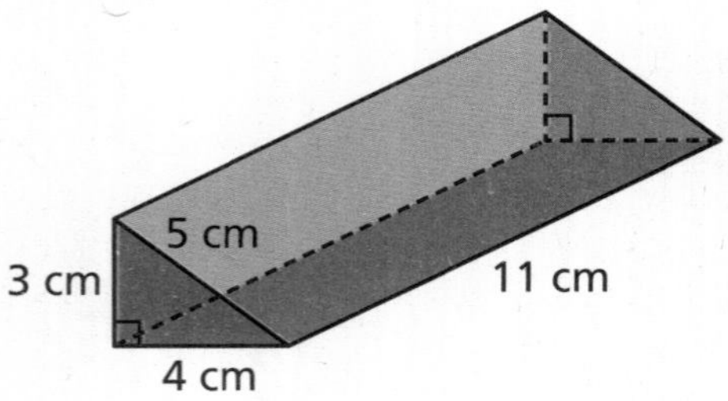

____

13. Find the approximate surface area of the regular pentagonal prism.

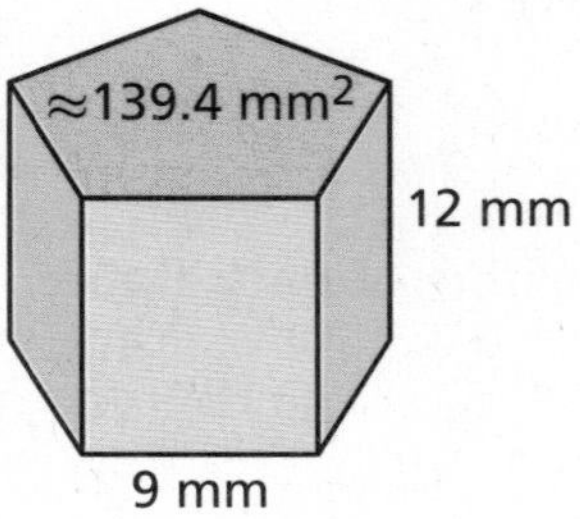

____

© Houghton Mifflin Harcourt Publishing Company

Name ______________________

Find Volume of Cylinders

I Can **find the volume of a cylinder or the dimensions of a cylinder given the volume.**

Spark Your Learning

SMALL GROUPS

You have seen that the volume of a rectangular prism is the area of the base times the height. This may be written as $V = Bh$. Since the area of the rectangular base is the length times the width, the formula can also be written as $V = \ell wh$.

Rectangular Prism

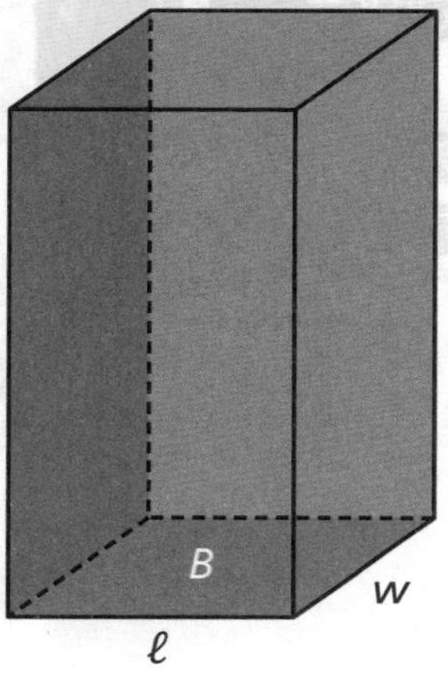

Cylinder

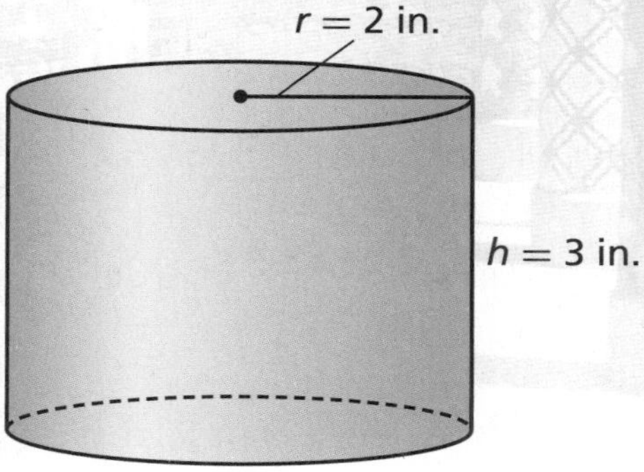

The base of a cylinder is a circle. What is the volume of the cylinder shown? (*Hint*: Recall that the formula for the area A of a circle is $A = \pi r^2$.) Show your steps.

Turn and Talk How is finding the volume of a cylinder similar to finding the volume of a rectangular prism? How is it different?

© Houghton Mifflin Harcourt Publishing Company • Image Credit: ©Sylvain Grandadam/Photographer's Choice/Getty Images

Build Understanding

The formula for the volume of a cylinder is similar to the formula for the volume of a rectangular prism. The formula states that the volume V is the product of the area of the base B and the height h. The only difference is in how to calculate B. You can use the fact that the base of a cylinder is a circle to write the formula in terms of the radius r.

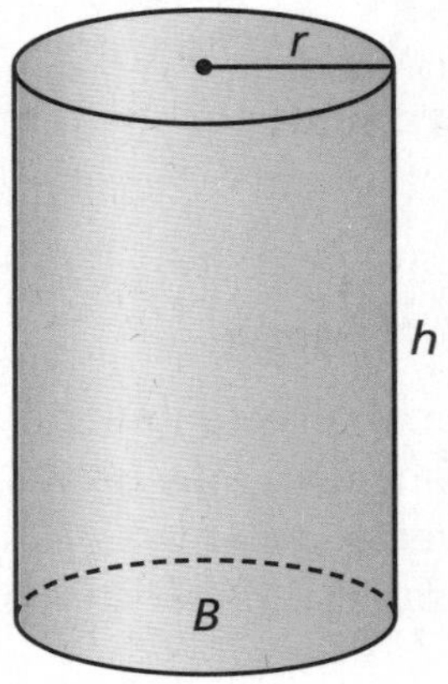

Connect to Vocabulary

A **cylinder** is a three-dimensional figure with two parallel, congruent circular bases connected by a curved lateral surface.

$V = Bh$

or

$V = \pi r^2 h$

1 Find the volume of the cylindrical can of tomato soup shown. Leave your answer in terms of π.

A. What information do you need to know in order to use the formula $V = \pi r^2 h$?

____

____

B. What are the radius and the height of the cylinder?

____

____

C. Show how to substitute for r and h in the formula. Then simplify and leave your answer in terms of π. Be sure to include an appropriate unit for the volume.

____

____

____

D. Now show how to use 3.14 as an approximation for π. Round the volume to the nearest tenth.

____

____

____

Turn and Talk How can you use estimation to show that the volume you found is reasonable?

© Houghton Mifflin Harcourt Publishing Company

Name ____________________

Step It Out

2 Find the volume of the cylinder shown. First write the volume in terms of π. Then substitute 3.14 for π, and express the volume in scientific notation with the first factor rounded to the nearest tenth.

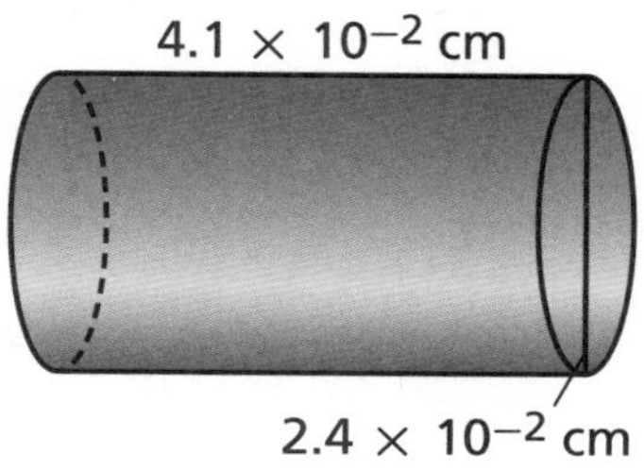

The diameter is 2.4×10^{-2} centimeter, so the radius is

____ $\times 10^{□}$ centimeter.

Now use the formula for the volume of a cylinder.

$V = \pi r^2 h$

$= \pi(\_\_\_\_ \times 10^{-2})^2(\_\_\_\_ \times 10^{-2})$

$= \pi(\_\_\_\_ \times 10^{-4})(\_\_\_\_ \times 10^{-2})$

$\approx (3.14)(\_\_\_\_ \times 10^{□})$

$\approx \_\_\_\_ \times 10^{-6}$

$\approx \_\_\_\_ \times 10^{-5}$ cubic centimeter

3 The volume of the cylinder shown is 602.88 cubic feet. Find the height of the cylinder. Use 3.14 for π.

Use the formula for the volume of a cylinder to solve for h.

$V = \pi r^2 h$

$\_\_\_\_ \approx (3.14)(\_\_\_\_)^2 h$

$\_\_\_\_ \approx (3.14)(\_\_\_\_)h$

$\_\_\_\_ \approx (\_\_\_\_)h$

$h \approx \frac{□}{□} = \_\_\_\_$ feet

Check Understanding

1. The volume of this cylinder is 32π yd^3. Find the height.

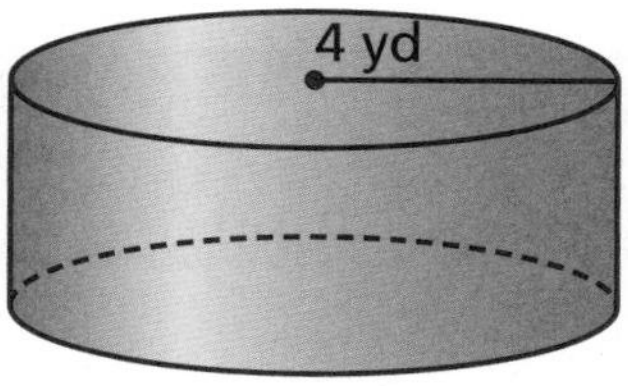

____

2. Find the volume to the nearest tenth. Use 3.14 for π.

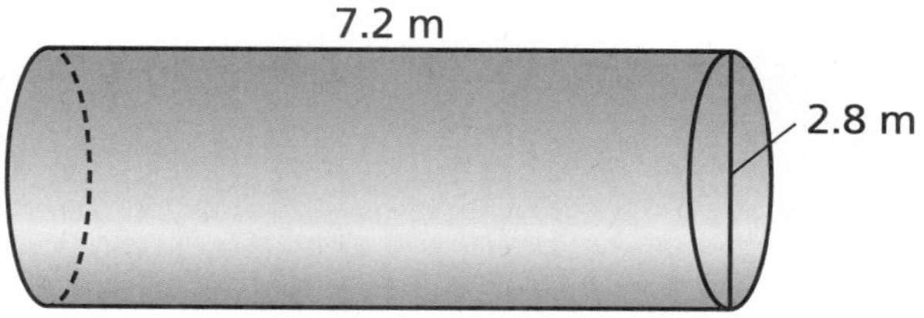

____

© Houghton Mifflin Harcourt Publishing Company • Image Credit: ©Reven T.C. Wurman/Alamy Images

On Your Own

For Problems 3–4, find the volume of each cylinder. Use 3.14 for π. Round the volume to the nearest tenth.

3.

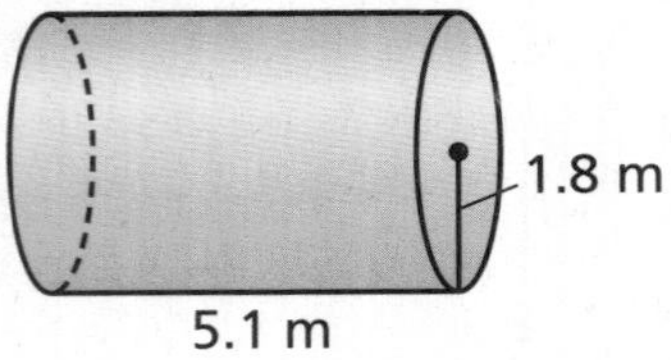

____

4.

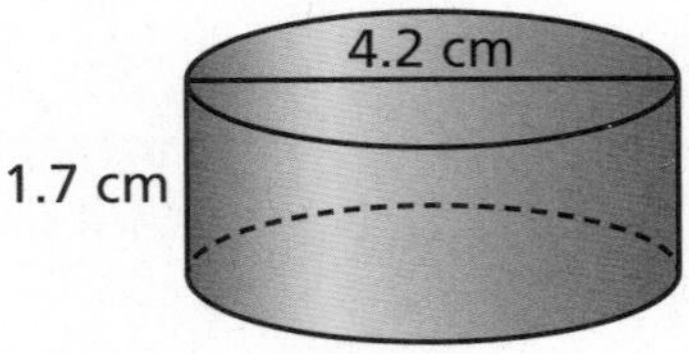

____

For Problems 5–6, find the approximate height of each cylinder. Use 3.14 for π.

5. Volume $= 37.68 \text{ in}^3$

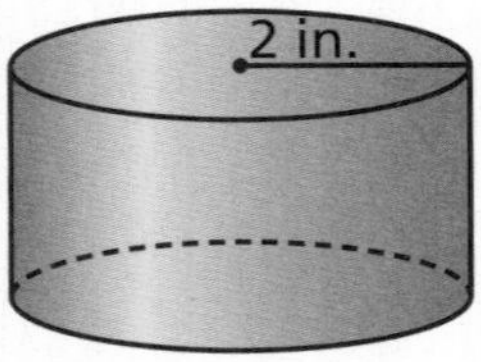

____

6. Volume $= 146.952 \text{ cm}^3$

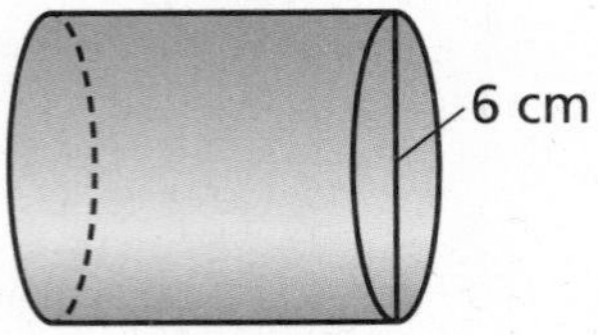

____

7. Find the approximate volume of the cylinder shown. Use 3.14 for π. Express the volume in scientific notation and round the first factor to the nearest tenth. ______________________

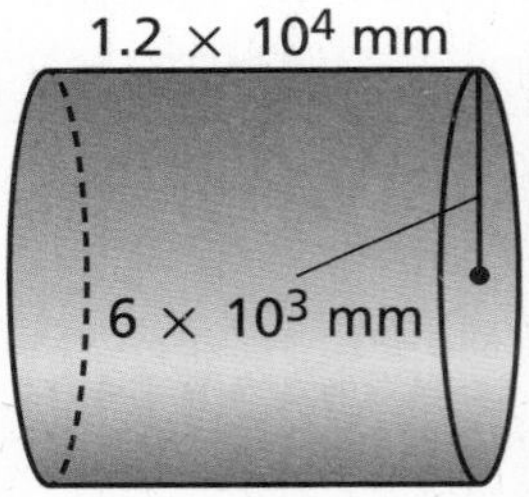

8. **Open Ended** Give the radius and height of a cylinder whose volume is greater than 1,000 cubic feet but less than 2,000 cubic feet. ______________________

9. (MP) **Attend to Precision** Consider a cylinder with the radius and height shown in the image.

A. Find the approximate volume of the cylinder using the π key on your calculator. Round your answer in a way that seems most appropriate.

____

B. Explain how you decided how many digits to include in your answer.

____

____

I'm in a Learning Mindset!

What methods are most effective in helping me use the formula for the volume of a cylinder?

____

© Houghton Mifflin Harcourt Publishing Company • Image Credit: ©arigato/Shutterstock

Name ______________________

ONLINE
Video Tutorials and Interactive Examples

Find Volume of Cylinders

1. The radius of a cylinder is 49 feet, and the height is 180 feet. Find the volume of the cylinder. Leave your answer in terms of π.

____

2. Math on the Spot Find the approximate volume of each cylinder. Use 3.14 for π. Round the volume to the nearest cubic unit.

A.

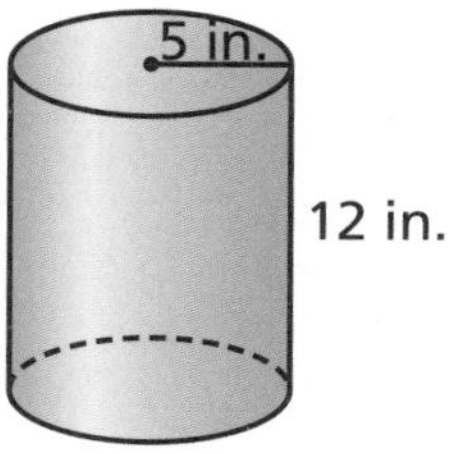

B.

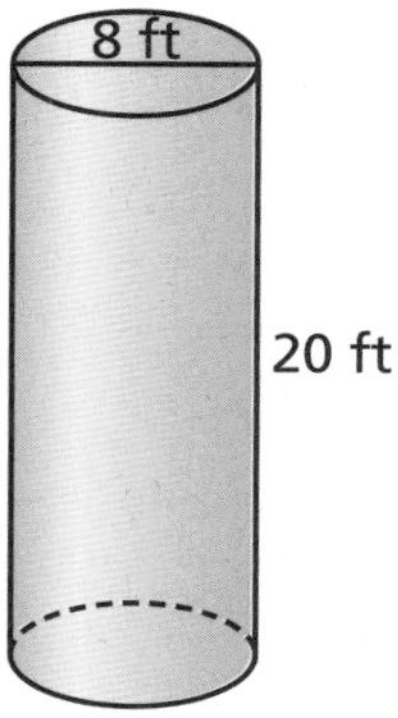

C.

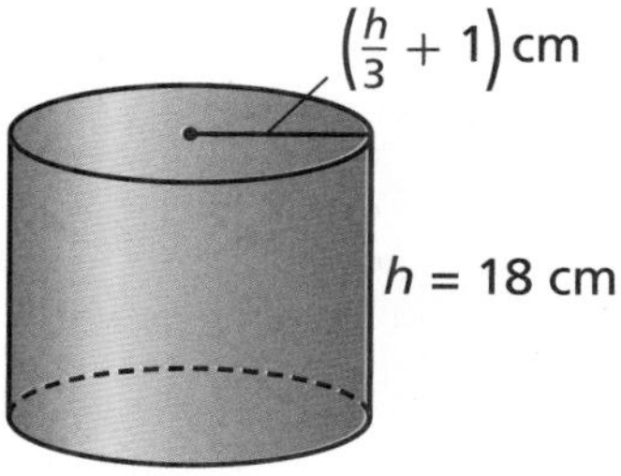

______________ ______________ ______________

For Problems 3–4, approximate the volume of each cylinder. Use 3.14 for π. Round the volume to the nearest cubic unit.

3.

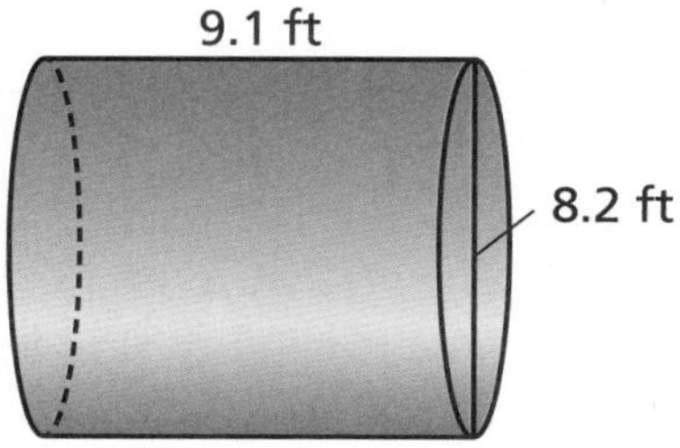

4.

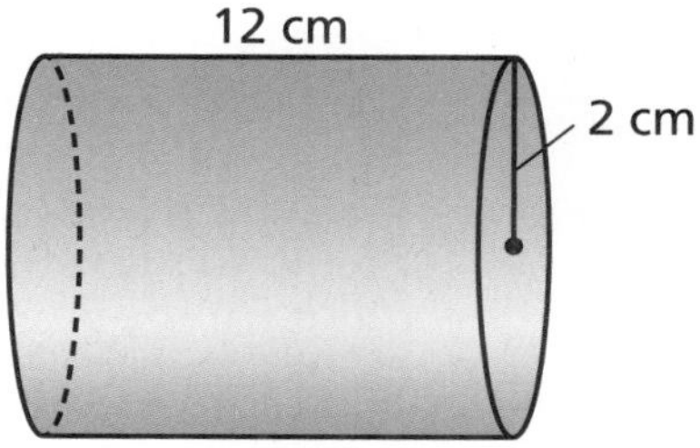

______________ ______________

5. A cylinder has diameter *d* and height *h*. Write a formula for the volume *V* of the cylinder in terms of *d* and *h*.

____

For Problems 6–7, find the approximate height of each cylinder. Use 3.14 for π.

6. Volume = 7.85 ft^3

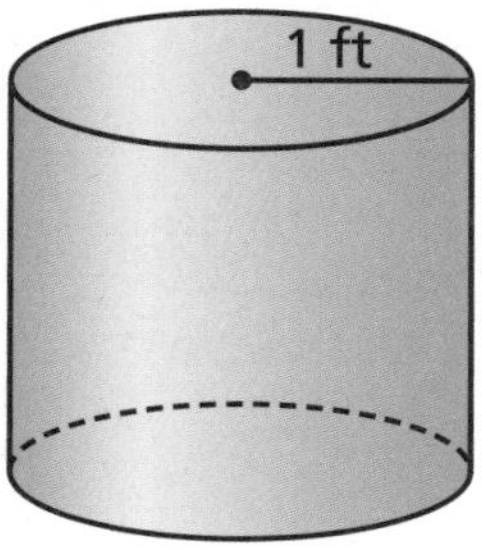

7. Volume = 668.6944 m^3

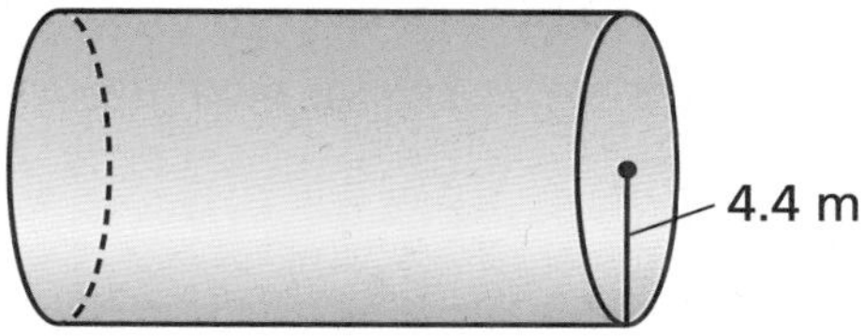

______________ ______________

© Houghton Mifflin Harcourt Publishing Company • Image Credit: ©Hans Georg Roth/Corbis Documentary/Getty Images

Test Prep

8. Which of the following values for the radius and height of a cylinder result in a cylinder with the greatest volume?

Ⓐ radius = 1 ft; height = 4 ft
Ⓑ radius = 2 ft; height = 3 ft
Ⓒ radius = 3 ft; height = 2 ft
Ⓓ radius = 4 ft; height = 1 ft

9. Which value or values for the radius of the cylinder shown result in a cylinder with a volume that is greater than 100 cubic centimeters but less than 600 cubic centimeters? Select all that apply.

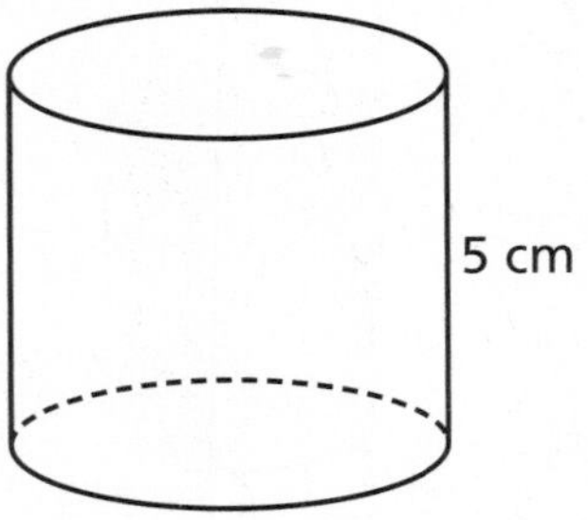

Ⓐ 1 cm
Ⓑ 3 cm
Ⓒ 5 cm
Ⓓ 6 cm
Ⓔ 8 cm
Ⓕ 10 cm

10. The cylinder shown has a volume of 62.8 cubic inches. Which of the following is closest to the height of the cylinder?

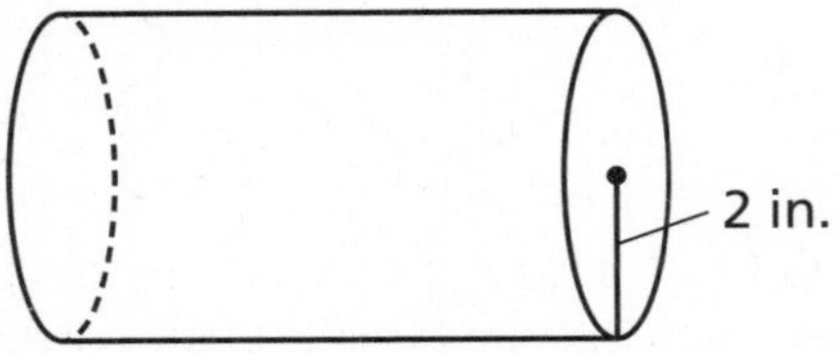

Ⓐ 5 in.
Ⓑ 10 in.
Ⓒ 20 in.
Ⓓ 30 in.

11. The radius of Cylinder *P* is 6 millimeters, and the radius of Cylinder *Q* is 3 millimeters. The cylinders have the same height. Which is a true statement about the cylinders?

Ⓐ The volume of Cylinder *P* is 2 times the volume of Cylinder *Q*.
Ⓑ The volume of Cylinder *P* is 4 times the volume of Cylinder *Q*.
Ⓒ The volume of Cylinder *P* is 18 times the volume of Cylinder *Q*.
Ⓓ The volume of Cylinder *P* is 36 times the volume of Cylinder *Q*.

Spiral Review

12. Find the height of the cone. Round your answer to the nearest tenth of a centimeter.

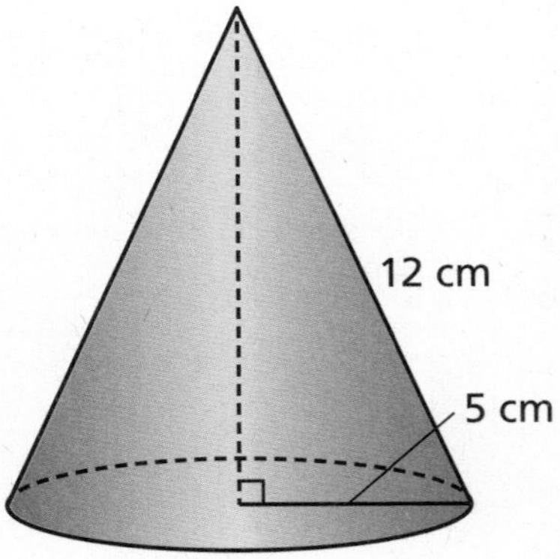

____

13. Write the number 0.0000000058 in scientific notation.

____

14. Find the difference and express your answer in scientific notation.

$(3.4 \times 10^6) - (4.9 \times 10^5)$

____

© Houghton Mifflin Harcourt Publishing Company

Name ____________________

Find Volume of Cones and Spheres

I Can **find the volume of a cone and a sphere, and find the dimensions of a cone and a sphere, given their volumes.**

Step It Out

1 In a **right cone**, a line drawn from the vertex perpendicular to the base passes through the center of the base. The distance from the vertex to the center of the base is the height of the right cone.

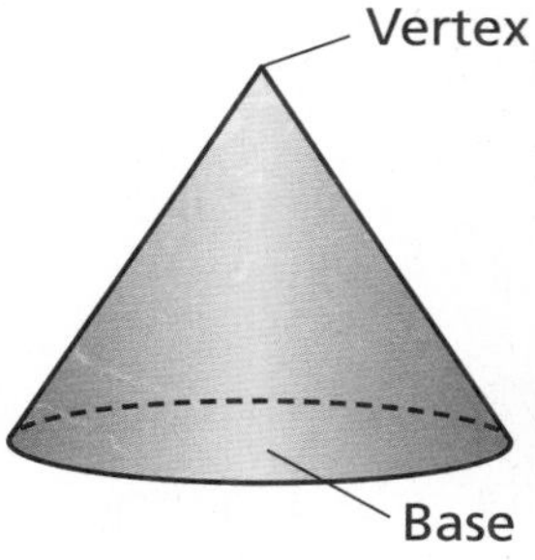

You can use the following reasoning to develop a formula for the volume of a cone.

A. Consider a cone with radius r and height h. Imagine that the cone is made of cardboard and has an open top, as shown. Also, consider a cylinder with the same radius and the same height.

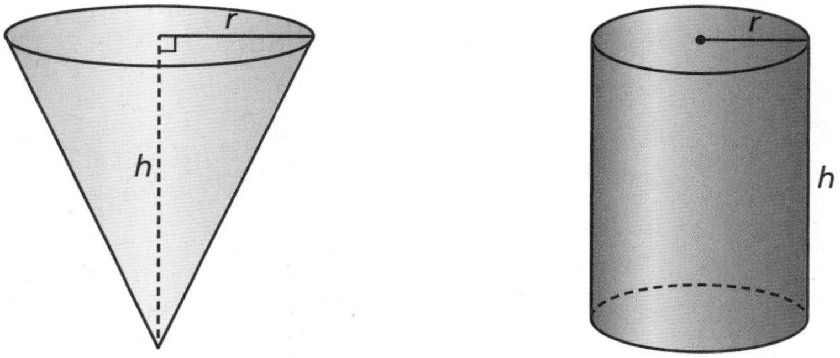

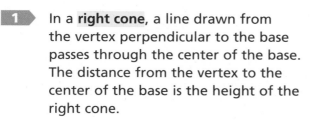

You can fill the cone with sand and pour the sand into the cylinder. It takes 3 cones full of sand to fill the cylinder completely.

This means the volume of the cone is ____ the volume of the cylinder.

B. Complete the following to write a formula for the volume of a cone.

volume of cone $= \frac{\square}{\square}$ volume of cylinder

$= \frac{\square}{\square} B \square = \frac{\square}{\square} \square \square^2 \square$

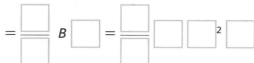

Turn and Talk How is the formula for the volume of a cone similar to the formula for the volume of a cylinder? How is it different?

© Houghton Mifflin Harcourt Publishing Company • Image Credit: ©David Moore/Australia/Alamy

2 A **sphere** is a three-dimensional figure with all points the same distance from the center. The radius of a sphere is the distance from the center to any point on the sphere.

You can use the following reasoning to develop a formula for the volume of a sphere.

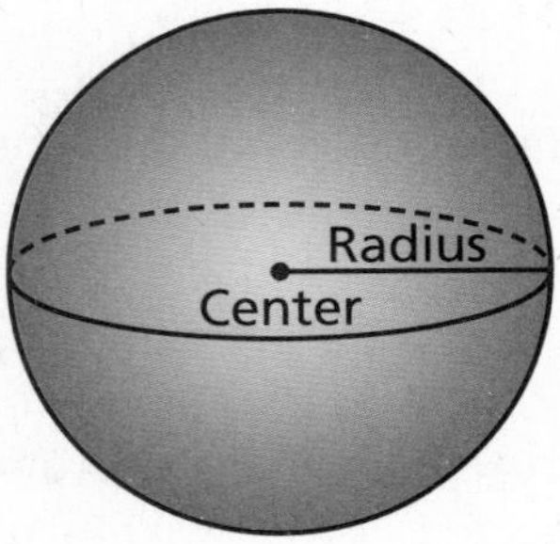

A. Start with a sphere of radius r. How is the height of the sphere related to the radius?

$h =$ ______ r

B. Consider a cylinder with the same radius and the same height as the sphere.

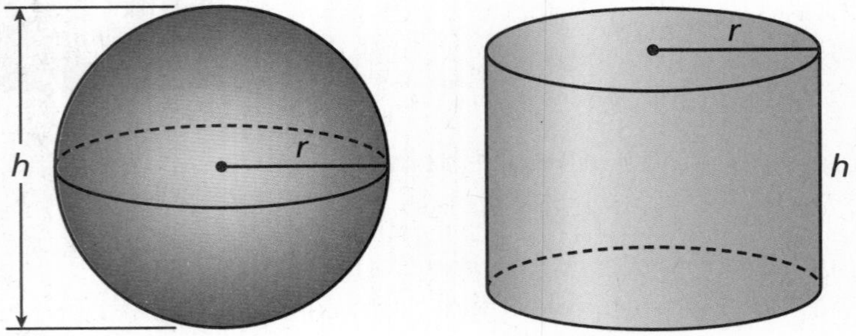

Imagine filling the sphere with sand and pouring the sand into the cylinder. The sand will fill $\frac{2}{3}$ of the cylinder.

volume of sphere $= \frac{\square}{\square}$ volume of cylinder

$= \frac{\square}{\square} \pi r^2 h$

$= \frac{\square}{\square} \pi r^2($______$)$

$= \frac{\square}{\square} \pi r^3$

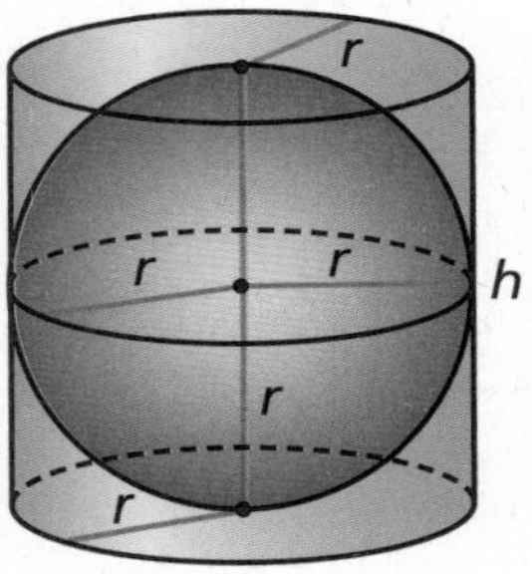

Turn and Talk How is the formula for the volume of a sphere similar to the formula for the volume of a cone? How is it different?

© Houghton Mifflin Harcourt Publishing Company

Name ___

3 You can use a formula to find the volume of a cone when you know, or can calculate, its radius and height.

The cone-shaped party hat shown here has a radius of 3 inches. Find the volume of the cone. Use $\frac{22}{7}$ for π.

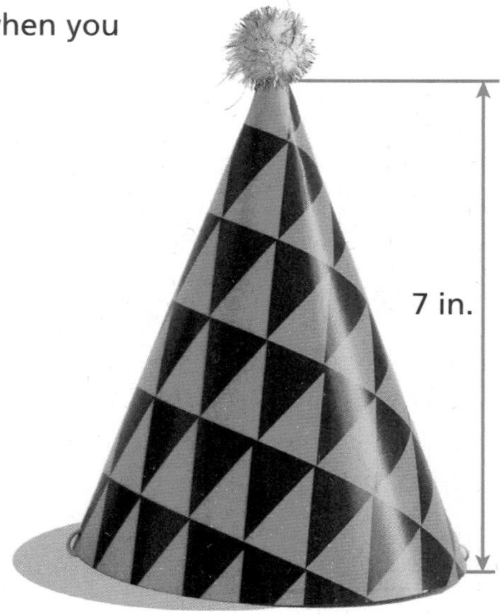

$V = \frac{1}{3}\pi r^2 h$

$\approx \frac{1}{3}\left(\frac{22}{7}\right)(\_\_\_\_\_\_)^2(\_\_\_\_\_\_)$

$= \frac{1}{3}\left(\frac{22}{7}\right)(\_\_\_\_\_\_)(\_\_\_\_\_\_)$

$= \_\_\_\_\_\_$

The volume of the cone is approximately ______ cubic inches.

4 You can use a formula to find the volume of a sphere when you are given or can calculate its radius.

Approximate the volume of the sphere. Use $\frac{22}{7}$ for π and leave your answer as an improper fraction.

To find the volume, use the volume formula with $r = \_\_\_\_\_\_$.

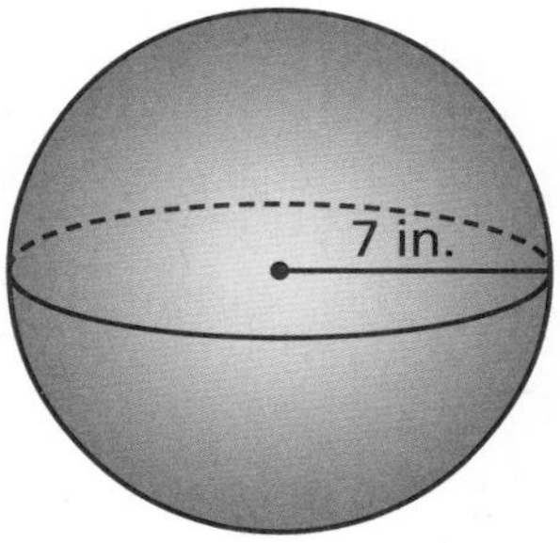

$V = \frac{4}{3}\pi r^3$

$\approx \frac{4}{3}\left(\frac{22}{7}\right)(\_\_\_\_\_\_)^3$

$= \frac{4}{3}\left(\frac{22}{7}\right)(\_\_\_\_\_\_)$

$= \_\_\_\_\_\_$

The volume of the sphere is approximately ______ cubic inches.

Check Understanding

1. **A.** A cone has a radius of 6 inches and a slant height of 10 inches. What is the height of the cone? ______

   B. What is the volume of the cone in Part A? Leave your answer in terms of π. ______

2. Approximate the volume of a sphere with a diameter of 20 meters. Leave your answer in terms of π. Then use 3.14 for π and round the volume to the nearest tenth.

______

© Houghton Mifflin Harcourt Publishing Company • **Image Credit:** ©yukihipo/Shutterstock

On Your Own

3. The cone-shaped candle shown has a radius of 6 centimeters.

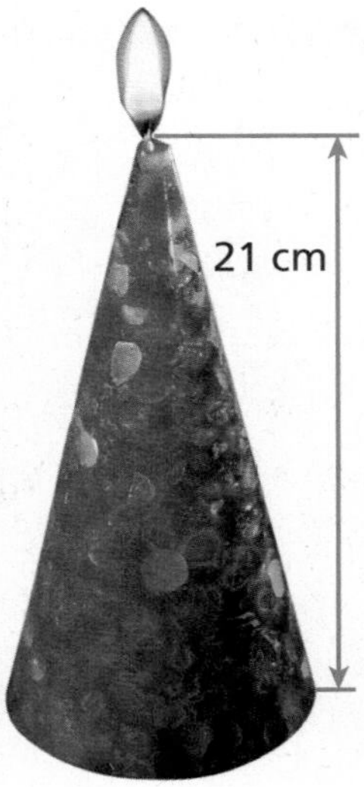

A. Find the volume of the cone. Leave your answer in terms of π.

____

B. (MP) **Construct Arguments** A cylinder has the same radius and height as the cone. What is the volume of the cylinder in terms of π? Explain how you know.

____

____

____

4. Consider the spherical marble shown in the photo.

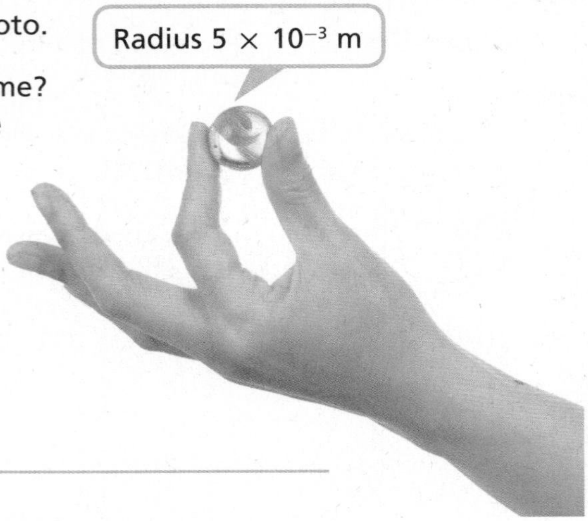

A. (MP) **Attend to Precision** What is the volume? Leave your answer in terms of π. Round the first factor in scientific notation to the nearest tenth.

____

B. Find the volume of the marble to the nearest cubic millimeter using $\frac{22}{7}$ for π. Explain your method.

____

____

____

For Problems 5–6, find the approximate volume of the cone. Use 3.14 for π and round the volume to the nearest tenth.

5.

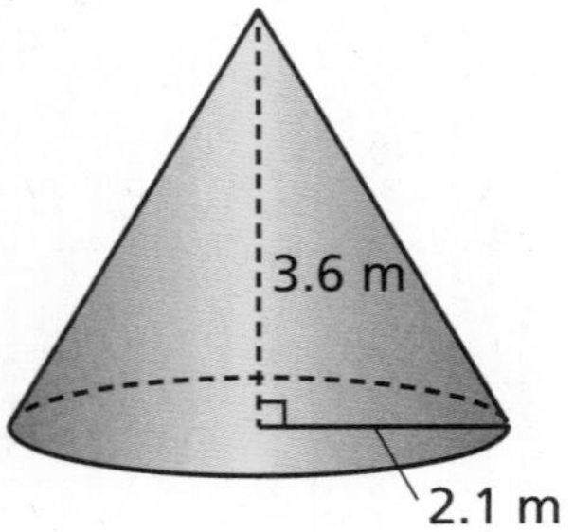

____

6.

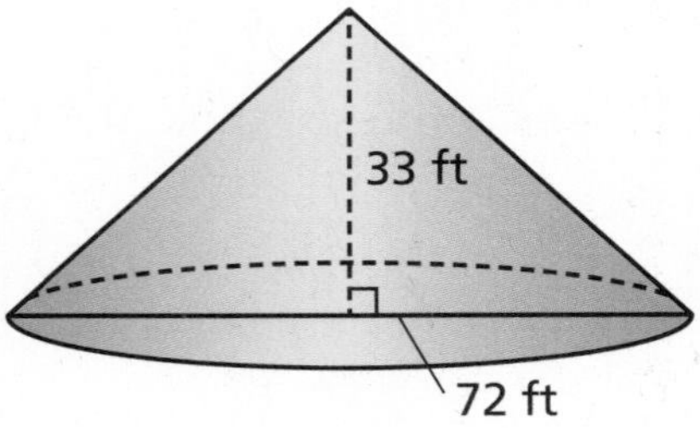

____

© Houghton Mifflin Harcourt Publishing Company • Image Credit: ©Martin Bond/Alamy

Name

Use the cone-shaped hedge shown to answer Problems 7–8.

7. What is the volume of the cone? Leave your answer in terms of π.

8. Find the approximate volume of the cone using $\frac{22}{7}$ for π. Round the volume to the nearest tenth.

9. The radius of a basketball is 12 centimeters. Approximate the volume of the basketball. Use $\frac{22}{7}$ for π and round the volume to the nearest tenth.

For Problems 10–12, find the approximate volume of each sphere. Use 3.14 for π and round the volume to the nearest tenth.

10.

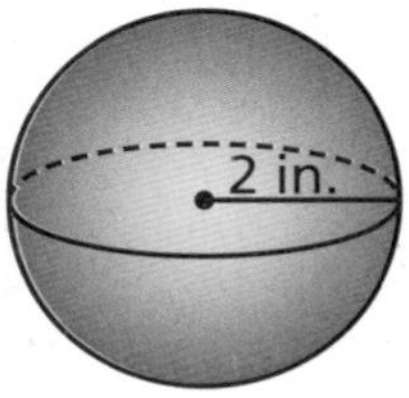

11.

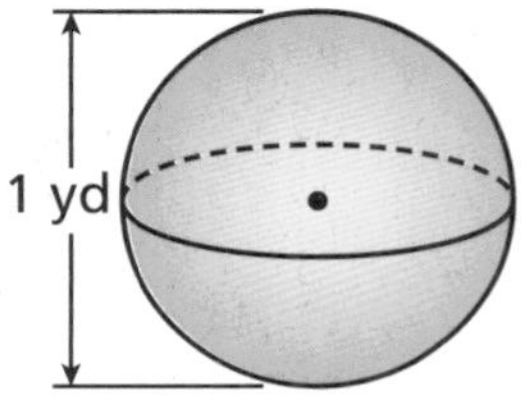

12.

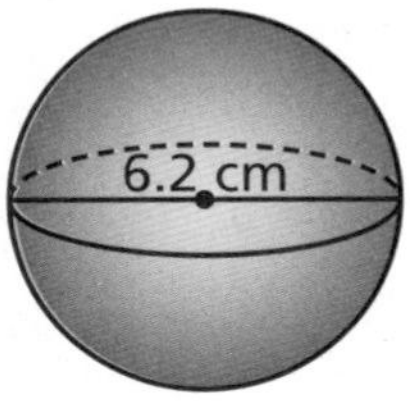

For Problems 13–14, find the approximate volume of each cone. Use 3.14 for π.

13.

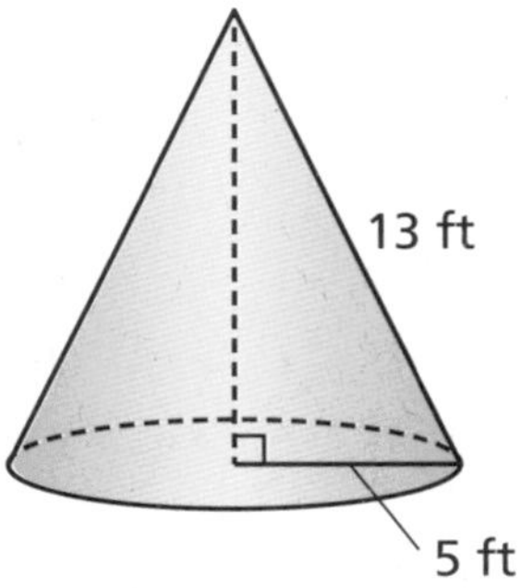

14.

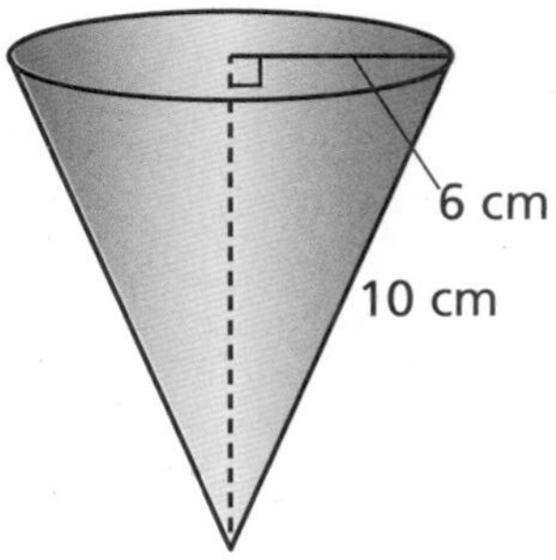

© Houghton Mifflin Harcourt Publishing Company • Image Credit: ©Aaron Amat/Shutterstock

15. Open Ended In the photo, V represents the volume of the spherical plant shown. Determine a possible radius for the sphere. Justify your answer.

16. (MP) **Critique Reasoning** The cone and cylinder shown have the same radius. The height of the cylinder is 3 times the height of the cone. Jared looked at the solids and concluded that the volume of the cylinder must be 3 times the volume of the cone. Therefore, he said the volume of the cylinder is 3×40, or 120 cubic centimeters.

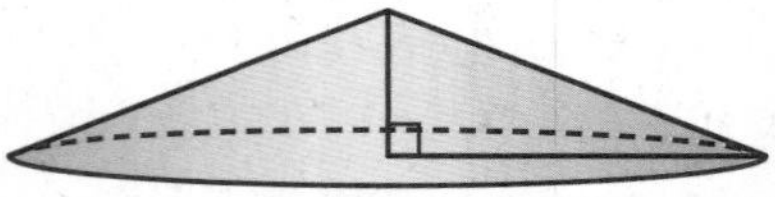

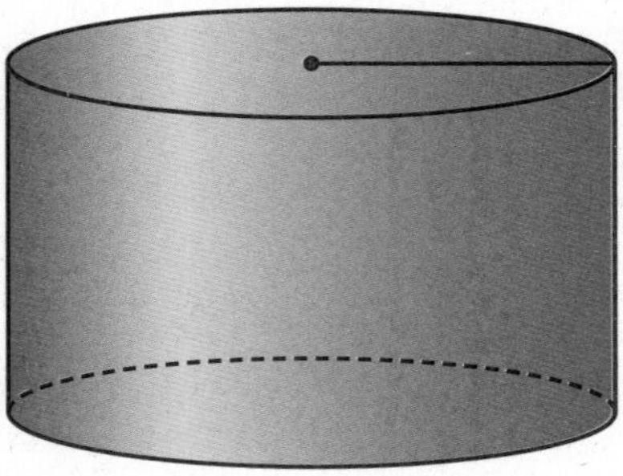

Do you agree with Jared's reasoning? Explain.

17. Consider a set of cones that all have a radius of 1 centimeter. The heights of the cones are 1 centimeter, 2 centimeters, 3 centimeters, 4 centimeters, and 5 centimeters.

A. Complete the table. Leave the volumes in terms of π.

Height (cm)	1	2	3	4	5
Volume (cm^3)					

B. (MP) **Model with Mathematics** Write an equation that gives the volume y of a cone with radius 1 centimeter if you know the height x of the cone. Describe the graph of the equation.

© Houghton Mifflin Harcourt Publishing Company • Image Credit: ©mikespics/iStock / Getty Images Plus/Getty Images

Name ______________________________

ONLINE
Ed
Video Tutorials and
Interactive Examples

Find Volume of Cones and Spheres

1. **Math on the Spot** Approximate the volume of a sphere with a radius of 7 feet, both in terms of π and to the nearest tenth. Use 3.14 for π.

____

2. A cone has a height of 6×10^3 millimeters and a radius of 2×10^3 millimeters. Find the volume of the cone. Leave your answer in scientific notation and in terms of π.

____

Approximate the volume of each cone. Use 3.14 for π and round the volume to the nearest tenth.

3.

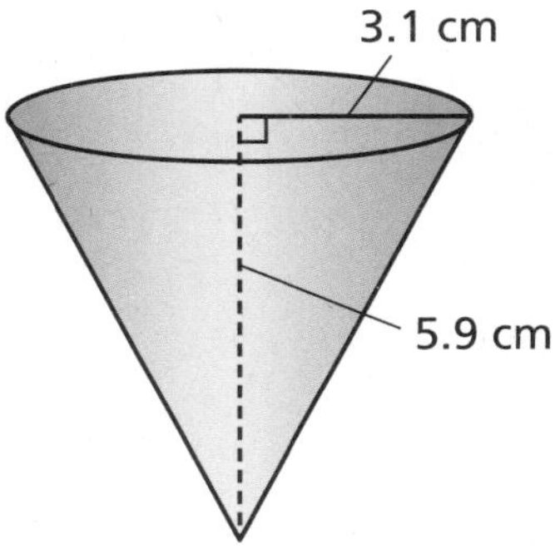

____

4.

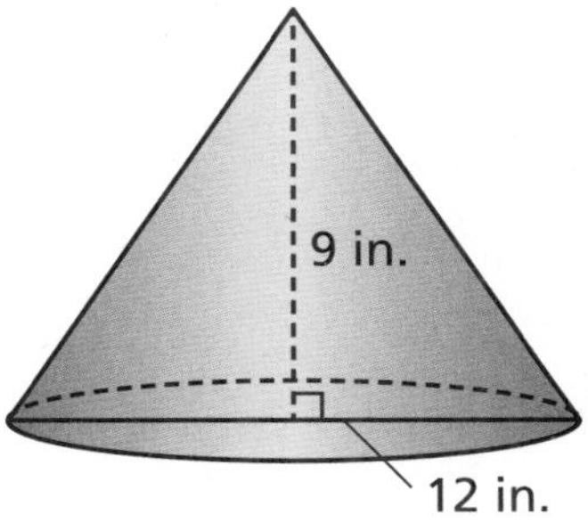

____

For Problems 5–6, approximate the volume of the sphere. Use 3.14 for π and round the volume to the nearest tenth.

5.

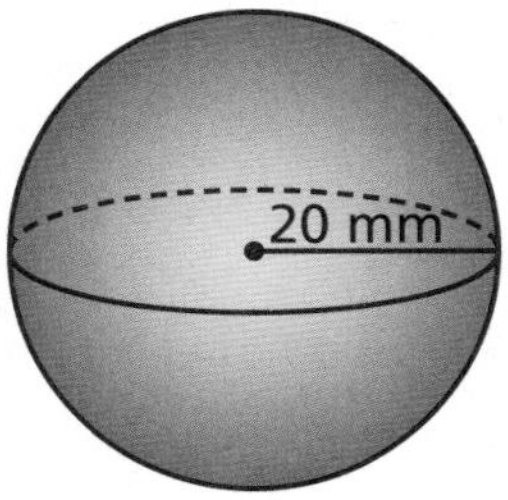

____

6.

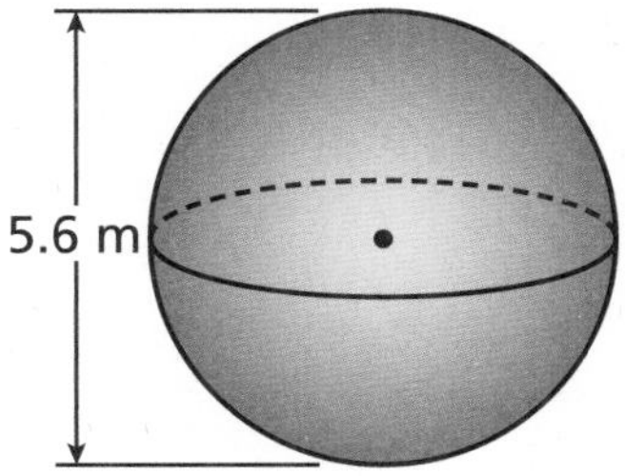

____

7. (MP) **Critique Reasoning** A student was asked to find the exact volume of the sphere shown, leaving the answer in terms of π. The student's work is shown. Explain the student's error.

$V = \frac{4}{3}\pi r^3 = \frac{4}{3}\pi(6)^3 = \frac{4}{3}\pi(216) = 288\pi \text{ ft}^3$

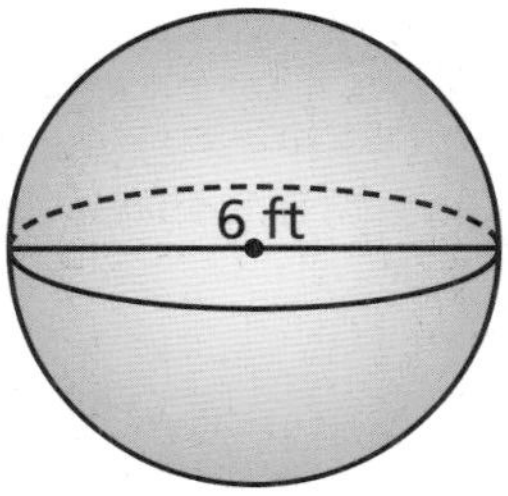

____

____

© Houghton Mifflin Harcourt Publishing Company

Test Prep

8. Fill in the formula for the volume of the cone shown here by writing a numerical value in each box.

$$V = \frac{\square}{\square}\pi\left(\square\right)^2\left(\square\right)$$

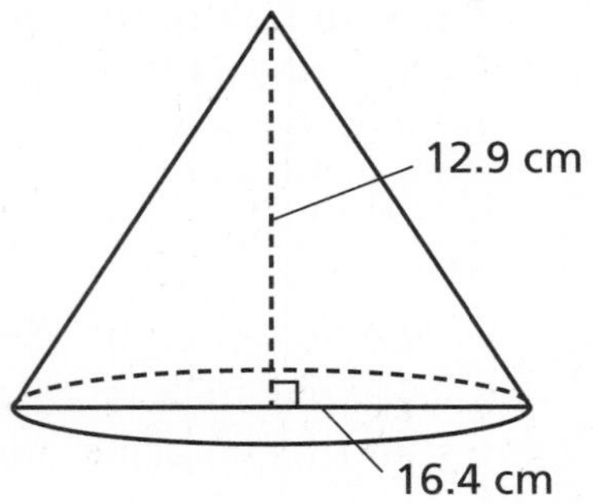

9. A student has a set of six spheres with radii 1, 2, 3, 4, 5, and 6 centimeters. Which of the following is the volume of a sphere in the set? Select all that apply.

Ⓐ $\frac{4}{3}\pi\ \text{cm}^3$

Ⓑ $\frac{8}{3}\pi\ \text{cm}^3$

Ⓒ $\frac{32}{3}\pi\ \text{cm}^3$

Ⓓ $36\pi\ \text{cm}^3$

Ⓔ $125\pi\ \text{cm}^3$

Ⓕ $288\pi\ \text{cm}^3$

10. Which radius and height result in a cone with the least volume?

Ⓐ radius = 7 m; height = 1 m

Ⓑ radius = 5 m; height = 5 m

Ⓒ radius = 3 m; height = 10 m

Ⓓ radius = 1 m; height = 15 m

Spiral Review

11. Latreesha collected data on the daily high temperature and the number of quarts of iced coffee sold at a cafe. She made a scatter plot of the data and then drew a trend line. Her trend line is shown. The line passes through the points (10, 50) and (30, 100). What is the slope of the line? What does it represent in this context?

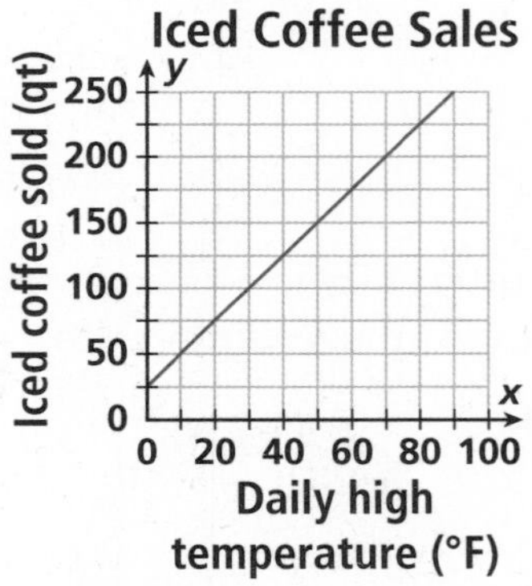

____

____

____

12. A triangle has sides of length 3 inches, 5 inches, and 6 inches. Is the triangle a right triangle? Explain how you know.

____

____

13. Approximate the volume of a cylinder with a radius of 3.4 meters and a height of 1.2 meters. Use 3.14 for π and round the volume to the nearest tenth.

____

© Houghton Mifflin Harcourt Publishing Company

Name ______________________

Solve Multi-Step Problems with Surface Area and Volume

I Can **solve multi-step surface area and volume problems.**

Step It Out

1 A toy manufacturer makes a game that they package in a cube-shaped carton with a surface area of 54 square inches. What is the volume of the shipping carton?

A. What information is given? surface area / volume

What information is needed? surface area / volume

B. Write the formulas for surface area and volume of a cube, where *s* is the length of an edge.

Surface area $= 6\square^2$ and Volume $= \square^3$

What do the two formulas have in common?

____

C. Use the given surface area to find the edge length, *s*.

	Surface area $= 6\square^2$
Substitute the surface area.	$\square = 6\square^2$
Divide both sides by 6.	$\square = s^2$
Find the number whose square is 9.	$\square = s$

D. Use the edge length to find the volume.

Volume $= \square^3$

Volume $= \square^3 = \square$ in^3

The volume is ________ cubic inches.

Turn and Talk If the carton were a rectangular prism instead of a cube, could you find its edge lengths from its surface area? Explain.

© Houghton Mifflin Harcourt Publishing Company • Image Credits: (tl) ©artpritsadee/Shutterstock, (tr) ©Sergei Kardashev/Shutterstock

2 Use what you know about surface area and volume to solve each problem.

A. The regular pentagonal prism shown has a surface area of approximately 191 square centimeters. Find the approximate volume of the prism.

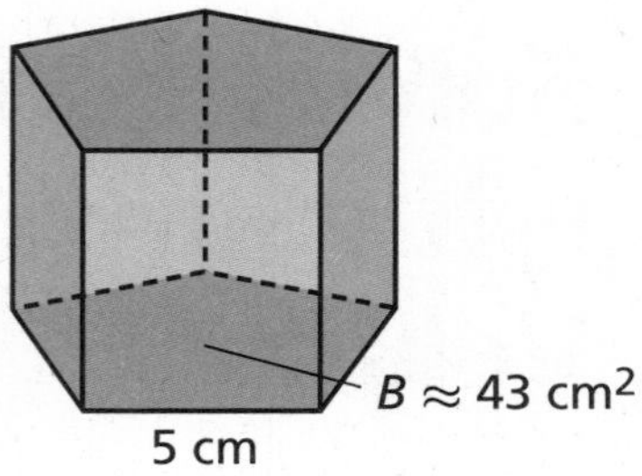

Use the surface area to find the approximate height.

Surface Area $= 2B + Ph$ $\quad \square \approx 2(\square) + \square h$

$191 \approx \square + 25h$

Subtract 86 from both sides: $\square \approx 25h$

Divide both sides by 25: $\square \approx h$

The approximate height h is ______ centimeters. Use the approximate height to find the volume.

Volume $= Bh \approx \square \times \square = \square$ cm^3

The volume is approximately ______ cubic centimeters.

B. Find the surface area of the rectangular prism with a square base.

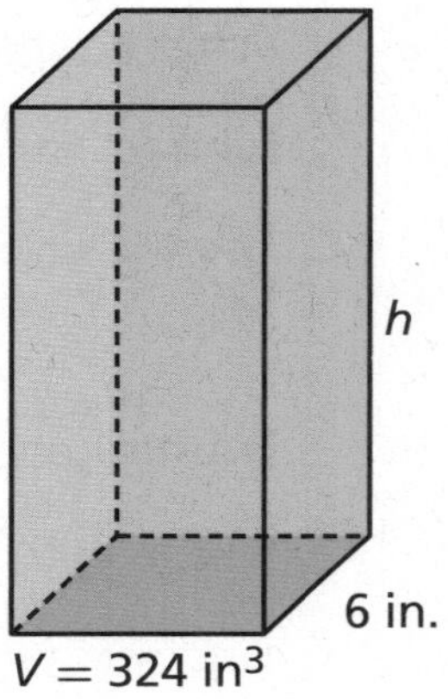

First use the volume to find the ______.

Volume $= Bh$

Substitute known values: $\square = (\square)h$

Divide both sides by $\square$: $\square = h$

The height is ______ inches.

Use the height you found to determine the surface area.

Surface Area $= 2B + Ph$

$= 2(\square) + (\square)(\square) = \square$

The surface area is ______ square inches.

Turn and Talk Make a list of strategies that help with setting up and solving word problems relating to surface area and volume. Explain each strategy.

© Houghton Mifflin Harcourt Publishing Company

Name ______________________________

3 Holly has an empty cylindrical container. She places four tennis balls, each with a diameter of 2.6 inches, inside the container. What is the approximate volume of air remaining inside the container?

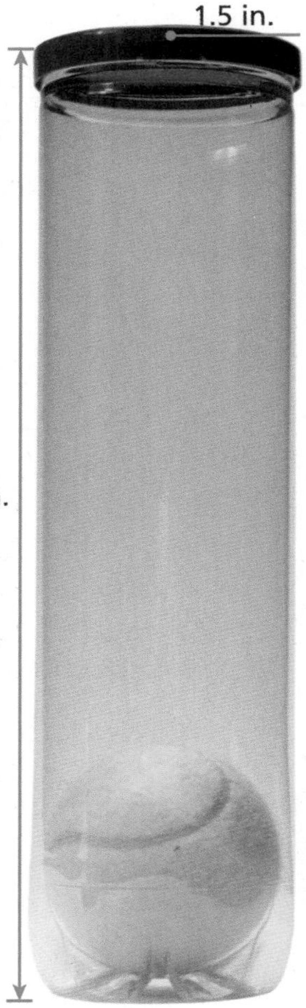

A. Find the volume of the cylindrical container to the nearest hundredth. Use 3.14 for π.

$V = \pi r^2 h$

$= \pi(\_\_\_\_\_\_)^2(\_\_\_\_\_\_)$

$\approx (\_\_\_\_\_\_)(\_\_\_\_\_\_)(\_\_\_\_\_\_)$

$\approx \_\_\_\_\_\_$ in^3

B. Find the volume taken up by the four tennis balls to the nearest hundredth. Use 3.14 for π.

$V = \frac{4}{3}\pi r^3 \cdot 4$

$= \frac{4}{3}\pi(\_\_\_\_\_\_)^3 \cdot 4$

$\approx \frac{4}{3}(\_\_\_\_\_\_)(\_\_\_\_\_\_)4$

$\approx (\_\_\_\_\_\_)4$

$= \_\_\_\_\_\_$ in^3

C. Subtract to find the difference.

____

Turn and Talk Find the volumes in Parts A and B in terms of π. In Part C, use 3.14 to complete the calculations. Why are the answers slightly different?

Check Understanding

1. The interior of a barrel used to store rice has a radius of 4 inches and a height of 7 inches.

   A. What is the interior volume of the barrel in cubic inches? Give your answer in terms of π. ______________

   B. How many scoops of rice can the barrel hold if each scoop is a hemisphere with radius 1 inch? ______________

2. A triangular prism with an equilateral triangle as its base has a volume of 64.98 cubic centimeters, a base area of 10.83 square centimeters, and a triangle edge length of 5 centimeters. What is the surface area of the prism in square centimeters?

____

© Houghton Mifflin Harcourt Publishing Company • Image Credit: (t) ©Houghton Mifflin Harcourt; (b) ©Denim Background/Shutterstock

On Your Own

$B \approx 23.4$ in^2

3. (MP) **Use Structure** Lonnie makes a regular hexagonal prism as shown with a surface area of approximately 244.8 square inches to collect his change. What is the approximate volume of change the prism will hold in cubic inches?

   A. What is the approximate height of the prism? ________

   B. What is the approximate volume of the prism? ________

4. **Social Studies** The USDA estimates that 15 million households in the United States were food insecure in 2017. To help people in their community who might be food insecure, a school has a fundraiser to fill a truck with canned goods for the local food bank. If the cube-shaped boxes used to store the canned goods have a surface area of 24 square feet and the truck will hold 128 boxes, what is the maximum volume of canned goods the students can collect?

   A. What is the edge length of 1 box?

   ____

   B. What is the volume of canned goods that the truck can carry?

   ____

5. A triangular prism has a base that is a right triangle with legs that measure 3 centimeters and 4 centimeters, and a hypotenuse of 5 centimeters. The volume of the triangular prism is 18 cubic centimeters. What is the surface area of the prism?

   ____

6. (MP) **Attend to Precision** Maribelle decorates candleholders in the shape of open-topped regular pentagonal prisms. Each candleholder holds an approximate volume of 275 cubic centimeters of wax. The area of the base of the holder is approximately 27.5 square centimeters and the edge length of the base is 4 centimeters. What is the approximate surface area of the candleholder (not including a top)?

   A. What is the approximate height of the candleholder? ________

   B. What is the approximate surface area of the candleholder? ________

7. (MP) **Reason** A rectangular prism has a 10-inch by 2-inch base and a surface area of 424 square inches. What is the volume of a column of 8 rectangular prisms with these dimensions, stacked base to base?

   ____

© Houghton Mifflin Harcourt Publishing Company • Image Credit: ©xiaorui/Shutterstock

Name

8. An ice cube from this ice tray has a surface area of 6 square inches. What is the total volume of all the ice in the tray?

A. What is the edge length of the ice cube?

B. MP **Use Structure** What is the total volume of all the ice in the tray?

9. MP **Use Structure** The tent shown is a triangular prism. What is the amount of space inside the tent?

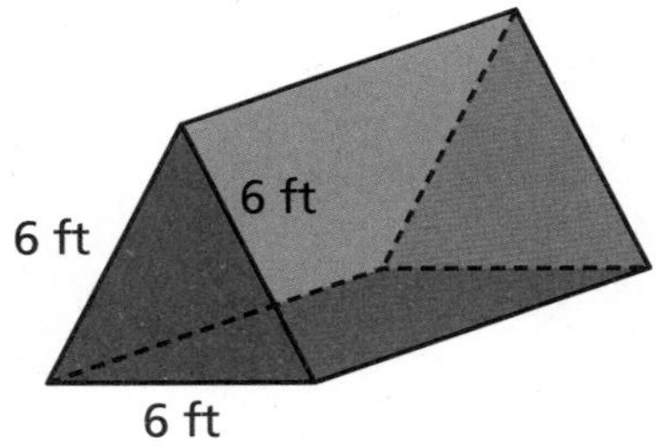

$B \approx 15.6$ ft^2
Surface area ≈ 157.2 ft^2

A. About how long is the tent from the front to the back?

B. What formula will find the space inside the tent? What is the space inside the tent?

10. MP **Use Structure** A company stores supplies in cube-shaped boxes in a warehouse. They are stored on pallets that hold 4 boxes wide, deep, and high. The total volume of boxes on a pallet is 512 cubic feet. Find the surface area of 1 box.

A. What is the volume of one cube? What is its edge length?

B. What is the surface area of one box?

11. A trapezoidal prism has a volume of 585 cubic centimeters. The area of the base is 39 square centimeters. If the base has sides measuring 4, 6.5, 6.5, and 9 centimeters, what is the surface area of the prism?

© Houghton Mifflin Harcourt Publishing Company • Image Credit: ©Anton Starikov/Alamy

12. **Reason** The conical cup, cylindrical cup, and hemispherical bowl shown have the same unknown radius *r*. If the height of each container is the same as that radius, which of the containers holds the most liquid? Explain.

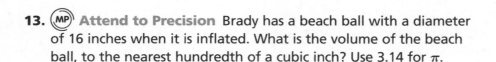

13. **Attend to Precision** Brady has a beach ball with a diameter of 16 inches when it is inflated. What is the volume of the beach ball, to the nearest hundredth of a cubic inch? Use 3.14 for π.

14. **Attend to Precision** A conical container can hold up to 654 cubic centimeters of sand. If the radius of the cone is 5 centimeters, what is the height of the cone? Round your answer to the nearest whole centimeter. Use 3.14 for π.

15. **Attend to Precision** A cylindrical water tank is 7 feet tall and has a diameter of 12 feet. If the tank is currently half full, how much more water can be poured into the tank? Use $\frac{22}{7}$ for π and round your answer to the nearest cubic foot.

16. **Attend to Precision** Brittany makes dough and packages it in cylindrical containers that each have a height of 4 inches. What is the radius of each container if a pack of 6 containers contains 169.56 cubic inches of dough? Use 3.14 for π and round the radius to the nearest tenth of an inch.

17. **STEM** Cinder cone volcanoes are roughly cone-shaped, with heights ranging between 300 feet and 1,200 feet. Approximate the volume of a cinder cone volcano with a height of 350 feet and a diameter of 1,100 feet. Use 3.14 for π, and round your answer to the nearest cubic foot.

18. **Attend to Precision** Sonia fills half of the spherical bowl shown with sand using the cylindrical scoop shown. How many scoops of sand will it take to fill half of the bowl?

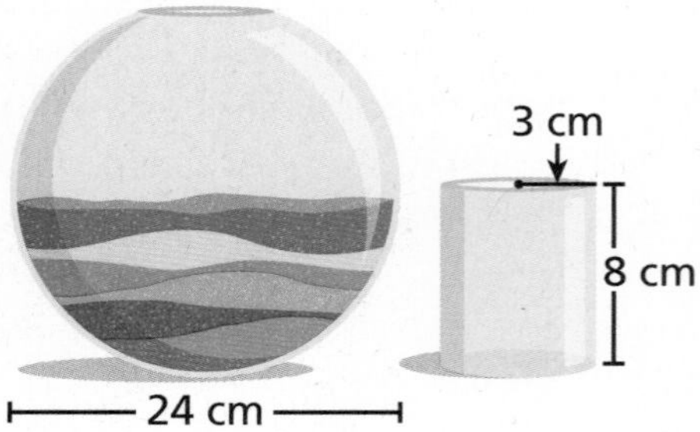

© Houghton Mifflin Harcourt Publishing Company

Name ______________________________

LESSON 18.6
More Practice/ Homework

ONLINE
Video Tutorials and Interactive Examples

Solve Multi-Step Problems with Surface Area and Volume

1. **Use Structure** The cargo area of the moving truck shown will be completely filled by 45 identical cube-shaped boxes with no empty space in the truck remaining. What will be the surface area of one layer of boxes on the floor of the truck bed?

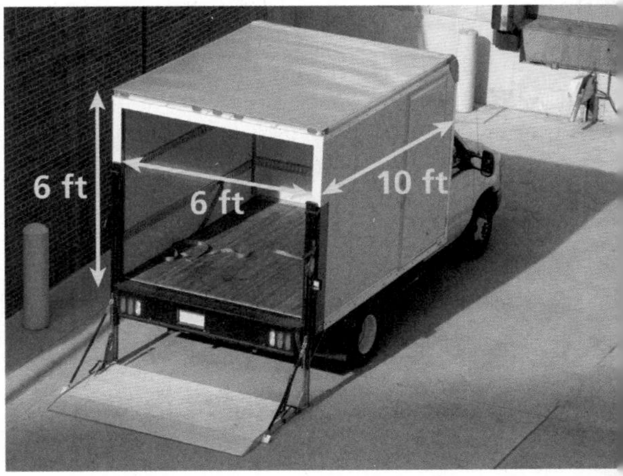

   A. What is the side length of one box? ____________

   B. What is the surface area of one layer of boxes on the floor of the truck bed?

   ____

   C. How many boxes make up this one layer?

   ____

2. **Math on the Spot** Find the volume of milk, in cubic inches, that the carton shown can hold when it is filled up to the top of the rectangular part of the carton.

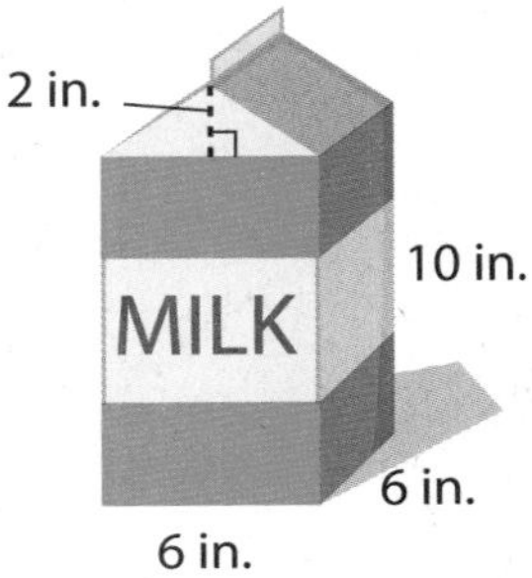

____

3. **Critique Reasoning** Eddie measures and finds the volume of the baseball shown. Does he approximate the volume correctly? Explain.

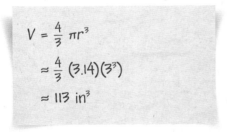

$$V = \frac{4}{3}\pi r^3$$
$$\approx \frac{4}{3}(3.14)(3^3)$$
$$\approx 113 \text{ in}^3$$

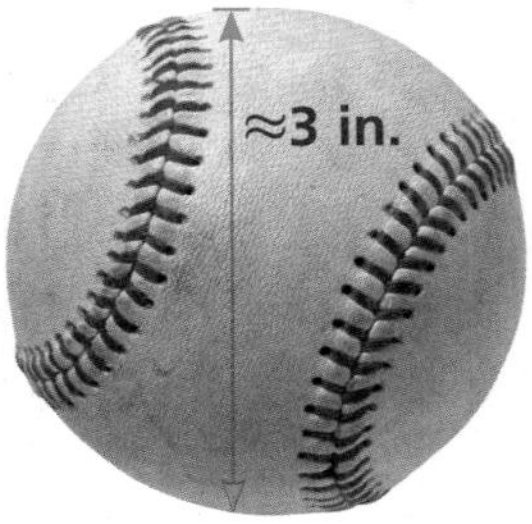

____

____

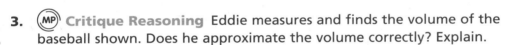

4. A grain silo is in the shape of a cylinder. The area of the circular roof is 803.84 square feet. If 13,665.28 cubic feet of grain fits in the silo, what is the height of the silo?

____

5. A funnel in the shape of a cone has a diameter of 4 centimeters and a height of 9 centimeters. What is the volume of the funnel, to the nearest cubic centimeter? Use 3.14 for π.

____

© Houghton Mifflin Harcourt Publishing Company • Image Credit: ©jweise/E+/Getty Images

Test Prep

6. A cube has a surface area of 1,176 square inches. What is the volume of the cube?

Ⓐ 14 in^3
Ⓑ 196 in^3
Ⓒ 1,728 in^3
Ⓓ 2,744 in^3

7. Ina makes cakes in a pan shaped like a rectangular prism. The base is an 8-inch by 12-inch rectangle, and the volume is 288 cubic inches. Find the surface area of a cake baked in this pan.

____

____

8. Suppose you are given the base area, the perimeter of the base, and the surface area of a triangular prism. Select all the steps needed to find the volume of the prism.

Ⓐ Find the height of the prism using the surface area formula.
Ⓑ Find the height of the prism using the volume formula.
Ⓒ Find the height of the triangle.
Ⓓ Use the area of the base and the height to find the volume.
Ⓔ Use the height of the base and the height of the prism to find the volume.

9. Alissa has an 8.2-inch-tall water bottle with a radius of 1.5 inches. Find the volume of the water bottle, rounded to the nearest hundredth of a cubic inch. Use 3.14 for π.

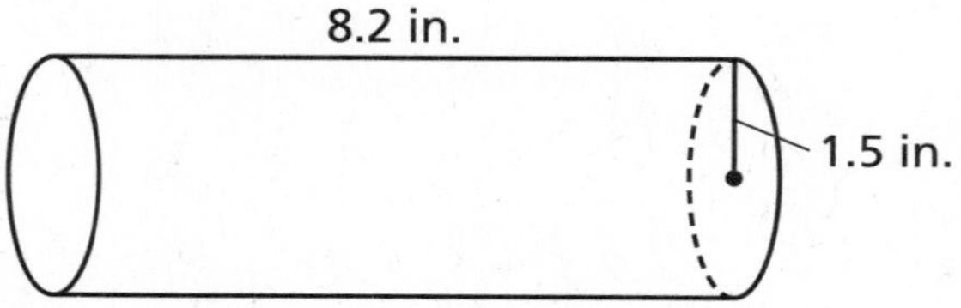

____

10. A waffle cone has a volume of 31.25π cubic centimeters and a radius of 2.5 centimeters. What is the height of the cone?

Ⓐ 5 cm
Ⓑ 6.25 cm
Ⓒ 15 cm
Ⓓ 30 cm

Spiral Review

11. Simplify.

$\frac{7^4 \cdot 7^3}{7^5} =$ ________

12. A bike wheel has a 16-inch diameter. Approximately how far will the wheel travel in three rotations? Use 3.14 for π.

____

© Houghton Mifflin Harcourt Publishing Company

Module
18 Review

Name ______________________________

Vocabulary

1. Select all three-dimensional figures that have each characteristic.

	Cylinder	Cone	Sphere
A vertex	☐	☐	☐
A curved surface	☐	☐	☐
Exactly one circular base	☐	☐	☐
Two parallel circular bases	☐	☐	☐

For Problems 2–4, tell whether each statement is true or false. If it is false, tell what word could replace the underlined word to make the statement true.

2. A cross section is a <u>two</u>-dimensional figure formed when a three-dimensional figure is cut. ______________________________

3. A <u>pentagon</u> is a polygon with six sides. ______________________________

4. A triangular prism has three faces that are <u>triangles</u>.

____

Concepts and Skills

5. (MP) **Use Tools** The cylinder shown has a radius of 8 centimeters and a height of 14 centimeters. What is the approximate volume of the cylinder? (Use $\frac{22}{7}$ for π.) State what strategy and tool you will use to answer the question, explain your choice, and then find the answer.

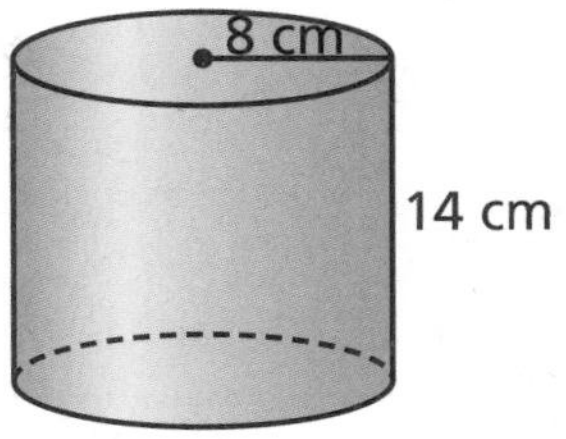

____

6. A school garden club is making the garden bed shown. It needs to hold 24 cubic feet of soil when full. Draw a rectangle on the grid that represents a possible length and width of the bed.

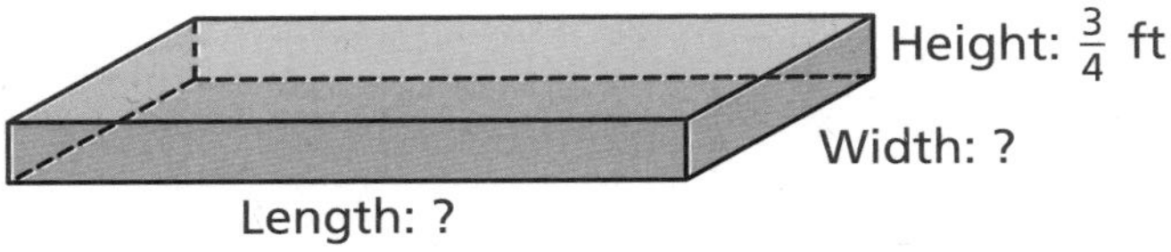

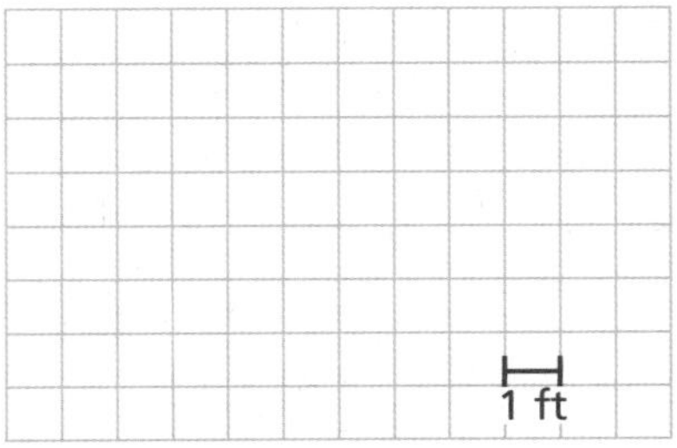

© Houghton Mifflin Harcourt Publishing Company

7. A cone-shaped pile of sand has a base diameter of 7 feet and a height of 2.4 feet, as shown. To the nearest tenth of a cubic foot, what is the volume of the pile of sand? (Use $\frac{22}{7}$ for π.)

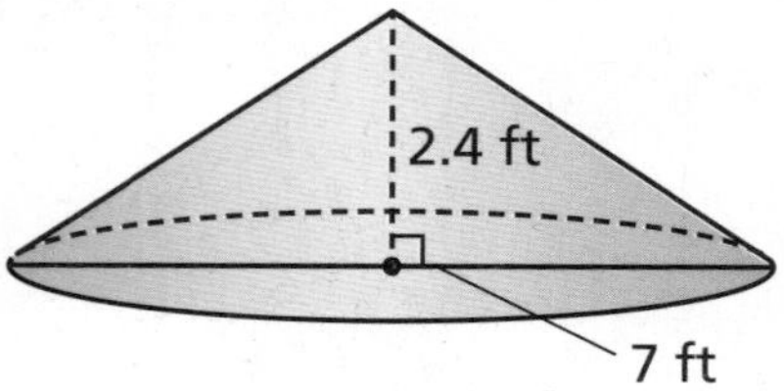

_________ cubic feet

8. The bases of the triangular prism are isosceles triangles. Darren and Riya each cut the prism to make a cross section. The cross section from Darren's cut is a triangle. The cross section from Riya's cut is a rectangle. How did each of them cut the prism?

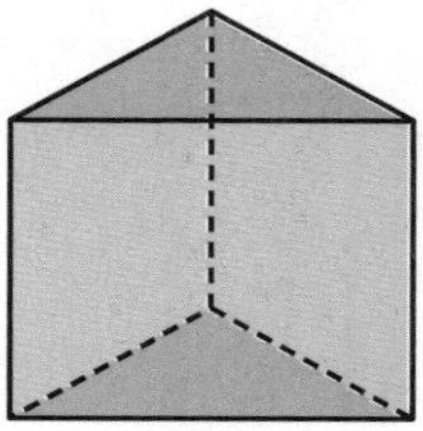

____

____

____

9. A sphere has a diameter of 12 inches, as shown. To the nearest cubic inch, what is the volume of the sphere? (Use 3.14 for π.)

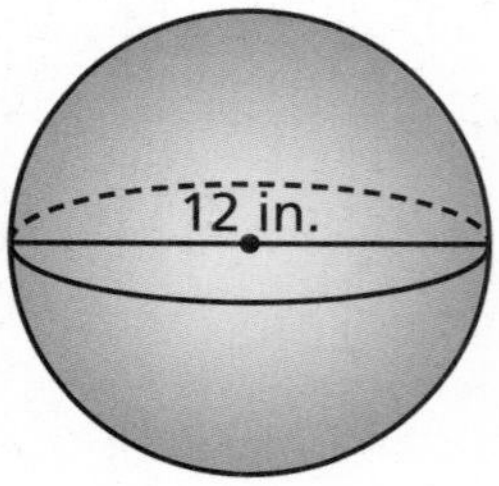

_________ cubic inches

10. The surface area of a cube is 150 square meters. What is the volume of the cube?

Ⓐ 25 m^3

Ⓑ 125 m^3

Ⓒ 15,625 m^3

Ⓓ 625 m^3

11. A frozen yogurt stand has two types of containers. To the nearest cubic centimeter, how much greater is the volume of the cylinder-shaped container than the cone-shaped container? (Use 3.14 for π.)

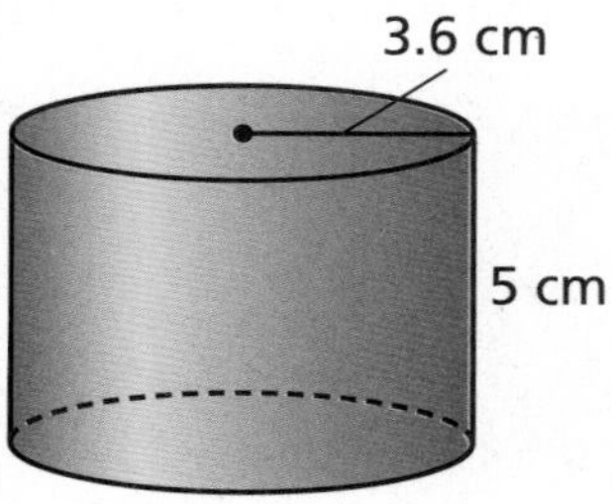

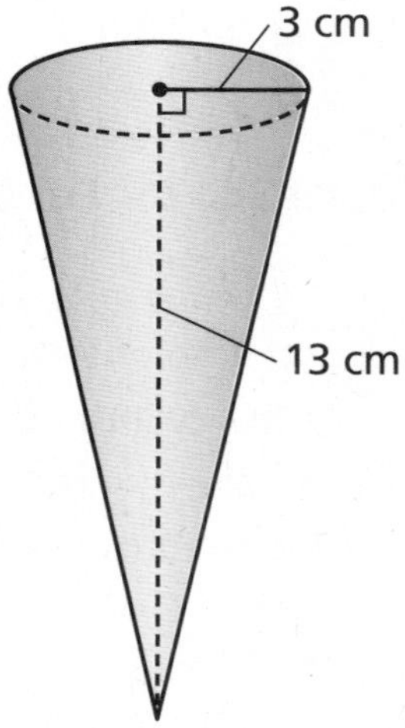

_________ cubic centimeters

12. The cylinder is sliced horizontally by a plane as shown. Select all reasonable statements for the figure.

Ⓐ The cross section is parallel to the base of the cylinder.

Ⓑ The cross section is a rectangle.

Ⓒ The cross section is a circle.

Ⓓ The cross section will have the same dimensions as the base of the cylinder.

Ⓔ The cross section in the figure would be the same if the cylinder were sliced vertically instead of horizontally.

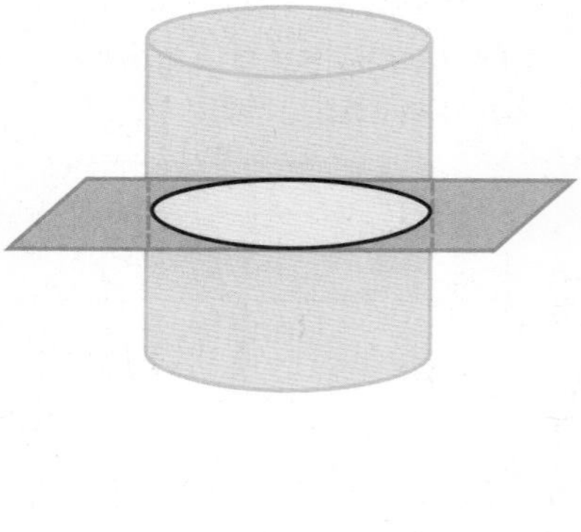

© Houghton Mifflin Harcourt Publishing Company

Unit 7 Probability

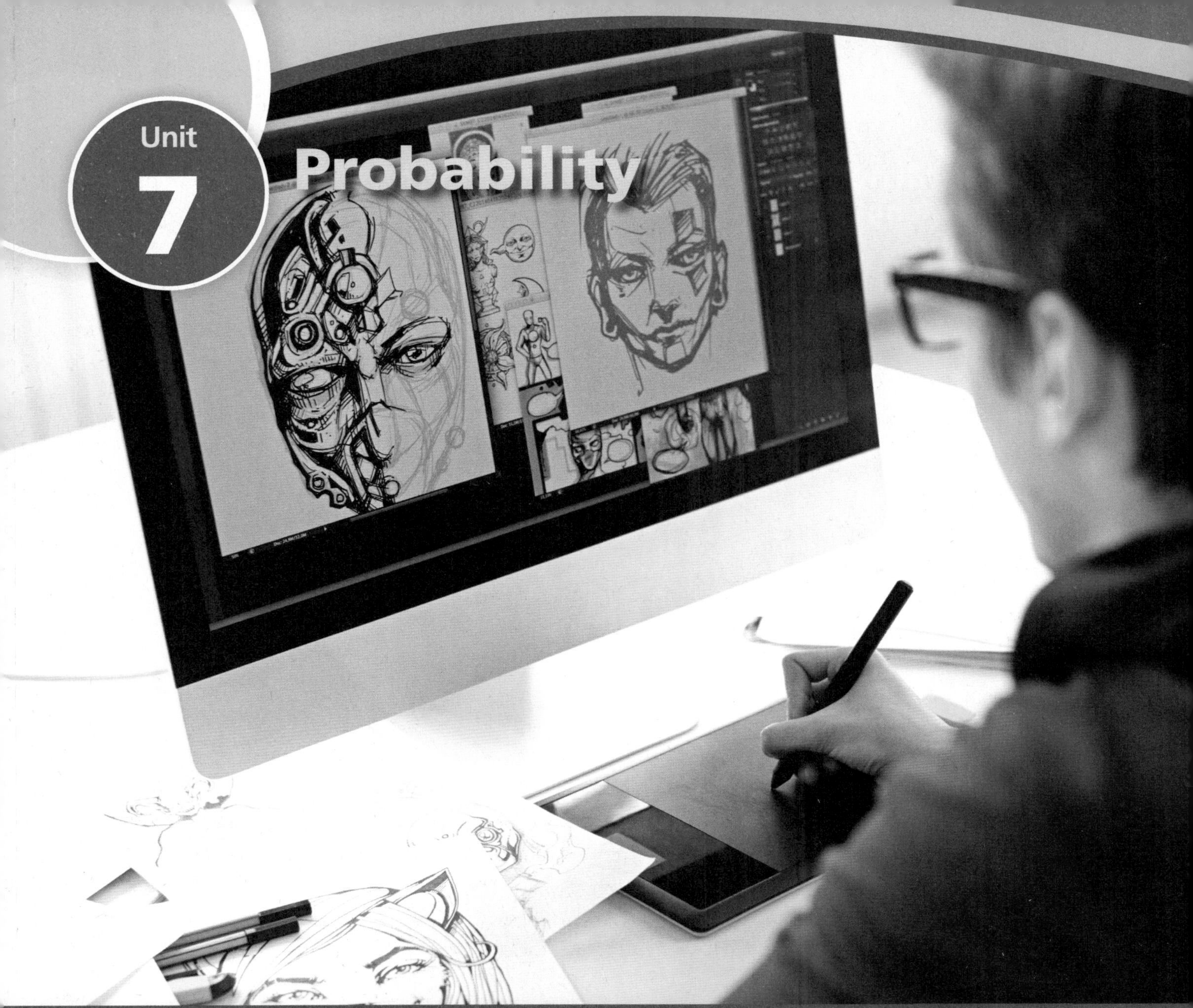

Game Designer

A game designer usually works as part of a team that designs games. Video game designers help develop computer games for a variety of platforms, from large consoles to mobile phones. Shigeru Miyamoto, sometimes called the father of modern video games, is a Japanese game designer who has invented some of the world's most famous and successful video games.

STEM Task:

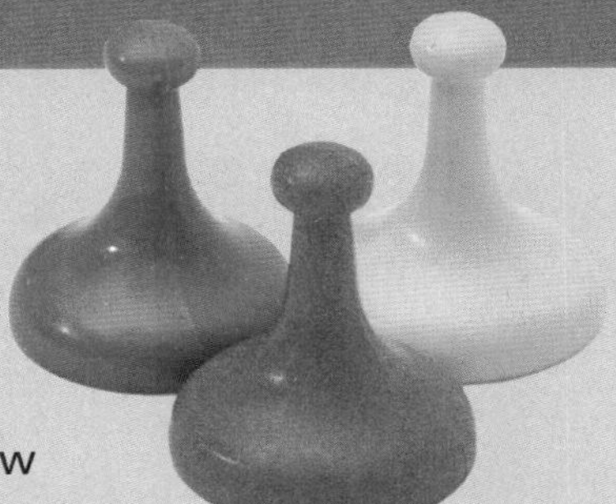

Work with a partner to invent a simple board game for two players. Your game should use up to ten cards and/or one or two number cubes. Choose the goal of the game and decide how players move on the board. Then play the game with your partner several times. Do you think you designed a fair game? Explain why or why not.

© Houghton Mifflin Harcourt Publishing Company • Image Credits: (t) ©mediaphotos/iStock/Getty Images Plus/Getty Images; (b) ©Diane Macdonald/iStock/Getty Images Plus/Getty Images

Learning Mindset

Challenge-Seeking Defines Own Challenges

A challenge is a problem that requires work and determination to solve. A challenging project may include both short- and long-term tasks. By definition, a challenge is not easy—that is why mastering a challenge is such a rewarding experience. You can feel a sense of pride because you know you accomplished something difficult. Here are some tips for tackling a challenge.

- Divide the challenge into smaller steps. Think about how each step leads to completion of the entire project or task.
- Decide how and where to find the information and knowledge you need to complete each step.
- Work with others to brainstorm, check work, share knowledge, and give and receive support.

© Houghton Mifflin Harcourt Publishing Company • Image Credit: ©ZargonDesign/Getty Images

Reflect

Q **What steps did you take to complete the STEM Task?**

Q **What challenges did you and your partner identify while working on the STEM Task? How did you address them?**

Module

19 Understand and Apply Experimental Probability

Go for the Gold!

In the first four levels of a video game, players roam through a castle collecting gold coins and bars. To reach Level D, a player must have a total of at least 10 more gold bars than coins. The table shows the number of coins or gold bars that Miguel collected in each of the first three levels.

Complete the table by sketching the missing gold coins and gold bars.

Level	Ratio of Coins to Gold Bars	Number of Coins Collected	Number of Gold Bars Collected
A	2:3	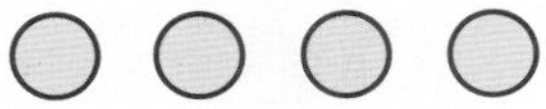	
B	6:8	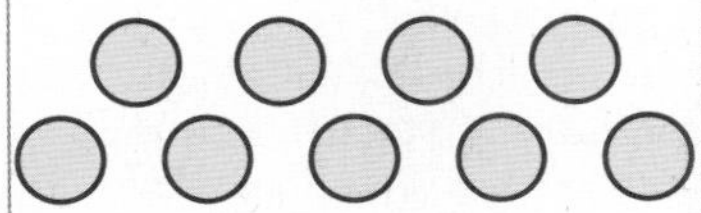	
C	4:10		

Turn and Talk

Does Miguel advance to Level D? Justify your answer.

© Houghton Mifflin Harcourt Publishing Company • Image Credit: ©Sergey Novikov/Shutterstock

Are You Ready?

Complete these problems to review prior concepts and skills you will need for this module.

Statistical Data Collection

The dot plot shows the heights of students in one class. Use this information for Problems 1–2.

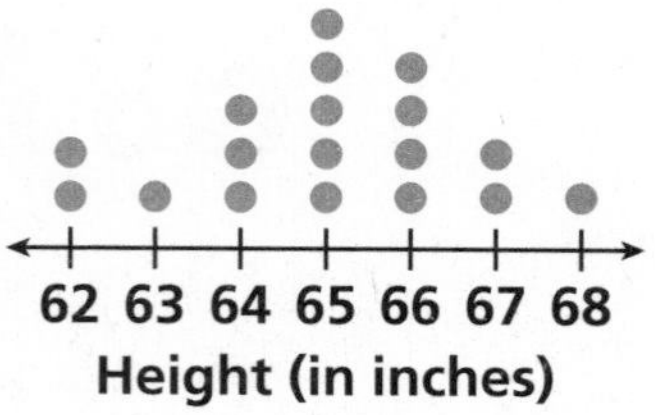

1. What unit of measure was used? How was it measured?

____

2. How many students are in the class? Explain.

____

____

Fractions, Decimals, and Percents

Write each fraction as a decimal and a percent.

3. $\frac{3}{5}$ ________ **4.** $\frac{12}{16}$ ________ **5.** $\frac{5}{8}$ ________

Write each decimal as a percent and a fraction in simplest form.

6. 0.35 ________ **7.** 0.7 ________ **8.** 0.125 ________

Use Ratio and Rate Reasoning

9. One out of every 3 players on a soccer team is new this season. There are 15 players on the team in all. How many of the players are new?

________ new players

10. There are 515 students who attend Central Middle School. Three out of every 5 students live within 1 mile of the school. How many students at Central Middle School live within 1 mile of the school?

________ students

11. How can you use proportional reasoning to write a ratio that is equivalent to another ratio?

____

____

© Houghton Mifflin Harcourt Publishing Company

Name ______________________________

Understand Probability of an Event

I Can describe the likelihood of an event.

Spark Your Learning

PAIRS

A gumball machine contains 50 gumballs. There are 25 blue, 10 red, 12 green, and 3 yellow gumballs in the machine. Bart puts a coin in and turns the wheel to receive a gumball. What is an outcome that is likely to occur? Not likely? As likely as not? Certain? Impossible?

© Houghton Mifflin Harcourt Publishing Company • Image Credit: ©RyanJLane/iStock/Getty Images Plus/Getty Images

Turn and Talk How would you describe the likelihood of receiving a red gumball, using the given phrases?

Build Understanding

© Houghton Mifflin Harcourt Publishing Company • Image Credit: ©Michael Burrell/iStock/Getty Images Plus/Getty Images

Connect to Vocabulary

The **probability of an event** measures the likelihood that the event will occur.

Probability describes how likely an event is to occur. It is a measure between 0 and 1 as shown on the number line, and can be written as a fraction, a decimal, or a percent. The probability of an event is written as *P*(event).

The closer the probability of the event is to 0, the less likely the event is to occur. The closer the probability of the event is to 1, the more likely the event is to occur. An event with probability 0 is impossible. An event with probability 1 is certain.

Impossible	Unlikely	As likely as not	Likely	Certain
0		$\frac{1}{2}$		1
0		0.5		1.0
0%		50%		100%

1 Tell whether each event is impossible, unlikely, as likely as not, likely, or certain. Then tell whether the probability is 0, close to 0, $\frac{1}{2}$, close to 1, or 1.

A. A bag contains pieces of paper labeled with the numbers 1 through 100. A piece of paper with the number 13 is selected at random.

____

B. Two standard number cubes are rolled. The sum of the numbers is 1.

____

C. A standard number cube is rolled, and the result is an even number.

____

____

D. A bowl contains 26 disks. Each disk is labeled with a different letter of the alphabet. A consonant is selected at random.

____

E. Twelve middle-school students are selected to complete a survey. None of the students are in tenth grade.

____

Turn and Talk What do you know about the value of the probability of an event that is likely?

Name

Often the same experiment is repeated many times. Each repetition of an experiment is called a **trial**, and each result of a trial is an **outcome**. A set of one or more possible outcomes for a trial is an **event**. A **sample space** is the set of all possible outcomes for an experiment.

Connect to Vocabulary

An **experiment** is an activity involving chance in which results are observed.

2 Roll a number cube 10 times. How likely is each event in the table?

A. What is the sample space of all possible outcomes when you roll the number cube once?

B. Roll a number cube 10 times and record the results in the table.

Event	Frequency
Roll a 2	
Roll a 1, 3, 4, 5 or 6	
Roll an odd number	
Roll a number less than 7	

C. How many trials did you perform? How many events did you record?

D. Judging from the results of your trials, which events are certain when rolling a number cube?

E. Judging from the results of your trials, which events are likely? Which events are unlikely? Which events are as likely as not?

Turn and Talk Based on your results from the table, what number or number range might you use to describe the probability of rolling a 2? Explain.

Check Understanding

1. Tell whether choosing a blue marble from a jar containing 4 blue marbles and 12 red marbles is unlikely, as likely as not, or likely. Is the probability closer to 0 or 1?

2. What number and what percent describe the probability of a certain event? What number and what percent describe the probability of an impossible event?

© Houghton Mifflin Harcourt Publishing Company

On Your Own

3. Mina opens a book 15 times and records whether the page number is even or odd. How many trials did she conduct? Name two events that she recorded.

4. Orlando has a bowl with 12 green disks and 8 yellow disks. Is the probability of randomly selecting a green disk unlikely, as likely as not, or likely?

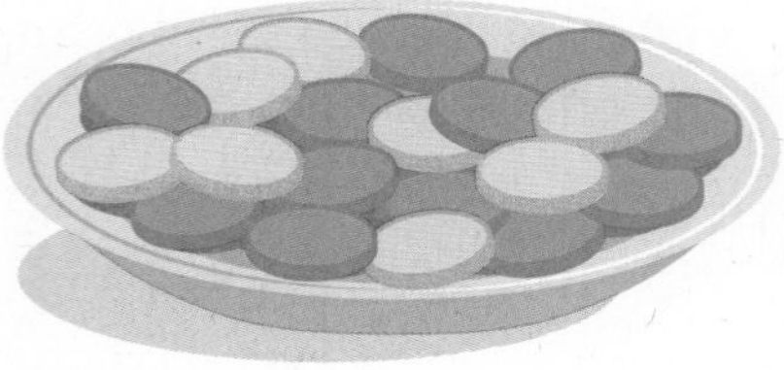

5. (MP) **Reason** A container holds 20 red, 20 blue, and 10 green marbles. Is the probability of choosing a blue marble greater than or less than the probability of choosing a marble that is not blue? Explain.

For Problems 6–7, describe the probability of each event in words. Then describe each probability with a number or a number range.

6. Roll a number greater than 5 on a standard number cube.

7. Pick a number less than or equal to 30 from a bag with 40 pieces of paper numbered 1 through 40.

8. **Open Ended** Ask 6 students their age and record the results. Pick one age from the results. How many students stated this age? Describe in words the probability that a student in your class is this age, judging from the results.

© Houghton Mifflin Harcourt Publishing Company

I'm in a Learning Mindset!

Did I select appropriate challenges as part of learning how to describe the probability of an event?

Name ______________________________

Understand Probability of an Event

1. Mia rolls two standard number cubes. Is a sum greater than 12 impossible, unlikely, as likely as not, likely, or certain?

____

2. A machine makes 50 parts. Out of the 50 parts, 3 are defective. Describe the probability that a randomly selected part is not defective, using a number or a number range.

____

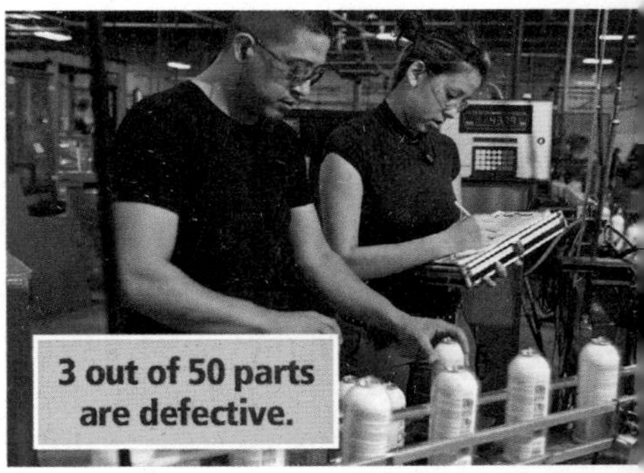
3 out of 50 parts are defective.

3. **Open Ended** Write a situation where the probability of an event occurring is unlikely.

____

____

____

4. Rocky has a box of pens. He has 11 black pens, 8 blue pens, and 6 red pens. He randomly selects a pen from the box. Use a number or number range to describe the probability that the pen he selects is blue.

____

Flip a coin eight times and record the results of *heads* or *tails*. Use the results for Problems 5–9.

5. List the sample space of all possible outcomes when you flip a coin once.

____

6. What experiment did you perform? How many trials of the experiment did you conduct? What events did you record?

____

7. How many times did the coin land heads up? Based only on these results, does getting *heads* seem to be impossible, unlikely, as likely as not, likely, or certain?

____

8. How many times did the coin land tails up? Based only on these results, does getting *tails* seem to be impossible, unlikely, as likely as not, likely, or certain?

____

9. (MP) **Reason** Are the results of your experiment what you would expect? Explain.

____

© Houghton Mifflin Harcourt Publishing Company • Image Credit: ©DreamPictures/Shannon Faulk/Blend Images/Getty Images

Test Prep

10. Adam has 10 blocks numbered 1 through 10. Which describes the probability of randomly choosing a block that has an even number?

Ⓐ impossible

Ⓑ unlikely

Ⓒ as likely as not

Ⓓ likely

Ⓔ certain

11. Bella finds some beach glass. She finds 14 pieces of brown beach glass, 12 pieces of white beach glass, 12 pieces of green beach glass, and 2 pieces of blue beach glass. She lets her sister pick one piece at random to keep. Describe the probability that her sister picks a piece of blue beach glass, using a number or a number range.

____

12. A bowl contains 4 blue marbles and 12 red marbles. Soo-jin picks a marble from the bowl. Describe a likely event.

____

13. A community service club has 12 seventh-graders and 12 eighth-graders. The name of each student is put in a hat, and a name is drawn at random. Which number or number range describes the probability that the student selected is a seventh-grader?

Ⓐ a number greater than 0 and less than $\frac{1}{2}$

Ⓑ a number greater than $\frac{1}{2}$ and less than 1

Ⓒ 1

Ⓓ $\frac{1}{2}$

Spiral Review

14. A patio is shaped as a composite figure consisting of two rectangles. One part of the patio is 20 feet long and 15 feet wide. The other part is 15 feet long and 10 feet wide. What is the area of the patio?

____

15. An aquarium is a rectangular prism. The volume of the aquarium is 6,480 cubic inches. The length of the aquarium is 30 inches, and the height is 18 inches. What is the width of the aquarium?

____

© Houghton Mifflin Harcourt Publishing Company

Name ______________________________

Find Experimental Probability of Simple Events

I Can find an experimental probability and its complement.

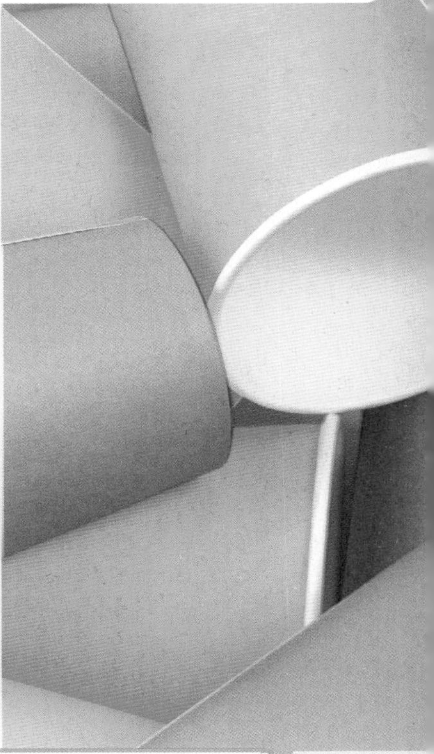

Spark Your Learning

Toss a paper cup a number of times and record the different ways that the cup lands on a table. Describe each way that the cup lands as likely or unlikely. Organize your results in a table.

Outcome	Frequency
Open end up	
Open end down	
On its side	

Turn and Talk How do you think increasing the number of times you toss the cup would change your results?

© Houghton Mifflin Harcourt Publishing Company • Image Credit: ©Yoki5270/Shutterstock

Build Understanding

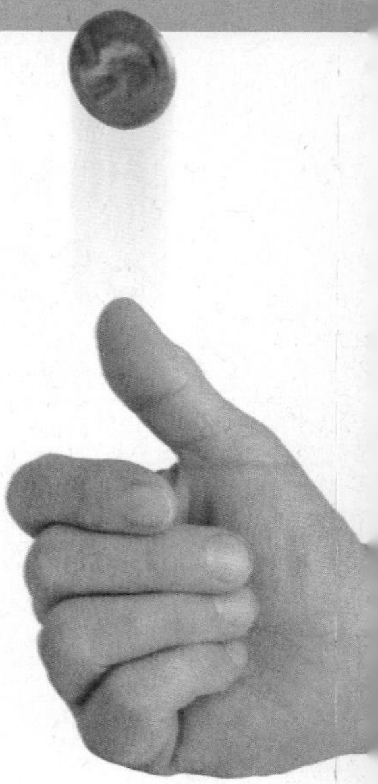

1 Conduct an experiment by flipping a coin. Record your results in the table. Repeat until you have conducted the experiment 20 times.

Outcome	Frequency
Heads	
Tails	

A. How many trials did you conduct?

____

B. Do the outcomes appear to be equally likely? Explain.

____

____

C. Use the number of times each event occurs compared to the number of trials to approximate the probability of each event.

Outcome	Probability
Heads	$\frac{\text{heads}}{20} = \frac{\square}{20}$
Tails	$\frac{\text{tails}}{20} = \frac{\square}{20}$

D. If you flip the coin only four times, do you think it is possible that you might record only *tails* and no *heads*? What if you flip a coin 100 times? Compare the chances of the two possibilities.

____

____

E. What happens to the number of times each outcome occurs as you perform more trials?

____

____

____

F. What is the sum of the probabilities in Part C?

____

Turn and Talk Are there any outcomes that did not occur in your set of trials? Explain why or why not.

© Houghton Mifflin Harcourt Publishing Company • **Image Credit:** ©Straublund Photography/Moment Open/Getty Images

Name ___

Step It Out

The **experimental probability** of an event is found by comparing the number of times an event occurs to the total number of trials.

$$\text{experimental probability} = \frac{\text{number of times the event occurs}}{\text{total number of trials}}$$

2 Muriel has a spinner with red, blue, and green sections. She spins the spinner 50 times and records the results in a table.

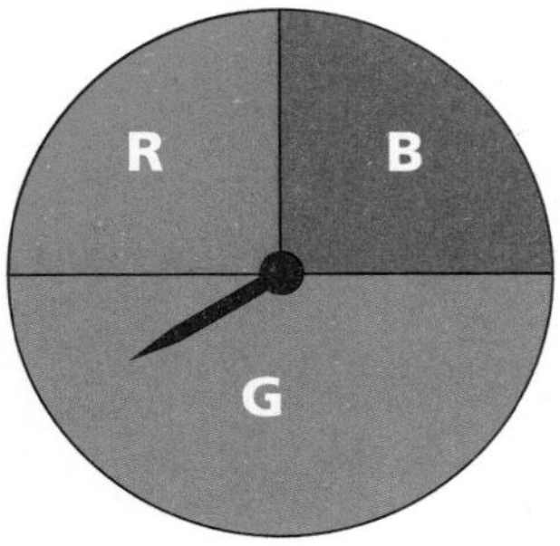

Event	Frequency
Red	14
Blue	12
Green	24

A. Find the experimental probability of each outcome.

___

B. What conclusions can you make about the spinner using the experimental probabilities?

___

___

___

C. How would you find the experimental probability of the spinner landing on a color that is not red, and what is that experimental probability in this example?

___

___

D. How is the experimental probability of the spinner landing on a color that is not red related to the experimental probability of the spinner landing on red?

___

Connect to Vocabulary

The **complement** of an event is the set of all outcomes in the sample space that are *not* included in the event. The sum of the probability of an event and the probability of its complement is 1.

© Houghton Mifflin Harcourt Publishing Company

A **simulation** is a model of an experiment that would be difficult to actually perform. A simulation can be used to find an experimental probability and make a prediction.

3 A softball player hits the ball and reaches base safely about 30% of the time. The player hits the ball but is called "out" about 50% of the time. The player strikes out about 20% of the time.

A. How could you use a random number generator to simulate what might happen the next 25 times the player comes up to hit the ball?

B. Perform the simulation. Record your results.

Event	Frequency
Hit - Safe	
Hit - Out	
Strikeout	

C. Make a prediction based on your simulation.

D. Combine the results of your simulation with the results of all the simulations. How do the total results of the class compare to your simulation?

Check Understanding

1. Allison rolls a standard number cube 30 times and records her results. The number of times she rolled a 4 is 6. What is the experimental probability of rolling a 4? What is the experimental probability of not rolling a 4?

2. Kelly averages 90% correct on her math assignments. She wants to perform a simulation to predict the number of questions she will answer correctly out of her next 70 questions. What is a simulation she could use to make this prediction?

© Houghton Mifflin Harcourt Publishing Company

Name

On Your Own

3. Andreas is performing an experiment involving rolling a number cube. He rolls the number cube 60 times and records the results in the table.

A. (MP) **Reason** Are the outcomes equally likely? Explain.

B. Find the experimental probabilities to complete the table.

Outcome	Frequency	Experimental Probability
1	8	
2	11	
3	10	
4	7	
5	11	
6	13	

4. **Open Ended** Ask 8 students how many letters are in their first name. Record the number of letters for each answer. Describe one event from your experiment and find the experimental probability of this event.

5. (MP) **Use Tools** A football quarterback completes 60% of attempted passes. Describe a simulation that you can perform in order to predict how many passes out of 40 this quarterback will complete.

6. Jean estimates that her friend completes a new level of a video game on the first try 20% of the time. She conducts a simulation to predict how many times out of 80 her friend would complete a new level on the first try. Jean uses a random number generator. Every digit that is 8 or 9 represents completing the level. What is the probability that her friend completes a new level on the first try, written as a percent?

Digit	0	1	2	3	4	5	6	7	8	9
Frequency	10	9	6	7	8	12	4	6	7	11

© Houghton Mifflin Harcourt Publishing Company • Image Credit: ©Houghton Mifflin Harcourt

7. Diego has a spinner that is divided into four sections labeled A, B, C, and D as shown. He spins the spinner many times and records the results. The results are shown in the table.

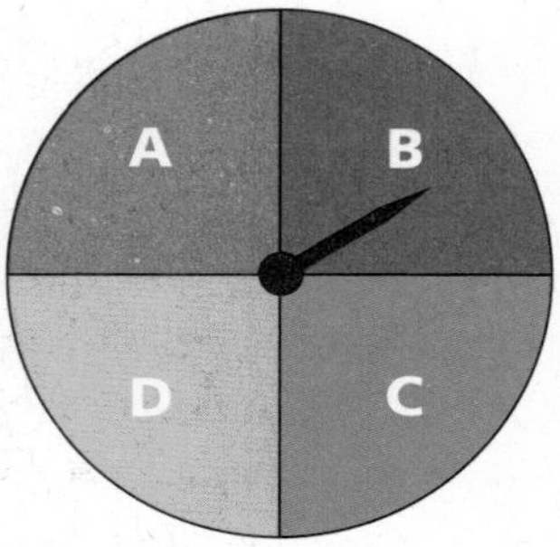

Letter	A	B	C	D
Frequency	14	24	14	12

A. Add the frequency of each event to find the total number of times that he spun the spinner. Then find the experimental probability of spinning each letter.

B. What is the probability of the complement of spinning D?

C. (MP) **Construct Arguments** What conclusion can Diego make about the bias of the spinner he used, based on the experimental probabilities? Explain your reasoning.

8. Dustin buys packs of trading cards. He reads that half of the packs contain a bonus card. Dustin uses a coin to perform a simulation to estimate how many packs will contain a bonus card if he buys 20 packs. He uses heads to represent a pack with a bonus card. The results of his simulation are shown.

H, H, T, H, T, T, T, H, T, H, H, T, T, H, T, H, H, T, H, H

How many packs in this simulation did not contain a bonus card?

© Houghton Mifflin Harcourt Publishing Company

I'm in a Learning Mindset!

Am I willing to accept new challenges while learning about probability?

Name ______________________

LESSON 19.2
More Practice/ Homework

ONLINE Ed Video Tutorials and Interactive Examples

Find Experimental Probability of Simple Events

1. Luther is performing an experiment involving a triangular pyramid with faces labeled 1–4. He shakes it in a jar and empties the jar without looking 80 times. Using a table, he records the number of the face it lands on. Find the experimental probabilities to complete the table.

Outcome	Frequency	Experimental Probability
1	19	$\frac{\square}{80}$
2	17	$\frac{\square}{80}$
3	23	$\frac{\square}{80}$
4	21	$\frac{\square}{80}$

2. (MP) **Use Tools** Marcela gets to school later than her friend Kim about half the time. Describe a way to simulate this event for 10 school days. Then perform the simulation. How many times does it show Marcela arriving later than Kim? What is the experimental probability of this event?

____

____

3. **Math on the Spot** For one month, Terry recorded the time at which her school bus arrived. She organized her results in a frequency table. Find the experimental probability that the bus will arrive between 8:20 and 8:24. Find the experimental probability that the bus will arrive after 8:19.

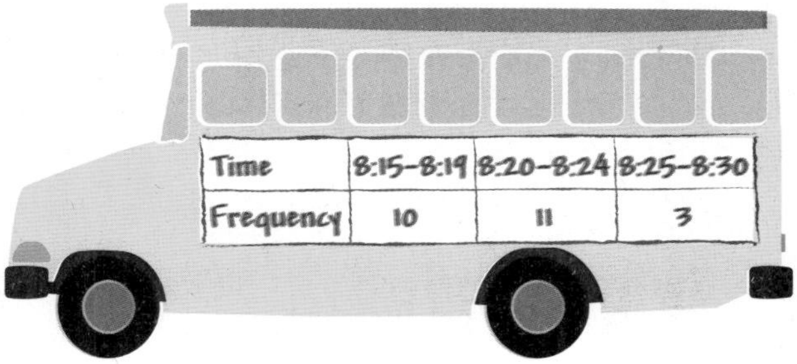

____

4. (MP) **Use Tools** Wei has two different routes he takes to a park. He labels the routes A and B. He takes route B about 33% of the time. Describe a simulation Wei could perform using a number cube to estimate the number of times he will take route B to get to the park if he goes to the park 60 times.

____

____

____

____

____

© Houghton Mifflin Harcourt Publishing Company

Test Prep

5. Asia has a jar of marbles. She randomly selects a marble from the jar, records its color, and returns it to the jar. She repeats this 74 times. Her results are shown in the table.

Outcome	Frequency
Red	13
Blue	20
Green	22
Yellow	19

What is the experimental probability of Asia choosing a green marble?

____

6. Jordan performed an experiment using a number cube. He rolled a number cube 50 times. He found that he rolled a 6 a total of 8 times. What is the experimental probability that he did *not* roll a 6?

Ⓐ $\frac{3}{25}$

Ⓑ $\frac{4}{25}$

Ⓒ $\frac{21}{25}$

Ⓓ $\frac{22}{25}$

7. Juan rolls a number cube 40 times. He rolls a 3 on the number cube 6 times. What is the experimental probability that he rolls a 3?

____

Spiral Review

8. Emma selects coins at random from a jar, putting the coin back each time after selecting it. She conducts 28 trials and selects 7 pennies, 12 nickels, and 9 dimes. Based on the results, describe in words the likelihood that she selects a penny.

____

9. Juana and Andy completed 10 math problems total. Juana completed 6 of the problems. Write an equation to determine the number of math problems that Andy completed, then solve the equation. How many of the math problems did Andy complete?

____

© Houghton Mifflin Harcourt Publishing Company

Name ______________________

Find Experimental Probability of Compound Events

I Can determine the experimental probability of compound events.

Spark Your Learning

PAIRS

Felix was attending an awards dinner and the menu had the choices shown for appetizer and entrée. What is the sample space for his dinner selection?

Awards Dinner

Appetizers:
- Shrimp Cocktail
- Garden Salad

Entrees:
- Roast Beef
- Chicken Marsala
- Vegetarian Lasagna

Turn and Talk The menu also had a choice of two drinks. When considering that choice, how does that affect the total number of combinations that are available to order?

© Houghton Mifflin Harcourt Publishing Company • Image Credit: ©Boris Kuznets/iStock/Getty Images Plus/Getty Images

Build Understanding

At Felix's awards dinner, T-shirts were being handed out to the award winners. The choices for the shirts are shown. The selection of a shirt is a compound event due to the available choices in different categories.

Connect to Vocabulary

A coin landing heads up when flipped or rolling a 6 on a number cube are simple events. A **compound event** is an event that includes two or more simple events.

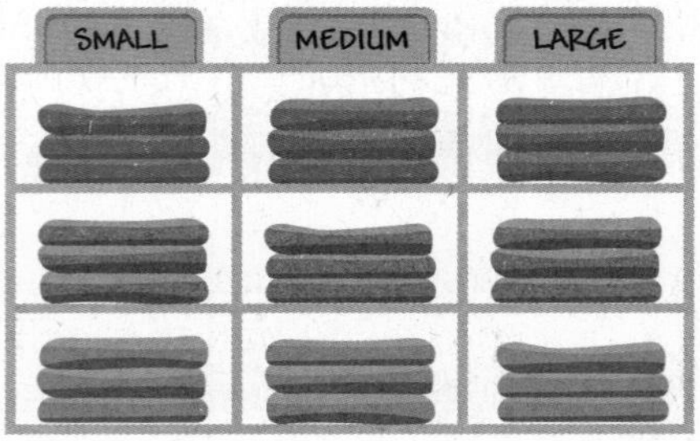

1 Define the sample space of the shirt choices.

A. How many colors are there? What are the choices?

____

B. How many sizes are there? What are the choices?

____

C. Write all the possible combinations of sizes and colors.

____

____

____

D. There are ____ possible outcomes for this compound event.

E. In the table, fill out the shaded boxes with headings for the sizes and colors of the shirts. Then fill in the table to show the sample space, all the possible outcomes when a shirt is selected.

F. Suppose a compound event includes two simple events. Explain how many rows and columns are needed in a table of the sample space.

____

____

____

____

____

Turn and Talk Does it matter whether sizes or colors are listed in rows or columns? Explain.

© Houghton Mifflin Harcourt Publishing Company

Name ______________________

Step It Out

Conducting a survey is a type of experiment. Each time a question is asked of one person counts as one trial. Each answer is an outcome. Compare the number of times one answer is given to the total number of times a question is asked to find the experimental probability that a new, randomly chosen person, if asked, will give this answer.

2 Guests at the awards were asked for their dinner order. The number of people who gave each answer is shown. Find the experimental probability that a dinner guest orders roast beef and salad.

	Roast beef	Chicken marsala	Vegetarian lasagna
Shrimp cocktail	15	32	12
Garden salad	24	22	15

Awards Dinner

Appetizers:
- Shrimp Cocktail
- Garden Salad

Entrees:
- Roast Beef
- Chicken Marsala
- Vegetarian Lasagna

A. Find the total number of dinner orders.

$15 + 32 + \square + 24 + 22 + 15 = \square$

B. Find the experimental probability.

$P(\text{roast beef, salad}) = \dfrac{\text{number of orders for roast beef with salad}}{\text{total number of orders (total trials)}}$

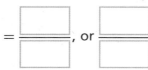

$= \dfrac{\square}{\square}$, or $\dfrac{\square}{\square}$

3 The T-shirt choices of some award winners are shown in the table. What is the experimental probability that an award winner does NOT select a medium green T-shirt?

	Small	Medium	Large
Red	4	8	8
Green	2	5	7
Blue	3	4	9

A. Find the experimental probability of choosing a medium green T-shirt.

$P(\text{medium, green}) = \dfrac{\text{number of medium green T-shirts selected}}{\text{total number of T-shirts selected (total number of trials)}}$

$= \dfrac{\square}{\square} = \dfrac{\square}{\square}$, or $\square$ %

B. Find the complement of the event in Part A, the experimental probability of NOT choosing a medium green T-shirt.

$P(\text{NOT medium, green}) = 1 - P(\text{medium, green})$

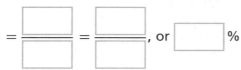

$= 1 - \dfrac{\square}{\square} = \dfrac{\square}{\square}$, or $\square$ %

© Houghton Mifflin Harcourt Publishing Company

4 A party bundle sold by an event planning company contains party favors and table decorations. The party favors are key chains, pens, and wristbands. The table decorations are flowers and candles. The company packs party bundles and stores them in a warehouse, choosing the party favor and decorations for each bundle at random. Tatiana simulates choosing a bundle from the warehouse and checking its contents.

A. List the compound events that occur when checking the bundles.

____

____

____

B. Describe the two choices that together make up each compound event.

____

C. How can you use a number cube and a coin to simulate the experiment?

____

____

D. Tatiana simulates 100 trials of the experiment and records the results shown in the table. What is the experimental probability that the next choice of a bundle includes pens and candles?

	Key chain	Pen	Wristband
Flowers	21	19	18
Candles	18	14	10

$$P(\text{pens, candles}) = \frac{\text{number of pens/candles bundles selected}}{\text{total number of party bundles selected (total trials)}}$$

$$= \frac{\square}{\square} = \frac{\square}{\square}\text{, or } \square\ \%$$

Check Understanding

The table shows the average daily breakfast orders for toast at a diner.

	Wheat	White	Rye
Butter	20	32	8
Dry	7	10	3

1. How many possible outcomes are in the sample space of toast choices?

____

2. What is the experimental probability that a customer orders buttered white toast? Write your answer as a fraction and a percent.

____

© Houghton Mifflin Harcourt Publishing Company • **Image Credits:** (t)©Vasilixa/Shutterstock; (b)©Susan Kinast/The Image Bank/Getty Images

Name ______________________________

On Your Own

3. A tea bar offers tea in the varieties shown.

A. How many rows and columns represent the sample space?

____

B. How many possible outcomes are in the sample space?

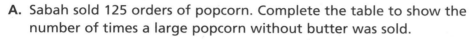

____

4. (MP) **Model with Mathematics** Sabah works at a movie theater. One evening, she tracks the popcorn orders at the concessions stand.

A. Sabah sold 125 orders of popcorn. Complete the table to show the number of times a large popcorn without butter was sold.

	Small	Medium	Large
With butter	18	15	36
Without butter	19	22	

B. Find the experimental probability of a new customer ordering a large popcorn without butter. ______________

5. (MP) **Construct Arguments** When simulating a compound event by rolling a number cube and flipping a coin, does it matter which one is done first? Explain your answer.

____

____

The table shows activities chosen. For Problems 6–9, use the table to determine the experimental probability of the choice and its complement.

	Swimming	Boating	Arts & Crafts	Field Sports
Morning	48	36	16	25
Afternoon	45	30	40	35

6. swimming in the afternoon ______________

7. field sports in the morning ______________

8. boating in the morning ______________

9. arts & crafts in the afternoon ______________

© Houghton Mifflin Harcourt Publishing Company • Image Credit: ©Granger Wootz/Blend Images/Alamy

(MP) Use Tools For Problems 10–12, tell how you could use the tools shown to simulate each compound event.

10. Choosing a pet at the animal shelter: a male or female; a cat, a dog, or a rabbit

11. Choosing colors for a shed: a red, blue, or yellow shed with white, gray, or black trim

12. Choosing an activity: going hiking or going swimming, traveling by bus or traveling by bicycle

13. Open Ended Write a word problem that includes finding the possible outcomes and the size of the sample space for a compound event. Then find the size of the sample space described in your problem.

© Houghton Mifflin Harcourt Publishing Company

I'm in a Learning Mindset!

If you want to adjust the level of challenge in a simulation, would changing the order of simple events work? Why or why not?

Name ______________________

Find Experimental Probability of Compound Events

1. **Math on the Spot** A compound event is simulated by flipping a coin (H or T) and rolling a number cube (1–6).

   A. List all the different possible outcomes.

   ____

   B. Represent the sample space using the table.

	1	2	3	4	5	6
H						
T						

Nico rolled two number cubes 250 times. The table shows his results. Use the table for Problems 2–4.

NC2 \ NC1	1	2	3	4	5	6
1	6	7	3	8	9	7
2	4	8	6	5	10	2
3	7	6	11	9	8	7
4	6	7	6	8	9	5
5	3	5	9	7	6	4
6	6	8	5	3	4	26

2. Find the experimental probability of rolling a 5 on the first number cube and a 2 on the second number cube.

   ____

3. A. Find the experimental probability of rolling a 1 on the second number cube.

   ____

   B. Use the complement to find the experimental probability of NOT rolling a 1 on the second number cube.

   ____

4. (MP) **Reason** Find the experimental probability of rolling double sixes. Is this experimental probability close to what you would expect? Explain.

   ____

   ____

   ____

© Houghton Mifflin Harcourt Publishing Company • Image Credit: ©Houghton Mifflin Harcourt

Test Prep

5. Carlotta is doing an experiment by flipping a coin and rolling a number cube. Select all that apply to the sample space of the experiment.
   - (A) The possible outcomes for the simulation can be represented in a table with 2 rows and 6 columns.
   - (B) The possible outcomes for the simulation can be represented in a table with 6 rows and 2 columns.
   - (C) The sample space of the simulation can only be represented by a table.
   - (D) The sample space has 36 total possible outcomes.
   - (E) The sample space has 8 total possible outcomes.

6. Ali runs a simulation using a coin and random number generator with output from 1 to 5. The table shows the results of the simulation.

	1	2	3	4	5
Heads (H)	12	8	11	14	8
Tails (T)	9	10	9	7	12

A. Find the experimental probability of the outcome *H-4*.

____

B. Use the complement to find the experimental probability of *not H-4*.

____

Spiral Review

7. Octavia found that in a population, 35% of customers bought socks. She took a random sample of 150 customers and found that 42 bought socks. Describe the sample ratio. Is it above or below the population ratio?

____

8. Using a number or number range, describe the probability of rolling a 3 on a number cube.

____

9. Is the graph of the distance a person has walked over time an example of a continuous graph or a discrete graph?

____

© Houghton Mifflin Harcourt Publishing Company

Name ______________________

Use Experimental Probability and Proportional Reasoning to Make Predictions

I Can use proportional reasoning or percent expressions to make a prediction based on an experimental probability.

Step It Out

1 Jessica bowls in several leagues, and she is very good at closing out frames. Over the past few years, she has closed out 8 of every 10 frames she has bowled. This season Jessica will bowl 35 games, or 350 frames. How many frames can Jessica expect to close out this season?

A. Method 1: Use a proportion.

Write a proportion. 8 out of 10 is how many out of 350?

$\frac{8}{10} = \frac{x}{\square}$

Multiply $\frac{8}{10}$ by a form of 1 to keep the equation true and to find the value of x.

$$\frac{8}{10} \cdot \frac{\square}{\square} = \frac{x}{\square}$$

The value of x is $8 \cdot \square = \square$.

B. Method 2: Use a percent expression.

Write $\frac{8}{10}$ as a percent and a decimal: $\square$% and $\square$.

Find $\square$% of 350: $\square \cdot 350$, or $\square$.

So Jessica can expect to close out about ________ frames.

C. If Jessica closes out 288 frames this season, was her average over the past few years a good predictor of her performance?

____

Turn and Talk Which method do you prefer for making a prediction, using a proportion or a percent?

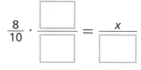

© Houghton Mifflin Harcourt Publishing Company • Image Credit: ©Slawomir Kruz/Alamy

2 The middle school that Carmen and Richard attend has 925 students. The schedule options for first period include only math and English. In order to find out whether students prefer first period math or first period English, Carmen and Richard took a poll of 100 randomly selected students. The results are shown.

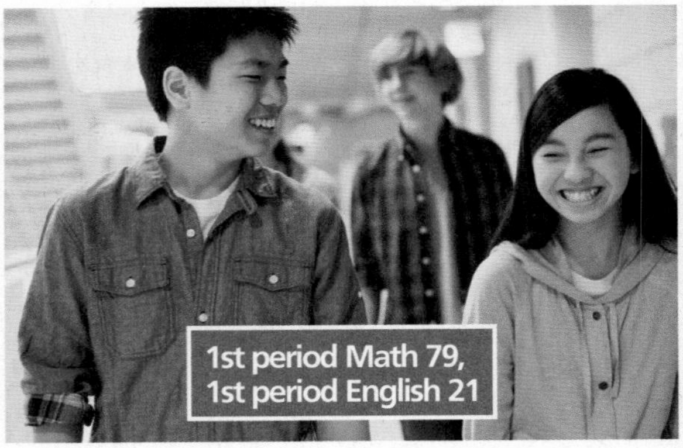

A. Method 1

Use proportional reasoning to predict the number of students in the whole school who will state that they prefer first period math.

______ out of 100 is how many out of 925? $\frac{\square}{100} = \frac{x}{\square}$

Multiply by a form of 1: $\frac{79}{100} \cdot \frac{\square}{\square} = \frac{x}{925}$.

The value of x is $79 \cdot \square = \square$.

About ______ students will state that they prefer first period math.

B. Method 2

Use a percent to predict the number of students in the whole school who will state that they prefer first period math.

79 out of 100 is ______%, so find ______% of ______, the number of students in the whole school.

$\square \cdot 925 = \square$

About ______ students will state that they prefer first period math.

Check Understanding

1. A doctor takes a random sample of her patients and finds that 40% are between the ages of 13 and 21. She has 1,100 patients in total. Use the experimental probability from the survey to predict how many of her patients are between the ages of 13 and 21.

______

2. A company sold 660 watches. A consumer advocate group found that 5% of this type of watch were defective, when the group conducted a random survey of 100 watches. Estimate the number of watches sold that were defective.

______

© Houghton Mifflin Harcourt Publishing Company • Image Credit: ©Sidekick/E+/Getty Images

Name

On Your Own

3. MP **Model with Mathematics** In a sample of 100 randomly selected concert attendees, the concert organizers find that 11 of them left the show early. The concert originally had 2,040 attendees.

   A. Use proportional reasoning to estimate how many of the total number of attendees left the concert early.

   B. MP **Attend to Precision** Explain why the answer in Part A cannot be a decimal.

4. MP **Model with Mathematics** In D'Andre's class, 5 of the 25 students are 5 feet tall or shorter. There are 400 students in D'Andre's grade at his school.

   A. Set up a proportional relationship to estimate the total number of students who are 5 feet tall or shorter in D'Andre's grade.

   B. Estimate how many students in D'Andre's grade are *over* 5 feet tall.

5. **STEM** According to the US Forest Service, the most common tree type found in timberlands in the state of Florida is the longleaf pine tree. In a sample population, 35% of trees were of this type.

There are approximately 17.4 million acres of forested land in Florida.

   A. Write a percent expression to estimate the number of acres of longleaf pine trees in Florida.

   B. Evaluate the percent expression to estimate how many acres of longleaf pine trees there are in Florida.

© Houghton Mifflin Harcourt Publishing Company • Image Credits: ©Gregg Vignal/Alamy; ©Jason Ross/Alamy

For Problems 6–7, the following samples were taken to see how many people preferred Candidate A. Predict the number of people who prefer Candidate A based on the information given.

6. Sample size: 200
Number of favorable responses: 100
Population: 1,000

____

7. Sample size: 100
Percent favorable: 35%
Population: 1,800

____

8. **Social Studies** Jiang was concerned about a busy intersection because it did not have a stop sign. She asked 100 people near the intersection. Seventy-five of the people supported putting in a stop sign. The town's population is 4,480. Write a percent expression and a proportion to estimate how many people in town support the stop sign. Then explain why the survey results might *not* represent opinions in town.

____

____

____

____

9. (MP) **Attend to Precision** Luis used proportional reasoning to predict that the number of people riding buses past his window each day would be 100.6 people. How should he express his answer? Explain.

____

For Problems 10–11 use this information.

The birthstones of a sample of 100 students and teachers in Claire's school are provided. The school has a total of 510 teachers and students.

Garnet (January): 6
Amethyst (February): 15
Aquamarine (March): 8
Diamond (April): 9
Emerald (May): 9
Pearl (June): 7
Ruby (July): 11
Peridot (August): 6
Sapphire (September): 8
Opal (October): 4
Topaz (November): 10
Tanzanite (December): 7

10. Write and evaluate a percent expression to estimate the total number of teachers and students at the school who have the amethyst as their birthstone.

____

11. Write and solve a proportion to estimate how many more teachers and students at the school have the garnet than the opal as their birthstone.

____

© Houghton Mifflin Harcourt Publishing Company • Image Credit: ©Derek Anderson/Alamy

Name ______________________

ONLINE
Video Tutorials and Interactive Examples

Use Experimental Probability and Proportional Reasoning to Make Predictions

1. Ms. Kalidova asked her class to use a percent expression to predict the result of the upcoming election for class president of the seventh grade. Results of a poll conducted of 50 students are provided in the graph. Assume the seventh grade has 350 students and everyone votes for one of the two candidates. Write a percent expression and evaluate it to find how many votes Andrew should expect to receive.

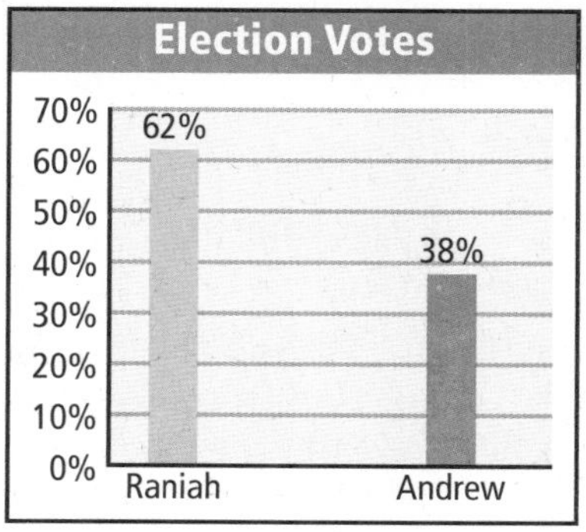

2. **Open Ended** Write a real-world problem involving a sample and a population that can be modeled by this proportion: $\frac{66}{100} = \frac{x}{2,500}$.

3. Shane plays baseball. The chart shows the results of his first 100 times at bat. Write a proportion and solve it to predict the number of home runs Shane will hit in his next 460 times at bat.

Out	63
Walk	8
Single	15
Double	8
Triple	1
Home run	5

4. **Math on the Spot** Professor Burger found that the experimental probability of his making a strike in bowling is 20%. Out of 400 throws, about how many could he predict would be strikes?

Model with Mathematics For Problems 5–6, use the following scenario.

In one weekend, 1,200 people attend a play at the theater downtown. A survey of 100 people who attended found that 45 gave the play at least 4 stars out of 5. Write and use the indicated model to estimate how many people in all would give the play at least 4 stars.

5. Solve using a proportion.

6. Solve using a percent expression.

© Houghton Mifflin Harcourt Publishing Company • Image Credit: ©Peter Kim/Shutterstock

Test Prep

Use the chart for Problems 7–8. The chart shows the number of hours each student spends training for their favorite sport, per 100 hours.

Simone	12
Javier	9
Robert	15
Natasha	8

7. Write a proportion and make a prediction for the number of hours Simone will spend training over a 2,000-hour period.

____

8. Write and use a percent expression to predict the number of hours Javier will spend training over a 2,000-hour period.

____

9. Jabrin was tossing a ball up in the air and catching it. He found that in 50 tries, he could catch it 45 times. He is going to do this 600 more times. Predict how many times Jabrin will catch the ball out of these 600 tosses.

____

10. Considering the proportions/percent equations and the corresponding values of *x* given, which combination is correct?

Ⓐ $\frac{40}{100} = \frac{x}{900}$; $x = 49$

Ⓑ $0.20(1{,}200) = x$; $x = 300$

Ⓒ $\frac{25}{100} = \frac{x}{750}$; $x = 175$

Ⓓ $0.70(500) = x$; $x = 350$

Spiral Review

11. A vegetarian restaurant offers 52 vegetarian meals on its menu. Four of the meals include eggplant. Shan picks a dish at random from the menu with his eyes closed. What is the probability that he orders a meal that does not include eggplant? Write the probability as a fraction.

____

12. Jake is saving for a new tablet. It costs \$250, and he has \$100. He earns \$5 per week for doing chores. Jake wants to figure out how many weeks it will take for him to have at least enough money to buy a new tablet. Write an inequality and solve it to determine the number of weeks it will take.

____

© Houghton Mifflin Harcourt Publishing Company

Module 19

Name ______________________

Review

Vocabulary

Complete each sentence using terms from the Vocabulary box.

Vocabulary
event experiment outcome probability sample space trial

1. The ______________ of an experiment is the set of all possible outcomes of the experiment.

2. The ______________ of an event is a number from 0 to 1, or from 0% to 100%, that describes its likelihood.

3. Each repetition of a probability ______________ is called a ______________.

4. Rolling a number less than 4 on a number cube is an ______________ that consists of more than one ______________.

Concepts and Skills

5. The chance that a baseball player will get a hit is estimated to be 23%. How would you describe this likelihood?

Ⓐ certain Ⓑ likely Ⓒ unlikely Ⓓ as likely as not

6. A news report states that a hurricane will reach land on Monday or Tuesday, but Tuesday is more likely. Give a number or number range to describe the probability that the hurricane will reach land on Tuesday.

____

7. Indira drew 3 animals: an eagle, a snake, and a shark. She drew each animal twice, once with green eyes and once with red eyes. Ten students chose their favorite drawing. Three of them chose the shark with red eyes. How many possible outcomes are in the sample space of the experiment? Based on the results, what is the experimental probability that a shark with red eyes is *not* picked, written as a percent?

____

8. (MP) **Use Tools** Sophia randomly selects a marble from a bag of marbles and then replaces it. The results of 300 trials are shown. Based on this data set, what is the experimental probability of selecting a red marble from the bag? State what strategy and tool you will use to answer the question, explain your choice, and then find the answer.

Red	57
White	105
Blue	138

____

____

© Houghton Mifflin Harcourt Publishing Company

9. In each cycle of a stoplight, the light is green for 30 seconds, yellow for 5 seconds, and red for 85 seconds. Liam conducts 500 trials of a simulation to estimate the likelihood that the stoplight will be a particular color when a car reaches it. Use the results to find the probability of each event.

Event	Experimental Probability
Getting a green light	
Getting a yellow light	
Not getting a red light	

Simulation Results	
Outcome	**Frequency**
Green light	115
Yellow light	15
Red light	370

10. A bag holds 6 plain bagels, 3 raisin bagels, 2 cheddar bagels, and 1 onion bagel. Grace chooses 4 bagels from the bag at random without replacing them. Select all possible compound events.

Ⓐ All of the bagels are raisin bagels.

Ⓑ There are exactly 2 plain bagels.

Ⓒ More than half the bagels are cheddar bagels.

Ⓓ There are more onion bagels selected than raisin bagels.

Ⓔ The number of cheddar bagels is equal to the number of plain bagels.

11. The experimental probability that Teresa will make a free-throw shot in basketball is 50%. Describe a simulation that can be used to estimate the probability that Teresa will make both of her next 2 free-throw shots.

____

____

____

12. The table shows the blood types of the last 300 people to donate blood at a blood bank. Use this information to answer each question.

Blood Donations	
Blood type	**Frequency**
O	144
A	93
B	49
AB	14

A. What is the experimental probability that the next person to donate blood will have type O blood?

____

B. If 50 people donate blood on Friday, how many can be expected to have type O blood? __________ people

13. The experimental probability of winning a prize when playing a carnival game is estimated to be 4%. Based on this information, approximately how many times would a player need to play the game to win 10 prizes?

Ⓐ 25 times Ⓑ 40 times Ⓒ 250 times Ⓓ 400 times

© Houghton Mifflin Harcourt Publishing Company

Module

20 Understand and Apply Theoretical Probability

ANALYZING ROCK-PAPER-SCISSORS

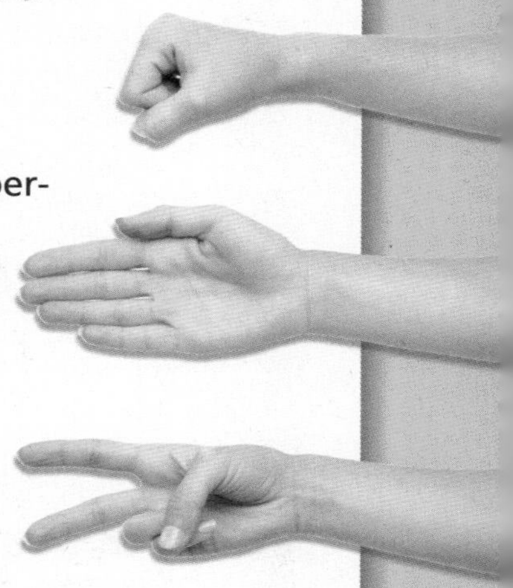

Destiny and Mateo are in the semi-finals of a Rock-Paper-Scissors tournament. Rock-Paper-Scissors is a game for two players, using the three hand signals shown. Players count, "1, 2, 3, go!" and then each player makes a hand signal for rock, paper, or scissors. Each player has an equal chance of winning.

Rock (R) beats scissors (S); Scissors (S) beat paper (P); Paper (P) beats rock (R)

A. The table shows the results of Destiny and Mateo's match. Complete the table by filling in the missing entries.

Destiny	R	P	S	S	S	P	P	P	P	R
Mateo	P	R	P	S	R	S	R	P	R	R
Winner	M	D	D	X						

The winner of this round of the semi-finals is ________!

B. Complete the statements. Write each experimental probability as a fraction and as a decimal.

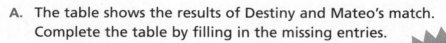

- Destiny (D) chose Rock _____ times. $P(DR) = \frac{\square}{10}$ or _____
- Mateo (M) chose Rock _____ times. $P(MR) = \frac{\square}{10}$ or _____
- Destiny chose Paper _____ times. $P(DP) = \frac{\square}{10}$ or _____
- Mateo chose Paper _____ times. $P(MP) = \frac{\square}{10}$ or _____

Turn and Talk

Calculate each player's experimental probability of choosing scissors. Explain your method of calculation.

© Houghton Mifflin Harcourt Publishing Company • Image Credit: ©LeventeGyori/Shutterstock

Are You Ready?

Complete these problems to review prior concepts and skills you will need for this module.

More Likely, Less Likely, Equally Likely

Use the spinner for Problems 1–3.

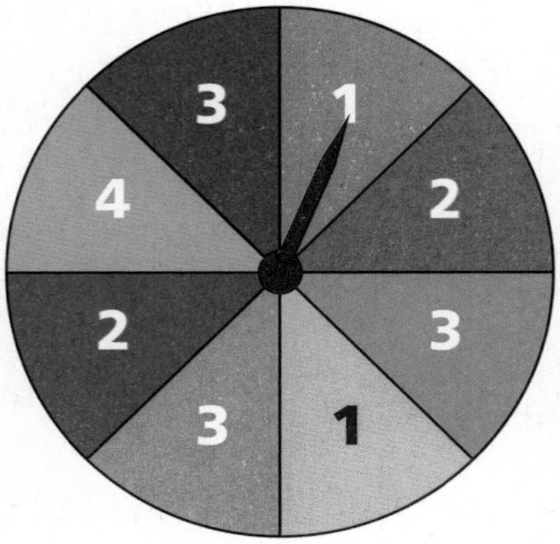

1. Which event is more likely than spinning a 1?

____

2. Which event is less likely than spinning a 1?

____

3. Which event is equally likely as spinning a 1?

____

Experimental Probability

The number of each type of bar in a variety pack of granola bars can vary. The table shows the number of peanut butter bars in a random sample of 300 variety packs. Use this information for Problems 4–6.

Number of Peanut Butter Bars per Pack	Frequency
0	11
1	29
2	60
3	75
4	71
5	39
6	15

4. What is the experimental probability that a variety pack will have exactly 3 peanut butter bars?

____

____

5. What is the experimental probability that a variety pack will have at most 4 peanut butter bars?

____

____

6. Esme buys 15 variety packs. How many packs can she expect will have more than 2 peanut butter bars? Explain your reasoning.

____

____

____

____

© Houghton Mifflin Harcourt Publishing Company

Name ____________________

Find Theoretical Probability of Simple Events

I Can find the theoretical probability of a simple event.

Spark Your Learning

SMALL GROUPS

Dominic wants to play a balloon dart game at the county fair. He can play Game 1 or Game 2. If he pops a blue balloon with a dart, he wins a prize. Which game should Dominic play if he wants a better chance of winning a prize? Assume that Dominic gets one throw, and it will hit a balloon in either game.

Turn and Talk Explain what changes could be made to Game 1 so that Dominic has the same chance of winning a prize when playing either game.

© Houghton Mifflin Harcourt Publishing Company • Image Credit: ©Goss Images/Alamy

Build Understanding

1 Clara is playing a game where she chooses to spin one of the spinners shown. If the spinner lands on a section labeled "A," she wins a pair of headphones. Which spinner will give her a better chance of winning?

Spinner 1

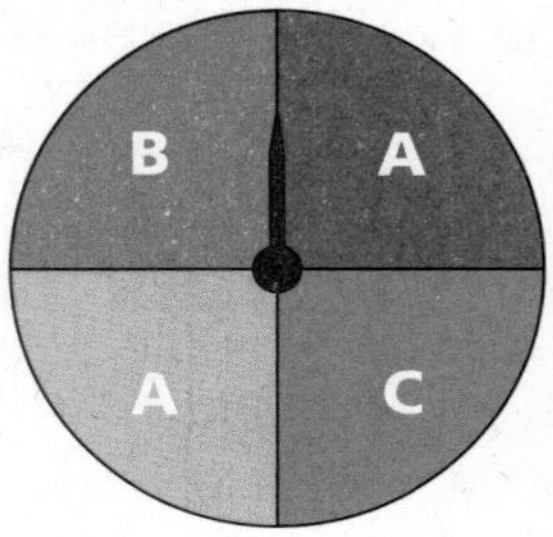

Spinner 2

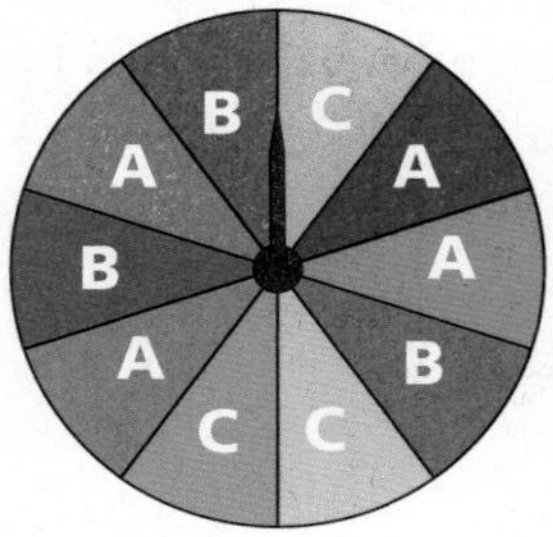

A. Total number of sections for each spinner:

Spinner 1 has a total of _______ sections of the same area.

Spinner 2 has a total of _______ sections of the same area.

B. Number of sections labeled "A" for each spinner:

Spinner 1 has _______ sections labeled "A."

Spinner 2 has _______ sections labeled "A."

C. What is the ratio of sections labeled "A" to total number of sections for each spinner?

Spinner 1: $\frac{\square}{4}$ Spinner 2: $\frac{\square}{10}$

D. How can you make the ratios in Part C easier to compare?

____

____

E. What is the ratio of sections labeled "A" to total number of sections for each spinner, written as fractions with a common denominator?

Spinner 1: $\frac{\square}{20}$ Spinner 2: $\frac{\square}{20}$

F. Which spinner should Clara spin to give her a better chance of winning a pair of headphones? Explain.

____

____

____

G. Which spinner should Clara spin to give her a better chance of landing on "C"? Explain.

____

____

Turn and Talk Describe another way to compare the ratios in Part C.

© Houghton Mifflin Harcourt Publishing Company

Name

Step It Out

If the outcomes of an experiment are equally likely, you can find the theoretical probability of an event without performing the experiment.

$$P(\text{event}) = \frac{\text{number of equally likely outcomes in the event}}{\text{total number of equally likely outcomes in the sample space}}$$

When a probability is given as a fraction, it is usually written in simplest form.

Connect to Vocabulary

If all possible outcomes are equally likely, the **theoretical probability** of an event is the ratio of the number of possible outcomes in the event to the total number of possible outcomes in the sample space.

2 Lindsay is going to draw one tile from the bag shown without looking. The tiles are the same size and cannot be told apart by touch, so each tile has an equal chance of being chosen. What is the theoretical probability that she selects a red tile?

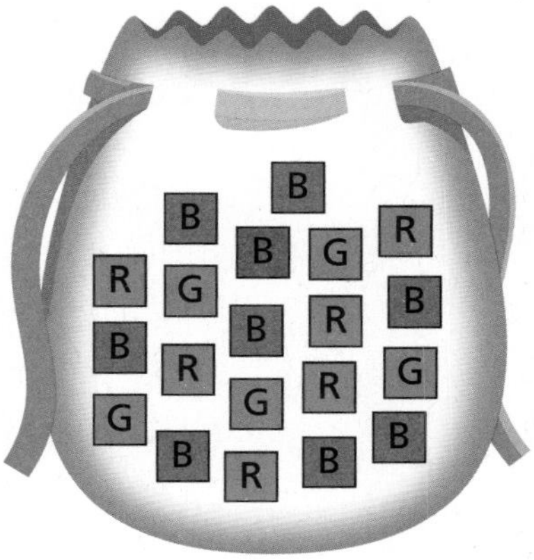

A. Identify the sample space.

5 red / blue / green tiles

6 red / blue / green tiles

9 red / blue / green tiles

B. Find the total number of equally likely possible outcomes in the sample space by adding.

green tiles + red tiles + blue tiles = total number of tiles

☐ + ☐ + ☐ = ☐

There are ______ equally likely outcomes in the sample space.

C. Identify the total number of possible outcomes included in the event "selects a red tile." Is each possible outcome equally likely?

There are ______ red tiles in the bag, so there are ______ possible outcomes included in this event. Each of these possible outcomes is / is not equally likely.

D. Find the theoretical probability that Lindsay will select a red tile. Then, write the ratio in simplest form.

$$P(\text{red tile}) = \frac{\text{number of red tiles}}{\text{total number of tiles}} = \frac{\square}{\square} = \frac{\square}{\square}$$

E. Probability can be written as a fraction, decimal, or percent. Write the theoretical probability that Lindsay draws a red tile from the bag as a fraction, a decimal, and a percent.

© Houghton Mifflin Harcourt Publishing Company

3 Miguel is deciding if he should do his chores or homework first. To help him decide, he flips a coin.

A. Miguel flips the coin once. Find the theoretical probability of the coin landing on heads and the theoretical probability of the coin landing on tails. Write each as a decimal.

P(Heads) = ☐ P(Tails) = ☐

B. Predict the number of times the coin will land on heads and tails out of 20 flips using the theoretical probability.

P(Heads)	×	Number of flips	=	Prediction: number of heads
______	×	______	=	______

P(Tails)	×	Number of flips	=	Prediction: number of tails
______	×	______	=	______

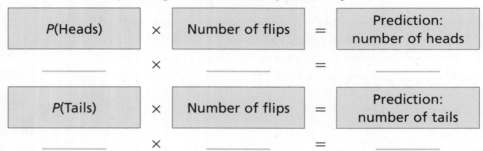

C. Flip a coin 20 times. Record the outcomes in the frequency column. Then give the experimental probability to the nearest percent.

Outcome	Heads	Tails
Frequency		
Experimental probability		

D. Compare the theoretical and experimental probabilities of the coin landing on heads and tails. Are the probabilities equal? Why isn't experimental probability always the same as theoretical probability?

____

____

____

Check Understanding

1. Eric's coach said he could spin a spinner with 4 equal sections labeled 1–4, or roll a number cube labeled 1–6. If Eric gets a 1, he does not have to run a sprint. If Eric does not want to run a sprint, which should he pick? Explain.

____

____

2. Pam tossed a coin 50 times. She found the probability of getting heads was 45%. Was this a theoretical or experimental probability? Explain.

____

© Houghton Mifflin Harcourt Publishing Company • **Image Credit:** ©Image Club/ Getty Images Royalty Free

On Your Own

3. (MP) **Use Structure** Amara has the choice to select one card from Pile 1 or Pile 2 without looking. If she selects a yellow card, she wins a game. Which pile should Amara pick from to give her a better chance of winning? Explain your reasoning.

Pile 1

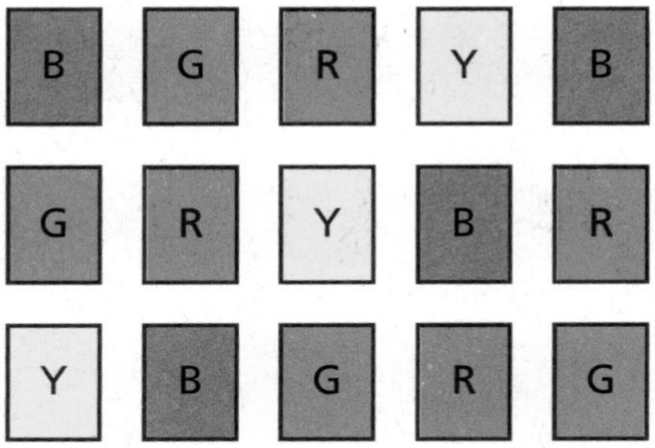

Pile 2

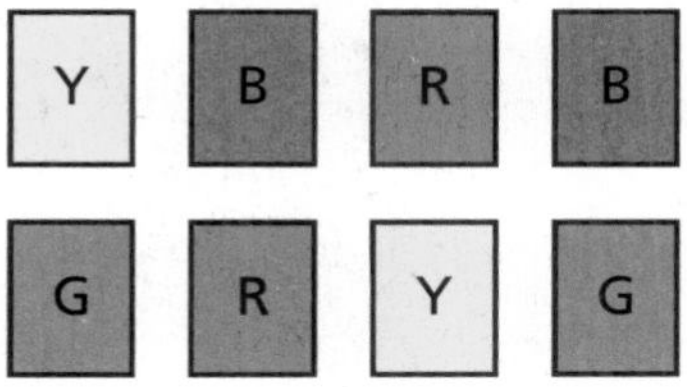

4. (MP) **Reason** The table shows the results of rolling a number cube 50 times. Compare the experimental probability and theoretical probability of rolling a 5. Give a possible reason why the probabilities are different. Explain your reasoning.

Outcome	1	2	3	4	5	6
Frequency	10	9	5	6	7	13

For Problems 5–8, use the gift boxes shown. Find the theoretical probability of randomly selecting each gift box. Write the probability as a fraction in simplest form.

5. yellow box: ☐ **6.** purple box: ☐

7. blue box: ☐ **8.** green box: ☐

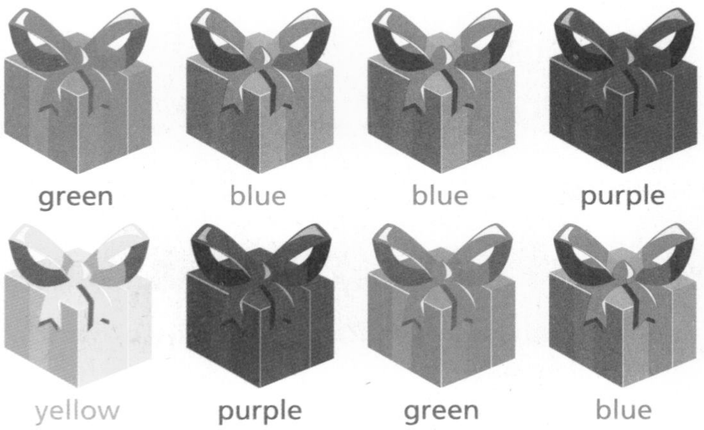

© Houghton Mifflin Harcourt Publishing Company

9. A bag contains 5 red balls, 8 white balls, and 7 black balls. What is the theoretical probability of randomly selecting a black ball from the bag?

____

10. Chase can spin a spinner centered on Board 1 or Board 2. He wants the spinner to land on a section labeled "R." Which board should he choose? Explain.

____

____

____

____

____

Board 1

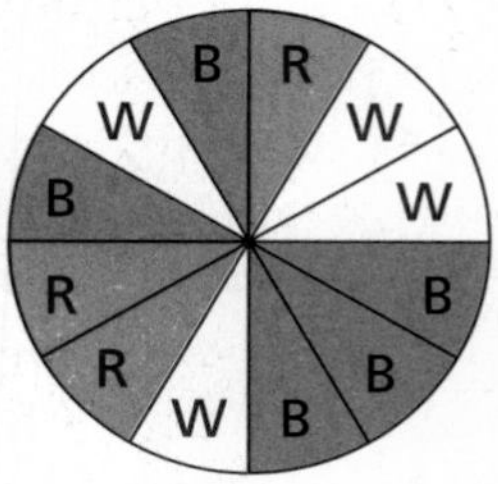

Board 2

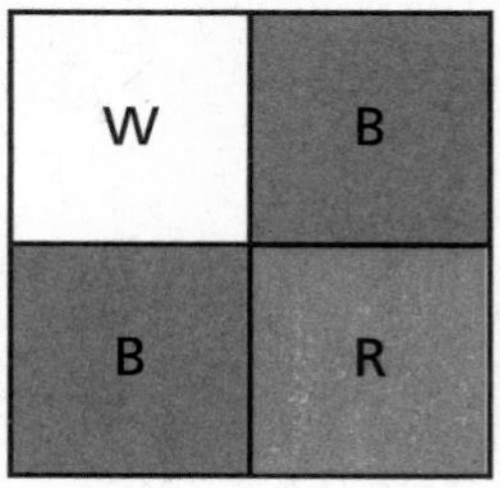

11. Edith spun a spinner with 5 equal sections labeled 1–5. The spinner landed on 1 five times, on 2 three times, on 3 four times, on 4 three times, and on 5 five times. For which number is the experimental probability the same as its theoretical probability? Explain.

____

____

____

____

(MP) Use Structure **For Problems 12–13, use the flowers shown. Find the theoretical probability of selecting the color listed. Write the probability as a fraction in simplest form, a decimal, and a percent.**

12. orange flower

____

13. purple flower

____

© Houghton Mifflin Harcourt Publishing Company

I'm in a Learning Mindset!

Was finding theoretical probabilities of simple events an appropriate challenge for me?

____

Name

Find Theoretical Probability of Simple Events

Luke has a bag of 52 beads. Half the beads are rough. The other half are smooth. There are 13 red beads, 13 blue beads, 13 green beads, and 13 black beads. Use this information for Problems 1–5. Write each probability as a fraction in simplest form.

1. What is the theoretical probability of selecting a smooth bead?

2. What is the theoretical probability of selecting a blue bead?

3. What is the theoretical probability of selecting a rough bead?

4. What is the theoretical probability of not selecting a red bead?

5. (MP) **Reason** One hundred times, Luke picks one bead then puts it back into the bag. The results are shown. What are the experimental probability and theoretical probability of picking a black bead? Name a possible reason why the probabilities are not the same.

Outcome	Red	Blue	Green	Black
Frequency	21	26	33	20

6. **Math on the Spot** Find the probability of the event. Write your answer as a fraction, as a decimal, and as a percent.

A. draw one of the 4 *L*'s from a bag of 100 letter tiles

B. roll a number less than 4 on a number cube

© Houghton Mifflin Harcourt Publishing Company

Test Prep

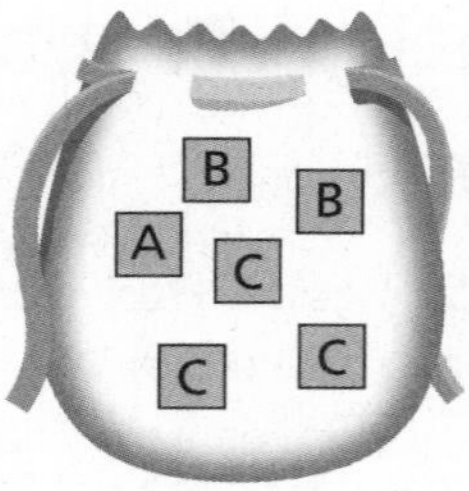

Bag 1

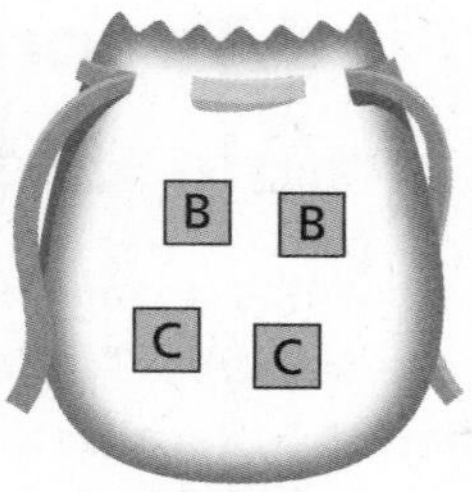

Bag 2

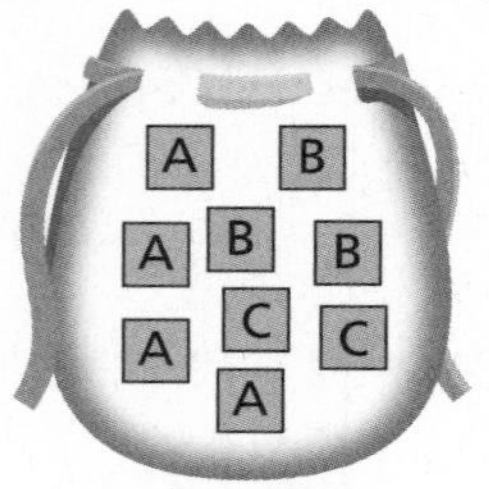

Bag 3

7. Brice can win a game by selecting a letter tile with the letter B from a bag. He wants to choose a bag that will give him the best chance of winning. Which statement is correct?

Ⓐ Brice has the best chance only with Bag 1.

Ⓑ Brice has the best chance only with Bag 2.

Ⓒ Brice has the best chance only with Bag 3.

Ⓓ Brice has the best chance with either Bag 1 or Bag 3.

8. Use the spinner shown to match the theoretical probability to the correct event.

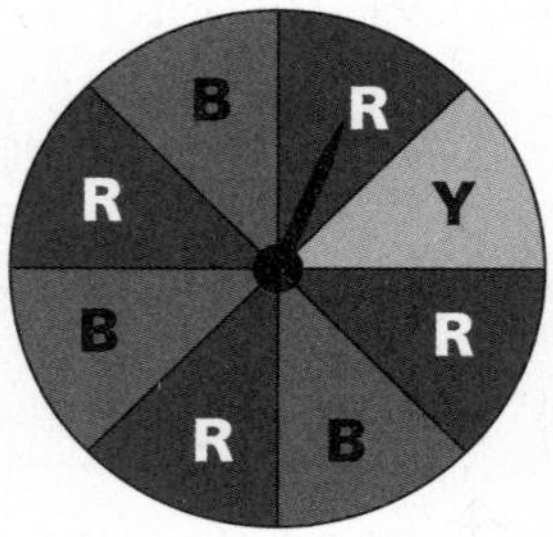

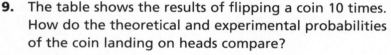

P(Y) •	• $\frac{1}{2}$
P(R) •	• 0.375
P(B) •	• 12.5%

9. The table shows the results of flipping a coin 10 times. How do the theoretical and experimental probabilities of the coin landing on heads compare?

Outcome	Heads	Tails
Frequency	3	7

____

____

Spiral Review

10. A soccer team made 2 goals out of 32 attempts in a game. What is the experimental probability that the team made a goal on any given shot? Write the probability as a decimal.

____

11. The experimental probability that Jason makes a free throw is 72%. If Jason shoots 50 free throws, about how many can you expect him to make? Explain.

____

© Houghton Mifflin Harcourt Publishing Company

Name ____________________

Find Theoretical Probability of Compound Events

I Can find the theoretical probability of a compound event.

Step It Out

1 Lucas spins the two spinners shown. Spinning each number on one spinner is equally likely. He wants to find the probability that the sum of the two numbers he spins is 3.

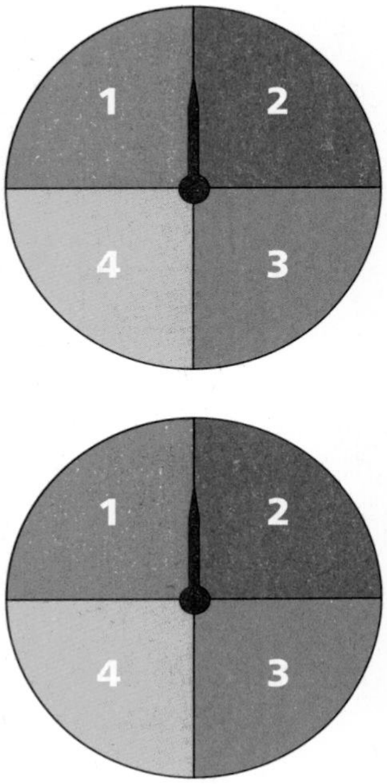

A. Lucas makes a table to represent the sample space of sums. Each entry in the table is the sum of the numbers in the corresponding row and column. Complete the remainder of the table.

+	1	2	3	4
1	2	3	4	
2	3	4		
3	4			
4				

B. The table in Part A shows:

- There are ______ possible outcomes with a sum of 3.
- There are ______ equally likely outcomes in the sample space.

C. Find the theoretical probability of spinning a sum of 3.

$$P(\text{sum of 3}) = \frac{\text{number of equally likely outcomes that add to 3}}{\text{total number of equally likely outcomes in the sample space}}$$

$$= \frac{\square}{16}$$

$$= \frac{\square}{\square}$$

D. Determine another possible outcome in the sample space that has the same probability as that of spinning a sum of 3.

$P(\text{sum of 3}) = P($____________$)$

Turn and Talk Explain why spinning a sum of 3 is a compound event.

© Houghton Mifflin Harcourt Publishing Company

2 Aria can choose one pair of shorts (black or white), one shirt (red, blue, or green), and one pair of shoes (brown or tan) as her outfit. Find the probability of choosing an outfit at random and getting white shorts, a blue shirt, and tan shoes.

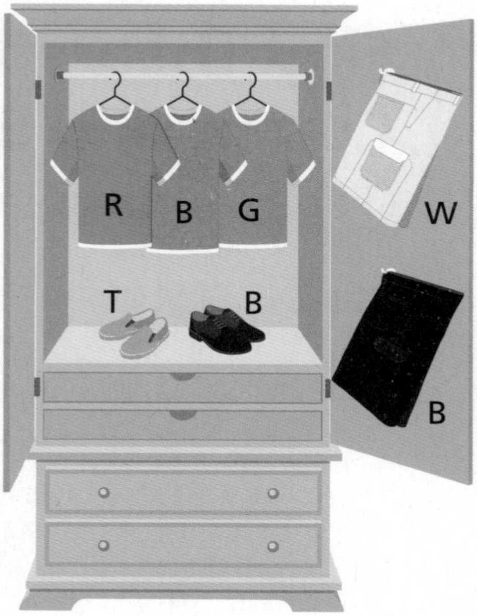

A. Complete the **tree diagram** to represent the sample space.

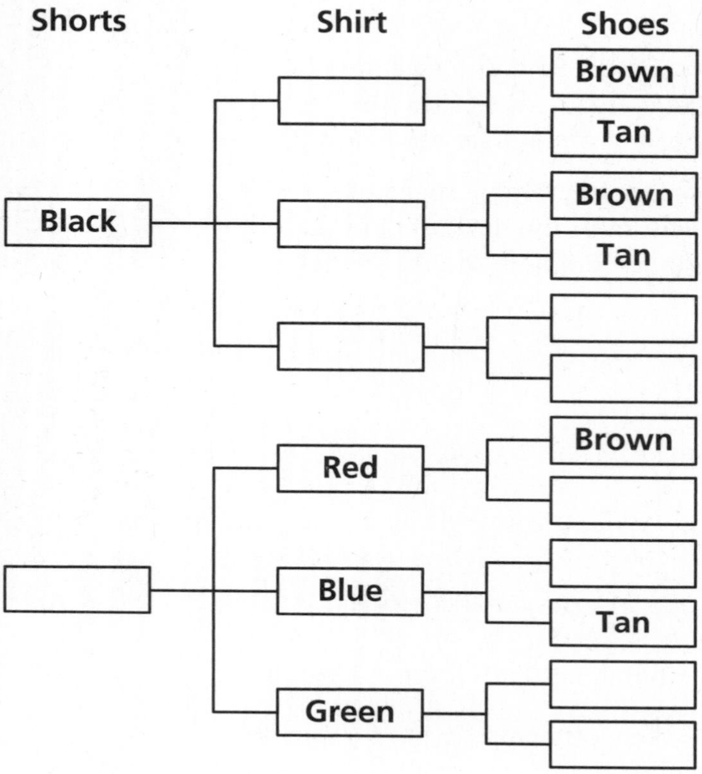

B. The tree diagram shows that there are _______ equally likely outcomes in the sample space.

C. Find the probability P(white, blue, tan).

$$P(\text{white, blue, tan}) = \frac{\text{number of equally likely outcomes in the event (white, blue, tan)}}{\text{total number of equally likely outcomes in the sample space}}$$

$$= \frac{\square}{\square}$$

D. Find the probability of selecting white shorts and a blue shirt when selecting clothes at random.

$$P(\text{white, blue}) = \frac{\text{number of equally likely outcomes in the event (white, blue)}}{\text{total number of equally likely outcomes in the sample space}}$$

$$= \frac{\square}{\square}$$

© Houghton Mifflin Harcourt Publishing Company

Name ______________________________

3 Ethan draws cards from a hat that contains three cards labeled A, B, and C. He has an equal chance of drawing each card. He draws one card at a time, records the result, and replaces it before the next draw. What is the probability that Ethan draws the A-card 3 times in a row?

Winning Combination

A	A	A

A. Complete the organized lists to represent the sample space.

A on first draw		
A	A	A
A	A	B
A	A	C
A	B	A
A	B	B
A	B	C
A	C	
A	C	
A	C	

B on first draw		
B	A	A
B	A	B
B	A	C
B	B	
B	B	
B	B	
B	C	
B	C	
B	C	

C on first draw		
C	A	
C	A	
C	A	
	B	
C		A
C		B
C	C	C

B. The organized lists show that there are ______ equally likely outcomes in the sample space.

C. Find the probability *P*(A, A, A). Write the probability as a fraction, decimal, and percent. Round to the nearest hundredth and whole percent.

$$P(\text{A, A, A}) = \frac{\text{number of equally likely outcomes in the event (A, A, A)}}{\text{total number of equally likely outcomes in the sample space}}$$

$$= \frac{\square}{\square} \text{ or } \square \text{ or } \square\,\%$$

The probability that Ethan draws the A-card 3 times in a row is about ______%.

Turn and Talk How do you think you could use the organized lists to find the probability of drawing 2 or more A-cards in any order?

Check Understanding

1. What are some ways that you can represent the sample space of a compound event?

____

2. Mila spins two spinners. One spinner has two equal sections labeled 1 and 2. The other spinner has three equal sections labeled 1, 2, and 3. What is the probability that the sum of the two spins is 4?

____

© Houghton Mifflin Harcourt Publishing Company

On Your Own

3. (MP) **Use Structure** Wyatt rolls two number prisms in the shape of triangular prisms, labeled 1 to 3 as shown.

A. Complete the table to represent the sample space for the sum of these two number prisms.

+	1	2	3
1			
2			
3			

B. What is the probability that Wyatt rolls a sum of 3?

____

C. What event has the same probability as rolling a sum of 3? Explain.

____

____

D. Name an event that is less likely than a sum of 3. Explain.

____

____

____

E. Name an event that is more likely than a sum of 3. Explain.

____

____

____

(MP) **Model with Mathematics** **Find each probability. Give your answer as a simplified fraction, a decimal to the nearest hundredth, and a percent to the nearest whole percent.**

F. *P*(sum of 4)

____

G. *P*(sum of 6)

____

H. *P*(sum $<$ 10)

____

I. *P*(sum $>$ 10)

____

© Houghton Mifflin Harcourt Publishing Company

Name

4. (MP) **Use Structure** Layla tosses three coins.

A. Complete the tree diagram to show the sample space for how the coins can land. H represent heads and T represent tails.

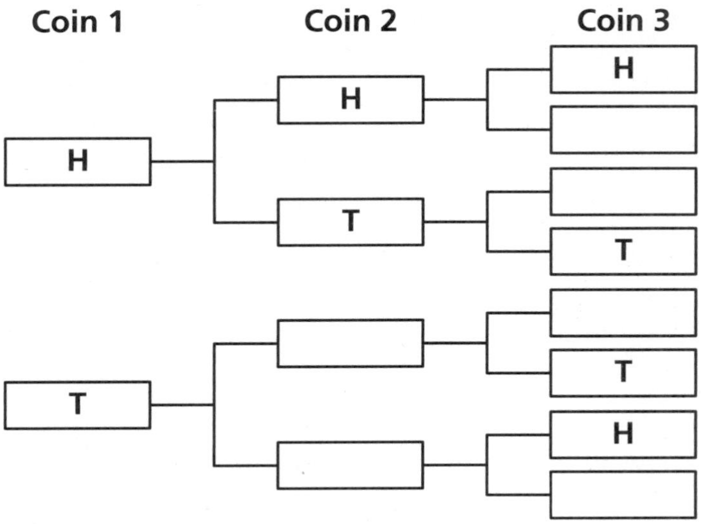

B. What is the probability that exactly two coins land heads up? Write the probability as a fraction, decimal, and percent.

____

C. What is the probability that exactly two coins land tails up? Compare this probability to the probability that exactly two coins land heads up.

____

D. What is the probability that exactly three coins land tails up? Write the probability as a fraction, decimal, and percent.

____

E. Name an event that has the same probability as that of three tails? Explain.

____

____

F. Compare the theoretical probability of getting at least one head and the theoretical probability of getting at least two tails.

____

____

____

____

© Houghton Mifflin Harcourt Publishing Company • Image Credit: ©P Maxwell Photography/Shutterstock

5. (MP) **Use Structure** Daniel is going to spin the spinner shown and roll a number cube.

A. Make an organized list to show the sample space for spinning the spinner and rolling the number cube.

B. What is the probability that Daniel gets a sum of 5?

C. What is the probability that Daniel gets a sum of 3?

D. Compare the probability of getting a sum of 5 and the probability of getting a sum of 3.

E. **Open Ended** Give an example of an event that is more likely than getting a sum of 8. Explain your reasoning.

F. **Open Ended** Give an example of an event that is as likely as getting a sum of 6. Explain your reasoning.

6. (MP) **Reason** How is finding the theoretical probability of a compound event similar to finding the theoretical probability of a simple event?

© Houghton Mifflin Harcourt Publishing Company

Name ______________________________

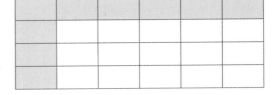

Find Theoretical Probability of Compound Events

1. MP **Use Structure** Christian has a red box with tiles numbered from 1 to 5 and a green box with tiles numbered from 1 to 3. He draws a tile from each box, and then finds the sum.

A. Make a table to represent the sample space for drawing a particular sum from the numbers in the two boxes.

B. What is the probability of drawing a sum of 7?

____

C. Name an event that is more likely than drawing a sum of 7.

____

2. MP **Use Structure** Lucy can choose one sandwich (ham or turkey), one side (apples or grapes), and one drink (milk or water). Lucy has an equally likely chance of choosing any combination.

A. Make a tree diagram to find the sample space.

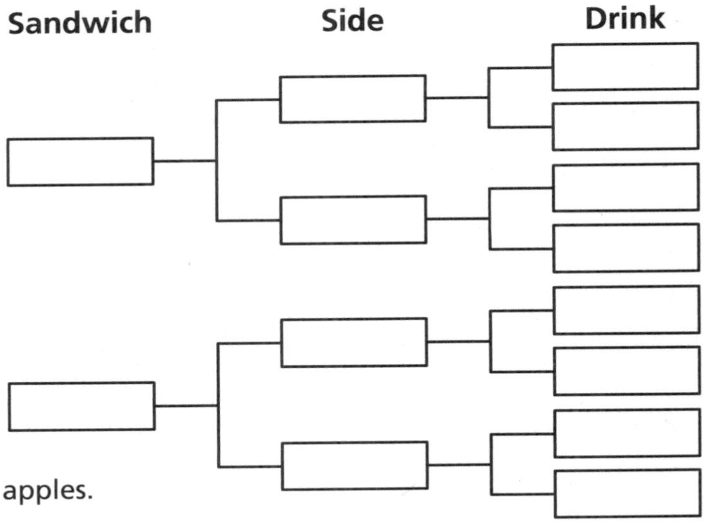

B. What is the probability Lucy picks a ham sandwich and grapes?

____

C. What is the probability Lucy chooses milk with a turkey sandwich and apples?

____

D. MP **Reason** Name an event that is equally as likely as choosing ham and apples.

____

3. MP **Attend to Precision** How many different possible outcomes are there for the experiment described here?

Step 1 Toss a number cube.

Step 2 Toss a fair coin.

Step 3 Spin the spinner.

There are __________ different possible outcomes.

© Houghton Mifflin Harcourt Publishing Company

Test Prep

4. Emma is going to flip a coin, resulting in H for heads or T for tails, and spin the spinner shown. Which list correctly represents the sample space?

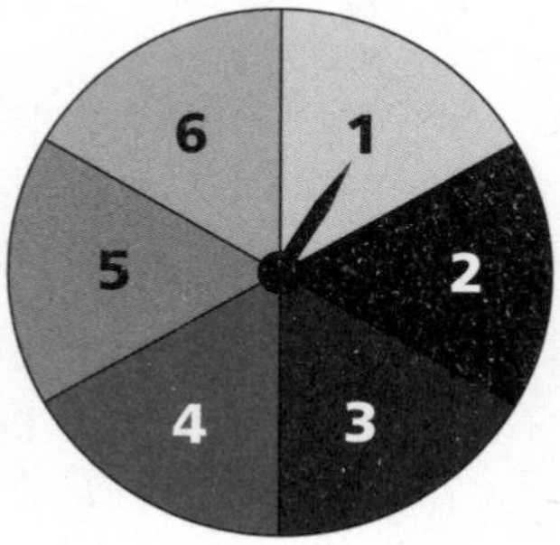

Ⓐ H, T, 1, 2, 3, 4, 5, 6

Ⓑ H-1, H-2, H-3, H-4, H-5, H-6

Ⓒ H-1, H-2, H-3, H-4, H-5, H-6, T-1, T-2, T-3, T-4, T-5, T-6

Ⓓ H-T-1, H-T-2, H-T-3, H-T-4, H-T-5, H-T-6

5. Luna rolls two number cubes labeled 1–6. Match the probability to the correct event.

P(sum of 5) •	• $\frac{1}{6}$
P(sum less than 4) •	• $\frac{1}{9}$
P(sum of 7) •	• $\frac{5}{18}$
P(sum greater than 8) •	• $\frac{1}{12}$

6. Carson can choose one type of vehicle (car or truck), one color (blue, red, or silver), and one type of transmission (standard or automatic). How many possible outcomes are there?

____

Spiral Review

7. Aaliyah spins the spinner shown. What is the theoretical probability that the spinner will land on an even number?

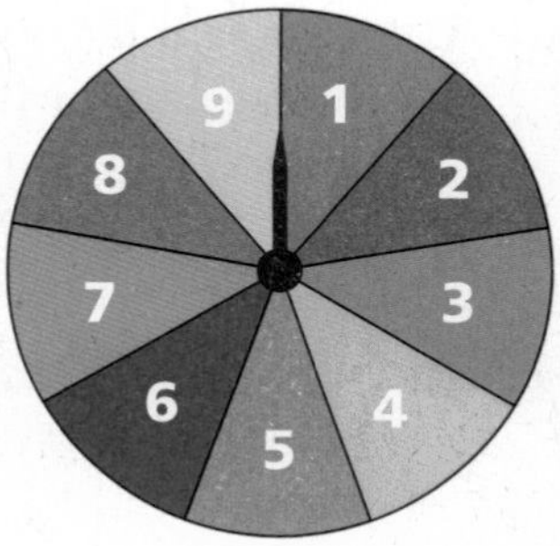

____

8. You and 19 other people are entered in a drawing. One person will be randomly selected to win a prize. What is the theoretical probability that you will win the prize? Explain.

____

____

____

____

____

© Houghton Mifflin Harcourt Publishing Company

Name ____________________

Use Theoretical Probability and Proportional Reasoning to Make Predictions

I Can use theoretical probability to make predictions about real-world situations.

Step It Out

1 Sadie spins the spinner shown 80 times. Predict how many times she will spin a 2 or 3.

A. The theoretical probability of spinning a 2 or 3 is ______, or ______%.

B. Solve by using proportional reasoning.

$\frac{1}{2} = \frac{x}{\square}$ $\quad 1 \times \square = x \quad$ So $x = \square$.
$\qquad\qquad\quad 2 \times 40 = 80$

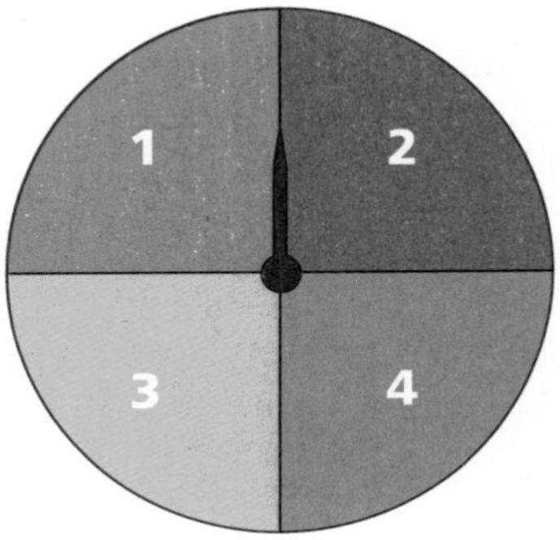

Sadie will spin a 2 or 3 about _____ times.

C. Solve by multiplying the probability by the number of trials.

P(spinning 2 or 3) × number of trials

$\square\% \quad \times \quad \square \quad = \square$

Sadie will spin a 2 or 3 about _____ times.

2 Jamie volunteers at an animal shelter. The types, colors, and genders of dogs are shown. Predict how many times out of 90 Jamie will randomly select a tan, male pug to walk. Assume an equal chance for her to select each dog.

Type	Color	Gender
Pug (P)	Black (Bl)	Male (M)
Beagle (B)	White (Wh)	Female (F)
Collie (C)	Tan (T)	

A. Make an organized list for the sample space.

B. The theoretical probability of selecting a tan, male pug is _____.

C. Solve by multiplying the probability by the number of trials.

$\square \times \square = \square$

Jamie will select a tan, male pug about _____ out of 90 times.

© Houghton Mifflin Harcourt Publishing Company • Image Credit: ©Camille Tokerud/The Image Bank/Getty Images

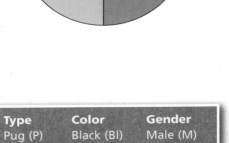

3 Ezekiel randomly draws a card from the stack shown. Which is more likely: drawing a card that is NOT red or drawing a green card?

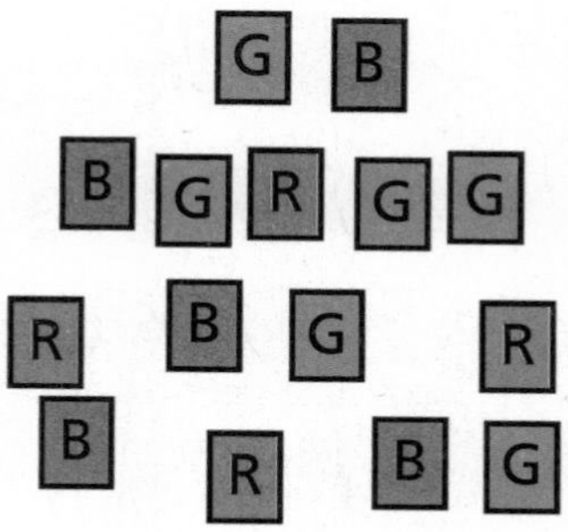

A. First find P(red). Then find the **complement**, P(NOT red).

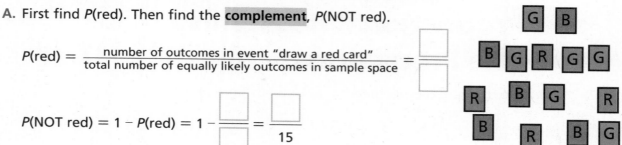

$$P(\text{red}) = \frac{\text{number of outcomes in event "draw a red card"}}{\text{total number of equally likely outcomes in sample space}} = \frac{\square}{\square}$$

$$P(\text{NOT red}) = 1 - P(\text{red}) = 1 - \frac{\square}{\square} = \frac{\square}{15}$$

B. Complete the inequality statement to compare P(NOT red) and P(green).

P(NOT red) ☐ P(green)

☐ ☐ ☐

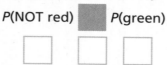

So drawing not red / green is more likely.

4 Isla is resetting her door code. The code is a 3-digit number made up of the digits 0 through 9. The digits can be repeated. Isla used a random number generator to select a code, so all possible codes are equally likely. Would you predict that the door code 567 will be generated more than 5 out of 8,000 times?

A. First find the number of equally likely outcomes in the sample space.

Imagine drawing a tree diagram. There are 10 possible outcomes for the first digit, and each of those has 10 possible outcomes for the second digit, and each of those 10 more for the third digit.

The sample space has $10 \times 10 \times 10 =$ ______ equally likely outcomes.

B. Find the probability of randomly generating the code 567, and use it to predict the number of times out of 8,000 you would expect code 567 to be generated.

$$P(567) = \frac{\square}{1{,}000}$$

$P(567) \times$ number of trials

$$\square \times \square = \square$$

I would / would not predict that the code 567 will be generated more than 5 out of 8,000 times.

Check Understanding

1. A bag of marbles contains 5 red, 3 blue, and 12 yellow marbles. Predict the number of times Hazel will select a blue marble out of 500 trials.

____

2. Kai flips a coin and spins a 3-sector spinner labeled 1–3. Predict the number of times Kai will get the outcome (heads, 2) in 300 trials.

____

© Houghton Mifflin Harcourt Publishing Company

On Your Own

3. (MP) Construct Arguments Bryson selects a folder from a pile. The folder is blue. There are 8 blue folders, 9 yellow folders, and 3 orange folders left in the pile. He selects a second folder without looking. Is it likely that Bryson selects matching folders? Explain your reasoning.

(MP) Model with Mathematics **An eight-sided game piece has 8 congruent triangular sides. The sides are labeled 1–8. Nevaeh rolls the game piece 400 times. Use this information for Problems 4–6.**

4. Write and solve a proportion to predict how many times the game piece will land on 7.

5. Write and solve a proportion to predict how many times the game piece will land on 3 or 5.

6. Write and evaluate an expression to predict how many times the game piece will land on a number less than or equal to 3.

Liliana spins a spinner with equal-sized sections numbered 1 through 4 a total of 300 times. Use this information for Problems 7–8.

7. Write and solve a proportion to predict the number of times Liliana can expect to spin a 3.

8. Write and evaluate an expression to predict the number of times Liliana can expect to spin an even number.

9. A box has 12 red tiles, 15 blue tiles, and 23 purple tiles. LaTanisha randomly selects a tile without looking 2,000 times. Each time a tile is selected, it is replaced before the next selection. Predict the number of times LaTanisha selects a blue or red tile.

© Houghton Mifflin Harcourt Publishing Company • Image Credit: ©Undorik/Shutterstock

10. Ezra is resetting the code on his safe. The code is a 3-digit number made up of the digits 0 through 5. The digits can be repeated. Ezra will randomly draw numbers from a hat to select a code, replacing the number after each draw. Is it likely that Ezra will randomly select the safe code 123 more than 10 times out of 4,320 random codes drawn from the hat? Solve using multiplication. Explain your reasoning.

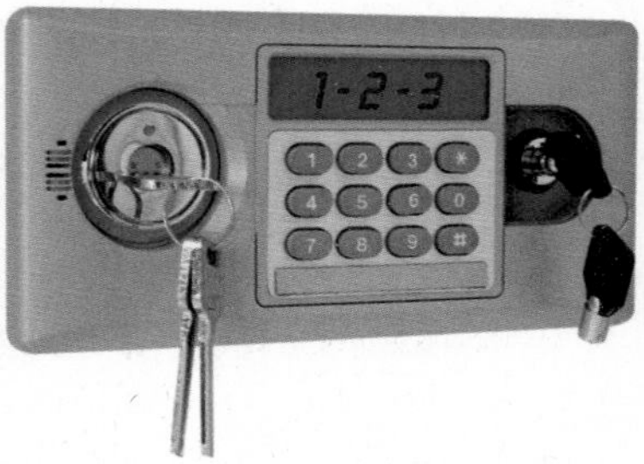

MP **Model with Mathematics** **Elliot rolls two number cubes 900 times. Their sides are labeled 1–6. Use this information for Problems 11–14.**

11. Write and solve a proportion to predict the number of times Elliot can expect to roll a sum of 11.

12. Write and solve a proportion to predict the number of times Elliot can expect to roll two odd numbers.

13. Write and evaluate an expression to predict the number of times Elliot can expect to roll one even number and one odd number.

14. Write and evaluate an expression to predict the number of times Elliot can expect to roll the same number on both cubes.

15. MP **Construct Arguments** The security desk for an office building has visitor's badges with codes consisting of one letter (A–Z) and 1 digit (0 through 9). A visitor can select a badge at random, and badges are returned at the end of each day. Is it likely that the badge L7 is the first badge selected more than 5 times in 365 days? Explain your reasoning. (*Hint*: Imagine making a a rectangular array. There would be 26 × 10 different badge codes.)

© Houghton Mifflin Harcourt Publishing Company • **Image Credit:** ©nartt/Shutterstock

Name ___________________________________

ONLINE
Video Tutorials and Interactive Examples

Use Theoretical Probability and Proportional Reasoning to Make Predictions

1. Oliver selects a glove from his drawer. The glove is blue. There are 3 red gloves, 6 black gloves, and 11 blue gloves left in the drawer. He selects a second glove from the drawer without looking. Is it more likely than not that Oliver selects a glove of the same color? Explain your reasoning.

____

____

2. If you roll a number cube 20 times, about how many times do you expect to roll a number greater than 4?

____

(MP) **Use Structure** **Victoria spins the two spinners shown 500 times. Use this information for Problems 3–5.**

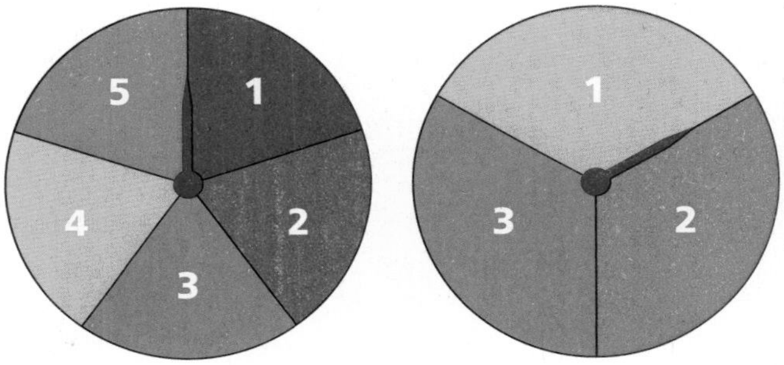

3. Solve a proportion to predict the number of times the sum is 4.

____

4. Solve a proportion to predict the number of times the sum is 4, 5, or 6.

____

5. Use a percent equation to predict the number of times the sum is less than or equal to 3.

____

(MP) **Model with Mathematics** **There are 5 red, 18 green, and 17 blue pens in a bag. Leah selects a pen 800 times without looking. After each selection, she replaces the pen in the bag. Use this information for Problems 6–7.**

6. Write and evaluate an expression to predict the number of times that Leah selects a pen that is red or green.

____

7. Write and evaluate an expression to predict the number of times that Leah selects a pen that is not red.

____

© Houghton Mifflin Harcourt Publishing Company

Test Prep

8. Leo has 10 red cards, 20 black cards, 20 yellow cards, and 25 white cards in a bag. He randomly selects a card 300 times. He replaces the card after each selection. Predict how often Leo will select a white card.

Ⓐ about 12 times

Ⓑ about 75 times

Ⓒ about 100 times

Ⓓ about 150 times

9. Scarlet rolls a number cube labeled 1–6 and spins the spinner shown 2,100 times. Match the prediction to the correct event.

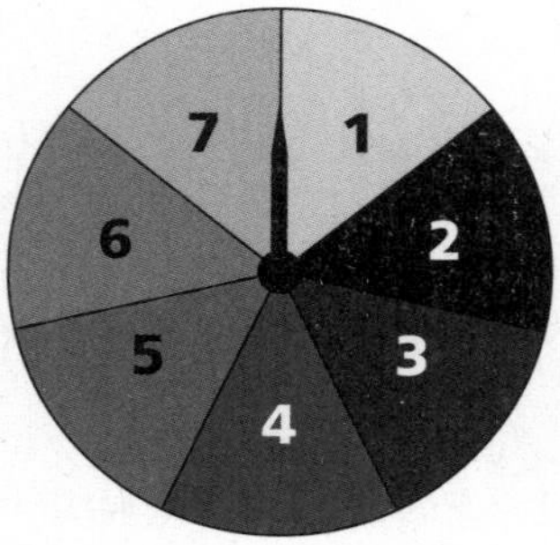

sum of 5 •	• about 300 times
sum less than 7 •	• about 50 times
sum of 13 •	• about 200 times
sum greater than 10 •	• about 550 times
sum of 8 or 9 •	• about 750 times

10. All 3,000 lockers at a school are randomly assigned 3-digit combination codes. The codes are made up of the digits 0 through 9. The digits can be repeated. Describe the likelihood that fewer than 5 of the lockers will have the code 000. Explain.

Spiral Review

11. Levi rolled a number cube. The number cube landed on 1 four times, 2 two times, 3 one time, 4 two times, 5 three times, and 6 six times. Which experimental probability is the same as the theoretical probability?

12. Brent rolls two number cubes labeled 1–6. What is the probability that Brent rolls a sum of 5?

© Houghton Mifflin Harcourt Publishing Company

Name ______________________________

Conduct Simulations

I Can use a simulation to test the probability of simple and compound events.

20% of the plates are winners!
WINNER

Step It Out

1 What is the experimental probability that you first find a winner on the second plate you check at the fundraiser dinner shown?

A. *P*(winning sticker) = ☐ % = $\frac{\square}{10}$

B. Carlos uses whole numbers from 1 to 10 to design a simulation. He generates one number at random to simulate checking one plate.

Winning: 1, 2

Non-winning: 3, 4, 5, 6, 7, 8, 9, 10

The table shows the results from Carlos's experiment: generating numbers for each trial until a winning number (1 or 2) appears. Complete the table.

Trial	Numbers generated	Plates checked
1	5, 8, 1	3
2	1	1
3	4, 8, 9, 2	4
4	5, 1	2
5	7, 8, 2	
6	8, 9, 10, 6, 2	
7	2	
8	3, 5, 7, 1	
9	9, 8, 2	
10	8, 6, 3, 4, 9, 2	

C. For Trial 1, a winning number appeared after ________ plate(s).

For Trial 2, a winning number appeared after ________ plate(s).

How many of the 10 trials showed a winner on the second plate?

____

D. The experimental probability of first finding a winner on the second plate is

$\frac{\square}{\square}$, or ________ %.

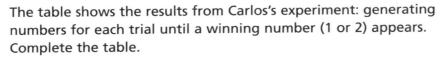

© Houghton Mifflin Harcourt Publishing Company • Image Credit: ©standby/iStock/Getty Images Plus/Getty Images

2 The chance that Amir will make a free throw at any given time is shown. Find the experimental probability that Amir will make at least 3 of the next 5 free throws he attempts.

A. Design a simulation to model this compound event. Use whole numbers from 1 to 5. Amir makes free throws _________ % of the time. Let 1, 2, and 3 represent a successful free throw, and let _________ and _________ represent a missed free throw.

B. Amir conducted 8 trials generating five random numbers from 1 to 5. Complete the table.

Trial	Numbers Generated	Successful Free Throws
1	3, 1, 4, 4, 5	2
2	5, 2, 1, 3, 2	4
3	2, 5, 4, 2, 4	
4	4, 3, 5, 4, 5	
5	2, 1, 3, 3, 4	
6	3, 4, 2, 3, 2	
7	1, 1, 5, 4, 5	
8	4, 5, 1, 2, 1	

C. Find the experimental probability that Amir makes at least 3 of the next 5 free throws he attempts.

$\frac{\square}{8} = \square\%$

Turn and Talk Design another simulation to find the probability that Amir makes at least 3 of his next 5 free throws. Explain your reasoning.

Check Understanding

There is a 70% chance that Reagan will catch an early bus home from work. A computer generated 8 sets of random numbers from 1 to 10. The numbers 1–7 represent a success and 8–10 represent a missed bus. The table shows the results. Use it for Problems 1 and 2.

Trial	Numbers Generated
1	1, 9, 1, 2, 10, 6, 5, 2, 7, 2
2	8, 10, 4, 10, 2, 2, 3, 6, 7, 10
3	6, 9, 9, 10, 4, 10, 10, 2, 6, 6
4	8, 8, 2, 3, 4, 6, 5, 6, 5, 3
5	1, 10, 1, 2, 5, 6, 9, 4, 10, 3
6	7, 1, 9, 1, 6, 3, 3, 7, 5, 6
7	2, 5, 2, 7, 5, 5, 10, 5, 6, 3
8	9, 6, 10, 4, 9, 6, 8, 9, 9, 9

1. Find the experimental probability that Reagan will miss the early bus twice but catch it the third time.

____

2. Find the experimental probability that Reagan will catch the early bus at least 7 of the next 10 times.

____

© Houghton Mifflin Harcourt Publishing Company • Image Credit: ©Monkey Business Images/Shutterstock

Name

On Your Own

Use the table and the information given for Problems 3 and 4.

Geography Over a 100-year period, the probability that a hurricane struck Reyna's city in any given year was 20%. Reyna performed a simulation to find the experimental probability that a hurricane would strike the city in at least 4 of the next 10 years. In Reyna's simulation, 1 represents a year with a hurricane.

Trial	Numbers Generated
1	2, 5, 3, 2, 5, 5, 1, 4, 5, 2
2	1, 1, 5, 2, 2, 1, 3, 1, 1, 5
3	4, 5, 4, 5, 5, 4, 3, 5, 1, 1
4	1, 5, 5, 5, 1, 2, 2, 3, 5, 3
5	5, 1, 5, 3, 5, 3, 4, 5, 3, 2
6	1, 1, 5, 5, 1, 4, 2, 2, 3, 4
7	2, 1, 5, 3, 1, 5, 1, 2, 1, 4
8	2, 4, 3, 2, 4, 4, 2, 1, 3, 1
9	3, 2, 1, 4, 5, 3, 5, 5, 1, 2
10	3, 4, 2, 4, 3, 5, 2, 3, 5, 1

3. According to Reyna's simulation, what was the experimental probability that a hurricane would strike the city in at least 4 of the next 10 years?

4. According to the simulation, what was the experimental probability that a hurricane strikes the city for the first time on the eighth year? Explain.

5. **Open Ended** Keith wants to use the spinner shown to simulate an event with a 75% chance of occurring. Describe a situation Keith could be simulating. Then describe how the spinner can be used.

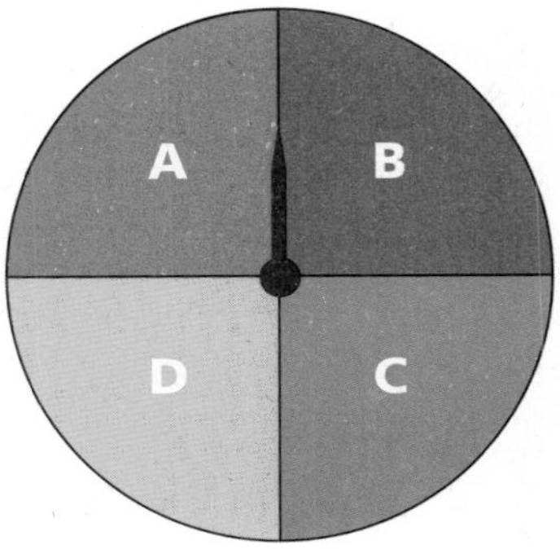

© Houghton Mifflin Harcourt Publishing Company • Image Credit: ©Warren Faidley/Corbis/Getty Images

6. (MP) **Use Tools** Dave wants to generate random numbers to simulate an event with a 25% chance of occurring. Describe a model he could use.

7. (MP) **Reason** Is it possible to perform a simulation several times and get different experimental probabilities for the same event? Explain.

8. **STEM** A quality control technician wants to determine how much variation can be expected in a random sample of light bulbs produced at a plant. The known rate of defective light bulbs is 5%. Describe a simulation the technician could use to find the experimental probability that a sample of 100 bulbs will include at least 5 defective bulbs.

9. (MP) **Use Tools** Allie is a softball player. She has a batting average of 0.600. This means that Allie gets a hit 60% of the time.

   A. Design a simulation using slips of paper and a box to find the experimental probability of Allie getting a hit at least 2 out of 5 times.

   B. Perform the simulation and use your results to predict the probability of Allie getting a hit at least 2 out of 5 times.

© Houghton Mifflin Harcourt Publishing Company

Name ______________________________

LESSON 20.4
More Practice/ Homework

ONLINE
Video Tutorials and Interactive Examples

Conduct Simulations

1. There is a card under 30% of the chairs at a booster meeting. Finn wants to find the probability that the first card he finds will be under the third chair that he checks. He generates 10 sets of random numbers from 1 to 10. The numbers 1–3 represent a chair with a card and 4–10 represent a chair without a card. Complete the table and find the experimental probability of the event.

Trial	1	2	3	4	5	6	7	8	9	10
Numbers Generated	6, 5, 1	8, 1	10, 1	7, 8, 4, 1	9, 3	5, 4, 2	3	9, 5, 8, 2	7, 3	9, 6, 8, 4, 7, 3
Chairs Checked										

____

2. Math on the Spot There is a 20% chance that a particular volcano will erupt during any given decade. A random number generator generated 10 sets of random numbers from 1 to 5 as shown. The number 1 represents the volcano erupting. Find the experimental probability that the volcano will erupt in 1 or 2 of the next 5 decades.

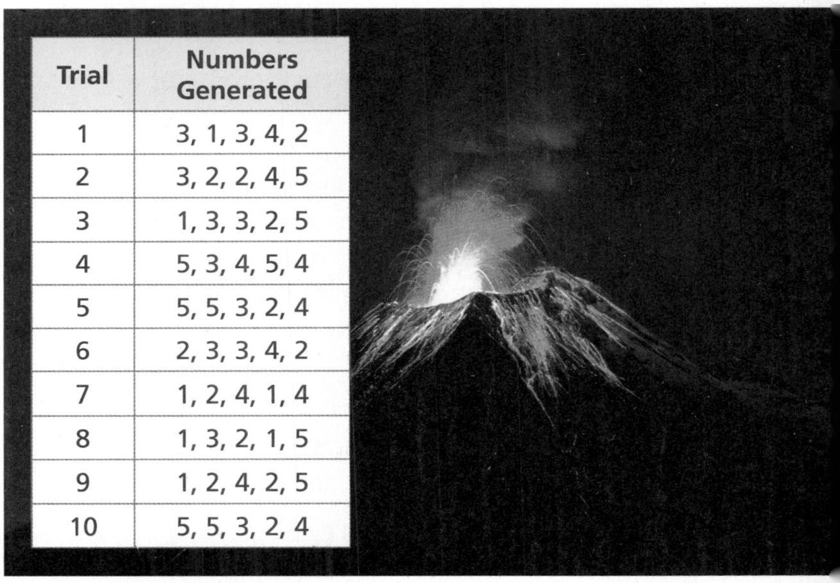

Trial	Numbers Generated
1	3, 1, 3, 4, 2
2	3, 2, 2, 4, 5
3	1, 3, 3, 2, 5
4	5, 3, 4, 5, 4
5	5, 5, 3, 2, 4
6	2, 3, 3, 4, 2
7	1, 2, 4, 1, 4
8	1, 3, 2, 1, 5
9	1, 2, 4, 2, 5
10	5, 5, 3, 2, 4

____

3. Sia makes 10% of the shots she attempts in soccer at any given time. A random number generator was used to generate 5 sets of random numbers from 1 to 10 as shown, where number 1 represents a successful shot and numbers 2–10 represent a missed shot. Find the experimental probability that Sia will make at least 2 of the next 10 shots.

Trial	Numbers Generated
1	5, 4, 8, 4, 8, 6, 7, 1, 7, 4
2	6, 9, 4, 6, 6, 4, 6, 8, 8, 6
3	10, 1, 8, 2, 3, 2, 9, 3, 5, 7
4	3, 6, 10, 5, 5, 4, 10, 6, 1, 5
5	8, 1, 9, 9, 3, 7, 4, 5, 1, 10

____

© Houghton Mifflin Harcourt Publishing Company • Image Credit: ©pxhidalgo/iStock/Getty Images Plus/Getty Images

Test Prep

4. There is a 25% chance that Jahil will hit an archery target on any given attempt. Which model can be used to find the experimental probability that Jahil will hit the target on at least 3 of the next 4 attempts?

Ⓐ Use a computer to generate whole numbers from 1 to 8 where numbers 1–2 represent hitting the target and numbers 3–8 represent not hitting the target.

Ⓑ Use a calculator to generate whole numbers from 1 to 8 where numbers 1–6 represent hitting the target and numbers 7–8 represent not hitting the target.

Ⓒ Use a computer to generate whole numbers from 1 to 4 where numbers 1–2 represent hitting the target and numbers 3–4 represent not hitting the target.

Ⓓ Use a calculator to generate whole numbers from 1 to 4 where numbers 1–3 represent hitting the target and number 4 represents not hitting the target.

5. At a gym, 50% of the customers get a free training session. Let the number 1 represent a customer receiving a free training session and the number 2 represent not receiving a free training session. A calculator generated random numbers, 1 and 2, until a number that represents a customer receiving a free training session appeared. The results are shown in the table. Find the experimental probability that you must ask exactly 2 customers before you find a customer that received a free training session.

Trial	Numbers Generated
1	1
2	2, 2, 1
3	2, 1
4	1
5	2, 2, 1

________ %

6. Out of 12 trials, a simulation showed Ming getting a place in a summer art program 10 times. What is the experimental probability of the event, according to the simulation?

____

Spiral Review

7. Vera is going to flip a coin 50 times. Write and evaluate an expression to predict the number of times the coin lands on heads.

____

8. Juan spins two spinners each with 4 equal sections labeled 1–4 and adds the results. What is the probability that Juan spins a sum greater than 3?

____

© Houghton Mifflin Harcourt Publishing Company

Module 20

Name

Review

Vocabulary

1. How is theoretical probability different from experimental probability?

2. What is a *simulation* in probability? Write a definition in your own words.

Concepts and Skills

3. A box contains 4 red pencils, 6 yellow pencils, and 5 blue pencils. What is the probability of randomly selecting a yellow pencil from the box?

4. Select the situation with a $\frac{1}{3}$ probability of randomly selecting a blue marble from a bag.

   (A) A bag containing 1 white, 4 red, 3 blue, 2 green, and 4 black marbles

   (B) A bag containing 2 white, 6 red, 8 blue, 5 green, and 5 black marbles

   (C) A bag containing 3 white, 2 red, 5 blue, 3 green, and 2 black marbles

   (D) A bag containing 3 white, 3 red, 3 blue, 3 green, and 3 black marbles

5. (MP) **Use Tools** A stack of cards contains 25 red cards, 25 blue cards, 25 green cards, and 25 yellow cards. A card is drawn from the stack at random and then replaced 300 times. The results are shown. Which experimental probability from this experiment is closest to the expected theoretical probability based on the sample space? State what strategy and tool you will use to answer the question, explain your choice, and then find the answer.

Experimental Results

Outcome	Frequency
Red	74
Blue	68
Green	78
Yellow	80

© Houghton Mifflin Harcourt Publishing Company

6. Ginny rolls two number cubes numbered 1 to 6. Complete the table by determining the theroretical probability of each event.

Event	Probability
Rolling double 3s	
Rolling a sum of 7	
Rolling two even numbers	

7. Harry spins the spinner shown 60 times. How many times can he be expected to get a number less than 3?

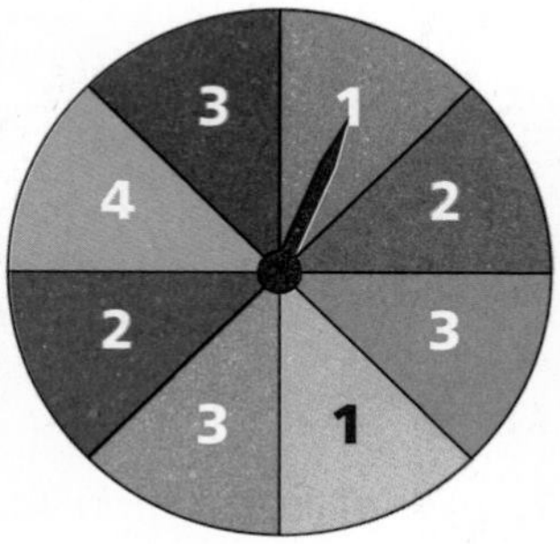

_________ times

8. A restaurant serves buttermilk, gingerbread, and pecan pancakes with strawberry, banana, or blueberry topping. Each week, the manager randomly selects one pancake type and one topping to be the breakfast special. There is an equal chance that each type and topping is picked. For about how many of the 52 weeks in a year can the restaurant be expected to have banana pecan pancakes as the breakfast special?

Ⓐ 6 weeks Ⓑ 9 weeks Ⓒ 12 weeks Ⓓ 17 weeks

9. Sula designs greeting cards for her friends. Each friend has a 30% chance to get a musical greeting card. Design a simulation that can be used to estimate the probability that a friend who receives 2 greeting cards will receive at least one musical greeting card.

____

____

____

____

____

10. A kitten has an equal chance of being male or female. In a litter of 3 kittens, the outcomes {MMM, MMF, MFM, MFF, FMM, FMF, FFM, FFF} are theoretically equally likely. Jaime used random numbers to simulate 400 litters of 3 kittens each. The table shows the result of the simulation. For which type of litter of 3 kittens is the frequency from the simulation less than the expected theoretical frequency?

Simulation Results	
Outcome	**Frequency**
3 males	63
2 males, 1 female	151
1 male, 2 females	130
3 females	56

Ⓐ 3 male kittens

Ⓑ 3 female kittens

Ⓒ exactly 2 male kittens

Ⓓ exactly 2 female kittens

© Houghton Mifflin Harcourt Publishing Company

UNIT 1

MODULE 1, LESSON 1

On Your Own

5. They stay the same measure.
7. 2 inches **9.** yes **11.** 1 pair of parallel lines
13.

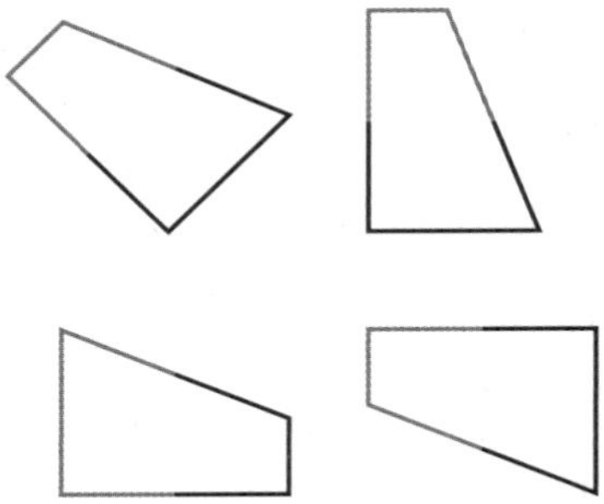

More Practice/Homework

1. on the bottom **3A.** yes; flip
B. no
5.

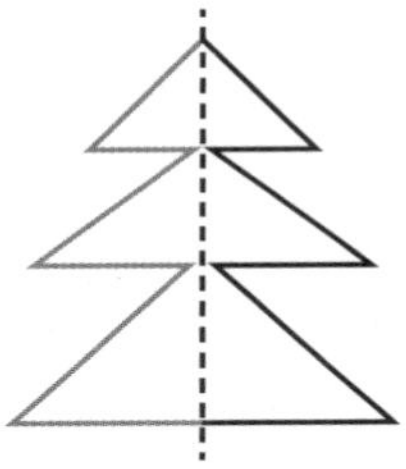

7. rhombus **9.** the same size
11. $32.10

MODULE 1, LESSON 2

On Your Own

5. Building *D* **7.** 60° **9.** Opposite sides are parallel and the same length. **11.** $(x, y) \rightarrow (x + 7, y + 1)$

More Practice/Homework

3. Figure *E* is not the same size or shape as Figure *C*.
5.

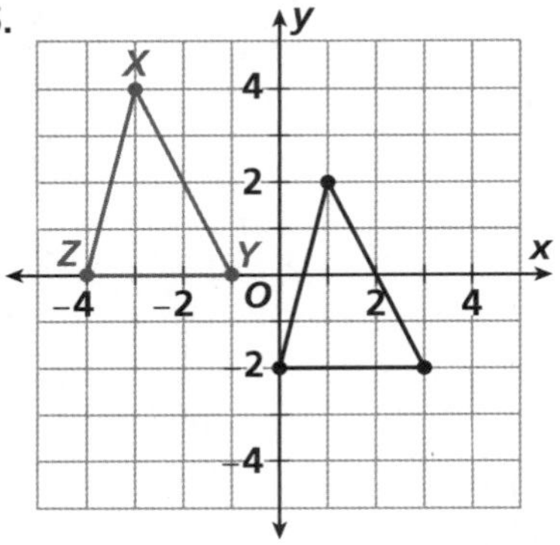

7. (−3, 3); (−1, 5); (1, 4)
9. 1 and 3 **11.** positive

MODULE 1, LESSON 3

On Your Own

5. 115°
7.

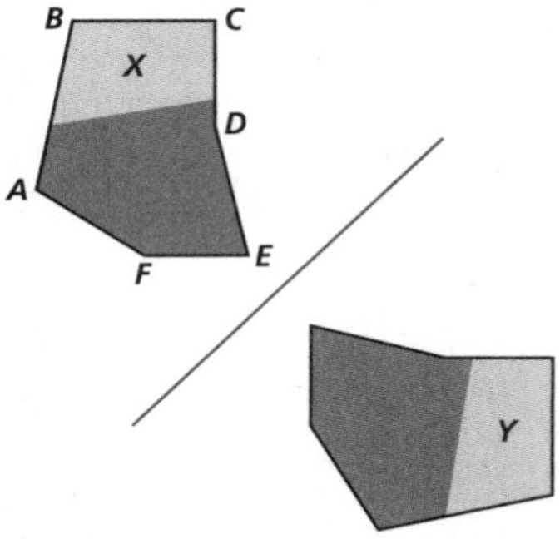

9A. yes **B.** yes **C.** yes **11A.** no; no
B. yes **C.** yes

More Practice/Homework

1. yes **3.** no **5.** A, C **7.** D
9. $6\frac{7}{8}$ cups

MODULE 1, LESSON 4

On Your Own

3. The size and shape of the letter stayed the same. The V now opens down instead of up.
5A.

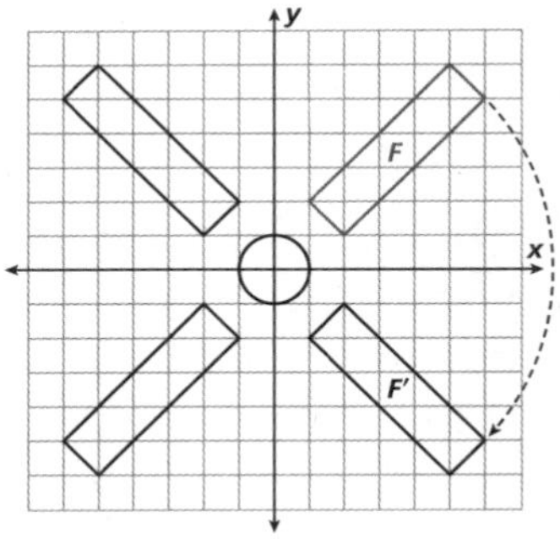

B. 90° clockwise about the origin **C.** $(x, y) \rightarrow (y, -x)$
7. $(x, y) \rightarrow (-y, x)$ **9A.** 90° clockwise **B.** (2, −1), (5, −2), and (3, −6)

More Practice/Homework

1. Figure *B*
3. (3, −4), (1, 0), (4, 0)

5.

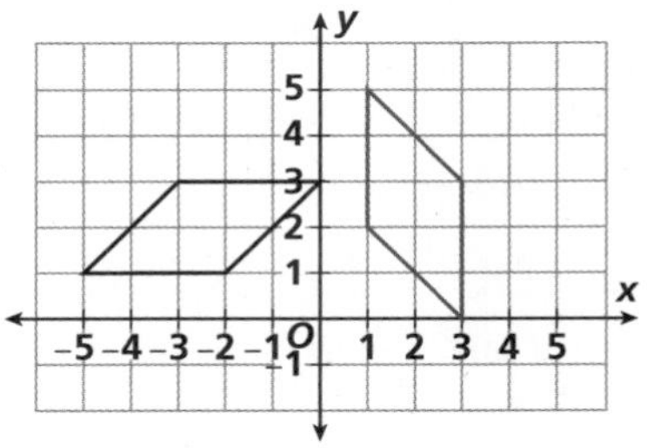

7. (1, 1), (5, 2), (6, 4), (4, 7), and (2, 3) **9.** Figure 4

MODULE 1, LESSON 5

On Your Own

3. no **5.** Figure *C* **9.** Possible answer: I can use a ruler to measure and compare the side lengths. I can use a protractor to measure and compare the angles. **11.** Figures 2, 4, and 5 are congruent; Figures 3 and 6 are not congruent. **13.** Figure 1
15. Figure *B*

More Practice/Homework

1. Trace Fig. 3 and place it over my figure to show that they match exactly in size and shape. **3.** no **5.** a translation 3 units down **7.** yes **9.** C
11. (4, −7), (4, −3), (9, −3)
13. 31% decrease

MODULE 2, LESSON 1

On Your Own

3. The quadrilateral is a parallelogram. **5.** The quadrilateral is a trapezoid that is not a parallelogram.

More Practice/Homework

3. Possible answer shown (reduced):

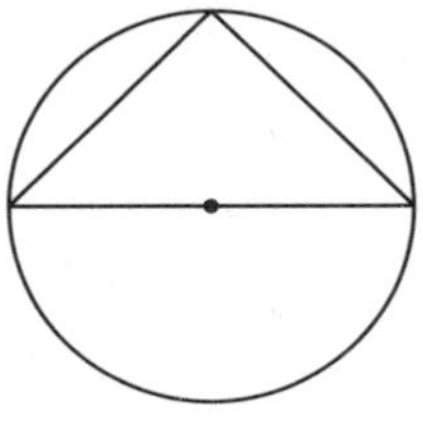

© Houghton Mifflin Harcourt Publishing Company

5A. The quadrilateral is a square. **B.** 1.5 units **7.** Possible answer: a rotation followed by a translation

MODULE 2, LESSON 2

On Your Own

3. $12 + 12 < 26$, so the pieces will not make a triangle.
5. $5 + 5 = 10$, so these pieces will not make a triangle. **7.** an infinite number of quadrilaterals **9.** no **15.** $4 + 5 < 10$, so these logs will not make a triangle.
17. no **19.** yes

More Practice/Homework

1. $6 + 8 > 13$, so these pieces will make a triangle. **3.** One possible side length is 5 ft; $3 + 3 = 6$, so the length of the third side must be less than 6 ft. **5.** no **7.** yes **11.** A **13.** B, C, E **15.** rectangle

MODULE 2, LESSON 3

On Your Own

3A.

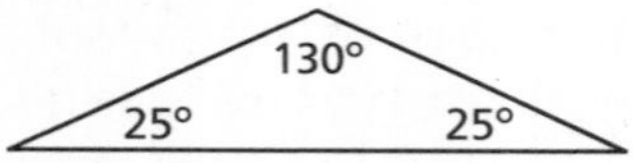

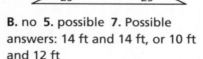

B. no **5.** possible **7.** Possible answers: 14 ft and 14 ft, or 10 ft and 12 ft

More Practice/Homework

1. yes **3.** possible **5.** not possible **7.** They may or may not be the same. **9.** B, C, E **11.** (−5, −3), (2, 5), (0, 6)

MODULE 2, LESSON 4

On Your Own

3. a diameter of the circle

5.

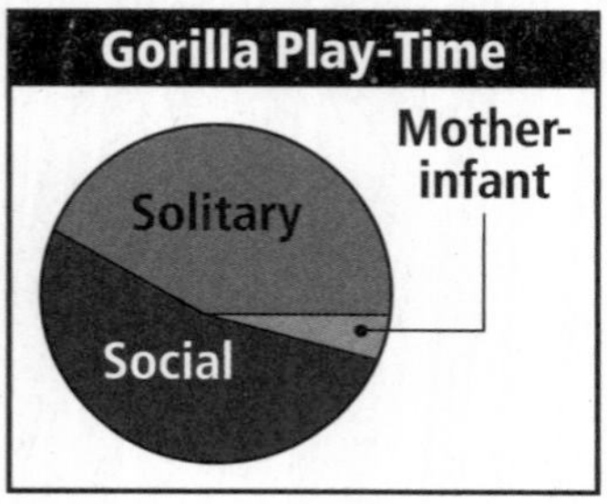

7.

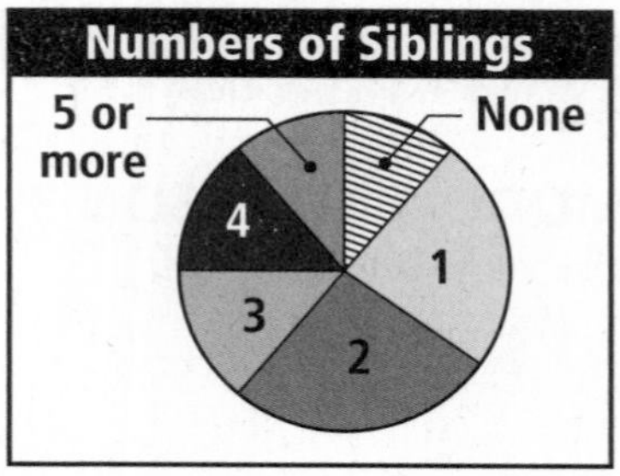

More Practice/Homework

3B. two triangles **5.** one; none; many; one; one; none **7.** B
9. none

MODULE 2, LESSON 5

On Your Own

3B. $\frac{5\text{ ft}}{1\text{ in.}}$ **C.** $y = 5x$ **D.** 17.5 ft
E. 8 in. **5A.** 7.5 feet per unit
B. $y = 7.5x$; about 47 ft

More Practice/Homework

1A. $y = 22.5x$ **B.** length:18 m; width: 9 m **3.** 14.7 in. **5.** 10; 18

7.

Hours	Parts
2	40
3	60
5	100
8	160

MODULE 3, LESSON 1

On Your Own

3. Left to right: reduction; enlargement; reduction **5.** no

7.

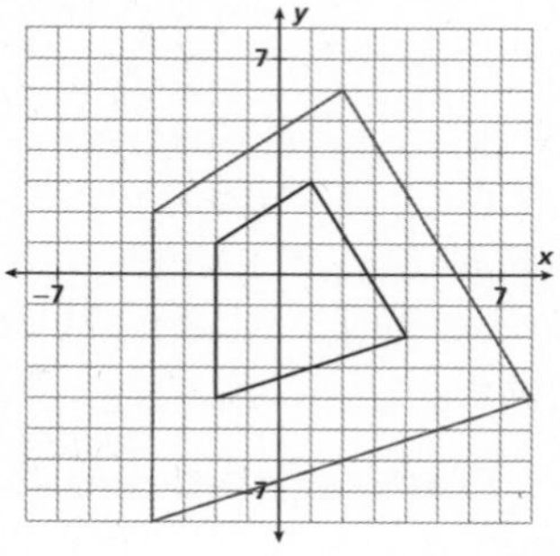

More Practice/Homework

3. no **5.** B **7.** reflection

MODULE 3, LESSON 2

On Your Own

3A. greater than 1 **B.** no **C.** no
5A. 3 **B.** $L'(21, 27)$; $M'(6, 15)$
C. $(x, y) \rightarrow (3x, 3y)$ **7A.** $\frac{2}{3}$

7B.

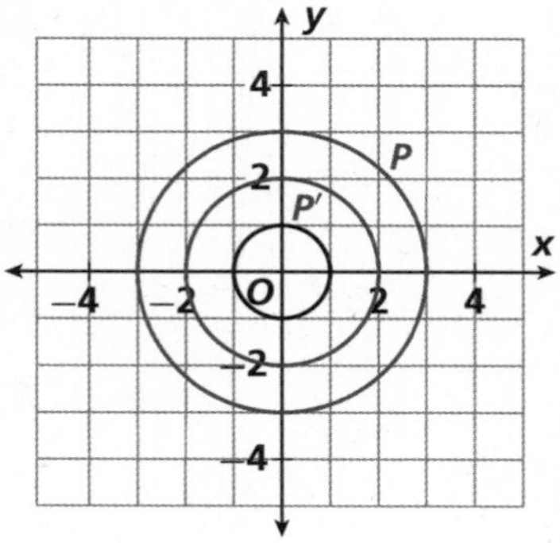

More Practice/Homework

1. Figure *B* is the correct shape. **3.** (7, −1)

5.

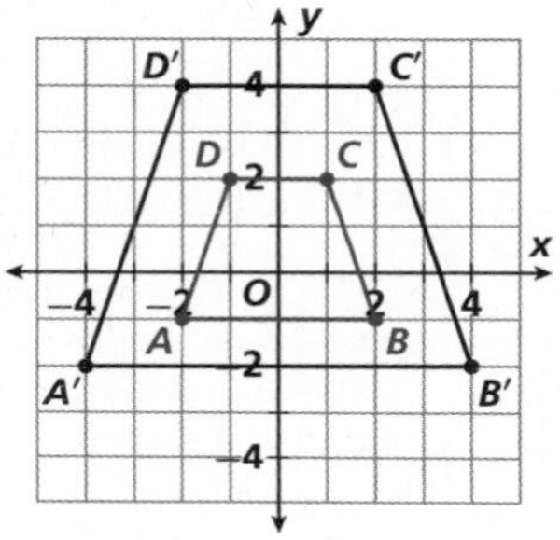

7. 30°, 60°, and 90°
9. rotation of 180° about the origin

MODULE 3, LESSON 3

On Your Own

3A, B.

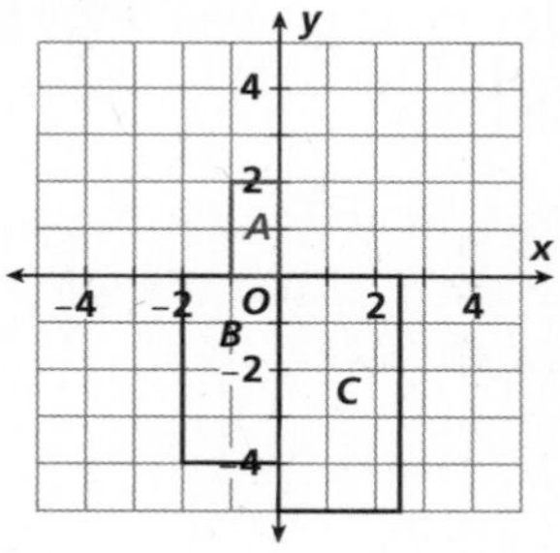

C. The flower beds are all similar.
5. Triangle *P* and Triangle *J*
7. Possible answer: dilation with scale factor 2 and center of dilation (0, 0), followed by a translation 1 unit left and 1 unit down **9.** Possible answer:

© Houghton Mifflin Harcourt Publishing Company

dilation with scale factor 4 and center of dilation (0, 0), followed by a reflection across the x-axis **11.** $(x, y) \rightarrow (243x, 243y)$

More Practice/Homework

1A, B.

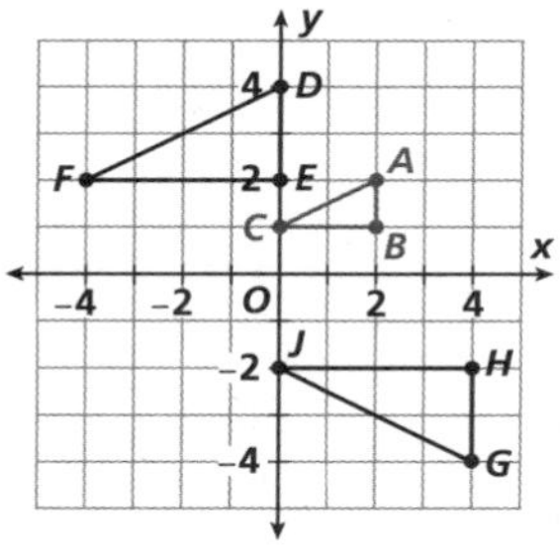

C. agree **3A.** Possible answer: dilation centered at (0, 0) with scale factor 2, translation $(x, y) \rightarrow (x + 6, y + 2)$; not congruent; similar **B.** Possible answer: reflection across the y-axis, dilation centered at (0, 0) with scale factor $\frac{1}{2}$, translation $(x, y) \rightarrow (x - 4, y + 4)$; not congruent; similar **5.** B, C, D

7.

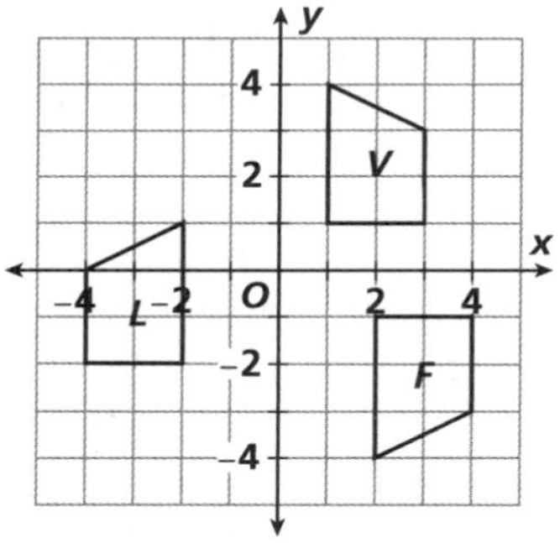

9. $A'(-5, -2.5)$, $B'(2.5, 5)$, $C'(5, -10)$

UNIT 2

MODULE 4, LESSON 1

On Your Own

3. Possible answer: $2x + 48 = 120$ **5.** Possible answer: $2(x + 2\frac{1}{2}) = 6\frac{1}{3}$ **7.** Possible answer: $0.70(x + 35) = \$44.80$

More Practice/Homework

1. Possible answer: $2x + 40.6 = 72.2$ **3.** $0.85x + 2.95 = 8.05$ **5.** Possible answer: $0.20(x + 25) = 13$ **7.** Possible answer: $19.50(x + 3) = 146.25$ **9.** $0.10x + 2 = 2.8$ **11.** A **13.** \$26.39

MODULE 4, LESSON 2

On Your Own

3A. Possible answer: $\frac{637.50 - 200}{17.50} = 25$ h **B.** $17.50x + 200 = 637.50$; 25 h **5.** $6(x + 5) = 72$; 12 in. **7.** $h = -12$ **9.** $y = -\frac{7}{15}$

More Practice/Homework

1. $0.50b + 4.50 = 22$; 35 bulbs **3.** $2\left(x + 1\frac{1}{2}\right) = 4\frac{1}{2}$; $\frac{3}{4}$ c nuts **5.** $m = 50$; $3 = 0.2(50) - 7$ (true) **7.** $t = -6$; $-3(-6 + 6) = 0$ (true) **11.** B **13.** $16.50(h + 4) = 123.75$; 3.5 h **15.** 5 apples for \$2.50

MODULE 4, LESSON 3

On Your Own

3. Glenna 45, Val 80, Kim 55 **5A.** $x + \left(\frac{1}{2}x + 4\right) = 10$ **B.** $x = 4$ **C.** 4 home runs **D.** 6 home runs **E.** Possible answer: Add the answers in Parts C and D. **9.** $p = 1$ **11.** $t = 0.4$ **13.** $n = -\frac{11}{7}$ **15.** $b = -4$

More Practice/Homework

1. 39 feet, 9 feet **5.** $a = 3$ **7.** $x = 30$ **9.** $x = 7.5$, $\frac{15}{2}$, and $7\frac{1}{2}$ **11.** C **13.** 3 hours **15.** \$39,500 **17.** 45°, 55°, and 80°

MODULE 4, LESSON 4

On Your Own

3. yes; one solution **5.** Alex is not correct. **7.** infinitely many solutions

More Practice/Homework

1. no **3.** Blake is not correct. **7.** 1 **9.** 3 **11.** one solution; $x = 4.2$ **13.** C **15.** $10.5x$ **17.** C **19.** 1 unit right and 2 units up

MODULE 4, LESSON 5

On Your Own

3A. $t = 30$ **B.** They are at the same height after 30 seconds. **C.** 45 feet **5.** $\ell + (\ell + 3) = 49$; Josh is 26 years old and Lynette is 23. **9.** $(2x + 11)°$ **11.** Ethan is incorrect. **13.** \$2,480 **15.** $x = 16$; 37° and 53° **17A.** $3x + 7 + 5x + 3 = 90$ **B.** $x = 10$ **C.** 53°

More Practice/Homework

1. any number of games of bowling **3.** 4.8 months **5A.** $2x + 45 + 3x + 55 = 135$; $x = 7$ **B.** 59° **7.** D **9.** $m = -3$

MODULE 5, LESSON 1

On Your Own

5. $4x \leq 24$; $x \leq 6$ ft

7. $x \geq 3$

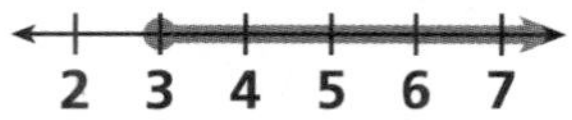

9. $x > -10$

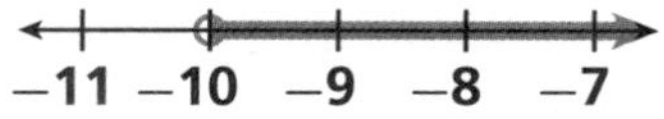

11. $4x \leq 24$; $x \leq 6$ **13.** no

15. $x > 11.2$

17. $x < -3\frac{3}{5}$

More Practice/Homework

1A. $12x > 72$; $x > 6$ ft **B.** $12x \leq 156$; $x \leq 13$ ft **C.** longer than 6 ft and no longer than 13 ft **3.** $-3t > -24$; $t < 8$ min **5.** B. **7.** at least 8 **9.** $x = 65°$

MODULE 5, LESSON 2

On Your Own

3. $23d + 20 \geq 140$ **5.** not a solution **7.** $22 - 0.25w < 18$ **9.** $\frac{1}{4}x - 3 < 6$

© Houghton Mifflin Harcourt Publishing Company

More Practice/Homework

1. $5t + 40 \geq 500$ **3.** Possible answer: $7x + 5 > 50$
5. 10 less than 2 times a number is greater than 22. **7.** $75b + 800 \leq 1{,}200$ **11.** $d - 31 \geq 15$; $d \geq 46$

MODULE 5, LESSON 3

On Your Own

3A. $2{,}100 - 25d < 1{,}500$; $d > 24$
B.

C. no, only whole numbers; The number of tables will be less than 1,500 after more than 24 days.
5. $x > 13$

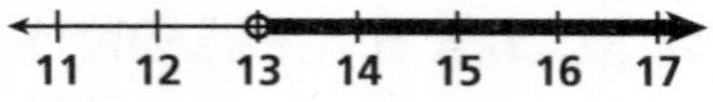

7. $d \geq -3$

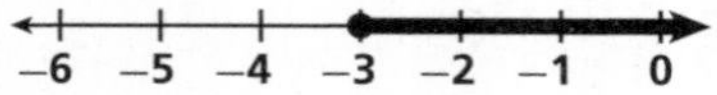

9A. $25 - 2p < 4$; $p > 10\frac{1}{2}$
B. at least 11 people
13. $m \leq -6$

15. $w < 16$

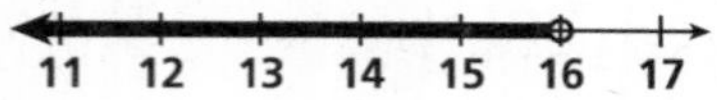

17. $b \geq -3$

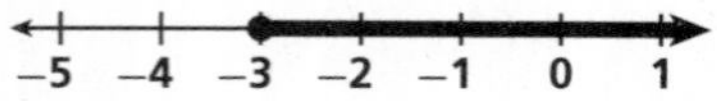

19. $y < 12$

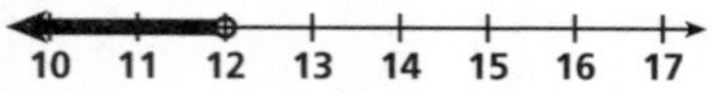

21. $g < -4$

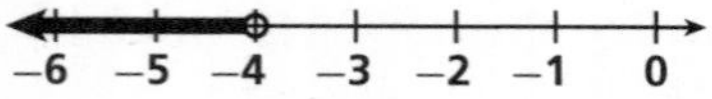

23. 9 games

More Practice/Homework

1. $x \leq 7$

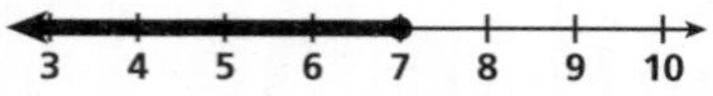

3. $r > \frac{1}{2}$

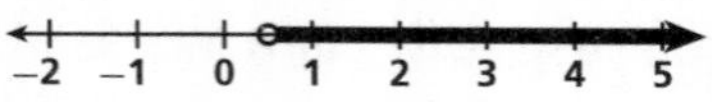

5. at least 50 tickets **7.** at least 7 pieces **9.** $36\frac{2}{3}$ mi **11.** $3f + 6 = 18$

UNIT 3

MODULE 6, LESSON 1

On Your Own

5. no **7.** 50°, 100° **9.** 125°
13. $x = 45$

More Practice/Homework

1. $x = 152.6$ **3.** no

7.

Triangle	Unknown angle
1	90°
2	115°

9. 60 **11.** equal **13.** one solution

MODULE 6, LESSON 2

On Your Own

5. yes **7.** no **9.** no **11.** no

More Practice/Homework

1A. yes **B.** yes **C.** 22 ft **3A.** 30
B. 60° **5.** Triangles *A*, *B*, and *C*
7. 8 oz **9.** Possible answer: a rotation and a reflection

MODULE 6, LESSON 3

On Your Own

3. 112° **5.** ∠*CBD* **7.** no
9. alternate exterior angles
11. none; ∠3 and ∠5; ∠1 and ∠5; ∠3 and ∠4; ∠2 and ∠4

More Practice/Homework

1. 125° **3.** 115° **7.** B **9.** (−3, −4)
11A. $3w + 4 = 22$ **B.** 6 ft

MODULE 7, LESSON 1

On Your Own

3. 2,250 ft **5.** yes **7.** $k = 48$
9. $k = -3$ **11.** 15 cm **13.** 18 cm
17. $n = -4$

More Practice/Homework

1. They are similar right triangles. **5A.** $\frac{5.5}{8.25} = \frac{x}{22.5}$
B. 15 feet tall; 14.25 feet away
7. A **9.** −3 **11.** Store A

MODULE 7, LESSON 2

On Your Own

3A. The slope is negative because the price is decreasing. **B.** $y = -5x$
5. Possible points shown.

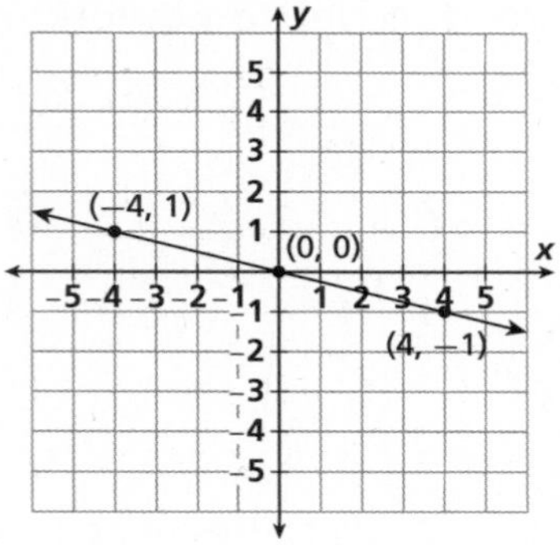

7. $y = \frac{1}{2}x$

More Practice/Homework

1A. \$80 **B.** $y = 20x$ **3.** $y = 5x$
5.

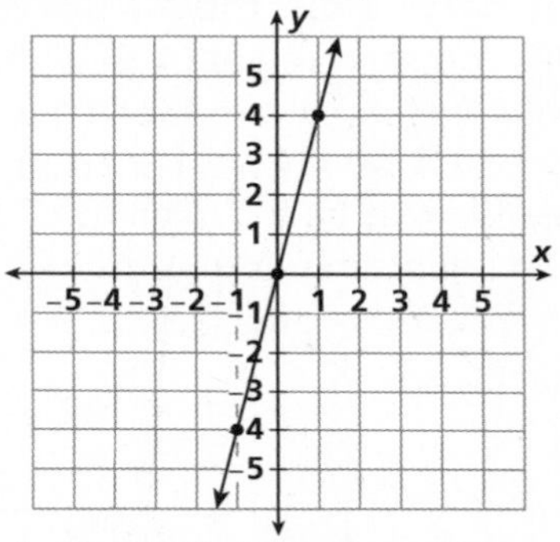

7. A **9.** 5,000 **11.** $A'(-1, 4)$, $B'(-5, 6)$, $C'(-3, 10)$ **13.** $x = 5$

MODULE 7, LESSON 3

On Your Own

3A.

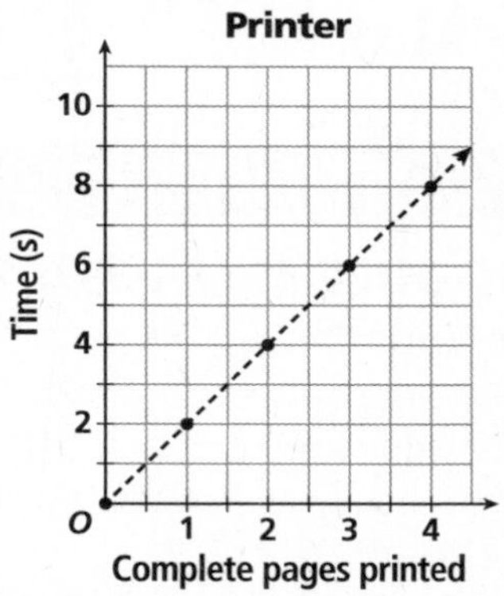

B. Possible answer: I drew a discrete graph because the number of complete pages printed is always a whole

© Houghton Mifflin Harcourt Publishing Company

number. **C.** Printing 3 complete pages takes 6 seconds. **5.** continuous graph **7A.** 75 gallons per hour; 200 gallons per hour **B.** rain barrel

More Practice/Homework

1A.

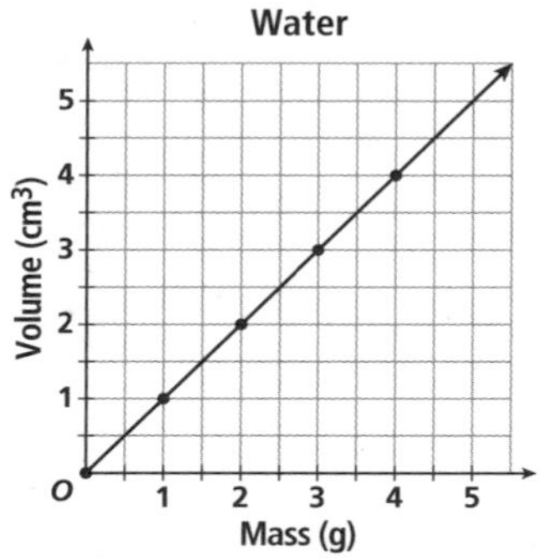

B. continuous **5.** continuous **7.** the field; 1.5 mm per year **9.** $x + 32 + 30 = 180$; $x = 118$

MODULE 8, LESSON 1

On Your Own

3A. \$4; \$7; \$10; \$13; \$16; \$19; \$22 **B.** numbers of minutes greater than or equal to 0 **5.** 1 to 41 **7.** no

More Practice/Homework

1. whole numbers from 0 to 20

3.

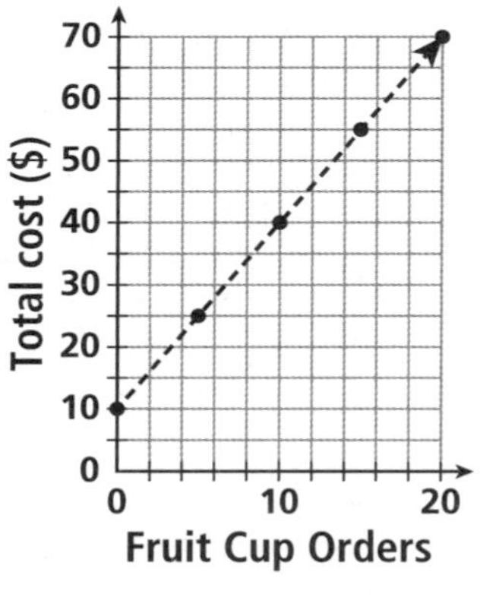

5. Possible answer: The section from $x = 0$ to $x = 1$ **7.** B, D **9.** 2 ft/s **11.** $x = 13$; 57° and 33°

MODULE 8, LESSON 2

On Your Own

3. 2 vertical yards per horizontal yard **5.** yes **9.** $y = -3x + 5$; negative slope; does not pass through the origin **11.** $y = -2x + 11$ **13B.** 3 units; slope **C.** no; 4 **D.** $y = 3x + 4$ **E.** yes; The lines have the same slope.

More Practice/Homework

1. Possible answer: $y = 3x + 2$; and $y = 3x - 2$ **3.** Substitute the coordinates of the given point and the slope into the equation $y = mx + b$. **5.** $y = 2x - 1$; y-intercept $= -1$ **7.** 3; rises **9.** linear **11.** -2; 3 **13.** yes **15.** A **17.** Distribute values on both sides of the equal sign. Then combine like terms. $y = -\frac{2}{5}$ **19.** 0 triangles

MODULE 8, LESSON 3

On Your Own

3. Option 1 **5.** positive **7A.** where the line crosses the y-axis **B.** \$10 **C.** 2 **D.** $y = 2x + 10$ **E.** \$60

More Practice/Homework

1. \$2 per muffin. **3.** Initial value represents the delivery fee. The rate of change represents the cost per muffin. **5.** \$115 **9.** B **11.** $x = -9$ **13.** 8

MODULE 8, LESSON 4

On Your Own

5. 13; how many gallons of gasoline Bridget had when she started mowing **7.** continuous **9.** $0 \le y \le 13$; She only has 13 gallons of gas, so she must use between 0 and 13 gallons. **11.** the cost of the charger; the price for each battery

More Practice/Homework

1. The slope is 3, which represents the amount of money charged to walk each dog. **3.** 87 dogs **5.** $y = 5x - 9$ **7.** 15 **9.** 4 **11.** D, E **13.** $x = 2$

MODULE 8, LESSON 5

On Your Own

3. increases rapidly at the beginning; is constant speed during the middle; gradually decreases near the end **11.** from 0 seconds to 6 seconds **13.** the ball staying at the same height as it rolls across the ledge **15.** It increases according to a nonlinear function.

More Practice/Homework

3. Bicycle A slows down at a constant rate. Bicycle B slows down rapidly at first, then gradually comes to a stop. **5.** Possible answer shown.

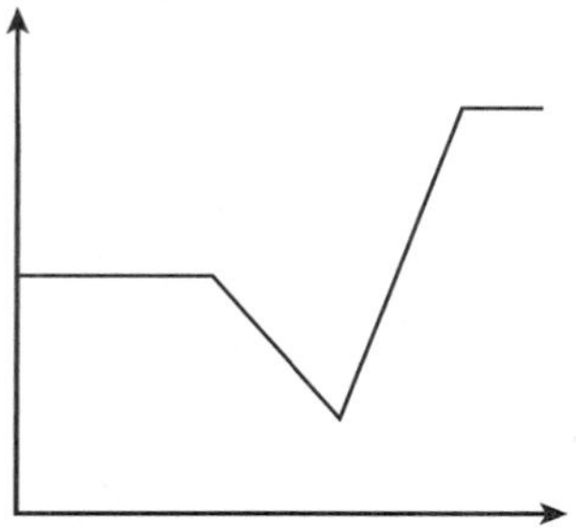

7. A, B, C, E **9.** Store A

MODULE 9, LESSON 1

On Your Own

3. Iceville's slope is 1, so it charges \$1 per hour for skating. Super Skate's slope is 0.5, so it charges \$0.50 per hour. **5.** If skating for more than 4 hours **7.** City B

More Practice/Homework

1. The slope for both services is 1.5. Both services charge \$1.50 per pound. **3.** Clean Machine **5.** D **7.** Shop X: intercept 3, fee 3;

© Houghton Mifflin Harcourt Publishing Company

Shop Y: intercept 0, fee 0 **9.** Both studios charge a monthly fee of $25 plus a charge of $10 per class. **11.** no solution

MODULE 9, LESSON 2

More Practice/Homework

1A.

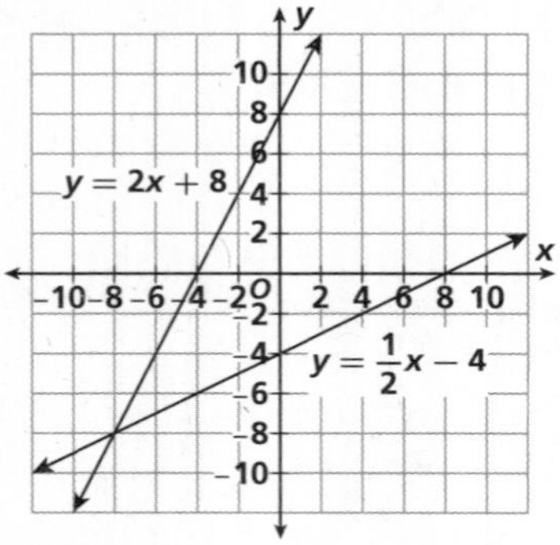

B. (−8, −8) **C.** Possible answer: Substitute (−8, −8) in each equation; both equations are satisfied. **3A.** (1, 3) **B.** (4, 2) **5.** (4, −8) **7.** $y = 50x + 20$ **9.** $x = 6$

MODULE 9, LESSON 3

On Your Own

3A. (10, 85) **B.** After 10 minutes, both drones are at a height of 85 meters. **7.** (−1, 6) **9.** $(\frac{1}{3}, -\frac{2}{3})$

More Practice/Homework

1. (4, 5); There are 4 trumpet players and 5 saxophone players in the jazz band. **3A.** Possible answer: $y = \frac{3}{2}x + 5$ **B.** (−4, −1) **5.** (−4, 5) **7.** D **9.** C **11.** (−6, 1) **13.** $x = 15$; $m\angle 3 = m\angle 6 = 61°$

MODULE 9, LESSON 4

On Your Own

3. Quarters: 4, $1.00; Dimes: 11, $1.10 **5A.** Possible answer: I would eliminate the y-terms. **B.** no **7.** (2, 0.5) **9.** (14, 11)

11A.

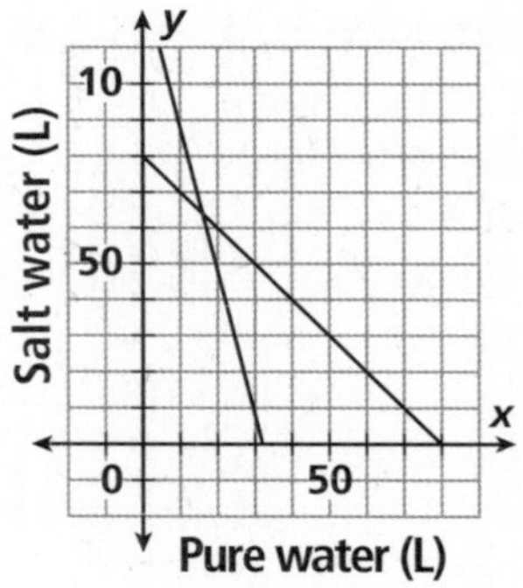

Possible answer: (15, 65)
B. 16 liters pure water and 64 liters salt water

More Practice/Homework

1. 20 inches by 18 inches
3. Possible answer: He did not multiply the y-term in the second equation by −2; (1, 6).
5. (−4, 0) **7.** (−1, 1) **9.** D
13. {−2, −1, 0, 1, 2}

MODULE 9, LESSON 5

On Your Own

5. Infinitely many **7.** no **9.** none **11.** 1 **13.** infinitely many **15.** infinitely many solutions **17.** no solution **19.** no solution

More Practice/Homework

1A. The system has no solution. **B.** yes; They did not because the system has no solution. **3.** no **5.** (0, 3) **7.** infinitely many solutions **9.** infinitely many solutions **11.** B **13.** infinitely many solutions; one solution; no solution; no solution; infinitely many solutions **15.** The candle starts at a height of 16 inches.

MODULE 9, LESSON 6

On Your Own

5A.

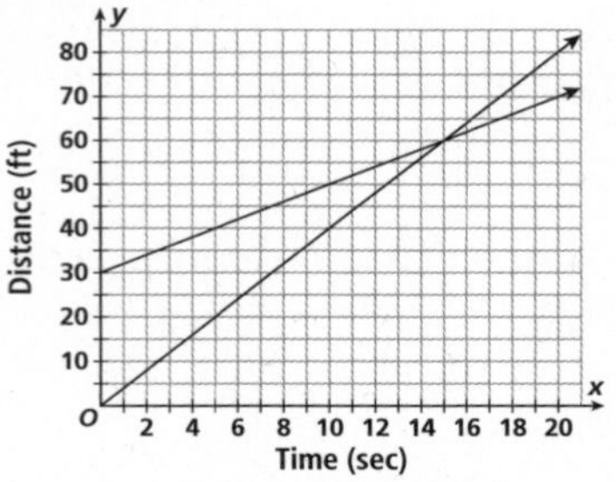

B. yes **7A.** $x + y = 90$ and $y = 2x + 15$ **B.** 25° and 65° **9.** no; Possible answer: The total number of questions on the test is needed. **11A.** $6b + 0.5g = 8$ and $30b + 7.5g = 60$ **B.** $b = 1$ and $g = 4$; Maya played 1 game of bowling and 4 holes of virtual golf. **13.** A sandwich costs $5.25 and a bowl of soup costs $3.50.

More Practice/Homework

1A. $x + y = 12$, $6x + 9y = 88$; $x = 6\frac{2}{3}$, $y = 5\frac{1}{3}$ **B.** 7 one-bedroom and 5 two-bedroom houses
3.

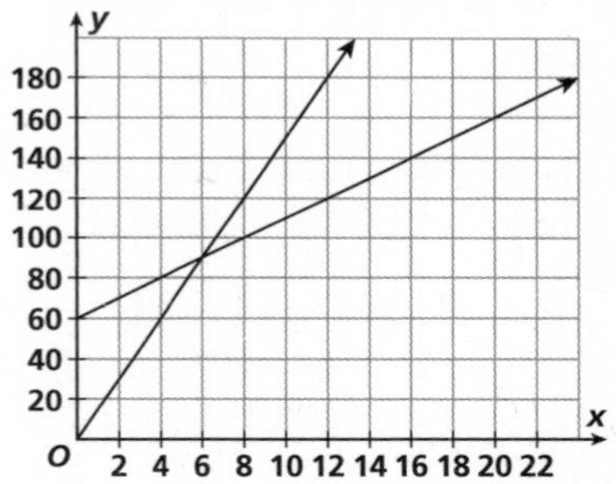

yes; after 6 seconds **5.** 17.50 **7.** 52
9. Triangles A and C
11. $y = -3x + 14$

© Houghton Mifflin Harcourt Publishing Company

UNIT 4

MODULE 10, LESSON 1

On Your Own

3. 6:30 p.m. **7.** nonlinear

More Practice/Homework

1A.

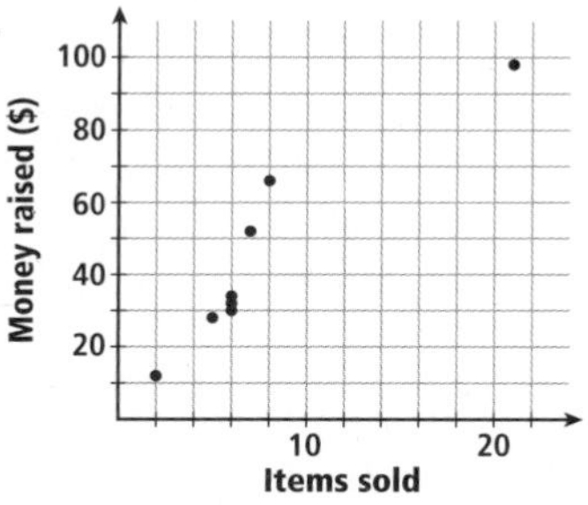

B. positive association; one outlier **3.** linear

5.

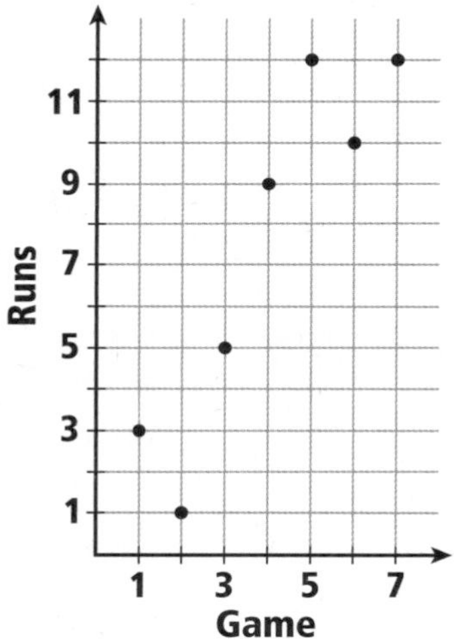

Possible answer: weak positive association **7.** positive linear association; negative nonlinear association; no association

9. $x = -2$, $y = 5$

MODULE 10, LESSON 2

On Your Own

3A. A trend line would be a good model. **B.** Possible answer:

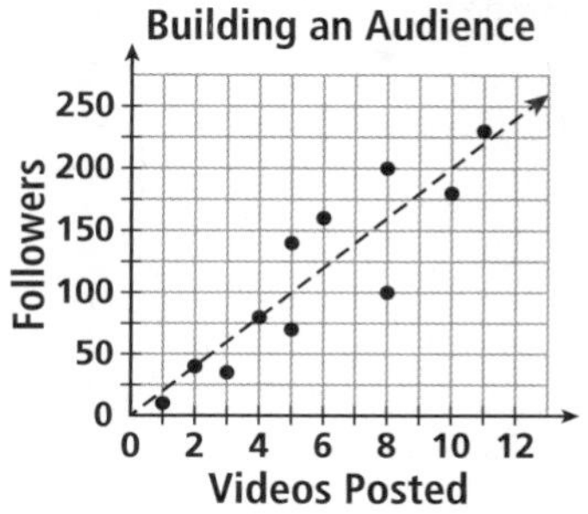

C. Possible answer: 400 followers

More Practice/Homework

1A. The trend line is not a good fit. **B.** The new line will be less steep and it will move farther away from many of the original points. **3.** Possible answer: not necessarily; One of the data points below the line might represent an outlier, pulling the trend line down. **7.** $x = 11$

9. $y = -2x + 3$

MODULE 10, LESSON 3

On Your Own

3A.

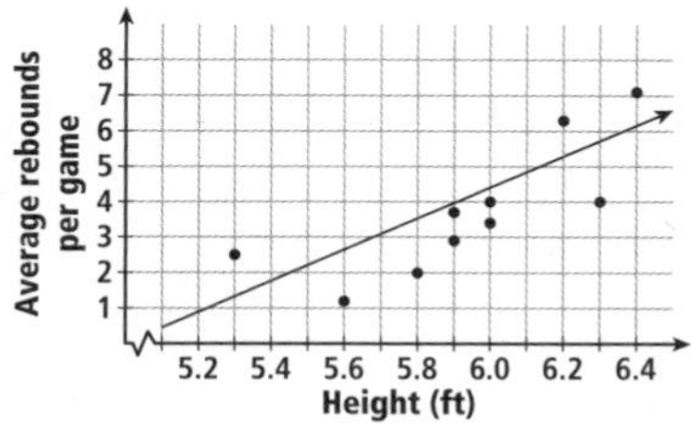

B. −22 **C.** It means that a person would get −22 rebounds if he or she were 0 feet tall. This is not possible. **D.** Possible answer: It is possible that the tallest player gets the most rebounds, but it is also possible for a shorter player to get the most rebounds.

5. 0.5 point

More Practice/Homework

1. Possible answer: Since the line trends down to the right, it shows that older people like the movie less. **3.** D **5.** D **7.** To be an outlier the data point would have to be far from the trend line, not just from the other points. 9. about 0.36 s less

MODULE 11, LESSON 1

On Your Own

5. yes; yes **7A.** all students in Cameron's school **B.** every tenth student that walks into school **C.** yes **D.** yes

More Practice/Homework

1A. Population: 10,000 members of the fan club; Sample: the 250 members chosen at random **B.** yes **C.** An overwhelming majority of club members are in favor. **3.** the sample of 200 students **5.** does not **7.** Julia's method **9.** 7 feet

MODULE 11, LESSON 2

On Your Own

3. at least **5.** yes **7.** 48 female athletes **9.** 90 letters **11.** 50 **13.** 25 **15.** Possible answer: 3,000 cars

More Practice/Homework

1A. 10th **B.** 9th **C.** 140 10th-graders **D.** 80 9th-graders **E.** Possible answer: 10th grade **3.** 270 students **5.** 12 laptop computers **7.** 64 steps per minute

MODULE 11, LESSON 3

On Your Own

3B.

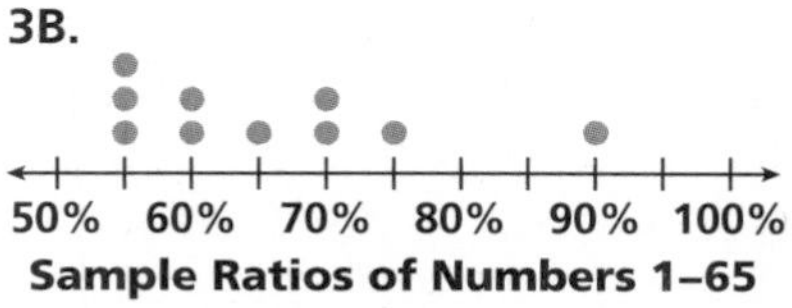

C. Slightly above the population ratio **D.** Possible answer: Most sample ratios are close to the population ratio.

© Houghton Mifflin Harcourt Publishing Company

More Practice/Homework

1A. above; below **B.**

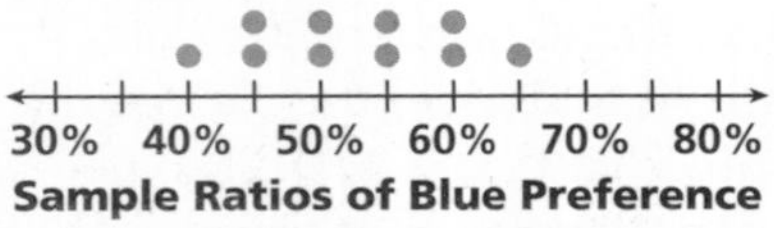

C. Possible answer: cluster around the population ratio of 55% or maybe slightly below it **D.** Possible answer: would cluster more tightly around 55% **3.** top down: 10% Below, 5% Below, 5% Above, 10% Above

MODULE 12, LESSON 1

On Your Own

5A. \$37,500; clustered from \$30,000 to \$40,000 **B.** \$50,000

More Practice/Homework

1. Tallahassee: 6°, Key West: 4°
3. Tallahassee: 87°, Key West: 85°
5. Tallahassee: 87°, Key West: 85°
7. Possible answer: The temperatures in Key West were more consistent and cooler than those in Tallahassee. Although Tallahassee is farther north, it got hotter in May than Key West. **9.** B **11.** Possible answer: HS students have more variation in the number of accounts than MS students. **13.** $y = 3x$

MODULE 12, LESSON 2

On Your Own

3A. Possible answer: On both teams, 25% of the players are ages 21–23, and 75% or more of the players are under 29.
B. Possible answer: I chose the interquartile range because it is less affected by outliers. The interquartile range for Team A is 2 yr, and the IQR for Team B is 5 yr. Team B has greater variability in players' ages.

C.

	Team A	Team B
Minimum	21	21
Lower quartile	23	23
Median	24	25
Upper quartile	25	28
Maximum	32	38

D. The centers are similar.
F. Possible answer: the data above the median

More Practice/Homework

1B. Possible answer: median A < median B; Store B prices vary more, but both stores have outlier high prices. **C.** Possible answer: The interquartile range for Store B is greater than the interquartile range for Store A. Both box plots have long right whiskers, so there may be high outliers at both stores.
D. Possible answer: 75% of the prices in the sample from Store B ≤ \$1,000, while all prices in the sample from Store A ≤ \$1,000. **E.** Possible answer: For Store A, the spread of the upper half of the data is 3 times the spread of the lower half. For Store B, the spread of the upper half of the data is a little less than $1\frac{1}{2}$ times the spread of the lower half. **3.** center; spread
5. Possible answer: Medians are close, but median Moesha < median Justin; Justin's times tend to be more varied. **7.** 1

MODULE 12, LESSON 3

On Your Own

3A. 14.7 h; 16.5 h **B.** Cross the Ocean **C.** 1 h; 3 h **D.** MAD for "Cross the Ocean" is 3 times as much. **E.** Possible answer: The variation for "Cross the Ocean" is greater. **5.** 1; some overlap
7. 3; little or no overlap
9A. Group A: 2; 1; **Group B:** 2.5; 1.25 **9B.** not much separation

More Practice/Homework

1A. 33.4; 39.2 **B.** 2.32; 2.56
C. yes **3.** C **5.** Colorado Springs was 2 °F higher. **7.** $x = 2$

MODULE 13, LESSON 1

On Your Own

3. yes

More Practice/Homework

1. Row 1: 51; 24; 75; Row 2: 119; 6; 125; Row 3: 170; 30; 200 **3.** C
5. A **7.** (2, −1)

MODULE 13, LESSON 2

On Your Own

3. $a + b = c$ **5.** 4%; 12 patients
7. $\frac{15}{30} = 0.5 = 50\%$ **9A.** 0.85 or 85% **B.** no

More Practice/Homework

1A. Row 1: 0.3; Row 2: 0.12; 0.63; Row 3: 0.81; 0.19; 1 **B.** 0.3 **C.** 0.63
3. D **5.** D **7.** Bucket B

UNIT 5

MODULE 14, LESSON 1

On Your Own

5. $\frac{43}{111}$ **7.** no **9.** $-1\frac{1}{9}$ **11.** $\frac{553}{900}$
13. $\frac{13}{18}$

More Practice/Homework

1A. $\frac{32}{60} = 0.533333...$ **B.** rational
3. $45\frac{2}{15}$ hourly visitors
5. 0.037037037... ; $0.\overline{037}$ **7.** $-8\frac{29}{40}$
9. $1\frac{119}{225}$ **11.** $\frac{19}{33}$ **13.** D
15A. Swimming: 18; 48; 66; No swimming: 6; 48; 54; TOTAL: 24; 96; 120 **B.** 45%

MODULE 14, LESSON 2

On Your Own

5A. yes **B.** 5 ft; $5^3 = 125$
7. $\frac{2}{5}$; Possible answer:
$\left(\frac{2}{5}\right)^3 = \frac{8}{125}$ **9.** $x = \pm 14$
13. yes; yes **15.** 9 **17.** $x = \pm\frac{1}{7}$
19. $y = \frac{3}{5}$

© Houghton Mifflin Harcourt Publishing Company

More Practice/Homework

1A. 6 in.; $6^3 = 216$ **B.** 343 in^3, 512 in^3, or 729 in^3 **3.** $y = \frac{4}{9}$ **5.** 17 **7.** $\frac{1}{10}$ **9.** $x = 7$ **11.** C **13.** B **15.** $8\frac{2}{3}$ **17.** Acme Parking

MODULE 14, LESSON 3

On Your Own

7A. 9; **B.** 9.2 **9.** $\sqrt{2} \approx 1.41$ **11.** $<$ **13.** $>$ **15.** 12 **17.** 19 **19.** $\sqrt{20} - 2$ **21.** $\sqrt{125}$ **23.** 12; 13 **25.** −2; −1 **27.** 6; 7 **29.** no

31.

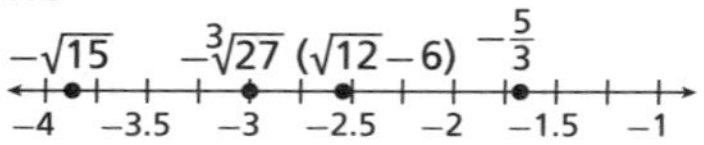

33. $\sqrt{27}, \sqrt[3]{70}, \pi, \frac{17}{6}, 1.8$ **35.** $(\sqrt{32} - 8), \left(4 - \frac{21}{4}\right), 0.\overline{7}, (-2 + \sqrt{19}), 2\sqrt{3}$ **37.** 9.9

More Practice/Homework

1. Kelsey's **3.** $<$ **7.**

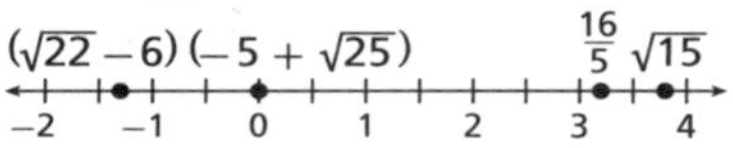

9. $(-\sqrt{45} + 9), \frac{12}{7}, (\sqrt{71} - 8), (\sqrt[3]{99} - 5), -\frac{8}{5}$ **11.** B **13.** least: $-\sqrt{130}$; greatest: $-3 - \sqrt{47}$ **15.** The relative frequency of owning a pet is about the same across the different music choices: 36%, 38%, and 35%. There does not appear to be a strong association.

MODULE 15, LESSON 1

On Your Own

3. Possible answer: For a right triangle with legs a and b, and hypotenuse c, $a^2 + b^2 = c^2$. **5.** yes **7.** Rafael is not correct. **11.** 17 ft

More Practice/Homework

3. 5; 16; 20; 25; 256; 400; no **5A.** 12 yards **B.** 120 yards **C.** The lengths in Part B are 10 times the lengths in Part A. **7.** A, D **9.** Possible answer: She did not use the correct formula for the Pythagorean Theorem. $3^2 + 6^2 \neq 9^2$ **11.** $-3, \frac{10}{4}, 2.7, \sqrt{8}$

MODULE 15, LESSON 2

On Your Own

3A. sidewalk route **B.** 11.9 m **5.** 10.77 m **7.** 28.8 **9.** 68.3 **11A.** Cone A **B.** 0.33 cm **13.** $\sqrt{12} \approx 3.46$ m

More Practice/Homework

1A. 1,336 km **B.** 553 km **3.** 7 in. **5.** C **7.** D

9.

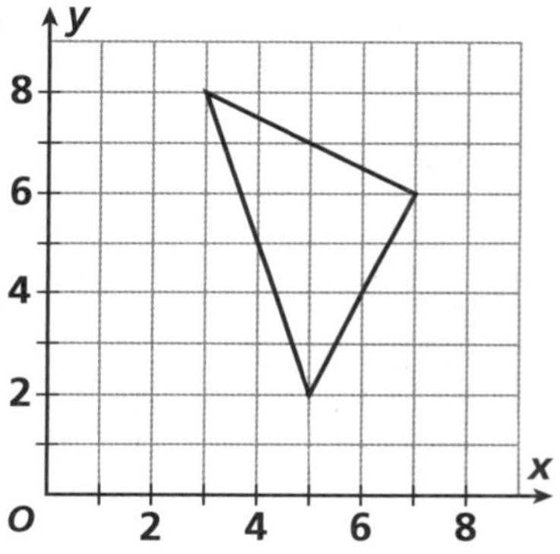

MODULE 15, LESSON 3

On Your Own

5. Point E **7A.** (−5, 2) or (4, 4) **B.** 9.2 units **C.** 20.2 units **9A.** (1, 0.5), (5, 3) **B.** 4.72 mi

More Practice/Homework

1. 4,270 ft **3A.** (−2, −1) or (4, −4) **B.** 3 units; 6 units **C.** 6.7 units **D.** 15.7 units **5.** A **7.** C **9.** $x = 3.5$

MODULE 16, LESSON 1

On Your Own

3A. 10^{11}; product of powers property **B.** 100,000,000,000 (one hundred billion) stars **5.** diameter of Milky Way disc; 10^{21} m **7.** distance from the Sun to Saturn, diameter of the Solar System, and diameter of Saturn **9B.** If $a \neq 0$ and $b \neq 0$ then $(ab)^m = a^m b^m$. **C.** $(3 \cdot 2)^5 = (6)^5 = 7{,}776$; $(3 \cdot 2)^5 = 3^5 \cdot 2^5 = 243 \cdot 32 = 7{,}776$ **11.** $\frac{1}{4}$ **13.** 65

More Practice/Homework

1A. 10^7; product of powers property, quotient of powers property **B.** 10,000,000 (10 million) **3.** Katie; 175 **5.** $\frac{1}{512}$ **7.** 81 **9.** A **11.** D **13.** $-2 < y < 10$

MODULE 16, LESSON 2

On Your Own

5A. negative **B.** 1.7×10^{-8} cm **7.** Car B, Car D, and Car E **9.** 3 times longer **11A.** Possible answer: 1.099511628E12; $1.099511628 \times 10^{12}$ **B.** 1,000,000,000,000 **13.** 4.71×10^7 **15.** 9×10^{-10} **17.** 320,000,000 **19.** 0.00106 **21.** 8×10^9 is 40,000 times as great as 2×10^5. **23.** 2.4×10^{10} is 1,000 times as great as 24,000,000. **25.** The first factor is not greater than or equal to 1 but less than 10. 1.54×10^8

More Practice/Homework

1. 7.5×10^{18} **3.** 186,000,000 **5.** 4.05×10^2 **7.** 6×10^{-14} **9.** 60,700,000 **11.** 0.000004 **13.** 2.8×10^{-4} is 20 times as great as 1.4×10^{-5}. **17.** B **19.** A **21.** 7.4 cm

MODULE 16, LESSON 3

On Your Own

5. 3.82×10^5 vehicles **7.** Golden Gate Bridge: 4.088×10^7 vehicles; San Francisco-Oakland Bay Bridge: 9.855×10^7 vehicles **9.** 2×10^6 sheets **11.** approximately 250 seeds **13A.** South Island; 3.7×10^4 km^2 greater **B.** approximately 18 people per square kilometer **15.** 5 meters

© Houghton Mifflin Harcourt Publishing Company

More Practice/Homework

1. 8.1×10^5 students **3.** 2.8×10^{-6} kg **5.** 1.595×10^8 km^2 **7.** 7.89×10^5 **9.** 9.6×10^{-8} **11.** 2×10^1 **13.** 1.3×10^{-9} **15.** B **17.** 2.875×10^3 or 2,875 attendees **19.** 5.8 units

UNIT 6

MODULE 17, LESSON 1

On Your Own

3A. about 176 ft **B.** about 2,640 ft **5.** 300 calories **7.** about 131.88 cm

More Practice/Homework

1A. about $\frac{55}{14}$ or 3.9 ft **B.** about 997 $\frac{6}{7}$ or 997.9 ft **3.** 48 years **5.** about 28.26 cm **7.** about 59.66 ft **9.** about 219.8 in. **11.** \$85.50 **13.** 27.63 in. **15.** 90°

MODULE 17, LESSON 2

On Your Own

3A. 176.63 in^2 **B.** 379.94 in^2 **C.** 203.31 in^2 or 203.32 in^2 **5.** Disagree; 4 times as large **7.** 254.34 m^2

More Practice/Homework

1. 200.96 ft^2 **3.** 153.86 in^2 **5.** 907.46 cm^2 **7.** 314 cm^2 **9.** 314 in^2 **11.** 28.26 mi^2 **13.** 132.665 cm^2 **15.** C **17.** 3,419.46 mm^2 **19.** 9.42 ft

MODULE 17, LESSON 3

On Your Own

3. 12 square units **5.** \$375.30 **7.** 8 square units **9.** 22 square inches

More Practice/Homework

1. 2,100 square feet **3.** 39 cm^2 **5.** about 1,757 square feet **7.** 6.25 square centimeters **9.** 113.04 cm^2 **11.** about 30.1 inches

MODULE 18, LESSON 1

On Your Own

5. parallel to the base **7.** circumference: 25.12 in.; area: 50.24 in^2 **9.** trapezoid **11.** pentagon **13.** square

More Practice/Homework

1. square **3.** parallel **5.** perpendicular **7.** Possible answer: circles **9.** A, B, D **11.** 108 in^2

MODULE 18, LESSON 2

On Your Own

5. 136 in^2 **7.** 640 cm^2 **9.** 2,194 in^2

More Practice/Homework

1. 486 in^2 **3.** 1,761 ft^2 **5.** 184 in^2 **7.** 672 cm^2 **9.** C **11.** 189.9 mm^2 **13.** 21 ft^2

MODULE 18, LESSON 3

On Your Own

3. 8,000 in^3 **5.** 3 m **7.** 645 mm^3

More Practice/Homework

1. 5,625 ft^3 **5.** 3,320 ft^3 **7.** 864 in^3 more **9.** $V = Bh$; $1{,}260 = 28h$; $h = 45$ m **11.** rectangle **13.** about 818.8 mm^2

MODULE 18, LESSON 4

On Your Own

3. 51.9 m^3 **5.** 3 in. **7.** 1.4×10^{12} mm^3 **9A.** Possible answer: 140.55 cm^3

More Practice/Homework

1. $432{,}180\pi$ ft^3 **3.** 480 ft^3 **5.** $V = \pi\left(\frac{d}{2}\right)^2 h$ or $V = \frac{\pi}{4} d^2h$ **7.** 11 m **9.** B, C, D **11.** B **13.** 5.8×10^{-9}

MODULE 18, LESSON 5

On Your Own

3A. 252π cm^3 **B.** 756π cm^3 **5.** 16.6 m^3 **7.** $\frac{3{,}887}{96}\pi$ ft^3 **9.** 7,241.1 cm^3 **11.** 0.5 yd^3 **13.** 314 ft^3

17A.

Height (cm)	1	2	3	4	5
Volume (cm^3)	$\frac{1}{3}\pi$	$\frac{2}{3}\pi$	π	$\frac{4}{3}\pi$	$\frac{5}{3}\pi$

B. $y = \frac{1}{3}\pi x$

More Practice/Homework

1. $\frac{1{,}372}{3}\pi$ ft^3; 1,436.0 ft^3 **3.** 59.3 cm^3 **5.** 33,493.3 mm^3 **7.** The student forgot to find the radius by taking half the diameter. **9.** A, C, D, F **11.** 2.5; For each increase of 1 degree in the daily high temperature, an additional 2.5 quarts of iced coffee are sold. **13.** 43.6 m^3

MODULE 18, LESSON 6

On Your Own

3A. 11 in. **B.** 257.4 in^3 **5.** 48 cm^2 **7.** 2,560 in^3 **9A.** 7 ft **B.** volume; 109.2 ft^3 **11.** 468 cm^2 **13.** 2,143.57 in^3 **15.** 396 ft^3 of water **17.** 110,815,833 ft^3

More Practice/Homework

1A. 2 ft **B.** 184 ft^2 **C.** 15 **3.** no **5.** 38 cm^3 **7.** 312 in^2 **9.** 57.93 in^3 **11.** 49

UNIT 7

MODULE 19, LESSON 1

On Your Own

3. 15 trials; opening to an odd page, opening to an even page **5.** less **7.** likely; a number greater than $\frac{1}{2}$ and less than 1

More Practice/Homework

1. impossible **5.** Possible answer: {heads, tails} or {heads, tails, lands on side} **11.** a number greater than 0 and less than $\frac{1}{2}$ **13.** D **15.** 12 inches

© Houghton Mifflin Harcourt Publishing Company

MODULE 19, LESSON 2

On Your Own

3A. yes **B.** The probabilities, in order, are $\frac{2}{15}, \frac{11}{60}, \frac{1}{6}, \frac{7}{60}, \frac{11}{60}$, and $\frac{13}{60}$. **5.** Possible answer: Use random integers 1–10, where 1–6 represent completed passes. Perform 40 trials. **7A.** $P(A) = \frac{7}{32}$; $P(B) = \frac{3}{8}$; $P(C) = \frac{7}{32}$; $P(D) = \frac{3}{16}$ **B.** $\frac{13}{16}$ **C.** The spinner is somehow biased in favor of the section labeled B.

More Practice/Homework

1. The probabilities, in order, are $\frac{19}{80}, \frac{17}{80}, \frac{23}{80}$, and $\frac{21}{80}$. **3.** between: $\frac{11}{24}$; after: $\frac{7}{12}$ **5.** $\frac{11}{37}$ **7.** $\frac{3}{20}$ **9.** $10 = 6 + x$; $x = 4$; four math problems

MODULE 19, LESSON 3

On Your Own

3A. 2 by 3 or 3 by 2 **B.** 6 possible outcomes **5.** no **7.** $\frac{1}{11}; \frac{10}{11}$ **9.** $\frac{8}{55}; \frac{47}{55}$ **11.** Possible answer: Random number generator, 1-2 for red, 3-4 for blue, 5-6 for yellow; Random number generator, 1-2 for white trim, 3-4 for gray trim; 5-6 for black trim

More Practice/Homework

1A. 1H, 1T, 2H, 2T, 3H, 3T, 4H, 4T, 5H, 5T, 6H, 6T **1B.** Row 1: 1H, 2H, 3H, 4H, 5H, 6H; Row 2: 1T, 2T, 3T, 4T, 5T, 6T **3A.** $\frac{4}{25}$ **3B.** $\frac{21}{25}$ **5.** A, B **7.** 28%; below **9.** continuous

MODULE 19, LESSON 4

On Your Own

3A. About 224 people **B.** because there cannot be partial people **5A.** 0.35(17,400,000) **B.** about 6.09 million acres **7.** 630 people **9.** 101 people; Possible answer: no such thing as 0.6 of a person **11.** about 10 more people

More Practice/Homework

1. 133 votes **3.** 23 home runs **5.** $\frac{45}{100} = \frac{x}{1,200}$; 540 people **7.** $\frac{12}{100} = \frac{x}{2,000}$; 240 h **9.** 540 times **11.** $\frac{12}{13}$

MODULE 20, LESSON 1

On Your Own

3. pile 2 **5.** $\frac{1}{8}$ **7.** $\frac{3}{8}$ **9.** 35% or $\frac{7}{20}$ **11.** 3 **13.** $\frac{3}{5}$, 0.6, 60%

More Practice/Homework

1. $\frac{1}{2}$ **3.** $\frac{1}{2}$ **5.** theoretical probability: $\frac{13}{52}$ or $\frac{1}{4}$; experimental probability: $\frac{1}{5}$ **7.** B **9.** The theoretical probability is greater. **11.** 36

MODULE 20, LESSON 2

On Your Own

3A. From left to right, top: 2, 3, 4; middle: 3, 4, 5; bottom: 4, 5, 6 **B.** $\frac{2}{9}$ **C.** rolling a sum of 5 **D.** Possible answer: Rolling a sum of 2 **E.** Possible answer: Rolling a sum of 4 **F.** $\frac{1}{3}$, 0.3, 33% **G.** $\frac{1}{9}$, 0.11, 11% **H.** 1, 1, 100% **I.** 0, 0, 0% **5A.** 1, 1; 1, 2; 1, 3; 1, 4; 1, 5; 1, 6; 2, 1; 2, 2; 2, 3; 2, 4; 2, 5; 2, 6; 3, 1; 3, 2; 3, 3; 3, 4; 3, 5; 3, 6 **B.** $\frac{3}{18}$ or $\frac{1}{6}$ **C.** $\frac{2}{18}$ or $\frac{1}{9}$ **D.** Possible answer: The probability of getting a sum of 5 is greater than the probability of getting a sum of 3.

More Practice/Homework

1A.

+	1	2	3	4	5
1	2	3	4	5	6
2	3	4	5	6	7
3	4	5	6	7	8

B. $\frac{2}{15}$ **C.** Possible answer: drawing a sum of 6 **3.** 48 **5.** From top to bottom: $\frac{1}{9}; \frac{1}{12}; \frac{1}{6}; \frac{5}{18}$ **7.** $\frac{4}{9}$

MODULE 20, LESSON 3

On Your Own

3. not likely **5.** $\frac{2}{8} = \frac{x}{400}$; about 100 times **7.** $\frac{1}{4} = \frac{x}{300}$; about 75 times **9.** about 1,080 times **11.** $\frac{1}{18} = \frac{x}{900}$; about 50 times **13.** about 450 times **15.** not likely; It would probably be chosen less than twice.

More Practice/Homework

1. yes **3.** about 100 times **5.** about 100 times **7.** about 700 times **9.** From top to bottom: about 200 times; about 750 times; about 50 times; about 300 times; about 550 times **11.** landing on 5

MODULE 20, LESSON 4

On Your Own

3. 20% **7.** yes **9A.** Possible answer: Use whole numbers 1–5. Let 1–3 represent Allie getting a hit and 4–5 represent Allie not getting a hit. Draw 5 slips of paper from a box with numbers 1–5, replacing the slip of paper after each draw. Repeat 10 times.

More Practice/Homework

1. Chairs Checked: 3; 2; 2; 4; 2; 3; 1; 4; 2; 6; experimental probability: 20% **3.** 20% **5.** 20 **7.** about 25 times

© Houghton Mifflin Harcourt Publishing Company

Interactive Glossary

As you learn about each new term, add notes, drawings, or sentences in the space next to the definition. Doing so will help you remember what each term means.

Pronunciation Key

ă	add, map	g	go, log	n	nice, tin	p	pit, stop	û(r)	burn, term
ā	ace, rate	h	hope, hate	ng	ring, song	r	run, poor	yo͞o	fuse, few
â(r)	care, air	hw	which	ŏ	odd, hot	s	see, pass	v	vain, eve
ä	palm, father	ĭ	it, give	ō	open, so	sh	sure, rush	w	win, away
b	bat, rub	ī	ice, write	ô	taught, jaw	t	talk, sit	y	yet, yearn
ch	check, catch	îr	tier	ôr	order	th	thin, both	z	zest, muse
d	dog, rod	j	joy, ledge	oi	oil, boy	*th*	this, bathe	zh	vision, pleasure
ĕ	end, pet	k	cool, take	ou	pout, now	ŭ	up, done		
ē	equal, tree	l	look, rule	o͝o	took, full	o͝o	pull, book		
f	fit, half	m	move, seem	o͞o	pool, food	o͝or	cure		

ə the schwa, an unstressed vowel representing the sound spelled *a* in *above*, *e* in *sicken*, *i* in *possible*, *o* in *melon*, *u* in *circus*

Other symbols:
- – separates words into syllables
- ′ indicates stress on a syllable

A

My Vocabulary Summary

acute triangle [ə-kyo͞ot′ trī′ăng′gəl] A triangle with all angles measuring less than 90°

triángulo acutángulo Triángulo en el que todos los ángulos miden menos de 90°

Addition Property of Equality [ə-dĭsh′ən prŏp′ər-tē ŭv ĭ-kwŏl′ĭ-tē] The property that states that if you add the same number to both sides of an equation, the new equation will have the same solution

Propiedad de Igualdad de la Suma Propiedad que establece que puedes sumar el mismo número a ambos lados de una ecuación y la nueva ecuación tendrá la misma solución

adjacent angles [ə-jā′sənt ăng′gəls] Angles in the same plane that have a common vertex and a common side

ángulos adyacentes Ángulos en el mismo plano que comparten un vértice y un lado

© Houghton Mifflin Harcourt Publishing Company

My Vocabulary Summary

alternate exterior angles [ôl′tər-nĭt′ ĭk-stîr′ē-ər ăng′gəls] For two lines intersected by a transversal, a pair of angles that lie on opposite sides of the transversal and outside the other two lines

ángulos alternos externos Dadas dos rectas cortadas por una transversal, par de ángulos no adyacentes ubicados en los lados opuestos de la transversal y fuera de las otras dos rectas

---

alternate interior angles [ôl′tər-nĭt′ ĭn-tîr′ē-ər ăng′gəls] For two lines intersected by a transversal, a pair of nonadjacent angles that lie on opposite sides of the transversal and between the other two lines

ángulos alternos internos Dadas dos rectas cortadas por una transversal, par de ángulos no adyacentes ubicados en los lados opuestos de la transversal y entre de las otras dos rectas

---

Angle-Angle Similarity Postulate [ăng′gəl-ăng′gəl sĭm′ə-lăr′ĭ-tē pŏs′chə-lāt′] Two triangles are similar if they have pairs of corresponding angles that are congruent

Postulado de Semejanza Ángulo-Ángulo Dos triángulos son semejantes si tienen dos pares de ángulos correspondientes y congruentes

---

association [ə-sō′sē-ā′shən] The description of the relationship between two data sets

asociación Descripción de la relación entre dos conjuntos de datos

---

axis [ăk′sĭs] A line of a coordinate plane that passes through the origin

eje Recta de un plano de coordenadas que pasa por el origen

© Houghton Mifflin Harcourt Publishing Company

Interactive Glossary

B

My Vocabulary Summary

base [bās] The number that is used as a factor when a number is raised to a power

base Cuando un número es elevado a una potencia, el número que se usa como factor es la base

base (of a polygon or three-dimensional figure) [bās (ŭv ā pŏl′ē-gŏn′ ôr thrē′dĭ-mĕn′shə-nəl fĭg′yər)] A side of a polygon; a face of a three-dimensional figure by which the figure is measured or classified

base (de un polígono o figura tridimensional) Lado de un polígono; cara de una figura tridimensional según la cual se mide o se clasifica la figura

bias [bī′əs] When a sample does not accurately represent the population

sesgada Cuando una muestra no representa precisamente la población

bivariate data [bī-vâr′ē-ĭt dā′tə] A set of data that is made of two paired variables

datos bivariados Conjunto de datos compuesto de dos variables apareadas

box plot [bŏks plot] A graph that shows how data are distributed by using the median, quartiles, least value, and greatest value; also called a box-and-whisker plot

gráfica de mediana y rango Gráfica que muestra los valores máximo y mínimo, los cuartiles superior e inferior, así como la mediana de los datos

© Houghton Mifflin Harcourt Publishing Company

C

My Vocabulary Summary

center of dilation [sĕn′tər ŭv dī-lā′shən] The point of intersection of lines through each pair of corresponding vertices in a dilation

centro de una dilatación Punto de intersección de las líneas que pasan a través de cada par de vértices correspondientes en una dilatación

center of rotation [sĕn′tər ŭv rō-tā′shən] The point about which a figure is rotated

centro de una rotación Punto alrededor del cual se hace girar una figura

circle graph [sûr′kəl grăf] A graph that uses sectors of a circle to compare parts to the whole and parts to other parts

gráfica circular Gráfica que usa secciones de un círculo para comparar partes con el todo y con otras partes

circumference [sər-kŭm′fər-əns] The distance around a circle

circunferencia Distancia alrededor de un círculo

clockwise [klŏk′wīz′] A circular movement in the direction of the typical forward movement of the hands of a clock

en el sentido de las manecillas del reloj Un movimiento circular en la dirección típica de las manecillas de un reloj

cluster [klŭs′tər] A set of closely grouped data

agrupación Conjunto de datos bien agrupados

© Houghton Mifflin Harcourt Publishing Company

My Vocabulary Summary

coefficient [kō'ə-fĭsh'ənt] The number that is multiplied by the variable in an algebraic expression

coeficiente Número que se multiplica por la variable en una expresión algebraica

common denominator [kŏm'ən dĭ-nŏm'ə-nā'tər] A denominator that is the same in two or more fractions

denominador común Denominador que es común a dos o más fracciones

complement of an event [kŏm'plə-mənt ŭv ən ĭ-vĕnt'] The set of all outcomes in the sample space that are *not* included in the event

complemento de un evento Conjunto de todos los resultados del espacio muestral que *no* están incluidos en el evento

complementary angles [kŏm'plə-mĕn'tə-rē ăng'gəls] Two angles whose measures add to 90°

ángulos complementarios Dos ángulos cuyas medidas suman 90°

composite figure [kəm-pŏz'ĭt fĭg'yər] A figure made up of simple geometric shapes

figura compuesta Figura formada por figuras geométricas simples

compound event [kŏm-pound' ĭ-vĕnt'] An event made up of two or more simple events

suceso compuesto Suceso que consista de dos o más sucesos simples

conditional relative frequency [kən-dĭsh'ə-nəl rĕl'ə-tĭv frē'kwən-sē] The ratio of a joint relative frequency to a related marginal relative frequency in a two-way table

frecuencia relativa condicional Razón de una frecuencia relativa conjunta a una frecuencia relativa marginal en una tabla de doble entrada

cone [kōn] A three-dimensional figure with one vertex and one circular base

cono Figura tridimensional con un vértice y una base circular

© Houghton Mifflin Harcourt Publishing Company

My Vocabulary Summary

congruence transformation [kŏng′grōō-əns trăns′fər-mā′shən] A transformation that results in an image that is the same shape and the same size as the original figure

transformación de congruencia Una transformación que resulta en una imagen que tiene la misma forma y el mismo tamaño como la figura original

---

congruent [kŏng′grōō-ənt] Having the same size and shape; the symbol for congruent is ≅

congruentes Que tienen la misma forma y el mismo tamaño expresado por ≅

---

constraint [kən-strānt′] A restriction of the value(s) of a quantity or variable

restricción Una restricción del valor de una cantidad o variable

---

continuous graph [kən-tĭn′yōō-əs grăf] A graph made up of connected lines or curves

gráfica continua Gráfica compuesta por líneas rectas *o* curvas conectadas

---

coordinate [kō-ôr dn-ĭt, -āt] One of the numbers of an ordered pair that locate a point on a coordinate graph

coordenada Uno de los números de un par ordenado que ubica un punto en una gráfica de coordenadas

---

coordinate grid [kō-ôr′dn-ĭt grĭd] A grid formed by the intersection of horizontal and vertical lines that is used to locate points

cuadrícula de coordenadas Cuadrícula formada por la intersección de líneas horizontales y líneas verticales que se usan por localizar puntos

---

coordinate plane [kō-ôr′dn-ĭt plān] A plane formed by the intersection of a horizontal number line called the *x*-axis and a vertical number line called the *y*-axis

plano cartesiano Plano formado por la intersección de una recta numérica horizontal llamada eje *x* y otra vertical llamada eje *y*

© Houghton Mifflin Harcourt Publishing Company

My Vocabulary Summary

corresponding angles (for lines) [kôr′ĭ-spŏn′dĭng ăng′gəls (fôr līns)] For two lines intersected by a transversal, a pair of angles that lie on the same side of the transversal and on the same sides of each of the other two lines

ángulos correspondientes (en líneas) Dadas dos rectas cortadas por una transversal, el par de ángulos ubicados en el mismo lado de la transversal y en los mismos lados de las otras dos rectas

corresponding angles (of polygons) [kôr′ĭ-spŏn′dĭng ăng′gəls (ŭv pŏl′ē-gŏn′s)] Angles in the same relative position in polygons with an equal number of sides

ángulos correspondientes (en polígonos) Ángulos en la misma posición formaron cuando una tercera línea interseca dos líneas

corresponding sides [kôr′ĭ-spŏn′dĭng sīds] Matching sides of two or more polygons

lados correspondientes Lados que se ubican en la misma posición relativa en dos o más polígonos

counterclockwise [koun′tər-klŏk′wīz] A circular movement in the direction opposite the typical forward movement of the hands of a clock

en sentido contrario a las manecillas del reloj Un movimiento circular en la dirección opuesta al movimiento típico de las manecillas del reloj

cross section [krôs sĕk′shən] The intersection of a three-dimensional figure and a plane

sección transversal Intersección de una figura tridimensional y un plano

cube (geometric figure) [kyo͞ob (jē′ə-mĕt′rĭk fĭg′yər)] A rectangular prism with six congruent square faces

cubo (figura geométrica) Prisma rectangular con seis caras cuadradas congruentes

cube (in numeration) [kyo͞ob (ĭn no͞o′mə-rā′shən)] A number raised to the third power

cubo (en numeración) Número elevado a la tercera potencia

© Houghton Mifflin Harcourt Publishing Company

My Vocabulary Summary

cube root [kyo͞ob ro͞ot] A number, written as $\sqrt[3]{x}$, whose cube is x

raíz cúbica Número, expresado como $\sqrt[3]{x}$, cuyo cubo es x

cylinder [sil′ən-dər] A three-dimensional figure with two parallel, congruent circular bases connected by a curved lateral surface

cilindro Figura tridimensional con dos bases circulares paralelas y congruentes, unidas por una superficie lateral curva

D

data set [dā′tə sĕt] A set of information collected about people or things, often to draw conclusions about them

conjunto de datos Conjunto de información recopilada sobre personas u objetos generalmente con el objetivo de obtener conclusiones acerca de los mismos

denominator [dĭ-nŏm′ə-nā′tər] The bottom number of a fraction that tells how many equal parts are in the whole

denominador Número que está abajo en una fracción y que indica en cuántas partes iguales se divide el entero

dependent variable [dĭ-pĕn′dənt vâr′ē-ə-bəl] The output of a function; a variable whose value depends on the value of the input, or independent variable

variable dependiente Salida de una función; variable cuyo valor depende del valor de la entrada, o variable independiente

diameter [di-am′i-tər] A line segment that passes through the center of a circle and has endpoints on the circle; or the length of that segment

diámetro Segmento de recta que pasa por el centro de un círculo y tiene sus extremos en la circunferencia, o bien la longitud de ese segmento

© Houghton Mifflin Harcourt Publishing Company

My Vocabulary Summary

dilation [dī-lā′shən] A transformation that enlarges or reduces a figure

dilatación Transformación que agranda o reduce una figura

discrete graph [dĭ-skrēt′ grăf] A graph made up of unconnected points

gráfica discreta Gráfica compuesta de puntos no conectados

Distributive Property [dĭ-strĭb′yə-tĭv prŏp′ər-tē] For all real numbers a, b, and c, $a(b + c) = ab + ac$, and $a(b - c) = ab - ac$

Propiedad Distributiva Dados los números reales a, b, y c, $a(b + c) = ab + ac$, y $a(b - c) = ab - ac$

domain [dō-mān′] The set of all possible input values of a function

dominio Conjunto de todos los posibles valores de entrada de una función

E

elimination [ĭ-lĭm′ə-nā′shən] Algebraic process of eliminating a variable in a system of equations by combining the equations through addition

eliminación Procedimiento algebraico que consiste en eliminar una variable en un sistema de ecuaciones sumando las ecuaciones

enlargement [ĕn-lärj′mənt] An increase in size of all dimensions in the same proportions

agrandamiento Aumento de tamaño de todas las dimensiones en las mismas proporciones

© Houghton Mifflin Harcourt Publishing Company

My Vocabulary Summary

equivalent expressions [ĭ-kwĭv'ə-lənt ĭk-sprĕsh'əns] Expressions that have the same value for all values of the variables

expresiones equivalentes Las expresiones equivalentes tienen el mismo valor para todos los valores de las variables

---

event [ĭ-vĕnt'] An outcome or set of outcomes of an experiment or situation

suceso Un resultado o una serie de resultados de un experimento o una situación

---

experiment [ĭk-spĕr'ə-mənt] In probability, any activity based on chance, such as tossing a coin

experimento En probabilidad, cualquier actividad basada en la posibilidad, como lanzar una moneda.

---

experimental probability [ĭk-spĕr'ə-mĕn'tl prŏb'ə-bĭl'ĭ-tē] The ratio of the number of times an event occurs to the total number of trials, or times that the activity is performed

probabilidad experimental Razón del número de veces que ocurre un suceso al número total de pruebas o al número de veces que se realiza el experimento

---

exponent [ĭk-spō'nənt] The number that indicates how many times the base is used as a factor

exponente Número que indica cuántas veces se usa la base como factor

---

expression [ĭk-sprĕsh ən] A mathematical phrase that contains operations, numbers, and/or variables

expresión Enunciado matemático que contiene operaciones, números y/o variables

---

exterior angle (of a polygon) [ĭk-stîr'ē-ər ăng'gəl (ŭv ā pŏl'ē-gŏn')] An angle formed by one side of a polygon and the extension of an adjacent side

ángulo extreno de un polígono Ángulo formado por un lado de un polígono y la prolongación del lado adyacente

© Houghton Mifflin Harcourt Publishing Company

My Vocabulary Summary

Exterior Angle Theorem [ĭk-stîr′ē-ər ăng′gəl thē′ər-əm] The measure of an exterior angle of a triangle is greater than either of the measures of the remote interior angles

Teorema del Ángulo Exterior La medida de un ángulo exterior de un triángulo es mayor que cualquiera de las medidas de los ángulos interiores no adyacentes

F

frequency [frē′kwən-sē] The number of times the value appears in the data set

frecuencia Cantidad de veces que aparece el valor en un conjunto de datos

function [fŭngk′shən] An input-output relationship that has exactly one output for each input

función Regla que relaciona dos candidates de forma que a cada valor de entrada corresponde exactamente un valor de salida

H

height [hīt] In a pyramid or cone, the perpendicular distance from the base to the opposite vertex

In a triangle or quadrilateral, the perpendicular distance from the base to the opposite vertex or side

In a prism or cylinder, the perpendicular distance between the bases

altura En una pirámide o cono, la distancia perpendicular desde la base al vértice opuesto

En un triángulo o cuadrilátero, la distancia perpendicular desde la base de la figura al vértice o lado opuesto

En un prisma o cilindro, la distancia perpendicular entre las bases

© Houghton Mifflin Harcourt Publishing Company

My Vocabulary Summary

hemisphere [hĕm′ĭ-sfîr′] A half of a sphere

hemisferio La mitad de una esfera

hypotenuse [hī-pŏt′n-o͞os′] In a right triangle, the side opposite the right angle

hipotenusa En un triángulo rectángulo, el lado opuesto al ángulo recto

I

My Vocabulary Summary

image [ĭm′ĭj] A figure resulting from a transformation

imagen Figura que resulta de una transformación

independent variable [ĭn′dĭ-pĕn′dənt vâr′ē-ə-bəl] The input of a function; a variable whose value determines the value of the output, or dependent variable

variable independiente Entrada de una función; variable cuyo valor determina el valor de la salida, o variable dependiente

indirect measurement [ĭn′dĭ-rĕkt′ mĕzh′ər-mənt] The technique of using similar figures and proportions to find a measure

medición indirecta La técnica de usar figuras semejantes y proporciones para hallar una medida

inequality [ĭn′ĭ-kwŏl′ĭ-tē] A mathematical sentence that shows the relationship between quantities that are not equivalent

desigualdad Enunciado matemático que muestra una relación entre cantidades que no son equivalentes

© Houghton Mifflin Harcourt Publishing Company

My Vocabulary Summary

infinitely many solutions [ĭn′fə-nĭt-lē mĕn′ē sə-lo͞o′shəns] Occurs when every value of the variable makes a true mathematical statement, or if the graphs of two linear equations overlap and therefore intersect at infinitely many points

soluciones infinitas Ocurre cuando cada valor de la variable sea un enunciado matemático verdadero, o si las gráficas de dos ecuaciones lineales se superponen y por tanto se intersecan en puntos infinitos

input [ĭn′po͝ot′] The value substituted into an expression or function

valor de entrada Valor que se usa para sustituir una variable en una expresión o función

intercept [ĭn′tər-sĕpt′] The coordinate of the point where the line of the graph intersects the axis

intersección Coordenada del punto en el cual la gráfica interseca el eje

interior angles [ĭn-tîr′ē-ər ăng′gəls] Angles on the inner sides of two lines cut by a transversal

ángulos internos Ángulos en los lados internos de dos líneas intersecadas por una transversal

interquartile range [ĭn′tər-kwôr′tĭl′ rānj] The difference between the upper and lower quartiles in a box-and-whisker plot

rango entre cuartiles La diferencia entre los cuartiles superior e inferior en una gráfica de mediana y rango

interval [ĭn′tər-vəl] The space between marked values on a number line or the scale of a graph

intervalo El espacio entre los valores marcados en una recta numérica o en la escala de una gráfica

© Houghton Mifflin Harcourt Publishing Company

My Vocabulary Summary

inverse operations [ĭn-vûrs′ ŏp′ə-rā′shəns] Operations that undo each other: addition and subtraction, or multiplication and division

operaciones inversas Operaciones que se cancelan mutuamente: suma y resta, o multiplicación y división

irrational number [ĭ-răsh′ə-nəl nŭm′bər] A number that cannot be expressed as a ratio of two integers or as a repeating or terminating decimal

número irracional Número que no se puede expresar como una razón de dos enteros ni como un decimal periódico o finito

isolate the variable [ī′sə-lāt′ thə vâr′ē-ə-bəl] To get a variable alone on one side of an equation or inequality in order to solve the equation or inequality

despejar la variable Dejar sola la variable en un lado de una ecuación o desigualdad para resolverla

J

joint relative frequency [joint rĕl′ə-tĭv frē′kwən-sē] The frequency in a particular category divided by the total number of data values

frecuencia relativa conjunta La frecuencia en una determinada categoría dividida entre el número total de valores

© Houghton Mifflin Harcourt Publishing Company

L

My Vocabulary Summary

legs [lĕgs] In a right triangle, the sides that form the right angle; in an isosceles triangle, the pair of congruent sides

catetos En un triángulo rectángulo, los lados adyacentes al ángulo recto. En un triángulo isósceles, el par de lados congruentes

like terms [līk tûrms] Terms that have the same variable(s) raised to the same exponent

términos semejantes Términos que contienen las mismas variables elevada a las mismas exponente

line of best fit [līn ŭv bĕst fĭt] A straight line that comes closest to the points on a scatter plot

línea de mejor ajuste La línea recta que más se aproxima a los puntos de un diagrama de dispersión

line of reflection [līn ŭv rĭ-flĕk'shən] A line that a figure is flipped across to create a mirror image of the original figure

línea de reflexión Línea sobre la cual se invierte una figura para crear una imagen reflejada de la figura original

line plot [līn plot] A number line with marks or dots that show frequency

diagrama de acumulación Recta numérica con marcas o puntos que indican la frecuencia

linear association [lĭn'ē-ər ə-sō'sē-ā shən] Two data sets have a linear association when their data values lie roughly along a line

assóciation lineal Dos conjuntos de datos tienen una asociación lineal cuando sus valores de datos se encuentran aproximadamente a lo largo de una línea

© Houghton Mifflin Harcourt Publishing Company

My Vocabulary Summary

linear equation [lĭn′ē-ər ĭ-kwā′zhən] An equation whose solutions form a straight line on a coordinate plane

ecuación lineal Ecuación cuyas soluciones forman una línea recta en un plano cartesiano

linear function [lĭn′ē-ər fŭngk′shən] A function whose graph is a straight line

función lineal Función cuya gráfica es una línea recta

lower quartile [lou′ər kwôr′tīl′] The median of the lower half of a set of data

cuartil inferior La mediana de la mitad inferior de un conjunto de datos

M

marginal relative frequency [mär′jə-nəl rĕl′ə-tĭv frē′kwən-sē] The sum of the joint relative frequencies in a row or column of a two-way table

frecuencia relativa marginal La suma de las frecuencias relativas conjuntas en una fila o columna de una tabla de doble entrada

mean [mēn] The sum of the items in a set of data divided by the number of items in the set; also called *average*

media La suma de todos loselementos de un conjunto de datos dividida entre el número de elementos del conjunto. También se llama *promedio*

mean absolute deviation (MAD) [mēn ăb′sə-lo͞ot′ dē′vē-ā′shən] Mean of the distances between the data values and the mean of the data set

desviación absoluta media (DAM) Distancias medias entre los valores de datos y la media del conjunto de datos

© Houghton Mifflin Harcourt Publishing Company

My Vocabulary Summary

median [mē′dē-ən] The middle number, or the mean (average) of the two middle numbers, in an ordered set of data

mediana El número intermedio, o la media (el promedio), de los dos números intermedios en un conjunto ordenado de datos

minuend [mĭn′yo͞o-ĕnd′] The first number in a subtraction sentence

minuend El primer número en una oración de resta

mode [mōd] The number or numbers that occur most frequently in a set of data; when all numbers occur with the same frequency, we say there is no mode

moda Número o números más frecuentes en un conjunto de datos; si todos los números aparecen con la misma frecuencia, no hay moda

multiple [mŭl′tə-pəl] The product of any number and any nonzero whole number is a multiple of that number

múltiplo El producto de un número y cualquier número cabal distinto de cero es un múltiplo de ese número

Multiplication Property of Equality [mŭl′tə-plĭ-kā′shən prŏp′ər-tē ŭv ĭ-kwŏl′ĭ-tē] The property that states that if you multiply both sides of an equation by the same number, the new equation will have the same solution

Propiedad de Igualdad de la Multiplicación Propiedad que establece que puedes multiplicar ambos lados de una ecuación por el mismo número y la nueva ecuación tendrá la misma solución

N

negative association [nĕg′ə-tĭv ə-sō′sē-ā shən] Two data sets have a negative association if one set of data values increases while the other decreases

asociación negativa Dos conjuntos de datos tienen asociación negativa si los valores de un conjunto aumentan a medida que los valores del otro conjunto disminuyen

© Houghton Mifflin Harcourt Publishing Company

My Vocabulary Summary

no association [nō ə-sō′sē-ā shən] Two data sets have no association when there is no relationship between their data values

sin asociación Caso en que los valores de dos conjuntos no muestran ninguna relación

no solution [nō sə-lo͞o′shən] Occurs when no value of the variable makes an equation true, or when a system of two equations has graphs that never intersect because lines are parallel

sin solución Ocurre cuando ningún valor de la variable hace que una ecuación sea verdadera, o cuando un sistema de dos ecuaciones tiene gráficas que nunca se intersecan porque son rectas paralelas

nonlinear association [nŏn-lĭn′ē-ər ə-sō′sē-ā shən] An association between two variables in which the data do not have a linear trend

asociación no lineal Una asociación entre dos variables en las que los datos no tienen una tendencia lineal

nonlinear function [nŏn-lĭn′ē-ər fŭngk′shən] A function whose graph is not a straight line

función no lineal Función cuya gráfica no es una línea recta

nonterminating decimal [nŏntûr′mə-nāt′ĭng dĕs′ə-məl] A decimal that never ends

decimal infinito Decimal que nunca termina

© Houghton Mifflin Harcourt Publishing Company

My Vocabulary Summary

number line [nŭm′bər līn] A line used to plot real numbers including integers, rational numbers, and irrational numbers

recta numérica Recta que se usa para marcar números reales que incluyen enteros, números racionales y números irracionales

numerator [no͞o′mə-rā′tər] The top number of a fraction that tells how many parts of a whole are being considered

numerador El número de arriba de una fracción; indica cuántas partes de un entero se consideran

O

obtuse angle [ŏb-to͞os′ ăng′gəl] An angle whose measure is greater than 90° but less than 180°

ángulo obtuso Ángulo que mide más de 90° y menos de 180°

origin [ôr′ə-jĭn] The point where the *x*-axis and *y*-axis intersect on the coordinate plane; (0, 0)

origen Punto de intersección entre el eje *x* y el eje *y* en un plano cartesiano: (0, 0)

outcome [out′kŭm′] A possible result of a probability experiment

resultado Posible resultado de un experimento de probabilidad

outlier [out′lī′ər] A value much greater or much less than the others in a data set

valor extremo Un valor mucho mayor o menor que los demás valores de un conjunto de datos

© Houghton Mifflin Harcourt Publishing Company

My Vocabulary Summary

output [out′po͝ot′] The value that results from the substitution of a given input into an expression or function

valor de salida Valor que resulta después de sustituir una variable por un valor de entrada determinado en una expresión o función

P

parallel lines [păr′ə-lĕl′ līns] Lines in a plane that do not intersect

líneas paralelas Líneas que se encuentran en el mismo plano pero que nunca se intersecan

parallelogram [păr′ə-lĕl′ə-grăm′] A quadrilateral with two pairs of parallel sides

paralelogramo Cuadrilátero con dos pares de lados paralelos

perfect cube [pûr′fĭkt kyo͞ob] A cube of a whole number

cubo perfecto El cubo de un número cabal

perfect square [pûr′fĭkt skwâr] A square of a whole number

cuadrado perfecto El cuadrado de un número cabal

© Houghton Mifflin Harcourt Publishing Company

My Vocabulary Summary

pi (π) [pī] The ratio of the circumference of a circle to the length of its diameter; $\pi \approx 3.14$ or $\frac{22}{7}$

pi (π) Razón de la circunferencia de un círculo a la longitud de su diámetro; $\pi \approx 3.14$ ó $\frac{22}{7}$

population [pŏp′yə-lā′shən] The entire group of objects or individuals considered for a survey

población Grupo completo de objetos o individuos que se desea estudiar

positive association [pŏz′ĭ-tĭv ə-sō′sē-ā shən] Two data sets have a positive association when their data values increase or decrease together

asociación positiva Dos conjuntos de datos tienen una asociación positiva cuando los valores de ambos conjuntos aumentan o disminuyen al mismo tiempo

power [pou′ər] A number produced by raising a base to an exponent

potencia Número que resulta al elevar una base a un exponente

preimage [prē′ĭm′ĭj] The original figure in a transformation

imagen original Figura original en una transformación

principal square root [prĭn′sə-pəl skwâr rōōt] The nonnegative square root of a number

raíz cuadrada principal Raíz cuadrada no negativa de un número

prism [prĭz′əm] A polyhedron that has two congruent polygon-shaped bases and other faces that are all parallelograms

prisma Poliedro con dos bases congruentes con forma de polígono y caras con forma de paralelogramo

© Houghton Mifflin Harcourt Publishing Company

My Vocabulary Summary

probability [prŏb′ə-bĭl′ĭ-tē] A number from 0 to 1 (or 0% to 100%) that describes how likely an event is to occur

probabilidad Un número entre 0 y 1 (ó 0% y 100%) que describe qué tan probable es un suceso

probability of an event [prŏb′ə-bĭl′ĭ-tē ŭv ən ĭ-vĕnt′] The probability of an event is the ratio of the number of outcomes in the event to the total number of outcomes in the sample space

probabilidad de un evento Razón del número de resultados del evento con respecto al número total de resultados del espacio muestral

properties of exponents [prôp′ər-tēz ŭv ĭk-spō′nənts] Rules for operations with exponents

propiedades de exponentes Reglas de operaciones con exponentes

proportional relationship [prə-pôr′shə-nəl rĭ-lā′shən-shĭp′] A relationship between two quantities in which the ratio of one quantity to the other quantity is constant

relación proporcional Relación entre dos cantidades en que la razón de una cantidad a la otra es constante

pyramid [pĭr′ə-mĭd] A polyhedron with a polygon base and triangular sides that all meet at a common vertex

pirámide Poliedro cuya base es un polígono; tiene caras triangulares que se juntan en un vértice común

Pythagorean Theorem [pĭ-thăg′ə-rē′ən thē′ər-əm] In a right triangle, the square of the length of the hypotenuse is equal to the sum of the squares of the lengths of the legs

Teorema de Pitágoras En un triángulo rectángulo, la suma de los cuadrados de los catetos es igual al cuadrado de la hipotenusa

© Houghton Mifflin Harcourt Publishing Company

My Vocabulary Summary

Pythagorean triple [pĭ-thăg′ə-rē′ən trĭp′əl] A set of three positive integers a, b, and c such that $a^2 + b^2 = c^2$

Tripleta de Pitágoras Conjunto de tres números enteros positivos de cero a, b y c tal que $a^2 + b^2 = c^2$

Q

quadrant [kwŏd′rənt] The x- and y-axes divide the coordinate plane into four regions. Each region is called a quadrant

cuadrante El eje x y el eje y dividen el plano cartesiano en cuatro regiones. Cada región recibe el nombre de cuadrante

quartile [kwôr′tīl′] Three values, one of which is the median, that divide a data set into fourths.

cuartiles Cada uno de tres valores, uno de los cuales es la mediana, que dividen en cuartos un conjunto de datos.

R

radical symbol [răd′ĭ-kəl sĭm′bəl] The symbol $\sqrt{}$ used to represent the nonnegative square root of a number

símbolo de radical El símbolo $\sqrt{}$ con que se representa la raíz cuadrada no negativa de un número

radius [rā′dē-əs] A line segment with one endpoint at the center of the circle and the other endpoint on the circle, or the length of that segment

radio Segmento de recta con un extremo en el centro de un círculo y el otro en la circunferencia, o bien se llama radio a la longitud de ese segmento

© Houghton Mifflin Harcourt Publishing Company

My Vocabulary Summary

random sample [răn′dəm săm′pəl] A sample in which each individual or object in the entire population has an equal chance of being selected

muestra aleatoria Muestra en la que cada individuo u objeto de la población tiene la misma oportunidad de ser elegido

range [rānj] In statistics, the difference between the greatest and least values in a data set

rango (en estadística) Diferencia entre los valores máximo y mínimo de un conjunto de datos

range (of a function) [rānj (ŭv ā fŭngk′shən)] The set of all possible output values of a function

rango (en una función) El conjunto de todos los valores posibles de una función

rate of change [rāt ŭv chānj] A ratio that compares the amount of change in a dependent variable to the amount of change in an independent variable

tasa de cambio Razón que compara la cantidad de cambio de la variable dependiente con la cantidad de cambio de la variable independiente

rational number [răsh′ə-nəl nŭm′bər] Any number that can be expressed as a ratio of two integers

número racional Número que se puede escribir como una razón de dos enteros

real number [rē′əl nŭm′bər] A rational or irrational number

.mero real Número racional o irracional

rectangular prism [rĕk-tăng′gyə-lər prĭz′əm] A polyhedron whose bases are rectangles and whose other faces are parallelograms

prisma rectangular Poliedro cuyas bases son rectángulos y cuyas caras tienen forma de paralelogramo

© Houghto. 'flin Harcourt Publishing Company

My Vocabulary Summary

reduction [rĭ-dŭk′shən] A decrease in the size of all dimensions of a figure

reducción Disminución de tamaño en todas las dimensiones de una figura

reflection [rĭ-flĕk′shən] A transformation of a figure that flips the figure across a line

reflexión Transformación que ocurre cuando se invierte una figura sobre una línea

relation [rĭ-lā′shən] A set of ordered pairs

relación Conjunto de pares ordenados

relative frequency [rĕl′ə-tĭv frē′kwən-sē] The frequency of a specific data value divided by the total number of data values in the set

frecuencia relativa La frecuencia de un valor dividido por el número total de los valores en el conjunto

remote interior angle [rĭ-mōt′ ĭn-tîr′ē-ər ăng′gəl] An interior angle of a polygon that is not adjacent to the exterior angle

ángulo interno remoto Ángulo interno de un polígono que no es adyacente al ángulo externo

repeating decimal [rĭ-pēt′ĭng dĕs′ə-məl] A decimal in which one or more digits repeat infinitely

decimal periódico Decimal en el que uno o más dígitos se repiten infinitamente

representative sample [rĕp′rĭ-zĕn′tə-tĭv săm′pəl] A sample that has the same characteristics of the population

muestra representativa Muestra que tiene las mismas características de la población

© Houghton Mifflin Harcourt Publishing Company

My Vocabulary Summary

right cone [rīt kōn] A cone in which a perpendicular line drawn from the base to the tip (vertex) passes through the center of the base

cono recto Cono en el que una linea perpendicular trazada de la base a la punta (vértice) pasa por el centro de la base

right triangle [rīt trī′ ăng′gəl] A triangle containing a right angle

triángulo rectángulo Triángulo que tiene un ángulo recto

rise [rīz] The vertical change when the slope of a line is expressed as the ratio $\frac{\text{rise}}{\text{run}}$, or "rise over run"

distancia vertical El cambio vertical cuando la pendiente de una línea se expresa como la razón $\frac{\text{distancia vertical}}{\text{distancia horizontal}}$, o "distancia vertical sobre distancia horizontal"

rotation [rō-tā′shən] A transformation in which a figure is turned around a point

rotación Transformación que ocurre cuando una figura gira alrededor de un punto

rotational symmetry [rō-tā′shən-əl sĭm′ĭ-trē] A figure has rotational symmetry if it can be rotated less than 360° around a central point and coincide with the original figure

simetría de rotación Ocurre cuando una figura gira menos de 360° alrededor de un punto central sin dejar de ser congruente con la figura original

run [rŭn] The horizontal change when the slope of a line is expressed as the ratio $\frac{\text{rise}}{\text{run}}$, or "rise over run"

distancia horizontal El cambio horizontal cuando la pendiente de una línea se expresa como la razón $\frac{\text{distancia vertical}}{\text{distancia horizontal}}$, o "distancia vertical sobre distancia horizontal"

© Houghton Mifflin Harcourt Publishing Company

S

My Vocabulary Summary

same-side exterior angles [sām-sīd ĭk-stîr′ē-ər ăng′gəls] A pair of angles on the same side of a transversal but outside the parallel lines

ángulos externos del mismo lado Par de ángulos que se encuentran del mismo lado de una transversal, pero por la parte exterior de las rectas paralelas

---

same-side interior angles [sām-sīd ĭn-tîr′ē-ər ăng′gəls] A pair of angles on the same side of a transversal and between two lines intersected by the transversal

ángulo internos del mismo lado Dadas dos rectas cortadas por una transversal, par de ángulos ubicados en el mismo lado de la transversal y entre las dos rectas

---

sample [săm′pəl] A part of the population that is chosen to represent the entire group

muestra Una parte de la población que se elige para representar a todo el grupo

---

sample space [săm′pəl spās] All possible outcomes of an experiment

espacio muestral Conjunto de todos los resultados posibles de un experimento

---

scale [skāl] The ratio between two sets of measurements

escala La razón entre dos conjuntos de medidas

---

scale drawing [skāl drô′ĭng] A drawing that uses a scale to make an object smaller than or larger than the real object

dibujo a escala Dibujo en el que se usa una escala para que un objeto se vea mayor o menor que el objeto real al que representa

© Houghton Mifflin Harcourt Publishing Company

My Vocabulary Summary

scale factor [skāl făk′tər] The ratio used to enlarge or reduce similar figures

factor de escala Razón empleada para agrandar o reducir figuras semejantes

scatter plot [skăt′ər plŏt] A graph with points plotted to show a possible relationship between two sets of data

diagrama de dispersión Gráfica de puntos que muestra una posible relación entre dos conjuntos de datos

scientific notation [sī′ən-tĭf′ĭk nō-tā′shən] A method of more conveniently writing very large or very small numbers by using powers of 10

notación científica Método que se usa para escribir números muy grandes o muy pequeños mediante potencias de 10

segment [sĕg′mənt] A part of a line between two endpoints

segmento Parte de una línea entre dos extremos

similar [sĭm′ə-lər] Figures with the same shape but not necessarily the same size

semejantes Figuras que tienen la misma forma, pero no necesariamente el mismo tamaño

© Houghton Mifflin Harcourt Publishing Company

My Vocabulary Summary

similarity transformation [sĭm′ə-lăr′ĭ-tē trăns′fər-mā′shən] A transformation that results in an image that is the same shape, but not necessarily the same size, as the original figure

transformación de semejanza Una transformación que resulta en una imagen que tiene la misma forma, pero no necesariamente el mismo tamaño como la figura original

simulation [sĭm′yə-lā′shən] A model of an experiment, often one that would be too difficult or too time-consuming to actually perform

simulación Representación de un experimento, por lo regular de uno cuya realización sería demasiado difícil o llevaría mucho tiempo

slant height (of a right cone) [slănt hīt (ŭv ā rīt kōn)] The distance from the vertex of a right cone to a point on the edge of the base

altura inclinada (de un cono recto) Distancia desde el vértice de un cono recto hasta un punto en el borde de la base

slope [slōp] A measure of the steepness of a line on a graph; equal to the rise divided by the run

pendiente Medida de la inclinación de una línea en una gráfica. Razón de la distancia vertical a la distancia horizontal

slope-intercept form [slōp-ĭn′tər-sĕpt′ fôrm] A linear equation written in the form $y = mx + b$, where m represents slope and b represents the y-intercept

forma de pendiente-intersección Ecuación lineal escrita en la forma $y = mx + b$, donde m es la pendiente y b es la intersección con el eje y

solution of an equation [sə-lo͞o′shən ŭv ən ĭ-kwā′zhən] A value or values that make an equation true

solución de una ecuación Valor o valores que hacen verdadera una ecuación

© Houghton Mifflin Harcourt Publishing Company

My Vocabulary Summary

solution of an inequality [sə-lo͞o′shən ŭv ən ĭn′ĭ-kwŏl′ĭ-tē] A value or values that make an inequality true

solución de una desigualdad Valor o valores que hacen verdadera una desigualdad

solution of a system of equations [sə-lo͞o′shən ŭv ā sĭs′təm ŭv ĭ-kwā′zhəns] A set of values that make all equations in a system true

solución de un sistema de ecuaciones Conjunto de valores que hacen verdaderas todas las ecuaciones de un sistema

sphere [sfĭr] A round three-dimensional figure with a central point and all points whose distance from the center is less than or equal to the radius

esfera Una figura redonda tridimensional con un punto central y todos los puntos cuya distancia desde el centro es menor o igual que el radio

square (numeration) [skwâr (no͞o′mə-rā′shən)] A number raised to the second power

cuadrado (en numeración) Número elevado a la segunda potencia

square root [skwâr ro͞ot] A number that is multiplied by itself to form a product is called a square root of that product

raíz cuadrada El número que se multiplica por sí mismo para formar un producto se denomina la raíz cuadrada de ese producto

standard form of a number [stăn′dərd fôrm ŭv ā nŭm′bər] A way of writing a number by using digits

forma estándar de un número Manera de escribir un número usando dígitos

straight angle [strāt ăng′gəl] An angle that measures 180°

ángulo llano Ángulo que mide exactamente 180°

substitute [sŭb′stĭ-to͞ot′] To replace a variable with a number or another expression in an algebraic expression

sustituir Reemplazar una variable por un número u otra expresión en una expresión algebraica

© Houghton Mifflin Harcourt Publishing Company

My Vocabulary Summary

Subtraction Property of Equality [səb-trăk′shən prŏp′ər-tē ŭv ĭ-kwŏl′ĭ-tē] The property that states that if you subtract the same number from both sides of an equation, the new equation will have the same solution

Propiedad de igualdad de la resta Propiedad que establece que puedes restar el mismo número de ambos lados de una ecuación y la nueva ecuación tendrá la misma solución

subtrahend [sŭb′trə-hĕnd′] The number that is subtracted from another number in a subtraction sentence

subtrahend el número que se resta de otro número en una oración de resta

supplementary angles [sŭp′lə-mĕn′tə-rē ăng′gəls] Two angles whose measures have a sum of 180°

ángulos suplementarios Dos ángulos cuyas medidas suman 180°

surface area [sûr′fəs âr′e-ə] The sum of the areas of the faces, or surfaces, of a three-dimensional figure

área total Suma de las áreas de las caras, o superficies, de una figura tridimensional

system of equations [sĭs′təm ŭv ĭ-kwā′zhəns] A set of two or more equations

sistema de ecuaciones Conjunto de dos o más ecuaciones

T

terminating decimal [tûr′mə-nāt′ĭng dĕs′ə-məl] A decimal number that ends, or terminates

decimal finito Decimal con un número determinado de posiciones decimales

© Houghton Mifflin Harcourt Publishing Company

My Vocabulary Summary

tessellation [tĕs′ə-lāt′shən] A repeating pattern of plane figures that completely covers a plane with no gaps or overlaps

teselado Patrón repetido de figuras planas que cubren totalmente un plano sin superponerse ni dejar huecos

---

theoretical probability [thē′ə-rĕt′ĭ-kəl prŏb′ə-bĭl′ĭ-tē] The ratio of the number of possible outcomes in the event to the total number of possible outcomes in the sample space

probabilidad teórica Razón entre el número de resultados posibles de un suceso y el número total de resultados posibles del espacio muestral

---

transformation [trăns′fər-mā′shən] A change in the size or position of a figure

transformación Cambio en el tamaño o la posición de una figura

---

translation [trăns-lā′shən] A movement (slide) of a figure along a straight line

traslación Desplazamiento de una figura a lo largo de una línea recta

---

transversal [trans-vûr′səl] A line that intersects two or more other lines

transversal Línea que cruza dos o más líneas

---

trapezoid [trăp′ĭ-zoid′] A quadrilateral with at least one pair of parallel sides

trapecio Cuadrilátero con al menos un par de lados paralelos

© Houghton Mifflin Harcourt Publishing Company

My Vocabulary Summary

tree diagram [trē dī′ə-grăm′] A branching diagram that shows all possible combinations or outcomes of an event

diagrama de árbol Diagrama ramificado que muestra todas las posibles combinaciones o resultados de un suceso

trend line [trĕnd līn] A line on a scatter plot that helps show the association between data sets more clearly

línea de tendencia Línea en un diagrama de dispersión que sirve para mostrar la asociación entre conjuntos de datos más claramente. *ver también* línea de mejor ajuste

trial [trī′əl] Each repetition or observation of an experiment

prueba Una sola repetición u observación de un experimento

Triangle Sum Theorem [trī′ăng′gəl sŭm thē′ər-əm] The theorem that states that the measures of the angles in a triangle add up to 180°

Teorema de la suma del triángulo Teorema que establece que las medidas de los ángulos de un triángulo suman 180°

triangular prism [trī-ăng′gyə-lər prĭz′əm] A polyhedron whose bases are triangles and whose other faces are parallelograms

prisma triangular Poliedro cuyas bases son triángulos y cuyas demás caras tienen forma de paralelogramo

two-way relative frequency table [to͞o-wā rĕl′ə-tĭv frē′kwən-sē tā′bəl] A two-way table that displays relative frequencies

tabla de frecuencia relativa de doble entrada Una tabla de doble entrada que muestran las frecuencias relativas

© Houghton Mifflin Harcourt Publishing Company

My Vocabulary Summary

two-way table [tōō-wā tā'bəl] A table that displays two-variable data by organizing it into rows and columns

tabla de doble entrada Una tabla que muestran los datos de dos variables por organizándolos en columnas y filas

U

unit rate [yōō'nĭt rāt] A rate in which the second quantity in the comparison is one unit

tasa unitaria Una tasa en la que la segunda cantidad de la comparación es la unidad

upper quartile [ŭp'ər kwôr'tīl'] The median of the upper half of a set of data

cuartil superior La mediana de la mitad superior de un conjunto de datos

V

vertex [vûr'tĕks'] On an angle or polygon, the point where two sides intersect; on a polyhedron, the intersection of three or more faces; on a cone or pyramid, the top point

vértice En un ángulo o polígono, el punto de intersección de dos lados; en un poliedro, el punto de intersección de tres o más caras; en un cono o pirámide, la punta

vertical angles [vûr'tĭ-kəl ăng'gəls] A pair of opposite congruent angles formed by intersecting lines

ángulos opuestos por el vértice Par de ángulos opuestos congruentes formados por líneas secantes

vertical line test [vûr'tĭ-kəl līn tĕst] A test used to determine whether a relation is a function: if any vertical line crosses the graph of a relation more than once, the relation is not a function

prueba de la línea vertical Prueba utilizada para determinar si una relación es una función. Si una línea vertical corta la gráfica de una relación más de una vez, la relación no es una función

© Houghton Mifflin Harcourt Publishing Company

My Vocabulary Summary

volume [vŏl′yo͞om] The amount of space enclosed within a three-dimensional region; or the number of cubic units needed to fill that space

volumen La cantidad de espacio dentro de una región tridimensional; o la cantidad de unidades cúbicas necesarias para llenar ese espacio

X

x-axis [ĕks′-ăk′sĭs] The horizontal axis on a coordinate plane

eje x El eje horizontal del plano cartesiano

x-intercept [ĕks-ĭn′tər-sĕpt′] The x-coordinate of the point where the graph of a line crosses the x-axis

intersección con el eje x Coordenada x del punto donde la gráfica de una línea cruza el eje x

Y

$y = mx$ [wī ē′kwəls ĕm ĕks] The form for a linear equation that passes through the origin and has a y-intercept of 0

$y = mx$ Ecuación que representa una ecuación lineal que pasa por el origen, la intersección con cada uno de los ejes es 0

© Houghton Mifflin Harcourt Publishing Company

My Vocabulary Summary

***y*-axis** [wī′-ăk sĭs] The vertical axis on a coordinate plane

eje *y* El eje vertical del plano cartesiano

***y*-intercept** [wī-ĭn′tər-sĕpt′] The *y*-coordinate of the point where the graph of a line crosses the *y*-axis

intersección con el eje *y* Coordenada *y* del punto donde la gráfica de una línea cruza el eje *y*

© Houghton Mifflin Harcourt Publishing Company

A

B

C

© Houghton Mifflin Harcourt Publishing Company

© Houghton Mifflin Harcourt Publishing Company

© Houghton Mifflin Harcourt Publishing Company

© Houghton Mifflin Harcourt Publishing Company

N

O

P

© Houghton Mifflin Harcourt Publishing Company

Q

R

© Houghton Mifflin Harcourt Publishing Company

© Houghton Mifflin Harcourt Publishing Company

Index

© Houghton Mifflin Harcourt Publishing Company

U

V

W

X

Y

Z

© Houghton Mifflin Harcourt Publishing Company

LENGTH

1 meter (m) = 1,000 millimeters (mm)	1 inch = 2.54 centimeters
1 meter = 100 centimeters (cm)	1 foot (ft) = 12 inches (in.)
1 meter ≈ 39.37 inches	1 yard (yd) = 3 feet
1 kilometer (km) = 1,000 meters	1 mile (mi) = 1,760 yards
1 kilometer ≈ 0.62 mile	1 mile = 5,280 feet
	1 mile ≈ 1.609 kilometers

CAPACITY

1 liter (L) = 1,000 milliliters (mL)	1 cup (c) = 8 fluid ounces (fl oz)
1 liter = 1,000 cubic centimeters	1 pint (pt) = 2 cups
1 liter ≈ 0.264 gallon	1 quart (qt) = 2 pints
1 kiloliter (kL) = 1,000 liters	1 gallon (gal) = 4 quarts
	1 gallon ≈ 3.785 liters

MASS/WEIGHT

1 gram (g) = 1,000 milligrams (mg)	1 pound (lb) = 16 ounces (oz)
1 kilogram (kg) = 1,000 grams	1 pound ≈ 0.454 kilogram
1 kilogram ≈ 2.2 pounds	1 ton = 2,000 pounds

TIME

1 minute (min) = 60 seconds (s)	1 year (yr) = about 52 weeks
1 hour (h) = 60 minutes	1 year = 12 months (mo)
1 day = 24 hours	1 year = 365 days
1 week = 7 days	1 decade = 10 years

© Houghton Mifflin Harcourt Publishing Company

SYMBOLS

$=$	is equal to	10^2	ten squared
$\neq$	is not equal to	10^3	ten cubed
$\approx$	is approximately equal to	2^4	the fourth power of 2
$>$	is greater than	$\|-4\|$	the absolute value of -4
$<$	is less than	%	percent
$\geq$	is greater than or equal to	(2, 3)	ordered pair (x, y)
$\leq$	is less than or equal to	°	degree

FORMULAS

Perimeter and Circumference

Polygon	$P =$ sum of the lengths of sides
Rectangle	$P = 2\ell + 2w$
Square	$P = 4s$
Circle	$C = \pi d$ or $C = 2\pi r$

Area

Rectangle	$A = \ell w$
Parallelogram	$A = bh$
Triangle	$A = \frac{1}{2}bh$
Trapezoid	$A = \frac{1}{2}h(b_1 + b_2)$
Square	$A = s^2$
Circle	$A = \pi r^2$

Volume

Right Prism	$V = \ell wh$ or $V = Bh$
Cube	$V = s^3$
Pyramid	$V = \frac{1}{3}Bh$
Cylinder	$V = \pi r^2 h$
Cone	$V = \frac{1}{3}\pi r^2 h$
Sphere	$V = \frac{4}{3}\pi r^3$

Surface Area

Right Prism	$S = Ph + 2B$
Cube	$S = 6s^2$
Square Pyramid	$S = \frac{1}{2}P\ell + B$

Pythagorean Theorem

$a^2 + b^2 = c^2$

© Houghton Mifflin Harcourt Publishing Company